HISTORY OF
THE SECOND WORLD WAR

UNITED KINGDOM MEDICAL SERIES

Editor-in-Chief :

SIR ARTHUR S. MacNALTY, K.C.B., M.A., M.D., F.R.C.P., F.R.C.S.

THE ARMY
MEDICAL SERVICES

BY

F. A. E. CREW, F.R.S.

Campaigns

VOLUME II

HONG KONG · MALAYA

ICELAND AND THE FAROES

LIBYA, 1942–1943

NORTH-WEST AFRICA

The Naval & Military Press Ltd

Published by

The Naval & Military Press Ltd
Unit 10 Ridgewood Industrial Park,
Uckfield, East Sussex,
TN22 5QE England

Tel: +44 (0) 1825 749494
Fax: +44 (0) 1825 765701

www.naval-military-press.com
www.military-genealogy.com

PREFATORY NOTE

BY THE EDITOR-IN-CHIEF

Professor F. A. E. Crew's second volume dealing with Campaigns in the Official Medical History of the Second World War might fittingly be sub-titled 'Disasters and Triumphs.' Chapter 1 relates the story of the Defence and Fall of Hong Kong— Chapter 2 the equally tragic and heroic story of the Campaign in Malaya and the Fall of Singapore.

These chapters will be read, I am sure, with mingled feelings of sorrow and admiration. Of sorrow that British forces, both men and women, had to endure such terrible ordeals, and that many died through the lack of necessary treatment and medicaments, for example, diphtheria antitoxin. In pride because of the nobility of men and women who endured 'the long years of captivity filled with suffering and humiliation' with courage, and while their bodies were imprisoned, kept the spirit of man free.

As Professor Crew observes in his preface, there was a complete lack of the normal source material for the narratives of Hong Kong and Singapore. The deficiency has been remedied by those members of the Army Medical Services who, while prisoners-of-war, maintained chronicles of the events in which they were participants. All readers will endorse the tribute of admiration and respect which Professor Crew accords to these contributors.

It will also be of interest to the readers to compare the accounts of Hong Kong by Sir Selwyn Selwyn-Clarke and of Malaya by Dr. R. B. MacGregor in Volume II *Civilian Health and Medical Services* with these two first chapters. They supplement the military narratives from the civilian health and medical aspects.

The occupation of Iceland and the Faroes, dealt with in Chapter 3, presented new medical problems which were solved by the Army Medical Services.

In Chapter 4 the successes in Libya and the turning of the tide at the Battle of Alamein are recorded. Much useful information is given in a review of the health of the troops in this campaign.

Chapter 5 contains an account of the campaign in North-west Africa, Operation 'Torch'. This was at first a hazardous adventure, but after a period of stalemate, the advance into Tunisia achieved complete victory. In the course of the campaign many problems of medical administration arose especially in connexion with the prevention, diagnosis and treatment of disease, and these are fully described and discussed.

I would also draw special attention to the Review of the Health of Middle East Force 1942–43 in Chapter 6, and to the accounts of the Army Psychiatric Service and the Army Pathology and Transfusion Service in the Middle East in Chapters 7 and 8. In many cases the medical lessons of war are hard, but as this volume shows they were learned and applied to the great benefit of the Armed Forces by the Army Medical Services.

This volume of the Official Medical History of the war has been prepared under the direction of the Editorial Board appointed by H.M. Government; but the author alone is responsible for the method of presentation of the facts and the opinions expressed.

August 1954.   ARTHUR S. MacNALTY

CONTENTS

Page

ILLUSTRATIONS

SKETCH MAPS AND DIAGRAMS

Facing Page

PLATES

Plates I–V were provided by Mr. J. D. Chalker, an artist who soldiered in Malaya, was taken prisoner and laboured on the Thailand-Burma railway. Plates VI–X are reproduced by permission of the author and the publishers from an article by Lieut. Colonel Ian Aird which appeared in the *Edinburgh Medical Journal*. Plates XI–XX are Crown copyright and were supplied by the Imperial War Museum. To Mr. Chalker, Professor Aird, Messrs. Oliver and Boyd and the Imperial War Museum acknowledgement is made.

TABLES

CONTENTS

Chapter 8: *The Army Pathology and Transfusion Service*

ABBREVIATIONS

A.	The Adjutant-General's Branch, dealing with personnel, discipline, documentation, chaplains', educational, medical services, selection of personnel and the like
A.A. . . .	Anti-aircraft
A.A.D.C. . .	The Australian Army Dental Corps
A.A.M.C. . .	The Australian Army Medical Corps
A.A.T.C. . .	Advanced Air Transport Centre
A.A.T.W. . .	Advanced Air Transport Wing
A.B.D.A. . .	The American, British, Dutch and Australian Area
A.B.S. . .	The Atlantic Base Section (U.S.)
A.B.S.D. . .	The Army Blood Supply Depot, Bristol
A.C.C. . .	Ambulance Car Company, R.A.S.C.
A.D. Corps or A.D.C.	The Army Dental Corps (now the Royal A.D. Corps)
A.D.H. . .	Assistant Director of Hygiene (now Health)
A.D. Lab. . .	Army Dental Laboratory
Admin. . .	Administration
A.D.M.S. . .	Assistant Director of Medical Services
A.D.P. . .	Assistant Director of Pathology
A.D.S. . .	Advanced Dressing Station
A.D.S. & T. .	Assistant Director of Supply and Transport
Adv. . .	Advanced
Adv. Depot Med. Stores . .	Advanced Depot of Medical Stores
A.E.C. . .	The Army Education Corps
A.F. . .	Army Form
A.F.H.Q. . .	Allied Force Headquarters
A.F.S. . .	American Field Service
A.F.V. . .	Armoured Fighting Vehicle
A.G.H. . .	Australian General Hospital
A.I.F. . .	The Australian Imperial Force
A.L.F.S.E.A. .	Allied Land Forces, South East Asia
Amb. . .	Ambulance
Amb. R.H. . .	Ambulance Railhead
Amb. Train .	Ambulance Train
A.M.P.C. . .	The Auxiliary Military Pioneer Corps
A.M.U. . .	Anti-malarial Unit
A.N.S. . .	The Auxiliary Nursing Service
A.O.R. . .	Australian Other Rank
A.P.T.C. . .	The Army Physical Training Corps
A.P.W. . .	Advanced Psychiatric Wing (of a General Hospital)
A./Q. . .	Adjutant-General's/Quarter-Master-General's Combined Branch
Armd. . .	Armoured
A. and S.H. .	The Argyll and Sutherland Highlanders
A/T or A.T. .	Anti-Tank
A.T.S. . .	The Auxiliary Territorial Service
A.Tr.S. . .	The Army Transfusion Service

Aust. . . .	Australian
Aux. Med. Depot. .	Auxiliary Medical Depot
Base Depot Med.	
Stores . .	Base Depot of Medical Stores
Bde. . . .	Brigade
Bedfords . .	The Bedfordshire and Hertfordshire Regiment
B.G.H. . .	British General Hospital
Black Watch .	The Black Watch (Royal Highland Regiment)
B.M.J. . .	The British Medical Journal
B.M.H. . .	British Military Hospital
Bn. . . .	Battalion
B.N.A.F. . .	The British North African Force
B.O.R. . .	British Other Rank
Br. or Brit. . .	British
B.R.C.S. . .	The British Red Cross Society
B.S.A. . .	Base Sub-area
Br.S.S. . .	British Staging Section
B.T.E. . .	British Troops in Egypt
B.T.S.D. . .	Base Transfusion Supply Depot
B.T.U. . .	Base Transfusion Unit
Bty. . .	Battery
Buffs. . .	The Royal East Kent Regiment
C.A.E.C . .	Casualty Air Evacuation Centre
Camerons .	The Queen's Own Cameron Highlanders
C.A.O. . .	Chief Administrative Officer (U.S.)
C.A.T.S. .	Cypriot Auxiliary Territorial Service
Cav. . .	Cavalry
C.B.R. . .	Crude Birth Rate
C.C.S. . .	Casualty Clearing Station
Cdo. . .	Commando
C.D.R. . .	Crude Death Rate
C.G.H. . .	Combined General Hospital (Indian Army)
C. in C. . .	Commander-in-Chief
Cln. . .	Clearing (U.S. Medical Corps, Clearing Platoon)
C.M.F. . .	The Central Mediterranean Force
C.M.P. . .	The Corps of Military Police or Civil Medical Practitioner
C.O. . .	Commanding Officer
C. of E. . .	The Church of England
Con. Depot .	Convalescent Depot
Con. Hosp. .	Convalescent Hospital
Coy. . .	Company
C.P. . .	Collecting Post = Casualty Collecting Post
C.P.L. . .	Central Pathological Laboratory
C.R.S. . .	Camp Reception Station
Cyrcom. . .	Cyrenaica Command
D.A.D.H. .	Deputy Assistant Director of Hygiene (now Health)
D.A.D.M.S. .	Deputy Assistant Director of Medical Services
D.A.D.O.S. .	Deputy Assistant Director of Ordnance
D.A.G. . .	Deputy Adjutant-General

D.A.P.	. . .	Director of Army Psychiatry
D.A.Q.M.G.	. .	Deputy Assistant Quarter-Master-General
D.D.D.S.	. .	Deputy Director of the Dental Service
D.D.H.	. . .	Deputy Director of Hygiene (now Health)
D.D.M.S.	. .	Deputy Director of Medical Services
D.D.P.	. . .	Deputy Director of Pathology
D.D.S.P.	. .	Deputy Director of Selection of Personnel
D.D.T.	. . .	Dichlor-diphenyl-trichlorethane
Detach.	. . .	Detachment
D.G.A.M.S.	. .	Director General Army Medical Services
D.I.	. . .	Dangerously Ill
Div.	. . .	Division or Divisional
Dj.	. . .	Djebel (Mountain)
D.L.I.	. . .	The Durham Light Infantry
D. of H.	. .	Director of Hygiene (now Health)
D.M.R.	. . .	Director of Medical Research
D.M.S.	. . .	Director of Medical Services
D.O.	. . .	Dental Officer
D.R.L.S.	. .	Despatch Rider Letter Service
D.U.K.W.	. .	A dual drive 2½ ton amphibious truck
D.W.R.	. . .	The Duke of Wellington's Regiment (West Riding)
E.B.S.	. . .	Eastern Base Section (U.S.)
E.I.	. . .	Enamelled Iron
E.M.O.	. . .	Embarkation Medical Officer
E.M.S.	. . .	The Emergency Medical Services
E.N.T.	. . .	Ear, Nose and Throat
E.P.I.P.	. . .	European Privates, Indian Pattern (tent)
Essex	. . .	The Essex Regiment
E.T.O.U.S.A.	. .	European Theatre of Operations, United States Army
Evac. Hosp.	. .	Evacuation Hospital (U.S.)
F.A.U.	. . .	Friends' Ambulance Unit = A.F.S.
Fd.	. . .	Field
Fd. Amb.	. .	Field Ambulance
F.D.U. or Fd. Dental Unit	.	Field Dental Unit
F.F.	. . .	Frontier Force
Fd. Hosp.	. .	Field Hospital
Fd. Hyg. Sec.	.	Field Hygiene Section
Fd. Lab.	. .	Field Laboratory
F.M.S.V.F.	. .	The Federated Malay States Volunteer Force
Fr.	. . . .	French
F.S.	. . .	Field Service
F.S.D.	. . .	Field Supply Depot
F.S.U.	. . .	Field Surgical Unit
F.T.U.	. . .	Field Transfusion Unit
F.W.D.	. . .	Four-wheel Drive
G.	. . .	General Staff, Branch dealing with Operations, Intelligence and Training

G.I. . . .	The General Staff Officer concerned with Intelligence
G.1098 . . .	Mobilisation Equipment Scale
G.B.D. . . .	General Base Depot
G.D.O. . . .	General Duty Officer or Orderly
Gds. . . .	Guards
Gen. Hosp. . .	General Hospital
G.H.Q. . . .	General Headquarters
G.O.C. . . .	General Officer Commanding
Gordons . . .	The Gordon Highlanders
Gp. . . .	Group
Gren. Gds. . .	The Grenadier Guards
G.S. . . .	General Service
G.S.W. . . .	Gun Shot Wound
H.A.A. . . .	Heavy Anti-Aircraft
Hamps. . . .	The Hampshire Regiment
H.K. . . .	Hong Kong
H.K.S.R.A. . .	The Hong Kong and Singapore Regt. R.A.
H.K.V.D.C. . .	The Hong Kong Volunteer Defence Corps
H.S. . . .	Hospital Ship
Hosp. Train . .	Hospital Train
H.Q. . . .	Headquarters
Hy. . . .	Heavy
Hy. Sec. . .	Heavy Section
I.1248 . . .	Scale of Medical Mobilisation Equipment, Apparatus and Drugs
I.A. . . .	The Indian Army
I.A.T. . . .	Inflammation of the Areolar Tissue
I.G.H. . . .	Indian General Hospital
I.H.C. . . .	The Indian Hospital Corps
I.J.A. . . .	The Imperial Japanese Army
I.M.D. . . .	The Indian Medical Department
I.M.H. . . .	Indian Military Hospital
I.M.R. . . .	Infant Mortality Rate
I.M.S. . . .	The Indian Medical Service
Ind. . . .	Indian
Inf. . . .	Infantry
I.O.R. . . .	Indian Other Rank
I.S.S. . . .	Indian Staging Section
J.A.G. . . .	The Judge Advocate General
K. . . .	Killed
K. Craft . .	A flat bottomed shallow craft with an outboard motor
K.D. . . .	Khaki Drill
K.D.G. . . .	1st King's Dragoon Guards
King's Own . .	The King's Own Royal Regiment (Lancaster)
L.A.D. . . .	Light Aid Detachment
L.C.A. . . .	Landing craft assault
L.C.I. . . .	Landing craft infantry
L.C.M. . . .	Landing craft mechanised

L.C.T. . . .	Landing craft tank
L./Cpl. . . .	Lance-corporal
L. of C. . . .	Lines of Communication
Leicesters . .	The Leicestershire Regiment
L.G. . . .	Landing Ground
L.O. . . .	Liaison Officer
Loyals . . .	The Loyal Regt. (North Lancashire)
L.R.D.G. . .	The Long Range Desert Group
L.S.T. . . .	Landing ship tank
Lt. . . .	Light
L./T. . . .	Line Telegraphy
Lt. Tk. Sqn. .	Light Tank Squadron
M. . . .	Medical or Missing
M.A.C. . . .	Motor Ambulance Convoy
Mal. . . .	Malayan
Mal. Fd. Lab. .	Malaria Field Laboratory
Mal. G.H. . .	Malayan General Hospital
M.A.P. . . .	Medical Aid Post
M.A.S. . . .	Motor Ambulance Section (Indian Army)
Max-Fac. Surg. Team	Maxillo-facial Surgical Team
M.B.S. . .	Mediterranean Base Section (U.S.)
M.B.U. . . .	Mobile Bath Unit
M.C.U. . . .	Malaria Control Unit
M.D.S. . . .	Main Dressing Station
M.D.U. . . .	Mobile Dental Unit
M.E. . . .	The Middle East
M.E.C. . . .	The Middle East Command
M.E.F. . . .	The Middle East Force
M.G. . . .	Machine Gun
Mil. Hosp. . .	Military Hospital
M.I. Room . .	Medical Inspection Room
M.N.O. . . .	Mental Nursing Orderly
M.O. . . .	Medical Officer
Mob. Bact. Lab. .	Mobile Bacteriological Laboratory
Mob. Dental Unit .	Mobile Dental Unit
Mob. Fd. Hyg. Sec. .	Mobile Field Hygiene Section
Mob. Hyg. Lab. .	Mobile Hygiene Laboratory
Mob. Mal. Fd. Lab. .	Mobile Malaria Field Laboratory
Mob. Mil. Hosp. .	Mobile Military Hospital
Mob. Ophthal. Unit .	Mobile Ophthalmic Unit
Mob. Surg. Unit .	Mobile Surgical Unit
Mov. & Tn. . .	Movement and Transport
M.R.C. . . .	The Medical Research Council
M.S.U. . . .	Mobile Surgical Unit
M.T. . . .	Mechanical Transport
M.T.C. . . .	Mechanical Transport Company
Mtn. . . .	Mountain
M. & V. . .	Meat and Vegetables
N.A.A.F.I. . .	Navy, Army and Air Force Institute
N.C.O. . . .	Non-commissioned officer
N.E. . . .	Non-European (South Africa)

Neur.-Surg.	Neurosurgical
N.O.	Nursing Orderly
Northamptons	The Northamptonshire Regiment
N.Y.D.	Not Yet Diagnosed
N.Y.D.(N.)	Not Yet Diagnosed (Neuro-psychiatric ?)
N.Z.	New Zealand
N.Z.A.S.C.	New Zealand Army Service Corps
N.Z.E.F.	The New Zealand Expeditionary Force
N.Z.G.H.	New Zealand General Hospital
O.C.	Officer Commanding
O.C.T.U.	Officer Cadet Training Unit
Ops.	Operations
O.Rs.	Other Ranks
O.R.A.	Operating Room Assistant
O.S.	Ordnance
P.A.C.	Prophylactic Ablution Centre
Para.	Parachute
Path. Lab.	Pathological Laboratory
P.A.T.S.	Palestinian Auxiliary Territorial Service
Pln.	Platoon
Pn.	Psychoneurotic
Pol.	Polish
Pol. G.H.	Polish General Hospital
P.o.W.	Prisoner-of-War
Pp.	Psychotic
Pr.	Pair
P.T.	Physical Training
Pte.	Private
P.U.O.	Pyrexia of Unknown Origin
Q.	The Quarter-Master-General's Branch dealing with food, quarters, clothing, equipment, stores and movement
Q.A.I.M.N.S.	Queen Alexandra's Imperial Military Nursing Service (now Q.A.R.A.N.C., Queen Alexandra's Royal Army Nursing Corps)
Q.L.(T.C.V.)	Quick Loading Troop Carrying Vehicle
Q.M.	Quartermaster
Queen's	The Queen's Royal Regiment (West Surrey)
R.A.	The Royal Regiment of Artillery
R.A.A.F.	The Royal Australian Air Force
R.A.C.	The Royal Armoured Corps
R.A.Ch.D.	The Royal Army Chaplains' Department
R.A.F.	The Royal Air Force
R.A.M.C.	The Royal Army Medical Corps
R.A.O.C.	The Royal Army Ordnance Corps
R.A.P.	Regimental Aid Post
R.A.P.C.	The Royal Army Pay Corps
R.A.P.W.I.	Released Allied Prisoners-of-War and Internees (Organisation)

R.A.S.C.	. .	The Royal Army Service Corps
R.C.A.M.C.	. .	The Royal Canadian Army Medical Corps
R.C.S.	. . .	The Royal Corps of Signals
R.C.T.	. . .	Regimental Combat Team (U.S.)
R.E.	. . .	The Corps of Royal Engineers
Recce.	. . .	Reconnaissance
Regt.	. . .	Regiment
R.E.M.E.	. .	The Royal Electrical and Mechanical Engineers
R.H.	. . .	Railhead
R.H.A.	. . .	The Royal Horse Artillery
R.I.A.S.C.	. .	The Royal Indian Army Service Corps
Rif.	. . .	Rifles
Rly. Stn.	. .	Railway Station
R.M.O.	. . .	Regimental Medical Officer
R.N.	. . .	The Royal Navy
R.Tks.	. . .	The Royal Tank Regiment
R.W.K.	. . .	The Queen's Own Royal West Kent Regiment
S.A.	. . .	South African or Sub-area
S.A.A.C. Regt.	. .	South African Armoured Car Regiment
S.A.C.S.E.A.	. .	Supreme Allied Commander South East Asia
S. & M.	. . .	Sappers and Miners (Indian Army)
S.A.M.C.	. .	The South African Medical Corps
S.A.S.	. . .	Special Air Squadron or Sub-Assistant Surgeon (Indian Army)
S.Bs.	. . .	Stretcher-bearers
S.D.F.	. . .	The Sudan Defence Force
S.E.A.C.	. .	South East Asia Command
Sec.	. . .	Section
Sergt.	. . .	Sergeant
Sherwood Foresters	.	The Nottinghamshire and Derbyshire Regiment
S.I.	. . .	Seriously Ill
S./L.	. . .	Search-light
S.M.O.	. . .	Senior Medical Officer
S.P.	. . .	Staging Post
Sp. Gp.	. . .	Support Group
Sqn.	. . .	Squadron
S.S.	. . .	Steamship
S.S.V.F.	. .	The Straits Settlements Volunteer Force
Surg. Hosp.	. .	Surgical Hospital (U.S.)
Surreys	. .	The East Surrey Regiment
T.A.N.S.	. . .	The Territorial Army Nursing Service
T.C.V.	. . .	Troop Carrying Vehicle
Tk.	. . . .	Tank
Tp.	. . .	Troop
Tpn.	. . .	Transportation (U.S. Medical Corps. Transportation Platoon)
Tps.	. . .	Troops
u/c.	. . .	Under command of
U.D.F.	. . .	The Union Defence Force (South Africa)
U.K.	. . .	The United Kingdom

U.S. or U.S.A.	The United States of America
U.S.A.A.F.	The United States Army Air Force
U.S.S.R.	The Union of Socialist Soviet Republics
V.A.D.	Voluntary Aid Detachment of the B.R.C.S.
V.C.O.	Viceroy's Commissioned Officer (Indian Army)
V.D.	Venereal Disease
V.D.T.C.	Venereal Diseases Treatment Centre
Vol.	Volunteer
W.	Wounded
W.A.A.F.	The Women's Auxiliary Air Force
W.D.	War Department
W.D.F.	The Western Desert Force
W.E.	War Establishment
West Yorks.	The West Yorkshire Regiment (The Prince of Wales' Own)
W.G.	The Welsh Guards
Worcesters	The Worcestershire Regiment
W.O.	Warrant Officer
W.O.S.B.	War Office Selection Board
W/T	Wireless Telegraphy
W.W.C.P.	Walking Wounded Collecting Post
Y. & L. or York and Lancaster	The York and Lancaster Regiment

BIBLIOGRAPHY

PUBLISHED SOURCES

Despatches

ALEXANDER, Field Marshal the Viscount, of Tunis. *The African Campaign from El Alamein to Tunis, from August 10, 1942, to May 13, 1943.* 1948. H.M.S.O.

ANDERSON, Lieut. General K. A. N. *Operations in North West Africa from November 8, 1942, to May 13, 1943.* 1948. H.M.S.O.

MALTBY, Major General C. M. *Operations in Hong Kong from 8th to 25th December, 1941.* 1948. H.M.S.O.

PERCIVAL, Lieut. General A. E. *Operations of Malaya Command. December 8, 1941–February 15, 1942.* 1948. H.M.S.O.

Books

BRADON, RUSSELL. *The Naked Island.* 1952. Werner Laurie.

BRADLEY, General OMAR N. *A Soldier's Story.* 1951. Eyre & Spottiswoode.

BRETT-JAMES, A. *Ball of Fire.* (*5th Indian Division in the Second World War*). 1951. Gale and Polden.

CHURCHILL, WINSTON S. *The Second World War.* Vol. 3. 1950. Cassell.

—— Ibid., Vol. 4. 1951. Cassell.

CLARK, General MARK. *Calculated Risk.* 1951. Harrap.

CLAY, E. W. *The Path of the 50th.* 1950. Gale and Polden.

COAST, JOHN. *Railroad of Death.* Commodore Press.

COPE, V. ZACHARY. *Medicine and Pathology* and *Surgery*, the two clinical volumes of the Official Medical History. 1952 and 1953. H.M.S.O.

CUNNINGHAM, Admiral Viscount, of Hyndhope. *A Sailor's Odyssey.* 1951. Hutchinson.

DE GUINGAND, Major General Sir FRANCIS. *Operation Victory.* 1947. Hodder and Stoughton.

EISENHOWER, General DWIGHT D. *Crusade in Europe.* 1948. Heinemann.

FERGUSON, B. *The Black Watch and the King's Enemies.* 1950. Collins.

J. A. R. *Memoirs of an Army Surgeon.* 1948. Blackwood.

JEFFREY, BETTY. *White Coolies.* 1954. Angus and Robertson.

KIPPENBERGER, Major General Sir HOWARD. *Infantry Brigadier.* 1949. O.U.P.

LINKLATER, ERIC. *The Northern Garrisons.* (M.O.I.). 1941. H.M.S.O.

MACKENZIE, COMPTON. *Eastern Epic. The Indian Army in the Second World War.* Vol. 1. 1951. Chatto and Windus.

McKINNEY, J. B. *Medical Units of 2 N.Z.E.F. in the Middle East and Italy.* 1952. War History Branch, Department of Internal Affairs, Wellington, New Zealand.

MARAVIGNA, General PIETRO. *Come abbiamo perduto la guerra in Africa.* 1949. Tosi, Rome.

MONTGOMERY, Field Marshal Viscount, of Alamein. *El Alamein to the River Sangro.* Hutchinson.

MOOREHEAD, A. *African Trilogy.* 1944. Hamish Hamilton.

PENIAKOFF, Lieut. Colonel VLADIMIR. *Private Army.* 1950. Jonathan Cape.

RAINIER, P. *Pipeline to Battle.* 1944. Heinemann.
RICHARDS, DENIS and SAUNDERS, H. St. G. Royal Air Force, 1939–45. Vol. 2. *The Fight Avails.* 1954. H.M.S.O.
RIVETT, ROHAN D. *Behind Bamboo.* 1946. Angus and Robertson.
ROMMEL, Field Marshal ERWIN. *Krieg ohne Hass.* 1950. Verlag Heidenheimer Zeitung.
SAUNDERS, H. St. G. *The Green Beret. The Story of the Commandos.* 1949. Michael Joseph.
—— *The Red Beret. The Story of the Parachute Regiment* 1940–45. 1950. Michael Joseph.
SALMOND, J. B. *The History of the 51st Highland Division* 1939–45. 1953. Blackwood & Son.
SCHMIDT, H. W. *With Rommel in the Desert.* 1951. Harrap.
SHAW, W. B. KENNEDY. *The Long Range Desert Groups.* 1945. Collins.
STACEY, Colonel C. P. *The Canadian Army* 1939–45. 1948. Kings Printer. Ottawa.
The Eighth Army (M.O.I.) 1944. H.M.S.O.
The Tiger Kills. (*4th and 5th Indian Divisions in North Africa*). 1944. H.M.S.O.
TUKER, Lieut. General Sir FRANCIS. *The Pattern of War.* 1948. Cassell.
WALKER, A. S. *Middle East and Far East.* Australia in the War of 1939–45. Medical Series. 1953. Australian War Memorial, Canberra.
WATTS, Lt. Col. J. C. *Surgeon at War.* 1955. Allen & Unwin.
WILSON, Field Marshal Lord, of Libya. *Eight Years Overseas.* 1950. Hutchinson.
YOUNG, DESMOND. *Rommel.* 1950. Collins.
A wide variety of papers published in the different medical journals, including *The Journal of the Royal Army Medical Corps.*

UNPUBLISHED SOURCES

War Diaries, Quarterly Reports and Other Official Documents.
Letters from officers of the Army Medical Services.
Provisional Narratives prepared by the Historical Section of the Cabinet Office.
Provisional Narratives prepared by the Australian, Canadian, Indian and New Zealand Official Medical Historians.

PREFACE

THIS VOLUME contains the narratives of (1) the defence and fall of Hong Kong, (2) the campaign in Malaya and the fall of Singapore, (3) the military occupation of Iceland and the Faroes, (4) the final phase of the campaign in Libya from the battle of Alamein to the passage of Eighth Army into Tunisia, and (5) the campaign in North-west Africa. It includes also sections that deal respectively with the health of the troops of Middle East Force 1942–43 and with the Army Psychiatric Service in the same force during 1940–43.

Though the Japanese invasion of Burma occurred during the war years covered by this volume, the narrative of this episode is not presented herein but is reserved for a later volume that will concern itself with the whole of the campaign in the Far East. The capitulations in Hong Kong and in Singapore marked the end of military operations in these theatres. These places were reoccupied without opposition following the surrender of Japan in 1945. The expulsion of the British-Indian force from Burma by the Japanese in 1942, on the other hand, was but the opening phase of a continuing campaign that, much later, ended in the complete defeat of the Japanese occupying force.

The complete lack of the normal source material, the official quarterly report and war diary, threatened to make the construction of the narratives of Hong Kong and Singapore impossible. This lack was more than made good, however. The writing of these narratives has been associated with the growth, in the mind of the writer, of admiration and respect for those members of the Army Medical Services who, during the long years of captivity, filled with suffering and humiliation, maintained chronicles of the events in which they themselves were participants, chronicles that are truly remarkable for their calm objectivity.

Nothing can be more impressive and more indicative of the nobility that lies within the grasp of man than documents such as these, the products of a sense of duty that overrides all considerations of self, written and maintained in circumstances designed to degrade and decivilise, hidden away and ultimately smuggled out of an abyss of despair to be presented to higher authority. Equally impressive has been the willingness of others to help by probing deeply into their painful memories in order that details enmeshed in uncertainty and obscurity might be checked.

Representative of the many to whom unrestrained gratitude is due are Colonel J. T. Simson, who served as A.D.M.S. China Command,

xxxiii

Lieut. Colonels C. O. Shackleton and Donald Bowie who, in succession, commanded the Bowen Road Military Hospital, and who helped greatly in the construction of the Hong Kong narrative, Lieut. Colonel S. W. Harris, O.B.E., R.A., who commanded 'F' Force, Colonel J. Huston, R.A.M.C., who was the S.M.O. of 'F' Force during the building of the Thailand-Burma railway, and Major Bruce Hunt, A.A.M.C., who was the medical specialist A.I.F. Malaya and commanded the Tanbaya P.o.W. hospital.

The account of the medical aspects of the occupation of Iceland owes much to a thesis presented for the degree of M.D. London by Colonel D. P. Holmes, who served as D.A.D.H. 'Alabaster' Force. To him grateful acknowledgement is made for his permission, readily given, to make use of this thesis.

In Libya in 1942 the Army Medical Services pursued a very rapid development. By this time they had attained a total size that was more or less commensurate with their immediate commitments and were now able to focus their main attention upon the achievement of an internal structure that would ensure that all relevant medical knowledge and skill could be made available when and where these were most needed. Growth now became succeeded by differentiation.

The mechanisation of the armies that fought in the Desert and the almost uninterrupted emptiness of the Desert itself evoked the elaboration of new tactics and imposed upon the Army Medical Services the necessity of devising new methods of utilising medical personnel and units in order to overcome the difficulties created by the great distances between the different links in the evacuation chain. Indeed the conditions and circumstances were such as to demand considerable refashioning of existing medical units and the creation of new ones. This mechanisation and the continuous introduction of new weapons created new medical problems. They were responsible for a disturbing rise in the incidence of accidental injury. As a cause of man-power wastage injuries not due to enemy action came to overtop wounds received in battle. The appearance in quantity of new therapeutic agents made possible certain theoretically desirable modifications of surgical and medical procedures.

New tactics and new medicaments create new needs and new opportunities and these in their turn are the agencies that mould medical policy and shape the instruments by means of which this policy is implemented. Much that was new came out of Libya, for the campaign lasted long enough for needs to be recognised and also to be satisfied.

During the course of the campaign in North-west Africa there was no comparable development. But it was in this campaign that the Army Medical Services cultivated and tested the skills that are exercised in the planning of a large scale assault landing and learnt the delicate and difficult business of working in close, warm and effective harmony with those of the other components of a large multi-national force. It was in Tunisia too that new measures for the control of malaria in the field were first tested on a large scale. The events recorded in this volume were pregnant with the promise of ultimate victory over the Germans and over the mosquito.

These campaigns saw the aeroplane, used as an instrument of evacuation, challenge the ambulance car (for long distance work), the ambulance train and the hospital ship. Its advantages were shown to be such that its increasing use had profound effects upon medical policy and created the need for new medical units. It also demanded the establishment of new working arrangements between the medical services of the Army and the Royal Air Force.

Heretofore the transport and the personnel to manage it had been supplied to the Army Medical Services by the R.A.S.C. (the field ambulance and the motor ambulance convoy), by G.H.Q. (ambulance train) or by the Sea Transport Department (hospital ship). But no matter what the transport was or who provided it, the casualties being transported remained at all times in the professional care of the Army Medical Services. But the arrangements made between the Army and the Air Force involved a division of this responsibility. The Army collected its casualties and delivered them to the airfield where they passed into the care of the medical services of the R.A.F. Only when they were deplaned at the end of their journey did they once again become a responsibility of the Army Medical Services. To many, both at this time and later, this development seemed to be uneconomical. It was inevitable that at the end of the war serious consideration should be given to the question of the possibility and the desirability of creating out of the three discrete medical services of the armed forces one single integrated service to satisfy the medical needs of all.

The preparation of the narrative of the campaign in North-west Africa was an introduction to novelty in so far as the writer is concerned. Operation 'Torch' was an enterprise undertaken conjointly by the United States and the British Governments and Staffs. A.F.H.Q. was a multi-national organisation, as was also its medical branch. Though each of the United States and British components of the invading force had its own medical service, administratively distinct and separate, the senior administrative medical officer in North-west Africa was the Surgeon (= D.M.S.) A.F.H.Q. He and his staff dealt with the affairs at G.H.Q. level of both United States and British Army Medical Services. The records maintained by the medical branch of A.F.H.Q. are not in the possession of the Army Medical Directorate of the War Office. It is fortunate, therefore, that the Surgeon A.F.H.Q. happened to be a British officer, Major General Sir Ernest Cowell,

K.B.E., C.B., D.S.O. Most generously he made available from his great store of memories a very great deal of precise information relating to the campaign as a whole. But this narrative does not attempt to deal with the campaign at the level of D.M.S., A.F.H.Q.; it is primarily concerned with the affairs of the medical services of First Army and refers to those of the United States and French Army Medical Services only in those instances in which U.S. and French medical units came to be administratively under the control of D.D.M.S. First Army.

It would appear that in so far as First Army was concerned Operation 'Torch' was regarded as, and indeed was, a highly hazardous enterprise. For the first two months or so of the campaign the outcome remained distinctly uncertain. It has to be assumed that in the circumstances that then obtained it was accepted that the major preoccupation of the Army Medical Services was the overcoming of the many serious impediments to the provision of adequate medical cover and that therefore there were far more urgent and important things to do than the writing of quarterly reports and the like. Be this as it may, they certainly are not to be found. Fortunately, the war diary maintained by D.D.M.S. First Army and his report on the campaign were available and several of the senior administrative medical officers who served with First Army, e.g. as D.D.M.S. V Corps and A.D.M.S. First Army, were able and willing to read the provisional narrative and remove from it some of its major flaws.

To the preparation of these narratives Mr. J. Basset Scott and Major General Sir Treffry O. Thompson made considerable contributions, the former to their earliest the latter to their penultimate forms. Full use has been made of the provisional narratives received from the Australian, Indian and New Zealand medical historians.

The Middle East was a theatre of war differing markedly in respect of its physico-climatic features from all the others. For this reason it is thought appropriate to present a comprehensive review of the health of Middle East Command. The chapter dealing with this topic is an adaptation of a paper on *The Health of the Middle East Forces*, 1942–43, by Colonel A. E. Richmond and Lieut. Colonel H. S. Gear, who served as D.D.H. and A.D.H. respectively in M.E.C., which appeared in the *Journal of the R.A.M.C.* in 1945. Their account, comprehensive and authoritative, provided an excellent picture of the interests and activities of the hygiene section of the medical branch of a G.H.Q. during the War of 1939–45. Acknowledgement is made to the authors and to the editor of the Journal for permission to make use of the paper.

There is reason to entertain the view that of all the branches of military medicine none developed more rapidly or further during the war years than did psychiatry. It was in the Middle East that the earliest phases of this development occurred. A comprehensive account of the

Army Psychiatric Service in M.E.F. is therefore given. The substance of the chapter on the Army Psychiatric Service in the Middle East was provided by Brigadier G. W. B. James who, during this period, served as Consulting Psychiatrist at Medical H.Q., M.E.F.

During the preparation of this volume great help has been received from the members of the staffs of the Historical Section of the Cabinet Office, of the Army Medical Directorate and of the Editor-in-Chief.

For the assistance, the advice and the criticism that have been given so generously the writer is indeed grateful. It is but fair, however, to make it clear that he alone is responsible for the decision as to whether or not that which was offered was accepted or disregarded, for the selection of the material and for such opinions as are expressed.

Edinburgh   F. A. E. C.
1954

CHAPTER 1

THE DEFENCE AND FALL OF HONG KONG

December 7 – 25, 1941

Précis

ON DECEMBER 8, 1941,* Japan abruptly entered the war. Her troops landed on the eastern Malayan coast and also invaded Hong Kong and her air force struck at Pearl Harbour, at the Philippines and at Hong Kong. The British Government and the Netherlands Government promptly declared war upon Japan, as did that of the United States of America. On December 11, Germany declared war upon the United States and so the war, extending, claimed its title of the Second World War.

The British Crown Colony of Hong Kong consisted of the island of Hong Kong, the Kowloon Peninsula on the mainland and Stonecutter's Island and the New Territories, the borders of which marched with that of the Chinese province of Kwantung. Canton, in this province and close to the border, had been occupied by the Japanese in 1938.

The garrison of Hong Kong, which included two British, two Canadian and two Indian battalions, was organised in two brigades, the Mainland and the Island Brigades. On the mainland the main defensive position was the Gin Drinkers Line running between the head of Gin Drinkers Bay and Tide Cove and thence to Port Shelter.

On December 8, Japanese columns crossed the Canton-New Territories border and the forward troops of Mainland Brigade, having carried out the pre-arranged demolitions, withdrew to the Gin Drinkers Line. It was expected that this line would be held for at least a week or ten days, but during the night of the 9th the Japanese captured the Shing Mun Redoubt and swiftly exploited their success. The decision was reached that Mainland Brigade should be withdrawn to Hong Kong island. This withdrawal was completed on December 13.

The garrison was now divided into East and West Brigades. During the next five days the Japanese guns on the mainland bombarded the gun positions and communications in the north-west sector of the

---

*The difference between local time and Greenwich mean time tends to confuse the day as well as the hour when Japan entered the war. Local time was 8 hours 30 minutes ahead of Greenwich mean time.

I

island. Batteries were put out of action, communications were cut and serious fires were started.

On the morning of December 18 the shelling grew ominously heavier while repeated air raids caused much havoc. Japanese troops in small boats crossed the narrow strait between Devil's Peak and the island, landed in the region of North Point, Taikoo and Aldrich Bay and overran the defences. By midnight the situation in the north-east sector was beyond control and the Japanese quickly infiltrated into the Tytam and the Wong Nei Chong Gaps, threatening to cut the island into two. East Brigade withdrew toward the Stanley Peninsula while West Brigade was slowly forced back toward the west. Attempts to reoccupy the Wong Nei Chong Gap were unsuccessful and by the morning of December 20 the situation had become desperate, for the Japanese had thrust between the East Brigade at Stanley and the rest of the island. By Christmas Day the garrison was exhausted after sixteen days of continuous fighting without relief. The ammunition for the few remaining guns was running out and the water supply was failing. At 1523 hours on Christmas Day the order to cease fire was issued and at 1800 hours the formal surrender of the garrison took place.

(i)
Preparations for War
STRATEGIC AND OTHER CONSIDERATIONS

From 1915 Japan had been pursuing an expansionist policy. In 1931 she occupied Manchuria; in 1937 the five northern provinces of China; in 1938 Canton. In 1941 she was still heavily involved in what she chose to call 'the China Incident'. She sought to establish a 'Greater East Asia Co-Prosperity Sphere' within which she herself would be the politically and commercially dominant power. She was far from being self-sufficient in respect of such commodities as oil, rubber, tin and bauxite. Having regard to her ambitions it was necessary for her to extend her dominion over Malaya, Borneo, Java and Sumatra. Since to do this by peaceful means seemed impossible, she had to plan on the assumption that the pursuit of her policy would, sooner or later, bring her into conflict with Great Britain and the Netherlands, possibly also with the United States of America.

In 1940 events in Europe favoured Japan. The collapse of France and the occupation of Holland by the Germans profoundly affected the possibilities of interference, should Japan make demands upon Indo-China and the Netherlands East Indies. Great Britain was exceedingly hard pressed and it could be expected that she would find it difficult to provide adequate protection for Hong Kong, Malaya and Burma.

Japan began to demand from the Vichy Government of France the right to establish airfields in Indo-China; from the N.E.I. special privileges in respect of supplies of oil, rubber and tin, and from Great Britain the closure of 'the Burma Road' along which supplies for China were passing. She entered into a tri-partite pact with Germany and Italy.

In an attempt to persuade Japan to bring 'the China Incident' to an end and to lighten her pressure upon Indo-China, the U.S.A., in October 1940, placed an embargo on all exports of iron and steel scrap to Japan.

In April 1941 Japan signed a neutrality pact with the U.S.S.R. This was interpreted as an attempt on her part to safeguard the north Manchurian border while she thrust to the south.

In a further attempt to dissuade Japan from continuing her expansionist adventures, the U.S.A., in July 1941, cut off all supplies of oil. The British and the Dutch Governments took similar action. As a result the whole of the Japanese economy was threatened with imminent collapse. Her government was called upon to make a most fateful decision, to seek a peaceful settlement or to have recourse to war. It chose war.

Suddenly, without any formal declaration of war, the poised forces of Japan struck. On December 7, at 1715 hours Greenwich mean time, a Japanese assault force began to land on the north Malayan shore; at 1825 hours Japanese aircraft from carriers attacked the U.S. Pacific fleet riding at anchor in Pearl Harbour; at 2100 and at 2330 hours respectively Japanese aircraft bombed the Philippines and Hong Kong.

Great Britain promptly declared war upon Japan. So also did the Dutch Government. On December 11 Germany declared war upon the U.S.A.

As the Japanese operations proceeded the strategic plan unfolded. It was to establish, with the utmost speed, a perimeter around the Japanese mainland and its satellites, running from the Kuriles through Wake Island, the Marshall and Gilbert Islands, the Bismarck Archipelago, New Guinea, Timor, Java, Sumatra and Malaya to Burma and the border of India. Included among these operations were:
1. The invasion of Hong Kong.
2. The occupation of Thailand as a stepping stone to Malaya and Burma.
3. The invasion of Malaya and British Borneo.
4. The invasion of Burma.
5. The occupation of the Andaman and Nicobar Islands.

Plans for the defence of Hong Kong had been prepared long before the war, based upon the assumption that the garrison would hold the invading force in check until relief came in the form of the fleet. But in

1941 circumstances were such that Hong Kong had to be regarded as a military liability, as an outpost to be held as long as possible. Adequate reinforcement of the garrison was as far beyond the powers of the British Commonwealth as was its relief.

THE BRITISH COLONY OF HONG KONG

This consisted of (1) the island of Hong Kong, formally ceded to Britain in 1842 by the Chinese Government of that day; (2) Stonecutter's Island and the Kowloon peninsula, ceded in 1860, and (3) the New Territories, held by Britain on a ninety-nine year lease obtained from the Imperial Chinese Government in 1898. The administration of the colony was vested in a governor who was assisted by an executive and a legislative council.

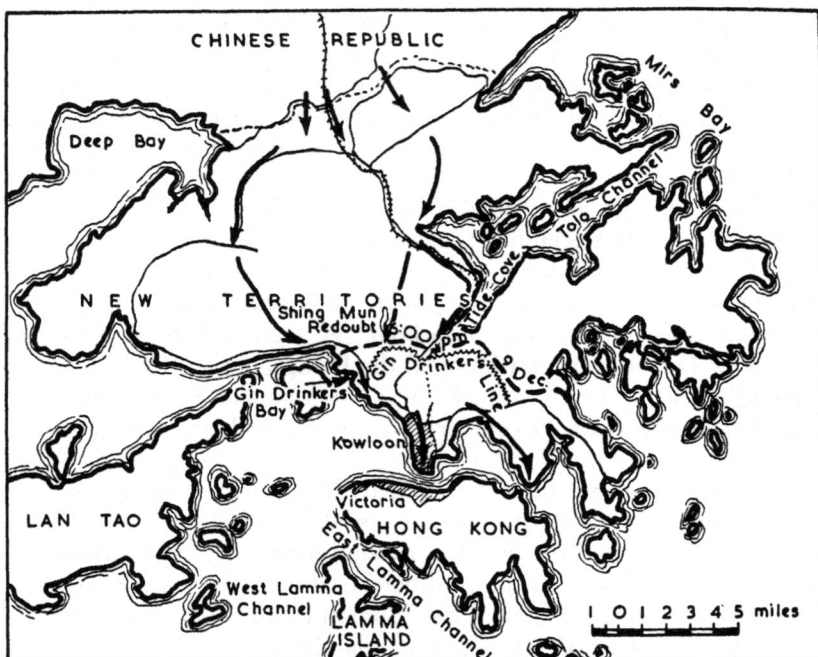

FIG. 1. The British Colony of Hong Kong. The paths of the Japanese invasion.

The area of the island of Hong Kong is about thirty-two square miles, that of the whole colony approximately four hundred square miles. The north-east end of the strait separating the island from the main-land—the Lye Mun Passage—is about a quarter of a mile across.

The mainland, except for a broad strip of swamp and irrigated land running south-west from the frontier, is mountainous and uncultivated, consisting of a series of steep grassy ridges strewn with granite boulders and intersected by scrub covered valleys. There were but two good roads, both starting at Fanling and running south to Kowloon, the eastern road by way of Taipo and the western one following the coastline. There were many mule tracks running through narrow mountain passes. All the approaches from the north were dominated by the high ground in the Golden Hill—Smugglers Ridge area.

The island, save for the coastal strip, consists of hilly country with heights ranging from five hundred to fifteen hundred feet and is divided into two almost equal parts, east and west, by the Wong Nei Chong Gap, through which runs a first-class road that connects the north and south parts of the island. In the north-west corner of the island lies the densely populated capital city, Victoria, sprawling along the coastal lowland and round the lower slopes of Victoria Peak (1,809 ft.). The population of the colony in December 1941 numbered more than 1,600,000, Chinese for the most part but with Indian, European and United States communities.

The hot weather extends for about seven months of the year. From May to October the temperature reaches 85–90° F, during December and January 60–75° F, although during these two months it can fall as low as 35° F. May to October is the rainy season.

Water was plentiful but usually was muddy and fouled. An elaborate system of storage reservoirs with catchment areas ensured an adequate water supply (under peace-time conditions). The reservoirs on which Victoria depended lay in the Tytam area, east of the Wong Nei Chong Gap. Outside Victoria and Kowloon the general level of sanitation was low and extensive soil pollution resulted in a high incidence of helminthiasis.

The malaria season extended from May to December with its peak in August, September and October. In the rural areas dysentery and diarrhoea were rife. Smallpox, cholera and the enteric group of fevers were endemic among the native population.

THE CIVIL MEDICAL SERVICES*

There was a Government Medical Department under a director of medical services with hospital, health and investigation divisions. Senior members of the staff of the medical school of Hong Kong University were associated with the department as consultants. In the investigation division were a bacteriological institute and a chemical analytical laboratory. In the hospital division were forty-two medical officers; in the health division twenty-four. In addition to the hospitals

*See *The Civilian Health and Medical Services.* Volume II. Chapter 3. Hong Kong.

of the department there were three Chinese hospitals and nine public
dispensary clinics. These were under the general direction of the
Director of Medical Services. There were also several missionary and
privately owned hospitals. In the Colony there were about three hundred
private practitioners, most of them Chinese. Altogether the D.M.S.
could call upon 2,939 general beds; 300 infectious diseases, 325 sick
children and 383 maternity beds.

In September 1939 the D.M.S. was appointed medical and sanitary
controller and established a close liaison with the military authorities.
He organised a civil medical service to cover the whole of the Colony
and recruiting for the St. John Ambulance Brigade and Ambulance
Nursing Division and for the Auxiliary Nursing Service became active.

THE GARRISON AND THE DEFENSIVE PLAN

The 1937 defensive plan was based on a chain of redoubts and fortified
positions on the mainland on a slightly convex line, about eleven miles
in length and some three miles distant from Kowloon, running between
the head of Gin Drinkers Bay in the west, north of Golden Hill, by
Smugglers Ridge to Tide Cove and thence southwards through the
hills to Port Shelter in the east. (*See* Fig. 1.) But this plan was abandoned
when the garrison became reduced in numbers. The new plan involved
a delaying action on the mainland while the necessary demolitions in
Kowloon were carried out and then a withdrawal to the island.

The garrison in September 1939 consisted of:

2nd Royal Scots
1st Middlesex Regt. (machine-gun battalion)
5/7th Rajput Regt.
2/14th Punjab Regt.

In 1941, in response to a request by the British Government, the
Canadian Government agreed to send to Hong Kong a brigade headquarters and two infantry battalions. On November 16, 1941, these
arrived:

The Winnipeg Grenadiers
The Royal Rifles of Canada

Unfortunately the carriers and lorries of this force were not shipped
with the troops. They sailed at a later date and the outbreak of war
prevented them from reaching Hong Kong.

With the arrival of the Canadians it became possible to revert to the
1937 defensive plan. The garrison consisted of the British, Canadian
and Indian units and detachments together with the Hong Kong
Volunteer Defence Corps (H.K.V.D.C.) and 1st Hong Kong Regt.

of the Hong Kong and Singapore Royal Artillery.* Out of the locally enlisted personnel artillery, engineer, signals, ordnance and other units had been formed. The garrison was grouped into two brigades. Its composition and strength are shown below:

CHINA COMMAND

Order of Battle. December 7, 1941. (abbreviated)
Mainland Brigade
2nd Royal Scots
5/7th Rajput Regt.
2/14th Punjab Regt.

Island Brigade
1st Middlesex Regt.
The Winnipeg Grenadiers
The Royal Rifles of Canada

Fortress Troops attached to Mainland Brigade
No. 1 Company Hong Kong Volunteer Defence Corps
Chinese (nucleus) Company
1st and 2nd Mountain Batteries, 1st Hong Kong Regt. (H.K.S.R.A.)
22nd Field Company, R.E.

Hong Kong Island
Nos. 2, 4, 6 and 7 Companies Hong Kong Volunteer Defence Corps
8th and 12th Coast Regiments R.A.
5th A.A. Regt., R.A.
3rd and 4th Medium Batteries, 1st Hong Kong Regt. (H.K.S.R.A.)
965th Defence Battery R.A.
40th Field Company R.E.

Stonecutter's Island
No. 3 Company Hong Kong Volunteer Defence Corps.

HONG KONG GARRISON STRENGTH†

		Strength	
	Officers	*O.Rs.*	
		British	*Indian*
H.Q. China Command . . .	33	—	—
H.Q. R.A.	6	—	—
8th Coast Regt. R.A. . . .	19	285	233
12th Coast Regt. R.A. . . .	16	200	187
5th A.A. Regt. R.A. . . .	23	231	332
1st Hong Kong Regt. H.K.S.R.A. .	24	30	830
965th Def. Bty. R.A. . . .	3	58	86
22nd Field Coy. R.E. . . .	7	213	—
40th Field Coy. R.E. . . .	7	220	—

*The H.K.S.R.A. was a unit raised to man the coastal batteries. The officers and many of the N.C.Os. were British; the remainder consisted of V.C.Os. and I.O.Rs. specially recruited. To bring the unit up to strength local Chinese were now enlisted.

†Despatch. C.O.C. B.T.C. *The London Gazette.* January 29, 1948.

	Officers	Strength O.Rs.	
		British	Indian
R.E. Services	18	54	—
2nd Royal Scots	35	734	—
1st Middlesex Regt. . . .	36	728	—
Canadian Staff	14	78	—
Winnipeg Grenadiers . . .	42	869	—
Royal Rifles of Canada . . .	41	963	—
5/7th Rajput Regt. . . .	17	—	875
2/14th Punjab Regt. . . .	15	—	932
R.C.S.	7	177	—
R.A.O.C.	15	117	—
R.A.S.C.	24	183	—
R.A.V.C.	2	3	—
A.D. Corps	4	6	—
R.A.M.C.	28	146	—
R.A.P.C.	5	25	—
Hong Kong Mule Corps . .	3	—	250
I.M.S.	5	—	—
H.K.V.D.C.	89	1,296	—
I.M.D. & I.H.C.	—	—	55
R.I.A.S.C.	—	—	13
Military Provost Staff Corps . .	—	3	—
C.M.P.	—	18	—
A.E.C.	—	8	—
	538	6,645	3,793

Other locally raised units brought the total strength of the garrison to about 14,500 of whom about 11,000 were combatants.

THE ARMY MEDICAL SERVICES, CHINA COMMAND

At Hong Kong, attached to H.Q. China Command, was an A.D.M.S. with his D.A.D.H. Under him were 10–12 officers R.A.M.C., 2 officers I.M.S. and from 8–12 nursing sisters Q.A.I.M.N.S. No. 27 Company R.A.M.C. had its headquarters in Hong Kong, where there was also a detachment of Indian medical orderlies. These formed the core of the staffs of two military hospitals, one British and one Indian.

The British Military Hospital (188 beds) was situated in Bowen Road, four hundred feet above sea level. The Indian Military Hospital (120 beds) was sited in Whitfield Barracks, Kowloon, on the mainland. It received, in addition to the Indian sick, such British patients as required segregation.

When, in the summer of 1940, the British troops in Shanghai, Tientsin and Pekin were withdrawn, the personnel of the British Military Hospitals in these places did not remain within China Command.

THE DEFENSIVE PLAN—MEDICAL ASPECTS

Since the defence scheme postulated that the garrison could expect no reinforcements and no replacements, the Army Medical Services were required out of their own limited resources, and making full use of local civil personnel and material, to provide (1) field medical units, (2) hospital accommodation sufficient to deal with the expected casualties, many of whom would have to be retained in hospital until hostilities ceased, and (3) an adequate quantity and variety of medical and hospital ordnance stores.

The Bowen Road Military Hospital was ill-suited for use in war. Standing four hundred feet above sea level on the north frontage of the island it was probably the most conspicuous landmark when the island was viewed from the mainland. Two roads led to it, Borrett Road, steep, ill-concealed and crossed by two bridges, both clearly visible from the mainland, and Bowen Road, suitable for light transport only. The hospital was a three-storied brick building with its operating theatre, X-ray department and kitchen on the upper floors. So vulnerable was the hospital to shell and bomb that strenuous efforts were made to obtain alternative accommodation. But these were unsuccessful and so it was reluctantly decided to carry out such structural alterations in the Bowen Road building as could be completed within a reasonable time. These, thanks to the energy and persistence of the officer commanding the hospital, were effected in good time and must have been the means of saving many lives. An underground operating theatre and X-ray annexe, a large underground shelter for walking wounded, a decontamination centre, a gas-proof ward and a system of alternative lighting were all constructed or installed. The accommodation was expanded to 400 beds and the hospital was earmarked for the reception of the more serious casualties.

For the reception of the less serious casualties and for the sick, St. Albert's Convent in Stubbs Road overlooking Happy Valley was selected as a suitable building to accommodate 400 beds. This stout building was also situated on the north frontage of the island, about two miles to the east of the Bowen Road B.M.H., and, like this, was a most obvious landmark from the mainland. However, this was almost equally true of every large building in the island.

The accommodation of the I.M.H. in Kowloon was quite unsuitable for use in war and so for it an alternative site had to be found. The D.M.S. of the Government Medical Department put at the Army's disposal the Tung Wah Eastern Hospital (300 beds) situated at Sookunpoo near Causeway Bay in the north-east sector of the island.

Additional accommodation, kept in reserve, in St. Stephen's College at the base of Stanley Peninsula (400 beds), in the Hong Kong Hotel, Victoria (200 beds), in Mount Austin Barracks, and in the Gethsemane and Nazareth Buildings between Aberdeen and Pokfulam, was also earmarked.

Scattered throughout the island were many civil hospitals, some permanent, some temporary, so that hospital beds were plentiful. But the difficulty that was foreseen was that owing to the very restricted area over which the fighting would take place, any of these could find itself engulfed in the vortex of battle.

A full year's normal peace-time supply of medical stores was held as a war-time issue. A mission school at Shaukiwan, in the north-east sector of the island half a mile from the sea front, was taken over as a medical store. Equipment required for hospital expansion was stored at Bowen Road and in St. Albert's Convent.

In the early summer of 1941, 6 officers R.A.M.C., 2 officers I.M.S., 6 sisters Q.A.I.M.N.S. and drafts of O.Rs. R.A.M.C. and of Indian medical orderlies reached Hong Kong. The strength of No. 27 Coy. R.A.M.C. was thus raised to 163.

With the Canadian 'C' Force there came to Hong Kong the R.M.Os. of the Winnipeg Grenadiers and of the Royal Rifles of Canada, two other R.C.A.M.C. officers, two nursing sisters (lieutenants R.C.A.M.C.) and two officers and five O.Rs. of the Canadian Dental Corps. On arrival on November 16, 1941, it was discovered that somewhere along the channel of communication Hong Kong—London—Ottawa a misunderstanding had arisen. The medical authorities in Hong Kong had suggested that a number of male N.Os. should accompany the Canadian Force, but these, as a result of misinterpretation or misunderstanding, had been transformed into two medical officers and two nursing sisters. Three of the R.C.A.M.C. officers were posted to the H.K. Field Ambulance, one to become second in command of the unit, one to serve in the medical aid post of the company in the area to be occupied by the Royal Rifles and one in that in the area of the Grenadiers. The fourth and the two nursing sisters were posted to the Bowen Road Military Hospital. The regimental S.Bs. began to accustom themselves to the novel terrain and thereafter were distributed among the Medical Aid Posts (M.A.Ps.) in the areas which contained the largest concentration of Canadian troops.

Valuable as these reinforcements were, the medical component of the garrison still remained far too small to provide more than a nucleus of the staffs of the many medical units that would be required in the event of war. Consequently, during the summer of 1941 the following arrangements were made:

Volunteers were called for from among the civil medical practitioners, British and Chinese, and from among the staff of the medical school. The response was immediate and most satisfactory. These medical men were allocated to one or other of the 'shadow' hospitals or else given temporary commissions in the medical section of the H.K.V.D.C. in which they underwent military training. They assisted in the instruction given to the V.A.Ds. and locally recruited orderlies.

A small V.A.D. had existed in Hong Kong for about five years prior to 1941. Active recruitment quickly brought its members up to about 120 and the majority of these agreed to serve through any crisis that might occur. Classes of instruction were organised, and by the end of the year there was a full complement of young women capable of acting as assistant nurses.

The officer commanding the medical section of the H.K.V.D.C. undertook to recruit and train a number of locally enlisted young men sufficient to complete the staffs of the medical units. A proportion of these volunteers were medical students.

A modified field ambulance consisting of a H.Q. and four companies was formed out of the medical section of the H.K.V.D.C. Its headquarters was to be in a house in Shui Fai Terrace, off Stubbs Road and near St. Albert's Convent. Of its companies one was to be attached to Mainland Bde., the other three to Island Bde. Each company was to be divided into three sections, each of which would serve one of the battalions of the brigade to which the company was attached. Motor ambulances would be attached to each section, while at H.Q. a pool of motor ambulances would be maintained. In the building occupied by the Indian Military Hospital in Kowloon, which would be vacated when hostilities commenced, an A.D.S. would be established. Evacuation from the mainland would be by ferry to the island, either to the B.M.H. at Bowen Road or to the I.M.H. in its new location in the Tung Wah Eastern Hospital near Causeway Bay. On the island No. 1 Company would have its H.Q. at Wanchai Gap to serve the east sector, No. 2 at Wong Nei Chong Gap (central) and No. 3 at Tytam Gap (west).

Since on the island the troops were to be deployed in numerous pillboxes and strong points it was arranged to provide a number of medical aid posts or collecting posts in the vicinities of the more important of these. Concrete casualty huts were constructed in relatively sheltered sites, as far as possible near to the roads leading to the hospitals. These shelters were not rifle proof but they gave some protection against blast and splinters and, what was not less important, protection against rain. It was hoped that it would be possible to evacuate casualties from these M.A.Ps., preferably by night, to whichever hospital was most accessible.

The field ambulance companies H.Qs. were linked by field telephone to Field Ambulance H.Q. When a loaded car left a M.A.P., H.Q. Field Ambulance would be notified by telephone and a replacement would then be sent to the M.A.P. An ambulance car, having delivered its patients to the hospital, would then join the ambulance car pool.

A hygiene section commanded by a British officer was also formed. Its headquarters was in the vicinity of H.Q. Field Ambulance near Stubbs Road.

4

Towards the end of 1941 field days were held during the weekends in order that those concerned might become familiar with the country in which they would have to operate.

(ii)
The Invasion

THE BATTLE ON THE MAINLAND

On December 7 information was received that Japanese troops were massing near the frontier. A state of emergency was declared, the regular troops moved to their war stations, the Canadian battalions left their barracks in Kowloon and crossed to the island and the local volunteers were mobilised.

In the mainland defensive position, from left to right, were 2nd Royal Scots, 2/14th Punjabis and 5/7th Rajputs. 1st Coy. H.K.V.D.C. was on the Kai Tak aerodrome and four troops of the H.K.S.R.A. were at the Filter Beds, Tai Wai, Custom's Pass and on the Kowloon Polo Ground.

Prior to moving into the Gin Drinkers Line the Royal Scots had been stationed in a highly malarious area and in consequence had suffered badly. At this time there were over a hundred of them in hospital or in a convalescent depot that had to be established for their benefit. Undoubtedly malaria had seriously sapped the efficiency of this battalion.

On the island the Royal Rifles manned the beach defences of the south-east sector, the Winnipeg Grenadiers those of the south-west and 1st Middlesex the machine-gun posts on the perimeter of the island.

On December 8 at 0800 hours (local time) Japanese aircraft attacked the Kai Tak airfield and destroyed or damaged all of the 5 R.A.F. and 8 civil aircraft grounded there. At the same time Japanese columns began to move towards the frontier and the pre-arranged demolitions north of Gin Drinkers Line were carried out and the covering force slowly withdrew, stubbornly resisting the Japanese advance. On the 9th the main defensive line was fully manned.

During the night of December 9–10 a platoon of the Royal Scots in the Shing Mun redoubt in the Gin Drinkers Line was overwhelmed and H.Q. 'A' Coy. 2nd Royal Scots and an artillery observation post nearby were overrun. The loss of this redoubt was fatal to any hope of prolonged defence of the Gin Drinkers Line. It was decided that in the circumstances that then existed there was no possibility of recapturing the redoubt by counter-attack. 'D' Coy. Winnipeg Grenadiers was sent from the island across to the Kowloon Polo Ground to form a reserve for Mainland Bde.

Then, on the morning of December 11, the left flank of the Royal Scots was assaulted and broken and the situation became critical. A complete break through was prevented by the stout resistance of a company of the Royal Scots and of the Rajputs.

It became necessary, however, to withdraw from the mainland. Under heavy and continuous pressure Mainland Bde. disengaged and was ferried across to the island. 5/7th Rajputs, less one company, withdrew by way of Devil's Peak peninsula and were withdrawn by motor torpedo boat and destroyer during the early morning of the 13th.

THE BATTLE ON THE MAINLAND—MEDICAL COVER

On December 7, when a state of emergency was declared, a beginning to the war-time expansion at the B.M.H. Bowen Road and St. Albert's Convent was made. The I.M.H. in Kowloon was cleared preparatory to its moving to the island and an A.D.S. was established in its place.

The mainland company of the field ambulance was deployed as follows:

H.Q. at the junction of Castle Peak–Taipo Road
1. Collecting Post (or M.A.P.) at Shing Mun redoubt in the rear of the Royal Scots
2. C.P. in the centre of Gin Drinkers Line in the rear of 2/14th Punjab Regt.
3. C.P. at Clear Water Bay in the rear of 5/7th Rajput Regt.

Casualties were evacuated from R.A.P. to C.P. to the A.D.S. at Kowloon, the bulk of the walking wounded making their own way back. The Star Ferry was running as usual and evacuation from Kowloon to the island proceeded smoothly. No trustworthy figure of the number of casualties evacuated from the mainland exists but it is known that the B.M.H. at Bowen Road admitted 163 wounded and sick up to and including December 13.

The policy now adopted was that Bowen Road should be reserved for surgical cases requiring operation, that St. Albert's Convent should deal with the less serious and less urgent surgical cases and ordinary sick, and that St. Stephen's College should function as a convalescent hospital, receiving cases from both Bowen Road and St. Albert's Convent. By the 14th the Indian Military Hospital was established at Tung Wah Eastern and was receiving patients.

From December 13 onwards the medical situation became increasingly difficult. The ability of the H.K. Fd. Amb. to carry out its essential rôle of evacuating the M.A.Ps. depended on the free movement of ambulance cars and on good telephone communications. But since moving transport invariably attracted enemy fire and aerial attack it soon became necessary to restrict the evacuation to the hours of darkness. Moreover, the roads quickly became cratered by artillery fire and bombardment from the air so that movement by night became as hazardous as evacuation by day.

When the 5/7th Rajputs were withdrawing from the Devil's Peak peninsula on the mainland after the rest of the Mainland Bde. had already been withdrawn to Hong Kong island, a Canadian medical officer, two ambulance cars and a number of O.Rs. R.A.M.C. were sent to the Lye Mun pier on the night of December 12–13. The Rajputs got away without enduring casualties, however, so the R.C.A.M.C. officer returned to the M.A.P. at Lye Mun Barracks to which he had been first posted on the 10th. But by this time the area was being heavily shelled and the barracks had been vacated. He therefore moved to a civilian first-aid post in the vicinity of the Army Medical Store on the southern edge of Shaukiwan, to the west of the Lye Mun Barracks.

THE BATTLE ON THE ISLAND

At 0900 hours on December 13 a launch, carrying a staff officer bearing a summons to surrender, crossed the harbour. The summons was refused. As a consequence of this the Japanese bombardment of the island defences, which had opened on the 11th, increased as the day wore on and continued throughout the following day. Gun emplacements were destroyed, roads and bridges wrecked, water mains broken, sewers and drains blocked, communications cut and in the city uncontrollable fires broke out. In the confusion fifth columnists carried out their stealthy tasks.

General Maltby, though expecting the Japanese assault to be launched from the mainland, had to reckon with the possibility that this might be combined with an assault from the sea. He therefore was obliged so to dispose his force that the whole perimeter of the island was defended. The island was divided into two brigade commands, East and West. The inter-brigade boundary was a line running roughly north and south through the centre of the island.

East Brigade

5/7th Rajputs	.	North shore waterfront from Pak Sha Wan to Causeway Bay.
Royal Rifles	.	Southern seaward defences from D'Aguilar Peak—Obelisk Hill—Stone Hill—Stanley Village. A reserve company covering the Lye Mun Gap.
H.K.V.D.C.	.	Two companies in reserve.

Two companies of 1st Middlesex were in the pillboxes from Saiwan Bay to West Bay.

West Brigade

| 2/14th Punjab Regt. | North shore waterfront from Causeway Bay to Belcher Point. |
| Winnipeg Grenadiers | Seaward defences of the south-west coast. One company in reserve at Wong Nei Chong Gap. |

1st Middlesex, less two companies, in the pillbox defences in the brigade area and in a defended locality on Leighton Hill.

Fortress Reserve

| 2nd Royal Scots | . | Wanchai Gap |
| H.K.V.D.C. | . . | Four companies. Near the Peak. |

1st Middlesex was directly under Fortress H.Q. for defence purposes but the detachments manning the pillboxes came under the operational command of the battalions in whose areas they were located.

At dawn on the 15th the Japanese began a systematic artillery and air bombardment, supplemented by mortar fire, which continued without abatement and with increasing intensity for the next four days. About 2100 hours they attempted to cross the Lye Mun passage, using rubber boats and rafts, and were sternly repulsed.

On the 17th a second summons to surrender was delivered and, like the first, was refused. It was noted that the Japanese were collecting barges and other craft in Kowloon Bay. By this time the defences on the north shore had become badly damaged by the constant bombardment.

On the 18th air raids increased in intensity. The oil tanks at North Point were set ablaze and great damage was caused in the centre of the city. In the late afternoon the bombardment shifted from Tytam Gap, Lye Mun Gap and Stanley Fort to the observation posts at Saiwan, which were shelled and bombed until destroyed. Just before dark the whole Lye Mun peninsula was drenched with artillery and mortar fire and a little later this was switched to Saiwan. Along the waterfront hung a heavy pall of smoke from the burning oil tanks and a paint factory. A burning rubber factory at Saiwan generated such heat that the nearby defences were threatened with disruption. At 2000 hours the Aldrich Bay defences were heavily shelled and from Taikoo docks ferry steamers towing small craft set out. The Japanese landed at Quarry Point, Braemar Point and at North Point. The resistance offered by the Rajputs did not check them for long and they quickly infiltrated towards Mt. Parker, Saiwan Hill, Lye Mun Gap, Mt. Butler and Jardine's Lookout. Saiwan Hill was lost but a Rajput detachment at Taikoo was not ejected until midnight when it withdrew to Sanatorium Gap between Mt. Butler and Mt. Parker. The reserve company of the Royal Rifles counter-attacked Saiwan Hill but was repulsed. When the commander of West Bde. heard of the landings he sent three platoons of the headquarters company of the Winnipeg Grenadiers forward from the Wong Nei Chong Gap, one towards Mt. Butler, another towards Jardine's Lookout and the third to the road junction near the Filter Beds. The first reached its objective but was forced back next morning; the second was forced to withdraw under heavy fire and the third secured and held the road junction throughout the night. He also ordered 'A' Company of the Grenadiers, which was holding the Brick Hill—Deep Water Bay area in the south, to counter-attack Jardine's Lookout and to advance towards Mt. Butler. At the same time General Maltby had taken steps to reinforce the troops in Wong Nei Chong Gap. A party of 70 British and 70 Chinese engineers was organised for use in this area and a company of 2/14th Punjab Regt. was directed to occupy the Mound west of Jardine's Lookout. Two hundred naval ratings at Aberdeen were assembled and ordered to report to H.Q. West Brigade at the Gap. The lines of advance of the Japanese forces between December 18 and 25 are illustrated in Fig. 2.

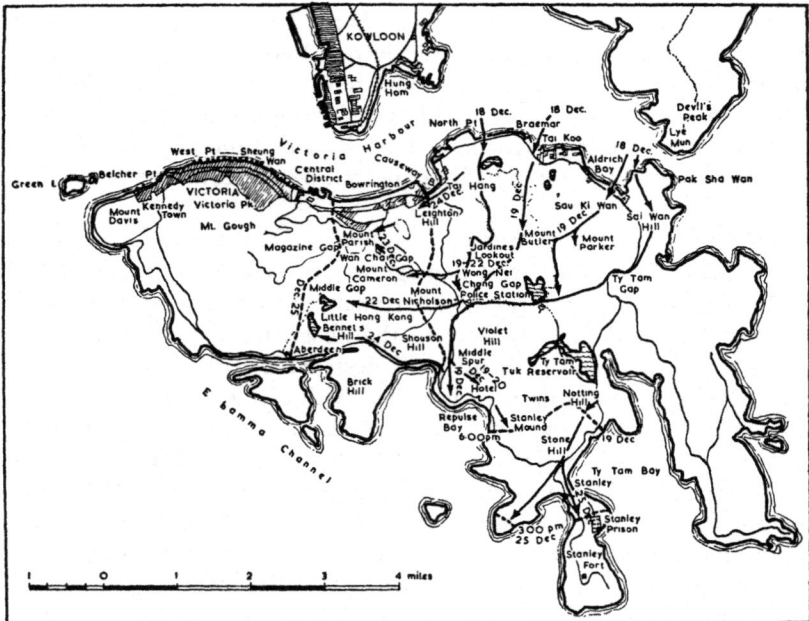

FIG. 2. Hong Kong Island. The paths of the Japanese invasion.

By dawn on the 19th the Japanese were in possession of Lye Mun Gap, Mt. Parker, Mt. Butler and Jardine's Lookout. The defence held Tytam Gap and a general line from Wong Nei Chong Gap to Causeway Bay. In East Bde's. sector the Royal Rifles, two companies of 1st

Middlesex and two companies of H.K.V.D.C. were in the vicinity of Tytam Gap. In West Bde's. sector a company of the Winnipeg Grenadiers (brigade reserve) held Wong Nei Chong Gap, a platoon of the Grenadiers was at the Filter Beds, the Mound was held by a company of the Punjabis and the survivors of the Rajputs and elements of 1st Middlesex occupied the line from Caroline Hill to the sea. Small bodies of troops were still holding out in isolated positions near the Power Station, Tai Hang Village and on the slopes of Jardine's Lookout.

It was decided that East Bde. must withdraw to the Stone Hill–Stanley Village area, there to reorganise preparatory to launching a properly mounted attack to retake Mt. Parker and Mt. Butler. During this withdrawal many of the guns of the brigade were lost.

The defences about North Point held out until the late afternoon of the 19th. The garrison of the Power Station continued to resist until the following day. It consisted of a small party of 1st Middlesex, all wounded, that had taken refuge there and the 'Hughsiliers', a detachment of the H.K.V.D.C. named after its commander, consisting of 4 officers and 66 O.Rs., including 2 officers and 6 O.Rs. of the Free French, all prominent business men and every one of them over 55 years of age. On the morning of the 19th the 'Hughsiliers' tried to cut their way through the ring of encircling Japanese but all were either killed or captured. The party of the Middlesex decided to stay where they were and fight it out. Ultimately they too were overwhelmed.

'A' Company of the Winnipeg Grenadiers which had been ordered to counter-attack Jardine's Lookout and to advance on Mt. Butler passed through Wong Nei Chong Gap just before dawn on the 19th. It won the crest of Mt. Butler and held it for several hours. But, suffering very heavy casualties, the company was forced off the hill, was surrounded and forced to surrender. Two platoons of the Grenadiers company in brigade reserve at Wong Nei Chong Gap were overwhelmed but the remainder of the company, holding a position immediately north-west of the Gap, withstood all attempts to eject them.

Fortress Command rushed up a company of Royal Scots with orders to counter-attack and secure the Gap. The company, suffering heavily, was repulsed. The naval party from Aberdeen moving towards the Gap was ambushed. At 1000 hours H.Q. West Bde. was overrun and the brigadier and most of his staff were killed.

General Maltby ordered two companies of the Punjabis from Victoria to advance eastward from Leighton Hill in order to enable the remnants of the Rajputs, fighting near Tai Hang Village, to disengage. He also ordered a general advance for 1500 hours ·by the Royal Scots and the Winnipeg Grenadiers. The first objective was to be the line Middle Spur—the reservoir east of Wong Nei Chong Gap—Sir Cecil's Ride—joining up with the two companies of the Punjabis who were to press on towards North Point. The Grenadiers were checked just short of the Police Station at the Gap. The Royal Scots, advancing north and south of Mt. Nicholson, were met with devastating fire and could make no headway. The Punjabis became involved in confused fighting about Tai Hang Village and were forced back. They were withdrawn into reserve at Victoria. The 19th ended with the Japanese in possession of Jardine's Lookout and astride the road at the Police Station in the Wong Nei Chong Gap. The defenders held the eastern slopes of Mt. Nicholson and the main road immediately north and south of the Gap with the Grenadiers and Royal Scots. Further north a company of · Punjabis held the Mound and the remnants of the Rajputs and elements of the Middlesex were on Leighton Hill; machine-gun posts on the western side of Causeway Bay were still in action. Just before dusk a machine-gun platoon of the H.K.V.D.C. on the slopes of Jardine's Lookout was overwhelmed. During the night of the 19th–20th repeated attempts to recapture the Police Station failed.

At 0800 hours on December 20, East Bde. advanced along the main Repulse Bay road towards Wong Nei Chong Gap. By 1000 hours the Royal Rifles had reached the Repulse Bay Hotel where a number of women and children had taken refuge under the protection of a subaltern of the Middlesex and a mixed party of sailors, soldiers and airmen. The Canadians cleared the Japanese out of the out-buildings and garages of the hotel but, advancing, were checked by fire from the direction of Middle Spur and Violet Hill. Leaving a company at the Repulse Bay Hotel they withdrew to their former positions in the Stone Hill–Stanley Mound area.

'A' Company 2/14th Punjabis of West Bde. from Victoria, with a platoon of Winnipeg Grenadiers from Aberdeen Island and a party of naval ratings, attempted to clear the road from Aberdeen to Repulse Bay. They succeeded in organising a defensive position about Brick Hill, Bennet's Hill and the magazine at Little Hong Kong.

The Commandant of the H.K.V.D.C. was appointed to the command of West Bde. and ordered to drive the Japanese from Wong Nei Chong Gap and the high ground beyond.

About midday the Japanese attacked the Punjabis holding the Mound. The attack was repulsed but a company of the Royal Scots sent up to cover their right suffered heavy losses. The Winnipeg Grenadiers, moving to occupy a position astride Mt. Nicholson, came under very heavy fire from this hill and had to be withdrawn to Middle Gap.

On December 21, East Bde. attacked, intending to break through Tytam Gap with the Royal Rifles and strike at the Japanese flank and rear. The leading troops, however, were soon held up in the area of Red and Bridge Hills. But, by the afternoon, they had gained a footing on Bridge and Notting Hills and had reached the crossroads at the southern end of the reservoir. Here the advance was finally halted and the brigade, now consisting of three companies of Royal Rifles, two companies H.K.V.D.C. and a small detachment of 1st Middlesex, was forced to withdraw.

While this attack was in progress another attempt was made to reach Wong Nei Chong Gap by a party of about forty men—Canadians, Volunteers and coast defence gunners—from the Repulse Bay Hotel area. The party reached the hotel about 1700 hours. There the Volunteers were left and the company of the Royal Rifles already at the hotel added to the party which pushed on up the road. Almost at once it came under fire and two trucks and an ammunition truck were knocked out. But three trucks eventually reached the vicinity of the Gap and an attack was at once launched on the Police Station. This was unsuccessful and the party withdrew to the hotel.

In West Bde's. area the Grenadier company launched its attack on Wong Nei Chong Gap. Half the company quickly became casualties and the rest were forced to withdraw to Middle Gap and thence to Wanchai Gap. Meanwhile the left flank of the Royal Scots was forced back and the flank of the Punjabis on the Mound exposed. The Punjabis held on until the afternoon when they too were forced to retire to the Filter Beds. The line from Leighton Hill to the sea still held. The remnants of the Grenadiers were reorganised and sent to establish a position on Mt. Cameron which they held throughout the rest of the day. A detachment of the Middlesex on Brick Hill repulsed repeated Japanese attacks.

General Maltby ordered that a senior officer of the Punjabis be sent to take control in the Aberdeen area. The commanding officer elected to go himself. To the 2 officers and 25 O.Rs. of his battalion now remaining he added an equal number of naval ratings and with this small force he launched an attack on Point 143. This last attempt to break through to Repulse Bay failed; the Punjabis and the naval ratings suffered very heavy casualties.

The 22nd saw the end of the defence of the Repulse Bay Hotel. The women and children had to be abandoned as they were unfit to walk and no transport could get through to them. It was considered that the surest way to save their lives was for them to surrender. The garrison attempted to get away in small groups but very few of them reached Stanley peninsula. About 30 men held the hotel until the following night and then got away by boat. On reaching Telegraph Bay they found that the garrison had surrendered.

In East Bde's. sector three defensive zones were organised. In the afternoon the Japanese attacked and drove the H.K.V.D.C. off the crest of Stone Hill and the Royal Rifles off that of Stanley Mound.

In the west of the island at daybreak the Japanese were holding
Brick Hill and Point 143, Mt. Nicholson, the Mound and the Tai Hang
road to the sea at the east end of Causeway Bay. West Bde., with small
garrisons, held the machine-gun post between Brick Hill and Point 143
and Little Hong Kong. The remnants of the Grenadiers held Mt.
Cameron, the Royal Scots held Stubbs Road facing Middle Gap and the
northern slopes of Mt. Nicholson, the Punjabis, only 35 strong, held
the Filter Beds and two weak platoons of the Rajputs, with elements
of 1st Middlesex, from Leighton Hill to the western side of Causeway
Bay. A small detachment of the Grenadiers, the survivors of the
company which was in the Gap area when H.Q. West Bde. was overrun,
was still holding out though surrounded. Early on the 22nd, when only
37 men, all wounded, were left and when food, water and ammunition
were exhausted, the party was forced to surrender.

During the day air raids and mortar fire became increasingly heavy
and as darkness fell the Grenadiers on Mt. Cameron were subjected
to a heavy artillery barrage. At 2000 hours they were attacked by
Japanese infantry who forced them from the hill. The loss of Mt.
Cameron necessitated the withdrawal of the mixed detachment, 34
Winnipeg Grenadiers, 14 airmen, 10 sailors and 43 men of the Dockyard
Defence Corps, from Bennet's Hill.

In West Bde's. area at dawn on December 23 a detachment of
Royal Marines was sent forward from the dockyard and reached the
northern slopes of Mt. Cameron, there to make contact with the Royal
Scots who were still in position on Stubbs Road facing the north-
western slopes of Mt. Nicholson. Mt. Kellett, north of Aberdeen, was
occupied by a detachment of the Royal Engineers and two companies
of H.K.V.D.C. were near Magazine Gap in reserve. At 0900 hours the
Japanese attacked the Royal Scots and were repulsed. Later in the day
the Royal Scots were withdrawn to a line facing the north-western
slopes of Mt. Cameron covering Wanchai Gap and Stubbs Road where
they were in touch with the Punjabis at the south-western end of the
racecourse. By evening the remnants of the Grenadiers were in position
south of them covering the reservoirs between Wanchai Gap and
Bennet's Hill. The garrison at Little Hong Kong continued to hold
out so that it was still possible during the hours of darkness to draw
ammunition from the magazines there. The Rajputs at the southern
end of Leighton Hill beat off several attacks during the day but
ultimately were forced to retire to the northern and western edges
of the racecourse. The Middlesex, however, still clung to their
position on Leighton Hill though they were forced to yield a little
ground.

On December 24, in the east, the Royal Rifles were withdrawn into
reserve, being relieved by composite units under Middlesex and

Volunteer officers. At noon a Japanese attack on the right flank near the coast was repulsed, but the water mains had been fractured and the water tanks at Stanley hit, all reserve water had been lost and water shortage had become serious.

On the western side of the island at dawn on the 24th most of Mt. Cameron was in Japanese hands. The Royal Scots, now only 175 strong, held its north-western slopes and the Wanchai Gap. Artillery and mortar fire was incessant and low-level air attack continuous. A Japanese attack south of Wanchai Gap was repulsed by the Grenadiers. On Leighton Hill the Middlesex were shelled, mortared and bombed throughout the morning and at about 1530 hours they were attacked and forced back to a line from Mt. Parrish across the north-western corner of the racecourse and thence to the coast, which they held along with the Rajputs.

During the night of December 24–25 there was heavy fighting at Stanley and the Japanese succeeded in overrunning the forward positions and in penetrating deeply into the Stanley peninsula.

Early on Christmas Day a retired R.A. officer who had been employed as manager of the Kowloon dockyard and a British civilian who was a member of the Hong Kong Executive Council were sent by the Japanese, under a white flag, across to the British line and were taken to Fortress H.Q. They were sent to describe, from their own observation, the Japanese superiority in respect of numbers and armament and to convey the suggestion that further resistance could not be other than futile. The Defence Council decided to ignore this suggestion. But by about 1430 hours Mt. Parrish and Wanchai Gap were in Japanese hands and the positions near the north shore, under very heavy shellfire, were beginning to disintegrate. At 1515 hours General Maltby informed the Governor that in his opinion there was no possibility of further effective resistance and shortly afterwards the signal to cease fire and to surrender was issued. The formal ceremony of surrender, without conditions, took place at 1800 hours.

Being unsure of these events East Bde. fought on. A company of the Royal Rifles launched a counter-attack on the Japanese positions in the vicinity of Stanley prison at 1330 hours. The attack failed and the company was almost completely wiped out. Shortly afterwards a car displaying a white flag appeared from the Japanese lines. It carried two British officers bringing verbal orders from General Maltby for the force to surrender. The brigadier demanded confirmation in writing and sent his brigade major back in the car for it. At 0230 hours on the 26th the white flag was hoisted and in this fashion the campaign ended.

THE BATTLE ON THE ISLAND—MEDICAL ASPECTS

No full and completely accurate account of the affairs of the medical units during the battle on the island can be given. The records out of which such an account might have been compiled do not exist.

The field medical units were no less static than were those which, in other circumstances, would have been on the L. of C. or at the base. The Japanese advance surged over M.A.P. and hospital alike and the staffs withdrew while the way was still open or else were taken prisoner.

The M.A.P. at the Wong Nei Chong Gap, where the fiercest and longest sustained fighting took place, consisted of two concrete huts. In one of these were a R.A.M.C. officer, one sergeant and three privates R.A.M.C.; in the other were ten Chinese stretcher-bearers. The M.A.P. was surrounded by the Japanese, who failed to break down the doors. After twenty-four hours, however, the staff were forced to surrender. They were wearing distinguishing Red Cross badges. These were torn off. The Chinese S.Bs. were butchered to a man. The British personnel were beaten and tied up but managed to escape during the night and, with the exception of the officer who was never seen again, reached the Bowen Road B.M.H.

After the island had been cut into two by the advance of the Japanese, all casualties in the eastern section were evacuated from the M.A.Ps.

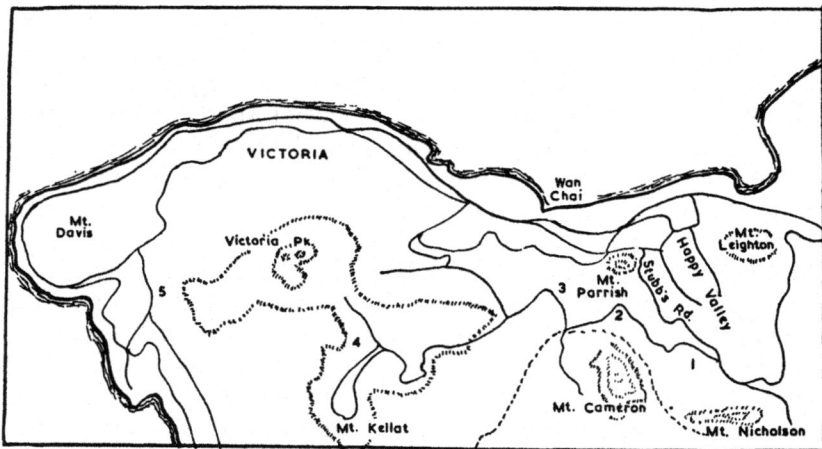

FIG. 3. The distribution of certain of the Medical Units on Hong Kong Island.

1. Hong Kong Field Ambulance, December 8–21.
2. St. Albert's Convent.
3. The Bowen Road British Military Hospital.
4. The War Memorial Hospital.
5. The Queen Mary Hospital.

to the hospital at St. Stephen's College. In the western sector H.Q. H.K. Fd. Amb. was obliged to move from Shui Fai Terrace, about three-quarters of a mile south-east of St. Albert's Convent, to the convent itself which was in the outskirts of Victoria and about halfway between Shui Fai Terrace and the Bowen Road Military Hospital, on December 21. On the following day it moved again, this time to the War Memorial Hospital under the west face of Mount Kellet, south-west of Victoria. As the western sector became increasingly contracted, casualties were evacuated to one or other of these hospitals or to the Bowen Road B.M.H. by whatever means could be devised. These arrangements continued until the final surrender. (*See* Fig. 3.)

During the night of December 18–19, following the landings on the island, the Japanese overran the Army Medical Store at Shaukiwan and the M.A.P. situated nearby. The staff of the store consisted solely of R.A.M.C. personnel, one W.O., 3 N.C.Os. and 6 privates. A Canadian medical officer and V.A.D. and A.N.S. personnel were at the M.A.P. The members of the staff of the medical store were forced to take off their boots and tunics and then, together with the nurses from the M.A.P., were marched away up the Island Road for some two hundred yards and then halted. While the nurses continued, the members of the staff of the store were taken for half a mile or so up a small path leading to the hills. Chinese civilians removed their rings and watches. The party was then marched to a small clearing and prodded into line with their backs towards their escort. There they were butchered with bayonet, sword and terminal revolver bullet. A corporal who had been struck on the back of the neck with a sword shammed dead and managed to roll down the slope into a nullah, along which he crawled in the direction of the medical store. Next morning he set off for Taikoo, which he reached, and hid in a deserted and looted house. Here he remained hidden until December 26. He had had only one pint of water and no food since the 19th. He had no alternative but to give himself up. He set off along Kings Road toward Causeway Bay and reached an internment camp at North Point, where interned medical and nursing personnel at once dressed his wounds. A Japanese officer gave him civilian clothes and a pass and sent him by car to the Queen Mary Hospital.

The Indian Military Hospital continued to function until December 20, when it was overrun. An Indian wing was thereupon opened in St. Albert's Convent and this continued to function until the capitulation.

The St. Stephen's College Hospital began to admit convalescent patients about December 20, first from Bowen Road B.M.H. and later from the Wong Nei Chong Gap, Tytam Gap and Shouson Hill areas direct. Many British and Chinese medical personnel made their way to St. Stephen's when their own units ceased to function. In order to relieve the growing congestion a number of the more serious cases were sent to the hospital at Stanley Prison, together with four medical officers and several orderlies.

On the evening of December 24, Canadian troops, withdrawing, set up machine-gun posts in the vicinity of the College, some actually on the verandah in front of the building. There was much firing all round the hospital through the night. Early on the following morning the troops withdrew, closely followed by the Japanese. The officer commanding the hospital and his second-in-command went forward to meet the Japanese. They were seized, made to take off their uniforms and marched away. Shortly afterwards shots were heard by those within the hospital. Subsequently the mutilated bodies of these two officers were found. The Japanese entered the hospital. All but one of the Chinese orderlies, who managed to escape, were butchered. Such patients as could not get out of their beds sufficiently quickly were bayoneted. The bodies of more than 60 patients and 25 orderlies were later collected for cremation.

THE BRITISH MILITARY HOSPITAL, BOWEN ROAD

The diary of the officer commanding the B.M.H. covering the period May 1940–June 1, 1942, which was begun in captivity on June 1, 1942, after all records had been destroyed deliberately by burning on December 25, 1941, and which was brought back to England by its author after remaining safely hidden until Hong Kong was reoccupied in 1945, gives a fairly clear picture of the work of the Army Medical Services during the battle.

When the personnel of the nursing detachment of the H.K.V.D.C. and the members of the St. John Ambulance Brigade had reported and had been despatched to their various stations, the staff of the Bowen Road B.M.H. consisted of:

13 Officers (9 R.A.M.C., 1 R.C.A.M.C., 2 H.K.V.D.C., 1 C.M.P.)
11 members of the Q.A.I.M.N.S./R. and T.A.N.S.
2 members of the Canadian Nursing Service
1 civilian
2 W.Os. and 29 O.Rs. R.A.M.C.

Three Japanese houses in Bowen Road, adjacent to the hospital, were taken over for the accommodation and messing of 60 members of the nursing detachment of the H.K.V.D.C. and two other Japanese houses in McDonnell Road were taken over for the accommodation and messing of the medical officers.

On December 9 one member of the Q.A.I.M.N.S. and three of the Q.A.I.M.N.S./R. were sent to St. Albert's Convent, the first to become acting matron of this hospital. On December 10 ordnance stores were sent to St. Albert's Convent and a beginning was made in the transformation of this place into a hospital.

On the 11th there was much shelling of the hospital area. One Chinese employee of the hospital was killed and several other Chinese employees were wounded, as was also a sergeant R.A.M.C. The company office, one of the wards and the sisters' quarters were hit. There were no casualties but a number of water pipes were burst.

On December 12 there was much dive-bombing and the road to the hospital was blocked by a large crater. It was now arranged that all nursing staff should sleep in the underground shelter. Drivers for motor vehicles were now becoming scarce and from this date onwards it was necessary to employ four to six O.Rs. R.A.M.C. for the drawing of rations, the conveyance of stores and the transport of patients. The ground floor of the hospital was now entirely reserved for the seriously ill and for such as were immobilised by surgical apparatus. All the windows on this floor on the harbour side were blocked up. The first floor was reserved for acute medical and walking wounded cases and, owing to the frequency of bombardment, it became necessary to retain such lying cases as could be moved continuously in the shelter throughout the day, taking them back to the wards only at night. The second floor was entirely evacuated. Twenty-nine O.Rs. R.A.M.C. proceeded to St. Albert's Convent for duty. Most of these had returned to the B.M.H. from the Indian Military Hospital at Kowloon.

On the 13th the commanding officer was instructed by H.Q. China Command to display more prominently the Red Cross emblem over the hospital. This was done, but it made no appreciable difference to the number of missiles landing in the vicinity of the hospital.

On the 14th the stores for St. Stephen's College were transferred and on the following day a small advance party proceeded to Stanley to begin the transformation of the College into a hospital. Upwards of 400 persons—patients, staff and Chinese servants—were now sleeping and spending some portion of the day underground.

On December 16 a Japanese plane made a direct hit upon the hospital kitchen and another upon the officers' mess in McDonnell Road. The sergeants' mess kitchen was enlarged in order to cook for approximately 500 persons. One of the nursing sisters Q.A.I.M.N.S./R. was killed by shellfire in the sisters' quarters of St. Albert's Convent and the acting matron was wounded. Eleven O.Rs. R.A.M.C. were despatched for duty at Stanley.

On the 17th 2 R.A.M.C. cooks were despatched to the headquarters of the field ambulance now at St. Stephen's College. Two large bombs were dropped on the Borrett Road producing a crater forty to fifty feet in circumference. That evening there was very heavy rain and an ambulance driver reported to the hospital that he had two seriously wounded patients in an ambulance which had become bogged at the bottom of Borrett Road. 20 S.Bs. proceeded to the place and attempted to carry these patients to the hospital, but owing to the steep gradient and the slippery mud found the task beyond their powers. The patients were taken to the Queen Mary Hospital. Early next morning a party from the hospital made the road passable for cars. This was the only occasion throughout the period of hostilities when the hospital was unable to take patients.

After December 17, owing to the almost constant artillery fire and dive-bombing, it was unsafe to permit patients in any wards except those on the ground floor, which were specially protected. Many British patients were transferred to St. Albert's Convent, the Queen Mary Hospital, Pokfulam, the University Hospital and the Royal Naval Hospital, Wanchai and many Indian patients to the Tung Wah Eastern Hospital at Sookunpoo. From December 17, therefore, the hospital ceased to function as a general hospital and became a C.C.S.

On December 18 the town electricity supply failed and from this date onwards the hospital emergency plant was used. Since its engine had to be rested for six to eight hours in every twenty-four the theatre staff was given time to relax and to restore order.

On December 19 the hospital was officially informed that the enemy had landed and that the hospital must be prepared for any eventuality. On this day the Army Medical Store at Shaukiwan was captured and the forts at Collinson and D'Aguilar were abandoned, the medical staffs of these two forts proceeding to Port Stanley. The A.D.S. at Tytam Gap and the C.P. at Windy Gap were also hurriedly evacuated. The staff of the former went to Stanley Fort, that of the latter to St. Stephen's College Hospital for duty. One hundred and forty-nine casualties were admitted to St. Stephen's Hospital from the Windy Gap–Tytam areas on this day. The officer commanding the Hong Kong Field Hygiene Section, together with 2 staff sergeants R.A.M.C. and 14 Chinese O.Rs. reported at the Bowen Road Hospital and were there accommodated.

On December 20 there were no less than 53 air raids and the town supply of water became so erratic that the hospital's own reservoir supply was taken into use for all purposes. Several O.Rs. R.A.M.C. from captured A.D.Ss. and C.Ps. and from abandoned ambulances and vehicles found their way to Bowen Road. These additions to the staff were most acceptable as practically all the Chinese employees had now left.

On the 21st a very ugly and awkward situation developed in the hospital. Numerous stragglers, both British and Indian, invaded the hospital in a state of complete exhaustion and demoralisation. After having been calmed and given food and drink they were conveyed to the H.Q. of the Middlesex Regt. As a result of this incident armed military police were posted for duty in the hospital.

From this time onwards, as the fighting grew nearer to the hospital, great difficulty was experienced in preventing violation of the Geneva Convention by units in the vicinity attempting to use the hospital telephone for tactical purposes.

By the 22nd the process of transferring patients was becoming increasingly difficult as road communications were extremely uncertain and most of the hospitals were filled to overflowing. As the Bowen Road Hospital was functioning as a C.C.S., so that the transfer of patients was essential to its successful working, it became imperative to find suitable and accessible additional hospital accommodation. The Hong Kong Hotel was taken over and sufficient bedding, equipment and stores to provide for 100 patients was supplied by the B.M.H. About midday the hospital at Stanley was hit, one shell landing in the operating theatre and killing a R.A.M.C. private. Another shell landed outside a ward, killing and wounding several of the patients who were being evacuated to another part of the building. The water supply failed.

On the 23rd St. Albert's Convent was becoming involved in the fighting. That day no telephonic communication was possible and after nightfall an attempt was made to send through a lorry load of rations, but without success. Between 50 and 60 patients were transferred from St. Stephen's Hospital to the hospital at Stanley Prison.

On December 24, 18 Chinese O.Rs. of the St. John Ambulance Brigade and the Hong Kong Field Hygiene Section donned civilian clothing and left the hospital. As reports were constantly coming in that Chinese personnel attached to British forces were receiving no consideration or protection from their Red Cross emblems, no attempt was made to oppose their leaving. By noon St. Stephen's Hospital was holding more than 400 patients. Its water supply was now exhausted, and, as no help could be given, the number of patients in the hospital was reduced to about 280, and the staff to about 60, by transfers to Stanley Fort and Stanley Prison. It was during the night of the 24th–25th that Canadian troops set up numerous machine-gun posts within the hospital grounds, one of these being located within six yards of the main hospital entrance and another quite close to the mast that carried the Red Cross flag.

On December 25, the final day of the battle, all available supplies, both public and private, of intoxicating liquors were destroyed. St. Stephen's College Hospital fell into the hands of the Japanese troops at dawn on Christmas Day. Reference has already been made to the shocking atrocities committed in this hospital, and among those killed were the officer commanding the hospital, a member of the medical section of the H.K.V.D.C., one officer and one sergeant R.A.M.C., three members of the nursing detachment of the H.K.V.D.C. and all the Chinese members of the St. John Ambulance Brigade.

During the 26th the Japanese made no appearance at the Bowen Road B.M.H., but on the morning of the 27th a Japanese officer accompanied by an officer of the H.K.V.D.C. (a P.o.W.) visited the hospital, asked no questions and gave no instructions. The staff began to clear the débris on the first and second floors and the wards were made habitable so that the pressure on the overcrowded ground floor and air-raid shelters was eased. The staff and patients of the Hong Kong Hotel Annexe were transferred to the B.M.H. At St. Stephen's Hospital water and food were running short but fresh supplies were sent from Stanley Fort on the following day. The evacuation of patients was commenced, British and Canadian being sent to Bowen Road B.M.H. and the Queen Mary, Indian to the Queen Mary, and all light cases being transferred to Stanley Fort.

On the 28th orders were issued by the Japanese military authorities through H.Q. China Command for all units to rendezvous at designated places. All R.A.M.C. personnel not on the strength of the B.M.H. were instructed to report at Bowen Road. Medical officers were detailed to take medical charge of troops that had been collected at various places. These medical officers later accompanied the troops under their care to the internment camps.

Up to the 29th very little restriction had been put upon the movements of such as wore the Red Cross emblem, so that the officer commanding the Bowen Road B.M.H. was able to visit all the hospitals in the Colony, collecting information regarding military wounded with a view to their ultimate transfer to Bowen Road. Lorries driven and manned by O.Rs. R.A.M.C. went out to the ration dumps, therefrom to bring back as much food as possible. This was permitted by the Japanese. Orders were received from H.Q. China Command that all R.A.M.C. and attached personnel surplus to the requirements of the B.M.H. were to go to the P.o.W. camp. Ten officers and 30 O.Rs. were instructed to do so.

On the 30th A.D.M.S. China Command and 2 O.Rs. R.A.M.C. from H.Q. China Command joined the hospital. Twelve O.Rs. R.A.M.C. reached the B.M.H. from Stanley Fort. These were originally members of the staff of St. Stephen's College Hospital. At Stanley Fort, looking after the wounded not yet fit for internment, were 2 officers and 12 O.Rs. R.A.M.C. and one officer A.D. Corps.

By the 31st no attempt had been made to take over or to interfere in any way with the administration of the B.M.H. at Bowen Road. There was still free movement between the various hospitals and consequently it was possible for the officer commanding to compile a list of the medical personnel known to have been killed during the fighting:

2 Officers R.A.M.C.
1 Officer of the medical section of the H.K.V.D.C.
1 member of the Q.A.I.M.N.S./R.
16 O.Rs. R.A.M.C.
3 V.A.Ds. (nursing detachment of the H.K.V.D.C.)

On the last day of the year the establishment of the B.M.H. Bowen Road consisted of:

A.D.M.S. China Command, attached
10 Officers (including 1 member of the H.K.V.D.C., 1 A.D. Corps and 1 C.M.P., together with a chaplain)
10 members of the nursing staff (2 Q.A.I.M.N.S., 5 Q.A.I.M.N.S./R., 2 R.C.A.M.C., 1 T.A.N.S.)
2 W.Os., 58 N.C.Os., and O.Rs. R.A.M.C.
35 members of the nursing detachment of the H.K.V.D.C.
6 senior O.Rs. of the R.E.
1 private of the Royal Scots (batman to the chaplain)

The distribution of the 163 O.Rs. of No. 27 Company R.A.M.C. was as follows:

At the B.M.H. Bowen Road	60
Hong Kong Hotel Annexe	11
Stanley Fort	12
Tung Wah Eastern I.M.H.	6
St. Albert's Convent	27
P.o.W. camps	29
Wounded and in hospital	2
Killed	16

The Japanese issued orders to the effect that all the hospitals that had been taken over by the Army were to be evacuated. The time-table was to be as follows:

January 18, 1942. *Royal Naval Hospital*: The P.M.O., nursing staff and patients to the B.M.H., Bowen Road. The rest of the staff to St. Albert's Convent Hospital. All patients fit for discharge to be sent to the North Point P.o.W. Camp.
January 22. *St. Stephen's College Hospital*: Patients to the B.M.H.
February 26. *St. Albert's Convent Hospital*: Part of staff to St. Theresa's Hospital in Kowloon to serve P.o.W. Camp. Patients to the B.M.H.
August 11. St. *Theresa's Hospital*: Patients to B.M.H.

Thus the B.M.H., Bowen Road became the only hospital admitting Service patients. Following the surrender it had been enclosed within a wire fence and members of the staff could leave and patients could enter or depart only by permission of the Japanese medical officer who was in administrative charge of the hospital under the Japanese Commandant of P.o.W. Camps, Hong Kong. Patients in the P.o.W. camps, irrespective of the urgency of their need for hospitalisation, were brought to the hospital only on days appointed by the I.J.A. The hospital was not permitted to send medical supplies to the P.o.W. camps, but small quantities were hidden on the persons of discharged patients returning to these camps. Until he himself was imprisoned, the D.M.S. Civil Medical Services rendered great service to the hospital by obtaining for it quantities of special foods and drugs.

Up to August 1942 the main task of the hospital staff was the treatment of the wounded as these were transferred from the other hospitals. Thereafter, until the relieving force arrived in 1945, it became the care of patients suffering from diphtheria, dysentery and the deficiency diseases.

On August 8, 1942, A.D.M.S. China Command and O.C. Hospital were transferred by the Japanese to the P.o.W. camp. The senior surgeon on the staff succeeded to the command of the hospital. Like his predecessor he maintained a chronicle of events, and that which follows derives from this.

On August 10 all the female nursing staff (Q.A.I.M.N.S., Canadian Army Nursing Service, T.A.N.S., Nursing Division of the H.K.V.D.C. and Auxiliary Nursing Service) were sent by the Japanese to the internment camp at Stanley. The staff then remaining consisted of 6 medical officers, 1 dental officer, 1 chaplain, 1 quartermaster, 55 O.Rs. R.A.M.C., 6 O.Rs. R.E. and 1 civilian engineer. The number of occupied beds was 211.

1943 opened with 327 patients and ended with 224. By the end of the year the number of dysentery cases had fallen. The troops had by now become more adjusted to a rice diet. The rations issued were:
Breakfast: Tea, bread, sugar (usually), syrup and Chinese dates (exceptionally).
Dinner: Boiled rice, fish (twice weekly), meat (once weekly), vegetables.
Supper: Boiled rice, sometimes with vegetables.

For the patients a little milk was commonly provided. 1944 ended with 145 occupied beds. During this year life was made more difficult by the progressive decline in the purchasing power of the military yen, which was the currency. For example, a tin of syrup, which in September 1943 could be bought for M.Y. 5.75, cost at the end of 1944 M.Y. 85.90. (By mid-1945 the cost had risen to M.Y. 528.00).

In March 1945 the I.J.A. ordered the B.M.H. to move to the Central British School, Kowloon. The majority of the staff proceeded thereto while the rest, together with the 124 patients, moved to the Shamsuipo

P.o.W. Camp where they remained until April 10 and 12, when they were transported to the B.M.H.

During June and July the rations progressively improved. The staff of the hospital was not greatly surprised, therefore, to learn from the Japanese guards on August 16 that the war was over. On August 17 the nurses rejoined the hospital, soon to be followed by R.N. and R.A.F. elements of the relieving force.

The following records of the work of the hospital, not the originals, for these were burnt by the Japanese on July 9, 1945, serve to illustrate the high quality of the service that the staff of this hospital rendered during the periods of battle and of captivity:

TABLE 1

Admissions, Discharges and Deaths. B.M.H. Bowen Road. December 8, 1941–March 23, 1945

	Admissions		Discharges		Deaths		Remaining at end of period	
	Officers	O.Rs.	Officers	O.Rs.	Officers	O.Rs.	Officers	O.Rs.
1941: December 8–31 .	32	536	19	298	2	29	11	209
1942: January 1–December 31	127	1,098	108	939	9	48	21	320
1943: January 1–December 31	30	275	30	352	1	29	20	214
1944: January 1–December 31	17	212	29	275	4	10	4	141
1945: January 1–March 23 .	—	—	1	22	—	3	3	116

TABLE 2

Battle Casualties Admitted to the B.M.H.

	Officers		O.Rs.		Total all ranks	Total deaths	Percentage mortality
	Totals	Deaths	Totals	Deaths			
British (all Services)	36	3	361	28	397	31	7·8
Canadian Army .	15	—	203	7	218	7	3·2
Indian Army . .	4	1	27	4	31	5	16·1
	55	4	591	39	646	43	6·6

TABLE 3

Classification of Wounds by Anatomical Region

1. *Gunshot Wounds of the Head:*
   Total cases 38
   Cases with fracture of cranium with or without depression, and with penetration or perforation of cranium 21
   Deaths 8

2. *Gunshot Wounds of the Face:*

Total cases	48
Cases with severe eye injury (19 eyes affected)	15
Penetrating injuries	17
Non-penetrating injuries	2
Eyes enucleated	9
Result better than $V=6/60$ . . .	4
Cases of fracture of frontal bone . .	6
Cases of fracture of maxilla . . .	4
Cases of fracture of mandible . . .	6
Deaths	2

3. *Gunshot Wounds of the Neck:*

Total cases (severe 2)	26
Deaths	1

4. *Gunshot Wounds of the Chest:*

Total cases	80
Cases with flesh wounds and contusions .	38
Cases with injury of bony and chest wall .	17
Cases with non-penetrating injury of chest contents	7
Cases with penetrating injuries . . .	1*
Cases implicating contents . . .	20
Deaths	2

* The case of an officer, a metal missile lodged in his heart wall; no attempt at surgery was made and he lived to return home in 1945.

5. *Gunshot Wounds of the Abdomen:*

Total cases	26
Simple flesh wounds and contusions . .	10
Non-penetrating with fracture of ilium .	3
Penetrating with lesion of:	
Mesocolon and vena cava . . .	1
Small gut	1
Mesentery	1
Caecum	1
Transverse colon	1
Small gut and rectum . . .	1
Transverse colon and liver . . .	1
Kidney and pancreas . . .	1
Unrecorded	5
Deaths (only 3 of the 13 cases with internal injury survived)	9

6. *Gunshot Wounds of the Back and Spine:*

Total cases	28
Simple flesh wounds and contusions . .	21
With fracture of vertebrae:	
Without cord lesion	2
With cord lesion	5
Deaths	4

7. *Gunshot Wounds of the Perineum, Genital and Urinary Organs, not involving Peritoneum:*

Total cases	11
Involving male genital organs . . .	6
Contusion of bladder	1
Involving:	
Rectum	1
Hip joint and ischium . . .	1
Os pubis	1
Deaths	2

8. *Gunshot Wounds of the Upper Extremities:*

Total cases (number of injuries 247) . .	208	
Flesh wounds and contusions . . .		149
With compound fractures		98
No. of amputations:		
Through shoulder		1
Through arm		5
Part of hand		1
Fingers		19
Deaths attributable to these injuries . .	4	

9. *Gunshot Wounds of Lower Extremities:*

Total cases (no. of injuries 313) . . .	247	
Flesh wounds and contusions . . .		227
Simple fractures		1
With compound fractures		85
No. of amputations:		
Through hip joint		1
Through thigh		6
Through leg		8
Through toes		4
Deaths attributable to these injuries . .	3	

10. *Gunshot Wounds with Direct Injury of Large Arteries without Compound Fractures:*

Total cases (axillary 3; popliteal 1) . .	4	
No. of aneurysms (axillary) . . .		2
Amputation through thigh . . .		1
Deaths	—	

11. *Gunshot Wounds with Penetration or Perforation of Larger Joints:*

Total cases	22	
Shoulder		4
Elbow		3
Wrist		4
Knee		9
Ankle		2
No. of amputations:		
For knee injury with compound fracture		2
For ankle injury		1
Deaths	1	

12. *Gunshot Wounds with Direct Injury to Large Nerves without Compound Fractures:*

Total cases	20*	
Brachial plexus		2
Median		1
Ulnar		2
Musculo-spiral		4
Sciatic		3
Multiples:		
Median, ulnar and internal cutaneous .		2
Median and ulnar		4
Ulnar and internal cutaneous . .		1
Ulnar, sciatic and anterior tibial . .		1
Deaths	—	

    * In addition nerve injuries with complicated compound fractures in a further 19 instances without fatality.

13. *Sword Wounds:*

Total cases	4	
Neck (severe)		1
Arm		1
Hand		3
Deaths	—	

14. *Bayonet Wounds:*
    Total cases   10
    With nerve injury   1
    Slight   9
    Deaths . . . .   —
15. *Burns:*
    Total cases   9
    Deaths . . . .   —
    Tetanus:
    Total cases   1
    Deaths . . . .   —
    Gas Gangrene:
    Total cases   2
    Deaths . . . .   —

TABLE 4

Classification of Wounds by Missile

	Per cent.
No record	42·2
G.S.W.	26·6
*Shrapnel	9·4
Shell	6·6
Mortar bomb . . .	5·2
Hand grenade . . .	4·6
Aerial bomb . . .	3·3
Bayonet	1·6
Sword	0·7

* The Japanese did not use shrapnel. The wounds so classified in this table were in the main caused by mortar bomb and hand grenade.

TABLE 5

Admissions to the B.M.H. on account of Dysentery, Diphtheria and Deficiency Diseases. August–December 1942

	Total admissions all causes	Dysentery	Diphtheria	Deficiency diseases	Deaths
August . .	82	37	18	17	6
September .	237	91	59	27	16
October .	82	16	—	58	5
November .	78	3	—	66	6
December .	67	7	—	50	9
	546	154	77	218	
		449			

These figures do not represent the incidence of these diseases among the troops for it is known that many patients suffering from these diseases were retained in the P.o.W. camps, their transfer to hospital being prohibited by the I.J.A.

During the course of the fighting in the island naval personnel fought alongside the troops and the Royal Naval Hospital at Wanchai admitted casualties irrespective of the Service to which they belonged. Army casualties were being admitted to this hospital from December 13. It is recorded in the Official Naval Medical History (Vol. II) that on December 21 the shelling around the Royal Naval Hospital was practically unceasing, so that it became necessary to keep a large number of the more seriously ill patients continuously under morphia. On Christmas Day this hospital was holding 120 patients.

CASUALTIES

The tables below record the total known battle casualties among British, Canadian and Indian troops. The figures are of course only approximate owing to the circumstances prevailing:

TABLE 6

Total Battle Casualties (*Killed, Died of Wounds, Wounded and Missing*). (*Approximate*)

	Number	Percentage of strength
Officers	212	39·5
B.O.Rs.	2,069	31·0
I.O.Rs.	1,164	30·0

	Killed. Died of wounds	Wounded	Missing
Officers	74	77	61
B.O.Rs.	595	778	696
I.O.Rs.	376	477	311
	1,045	1,332	1,068

The figure for wounded does not include the lightly wounded or those wounded but returned to duty. A.D.M.S. states that 2,000 wounded men passed through the hospitals and that, in addition, many of the wounded of 5/7th Rajputs fell into Japanese hands and were not recorded.

The figures given by the then Director of the Hong Kong Medical Department differ from the above. He records that 1,400 of the garrison were killed, died of wounds, believed killed or missing, and that 1,678 were wounded.

TABLE 7

Canadian Casualties

Of the 1,972 Canadians who landed in Hong Kong, 1,416 eventually got back to Canada.

Killed, died of wounds, or killed while P.o.W. . . . 290
Died of disease 253
Died of accident or injury 11
Died subsequent to release at the end of the campaign . . 2

556
Wounded (up to the time of the surrender) . . . 290

TABLE 8

Casualties (*Indian Records*)

Unit or formation	Total strength			Killed, or died of wounds		Missing		Wounded	
	Officers	I.O.Rs.	B.O.Rs.	Officers	I.O.Rs.	Officers	I.O.Rs	Officers	I.O.Rs.
5/7th Rajputs .	17	875	—	6	150	4	109	7	186
2/14th Punjabis .	15	932	—	3	52	—	69	5	156
I.M.S. . .	5	55	—	—	—	1	2	—	—
R.I.A.S.C. . .	—	13	—	—	—	—	—	—	1
1 H.K. Regt. .	24	830	30	3	144	7	45	3	103
H.K.S.R.A. . .									
5 A.A. Regt. R.A.	23	332	231	—	24	8	80	1	15
8 Coast Regt. R.A.	19	233	285	—	—	—	1	3	4
12 Coast Regt. R.A.	16	187	200	1	3	1	—	1	3
965 Def. Bty. R.A.	3	86	58	—	2	—	—	1	4
H.K. Mule Corps .	3	250	—	—	1	—	5	1	5
	125	3,793	804	13	376	21	311	22	477

All officers (save two or three Indian officers) were British.

Indian Medical Services Casualties

	Officers	I.O.Rs.
Killed, or died of wounds .	—	—
Missing	1	2
Wounded	—	—

No information concerning the number of casualties incurred by the locally enlisted Chinese exists.

REFLECTIONS UPON THE MEDICAL ASPECTS OF THE BATTLE

The collection and evacuation of the wounded was not, and could not be, according to plan. The battle developed so rapidly and so disastrously that most of the M.A.Ps. were overrun and lost their usefulness within a few hours. The medical services did not break down. The reason for this was the number of the civil hospitals in the island. All of these admitted military patients. The Bowen Road B.M.H. worked to capacity from start to finish and it says much for the ability of its commanding officer that not a single patient was killed by enemy action though the hospital area received much attention from the Japanese guns.

The whole of the island was the battlefield and there was no L. of C.

and no base. A medical unit was inevitably amid combatant units. When forming judgments concerning the killing of medical officers and orderlies by the Japanese it must be borne in mind that in the heat of battle it must sometimes have been difficult to recognise a M.A.P. or a hospital when the buildings occupied by medical personnel, or others adjacent to these, were at the same time being used as strong points by combatant troops. In the circumstances that existed, mistakes of this kind could easily happen. But the killing of male protected personnel was, in one instance, associated with the criminal assault of the female nursing staff, some of whom were subsequently murdered. For such behaviour there can be no possible excuse for it was displayed, not in the heat of battle but during the night following the capitulation.

After the capitulation the Japanese allowed the Army Medical Services to send out parties to look for wounded. It is of interest to note that very few were discovered. It would seem that in spite of all the difficulties the majority of the casualties had been admitted to hospital without serious delay.

THE CONDITIONS OF CAPTIVITY*

Following the formal surrender there began for the survivors of the garrison an interminable period of dreary captivity filled with spiteful humiliations amid conditions that were almost beyond description. For nearly four years they were herded in prison camps, kept on a near starvation diet yet compelled to perform hard manual labour. With few exceptions their captors were largely indifferent to the needs of the sick, and such medical facilities as they supplied were hopelessly inadequate. Had not the British, Canadian and Indian medical officers among them been able by various stratagems to obtain the means to provide medical care it is questionable whether many of the prisoners-of-war would have survived this cruel experience.

On the island of Hong Kong there was but one camp, formerly occupied by Chinese refugees, at North Point. On the mainland there were three, one at Shamshuipo, three miles north of Kowloon in the British barracks which the Canadian battalions had occupied after their arrival in Hong Kong, the second at Argyle Street close to the Kai Tak airfield, and the third half a mile away from this.

At the North Point camp three R.A.M.C. and a R.N. surgeon established a small hospital of 30 beds for the Canadian Royal Rifles and the naval ratings incarcerated there. The accommodation in the camp consisted of frame huts 125 ft. × 18 ft. Into each of these 120 or more were crowded. The whole of the area about the camp was black with flies for near the camp were former Japanese horse lines and the

---

*See *The Civilian Health and Medical Services*. Volume II. Chapter 3.

garbage dump for the city of Victoria. On the nearby beaches the rotting dead lay unburied.

In January 1942 all the Canadians were concentrated at North Point and the Canadian sick and wounded were collected in the Bowen Road Military Hospital. The main advantage of this transfer was that the senior R.C.A.M.C. officer in the camp was enabled to maintain close contact with the hospital. In the camp itself the small hospital was extended, a M.I. room established and a dental clinic opened. The horse lines were cleared up and the dead buried. About the middle of April all the naval personnel were transferred elsewhere and North Point became a Canadian camp. The Canadian officers now began to receive pay and a monthly contribution was levied according to rank and a fund for the purchase of medical supplies established.

The Canadian sick rate in the North Point camp remained high. During March 1942, for example, the daily sick parade ranged between 140 and 250. By June the Japanese were demanding working parties of 200 and in July of 400. They refused to accept any excuse for non-compliance with this order. It became necessary therefore to send out men who were sick in order to spare those who were sicker still. The inevitable result was a considerable increase in the incidence of physical exhaustion.

By August a few cases of diphtheria made their dreaded appearance. The Japanese refused to provide the means for immunisation. Towards the end of September the Canadians were moved back to the Shamshuipo camp along with their diphtheria cases, for the removal of these to the Bowen Road Military Hospital had not been permitted. Within three days of the arrival in the Shamshuipo camp there were 35 fresh cases. Throughout the autumn the epidemic raged. Some 500 men were affected and of these 46 died.

In this camp the R.A.M.C. had established a well organised hospital; but the Japanese insisted that the Canadians and the British must remain apart and so a Canadian hospital of 300 beds was opened with separate sections for general cases, dysentery cases and diphtheria cases. There had been a diphtheria epidemic among the British P.o.W. but fortunately this was drawing to its end as the Canadian one started.

At the end of November the first Red Cross parcels arrived to revive morale and to refresh hope. Thereafter they continued to arrive with a certain regularity, though the Japanese were responsible for delays and interruptions. Here, as elsewhere, these parcels alone made continued survival possible.

In January 1943 a draft of 650 Canadians was sent to Japan, there to work in the mining and shipbuilding industries. Subsequently other drafts were sent, to bring the total of Canadians in Japan to 1,183 O.Rs. With the first draft went a R.C.A.M.C. officer.

The two Canadian nursing sisters working in the Bowen Road Military Hospital remained there until August 1942 when they were transferred to a civilian internment camp on Stanley peninsula. In November 1943 they were repatriated.

The conditions in the Shamshuipo camp, into which some 6,000 British, Canadian, Indian and H.K.V.D.C. prisoners-of-war were herded, beggared description. Chinese looters had wrecked the place. All the doors had been taken away, all the windows broken, all the plumbing fixtures removed. Much of the flooring of the huts had been torn up. Indeed nothing remained but the walls and the roofs. The Japanese provided rice, a small amount of meat, a few vegetables and a little firewood. The captives had no cooking utensils. Out of the materials provided they were able to produce two meals, very inadequate in respect of both quantity and quality, a day. It was not long before an epidemic of dysentery broke out. The building that had been the officers' mess was transformed into a hospital. The Japanese were persuaded to provide rice sacks wherewith to block the broken windows, about fifty canvas beds and a meagre quantity of medical supplies. The billiard table became the operating table and the steriliser the pot on the kitchen fire. Chloroform was the only available anaesthetic and sulpha drugs the principal antiseptic.

The weather was trying, the night temperatures ranging between 40 and 50 degrees. The troops had no blankets. Everywhere the wind whistled through the holes that once had been windows and in the pursuit of warmth the men had to sleep huddled on the floor.

Officers were confined in the Argyle Street camp together with a number of other ranks who served as batmen and cooks. It housed in all about 600, but this number decreased as drafts were sent from time to time to Japan and Formosa. The camp consisted of a number of wooden huts with concrete floors which had been built to accommodate Chinese internees. The average number of officers in a hut was 40. Latrines were of the Asiatic type and were flushed with water.

The dietary was poor, its principal ingredient being white rice, varying in quantity from 700 to 375 grammes daily. Meat was available for the first few weeks only. Green vegetables were issued in sufficient quantity to supply soup with the rice twice daily. In addition peanut oil was issued fairly regularly. Fish, sufficient to supply a man with a ration every ten days, was also included. Every effort was made to preserve the vitamin content of the vegetables by cooking them for as short a time as possible. The calorie value of the diet varied from time to time; in June 1942 it sank to 1,400 and seldom if ever did it exceed 2,000.

Officers were paid according to rank and were allowed to purchase some few foodstuffs and necessaries from the canteen. During 1943 prices were reasonable, but from 1943 onwards they became increasingly exorbitant, so much so that it became more and more difficult to augment the ration. All the officers sent money regularly to the other camps to pay for foodstuffs for the men who were threatened with malnutrition. Red Cross parcels to the scale of a parcel a man were first received in November 1942 and did much to enrich the basic diet. In April 1943 parcels additional to the above were received. They arrived at a critical time and were directly responsible for a significant fall in the incidence of malnutrition which had been causing much anxiety. In addition small but regular supplies of foodstuffs were sent into the camp to many of the prisoners-of-war by Chinese friends.

A small but totally inadequate quantity of medical supplies was issued monthly by the Japanese. They consisted of such simple drugs as iodine, aspirin, magnesium sulphate and bicarbonate of soda.

The transfer of surgical cases to the Bowen Road Hospital was invariably refused by the Japanese so that such patients had to be carried by stretcher to the Indian P.o.W. camp half a mile away. The stretcher-bearer party consisted of the surgeon, his assistant, the anesthetist and one other. In this camp there was a proper hospital and it chanced that among the prisoners there were four medical officers of the Colonial Medical Service and of these one was a surgeon of considerable experience. These medical officers had outside contacts and were thus able to obtain small supplies of essential drugs. Thus it was that the patients admitted from the officers' camp suffered no great hurt because of the Japanese refusal to allow them to be taken to Bowen Road. Of four perforated gastric ulcers and four cases of acute appendicitis all recovered.

A Japanese medical officer paid periodic visits to the camp, usually at about six weeks intervals, for the purpose of selecting cases for transfer to Bowen Road. He seldom proceeded beyond the main gate of the camp where he would select perhaps four out of the seven cases suggested to him. It was the considered opinion of the P.o.W. medical officers that this officer did little to alleviate the conditions in this camp and that his attitude towards the sick was one of complete indifference.

CHAPTER 2

THE CAMPAIGN IN MALAYA
December 8, 1941 – February 15, 1942

Précis

A STRONG Japanese expeditionary force landed on December 8, 1941, in the Singora–Patani area in southern Thailand and on the beaches at Badang and Sabak in northern Kelantan, in the north-east of the Malayan peninsula. Their air force bombed Singapore city and the main airfields on the mainland.

At this time Malaya Command consisted of Indian III Corps with Indian 11th Division deployed in the north of Kedah and Indian 9th Division with one brigade in the Kota Bharu area of northern Kelantan and another at Kuantan; the A.I.F. Malaya, Australian 8th Division, also of two brigades, in Johore and Malacca; garrisons in the fortresses of Penang and Singapore and the Federated Malay States Volunteer Force and the Straits Settlement Volunteer Corps. Indian 45th and 44th Brigades of Indian 17th Division and British 18th Division were shortly to arrive.

In Kelantan the Japanese quickly overran the defences round Kota Bharu and forced Indian 8th Brigade to withdraw to the area of Kuala Lipis in Pahang. Later the Japanese, moving south to Kuala Trengganu and Kuantan, caused Indian 22nd Brigade to withdraw to the west. The main Japanese thrust was from the Singora–Patani area across to the west coast and thence down the west side of the peninsula along the line of the main trunk road and the railway. Indian 11th Division vainly attempted to oppose their advance on a series of defensive positions at Jitra, Gurun, Kampar and the Slim River. The Japanese would not be denied; they were highly trained in the techniques of jungle fighting, they were strongly supported by armour and in the air they enjoyed undisputed mastery. Indian 11th Division, resisting valiantly, endured crippling losses and had to be withdrawn into Johore through a defensive line Segamat–Mount Ophir–Muar, manned by 'Westforce', consisting of Australian 27th Brigade, Indian 9th Division (withdrawn from the east) and Indian 45th Brigade. 53rd Brigade of 18th Division, on arrival at Singapore, was sent forward to join 'Westforce'.

On January 15 and 16 the Japanese pierced this line and also landed on the west coast in its rear. The withdrawal from this line was associated with very grievous casualties and it became necessary to withdraw from the mainland altogether. While Indian 11th Division held the Skudai corner the rest withdrew into Singapore island, Australian 22nd Brigade, which had been opposing further Japanese landings in the Endau area, moving across country to do so. On the morning of January 31, the last units of the rearguard passed across the causeway, which was then destroyed.

For its defence Singapore island was divided into three sectors. 18th Division and Indian 11th Division, into which the remains of Indian 9th Division had been incorporated, held the northern sector with its coastline from the causeway to Changi; the southern sector, from Changi to the mouth of the river Jurong, was defended by 1st and 2nd Malayan Brigades and the Straits Settlement Volunteer Force, and the western sector, the River Jurong to the causeway, by Australian 8th Division and Indian 44th Brigade. In reserve was Indian 12th Brigade.

On February 8, following an intense and prolonged bombardment, the Japanese landed in the sector held by Australian 22nd Brigade and, on the 9th, in that held by Australian 27th Brigade. Greatly favoured by the nature of the terrain and by the destruction of communications by shellfire and bombing, the Japanese quickly thrust inland to gain possession of the Tengah airfield and of the supply dump area round Bukit Timah. Much bitter and confused fighting occurred during the next two days but the Japanese, continuously reinforced, could not be halted. By the 13th the defenders had been withdrawn to a perimeter line around Singapore city. This remained intact, but continued resistance quickly became impossible. The overcrowded city was being mercilessly bombed and shelled and the water supply had failed. At 2030 hours on February 15 the campaign ended in unconditional surrender.

Below is a glossary of Malay words used in this chapter:

Alor	River channel, pool
Ampang . . .	Dam
Bagan . . .	Landing place
Bukit (Bt) . .	Hill
Kampong (Kg) .	Village
Kota	Castle, fort
Kuala (K) . .	Mouth of a river
Padang (Pdg) .	Open space, moorland
Parit (Pt) . .	Ditch or drain
Paya	Permanent swamp

Note.—As the Australian and Indian Medical Services were heavily involved in this campaign the Official Australian and Indian Medical Histories should be consulted for more detailed information.

Pulau (P)	.	.	Island
Simpang	.	.	Crossroads
Sungei (S)	.	.	River or stream
Tanjong (Tg)	.	.	Promontory, cape
Tinggi	.	.	High
Ulu	.	.	Upper reaches of a river

(i)
Preparations for War

STRATEGIC AND OTHER CONSIDERATIONS

As an outcome of the War of 1914–18 Japan came to rank third among the great naval powers. In the region that includes India, Burma, Malaya, Australia and New Zealand, Great Britain had many interests and many commitments and it became essential that a British fleet should be stationed somewhere within it. The area running from Malaya through the N.E.I. was recognised by the Indian and Australian governments as being of special importance in the defence plans of their countries. The base at Hong Kong was too near the Japanese mainland and too remote from sources of reinforcement. In 1921 the Committee of Imperial Defence decided that Singapore was strategically best situated for the control of sea communications in the Indian Ocean and southern Pacific and recommended that Keppel Harbour on Singapore island should be converted into a large naval base. But for a variety of reasons, political and economic, nothing was done. In 1924 it was decided that the proposed naval base should be constructed in the north of the island in the Strait of Johore. At this time it was accepted that any assault upon this base would come from the sea. The London Naval Treaty for the limitation and reduction of armaments, signed in 1930, resulted in a postponement of the project. Then in 1931 Japan occupied Manchuria and in 1932 sent an expeditionary force to Shanghai and the need for a British naval base in the Far East gained in urgency. This need became further increased when in 1935 Japan withdrew from the League of Nations and from the pacts relating to the mutual limitation of armaments.

By 1937 opinion concerning the possibility of a large force attacking Singapore from the mainland of Malaya had undergone a profound change. It was now thought that a force landing on the east coast of Thailand could make its way through the thick jungle country with comparative ease, even during the monsoon season. Acceptance of this opinion meant that the whole of the defence plan had to be modified. For a Japanese invading force there were five possible lines of attack. Landings could be effected (1) on the Kra Isthmus near Singora in southern Thailand, (2) at Kota Bharu, (3) at Kuantan, (4) in the

6

Endau-Mersing area and (5) on Singapore island itself. It was no longer sufficient to have a garrison on the island strong enough to hold out against an assault from the sea until the fleet could come and relieve it. The naval base had to be defended against a land attack from the north, defended by the R.A.F. from a series of airfields strategically sited throughout the mainland of Malaya and by the Army covering these airfields and holding prepared defensive positions far removed from the naval base itself.

Skeleton defences were constructed in Johore during 1938, and by the time of the outbreak of war with Germany, the great naval base of Singapore had been completed.

The Malay Peninsula, thrusting southwards from the southern border of Siam (Thailand), is about 400 miles long and varies in breadth from about 200 in its central part to about 60 miles in its northern and southern ends. Its area is about 50,000 square miles. At its southern tip is Singapore island, not unlike the Isle of Wight in shape and size (220 square miles). The island is separated from the mainland by the Strait of Johore. The tip of the peninsula lies between the islands of Sumatra in the west and Borneo in the east.

Politically the peninsula was divided into:

(1) The British Colony of the Straits Settlements—Malacca, Penang, Province Wellesley and Singapore—the first of these having been obtained by exchange with the Dutch for an area in Sumatra, the others by purchase from local Sultans.

(2) The Federated Malay States—Perak, Selangor, Negri Sembilan and Pahang—each with its own Sultan and a British resident and the whole administered by a federal government at Kuala Lumpur.

(3) The Unfederated Malay States—Johore, Kedah, Perlis, Kelantan and Trengganu—each governed by its own Sultan aided by a British resident.

The Governor of the British Colony was at the same time the High Commissioner for both the Federated and the Unfederated States. The British Government had by various treaties undertaken to afford protection against external aggression to most of these States.

POPULATION, TERRAIN, COMMUNICATIONS AND CLIMATE

In 1939 the population of Malaya numbered about 5,000,000; 2,200,000 Malays, 1,800,000 Chinese, 700,000 Indians (mostly Tamils) and 15,000 Europeans. The population of Singapore island was about 750,000, of whom 600,000 were Chinese, 48,000 Eurasians and 12,000 Europeans.

The middle part of the peninsula is occupied by a great ridge of mountains covered with jungle and was devoid of communications. On either side of this massif are coastal plains through which roads

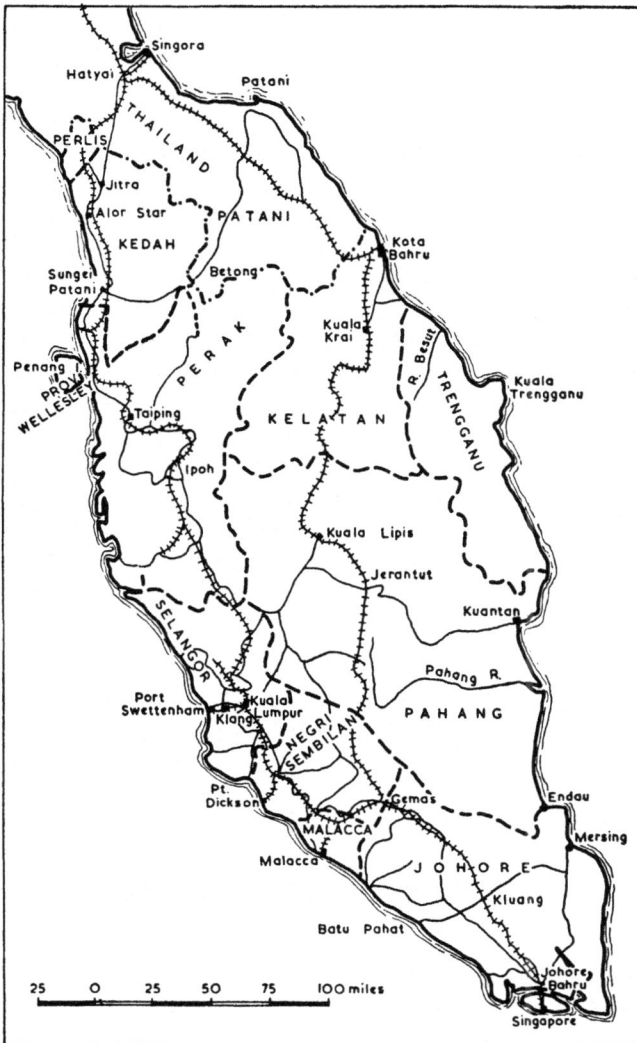

FIG. 4. Malaya.

and the railway run and on which rubber was grown and tin was mined. In the northern parts of these coastal strips rice was extensively cultivated. In the main, the west coast is lined with mangrove swamps penetrated by many rivers. The east coast consists of an almost continuous series of sandy beaches.

A good trunk road ran from Johore Bahru at the southern tip of the peninsula roughly parallel to the western coast line to the Siamese frontier, 585 miles to the north, and thence to Singora (Songkhla) on the east coast of Siam. The railway, running northwards from Singapore, forked at Gemas. The western branch followed the route of the western trunk road. The eastern branch, running up the centre of the peninsula through Jerantut and Kuala Lipis reached Kuala Krai, near Kota Bharu on the east coast in the far north of Malaya, crossed the border into Siam, fused with the western branch and ran on to Bangkok.

There was no continuous road on the eastern side of the peninsula and lateral roads joining the east and west sides of the country were few. A road from Patani on the east coast of Siam crossed the Siam-Malaya border near its mid-point and ran to Sungei Patani, north of Butterworth in Kedah. A road from Kuala Kubu Bharu, north of Kuala Lumpur on the west trunk road, ran to Kuantan on the east coast. A road from Mersing on the east coast ran across to Batu Pahat on the west coast. A road from Kroh, on the Siam border and on the Patani–Sungei Patani road, ran southwards to Grik and on to Kuala Kangsar on the main trunk road north of Ipoh.

The climate is equatorial, hot, humid, with an annual rainfall of 100 inches and an average temperature of 85° F.

The prevailing diseases of military importance were malaria, dysentery and hookworm. Mite-borne typhus occurred but was not common.

THE PRE-WAR GARRISON

In August 1939, when the clouds of war began to darken the European skies, Ind. 12th Inf. Bde. and Indian 22nd Mountain Battery were sent from India to Singapore to reinforce the small pre-war garrison which consisted of:

Singapore Island:
> Two coast regts. R.A.
> Three heavy A.A. regts. Hong Kong and Singapore Royal Artillery (H.K.S.R.A.)
> One heavy A.A. regt. R.A.
> Two British infantry battalions
> One British M.G. battalion
> One Indian infantry battalion
> One Malayan infantry battalion
> Three fortress companies R.E.

Penang Island:
> One coast regt. R.A.
> One Indian infantry battalion

Taiping:
> One Indian infantry battalion

Ind. 12th Inf. Bde. consisted of 2nd A. & S.H., 5/2nd Punjab Regt., 4th Hyderabad Regt. and 15th Coy. Sappers and Miners. The British battalions already in Malaya were 2nd The Loyal Regt. (North Lancashire), 2nd Gordon Highlanders and 1st Manchester Regt. (M.G.).

Medical

A.D.M.S. and D.A.D.M.S. Malaya Command
Tanglin Hospital (240 beds) Singapore
Reception Stations at Changi, Blakang Mati and Pulai Brani
Alexandra Hospital, under construction, Singapore
Federated Malay States Volunteer Force Field Ambulance at
    Kuala Lumpur
Straits Settlements Volunteer Force Field Ambulance.

With Ind. 12th Inf. Bde. came 12 I.G.H., 18 (Ind.) Fd. Amb., 5 (Ind.) Fd. Hyg. Sec. and 2 M.A.S. Initially these were accommodated in the private park of the Sultan of Johore on Singapore island. The F.M.S.V.F. Fd. Amb. and the S.S.V.F. Fd. Amb. were incomplete, only partially equipped and untrained. The latter unit consisted in the main of medical students from the Medical College in Singapore.

The Civil Hospital Services were well developed.* The nine larger towns in the Peninsula each had a hospital of 400–500 beds. In twenty-eight smaller towns there were district hospitals of 100–200 beds. Excluding mental and leper institutions there were just over 10,000 beds in government hospitals. The medical staff included 120 European and 180 Asiatic medical officers; the nursing staff 100 matrons and sisters, 700 nurses and 1,000 hospital assistants (male). On the rubber estates there were some 150 small private hospitals with a total of 6,000 beds. Private medical practitioners in Malaya, excluding Singapore, numbered about 200.

In Singapore there were a large government general hospital of 850 beds, a maternity hospital of 200 beds and a pauper hospital of 800 beds. There were 30 European and 60 Asiatic medical officers, 60 matrons and sisters, 280 nurses and 180 hospital assistants. Private practitioners numbered over 150. The College of Medicine provided a reserve of specialists.

Following the outbreak of war in September 1939, permission was sought to permit the recruitment of civilian medical practitioners and nurses and the formation of further military medical units. Many difficulties were encountered and War Office sanction had to be obtained for all increases of establishment and for the raising of new units. Permission to commission Asiatic medical men was obtained in November 1940 but a decision concerning the rates of pay was not

---

*See The Civilian Health and Medical Services, Volume II. Chapter 5. Malaya.

received until July 1941. In June 1940 the Straits Settlements government issued an ordinance that made all males in the Colony liable for service during the emergency, but, in so far as medical men were concerned, almost all those affected claimed and obtained exemption.

THE REINFORCEMENT OF MALAYA COMMAND

In August 1940, 2nd East Surrey Regt. reached Singapore from Shanghai when this place was abandoned. In October 1940, Ind. 6th Inf. Bde. of Indian 11th Division arrived from India, to be followed in November by H.Q. Indian 11th Division, Ind. 8th Inf. Bde. and a number of sappers and miners and administrative units. In March 1941, Ind. 15th Inf. Bde. came from India and was posted to Indian 11th Division in place of Ind. 8th Inf. Bde. which was assigned to Indian 9th Division, the H.Q. of which had also reached Malaya in March. In April, Ind. 22nd Inf. Bde. of Indian 9th Division arrived, as did also 1st Leicestershire Regt. In May, H.Q. Indian III Corps was established at Kuala Lumpur and assumed command of Indian 9th and 11th Divisions, the Penang Fortress and the Federated Malay States Volunteer Force.

The disposition of the troops in May 1941 is given below:

Disposition of Troops—May 1941

Northern Area . .	Indian III Corps
East Coast Sub-area .	Indian 9th Division of two brigade groups less one battalion
Kelantan area .	Ind. 8th Inf. Bde.
Kuantan area .	Ind. 22nd Inf. Bde. less one battalion
Northern Sub-area .	Indian 11th Division of two brigade groups
Sungei Patani .	H.Q. Indian 11th Division and Ind. 15th Inf. Bde.
Tanjong Pau . .	Ind. 6th Inf. Bde. less one battalion
Perlis, Penang and Kroh . .	One Indian infantry battalion at each.
Penang	
Penang garrison .	One infantry volunteer battalion (S.S.V.F.)
	Two 6-in. batteries
	R.E. and administrative units.
L. of C.	
The west coast area south of the river Perak . .	F.S.M.V.F. (4 infantry battalions and some supporting units).
Corps Reserve . .	One infantry battalion at Mantin.
Singapore Island and Eastern Johore .	Singapore Fortress Troops.

Fixed defences of two fire commands.
A.A. defences
  Three A.A. regts.
  One light A.A. regt.
  One S.L. regt.
Field troops
  Three infantry brigades
    1st Malaya
    2nd Malaya
    Ind. 12th Inf. Bde.
Fortress Troops, Fortress companies
R.E., etc.
S.S.V.F. less the battalion at Penang.
Equal to a weak brigade in strength.
Malaya Command H.Q. and base units.

Malaya Command Reserve Australian 8th Division less two infantry brigade groups.

Borneo .   .   . One infantry battalion, less one company at Miri, at Kuching in Sarawak.

Christmas Island .   . A coast artillery detachment.

Guarding the aerodromes in Malaya were units of the forces of certain of the Indian States.

In September 1941, Ind. 28th Inf. Bde. from India joined Indian III Corps, as did Indian 3rd Cavalry in December to serve as its reconnaissance regiment. On January 3, 1942, Ind. 45th Inf. Bde., diverted from Iraq, arrived, as did Ind. 44th Inf. Bde., also of Indian 17th Division, on January 21, and Ind. 100th Lt. Tk. Sqn. on January 29.

On February 4, 1941, 'Elbow' Force, 6,000 strong consisting of the nucleus of H.Q. Australian 8th Division and Australian 22nd Inf. Bde., sailed from Sydney for Malaya, to be followed in August by Aust. 27th Inf. Bde., when the Australian Imperial Force, Malaya, was constituted with two brigades and divisional troops. On January 24, 1942, Aust. 2/4th M.G. Bn. and A.I.F. reinforcements arrived. On January 13, 1942, 53rd Inf. Bde. of 18th Division reached Singapore from the United Kingdom, to be followed on the 29th by 54th and 55th Bdes of the same division.

The Order of Battle of Malaya Command as on December 8, 1941,* is given below:
H.Q. Malaya Command
  Singapore Fortress
    1st Malaya Inf. Bde.
      2nd Loyals
      1st Malaya Regt.
    2nd Malaya Inf. Bde.
      1st Manchesters (M.G.)

---

*Despatch G.O.C. Malaya. *The London Gazette*, February 26, 1948.

       2nd Gordons
       2/17th Dogras
  Coast Defences
       7th Coast Regt. R.A.
       9th Coast Regt. R.A.
       16th Defence Regt. R.A.
       35th Fortress Coy. R.E.
       41st Fortress Coy. R.E.
  S.S.V.F.
A.A. Defences
       3rd A.A. Regt. R.A.
       1st Hy. A.A. Regt. (H.K.S.R.A., less one bty.)
       2nd Hy. A.A. Regt. (H.K.S.R.A., less one bty.)
       3rd Lt. A.A. Regt. (H.K.S.R.A.)
       1st A.A. Regt. I.A.
       5th S/L Regt. R.A.
Indian III Corps
  H.Q. L. of C. Area
  H.Q. F.M.S.V.F.
  Penang Fortress
       11th Coast Regt.
       36th Fortress Coy.
       5/14th Punjab Regt.
  Indian 9th Division
       5th Fd. Regt.
       88th Fd. Regt.
       80th A./Tk. Regt., one bty.
       42nd Fd. Park Coy.
       Ind. 8th Inf. Bde.
           21st Mtn. Bty., less one section
           19th Fd. Coy. S. and M.
           2/10th Baluch Regt.
           2/12th F.F. Regt.
           3/17th Dogras
           1/13th F.F. Rifles
       Ind. 22nd Inf. Bde.
           21st Mtn. Bty., one section
           22nd Fd. Coy. S. and M.
           5/11th Sikhs
           2/18th R. Garhwal Rif.
  Indian 11th Division
       Ind. 3rd Cav., less one sqn.
       137th Fd. Regt.
       155th Fd. Regt.
       80th A/Tk. Regt., less one bty.
       23rd Fd. Coy.
       43rd Fd. Park Coy.
       Ind. 6th Inf. Bde.

22nd Mountain Regt., less 21st Mtn. Bty.
17th Fd. Coy. S. and M.
2nd Surreys
1/8th Punjab Regt.
2/16th Punjab Regt.
Ind. 15th Inf. Bde.
3rd Fd. Coy. S. and M.
1st Leicesters
2/9th Jat
1/14th Punjab Regt.
3/16th Punjab Regt.
Ind. 28th Inf. Bde.
2/1st Gurkhas
2/2nd Gurkhas
2/9th Gurkhas
A.I.F. Malaya
2/10th Fd. Regt.
2/15th Fd. Regt.
4th A/Tk. Regt., less one bty.
2/10th Fd. Coy.
2/12th Fd. Coy.
2/6th Fd. Park Coy.
Aust. 22nd Inf. Bde.
Aust. 2/18th Bn.
Aust. 2/19th Bn.
Aust. 2/20th Bn.
Aust. 27th Inf. Bde.
Aust. 2/26th Bn.
Aust. 2/29th Bn.
Aust. 2/30th Bn.
Ind. 12th Inf. Bde. (Malaya Command Reserve)
122nd Fd. Regt.
15th Fd. Coy. S. and M.
2nd A. and S.H.
5/2nd Punjab Regt.
4/19th Hyderabad
O.C. Troops Sarawak and Brunei
2/15th Punjab Regt.
R.A. Det.
O.C. R.A. Det. Christmas Island
Strength

Australian	15,200
British	19,600
Indian	37,000
Locally enlisted Asiatics .	16,800
	88,600

THE TACTICAL PLAN

In October 1940 Air Chief Marshal Sir Robert Brooke-Popham was appointed C. in C. Far East. He was to be responsible to the Chiefs of Staff for operational control in Malaya, Burma and Hong Kong and was informed that the policy of the Government was to avoid war with Japan and to rely on air power to defend the Far East until the fleet became available for employment in this region. The local commanders estimated that for the defence of Malaya 566 first line aircraft and 26 infantry battalions with supporting arms and ancillary services were required. The Chiefs of Staff cut down the number of aircraft to 336. On the mainland there were twenty-two airfields and on Singapore island a further four. When the Japanese invaded Malaya there were only 158 aircraft, mostly obsolescent, to oppose them and these airfields to be denied to them.

In April 1941 General Percival arrived in Singapore to assume the post of G.O.C. Malaya. He was required by the C. in C. Far East to prepare a detailed plan for forestalling any attempted Japanese landing upon the beaches of Singora and Patani in southern Thailand by an advance beyond the Malaya–Thailand border (Operation 'Matador'). The idea was that as soon as it was known that the Japanese were approaching the shores of Thailand, Indian 11th Division would be rushed northwards by road and rail to capture Singora and hold a defensive position north of Hatyai Junction. At the same time an advance would be made from Kroh to a defensive position known as 'The Ledge', on the road to Patani and about forty miles north of the Thailand–Malaya border. Here the road is cut out of the steep side of a hill and so could easily be blocked. Should Operation 'Matador' turn out to be impracticable, a defensive position in front of the village of Jitra, eighteen miles south of the frontier where the branch road from Perlis joins the main trunk road, would be manned.

The defence of the east coast of Malaya presented many difficulties, for along it were many miles of beaches suitable for assault landings. The aerodromes at Kota Bharu, Gong Kedah and Machang in the north-east and at Kuantan halfway down the coast and the ports at Mersing and Endau, from which good lateral roads ran across the peninsula to Batu Pahat, all had to be denied to the enemy. So also had the landing ground at Kuching and the oilfields and refinery at Miri, Leria and Latong in Sarawak.

The following decisions were reached:

1. Indian III Corps (H.Q. at Kuala Lumpur) would be responsible for the defence of Malaya north of Johore and Malacca.
2. Indian 11th Division would undertake Operation 'Matador'.
   H.Q. Indian 11th Division at Sungei Patani;

Ind. 6th Inf. Bde. at Tanjong Pau (on the west trunk road halfway between Alor Star and Jitra);

Ind. 15th Inf. Bde. at Sungei Patani.

3. For the advance to 'The Ledge', 'Krohcol' would be responsible.

3/16th Punjab Regt. of Ind. 15th Inf. Bde.;

5/14th Punjab Regt. from Penang Fortress;

Lt. Bty. of the F.M.S.V.F. (replaced by 10th Mtn. Bty.);

a company of sappers and miners.

4. Ind. 8th Inf. Bde. of Indian 9th Division would guard the Kelantan area, including the Kota Bharu, Gong Kedah and Machang airfields.

2/12th F.F. Regt. from Ind. 22nd Inf. Bde. would be assigned to Ind. 8th Inf. Bde. as a reinforcement.

The Hyderabad State Infantry of Ind. 8th Inf. Bde. would defend the Kota Bharu airfield and the Mysore Infantry of the same brigade those at Gong Kedah and Machang.

5. Ind. 22nd Inf. Bde. of Indian 9th Division (less one battalion) would defend the Kuantan airfield.

6. Australian 8th Division would be responsible for the defence of all Johore and Malacca.

7. To Sarawak 2/15th Punjab Regt. would be sent.

THE BUILD-UP OF THE MEDICAL SERVICES

Towards the end of 1940 the medical position was as follows:

A.D.M.S. Malaya Command became D.D.M.S. Malaya Command as his responsibilities enlarged and an A.D.M.S. Singapore Fortress was appointed.

18 (Ind.) Fd. Amb., less one coy. at Singapore

18 (Ind.) Fd. Amb., one coy. at Penang

S.S.V.F. Fd. Amb. at Singapore

F.M.S.V.F. Fd. Amb. at Kuala Lumpur

5 (Ind.) Fd. Hyg. Sec.

2 M.A.S.

Tanglin Hospital (200 beds) at Tanglin, Singapore Island

Alexandra Hospital (356 beds) at Singapore

12 I.G.H. (210 beds) at Singapore

A reception station functioning as a hospital at Blakang Mati

Reception station at Taiping

Reception station at Pulai Brani (a small island lying between Singapore Island and Blakang Mati)

Reception station at Changi, Singapore Island.

Early in 1941 the military hospital beds numbered 614 for British and 1,100 for Indian troops. The Civil Medical Services had undertaken to make available 1,500 beds for British and 2,900 for Indian troops in the event of hostilities, but this arrangement was under revision as the Army had already taken over certain of the civil hospitals. In Malacca, for example, 1,000 beds had been earmarked for military patients but the hospital was accommodating 2/10 A.G.H. In July it was decided that only the Alexandra Hospital (now 450 beds) and 12 I.G.H. should be further expanded and that a general policy of dispersal of hospital beds should be adopted. In August it was arranged that the Indian hospital ship, H.S. *Karapara*, would call at Singapore monthly to evacuate patients, estimated to be 100 per month. The *Wu Sueh*, a Yangtse river boat, was converted into a carrier for evacuation from Penang and other ports to Singapore. In August approval was given to recruit locally 25 per cent. of the personnel for a C.C.S., a field ambulance and two M.A.Cs., the equipment and vehicles to be supplied and the remaining personnel provided by the United Kingdom. A Malayan field ambulance, a field hygiene section and an auxiliary medical depot had already been formed. The last of these was for the training of locally enlisted Tamils, Chinese and Indians and was the parent unit of three ambulance trains, a bearer corps unit of 210, 150 Chinese rickshaw pullers and 86 ambulance car orderlies of the Malayan M.A.Cs. By October, 6 Malaria Field Laboratory had been formed, three malariologists and an entomologist from the Civil Medical Services constituting its staff. It was accommodated in the New General Hospital, South Johore. Six months reserves of medical stores had now been accumulated in Malaya.

When, in November 1940, Indian 11th Division became responsible for the northern area:

16 (Ind.) Fd. Amb. moved with Ind. 6th Inf. Bde. to Ipoh
15 (Ind.) Fd. Amb., less one coy., was at Kota Bharu
15 (Ind.) Fd. Amb., one coy., was at Kuantan
5 (Ind.) C.C.S. (no equipment) functioning as an improvised field ambulance was at Singapore.
13 (Ind.) Fd. Hyg. Sec. was at Kuala Lumpur
1 M.A.S., less 11 cars in Singapore, was at Maha Stadium, Kuala Lumpur
5 M.A.C. was at Kuala Lumpur
Two secs. of an I.G.H. were at Batu Road School, Kuala Lumpur, there to open 124 beds for minor cases. Serious cases were admitted to civil hospitals.

At this time there was no adequate accommodation in military hospitals outside Singapore itself for British patients. These were admitted to civil hospitals where their documentation created difficulties for the staffs of these hospitals and where patients tended to become demilitarised. The lack of ambulance car trains and coaches made it impossible to evacuate any but the most urgent cases to Singapore.

The troops were accommodated in buildings, tented camps and partially hutted camps, while vast hutted camps were being constructed. There was no D.A.D.H. on the medical establishment of this force and it was necessary to borrow one from Malaya Command to attend to the medico-sanitary aspects of this construction.

The Indian field ambulance was so organised that it could not move all its personnel and equipment without additional transport. It was well suited for the establishment of a M.D.S. and two A.D.Ss. but not to provide cover for troops operating in such a terrain as Malaya. It was therefore decided to divide the headquarters of the field ambulance into heavy and light sections and each company into a headquarters and three light A.D.Ss., all capable of operating independently. Much of the heavy ordnance equipment was discarded.

In March, Ind. 15th Inf. Bde., arriving with 28 (Ind.) Fd. Amb., was sent to Ipoh. In April, 27 (Ind.) Fd. Amb. with Ind. 22nd Inf. Bde. arrived. In May, Indian 11th Division took over from H.Q. Northern Area. The divisional H.Q., divisional troops and Ind. 15th Inf. Bde. moved to the hutted camp at Sungei Patani.

A hutted camp hospital was now available in each brigade area, at Sungei Patani, Kelantan and Kuantan, staffed by a field ambulance. In the east evacuation was by road or passenger train to Kuala Lipis; in the west to Tanjong Malim, on the trunk road north of K. Kubu. By the beginning of June an ambulance coach service to Tanjong Malim was in operation.

On July 1, 1941, the distribution of the medical units of Indian III Corps was as follows:

Indian 11th Division
 16 (Ind.) Fd. Amb. (Ind. 6th Bde.) . . Tanjong Pau
 28 (Ind.) Fd. Amb. (Ind. 5th Bde.) . . Sungei Patani
 27 (Ind.) Fd. Amb., less one coy. . . Kroh
 5 (Ind.) M.A.S. (25 cars) . . . Kroh
 6 (Ind.) A.M.U. . . . . Tanjong Pau
 13 (Ind.) Fd. Hyg. Sec. . . . Sungei Patani
Penang Fortress
 Reception station (14 Br. beds)
 18 (Ind.) Fd. Amb., one coy. (Ind. 12th Bde.)
 Sub-depot Med. Stores
L. of C. Area
 17 C.G.H. (11 Br., 500 Ind. beds) . . Tanjong Malim
 M.A.S. (24 cars) . . . . Tanjong Malim
 12 I.G.H., one sec. (100 beds) . . Kuala Lumpur
Indian 9th Division Area
 15 (Ind.) Fd. Amb. (Ind. 8th Bde.) . . Kota Bharu
 27 (Ind.) Fd. Amb., one coy. (Ind. 22nd Bde.) Kuantan
 10 I.S.S. . . . . . Maran
 2 I.S.S. . . . . . Jerantut
 12 I.G.H., one sec. (100 beds) . . Kuala Lipis
 5 (Ind.) A.M.U. . . . . Kota Bharu

In September, 36 (Ind.) Fd. Amb. arrived with Ind. 28th Inf. Bde. and moved to Ipoh. In August 1941, 27 I.G.H. (400 beds) arrived in Penang and, in September, 19 I.G.H. in Mantin, near Seremban, where it was located temporarily pending the completion of its accommodation at Segamat, South Johore. By October it had opened 200 out of its 1,000 beds.

The Indian hospitals were short of nurses. The policy adopted was one that entailed the recruitment of nurses locally and this was not successful. Owing to shortages in India, they lacked specialist staff, laboratory and X-ray facilities. They had no dental establishment and so British A.D. Corps officers and O.Rs. were used for the staffing of dental centres at Bedong, Penang, Kuala Lumpur, Kota Bharu and Tanjong Malim. For a blood transfusion service they depended on the Malaya Civil Medical Services. On December 1, two sections of 19 I.G.H. were warned to be prepared to move, together with a surgical team, to Kuala Krai and the hospitals at Kuala Krai and Kuala Lipis were ordered to evacuate their patients to Singapore, as was also 5 (Ind.) C.C.S. at Bedong which had been functioning as a stationary hospital.

A.I.F. MALAYA MEDICAL SERVICES

The medical units that accompanied 'Elbow' Force were 2/9 (Aust.) Fd. Amb., 2/4 (Aust.) C.C.S., a transport section of 2/2 (Aust.) M.A.C., 2/10 A.G.H., 2/2 (Aust.) Mob. Bact. Lab., 17 (Aust.) Dental Unit, 2/5 (Aust.) Fd. Hyg. Sec. and a detachment of 2/3 (Aust.) Adv. Depot Med. Stores. The divisional headquarters and attached units proceeded to Kuala Lumpur. 2/9 (Aust.) Fd. Amb. went with Aust. 22nd Inf. Bde. to the Seremban–Port Dickson area, 2/4 (Aust.) C.C.S. and the section of 2/2 (Aust.) M.A.C. were stationed at Kajang and 2/10 A.G.H. (400 beds) was sited at Malacca. 2/3 (Aust.) M.A.C. was recruited in Australia for the Medical Services of Malaya Command. The remainder of 2/3 (Aust.) Adv. Depot Med. Stores arrived in April 1941 and was attached to 2/10 A.G.H. at Malacca. On April 24, 2/2 (Aust.) Con. Depot and 2/3 (Aust.) M.A.C. arrived, as did the medical wing of 2/2 (Aust.) M.A.C. in June. On August 15, 2/10 (Aust.) Fd. Amb. and further dental units arrived with Aust. 27th Inf. Bde. On September 15, 2/13 A.G.H. reached Singapore and was billeted in St. Patrick's School. On August 29 to the Australian division was assigned the responsibility of defending Johore and Malacca.

A.D.M.S. Australian 8th Division acted also as A.D.M.S. A.I.F. Malaya and an administrative medical headquarters with a D.A.D.M.S. was formed to control the base organisation.

Aust. 22nd Inf. Bde. prepared defensive positions in the Mersing area. The attached field ambulance, 2/9 (Aust.) Fd. Amb., constructed an A.D.S. capable of accommodating 600 stretcher cases in blast-proof shelters. 2/10 (Aust.) Fd. Amb. at Kahang constructed a M.D.S. 2/4 (Aust.) C.C.S. at Kajang had attached to it a section for venereal diseases staffed by personnel of 2/10 A.G.H. In September the C.C.S. moved to Johore Bahru, there to function as a small hospital of 150–200 beds. When 2/13 A.G.H. (1,200 beds) arrived the C.C.S. moved to Kluang where it was conveniently sited to receive casualties from Segamat, Mersing, Muar and Batu Pahat and to evacuate to 2/13 A.G.H. which was in an unfinished mental hospital at Tampoi, seven miles from Johore Bahru, by road and rail. 2/10 A.G.H. (600 beds) at Malacca was accommodated in the civil hospital there. Though Malacca was on the coast, evacuation by hospital ship was not feasible since the port did not permit ocean going ships to approach within several miles of the shore. 2/2 (Aust.) Con. Depot at Tanjong Bruas provided accommodation for 600 men. At the beginning medical supplies were very deficient for the reason that Malaya Command assumed that Australia would provide all stores and replacements.

DISTRIBUTION OF MEDICAL UNITS—DECEMBER 1, 1941

Malaya Command
D.D.M.S. and A.D.M.S.
Singapore Fortress
A.D.M.S.
Indian III Corps
D.D.M.S.

Approximate strength Indian 11th Division Area		20,000
Indian 9th Division Area		
Kelantan .	.	10,000
Kuantan .	.	8,000
Penang Fortress .	.	3,000
L. of C. Area	.	15,000

Indian 11th Division Area

36 (Ind.) Fd. Amb. (Ind. 28th Bde.)	.	. Ipoh
28 (Ind.) Fd. Amb. (Ind. 15th Bde.)	.	. Sungei Patani
16 (Ind.) Fd. Amb. (Ind. 6th Bde.)	.	. Tanjong Pau
13 (Ind.) Fd. Hyg. Sec.	. .	. Sungei Patani
6 (Ind.) A.M.U.	. . .	. Tanjong Pau
5 M.A.S.	. . . .	. Bedong
10 I.S.S.	. . . .	. Kroh

Indian 9th Division Area

15 (Ind.) Fd. Amb. (Ind. 8th Bde.)	.	. Kota Bharu
M.A.S. (25 cars)	. . .	. Kota Bharu
5 (Ind.) A.M.U.	. . .	. Kota Bharu
10 (Ind.) Fd. Hyg. Sec., one sub-sec.	.	. Kota Bharu
27 (Ind.) Fd. Amb. (Ind. 22nd. Bde.)	.	. Kuantan
M.A.S. (25 cars)	. . .	. Kuantan

    2 I.S.S. . . . . Kuantan
    10 (Ind.) Fd. Hyg. Sec., one sub-sec. . . Kuantan
Penang Fortress
    27 I.G.H. (400 beds)
    Reception station (14 (Br.) beds.)
    18 (Ind.) Fd. Amb., one coy. (Ind. 12th Bde.)
    Sub-depot Med. Stores
L. of C. Area (A.D.M.S. attached H.Q. Indian III Corps)
West Coast
    5 (Ind.) C.C.S. (300 beds) . . . . Bedong
    8 (Ind.) Adv. Depot Med. Stores . . Bedong
    20 C.G.H. (100 Br., 500 Ind. beds) . . Taiping
    17 C.G.H. (900 beds) . . . . Mantin
    Reception station (40 Ind. beds) . . . Kuala Lumpur
    Ind. Con. Depot (500) . . . . Morib
    2 Adv. Depot Med. Stores . . . . Kuala Lumpur
    1 Amb. Train . . . . . . Tanjong Malim
    F.M.S.V.F. Fd. Amb. . . . Kuala Lumpur
    2/3 (Aust.) M.A.C. (75 cars) . . . Ipoh
    M.A.S. (25 cars) . . . . . Tanjong Malim
    M.A.S. (25 cars) . . . . . Kajang
East Coast
    12 I.G.H. one sec. (100 beds) . . . Kuala Krai
    12 I.G.H. one sec. (100 beds) . . . Kuala Lipis
    Sub-depot Med. Stores . . . . Kuala Krai
    Sub-depot Med. Stores . . . . Kuala Lipis

Provisional arrangements had been made with the civil medical authorities whereby the following numbers of beds for military patients would be made available:

	British	*Indian*
Penang . .	300	200
Taiping . .	300	200
Kuala Lumpur .	200	200
Seremban . .	100	300

Australian Imperial Force—Malaya
    H.Q. Australian 8th Division . . Kuala Lumpur
    Aust. 22nd Inf. Bde. . . Mersing
    Aust. 27th Inf. Bde. . . . Malacca and West Johore
        attached
    Johore Military Forces
    Johore Volunteer Forces
    Johore Volunteer Engineers (European)

2/9 (Aust.) Fd. Amb. (Aust. 22nd Bde.)

        M.D.S. Kota Tinggi

        'B' Coy. Mersing

        'A' Coy. in reserve

2/10 (Aust.) Fd. Amb. (Aust. 27th Bde.)

        in reserve at Jasin

2/5 (Aust.) Fd. Hyg. Sec. . .	Kota Tinggi
2/4 (Aust.) C.C.S. . . .	in civil hospital Kluang; detachs. at Segamat with Aust. 2/29th Bn. and at Batu Pahat with Aust. 2/30th Bn.
2/2 (Aust.)M.A.C. . . .	Tampoi Hill, Johore Bahru
2/3 (Aust.) M.A.C. . . .	Attached 2/10 (Aust.) Fd. Amb. at Jasin
2/2 (Aust.) Mob. Bact. Lab. .	Attached M.D.S. 2/9 (Aust.) Fd. Amb. at Kota Tinggi
2/10 A.G.H.	Civil General Hospital, Malacca
2/13 A.G.H.	Tampoi (Johore Bahru)
2/2 (Aust.) Con. Depot . . .	Tanjong Bruas, on the coast eight miles north of Malacca
2/3 (Aust.) Adv. Depot Med. Stores	Johore Bahru

The following locally raised medical units were not yet ready to function:

    1 (Mal.) G.H.

    1 (Mal.) C.C.S.

    1 (Mal.) Fd. Amb.

    4 (Mal.) Fd. Amb.

    1 (Mal.) M.A.C.

    2 (Mal.) M.A.C.

    H.S. *Wu Sueh* (for coastal work)

On December 6 the Australian troops began to move to their deployment areas and the regular administration of suppressive quinine, 8 grains daily, was begun. All detachments of the C.C.S. were recalled. 2/10 (Aust.) Fd. Amb. moved from reserve with Aust. 27th Inf. Bde. to establish a M.D.S. a mile and a half from Kluang, on the Rengam road, and an A.D.S. at Kahang. When 2/4 (Aust.) C.C.S. was fully established at Kluang, 2/10 (Aust.) Fd. Amb's. M.D.S. was moved to Kahang, where an underground dressing station and a blast-proof operating theatre were constructed for the use of the mobile surgical team of 2/4 (Aust.) C.C.S. Rickshaws were converted into wheeled stretchers for the quick transport of casualties from Aust. 2/29th Bn. at the Kahang airfield. An A.D.S. was established by 'B' Coy. near the Jemaluang crossroads and a small detachment was stationed at a

7

Japanese tin mine near Endau. Evacuation from this post was to be by boat down the Kahang river. 2/4 (Aust.) C.C.S. was moved from its site near—too near—the Kluang airfield to another on the Mengkibol rubber estate where tents and marquees were erected amid the plantations.

The medical evacuation plan for the A.I.F. was now as follows: 2/9 (Aust.) Fd. Amb. serving Aust. 22nd Inf. Bde. would provide A.D.Ss. to cover Aust. 2/20th and 2/18th Bns. and Aust. 2/10th Fd. Regt. From these A.D.Ss. evacuation would be by road to the M.D.S. at Kahang on the Kota Tinggi road. Thence 2/2 (Aust.) M.A.C. would clear to 2/13 A.G.H. at Tampoi. Aust. 27th Bde's. casualties from Aust. 2/30th, 2/19th Bns., Adv. H.Q. and the attached battery at Kahang and from 2/29th Bn. guarding the Kluang airfield would be taken direct to 2/4 (Aust.) C.C.S. at Kluang. Thence by (Aust.) 2/3 M.A.C. casualties would be cleared to 2/10 or 2/13 A.G.Hs.

THE HEALTH OF THE TROOPS

Indian

The health of the troops remained surprisingly good. The malaria rate per 1,000 for the month of September 1941 was British 34·28, Indian 36·15. The incidence of venereal diseases, indolent sores, body ringworm and *otitis externa*, 'Singapore ear', was high and caused much disability.

Australian

The daily average of sick moved from 5·9 per 1,000 soon after disembarkation to 2·0 shortly afterwards. It eventually became stabilised at 3·5. Skin diseases caused much sick wastage and prickly heat much discomfort; septic abrasions and ulcers were common and *otitis externa*, 'Singapore ear', was troublesome.

(ii)

The Japanese Invasion of Malaya

On December 5, Far East Command was notified by the Chiefs of Staff that if it received information of a Japanese expedition approaching with the intention of landing on the Thailand coast Operation 'Matador' might be put into effect immediately without reference to London. On December 6, at about 1130 hours, air reconnaissance sighted Japanese warships and transports 156 miles south-east of Point Camo in Indo-China, steaming west. At 1500 hours it was established that two Japanese convoys were about 80 miles east-south-east of Pul Obi. At 1515 hours Indian 11th Division was instructed to be ready to move at a moment's notice to carry out Operation 'Matador'.

On the morning of December 7 the aircraft shadowing the Japanese convoys failed to return. Other aircraft sent out to search for them failed to find them, but at 1730 hours one was picked up again steaming towards Singora.

Since at this time it seemed doubtful whether the Indian 11th Division, if unleashed, could reach the Singora area before the Japanese had landed, if this was their intention, instructions for the division to move were not issued. At 0820 hours on December 8 the Chiefs of Staff gave approval for Operation 'Matador' if the Japanese attacked Kota Bharu. But this the Japanese had already done. Operation 'Matador' was finally cancelled at 1330 hours on the 8th, when Indian 11th Division was ordered to man the Jitra position.

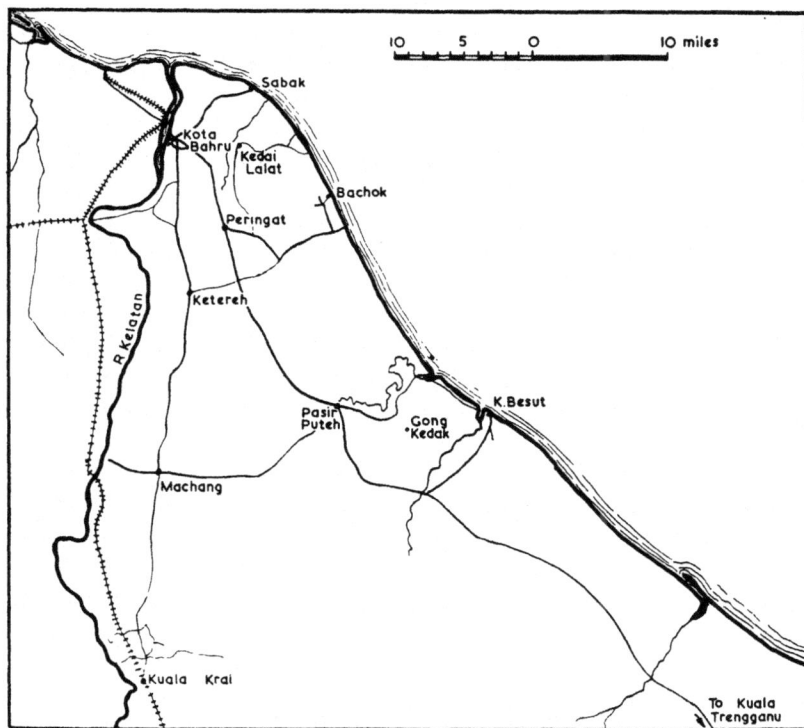

FIG. 5. North Kelantan.

On December 8 a strong Japanese force landed in the Singora–Patani area in Thailand unopposed and the Japanese air force occupied the Singora airfield. Singapore endured its first air raid shortly after 0400 hours and the airfields at Kota Bharu, Gong Kedak, Machang, Sungei Patani, Penang and Butterworth were attacked by Japanese bombers and low-flying fighters, these attacks continuing throughout the day.

At Kota Bharu, just before midnight on December 7/8, Japanese ships were observed to be anchoring off the Badang and Sabak beaches. Shortly afterwards assault barges began to land troops in ever increasing numbers. By 1300 hours on the 8th these had overrun many of the strong points held by 3/17th Dogra Regt. of Ind. 8th Inf. Bde. By 1900 hours the Japanese were penetrating through the defensive posts all over the Kota Bharu area and the brigade was forced to withdraw to the line Kedai Lalat–Kota Bharu. The Japanese pressure increased and, on the 9th, Ind. 8th Bde. was compelled to fall back to Peringat. The Kota Bharu airfield could no longer be used by the R.A.F. and the aircraft and ground staff were withdrawn to Kuantan. Further Japanese landings at Besut on the 10th threatened the airfields at Gong Kedak and Machang and on the following day it became necessary to abandon them. Ind. 8th Inf. Bde. withdrew to new positions south of Machang.

During the next few days it became apparent that the main Japanese thrust would be down the west coast. Ind. 8th Bde. was fighting in an area at the end of a roadless line of communication to the south. The single-track railway linking the area with the south had many bridges, easily destroyed by air attack. Ind. 8th Bde. could easily find itself cut off by a Japanese advance down the main trunk road in the west. It was therefore withdrawn step by step, the Japanese pressing hard all the time. By December 16 all surplus stores had been sent back and the withdrawal by rail had begun. Three days later the rearguard withdrew on foot, the bridges south of Kuala Krai having been destroyed. On December 22, Ind. 8th Bde. concentrated at Kuala Lipis with the exception of 2/12 F.F. Regt. which rejoined its brigade (22nd).

IND. 8TH INF. BDE. NORTH KELANTAN. MEDICAL COVER

15 (Ind.) Fd. Amb. had its M.D.S. on a rubber estate north of Kuala Krai and A.D.Ss. in the schools at Kota Bharu and at Ketereh. Local buses were requisitioned to serve as ambulances. Between the R.A.Ps. and the A.D.Ss. subsections of the field ambulance were placed to act as light A.D.Ss. Evacuation from the M.D.S. was by field ambulance cars to a section of 12 I.G.H. at Kuala Krai, the ambulance railhead. Only one ambulance train was available at this time in Indian III Corps area. Evacuation from Kuala Krai by rail was to Kuala Lipis where another section of 12 I.G.H. was functioning.

On December 9 the A.D.S. at Kota Bharu moved back to join the M.D.S. at Kuala Krai. The A.D.S. at Ketereh withdrew by stages, moving at night. Two sections of 19 I.G.H. were moved from Mantin to Kuala Krai together with a surgical team and the unit's equipment. On the 12th a second ambulance train became available and cleared Kuala Lipis to Singapore. On December 14 the section of 12 I.G.H. at Kuala Krai joined the other section of this unit at Kuala Lipis. By the

16th a third ambulance train became available. On the 19th the two sections of 19 I.G.H. returned from Kuala Krai to Mantin. The mobile surgical team was attached to the sections of 12 I.G.H. at Kuala Lipis and the advanced depot of medical stores went back to Singapore.

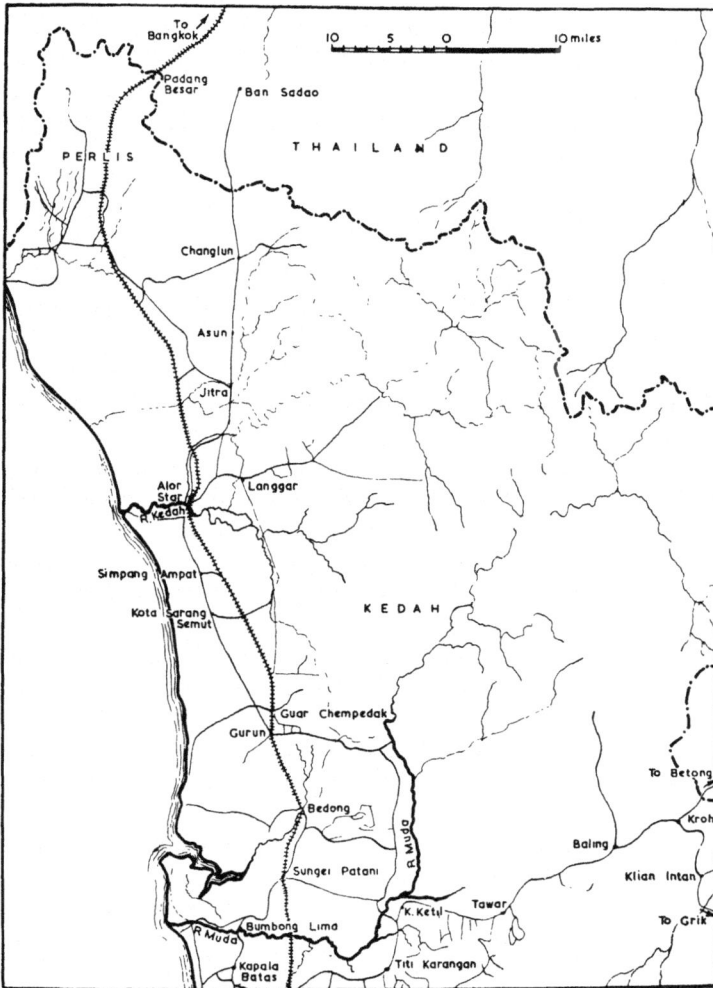

FIG. 6. Kedah.

15 (Ind.) Fd. Amb. took over the work of these sections of 19 I.G.H. and when it was pulled back left a detachment to serve the rearguard of the brigade, converting one truck of the last train out of Kuala Krai into an emergency operating theatre. One ambulance rail coach, without Red Cross markings, was destroyed by Japanese air action while on its way up to the rearguard.

On December 21, while Ind. 8th Inf. Bde. was concentrating in the Kuala Lipis–Jerantut area, 15 (Ind.) Fd. Amb. reorganised at Kuala Lipis and thereafter proceeded to Raub to rest. Here it was joined by a M.A.S. On December 24 one section of 12 I.G.H. at Kuala Lipis was ordered to join its parent unit at Singapore and the second section was instructed to proceed to Bahau and open there. There were now 100 beds at Jerantut (19 I.G.H.) and 100 at Bahau (12 I.G.H.). Evacuation therefrom was by rail to Singapore. Should the rail be blocked then evacuation would be by the M.A.S. at Tanjong Malim, either to 17 I.G.H. at Tanjong Malim or to 20 C.G.H. at Kajang.

INDIAN 11TH DIVISION

THE ACTIONS AT JITRA, KROH, GURUN, KAMPAR AND SLIM RIVER AND THE WITHDRAWAL INTO JOHORE

The Japanese troops landing at Singora pushed southwards without delay, using the Singora–Alor Star and the Patani–Kroh roads. Indian 11th Division in the Jitra position covering the Alor Star airfield hurriedly strengthened its defences. 'Krohcol', less 5/14th Punjab Regt. which did not arrive until later, moved across the frontier on December 8 to seize 'The Ledge' on the Patani road and a small mechanised column provided by 1/8th Punjab Regt., with a detachment of 16 (Ind.) Fd. Amb. attached, went forward to Sadao, eight miles beyond the frontier, to delay the Japanese advance. Three bridges were blown and the column returned safely. An armoured train at Padang Besar, manned by a platoon of 2/16th Punjab Regt., also crossed the border, destroyed a bridge and returned safely. 'Krohcol' encountered unexpected opposition from Thai armed constabulary at the frontier but overcame it and entered Betong at 1500 hours. Three and a half miles from 'The Ledge' 'Krohcol' met and checked a Japanese column led by tanks moving south from Patani.

The Jitra position was just north of the little town of this name and lay astride the west trunk road at the point where the road to Perlis leaves it. The line was held by Ind. 15th Bde. on the right and Ind. 6th Bde. on the left. It was covered by an outpost line running through Asun, on the trunk road about halfway between Jitra and Changlun, and Kampong Imam. In this outpost line were 1/14th Punjab Regt. of Ind. 15th Bde. and 1/8th Punjab Regt. of Ind. 6th Bde. Ind. 28th Inf. Bde. was in reserve.

It was not long before the Japanese leading elements began to press against the outpost line, to be halted by 1/14th Punjab Regt. 2/1st Gurkhas of Ind. 28th Bde. was sent forward to take over the Asun position and Ind. 6th Bde. was pulled back to Kodiang just north of Jitra on December 10. On the 11th, the outpost line of Ind. 15th Bde.

was strongly attacked and pierced by Japanese tanks. 1/14th Punjab Regt. and 2/1st Gurkhas suffered heavy casualties. The Japanese then pressed hard against the positions held by 2/9th Jats and 1st Leicesters. During the 12th the pressure increased and the general situation progressively deteriorated. At 2030 hours permission was given for Indian 11th Division to withdraw. The disengagement and withdrawal to the area of Gurun, fifteen miles to the south, constituted a most difficult operation. Rain fell incessantly, there was but a single road and the morale of the troops had been badly shaken. Ind. 15th Bde. became reduced to a quarter of its strength; Ind. 6th Bde. became grievously depleted; in Ind. 28th Bde. two of the battalions each endured 100 casualties and the third, 2/1st Gurkha Rifles, became reduced to the strength of a single company.

During these events the situation on the Kroh front, far away to the east, had been causing considerable anxiety. A Japanese thrust along the Betong–Kroh–Baling road would seriously threaten the communications of Indian 11th Division. 'Krohcol' was facing a numerically superior force and could not be expected to delay the Japanese in the Kroh–Baling area for more than two or three days. At dawn on December 12 the Japanese attacked 3/16th Punjabis and forced them to withdraw. Reduced to about half its strength the battalion passed through 5/14th Punjabis north-east of Betong to occupy a prepared position three miles west of Kroh on the Baling road.

At midnight on December 12/13, III Corps took over command of 'Krohcol' and the responsibility for the vitally important Kroh–Baling road. At the same time G.O.C. Malaya Command placed Ind. 12th Inf. Bde., less 4/19th Hyderabad Regt. in Kelantan, at the disposal of III Corps and arranged to send it by rail to Ipoh. The leading battalion, 2nd A. & S.H., was due to arrive at 1600 hours on the 13th.

During the night of December 12–13 the Japanese began to press against 5/14th Punjabis and to infiltrate around both flanks of the position they were holding. The Punjabis were obliged to withdraw to Betong and thence to join 3/16th Punjabis in the defensive position west of Kroh. This withdrawal uncovered the road from Kroh to Grik which led to Kuala Kangsar. To cover this a company of 2nd A. & S.H. with a number of armoured cars of the F.M.S.V.D.F. was sent forward while the rest of the Argylls moved to Baling.

'Krohcol' now passed u/c Ind. 12th Inf. Bde. 5/2nd Punjabis were moved to Merbau Pulas. 'Krohcol' was instructed to withdraw through 2nd A. & S.H. during the night of December 14/15.

By daybreak on December 13, Indian 11th Division had withdrawn south of the Kedah river. Ind. 6th Bde. was astride the railway and road at Simpang Ampat, covered by rearguards on the river south of Alor Star and at Langgar on the right flank. During the day the Japanese pressure increased and during the night of December 13–14, Indian 11th Division withdrew to the area of Gurun. The Gurun position lay astride the main road and railway about three miles north of Gurun village, between the jungle covered slopes of Kedah Peak in the west and the jungle area two miles further east. The troops, who had been fighting and withdrawing for the past week, at once began to prepare the position for defence. Ind. 6th Bde. was on the left with Ind. 28th Bde. on its right. The greatly depleted Ind. 15th Bde., now only about 600 strong, was in reserve.

The troops had no sooner taken up their positions than the Japanese attack opened. During the 14th they gained but little success, but on the 15th they broke through. H.Q. 2nd East Surrey and H.Q. Ind. 6th Inf. Bde. were overrun and 13 officers killed. The tactical situation quickly became dangerous and Indian 11th Division withdrew to a position about seven miles south of Gurun which was already held by 1st Independent Company* and Ind. 3rd Cav. and thence, during the night of December 15–16, behind the Muda river.

On the 16th the airfield at Butterworth was abandoned and the evacuation of Penang begun. Before leaving, the small garrison carried out much demolition but, unfortunately, the broadcasting station was not destroyed and some 24 self-propelled boats and many large barges and junks were not scuttled. The evacuation of the European residents was completed by midnight on December 17–18. Retaining their arms and equipment, 500 Asiatics of the S.S.V.F. chose to remain behind.

On the 16th it was decided that Indian 11th Division must be given a respite and that since a Japanese thrust through Baling would turn the Muda line and, since it was unlikely that Ind. 12th Inf. Bde. would be able to check such a thrust, the division should be withdrawn behind the Krian river which, with its extensive swamps, provided a good tank obstacle. Ind. 6th and 15th Bdes. were ordered to move to Taiping, there to rest and refit while Ind. 28th Bde. was ordered to move back to Simpang Lima, there to occupy a position covering the Krian river line from the bridge at Nibong Tebal westwards to the sea. 'Krohcol' was disbanded. 3/16th Punjab Regt., with 10th Mtn. Bty., was ordered to hold the river crossing at Selama. 5/14th Punjab Regt. was withdrawn to Taiping. To cover the withdrawal from the Muda to the Krian, Ind. 12th Bde. was ordered to fight a rearguard action through Titi Karangan to Selama, passing through 3/16th Punjab Regt. and joining Indian 11th Division at Taiping. 5/2nd Punjab Regt. held the bridge over the Muda at Batu Pekaka and 2nd A. & S.H. withdrew to Kupang and thence, on December 16, to Titi Karangan. The Japanese attempted

---

*This independent company consisted of one British and three Indian platoons and had been organised for employment behind the enemy's lines. It was never used for this purpose.

to rush the bridge at Batu Pakaka but were repulsed and the bridge was blown. By midnight on the 17th, Ind. 12th Inf. Bde. reached Selama, to pass u/c Indian 11th Division. By dawn on the 18th the whole force was south of the Krian.

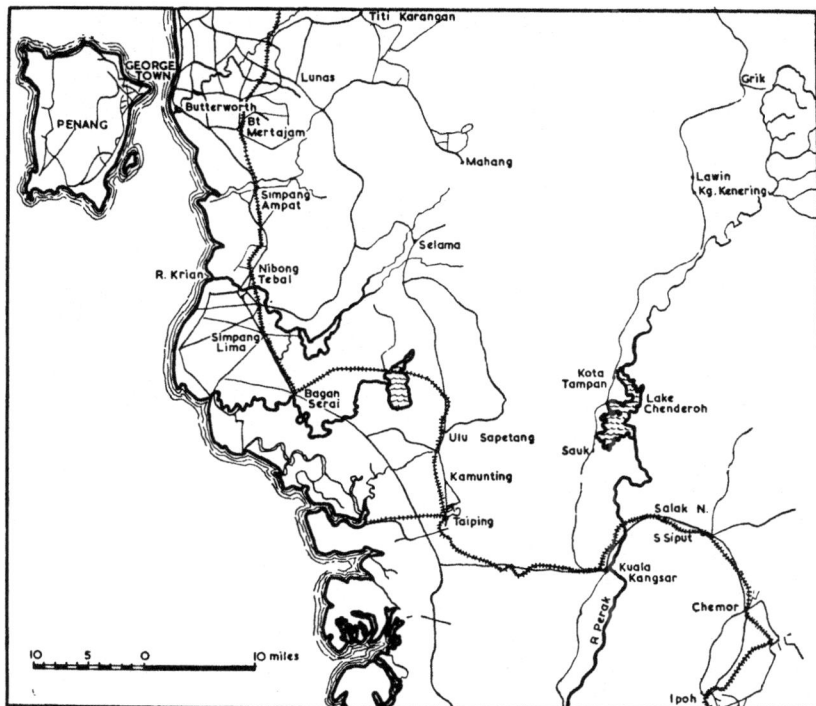

FIG. 7. Butterworth–Ipoh.

On December 16 the company of the Argylls and the detachment of armoured cars of the F.M.S.V.D.F. north of Grik were attacked and compelled to fall back to Kuala Kenering, and on the 17th to Sumpitan. This thrust towards Kuala Kangsar constituted a threat to the communications of the troops on the Krian river line. The rest of the Argylls were sent up to Lenggong on the 19th, and a company of 5/2nd Punjab Regt. to Kota Tampan, four miles farther south. Almost immediately the Japanese attacked and a fierce engagement resulted. On the 20th Lenggong and Kota Tampan were abandoned. The remainder of 5/2nd Punjab Regt. was sent forward to occupy a position covering the western shore of Lake Chenderoh.

On December 20 the Japanese, advancing southwards from Mahang, tried to cross the Krian at Selama but were repulsed by 3/16th Punjab Regt. It became necessary, however, to give up the river line and Ind.

28th Bde. withdrew during the night of December 20–21 through Bagan Serai to the vicinity of Ulu Sapetang. From midnight December 21–22 Ind. 12th Inf. Bde. and all troops west of the Perak river were placed u/c Indian 11th Division. G.O.C. Indian 11th Division now decided that a withdrawal behind the Perak could not long be delayed. He pulled back Ind. 28th Bde. to the Lawin area and ordered 2/1st Gurkha Rifles to hold a bridgehead at Blanja. On the 22nd, Indian 11th Division withdrew behind the Perak. Ind. 12th Bde. withdrew to Sungei Siput, Ind. 28th Bde. to Siputeh in support of the Blanja bridgehead.

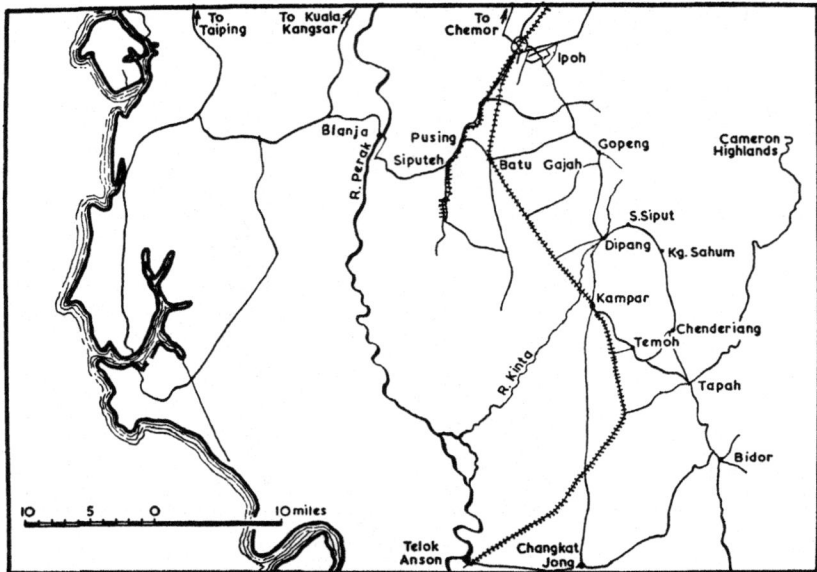

FIG. 8. Ipoh–Telok Anson.

III Corps selected a series of defensive positions south of Ipoh, at Kampar, near Tanjong Malim and at Tapah, Bidor and in the Slim river area. The amalgamated Ind. 6th and 15th Bdes. (Ind. 6/15th Bde.):
    1st Leicesters and 2nd East Surrey (the British battalion)
    1/8th Punjabis and 2/9th Jats (the Jat/Punjabi battalion)
    1/14th, 2/16th and 3/16th Punjabis,
was to occupy the Kampar position while Ind. 12th and 28th Bdes. fought delaying actions on the main road north and south of Ipoh and on the Blanja front respectively. Ind. 12th Bde. was disposed in depth on the trunk road covering Chemor. In the afternoon of December 26 the Japanese attacked and Ind. 12th Bde. was forced back some three miles, suffering heavy loss including a whole company of 4/19th

Hyderabad Regt. Both Ind. 12th and 28th Bdes. were withdrawn south of Ipoh during the night of December 27–28, 28th Bde. to Sahum and 12th Bde. to positions between Gopeng and Dipang. 'Roseforce', which included a specially selected party of 50 Australians, was transported in lightly armed naval craft to raid the Japanese communications west of

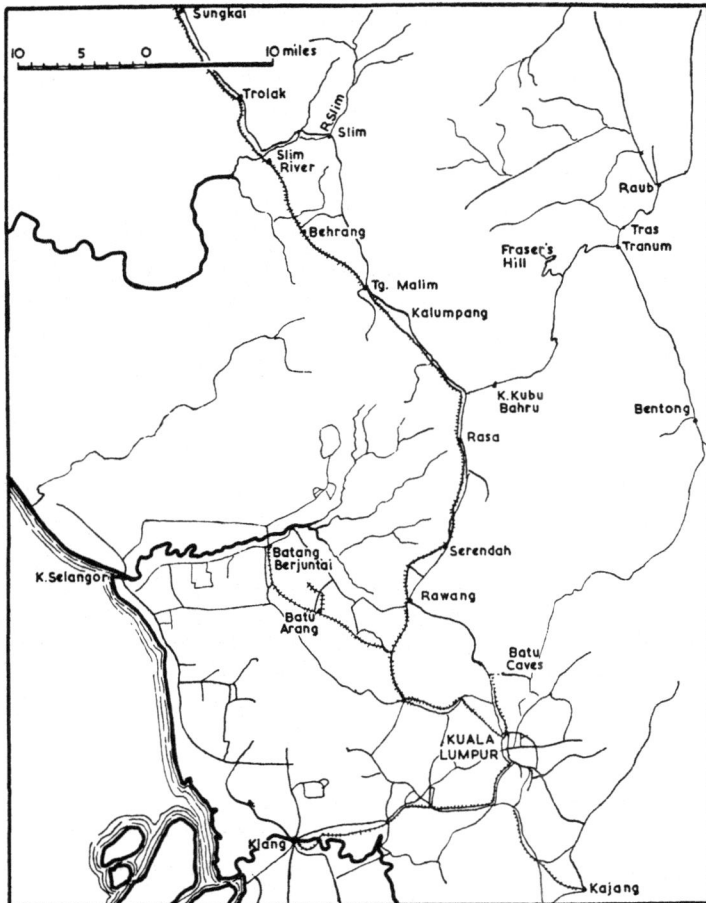

FIG. 9. Sungkai–Kajang.

the Perak river. The force landed near Trong, ambushed motor transport and staff cars and then returned to Port Swettenham.

The Kampar position was semi-circular with a perimeter of about four miles covering the town of Kampar. It could be turned either from Telok Anson by a force transported by sea and river or from Sahum. 6/15th Bde. was disposed in depth in the Kampar position. Ind. 28th Bde. held the Sahum road, being likewise disposed in depth. Ind. 12th

Bde. was withdrawn to Bidor. 1st Independent Company was sent to Telok Anson. 5/14th Punjab Regt. was in reserve at Temoh.

On December 28 the Japanese began to press against the positions at Gopeng and by midday on the 29th it became necessary for 12th Bde. to withdraw through Dipang. 28th Bde. established a bridgehead at the Dipang bridge. Ind. 12th Bde., now utterly exhausted, passed through this bridgehead and moved to Bidor. The Dipang bridge was then blown.

On January 1 the Japanese launched a strong attack on the main Kampar position, but this held. 2/2nd Gurkha Rifles of Ind. 28th Bde. were moved to the Slim river area to guard the communications from the direction of Telok Anson and the Bernam river. Japanese troops landing at Utan Melintang were engaged by Ind. 3rd Cav. Ind. 12th Bde. was ordered to hold the approaches from Telok Anson to Bidor and Tapah. 1st Independent Company withdrew through Ind. 12th Bde., which took up a position on the road about two miles west of Changkat Jong. The Kampar position was then abandoned, Ind. 28th and 12th Bdes. withdrawing through Ind. 6/15th Bde. to the Slim river area.

By January 4, Indian 11th Division was in the Sungkai–Trolak area, with Ind. 12th Bde. in the Trolak sector, Ind. 28th Bde. in the Slim river sector and 6/15th Bde. at Tanjong Malim. Shortly after midnight on January 6–7 a Japanese mechanised force led by tanks attacked straight down the road and overran 4/19th Hyderabad Regt., 5/2nd Punjab Regt. and 2nd A. & S.H. in rapid succession. The Japanese continued southwards, to run into and scatter 5/14th Punjab Regt. about a mile north of Kampong Slim. Further to the south 2/9th Gurkhas were beginning to occupy their positions near Kampong Slim when the leading Japanese tanks drove through them to overtake 2/1st Gurkha Rifles, moving in column of route towards the Cluny Estate. The battalion disintegrated.

Of Ind. 28th Bde. only 2/2nd Gurkha Rifles were left to take up their position covering the railway. The Japanese tanks then swept through 349th and 501st Batteries of 137th Fd. Regt. onwards towards the vital bridge across the Slim river. The bridge was captured and the tanks continued on their way until about two miles farther south they ran into 155 Fd. Regt., moving north to support Ind. 28th Bde., and were checked. They had destroyed one brigade and part of another in their headlong rush of some nineteen miles.

The remnants of Indian 11th Division assembled at Tanjong Malim. On January 8, of 5/2 Punjab Regt. there remained the quartermaster and 80 I.O.Rs.; of 5/14th Punjab Regt. 6 officers and 135 O.Rs.; of 2/1st Gurkha Rifles 4 Gurkha officers and 20 O.Rs. and of Ind. 28th Inf. Bde. 700 all ranks (2/2nd Gurkha Rifles 400, 2/9th 300).

On January 8 General Wavell, on his way to the headquarters of the newly created South West Pacific Command (Abdacom.), stopped at Singapore and, having inspected Indian 11th Division, realised that it was in no condition to fight any more delaying actions and must be withdrawn immediately to Johore.

General Wavell decided on the following general plan for the defence of southern Malaya:

(1) Australian 8th Division, less Aust. 22nd Bde. which was to remain in the Mersing area, to move immediately to north-west Johore to fight a decisive action on the general line Segamat—Mount Ophir—Muar. When Aust. 22nd Bde. was relieved by troops sent from Singapore it would move to the same general line.

(2) Indian 9th Division (Ind. 8th and 22nd Bdes., each of two battalions since 3/17th Dogras and 5/11th Sikhs had been sent to reinforce Indian 11th Division) to be placed u/c A.I.F. Malaya and to be reinforced by Ind. 45th Bde. recently arrived from India (7th Rajputana Rifles, 4th Jat Regt., 5th Royal Garhwal Rifles).

(3) III Corps, less Indian 9th Division, to be withdrawn into Johore and to take over operational command in south Johore.

(4) Troops from the southern defences of Singapore Island to be used to reinforce the Johore front.

On January 10 G.O.C. Malaya Command decided that the Segamat–Muar line should be held by 'Westforce', Australian 8th Division, less Aust. 22nd Bde. and Indian 9th Division, and that III Corps should include 'Eastforce':

Aust. 22nd Bde., less one battalion
5th Norfolks (did not join)
The Jat/Punjabi battalion of Ind. 6/15th Bde. at Kahang
2/17th Dogras at Kota Tinggi
The Johore State Forces

and accept responsibility for the defence of south Johore including the line of the lateral road Endau–Kluang–Batu Pahat.

Indian 11th Division was to be rested in Johore and Ind. 12th Bde. was to be sent to Singapore Island. He required Indian 11th Division to hold Kuala Lumpur until midnight of January 10–11 and thereafter to fall back thirty-two miles to the area of Seremban.

The defence of Kuala Lumpur was organised in three sectors: (1) the trunk road sector, covered by Ind. 28th Inf. Bde.; (2) the central sector including the Batang Berjuntai road, covered by Ind. 6/15th Bde. and (3) the coastal sector, covered by L. of C. Command. It was proposed to hold on to Rawang, Sungei Buloh and Klang until 1600 hours on the 10th and thereafter to deny Kuala Lumpur to the Japanese, either by Ind. 6/15th or 28th Bde., until midnight.

In the coastal sector the Japanese crossed the Sungei Selangor and moved on Kapar, pressing Ind. 3rd Cav. patrols back to the bridge over the river at Klang, held by the Jat/Punjabi battalion. On the 10th they attacked the bridgehead and surrounded one company of the Jat/Punjabis. The rest of the battalion withdrew to Batu Tiga and thence southwards through Kajang. A Japanese force landed at Port Swettenham unopposed on January 10 and moved on Kajang, reaching there a few hours after the last elements of Indian 11th Division had passed through.

Kuala Lumpur, the capital of the Federated Malay States, was entered by the Japanese at 2000 hours on January 11.

On the night of January 13–14, Indian 11th Division passed through 'Westforce' at Gemas and Batu Anam and moved into the Kluang–Rengam area. Indian 9th Division conformed, moving through Bentong and Bahau to reach the Segamat area on the 13th.

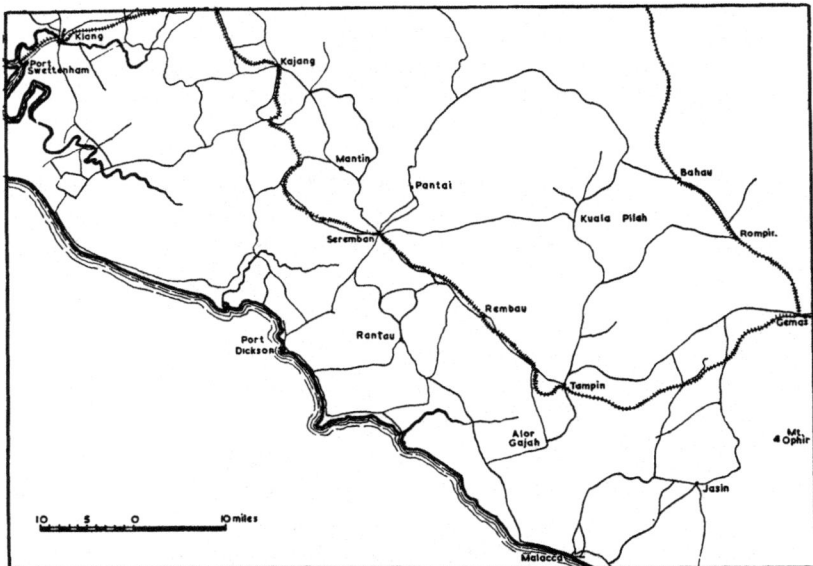

FIG. 10. Kajang–Malacca.

THE ACTION AT JITRA. MEDICAL COVER

16 (Ind.) Fd. Amb. :	.	M.D.S. at Alor Star
		A.D.S. at Puntai Johore
28 (Ind.) Fd. Amb. .	.	H.Q. at Langgar
		A.D.S. at Tanjong Pau
5 M.A.S.	. .	. at Alor Star

Evacuation from the M.D.S. was to 5 (Ind.) C.C.S. at Bedong, the ambulance railhead.

On the 12th, 13 (Ind.) Fd. Hyg. Sec. and 6 Indian A.M.U. were sent back to Sungei Patani and Hy. Sec. 5 (Ind.) C.C.S. and 8 (Ind.) Adv. Depot Med. Stores were ordered by Indian III Corps to move to Bagan Serai. Lt. Sec. 5 (Ind.) C.C.S. remained at Bedong. During the withdrawal to Gurun 28 (Ind.) Fd. Amb. got back safely across the Kedah river. 16 (Ind.) Fd. Amb. moved back in stages, opening an A.D.S. at Guar Chempedak, an A.D.S. at Kota Sarang Semut and a M.D.S. at Sungei Patani. Lt. Sec. 5 (Ind.) C.C.S. moved back to join its heavy section at Bagan Serai. Evacuation was now by M.A.C. to the civil hospital at Taiping, one hundred miles away.

'KROHCOL'. MEDICAL COVER

Though 'Krohcol' was u/c Indian 11th Division it was decided by D.D.M.S. Indian III Corps, when hostilities began, to keep all medical units under his own control, since Indian 11th Division might become involved in Operation 'Matador'. 36 (Ind.) Fd. Amb., attached to Ind. 28th Inf. Bde., only moved up from Ipoh when this brigade joined Indian 11th Division and passed u/c 'Krohcol' on arrival. A company of this field ambulance had been serving troops engaged on aerodrome protection on the L. of C. in Kedah. This company reached Sungei Patani on December 9 and established itself in the camp hospital.

36 (Ind.) Fd. Amb. established a light section A.D.S. at the R.A.P. of 3/16th Punjab Regt. and a M.D.S. at Kroh. Evacuation was by 2/3rd (Aust.) M.A.C. to 5 (Ind.) C.C.S. at Bedong, sixty miles away. On the 10th, 5/14th Punjab Regt. and 10th Mtn. Bty. reached Kroh and were ordered up to a point ten miles north of Betong. A section of 36 (Ind.) Fd. Amb. accompanied this column and opened a light A.D.S. six miles to the north of Betong with two ambulance cars forward at the R.A.P. of 3/16th Punjab Regt. As the Japanese pressure increased O.C. 36 (Ind.) Fd. Amb. ordered an I.S.S. and a field hygiene section to move back from Kroh to Sungei Patani.

On December 11, as 'Krohcol' was withdrawing, the medical cover was as follows: light A.D.S. five miles north of Betong; M.D.S. at Kroh; evacuation to Taiping as 5 (Ind.) C.C.S. was leaving Bedong. When 'Krohcol' fell back to a prepared position three miles west of Kroh on December 13, the light A.D.S. of 36 (Ind.) Fd. Amb. opened in Kroh and the M.D.S. on the Baling Estate. The company at Sungei Patani left to join its parent unit at Titi Karangan. On the 14th 'Krohcol' passed u/c Ind. 12th Inf. Bde., ceasing to exist as an independent force, and was moved to Baling, nine miles south-west of Kroh.

THE ACTION AT GURUN. MEDICAL COVER

16 (Ind.) Fd. Amb. .   . A.D.S. at Estate hospital, Bedong
                          M.D.S. at Sungei Patani

On December 14, because of the Japanese advance, Indian III Corps decided to move 27 I.G.H. from Penang to Seremban, its patients being transferred to Tanjong Malim. Ambulance Railhead was moved to Prai, just south of Butterworth. 6 A.M.U., 13 (Ind.) Fd. Hyg. Sec. and 10 I.S.S. also moved back to Taiping. 16 (Ind.) Fd. Amb., leaving car posts with the brigades and an A.D.S. at Sungei Patani, moved back to Kepala Batas where it established a M.D.S. Evacuation therefrom was by cars of 28 (Ind.) Fd. Amb. and 5 (Ind.) M.A.S. 28 (Ind.) Fd. Amb. opened a M.D.S. at Butterworth and the rest of the unit proceeded to Bt. Mertajam in reserve. 2/3rd (Aust.) M.A.C. evacuated casualties from this M.D.S. to Taiping, now the railhead for 17 C.G.H. at Tanjong Malim.

On December 16, when Indian 11th Division was south of the Muda river, 16 (Ind.) Fd. Amb., leaving an A.D.S. at Kepala Batas and a light A.D.S. at Bumbong Lima with the rearguard at the main road bridge over the Muda, moved to Simpang Ampat, south of Bt. Mertajam, where it opened a M.D.S. 28 (Ind.) Fd. Amb. withdrew to Taiping, its M.D.S. functioning as a C.C.S. An A.D.S. was established at Kamunting to serve stragglers.

When Ind. 28th Bde. moved back to Simpang Lima to take up a line behind the Krian river from Nibong Tebal to the sea with Ind. 12th Inf. Bde. on its right and Ind. 6th and 15th Bdes. were withdrawn to the Taiping area in reserve, 16 (Ind.) Fd. Amb. opened an A.D.S. at Simpang Lima, another at Kuala Kangsar and a M.D.S. at the cross-roads four miles south of Taiping.

20 C.G.H. evacuated all its patients (some 600) on December 15 by ambulance train to Tanjong Malim and Singapore. Its surgical team and four sisters proceeded to the civil hospital in Seremban and 20 C.G.H. itself moved on the 17th to Kajang. With it went 8 (Ind.) Adv. Depot Med. Stores which had been moved from Bedong to Taiping. Lt. Sec. 5 (Ind.) C.C.S. left Taiping the same night for Batu Gajah.

On the night of December 16–17 the evacuation of Penang was completed. The island had been mercilessly bombed and casualties among the civil population had been exceedingly heavy. The troops were moved to the mainland and the company of 18 (Ind.) Fd. Amb. that had been serving them joined its parent unit at Ipoh. The orders for 27 I.G.H. to move from Penang to Seremban failed to reach the unit but the Fortress Commander on his own initiative ordered it to clear its patients to the mainland and then to move to Seremban on the 17th.

These moves of 20 C.G.H. and 27 I.G.H. caused a shortage of hospital beds in Indian III Corps area and so, in accordance with arrangements previously made with the Civil Medical Services, 100 British and 300 Indian beds were provided in the civil hospital in Seremban. A registrar, a Q.M., nursing and clerical staff were provided by 27 I.G.H., a surgical team and sisters by 20 I.G.H. All cases not requiring surgical treatment or expert nursing were sent to 19 I.G.H. (600 beds), which could not itself accept serious cases for the reason that its surgical team and equipment had been sent to Jerantut. It had been dealing mainly with exhausted men suffering from minor injury or ailment and lack of food.

At Taiping all the civil services had now broken down and the field ambulances were instructed by Malaya Command to salvage medical stores from abandoned civil and estate hospitals and to send these back to Singapore. Some two million atebrin tablets were recovered in this way. 30 (Ind.) Fd. Amb. alone salvaged 150,000 tablets at Baling Estate hospital on December 14. Great quantities of these salvaged stores were loaded into railway trucks which were sent back attached to a train carrying ammunition. The train was bombed and set on fire and so the stores were lost.

13 (Ind.) Fd. Hyg. Sec. and 6 A.M.U. were now sent to Kuala Lumpur to pass u/c Indian III Corps. 10 I.S.S. was sent to Seremban and was there attached to 27 I.G.H. On December 18, 5 (Ind.) C.C.S. opened in the civil hospital at Batu Gajah which had been vacated by the civilian staff. The heavy section was sent back to Singapore for the reason that it had been found that the light section, using the extra equipment available in the civil hospitals, was adequate for all possible commitments.

When 'Krohcol' withdrew to Baling it left the jungle road through Klian Intan to Grik unguarded so a company of 2nd A. & S.H. and a detachment of the F.M.S.V.F. were sent to Grik. 36 (Ind.) Fd. Amb. moved to the Mountjoy Estate, about six miles south of Titi Karangan, leaving a light section at Kupang. The company of this unit then at Sungei Patani rejoined the field ambulance. Evacuation was to Bagan Serai. When, on December 15, 5/2nd Punjab Regt. was covering the bridges across the Muda river at K. Ketil and Bata Pekaka and 2nd A. & S.H. were at Titi Karangan, these units were served by 36 (Ind.) Fd. Amb. which opened a light A.D.S. at Titi Karangan.

Ind. 12th Inf. Bde. on December 16 was holding a position north of Lunas, where a company of 18 (Ind.) Fd. Amb. was functioning. That night this company moved to Taiping. Ind. 12th Bde. and 36 (Ind.) Fd. Amb. withdrew to Selama. On December 17, Ind. 12th Bde. was resting south of Selama and that night, with 36 (Ind.) Fd. Amb., left for Taiping, moving thence next day to Kuala Kangsar, when 36 (Ind.)

8

Fd. Amb. opened in the civil hospital, from which the civil medical staff had been withdrawn. On the 18th, Ind. 12th Bde. moved up the Grik road to give aid to the Argylls and Punjabis and to attempt to check the Japanese advance along this road.

On December 19, 2nd A. & S.H. were in position near milestone 42 on the Grik road sealing the exits from dense jungle beyond Kenering and 5/2nd Punjab Regt. in position south of Lake Chenderoh. 36 (Ind.) Fd. Amb., its M.D.S. in the civil hospital at Kuala Kangsar, opened light section A.D.Ss. at Kota Tampan and Sauk for 5/2nd Punjab Regt. and 2nd A. & S.H. respectively. Evacuation from the M.D.S. was to Batu Gajah. On the 21st, 2nd A. & S.H. were obliged to withdraw through the Punjabis and the Japanese reached a point twelve miles from Lawin. 36 (Ind.) Fd. Amb. moved to Sungei Patani and remained closed since 16 (Ind.) Fd. Amb. already had a functioning A.D.S. in Kuala Kangsar. On the 22nd, Ind. 12th Bde. withdrew across the Perak river covered by Ind. 28th Inf. Bde. and went into rest at Salak North. 30 (Ind.) Fd. Amb. moved into the Chinese Maternity Hospital at Ipoh, leaving a light section A.D.S. at Sungei Siput. On the 23rd, 36 (Ind.) Fd. Amb. passed u/c A.D.M.S. Indian 11th Division.

During December 19 and 20, when Ind. 28th Inf. Bde. was withdrawing to the line Ulu Sapetang–Bagan Serai and when Ind. 12th Bde. was in action astride the Grik road, the dispositions of 16 and 28 (Ind.) Fd. Ambs. remained unaltered. On December 21, 16 (Ind.) Fd. Amb. took over from 28 (Ind.) Fd. Amb. the A.D.S. at Kamunting and opened a light A.D.S. at Sungei Siput to serve 4/19th Hyderabad Regt. guarding the railway bridge there. On the following day this A.D.S. was taken over by 36 (Ind.) Fd. Amb. and moved its M.D.S. to the Daventy Estate, fourteen miles north of Ipoh, leaving its light A.D.S. still open at Kuala Kangsar. 28 (Ind.) Fd. Amb. withdrew to Ipoh, there to open in the civil hospital, taking over from 18 (Ind.) Fd. Amb. which had been left in Ipoh by Ind. 12th Inf. Bde. when this brigade moved to the support of 'Krohcol'.

When Ind. 12th Inf. Bde. was forced back on the Grik road towards Lawin, Ind. 28th Bde. was compelled to withdraw from the Ulu Sapetang–Bagan Serai line to cover the withdrawal of 12th Bde. 16 (Ind.) Fd. Amb. opened an A.D.S. at Blanja, on the Perak river about twenty-one miles south of K. Kangsar, while still maintaining its A.D.S. at Kuala Kangsar.

By the morning of the 23rd all troops, save those holding the bridge-head at Blanja, were east of the river, Ind. 12th Bde. in Salak North and Ind. 28th Bde. at Siputeh. 16 (Ind.) Fd. Amb. now opened an A.D.S. at Pusing and withdrew the A.D.Ss. from Blanja and Kuala Kangsar. Its M.D.S. was at Batu Gajah. Evacuation was to 5 (Ind.) C.C.S., now in the civil hospital at Sungkai.

THE ACTION AT KAMPAR. MEDICAL COVER

On December 26, 28 (Ind.) Fd. Amb. opened a M.D.S. in the civil hospital Tapah and an A.D.S. at Chenderiang, nine miles to the north. 16 (Ind.) Fd. Amb's. M.D.S. was still at Batu Gajah and its A.D.S. at Pusing. 36 (Ind.) Fd. Amb. had its M.D.S. in the civil hospital Ipoh and a light section A.D.S. with Ind. 12th Bde. five miles to the north of Ipoh. 18 (Ind.) Fd. Amb., corps reserve, was withdrawn to Kuala Lumpur and 5 (Ind.) C.C.S. moved from Sungkai to Tanjong Malim on December 27 to take over the accommodation vacated by 17 C.G.H. This hospital had been closed on Christmas Day, its 950 patients having been transferred to the civil hospital Seremban and to 19 I.G.H. at Mantin. On the 27th the unit moved to Singapore by rail. The hospital facilities in Indian III Corps area now became somewhat unsatisfactory. 20 C.G.H. at Kajang was functioning as a C.C.S. and 19 I.G.H. was only capable of dealing with relatively minor cases. Indian III Corps was far from being self-contained; it could not hold in its area such as were likely to be fit to return to their units in a reasonable time—two months. Arrangements were therefore made to take over 400 beds in the civil hospital at Kuala Lumpur (100 British, 300 Indian) which was being vacated by the civil medical authorities. Personnel of 27 I.G.H. were moved up there from Seremban. There were then in Indian III Corps area:

	British	Indian
Kuala Lumpur . .	100	300 beds
Kajang . .	100	500
Seremban . .	100	300
Mantin . .		600
	300	1,700

When the withdrawal of Ind. 12th and 28th Bdes. to the Kampar position took place on December 27–28, 36 (Ind.) Fd. Amb. moved to an estate hospital at Sungkai, leaving a light section A.D.S. four hundred yards south of Dipang bridge. Evacuation was to 28 (Ind.) Fd. Amb. at Tapah. 16 (Ind.) Fd. Amb., less one company, moved into reserve at the Tong Landen Estate, the company taking over the A.D.S. north of Chenderiang from 28 (Ind.) Fd. Amb. 28 (Ind.) Fd. Amb., with its M.D.S. at Tapah, opened an A.D.S. at Kampar.

When, on December 29, Ind. 12th Bde. was heavily attacked and withdrew to Bidor in reserve, the A.D.S. at Dipang was dive-bombed and got away with difficulty. 2/3rd (Aust.) M.A.C. moved to Tanjong Malim and the M.A.S. at Kuala Lumpur to Kajang alongside 20 C.G.H. When, on the 30th, Ind. 28th Bde. was threatened by Japanese infiltration across the Kinta river, 28 (Ind.) Fd. Amb. opened an additional A.D.S. on the brigade's left flank, north-west of the Tapah road.

On January 1, 1942, the Japanese thrust hard against Ind. 6/15th Bde. but were repulsed. Late in the day when Japanese landings were reported at Ulu Melintang, near the mouth of the Bernam river, Ind. 12th Bde. at Bidor was moved to meet this threat. 16 (Ind.) Fd. Amb., leaving one company with Ind. 28th Bde., opened a M.D.S. one mile south of Bidor. The withdrawal from the Kampar position to the Tapah–Bidor area was associated with a sharp rise in the incidence of malaria. The British battalion of Ind. 6/15th Bde. alone lost over 100 officers and men from this cause.

28 (Ind.) Fd. Amb. moved its H.Q. to Sungkai in reserve. While at Kampar the M.D.S. had been twice bombed and hit. 36 (Ind.) Fd. Amb. opened an A.D.S. at Sungkai and a light section A.D.S. at the junction of the Ct. Jong–Bidor roads. A detachment was sent back to the Slim river area. When Ind. 28th Bde. withdrew through Temoh to occupy a position two miles south of Kampar, one company of 28 (Ind.) Fd. Amb. was placed u/c 2/9th Gurkhas.

With the small force that was sent to the Kuala Selangor area to guard against Japanese landings went 3 (Vol.) Fd. Amb., rapidly becoming ineffective through desertions, 18 (Ind.) Fd. Amb. from corps reserve and a M.A.S. u/c A.D.M.S. Force. Evacuation was to the civil hospital at Kuala Lumpur.

Intensified efforts were being made at this time to collect and send back to base medical stores from civil sources, but owing to shortage of labour the loaded trains could not be accepted at Singapore and so were sent to Malacca. There they fell into the hands of the Japanese.

On January 3, 16 (Ind.) Fd. Amb. had one company with 2/9th Gurkha Rifles and its M.D.S. one mile south of Bidor. 36 (Ind.) Fd. Amb. had its A.D.S. at Sungkai and its M.D.S. at Slim river. 28 (Ind.) Fd. Amb. moved to a site five miles south of Tanjong Malim in reserve.

At dawn on January 4, Ind. 12th Bde. moved into position at Trolak with Ind. 28th Bde. six miles farther back near Slim River. The battalions had become greatly reduced in strength; none of them had more than three poorly armed companies. 16 (Ind.) Fd. Amb. placed an A.D.S. with Ind. 28th Bde. three miles east of Slim River and opened a M.D.S. one mile south of Tanjong Malim. 36 (Ind.) Fd. Amb. established a light section A.D.S. to serve Ind. 12th Bde. in the Trolak sector and a M.D.S. near the Slim river, half a mile south of Slim village. Evacuation from the M.D.S. was by 2/3rd (Aust.) M.A.C. to the civil hospital at Kuala Lumpur.

On January 5, to meet a Japanese threat from Kuala Selangor to the main road communications at Rawang, Ind. 6/15th Bde. moved to this area. 28 (Ind.) Fd. Amb. moved to Serendah and established an A.D.S. two miles west of Rawang and a M.D.S. eight miles south of this town. H.Q. 28 (Ind.) Fd. Amb. and 5 M.A.S. moved to Skeet Club near Kuala Lumpur.

Because of the threat of Japanese landings on the west coast in the rear of Indian 11th Division, it was now decided not to stand at Tanjong Malim but in front of Kuala Lumpur. This, it was assumed, would give time for Indian 9th Division, from the east coast, Australian 8th Division and the newly arrived 18th Division to prepare for a decisive battle on the line Batu Anam–Mount Ophir–Muar. This being done, the weary and much depleted Indian 11th Division would withdraw into Johore to rest.

D.D.M.S. Indian III Corps thereupon decided to send back to Singapore the following medical units:

2 (Mal.) M.A.C. . .	H.Q. and two secs. at Kuala Lumpur
20 C.G.H. . . .	Kajang
19 I.G.H. . . .	Mantin
1 (Ind.) Con. Depot .	Morib

5 (Ind.) C.C.S. was moved from Tanjong Malim to Kajang on January 4–5, having cleared its 406 patients by road and rail to 27 I.G.H. in the civil hospital Kuala Lumpur. 2 and 8 (Ind.) Adv. Depots Med. Stores were also sent to Kuala Lumpur. A.D.M.S. Indian 11th Division, to lighten his field ambulances, sent back to the vicinity of Rasa two officers, a hundred I.O.Rs. and the bulk of the heavy equipment.

THE ACTION AT SLIM RIVER AND THE WITHDRAWAL OF INDIAN 11TH DIVISION INTO JOHORE. MEDICAL COVER

During the fighting on the Slim river 36 (Ind.) Fd. Amb. and one company of 16 (Ind.) Fd. Amb. were overrun and lost. The experience of the officer commanding the former unit illustrates the confusion that prevailed. At 0715 hours on January 7 he set out on his motor cycle to visit his A.D.S. in the Trolak sector. On a narrow winding road he encountered a column of thirteen Japanese tanks. Flinging himself off his cycle he plunged into the rubber that edged the road and made his way to H.Q. Ind. 28th Bde. Thence he proceeded to H.Q. Ind. 12th Bde. Picking up an ambulance car he then went on to the A.D.S. and took the six men there to H.Q. 2nd Gurkha Rifles, where he left them. He had to swim across the river to get to his M.D.S. He found that it had been shot to bits but that its personnel were safe and were carrying on. He then returned to H.Q. Ind. 28th Bde., arriving there just in time to see Japanese tanks shoot up its transport. Here he met the commander of Ind. 12th Bde. who told him that evacuation of casualties from the Trolak sector was now impossible. Returning to the M.D.S. he organised the evacuation of casualties therefrom by stretcher-bearer parties. These, moving back, soon came under fire and were obliged to separate. That night they were forced to leave their wounded by the roadside and to take to the jungle in an attempt to get past a road block on the Slim river bridge road. Few got past. One party eventually reached the coast at Kuala Selangor only to be betrayed to the Japanese. The second in command of the field ambulance and his party were picked up by the Japanese two months after the capitulation 250 miles south of the Slim river. He was viciously sentenced to a long term of solitary confinement in Outram jail.

When Indian 11th Division withdrew to Rasa 16 (Ind.) Fd. Amb. moved thereto and opened a M.D.S., leaving a light section A.D.S. at Tanjong Malim until midnight January 7–8. On the 8th the survivors of 16 (Ind.) Fd. Amb. were at Batu Caves Estate, 28 (Ind.) Fd. Amb. was still at Rawang and the few who remained of 36 (Ind.) Fd. Amb. were sent to Kajang. 18 (Ind.) Fd. Amb. (corps reserve) had a M.D.S. in the civil hospital at Kuala Lumpur. Ambulance trains could no longer come farther north than Kajang and so evacuation from Kuala Lumpur was by road to Kajang.

27 I.G.H. at Kuala Lumpur moved with its patients and equipment to Singapore on the night of January 8–9. 2/3 (Aust.) M.A.C. at Kajang was now clearing field ambulances direct to Seremban, a return journey of some seventy miles. 2 and 8 (Ind.) Adv. Depots Med. Stores left Kuala Lumpur to reach Singapore on the 6th, but during the journey the stores of the former went astray and were never seen again. 5 (Ind.) C.C.S. was ordered to move from Kajang to Tampin on January 8.

The withdrawal in Johore was associated with a great reduction in the number of civil hospitals available for use by the Army Medical Services. Previously it had been possible to use them to form a series of improvised C.C.Ss., staffing them with sections of 27 I.G.H., and this had meant that the military hospitals on the mainland had not been overtaxed and could retain their patients. It was necessary, therefore, to arrange that patients should not be so retained in hospitals north of Johore Bahru and also to request that a C.C.S.—1 (Mal.) C.C.S.—should be sent forward. Unfortunately this unit could not be sent forward by rail at this time, the railway being overtaxed, and road transport could not be provided. This policy of evacuation to the base threw a very heavy additional strain upon the ambulance train service. This had been improvised out of ordinary rolling stock, the carriages being gutted and fitted with sling stretchers. The trains lacked adequate kitchen and lavatory facilities and were not really suitable for long journeys, long especially in respect of time. The journey of two hundred miles commonly took eighteen hours. They were being driven for the most part by survivors from H.M.S. *Repulse* and H.M.S.

Prince of Wales, sunk by Japanese aircraft on December 10, 1941, off the east coast of Malaya when searching for Japanese transports reported to be off Kuantan.

When Ind. 6/15th Bde. withdrew to the Batu Arang area and Ind. 28th Bde. to Serendah, 16 (Ind.) Fd. Amb. at the Batu Caves Estate opened a M.D.S. and placed detachments u/c Ind. 28th Bde. while 28 (Ind.) Fd. Amb. provided detachments for Ind. 6/15th Bde. H.Q. 2/3 (Aust.) M.A.C. moved to Seremban, now ambulance railhead, and the M.A.S. at Seremban moved to Tampin.

On January 10, 16 (Ind.) Fd. Amb. (Ind. 28th Bde.) was ordered to Seremban and 28 (Ind.) Fd. Amb. (Ind. 6/15th Bde.) to the vicinity of Jasin. Evacuation was by 2/3 (Aust.) M.A.C. to 5 (Ind.) C.C.S. at the civil hospital at Tampin. On the 11th, 16 (Ind.) Fd. Amb. established a M.D.S. at the junction of the trunk road and the Rantau road and an A.D.S. at Seremban and 28 (Ind.) Fd. Amb., with the remnants of 36 (Ind.) Fd. Amb. and 13 (Ind.) Fd. Hyg. Sec. from Kajang, which was at Rantau, nine miles to the south of Seremban, closed. 18 (Ind.) Fd. Amb., now u/c Indian 11th Division, had its A.D.S. near Port Dickson and a M.D.S. south of Seremban. Ambulance railhead was now at Gemas.

When, on January 12 and 13, L. of C. troops were covering Malacca and Ind. 6/15th Bde. was in the Alor Gajah area, 28 (Ind.) Fd. Amb. moved into reserve at Jasin with A.D.Ss. at Alor Gajah and Tampin. 5 (Ind.) C.C.S. at Tampin closed and moved to the vicinity of Rengam on January 12–13. Its patients had been evacuated to the civil hospital at Segamat which was occupied by 15 (Ind.) Fd. Amb. of Indian 9th Division. On the 13th, 16 (Ind.) Fd. Amb. withdrew to Ayer Hitam. 28 (Ind.) Fd. Amb. was at Jasin, 15 at Segamat and 18, with its H.Q. ten miles south of Tampin, had two A.D.Ss. operating independently and out of touch. The last of these units was ordered to send a light section M.D.S. to Malacca and relieve the detachments of 28 (Ind.) Fd. Amb. there.

By January 10, 2/10 A.G.H. had been withdrawn from Malacca and had moved to a site on the northern outskirts of Singapore city but was closed for the time being. 2/13 A.G.H. at Tampoi Hill, seven miles north of Johore Bahru, expanded from 600 to 1,200 beds to cover this move. 1 Mal. G.H. was moved up to the civil hospital at Johore Bahru, there to provide 200 beds. Only two C.C.Ss., 2/4 (Aust.) at Kluang and 5 (Ind.) at Rengam estate hospital, were functioning at this time. Evacuation from the east coast was direct to Johore Bahru.

INDIAN 22ND INFANTRY BRIGADE

THE WITHDRAWAL TO JERANTUT

Meanwhile, in the east, Ind. 22nd Inf. Bde., less 2nd F.F. Regt., had been guarding the airfield at Kuantan. A Japanese coastal column moving southwards from Kelantan had reached Kuala Trengganu by December 20 and on the 27th was challenged by Ind. 22nd Inf. Bde. On December 31 the Japanese were on the east bank of the Kuantan river and had occupied Kuantan town. On January 3 the G.O.C. Indian 9th Division ordered the brigade to withdraw to Jerantut. The withdrawal was costly, for the Japanese pressure grew in strength.

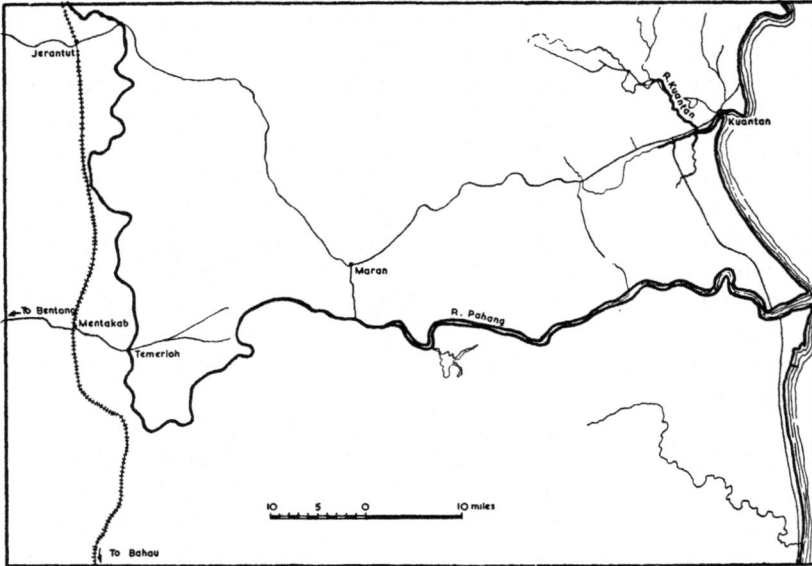

FIG. 11. Kuantan–Jerantut.

Kuantan on the east coast of Malaya is one hundred miles away from Jerantut on the railway in central Malaya and one hundred and sixty miles from Raub where H.Q. Indian 9th Division was located. To it a road ran through desolate jungle. 2/12th F.F. Regt., after serving with Ind. 8th Bde. in Kelantan had rejoined the brigade. 2/18th Garhwal Rifles were guarding twelve miles of coastline and 5/11th Sikh Regt. was west and south of the Kuantan river guarding the aerodrome. The only means of crossing the river was by the local ferry.

MEDICAL COVER

27 (Ind.) Fd. Amb. established a M.D.S. at the camp hospital at the 11th milestone on the Kuantan–Jerantut road. Evacuation therefrom was by a section of 1 (Mal.) M.A.C. to 19 I.G.H. at Jerantut. An A.D.S. was opened in Kuantan and two light section A.D.Ss. on the coastline. D.D.M.S. Malaya Command sent up a number of Chinese stretcher-bearers from the Aux. Med. Depot Singapore for use on the beaches but they were employed first at the M.D.S. and later at 19 I.G.H. at

Jerantut. A further light section A.D.S. was established on the airfield and a car post attached to the R.A.P. of 5/11th Sikh Regt. An advanced surgical centre was prepared at the M.D.S. to meet the possibility that the L. of C. might be cut. It was to be staffed when required from the Kuantan civil hospital.

When the Japanese reached Kuala Trengganu it was decided to withdraw the bulk of the brigade to the west of the river. When the brigade withdrew to Jerantut, light section A.D.Ss. moved with the two battalions. The A.D.S. took over from the M.D.S., which then moved back to Jerantut, leaving a light section M.D.S. and the M.A.C. at Maran. When 2/12th F.F. Regt. rejoined the brigade a light section A.D.S. was attached to it. When the brigade reached Maran the A.D.S. took over from the light section M.D.S. which then moved back to open about fifteen miles east of Jerantut. When the rearguard crossed the Jerantut ferry on the night of January 6–7, the brigade moved to the area Raub–Tras–Tranum.

On January 5 the section of 19 I.G.H. (100 beds) at Jerantut with a surgical unit from its parent unit was sent back to Mantin and 15 (Ind.) Fd. Amb. opened, to function as a modified C.C.S. in Raub to serve both Ind. 8th and 22nd Bdes. Evacuation was by M.A.S. u/c A.D.M.S. Indian 9th Division either to Bahau or else to Seremban, as 17 C.G.H. at Tanjong Malim was now closed. It was arranged that, should the railway south of Bahau be cut, evacuation would be to the civil hospital at Seremban which was functioning as a C.C.S.

INDIAN 9TH DIVISION

THE WITHDRAWAL FROM JERANTUT TO GEMAS

While Indian 11th Division was fighting delaying actions in front of Kuala Lumpur, Indian 9th Division was withdrawing from the Jerantut area to take its place in 'Westforce' for the coming battle on the Segamat–Mount Ophir–Muar line alongside Australian 8th Division and Ind. 45th Bde. Ind. 22nd Bde. held the Kuala Lipis–Raub area while Ind. 8th Bde. passed through. The division reached Gemas safely.

MEDICAL COVER

On January 7, 27 (Ind.) Fd. Amb. opened a M.D.S. at Bentong, leaving light section A.D.Ss. with the battalions of Ind. 22nd Bde. 15 (Ind.) Fd. Amb., leaving an A.D.S. at Mentakab, moved to Kuala Pilah and by the 9th had opened in Segamat to function as a modified C.C.S. The section of 12 I.G.H. at Bahau was ordered to move to Segamat but through some error was taken to Singapore. The A.D.S.

of 15 (Ind.) Fd. Amb. then moved from Mentakab to Batu Anam and opened on a rubber estate, to be promptly machine-gunned from the air. Next day it moved to Buloh Kasap.

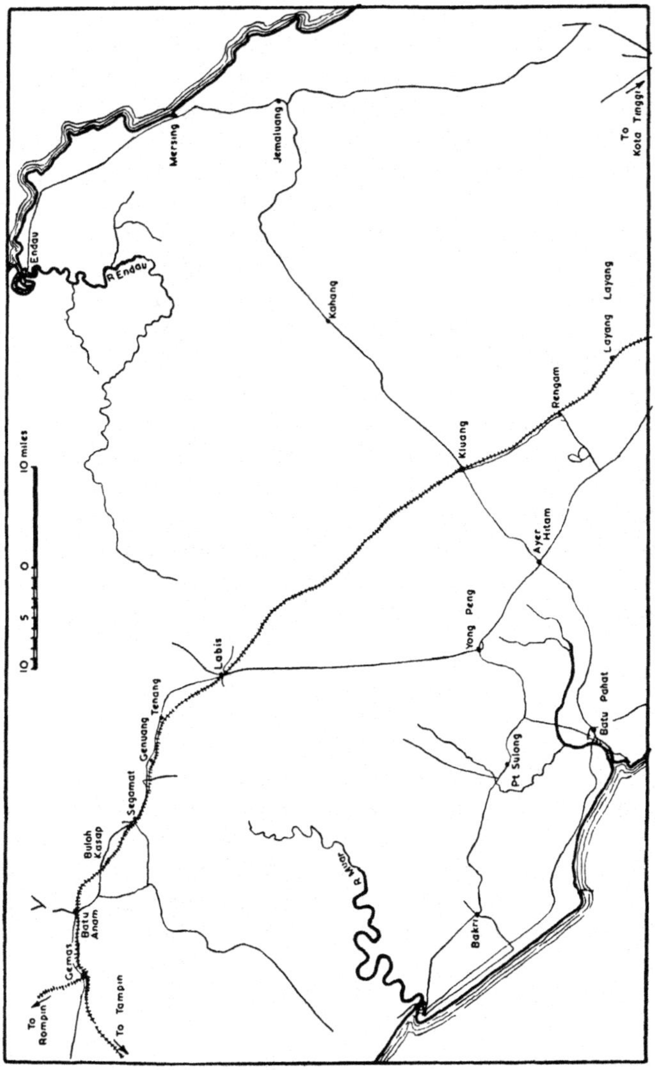

FIG. 12. Johore.

When Ind. 22nd Bde. moved back in its turn to Bentong, 27 (Ind.) Fd. Amb., leaving a light section A.D.S. at Karak, halfway between Mentakab and Bentong, moved back to the Batang Malaka Estate. Evacuation therefrom was to 15 (Ind.) Fd. Amb. at Segamat. On January 12, the A.D.S. having rejoined, 27 (Ind.) Fd. Amb. moved to the Socfin Estate, Labis, to open in the estate hospital as a staging post on the route of evacuation of 15 (Ind.) Fd. Amb. at Segamat.

THE ACTION ON THE SEGAMAT–MOUNT OPHIR–MUAR LINE– WITHDRAWAL FROM THE MAINLAND

Holding this line was 'Westforce', Aust. 27th Bde. (2/26th, 2/29th and 2/30th Bns.) of Australian 8th Division, 8th and 22nd Bdes. of Indian 9th Division and Ind. 45th Bde. of Indian 17th Division. General Wavell suggested that 53rd Bde. of 18th Division should be attached to 'Westforce'. The G.O.C., A.I.F. Malaya, would have preferred to have had his Aust. 22nd Bde. from Mersing and his 2/19th Bn. from Jemaluang but there was no time available for the carrying out of their relief by 53rd Bde. (1st Cambridgeshire, 5th Norfolks, 6th Norfolks). Aust. 27th Bde. covered the main trunk road west of Gemas; Indian 9th Division was in rear of the Australians with Ind. 8th Bde. on the trunk road at Batu Anam and Ind. 22nd Bde. astride the Segamat–Malacca road. Ind. 45th Bde. was on the Muar river line in the coastal sector.

The Japanese assault on this line opened on January 14. In the Gemas–Segamat area Aust. 2/30th Bn. neatly ambushed and destroyed several hundreds. On this and the following day the Japanese met fresh troops for the first time in six weeks and were checked, suffering heavy losses. In the Muar sector on the left of the line Ind. 45th Bde., new and untried, had been assigned a difficult task. It was holding a front of twenty-five miles along a tortuous river line. On the 15th it was fiercely attacked and by the 16th the Japanese were across the Muar river and part of the brigade was forced back towards Bakri. Aust. 2/29th Bn. of Aust. 27th Bde. was sent to Bakri to reinforce Ind. 45th Bde., reaching there on the 17th. So also was Aust. 2/19th Bn. of Aust. 22nd Bde. from Jemaluang. Indian 11th Division was placed on four hours' notice to move to the Yong Peng area.

When, on January 16, it was learnt that the Japanese had landed at the Telaga jetty, Batu Pahat, 53rd Bde. was sent forward to Ayer Hitam and one of its battalions, 6th Norfolks, took up a position at Bukit Pelandok, guarding the defile some eleven miles west of Yong Peng.

At dawn on January 18, Japanese tanks attacked Aust. 2/29th Bn. but were sharply repulsed. Aust. 2/19th Bn., arriving, moved up to support 2/29th. Ind. 6/15th Bde. organised the defence of Batu Pahat and 3/16th Punjab Regt. was sent to reinforce 53rd Bde. which, with 2nd Cambridgeshire at Batu Pahat and 5th Norfolks at Ayer Hitam, now consisted solely of 6th Norfolks. 2nd Loyals, who had recently joined Ind. 22nd Bde. from Singapore, were also sent to 53rd Bde.

The Japanese surprised a company of 6th Norfolks at Bukit Pelandok and thus gained control over the road to Bakri. 3/16th Punjab Regt.,

6th Norfolks and a company of 2nd Loyals attempted to recapture the defile at dawn on the 20th but failed. At dawn on the 19th, Aust. 2/19th Bn. was heavily attacked from the south. The attack was repulsed but the Japanese overran the battalion transport and cut the road to Yong Peng. Aust. 2/29th Bn. withdrew towards Bakri, meeting strong opposition on the way. The battalion, losing heavily, fought its way to Aust. 2/19th Bn's. perimeter, only 7 officers and 190 O.Rs. getting through, the rest taking to the swamps in an attempt to make their way back to Yong Peng; they were all lost or captured.

'Baker' Force, consisting of the remains of Aust. 2/19th and 2/29th Bns. and Ind. 45th Bde., began to withdraw towards Yong Peng on the 20th. At 2000 hours the head of the column was checked by a road block. This was cleared by a bayonet charge but the column was soon checked again. After fierce fighting the opposition was thrust aside and the column headed for the bridge at Parit Sulong. This was in Japanese hands, for the two platoons of 6th Norfolks, being of the opinion that they had become isolated, had left the bridge on the morning of the 20th and had moved across country to Batu Pahat.

In the meantime the withdrawal of 'Westforce' had been proceeding according to plan. By the morning of the 21st, Ind. 22nd Bde. was a few miles north of Labis, Ind. 8th Bde. some miles farther south and Aust. 27th Bde. in a position covering the road junction at Yong Peng. In order that the movements of 'Westforce', Ind. 45th and 53rd Bdes. might be co-ordinated, all troops in the Muar–Yong Peng area were placed u/c 'Westforce' with effect from 0800 hours on the 21st.

An attempt by 53rd Bde. to recapture Parit Sulong bridge on the morning of the 21st failed. By nightfall 45th Bde. had been cooped up in a very restricted area immediately west of the bridge and early on the 22nd an aircraft from Singapore dropped supplies of food for the beleaguered brigade. A request that the wounded might pass through the Japanese lines was refused. Destroying its heavy equipment and leaving its seriously wounded in charge of volunteers, the brigade made its precarious way to Yong Peng through the jungle. At Parit Sulong the Japanese massacred all those who had been left behind.

Meanwhile, patrols of Aust. 22nd Bde. had made contact with the Japanese north of Endau on January 14. On the 16th Endau and Mersing were bombed. On the night of January 17–18, having destroyed all the bridges and culverts on the Endau–Mersing road, the brigade withdrew behind the Mersing river.

On January 23, 53rd Bde. was instructed to withdraw through Aust. 27th Bde. at Yong Peng and move to Ayer Hitam, reverting to the command of Indian 11th Division. At the same time 'Westforce' was to withdraw from Yong Peng to positions covering the Kluang–Ayer Hitam road. 53rd Bde. began to move back from the Bukit Pelandok area at noon on the 23rd. Reaching Ayer Hitam on the 24th, it was sent on to Skudai, *en route* for Benut.

In the Batu Pahat area on the 21st the Japanese were in contact with Ind. 6/15th Bde. and cut the Batu Pahat–Ayer Hitam road. 5th Norfolks were unable to reinforce Batu Pahat and so were withdrawn to Ayer Hitam and thence to Pontian Kechil so that they could reach Batu Pahat by the coast road.

On January 24 the dispositions of Malaya Command were:

'Eastforce' was in contact with the Japanese on the line of the Mersing river.
'Westforce:' Ind. 8th and 22nd Bdes. were in the area of Kluang
        Aust. 27th Bde. at Ayer Hitam was temporarily out of
        touch with the Japanese.
Indian 11th Division was on the west coast:
        Ind. 6/15th Bde. at Batu Pahat
        Ind. 28th Bde. at Pontian Kechil
        53rd Bde. (now consisting of 6th Norfolks, and 3/16th
        Punjabis) was *en route* for Benut from Skudai.
All three fronts were u/c III Corps.

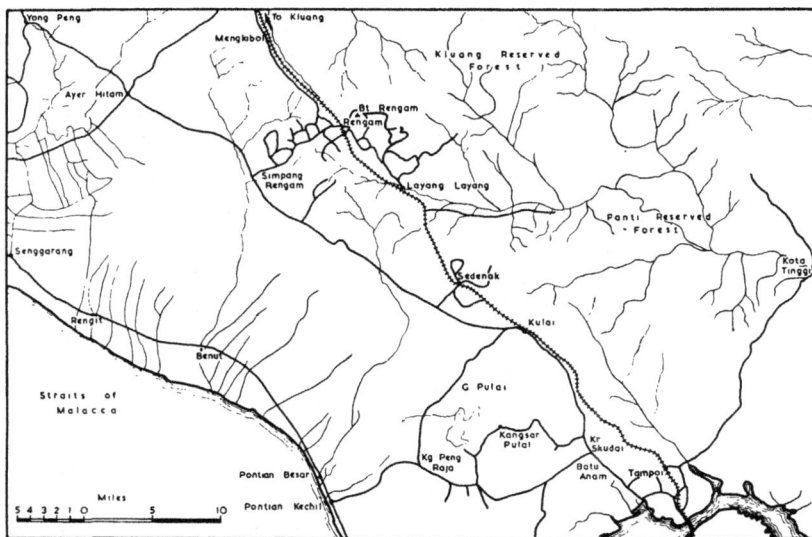

FIG. 13. Yong Peng–Batu Anam.

On the 25th the Japanese pressure north of Batu Pahat increased. 53rd Bde. reached Benut and 6th Norfolks was sent on to Senggarang, leaving a company at Rengit. The Japanese established a number of road blocks between Senggarang and Rengit. 6/15th Bde. was instructed to move to Benut but encountered road blocks south of Senggarang and was forced to leave its wounded in charge of a chaplain, 2 officers and 26 O.Rs. of 198 Fd. Amb., to destroy its guns and vehicles and to attempt to make its way across country. One column of 1,200 reached Benut on the afternoon of the 27th. The remainder of the brigade managed to reach the coast some three miles west of Rengit and were lifted by naval units during the nights of January 29–30, 30–31 and January 31–February 1. About 2,700 all ranks of 6/15th Bde. reached safety.

On January 25, Indian 9th Division reached the area Sungei–Sayong Halt–Rengam and Aust. 27th Bde. the vicinity of milestone 48 on the trunk road. 'Eastforce' conformed. Aust. 2/20th Bn. withdrew to Jemaluang and with Aust. 2/18th Bn. prepared an ambush ten miles north of the village. The leading Japanese troops fell into the trap and were severely mauled. The Australians then withdrew to Jemaluang and thence, on the 28th, moved southwards, to reach Johore Bahru on the 30th.

On January 25, 'Westforce' issued orders for a general withdrawal southwards, Indian 9th Division down the axis of the railway, Aust. 27th Bde. down the trunk road. Since there was no road between Layang–Layang and Kulai, the retirement down the railway meant that all the vehicles and guns of Indian 9th Division had to move by the track from Rengam through the Namazie Estate to the trunk road while this track was still covered by Aust. 27th Bde.

Ind. 8th Bde. (1/13th Frontier Force Regt., 2/10th Baluch and a company of 3/17th Dogras) moved back to the Layang–Layang area and Ind. 22nd Bde. (5/11th Sikhs and a composite battalion from 2/12th F.F. Regt. and 2/18th Garhwalis) to Rengam. But Aust. 27th Bde. had found it necessary to withdraw from the Namazie Estate twenty-four hours ahead of schedule and Ind. 8th Bde. had been pushed back down the line of the railway towards Sedenak. Between Ind. 8th and 22nd Bdes. a wide gap developed and into it the Japanese thrust. Ind. 22nd Bde. attempted to link up again with Ind. 8th Bde. by moving down the western side of the railway line at 1015 hours on the 28th.

G.O.C. Indian 9th Division went forward to see how his two brigades were faring. He found 8th Bde. halfway between Layang–Layang and Sedenak and learnt that the railway bridge at milestone 439¼ had been blown prematurely. He sent 2/10th Baluch to occupy a position at milestone 439½ near Layang–Layang and then, moving farther forward, he was ambushed and killed.

Aust. 27th Bde. moved farther back and Indian 9th Division with Ind. 8th Bde. conformed. Ind. 22nd Bde. thus became completely isolated. Encountering stubborn opposition at Layang–Layang station, it made the fatal decision to move through the jungle. With 5/11th

Sikhs and a platoon of 2/18th Royal Garhwal Rifles in the van and carrying twelve stretcher cases, it struggled on for the next four days through jungle and swamp, lacking rations and deprived of sleep. On January 31 the wounded were left in the care of a dispensary doctor and the brigade lightened its loads. Losses mounted as sleep, too long denied, claimed its victims. Small parties, numbering about a hundred in all, reached the coast, there to be rescued, but the bulk of the brigade was forced to surrender on February 1.

On January 27 General Wavell gave General Percival permission to withdraw the whole force to Singapore island if he considered this to be necessary. In the early morning of the 28th orders were issued that all troops in Johore would cross the causeway on the night of January 30–31. H.Q. Indian III Corps was made responsible for the conduct of the operation which involved the retiral of 'Eastforce' from Mersing, the retiral of 'Westforce' down the central road and that of Indian 11th Division down the west coast.

It was on January 30 that the first troops of Australian I Corps (Australian 6th and 7th Divisions) sailed from Suez (Movement 'Stepsister'). At this time it was intended that this corps should be used for the reinforcement of Malaya Command.

At 0530 hours on January 31 the last battalion on the mainland crossed the causeway. Two hours later the last troops of the inner bridgehead crossed. At 0815 hours on the 31st a seventy foot gap was blown in the causeway. During these events the Japanese air and land forces displayed no particular activity.

THE ACTION ON THE SEGAMAT–MOUNT OPHIR–MUAR LINE AND THE WITHDRAWAL FROM THE MAINLAND.
MEDICAL COVER

In the Segamat–Muar position Aust. 27th Bde. was served by 2/10 (Aust.) Fd. Amb. which established its M.D.S. on the Genuang Estate and its A.D.S. at Batu Anam. 38 (Ind.) Fd. Amb. covered Ind. 45th Bde. Evacuation was by 2/5 (Aust.) M.A.C. to 2/4 (Aust.) C.C.S. at Kluang and to Lt. Sec. 5 (Ind.) C.C.S. at Rengam.

When, on January 15, the Japanese had penetrated to the Muar position and had landed in the vicinity of Batu Pahat, 2/2 (Aust.) Con. Depot at Batu Pahat withdrew to Johore Bahru.

15 (Ind.) Fd. Amb. was still at Segamat receiving casualties from Ind. 8th and 22nd Bdes. of Indian 9th Division, to each of which an A.D.S. was attached. The A.D.S. with Ind. 8th Bde. was at Buloh Kasap. 28 (Ind.) Fd. Amb., Indian 11th Division, was at Mengkibol with an A.D.S. at Jemaluang; 16 (Ind.) Fd. Amb. was at Rengam.

On January 16, 198 Fd. Amb. with 53rd Bde. at Ayer Hitam established its M.D.S. at Simpang Rengam and A.D.Ss. at Ayer Hitam and Yong Peng. To this M.D.S. a detachment of 28 (Ind.) Fd. Amb. was attached.

On the 18th, during the fighting in the Muar sector, 38 (Ind.) Fd. Amb. with Ind. 45th Bde. dealt with 210 casualties. During the withdrawal of Ind. 45th Bde. one company of 38 (Ind.) Fd. Amb. was cut off and lost. The M.D.S. of this unit moved to three to four miles from the Yong Peng–Muar road junction and later withdrew to Ayer Hitam to rest, leaving the A.D.S. of 198 Fd. Amb. at Yong Peng.

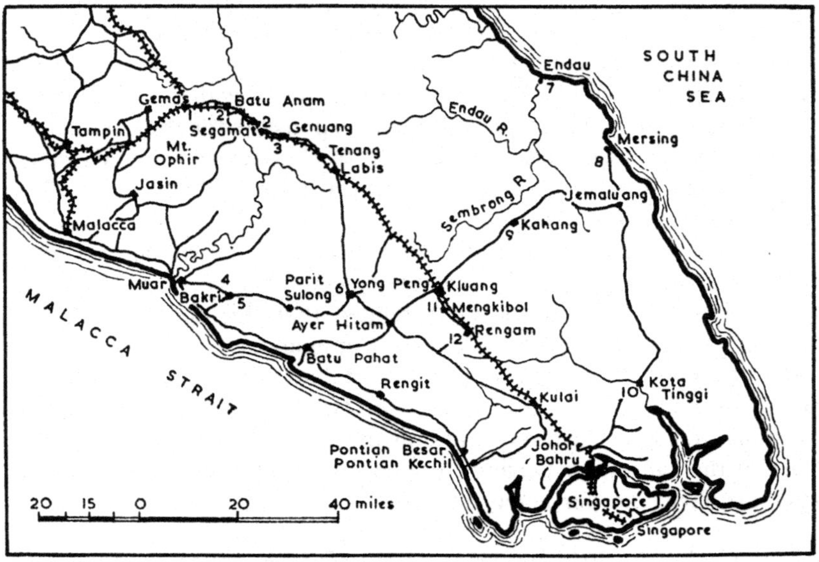

FIG. 14. The distribution of certain of the Australian Medical Units as on January 16.

1. R.A.P. Aust. 2/30th Bn.
2. 2/10 (Aust.) Fd. Amb.
3. „ „ „ M.D.S.
4. R.A.P. Aust. 2/19th Bn.
5. „ „ 2/29th Bn.
6. A.D.M.S. Australian 8th Division.
7. R.A.P. Aust. 2/22nd Bn.
8. A.D.S. 2/9 (Aust.) Fd. Amb.
9. „ „ „ „
10. M.D.S. 2/9 (Aust.) Fd. Amb.
11. 2/4 (Aust.) C.C.S.
12. 5 (Ind.) C.C.S.

On this day A.D.M.S., A.I.F. Malaya, recommended that all nursing sisters and masseuses should be evacuated from Malaya, but G.O.C. A.I.F. Malaya refused to accept this suggestion because of the effect it would have upon civilian morale.

2/10 (Aust.) Fd. Amb. moved to a site one mile north of Labis. 15 (Ind.) Fd. Amb. moved to a school in the vicinity of Labis and its A.D.S. moved from Buloh Kasap to Segamat.

On January 19, 16 (Ind.) Fd. Amb. moved to the Skudai–Pontian Kechil area to come u/c Ind. 28th Bde. 198 Fd. Amb. opened an A.D.S. two miles west of Ayer Hitam on the Ayer Hitam–Batu Pahat road and a M.D.S. at Simpang Rengam.

On the night of January 19–20, Indian 9th Division withdrew to the Tenang area, 15 (Ind.) Fd. Amb. opening an A.D.S. in the Socfin Palm Oil Estate, Labis, moving its M.D.S. to Rengam by stages. 27 (Ind.) Fd. Amb. moved from Labis to Sedenak.

On January 20 the M.D.S. of 2/10 (Aust.) Fd. Amb. moved to the Socfin Estate together with a relay post of 2/3 (Aust.) M.A.C., but as the withdrawal of 'Westforce' continued the medical units were pulled back to the Mengkibol Estate near Kluang. 198 Fd. Amb. moved to Yong Peng.

The situation in North Johore at this time is clearly revealed by the movements of the forward medical units. 2/10 (Aust.) Fd. Amb. at Mengkibol was retiring. 38 (Ind.) Fd. Amb. was withdrawing under continued pressure. 2/13 A.G.H. at Tampoi was closing and moving to Singapore island. 2/4 (Aust.) C.C.S. was moving from the Fraser Estate, Kulai into the mental hospital at Johore Bahru thus made available. 15 (Ind.) Fd. Amb's. M.D.S. was moving to the Fraser Estate, Kulai from Rengam. 5 (Ind.) C.C.S. was moving from Rengam to Singapore, being replaced by 1 (Mal.) C.C.S. which reached the Fraser Estate, Kulai on the 21st and opened alongside 2/4 (Aust.) C.C.S. It dealt with 193 cases before moving to Johore Bahru on the 26th.

On the 20th, 70 men of 198 Fd. Amb. were sent back to Singapore in order to increase the mobility of the unit. 16 (Ind.) Fd. Amb. opened an A.D.S. at Pontian Kechil and another at Kg. Peng Raja. At Skudai 18 (Ind.) Fd. Amb. opened in the Chinese school.

On the 22nd, 28 (Ind.) Fd. Amb. withdrew from Mengkibol to a mile south of Skudai and, on the 23rd, 16 (Ind.) Fd. Amb. sent one company from Pontian Kechil to Kota Tinggi to serve 'Eastforce'. On the 24th, 198 Fd. Amb. moved to an estate south of Skudai and on the following day established an A.D.S. at Benut. On the 25th, 16 (Ind.) Fd. Amb. at Skudai handed over to 28 (Ind.) Fd. Amb. and prepared to move south. 28 (Ind.) Fd. Amb. opened an A.D.S. at Pulai with car posts at Raja and Pontian Kechil.

On the 27th, 16 (Ind.) Fd. Amb. and H.Q. 198 Fd. Amb. moved to Singapore and 28 (Ind.) Fd. Amb. took over all commitments on the Skudai–Pontian Ketchil road.

By relays the patients of 2/4 (Aust.) C.C.S. were moved back to the A.G.Hs. in Singapore island and the C.C.S. itself took over the Bukit Panjang school from the R.A.F. A light surgical section of the C.C.S. was left behind on the mainland.

9

Aust. 22nd Bde., 2/17th Dogras and detachments of the Johore State Force, withdrawing from Jemaluang and Endau, had been served by 2/9 (Aust.) Fd. Amb. with an A.D.S. at Mersing and its M.D.S. at Kota Tinggi. From January 16–20, 28 (Ind.) Fd. Amb. had a car post at Jemaluang and an A.D.S. at Kahang aerodrome. This A.D.S. was withdrawn east of Kluang on January 21. From January 22, 16 (Ind.) Fd. Amb. had a company at Kota Tinggi.

The withdrawal went according to plan, the final move taking place in M.T. from Kota Tinggi to Singapore island.

2/9 (Aust.) Fd. Amb. was still receiving up to 80 casualties a day from 2/18th Aust. Bn. but its H.Q. moved on the 27th to Singapore, there to set up a 200 bedded hospital at Hill 80. The M.D.S. of 2/10 (Aust.) Fd. Amb. moved on the following day to a site at Bukit Panjang opposite 2/4 (Aust.) C.C.S. A light mobile section maintained an A.D.S. at the former site of 2/4 (Aust.) C.C.S. at Johore Bahru while the withdrawal was proceeding. A detachment of the field ambulance moved with Aust. 27th Bde.

On the 29th, 18 (Ind.) Fd. Amb. at Skudai moved to Singapore island. On the night of January 30–31, 28 (Ind.) Fd. Amb. moved to the mental hospital Paya Lebar in Singapore island.

When Indian 9th Division was withdrawn from Kluang down the railway line, Ind. 22nd Bde. moved to Rengam. When Ind. 22nd Bde. moved back to Rengam, casualties were evacuated by trolley cars pushed down the line. With Ind. 22nd Bde. an A.D.S. of 15 (Ind.) Fd. Amb. was lost. Ind. 8th Bde. moved down the line to Sedenak carrying its wounded until the road was reached, when they were transferred to ambulance cars. The A.D.S. of 15 (Ind.) Fd. Amb. with the brigade moved from Kulai by M.T. to Singapore island. During the withdrawal 15 (Ind.) Fd. Amb. had lost three medical officers, one sub-assistant surgeon and some 60 I.O.Rs. and a considerable proportion of its equipment and transport. It had evacuated some 1,500 casualties.

Aust. 27th Bde. and 2nd Gordons, withdrawing down the trunk road, fought many rearguard actions. They were served by 2/10 (Aust.) Fd. Amb. which, on January 26, moved back from a position at the 40¾ milestone on the Johore Bahru–Ayer Hitam road to a position at the 23½ milestone and, on the 29th, to Bt. Panjang in Singapore island. Evacuation during the withdrawal was by M.A.C. to 2/13 A.G.H. (2/4 (Aust.) C.C.S. from January 25) and 1 Mal. G.H. (1 (Mal.) C.C.S. from January 25).

38 (Ind.) Fd. Amb., reinforced by a resuscitation team from 2/10 (Aust.) Fd. Amb., served the bridgehead defence force. It had 24 wheeled stretchers and additional Chinese stretcher-bearers. A M.D.S. was established half a mile south of the causeway. The total number of casualties from the bridgehead was about 75, caused by bombing.

When all the troops from the mainland had crossed and the causeway had been blown, 38 (Ind.) Fd. Amb. moved to Rideout Camp.

The major medical losses during these events were endured by 36 (Ind.) Fd. Amb. and one company of 16 (Ind.) Fd. Amb. at the Slim river, one company of 38 (Ind.) Fd. Amb. at the Muar river, one A.D.S. of 15 (Ind.) Fd. Amb. at Layang–Layang and two light A.D.Ss. of 198 Fd. Amb. at Batu Pahat.

THE LAST PHASE

The island of Singapore, its greatest length fifteen miles and its greatest width twenty-six miles, is separated from the Malayan mainland by the narrow Strait of Johore, across which stretches the Causeway, about a thousand yards long carrying the road and railway that run across the

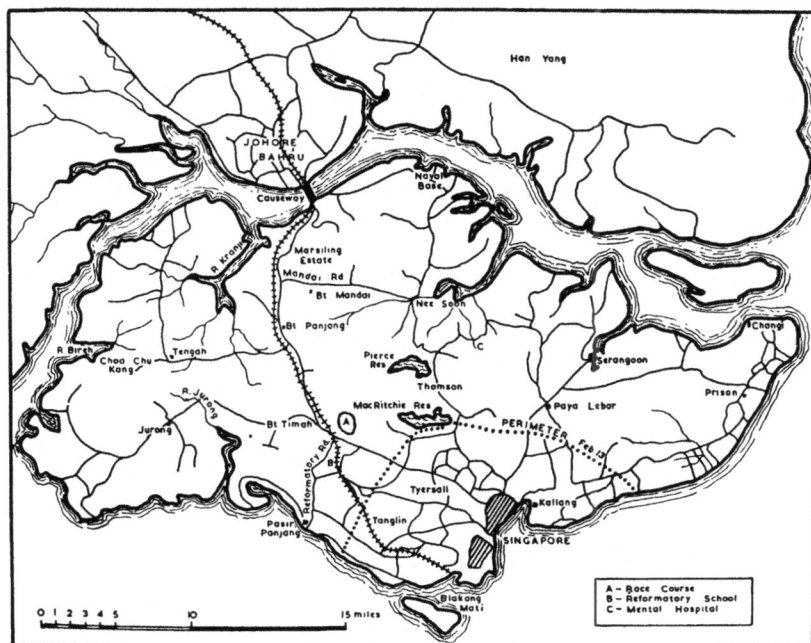

FIG. 15. Singapore Island.

island to Singapore City. The surface of the island is undulating with many low hills, the highest of these being Bukit Timah, 581 ft. In the western part the coastline generally is low and fringed with mangrove swamps pierced by many creeks. In the eastern part the coast offers many miles of sandy beach. The island was traversed by many excellent roads. Its population had become greatly swollen by refugees from the mainland. Food stocks, however, were satisfactory both for the garrison and for the civil population. This was not so as regards water, for about fifty per cent. of the supply came from the mainland, now in Japanese hands.

For its defence the island was divided into three sectors which, according to their coastline boundaries, were:

1. Northern Area. The Causeway to Changi.
   On the right:　18th Division, 54th and 55th Bdes.,
   　　　　　　196 and 197 Fd. Ambs.
   On the left:　Indian 11th Division into which the remnants
   　　　　　　of Indian 9th Division had been incorpor-
   　　　　　　ated, with 53rd Bde. of 18th Division.
   　　　　　　28 and 38 (Ind.) Fd. Ambs.
   　　　　　　198 Fd. Amb. (with 53rd Bde.)
2. Southern Area. Changi to the mouth of the R. Jurong.
   On the right:　1st Mal. Bde.
   　　　　　　1 (Mal.) Fd. Amb.
   In the centre: S.S.V.F.
   (Singapore City)　2 and 3 (Vol.) Fd. Ambs.
   On the left:　2nd Mal. Bde.
   　　　　　　4 (Mal.) Fd. Amb.
3. Western Area. R. Jurong to the Causeway
   　　　　　　Australian 8th Division with Ind. 44th Bde.
   On the right:　Aust. 27th Bde. (R. Kranji–Causeway)
   　　　　　　2/10 (Aust.) Fd. Amb.
   In the centre:　Aust. 22nd Bde. (R. Berih–R. Kranji)
   　　　　　　2/9 (Aust.) Fd. Amb.
   On the left:　Ind. 44th Bde. (R. Jurong–R. Berih)
   　　　　　　40 (Ind.) Fd. Amb.
Malaya Command Reserve.
   　　　　　　Ind. 12th Bde.
   　　　　　　18 (Ind.) Fd. Amb.

THE DISTRIBUTION OF THE MEDICAL UNITS

15 (Ind.) Fd. Amb.	Somapah Village		
16 (Ind.) Fd. Amb.	Teck Hock (corps reserve)		
18 (Ind.) Fd. Amb.	Rideout Road		
27 (Ind.) Fd. Amb.	Yck Road (Yio Chu Kang)		
28 (Ind.) Fd. Amb.	Serangoon Road, Ind. 6/15th and 28th Bdes. near Paya Lebar		
38 (Ind.) Fd. Amb.	Rideout Camp		
40 (Ind.) Fd. Amb.	Jurong Brick Works		
43 (Ind.) Fd. Amb.	Pearls Hill School		
196 (Br.) Fd. Amb.	Tented camp, Tampines Rd.	.	54th Bde.
197 (Br.) Fd. Amb.	Haigh Road	. . .	55th Bde.
198 (Br.) Fd. Amb.	Nee Soon Village	. .	53rd Bde.
1 (Mal.) Fd. Amb.	Ayer-Raja Reformatory and MacArthur Camp		
4 (Mal.) Fd. Amb.	Fowler Camp		
2 (Vol.) Fd. Amb.	One Tree Hill		
3 (Vol.) Fd. Amb.	Nan Yang Girls School		

2/9 (Aust.) Fd. Amb.	.	Choa Chu Kang			
2/10 (Aust.) Fd. Amb.	.	Bukit Panjang Village			
5 (Ind.) C.C.S.	.	Chinese High School	.	.	. 200 beds
1 (Mal.) C.C.S.	.	Chinese High School	.	.	. 200 beds
2/4 (Aust.) C.C.S.	.	Swiss Rifle Club	.	.	. 200 beds
Alexandra Mil. Hosp.	.	Singapore	.	.	. 450 beds
Aux. Mil. Hosp.	.	Singapore	.	.	. 140 beds
Tanglin Mil. Hosp.	.	Tanglin	.	.	. 250 beds (V.D. and Skin)
12 I.G.H.	. .	Tyersall	.	.	. 1,000 beds
19 I.G.H.	. .	Marsiling Road	.	.	. 900 beds
27 I.G.H.	. .	Bidadari	.	.	. 400 beds
40 I.G.H.	. .	Robertson's Old Bldgs.	.	.	1,000 beds
17 C.G.H.	. .	Changi	.	.	. 1,000 beds
20 C.G.H.	. .	Gilman Barracks	.	.	. 650 beds
1 Mal. G.H.	. .	Selerang	.	.	. 600 beds
2/10 A.G.H.	. .	Oldham Hall School	.	.	. 600 beds
2/13 A.G.H.	. .	St. Patrick's School	.	.	. 600 beds
2/2 (Aust.) Con. Depot	.	Island Golf Course	.	.	. 500 beds

8,690 beds

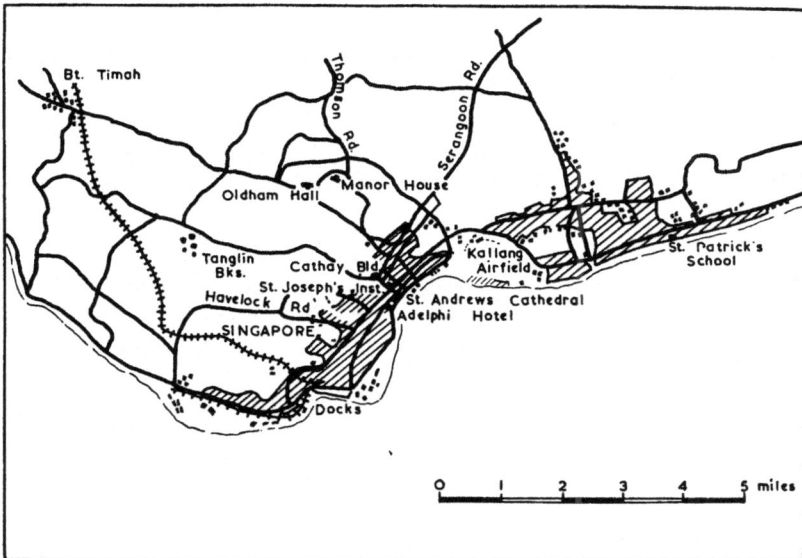

FIG. 16. Singapore City and its environs.

The statement that 8,690 hospital beds were available is misleading. Save for one group of 114 Australians invalided home on New Year's Eve there had been no evacuation of casualties out of Malaya since the campaign started. The hospital beds at this time therefore were mostly occupied. Certain of the hospitals had been involved in the withdrawal from the mainland and had become separated from their equipment. 40 I.G.H. only reached Singapore in late January and was not yet fully established. The civil hospitals on the island were in like condition.

THE FALL OF SINGAPORE

On February 5 the Japanese guns on the mainland opened a desultory bombardment of the naval base and of the gun positions in Aust. 27th Bde's. sector. For two days and three nights this continued while Japanese bombers came over in successive waves. Then on the 8th, the shelling extended to the area held by Aust. 22nd Bde. between the rivers Kranji and Berih. During the night of February 8–9 Japanese assault troops landed and quickly infiltrated between the defended localities in Aust. 22nd Bde's. sector. It became necessary to order the forward troops to make their way back to the main battalion perimeters. This withdrawal was attended by much difficulty and many small parties failed to get back. To restore the situation Aust. 2/29th Bn. and a special reserve battalion composed of Australian reinforcements were placed u/c Aust. 22nd Bde. and sent to Tengah airfield. Ind. 12th Bde. was placed u/c Western Area.

Aust. 2/18th Bn., under considerable pressure, withdrew to Tengah airfield. Aust. 2/20th Bn. found its path obstructed and suffered heavy casualties in attempts to break through. Aust. 2/19th Bn. became surrounded and had to cut its way through, enduring severe loss. Ind. 12th Bde. took up a position in the northern part of the line along the Jurong river and Aust. 22nd Bde. fell back to Bulim village.

It was decided that:

(1) Aust. 27th Bde. should continue to hold the Causeway sector.
(2) Ind. 44th Bde. should withdraw from its coastal positions and move into the southern part of the Jurong line.
(3) Ind. 12th Bde. and Aust. 22nd Bde. should occupy the northern part of the Jurong line.
(4) Ind. 6/15th Bde. should pass u/c Western Area and move to the area of the Racecourse, there to safeguard the dumps in the Bukit Timah area.
(5) The dumps at Kranji, Woodlands and the naval base should be destroyed.

By nightfall of the 9th the Jurong line was held by Ind. 12th Bde. on the right, by the special reserve Australian battalion in the centre and by Ind. 44th Bde. on the left. Aust. 22nd Bde. was in a covering position at Bulim and Ind. 6/15th Bde. was in reserve. It was decided that should the Japanese succeed in piercing the Jurong line Singapore City would be defended on a perimeter Kallang—hills west of Bukit Timah village—Pasir Panjang.

At 2030 hours on the 9th, Japanese assault troops landed in Aust. 27th Bde's. sector and quickly forced the forward troops back. The brigade withdrew to the vicinity of Bukit Mandai. This withdrawal resulted in the abandonment of the causeway, in the uncovering of the main road to Singapore City and in the creation of a gap of some 4,000 yards between Aust. 27th Bde. and Indian 11th Division.

Aust. 22nd Bde. withdrew from Bulim to the Jurong line and part of it thence to the Singapore City perimeter defence line. Ind. 12th Bde. fell back to Bukit Panjang because its right flank had become uncovered by the withdrawal of Aust. 27th Bde. Ind. 12th Bde., being attacked, found it necessary to withdraw towards Passir Panjang. By dusk on the 10th the Jurong line had been abandoned and the remnants of Western Area's four brigades had become widely dispersed. There was now no natural physical barrier in the path of the Japanese advancing upon Singapore City.

On February 10 General Wavell again visited Singapore, directed that a counter-attack should be made by all available troops on the west front and gave orders that there was to be no thought of surrender but that all troops were to continue fighting to the end.

G.O.C. Malaya Command formed 'Tomforce' which consisted of a battalion from each of the brigades of 18th Division (18th Bn. Recce Corps, 4th Norfolks, 1/5th Sherwood Foresters) and placed it u/c Western Area for the purpose of defending the Bukit Timah area where much confused fighting was taking place and where the Japanese had succeeded in penetrating between Ind. 28th and 8th Bdes. towards Nee Soon village.

During the night of February 12–13 all the troops were withdrawn into the Singapore City perimeter defence line which ran from the Kallang airfield–Paya Lebar airstrip–Woodleigh crossroads–Thomson village–Adam road–Farrar road–Tanglin halt–to the sea west of Buona Vista village.

2nd Mal. Bde . .	Kallang–Paya Lebar
Indian 11th Div. . .	Paya Lebar–Woodleigh crossroads
18th Div. . .	Woodleigh crossroads–Bukit Timah road
A.I.F. Malaya . .	Bukit Timah road–Tanglin halt
Ind. 44th Bde. and 1st Mal. Bde. . .	Tanglin halt–sea

On the 14th, 1st Mal. Bde. was heavily attacked and forced back. Other Japanese attacks upon the perimeter line were held, but the end was very near for the conditions within the city were fast becoming unendurable. The water supply failed for bomb and shell had wrecked the mains and their repair was impossible. The city had been mercilessly bombed and shelled and panic raced through its streets in which the many dead lay unburied.

On the 15th G.O.C. Malaya Command received permission from General Wavell to surrender when he was satisfied that continued resistance was no longer possible. At 2030 hours on this day the campaign ended in the unconditional surrender of the garrison.

THE ARMY MEDICAL SERVICES DURING THE LAST PHASE

Never in their history were the Army Medical Services called upon to discharge their functions in circumstances more difficult and more disadvantageous than those that obtained in the island and city of Singapore. The swiftness of the withdrawal from the coast to the perimeter and the confusion that attended it meant that most of the medical units were compelled time after time to close, move and open again. Only at the beginning could it be assumed that a unit designated as open and admitting casualties would in fact be able to receive them. Toward the end casualties had to be taken from unit to unit until accommodation for them was found. At the time when casualties were most numerous hospital accommodation for them was most scarce, for hospitals were bombed, burnt and destroyed. There was soon no place in the island where the wounded man could be safeguarded from further hurt, no place where he could feel at rest. The surgical team and the operating theatre shared the hazards of the machine-gun crew and the gunpit; the nursing orderly in the ward was alongside the rifleman in his trench. The congestion was such that the Red Cross could provide no protection, for if it flew over a hospital its shadow encroached on a battery site. The piped water supply of the hospitals quickly became utterly insufficient; water had to be carried to the wards and theatres in buckets, and in buckets the refuse and the excrement had to be carried out. For the patient gravely hurt there was no healing hope of evacuation; amid the noise of battle he breathed the anxiety and the hopelessness that tinctured the air and waited for the coming of horror magnified by his stimulated imagination.

15 (Ind.) Fd. Amb. moved from Somapah village to Tyersall Park on February 10, there to be involved in the catastrophe that overtook 12 I.G.H. It then moved to Mount Emily on the 12th and to the Outram Road Civil Hospital on the following day.

16 (Ind.) Fd. Amb. established an A.D.S. 12½ miles west of Nee Soon on February 2 and a M.D.S. of 200 beds in Teck Hock village. On the 7th the unit moved to Rideout Road and on the 10th opened an A.D.S. to serve Ind. 6/15th Bde. in the Bukit Timah area. On the 11th it moved again to Serangoon Road, on the 12th to the vicinity of the Raffles Institute and on the 13th to the Recreation Club. On February 14 its personnel were distributed among other medical units—to 27 I.G.H., to 44 (Ind.) Fd. Hyg. Sec. (for grave digging) and to 197 Fd. Amb.

18 (Ind.) Fd. Amb. 'B' Coy. served Ind. 12th Bde. in the Bukit Timah area on February 9. Losing touch with the brigade it moved

to the Kandang Kerbau Hospital on the 11th, there to deal with over 1,000 casualties, civil and military, before hostilities ceased.

27 (Ind.) Fd. Amb. moved to Fort Tekong on February 4 and there it remained until the capitulation.

28 (Ind.) Fd. Amb. on February 2 established a M.D.S. at Kah Hoe San, Yck Road, to serve Ind. 6/15th Bde., an A.D.S. two hundred yards south of Nee Soon village and another A.D.S. at Chong Peng, in association with the A.D.S. of 198 Fd. Amb. On the 10th the unit moved from Yck Road to Thomson Road and on the 12th to the Tan Tock Sen Hospital where it remained for the rest of the period.

30 (Ind.) Fd. Amb. left Rideout Camp on February 7 and relieved 16 (Ind.) Fd. Amb. at Nee Soon and Teck Hock. On the 12th the unit moved to Tan Tock Sen Hospital and on the 13th to the Civil General Hospital.

40 (Ind.) Fd. Amb. with Ind. 44th Bde. moved from the Jurong Brickworks on February 9 to the junction of the Bukit Timah–Hollang roads. Losing touch with its brigade it moved to the vicinity of 2/13 A.G.H. at St. Patrick's School. On the 11th it rejoined its brigade and later moved to Oldham Hall School, evacuated by 2/10 A.G.H. and on the 13th to the Raffles Institute.

43 (Ind.) Fd. Amb. at Pearls Hill School opened a hospital of 300 beds as well as providing an A.D.S. to serve 1st and 2nd Mal. Bns. On the 12th this A.D.S. was in Tanglin Military Hospital, vacated by the staff and patients, and on the 15th opened in the ballroom of the Raffles Hotel.

196 Fd. Amb. opened its M.D.S. at the tented camp Tampines Road and an A.D.S. in the mental hospital at Paya Lebar. On the 12th the unit moved to Thomson Road. Losing contact with 54th Bde. it moved to the City High School, there to open a M.D.S., and established an A.D.S. at the junction of the Balmoral–Bt. Timah roads. Another A.D.S. served with 'Tomforce'. On the 15th the unit moved into the Goodwood Park Hotel.

197 Fd. Amb. arrived in Singapore on February 5 and became separated from its equipment. From billets in Haigh Road it moved on the 10th to establish a M.D.S. on the Tanjong–Kampong Road and provided an A.D.S. to accompany 'Tomforce'. On the 13th it opened in the Municipal Buildings, Singapore.

198 Fd. Amb. established its M.D.S. at Nee Soon and its A.D.S. near the naval base. A detachment of the unit served with 28 (Ind.) Fd. Amb. On the 12th the unit moved to Bidadari.

1 (Mal.) Fd. Amb. had one section at MacArthur Camp, Bt. Timah, 'A' Coy. at the Ayer Raja–Reformatory road junction and an A.D.S. a mile from the Jurong river on the west coast road serving 1st Mal.

Bde. The unit first moved to Tanglin and then, on the 14th, to St. Andrew's Cathedral.

4 (Mal.) Fd. Amb. with 2nd Mal. Bde. moved from Fowler Camp on the 12th to Singapore Recreation Club Building and sent a detachment to help at the Alexandra Mil. Hosp. On the 13th the unit moved to the Nan Wah School and opened 200 beds.

2 (Vol.) Fd. Amb. moved from One Tree Hill to the outskirts of Singapore. 3 (Vol.) Fd. Amb. moved on the 11th from the Nan Yang Girls School to St. Joseph's Institute, its personnel being sent to help 1 (Mal.) C.C.S.

2/9 (Aust.) Fd. Amb. opened its M.D.S. on the road running west from Bt. Panjang and its A.D.S. on the crossroad from Bt. Timah. Owing to the shortage of hospital beds this unit, like the rest, was required to expand so that it could accommodate 150–200 patients. Malaria was now rife, for all anti-malarial work had ceased and the quinine administered to the Australian troops as a suppressive had not been effective. The unit was soon admitting many men suffering from exhaustion. On the morning of February 8 the A.D.S. was heavily shelled and throughout the day was continuously bombed. The unit moved on the 9th to the area of the race course, on the 10th to the Swiss Rifle Club, on the 11th to Barker Road and on the 12th to the Oldham Hall School, vacated by 2/10 A.G.H., and within an hour to the grounds of St. Andrew's Cathedral. On the 14th the unit established an operating theatre in the Adelphi Hotel in conjunction with 2/10 (Aust.) Fd. Amb.

2/10 (Aust.) Fd. Amb. at first was near 2/4 (Aust.) C.C.S. at Bt. Panjang. Between January 28 and February 8 the unit treated 667 Australian, 15 British and 25 Indian casualties in addition to some 250 Malayans. On the 8th the unit's A.D.S. was heavily shelled and bombed and on the 10th the unit moved, along with 2/9 (Aust.) Fd. Amb., to the Swiss Rifle Club. On the 11th, in company with 2/9 (Aust.) Fd. Amb. and 2/2 (Aust.) M.A.C., it moved to Barker Road and on the 12th, with 2/9 (Aust.) Fd. Amb., to Oldham Hall and on to St. Andrew's Cathedral. On the 14th the unit, again in conjunction with 2/9 (Aust.) Fd. Amb., set up an operating theatre in the Adelphi Hotel.

5 (Ind.) C.C.S. moved from the Chinese High School on February 9 to the bungalows of the Asiatic Petroleum Company at Pierce Road. 1 (Mal.) C.C.S. moved from the Chinese High School on February 11 to St. Joseph's Institute.

2/4 (Aust.) C.C.S., at Bt. Panjang with the Australian M.A.C. nearby, was soon busy dealing with exhausted men. A party of 33 from 4th Norfolk Regt. which had been cut off at Yong Peng after the fighting at Parit Sulong reached the C.C.S. in a condition of extreme exhaustion. On February 5 the unit was under fire from the Japanese guns and moved to the Swiss Rifle Club. As the Japanese advance proceeded the C.C.S. moved to houses in Gilstead Road, leaving a surgical team with 2/9 and 2/10 (Aust.) Fd. Ambs. which moved into the Swiss Club. When 2/9 and 2/10 (Aust.) Fd. Ambs. moved to Barker Road the C.C.S. provided a medical staff for an improvised battalion formed out of ordnance personnel and the rest of its staff and its equipment were distributed between 2/10 and 2/13 A.G.Hs.

Tanglin Mil. Hosp. closed on February 11 and its personnel joined 1 Mal. G.H. in the Victoria Theatre.

1 Mal. G.H. moved from Selerang to the Victoria Theatre on February 10.

19 I.G.H. moved to Oxley Road near Fort Canning on February 9.

27 I.G.H. moved on February 10 from Bidadari to Raffles College and on the following day to the Raffles Institute.

40 I.G.H. moved on February 10 to Tyersall and on the 12th to the Raffles Institute.

17 C.G.H. moved from Changi to Tyersall on the 11th and on the following day opened in the Union Jack Club.

20 C.G.H. remained at the Gilman Barracks throughout the period.

On the afternoon of February 11, 12 I.G.H. at Tyersall was bombed and set on fire. 15 (Ind.) Fd. Amb. and Marines and Argylls of Ind. 12th Bde. helped the staff of the hospital to rescue the patients from the blazing huts under a hail of machine-gun fire from Japanese planes overhead. Some 200 patients died in this holocaust.

12 I.G.H. moved from Tyersall on February 12 to the building of the Registrar of Vehicles.

On February 7, 17 I.G.H. in the Roberts Barracks, Changi, received three direct hits. Eight of the unit's personnel were killed and six wounded. On the 8th the hospital was again bombed. On the 9th, 1 Mal. G.H., a mile away, was bombed and badly damaged. On the 11th, 17 I.G.H. transferred its British patients to 1 Mal. G.H. and its Indian patients to 12 and 19 I.G.Hs. and then moved to Tyersall where it was promptly bombed again and set on fire. Salvaging as much of its equipment as it could, the unit hurriedly moved into Singapore.

1 Mal. G.H. with a nursing staff of 8 Q.A.I.M.N.S. and 35 V.A.Ds. in Selerang Barracks, Changi, found itself between the lines when 2nd Mal. Bde. withdrew without warning the hospital. It hurriedly moved with its patients on February 10 to the Singapore Cricket Club where it remained closed, its nursing staff being sent to the Alexandra Military Hospital. Then it opened 200 beds in the Victoria Hall where it was joined by the staff of the Tanglin Military Hospital which opened 200 beds in the Victoria Theatre. On the 13th, 1 Mal. G.H. took over further accommodation in the Government Buildings and Fullerton

Buildings and was reinforced by teams from 197 and the S.S.V.F. Fd. Ambs. On the 14th over 200 operations under general anaesthesia were performed by the five surgical teams.

2/10 A.G.H. in the Oldham Hall School and Manor House, like 2/13 A.G.H., was already full by February 5. By taking over private houses and erecting tentage it had 745 beds available, and of these 709 were occupied. On the 7th two members of the staff were killed and others wounded. The fighting from the 8th onwards yielded great numbers of casualties and the operating theatre was soon working day and night. Civilian labour disappeared, however, and the sanitary service became disrupted. The hospital was obliged to move on the 12th to the Cathay Building. One hundred of the most seriously ill surgical cases together with some of the staff were transferred to the Singapore General Hospital. Another 300 patients were transferred to St. Joseph's Institute. About 500 patients with the balance of the staff took over the lower floors of the Cathay Building. On the floors above was H.Q. Indian III Corps, so that the Red Cross could not be flown though the building was under frequent shellfire and bombing. Fortunately the lower floors escaped serious damage.

2/13 A.G.H. at St. Patrick's School on the south coast by February 5 had accommodation for 825 and 522 beds occupied. It was quickly filled and thereafter worked without ceasing. On February 13 the officer commanding conferred with his officers, for by this time the hospital was outside the perimeter and the Japanese were expected to appear at any moment. Red crosses were being displayed prominently and illuminated at night. The hospital was holding over 900 patients. The unit could not move to another site within the perimeter for there was nowhere within the perimeter where it could go. Indeed there was nothing to be done save to carry on with the task of tending the patients in its charge.

As the end drew near orders were issued to the effect that most of the hospitals were to remain where they were unless suffering too severely. On February 14 the Alexandra Mil. Hosp. was outside the perimeter. By 1300 hours on this day the Japanese were attacking along the Ayer Raja road and entered the hospital grounds. An officer, carrying a white flag, went out to meet them and to claim protection for the hospital. He was bayoneted and killed. The Japanese troops then entered the hospital and promptly killed two officers, a N.C.O., a B.O.R. and a patient then lying on the operating table. The staff and patients were rounded up and tied together by the wrists in groups of 3 to 5. During this procedure several other patients were bayoneted. The rest were confined in three small rooms. During the night many of the more seriously ill died. At intervals successive groups were taken out into the open and slaughtered. On the 15th the Japanese put their prisoners, still manacled, into an open drain, presumably for their protection, and on the 16th a Japanese senior medical officer appeared and thereafter the treatment of the prisoners quickly improved. Four officers and six B.O.Rs. were known to have been killed after surrender. Ten officers and 73 B.O.Rs. were missing, but concerning their fate their colleagues had no doubt.

20 C.G.H. in the Gilman Barracks half a mile away from the Alexandra Mil. Hosp. could not display the Red Cross emblem until, on February 12, the Loyals who had been occupying one of the barrack blocks had moved out. At 1830 hours on February 15, Japanese troops entered the hospital. All the staff were locked up in a godown. There they remained until the 17th when they were released to find their neglected patients in a most pitiable state.

2/2 (Aust.) Con. Depot was first at the Island Golf Club off Thomson Road, north of the Manor House, and then after two moves at Tanjong Katong on February 11 moved again on the 13th to the Cathay Cinema. On the morning of the 15th a shell penetrated the roof and killed 16 and wounded 30 of the 1,000 patients.

1 (Ind.) Base Depot Medical Stores at Tanglin moved on February 10 to a godown in River Valley Road and on the 12th to the Cathay Building. 2 (Ind.) Adv. Depot Med. Stores, having lost all during the withdrawal from Kuala Lumpur, was attached to the Base Depot. The Australian Adv. Depot Med. Stores moved along with 2/4 (Aust.) C.C.S. and 8 (Ind.) Adv. Depot Med. Stores moved on the 9th from Serangoon to Tanglin and thereafter was with the Base Depot.

In this fashion the medical services attempted, and to a considerable extent succeeded in spite of difficulties beyond the limits of verbal description, to give succour to the hurt and exhausted. The fragmentary records that miraculously survived the catastrophe fail to convey a true measure of the volume or of the quality of the work they performed. It would appear that some 10,000 sick and wounded were evacuated to Singapore island from the mainland and that at the time of the capitulation there were in the care of the Singapore military medical units some 9,000.

Following the withdrawal to Singapore island it was quickly decided that the female nursing staffs of the military hospitals should be sent out of the country. On February 10, six Australian nurses and 47 patients embarked in a transport bound for Australia. Surviving a vicious attack from the air soon after sailing, the ship reached Batavia safely. On the 11th, 59 more nurses from the Australian hospitals embarked on the cargo steamer *Empire Star*. The ship had accommodation for 16 passengers. Two thousand, one hundred and fifty-four persons, mostly Australian, Indian and British (Army and R.A.F.) nurses, were packed aboard. In spite of persistent air attack the ship reached Batavia on the 14th and three days later sailed for Fremantle. The *Wu Sueh* embarked 306 patients (including 120 A.I.F. and 93 Indians) and 22 nurses and V.A.Ds. and also sailed for Batavia where her patients were transferred to H.S. 36 (*Karapara*) for Colombo and Bombay. On February 12 the rest of the nurses (65 Australian nurses and physiotherapists) on the island were embarked on S.S. *Vyner Brooke*. She was hit off Banka Island and sunk. Those of the 300 passengers, mostly women and children, who were not drowned were taken prisoner.*

On the 13th the arrangements whereby some 1,000 nominated individuals were to be evacuated to Java before the surrender of the garrison were put into effect. Those ordered to go were key men, specialists, technicians, surplus staff officers, nurses and others whose services would be of special value for the prosecution of the war. Included in the party were several medical officers, each representing a clinical or administrative specialty. Only about half of those selected sailed. The eighty or so small ships that left Singapore encountered the Japanese naval force escorting the expedition against Sumatra and almost all of them were sunk or captured.

Capitulation was not followed by any improvement in the circumstances of the sick and the wounded for food shortage at once became acute and there was much interference in the affairs of the medical units by their captors. But the surrender did check the torrent of casualties that had threatened to overwhelm the medical services. The medical units were greatly overcrowded, the operating teams were nearing exhaustion and the maintenance of asepsis had become impossible. The failure of the water supply had brought in its train the threat of epidemic. Indeed the conditions were such as fully to justify the advice given by the military medical authorities to General Percival as early as February 11 to the effect that from the medical point of view capitulation was desirable before the situation passed completely out of control.

REFLECTIONS UPON THE MEDICAL ASPECTS OF THE CAMPAIGN IN MALAYA

Nothing new and nothing of any significance within the field of military medicine emerged from this campaign. As has already been observed in connexion with the campaigns in France and Belgium, Norway, Greece and Crete, the circumstances that lead up to and end in swift disaster are not conducive to the development of advantageous modifications of medical policy or practice.

Medical tactical planning prior to the outbreak of hostilities was greatly impeded by uncertainty regarding both the likelihood of war

---

* An account of their experiences is given later in this Chapter.

and the forces which, in the event of war, would be available for the defence of Malaya.

The A.I.F. Malaya was to a considerable extent a self-contained force. Its medical component, in size and variety, was adequate. Even in the final stages of the campaign the Australian medical units, though working in conditions that made the exhibition of medical skill almost impossible, continued to provide a service of outstanding value.

The medical affairs of Malaya Command generally were complicated by the dependence of the military upon the civil medical services. The arrangements made would doubtless have been satisfactory had the civil hospitals not been fully extended by the great influx of civilian casualties and had the civil hospitals on the mainland not been submerged by the tide of the Japanese advance. In the event, the civil hospitals could not, and did not, admit military patients in any systematic fashion. What seems to have happened is that as Indian III Corps withdrew down the Malayan peninsula the subordinate and domestic staffs of each civil hospital in turn decamped, seeking safety. The hospital was then used successively as an improvised C.C.S., a M.D.S. and an A.D.S. as the line fell back. Then in many an instance the civil staff, or part of it, returned as the battle moved on and the work of the civil hospital was resumed.

In Singapore island military and civil hospitals were equally engulfed in the maelstrom of war and no effective system of mutual aid could be maintained. Each functioned as best it could for as long as it could.

The shortage of C.C.S. facilities on the mainland, acutely felt, was not made good by the improvisation of such by the placement of sections of an I.G.H. in a succession of civil hospitals.

As would be expected, the value of the R.M.O. was greatly magnified during the withdrawal by the acquisition from some civil source of a motor-van which was converted into a mobile R.A.P.

In the final stages of the Malaya campaign the creation of a designated hospital area would have been the only method of providing the conditions that are essential for the practice of medicine. The Australian Medical Services presented this view to A.I.F. H.Q. at the beginning of the fighting on the island, but the general situation was such that it could not be accepted. Later the setting aside of a site in the Tyersall area was considered, but the great congestion everywhere made any such scheme impracticable.

In retrospect it would seem that evacuation from Singapore by hospital ship could have been carried out with great advantage. While it is true to say that the behaviour of the Japanese was to a large extent unpredictable, there were several instances in which they certainly respected the Red Cross. In many instances when they bombed or shelled medical units these were closely adjacent to artillery sites or dumps or were occupying barracks only recently vacated by combatant units. When they slaughtered medical staff and patients the explanation offered was that they had been fired on from hospital buildings. On the whole it seems possible that a hospital ship, clearly marked as such and docking well away from all other shipping, might have been unmolested. Certainly it would have been greatly to the advantage of all if the hospitals on the island could have been cleared when the withdrawal from the mainland took place. Had this been done, it is possible that very many lives would have been saved and much suffering avoided.

CASUALTIES

A summary of the casualties which occurred among British, Australian and Indian troops during the Campaign is given below. The British figures may be taken to be as accurate as can be expected; the Australian figures are those recorded at the time of the movement of the A.I.F. to Changi P.o.W. Camp after the capitulation; the Indian figures are also those known at this time but will probably be subject to a good deal of correction when accurately checked figures become available.

TABLE 9

British Casualties

December 8, 1941–February 15, 1942

	Killed	Wounded	Missing and prisoners	Totals
Officers	47	32	2,431	2,510
O.Rs.	260	64	35,463	35,787
	307	96	37,894	38,297

TABLE 10

A.I.F. Casualties

December 8, 1941–February 15, 1942

Killed in action	405
Died of wounds	111
Wounded	1,364 (approx.)
Missing	1,919 (33 A.A.N.S.)
Illness (death)	8
Illness (admission to hospital)	6,000 (approx.)
Accidents (death)	25

Strength 15,000 (approx.)

Battle casualties:
Deaths . 516
Wounded . 1,364
Missing . 1,919

3,799

Illness and accidents:
Deaths . 33
Hospital admissions 6,000

6,033

Total 9,832

TABLE 11

Indian Casualties

December 8, 1941–February 15, 1942

	Killed	Wounded	Missing	P.o.W.	Totals
Officers .	42	29	76	978	1,125
V.C.Os. .	33	52	158	1,217	1,460
I.O.Rs. .	265	726	4,675	55,487	61,153
Totals .	340	807	4,909	57,682	63,738

SARAWAK

2/15th Punjab Regt., together with a small number of administrative and other personnel, was sent to Borneo, there to reinforce the Sarawak State Forces. Their task was that of denying to the Japanese the airfield at Kuching and the oilfield and refinery at Lutong and Miri, 400 miles to the north near the Sarawak–Brunei border. Rather than let these fall into Japanese hands they were to be destroyed before the force withdrew into Dutch Borneo to place itself under the command of the Dutch military authorities. The total force numbered 85 officers and 2,480 O.Rs.

To Sarawak were sent from India 3 medical officers, 4 sub-assistant surgeons and 42 I.O.Rs. In the last week of December 1940 one S.A.S. and one nursing sepoy I.H.C. reached Miri and one nursing naik and one cook I.H.C. arrived at Kuching. On May 12, 1941, a medical officer arrived at Kuching, to become S.M.O. Sarawak and Brunei. On December 11, 1941, 'G' detachment 19 I.G.H., consisting of 2 medical officers, 3 S.A.Ss. and 39 I.O.Rs. I.H.C., reached Kuching.

On December 8 the company of 2/15th Punjab Regt. at Miri destroyed the oilfield and refinery and on the 13th embarked on a small coastal steamer for Kuching. One officer and some 60 Straits Settlement Police left Miri for Singapore.

On December 24 Japanese warships and transports anchored in Santubong Bay. Their landing craft proceeded up the Santubong river as far as Kuching. On Christmas Day 2/15th Punjab Regt. was forced to withdraw from the airfield and set out on its trek to Dutch Borneo. Of the rearguard of two companies, 4 officers and some 230 O.Rs. were either killed or captured. At Kuching the road ended. Transport and heavy equipment were abandoned and the Sarawak State Forces were released to return to their homes. Thereafter 2/15th Punjab Regt. carried on alone. On the 27th it crossed the border into Dutch Borneo and two days later arrived at Sinkawang II airfield. The regiment, along with Dutch native troops, took part in savage fighting around the airfield before being forced to withdraw. It now set out for the south coast of Dutch Borneo through virgin jungle, carrying its wounded. Travelling by forest track and by raft and boat on treacherous rivers, short of food and moving through almost unexplored swamp and jungle, the two columns into which the battalion was divided finally reached the coast, 800 miles away from Kuching.

On March 9, following the surrender of the Dutch East Indies, there was for 2/15th Punjab Regt. no other course than to lay down its arms.

The medical component of this force took part in these events. Use was made of the local hospital facilities in Sarawak and Dutch Borneo when this was possible, but for the most part the casualties were carried and tended as the column proceeded on its 800 mile trek that ended in a prisoner-of-war camp.

(iii)

Captivity

It was officially reported in 1946 that the total number of British Army personnel taken prisoner by the Japanese during the war was 42,610 and that of these 10,298 either died or else were killed in captivity. These figures do not relate solely to the campaign in Malaya for Hong Kong and Burma also made their contributions. Nor do they represent the total number of those taken captive for to them must be added those that refer to the other components of the land forces involved, the A.I.F., Canadian Army, Indian Army and local volunteer units.

In this account attention is focused upon British Army personnel. The affairs of the Australian, Canadian and Indian army P.o.W. are considered in the Official Australian, Canadian and Indian Medical Histories respectively. In so far as the Malayan campaign is concerned the Australian account is of particular interest and value by reason of its comprehensiveness and wealth of detail and should certainly be consulted.

Since the story of the Australian P.o.W. is essentially the same as that of the British it is unnecessary in this volume to present an equally detailed and equally comprehensive account. That which follows can be regarded as supplementary to the Australian narrative. It is intended (1) to describe a typical example of a temporary P.o.W. camp (= cage) established by the Japanese on the mainland of Malaya during the later stages of the campaign, that at Kuala Lumpur being chosen solely for the reason that concerning it fairly full records were available; (2) to record the experiences of the P.o.W. in Changi and Kranji camps on Singapore Island; (3) to follow one of the larger 'forces'—'F' Force—that were sent from Changi to be employed in the construction of the

Thailand–Burma railway, from the time of its departure to the time of its return and (4) to make but brief reference to all other matters that have been given adequate attention in the Australian account.

It is true that the conditions that obtained in the different labour camps, camp hospitals and base hospitals varied, some being better than others, and that the attitude and behaviour of the I.J.A. personnel in command of the different camps and hospitals also varied. But these differences were not of such an order as to make an account of one of them unrepresentative of the whole. Everywhere and at all times there was the same insensate cruelty and the same stupid inefficiency on the part of the Japanese and the same cohesion of spirit, the same courage and the same charity shown by the captives.

Of the large 'forces' that were sent from Changi, 'A' Force went to Burma to be employed on the Burma end of the railway. 'D', 'F', 'H', 'K' and 'L' Forces went to Thailand to be employed on the northern, central or southern Thailand sections of the railway. 'B' and 'E' Forces went to Borneo to swell the labour gangs there and 'C', 'G' and 'J' Forces were sent to Japan for the same purpose.

The Thailand–Burma railway project was undertaken by the I.J.A. Engineers to provide a land route along which the Japanese formations in Burma could be supplied. The line of the railway to be built ran from Non Pladuk, near Bampong and on the railway running from Bangkok southwards into Malaya, through some 270 miles of dense, malarious, roadless jungle along the valley of the Kwai Noi river, across the Thailand–Burma border near the Three Pagodas Pass, to Thanbyuzayat on the Burmese railway that runs from Moulmein southwards along the coast line to Ye.

Construction began at both ends of the line along which a series of working camps was constructed. In addition to the P.o.W. there was an unnumbered, uncared-for host of native Asian labourers. From this vast reservoir of infection the P.o.W. were in constant danger. In addition to the P.o.W. from Changi others were brought from the N.E.I.

The first of the forces left Changi in May 1942. The railway was finished in October 1943. Thereafter the survivors of these forces began to return to Singapore Island. Some were sent to Japan. A transport carrying them was torpedoed and from those that were rescued the world first heard the monstrous story of their experience.

THE KUALA LUMPUR P.O.W. CAMP

The P.o.W. camp at Kuala Lumpur was established on January 22, 1942, when 13 British officers and 43 B.O.Rs. of Indian 11th Division who had fallen into the hands of the Japanese during the retreat were moved from the police barracks in Kuala Lumpur to the Pudu gaol. This was a massive stone and concrete building with 600 cells and was in the form of a St. Andrew's Cross. At the main entrance to the gaol was a two-storeyed building which had housed the administration on the ground floor and had six cells (each 13 × 6 ft.) and two small store rooms on the upper floor. Within the grounds were a female block and the prison hospital.

These P.o.W. were housed in the female block, which consisted of a small building of six cells and two small storerooms within a walled-in area 60 yards square. Other parties of varying sizes which had been rounded up in the jungle soon arrived, Australians, Argylls, Leicesters and Volunteers among them, utterly fatigued, half starved and in tatters. Officers and men were herded together and, in accordance with the policy of the Japanese, the senior officer among them—the officer commanding 5/2nd Punjab Regt.—was made responsible for discipline and for the administration of the camp. He and the staff he appointed were responsible for the implementation of orders issued by the I.J.A. But for the first week or so there was no one Japanese officer with whom this senior officer could communicate. Authority passed from one to another and it seemed as though there was a Japanese administrative organisation parallel to that within the camp whose pleasure it was to countermand any instruction issued by the senior officer among the P.o.W. At length a Japanese medical officer visited the camp and to him was given a letter containing requests for better accommodation, better food and medical attention and for the appointment of someone with whom the senior officer could deal. A permanent guard commander, a Japanese sergeant, duly arrived and quickly displayed his enjoyment of authority by doing everything possible to undermine that of the senior officer of the camp.

On January 26 there were 126 P.o.W. in the camp and the guard commander allowed the upper floor of the administrative block to be opened for accommodation. By the middle of the first week of February the population of the camp had risen to 337, by February 9 it was 446 and by February 18, 550. The guard commander reluctantly allowed the officers to move into the prison hospital building. On March 26 the roll-call was 724 Australians, British and political prisoners, mainly Chinese, and sickness was now very rife, dysentery was prevalent and mortality was mounting. Insistent requests for additional space were ultimately successful and the guard commander allowed 300 Australians to move into the prison hospital building and 60 invalids to occupy cells in the main block. Finally, on April 6, owing to the growing congestion and to the verminous condition of the cells in the administrative block, three wings of the main block were opened and the P.o.W. redistributed themselves. The female block became a convalescent ward.

On July 8, 323 P.o.W., most of them acutely ill, arrived from a P.o.W. camp at Taiping which was closing. In August all the civilian

P.o.W. and 40 selected technicians from the Army personnel were sent to Singapore. On October 2, 300 Australians and 140 sick and on the 13th 160 sick were moved to Changi. On October 14, 1942, the camp was closed, 400 of the P.o.W. being sent to Thailand and 96 going south for use in the making of a Japanese film of the campaign in Malaya.

KUALA LUMPUR P.O.W. CAMP. MEDICAL ASPECTS

Three British Army medical officers were included among the P.o.W. At first there was only one of these in the camp and he at once took over one of the small rooms in the female block for use as a hospital. Over 80 per cent. of every batch of prisoners that arrived needed his urgent attention for they were suffering from wounds, sores, exposure and starvation. Fly-proof latrine pits were constructed with such tools, wood and rice bags as could be found. But in the beginning every rule of elementary sanitation was repeatedly broken and the compound became fouled. Two of the original inmates came in with dysentery and after a few days there were dozens more. By the beginning of February, dysentery was present in epidemic proportions. No drugs and no dressings were available. Out of 500 P.o.W. 140 were sick, many of them seriously so. At the end of February two officers and 15 O.Rs. R.A.M.C. of a field ambulance arrived, bringing with them two panniers with a fair stock of drugs and dressings; but there was still only one bed pan and no bucket. The mortuary was but one end of the room that was the hospital. The squalor, the filth and the smell were abominable. Swarms of flies covered everyone and everything.

By April the I.J.A. was developing some kind of P.o.W. administration and permission was obtained to use the prison hospital building as the camp hospital. It consisted of two fly-proofed wards and an annexe with bathroom and lavatory. The dysentery cases could now be segregated.

When the camp opened all that was available was one bed and a few rags of prison clothing. The latter, together with a few first field dressings, constituted the medical stores. Then the prison dispensary was discovered and the guard commander permitted it to be used. It had been looted, however, and little remained, but a bed, two mattresses, a few bottles of stock medicines, a drum of disinfectant, a small quantity of soap, some eating utensils and some prison clothing were acquired. In March the senior medical officer among the P.o.W. was permitted to go into Kuala Lumpur and bring away all that he could carry from a looted and abandoned pharmacy—mostly Mag. Sulph. and dressings. In April an Indian dresser from one of the rubber estate hospitals was appointed 'liaison officer' between the I.J.A. medical authorities and the camp. His main duty seemed to be that of spreading despondency and engaging in black market activities. In June the Japanese made an issue of drugs and dressings to the hospital:

Acid Sod. Sal . .	2 oz.
Quinine Sulp. . .	4 oz.
Aspirin . .	4 oz.
Phenacetin . .	4 oz.
Alcohol . .	8 oz.
Sod. Phosphate .	1 lb.
Cotton wool . .	4 oz.
Lint . .	2 oz.
Gauze . .	4 oz.
Bandages . . .	8

But from March onwards the local Roman Catholic priest had been permitted to visit the camp weekly and he and his Eurasian community regularly supplied the hospital with drugs, dressings and comforts which the priest brought in.

As more of the buildings were made available more blankets, prison clothing and utensils were discovered. Ultimately about 100 blankets were in use. When, in March, working parties were in demand these were able to equip themselves with odds and ends which they smuggled back into camp.

In June the Japanese had semi-permanent latrines constructed and introduced the bucket system using local Tamil labour.

The water supply was good but was insufficient for so large a population and so had to be rationed to a pint a day.

Refuse was incinerated right from the beginning.

Rations during the early weeks were irregular and uncertain. Rice and vegetable stew was served in rubber latrine buckets. Later the camp had to prepare its own food. A fluctuating quantity of rice and green vegetables daily and a microscopic amount of meat every other day were sent in to the camp. One large cauldron was provided for cooking the rice and fuel was scarce; it had to be supplemented from the floorboards and the like. There were no trained cooks among the P.o.W. Permission was given to use the kitchen of the prison hospital. Early in March the electric current was restored in the town and the town cold storage plant brought into use. A daily meat ration of a quarter of beef or four pigs was now provided for the 700 P.o.W. In April the I.J.A. introduced an individual daily ration scale which was:

Rice	500 g.
Vegetables . . .	100 g.
Meat or dried fish .	40 g.
Tea	4 g.
Salt	10 g.

In May working pay was introduced, 10 cents a day (3 dollars a month) for O.Rs. and 35 cents for officers. Rations were now issued only for such as worked but were given, of course, to all. The sick, the non-workers, constituted at least 20 per cent. of the population and so the food intake of the individual became so small that progressive starvation was inevitable. Officers worked with the men and lived their lives.

Food could be bought in the town by the working parties but it had to be smuggled past the guards. Towards the end of June the purchase of food was systematised. An officer was permitted to visit the local market. But when in August eight prisoners escaped this system was changed and a Chinese contractor visited the camp twice a week. (The escapees were recaptured and shot.) In September officers received allowances and a fund was started with compulsory stoppages. O.Rs. contributed 25 cents per month. With this central fund 200 ill-nourished men received extra nourishment in the form of a daily meat stew and hospital patients eggs and meat.

In February four tins of unsweetened milk were issued daily to the hospital and in March 30 loaves of bread were added. Insistent requests for more ultimately resulted in 200 loaves being issued. In August an extra ration of dried fish was issued to the hospital but its quantity varied considerably.

In August the senior officer of the camp was informed by the Japanese commandant that all P.o.W. were to be required to sign an undertaking not to attempt to escape. He explained the position to all the other officers in the camp. On August 27 all officers other than the sick were paraded and addressed by the Japanese commandant. The officers refused to sign and were thereupon confined to their cells.

One medical officer was instructed by the senior medical officer to sign the declaration in order that he might continue to attend the sick, which, however, he was not permitted to do. The C. of E. chaplain was likewise given permission to sign. Officers who were sick were not allowed to leave their cells unless they signed. They refused to do so. On the 28th the senior officer of the camp was warned that unless the declaration was signed they would be punished. It was explained that under Japanese military law the I.J.A. could issue orders to P.o.W. and that such as refused could be punished as would Japanese officers and men who disobeyed an order. The officers concerned then debated the matter. By refusing to sign, the health, even the lives, of 80 officers would become endangered; they certainly would not be able ever again to bear arms. According to International Law signature of a document could be regarded as valid only if it were made voluntarily. Therefore neither the officers nor their government need consider the signed document binding. The officers, though signing, were not giving their parole since they were signing under duress. The senior officer thereupon stated that if the Japanese authorities would give to him a statement in writing that the signing of this document was in accordance with Japanese military law and not International Law and that the Japanese military authorities ordered all officers to sign, he would advise his colleagues to sign the declaration.

On the 30th the officers were released from close confinement and paraded. The commandant had communicated with the Japanese H.Q. in Singapore and had been informed of Article VII of the Hague Convention of 1907 in which it was laid down that P.o.W. must obey the orders of the nation that held them captive. The senior officer of the camp called attention to Article VIII which stated that a parole could only be given voluntarily. The Japanese commandant ultimately agreed to give a statement in writing to the effect that he as the Japanese commandant of the camp ordered all officers to sign the declaration. The four senior officers among those in the camp then agreed to sign and to advise the rest to do the same. This they did.

PRINCIPAL DISEASES AFFECTING THE TROOPS

Detailed records could not be maintained under the conditions that obtained in the camp. Paper was allowed only for the returns that had to be submitted to the I.J.A. The strength of the camp fluctuated so violently by reason of the arrivals of fresh batches of prisoners and of the departure of others that it is difficult to expose such figures as are available to any statistical analysis.

From a copy of a letter from the senior officer of the camp to the Japanese officer i/c P.o.W. camp, Kuala Lumpur, it is learnt that 110 out of the 740 P.o.W. in the camp on April 16 were either in hospital or else were attending for treatment and that 48 deaths had occurred since the camp opened, the cause being either dysentery or malaria. From another letter dated May 3 it is learnt that there were 1,006 P.o.W. in the camp, that among them there were 25 cases of advanced beriberi, 180 cases of the same disease in not so severe a form and 100 others showing early signs, that there were 60 cases of chronic dysentery and 25 cases of long-standing malaria, and that the incidence of pellagra was steeply rising.

The record of deaths shows that the major causes were defined as: Dysentery 50, Malaria 26, Beriberi 6, Heart Failure 3, Jaundice 2.

The medical officers in the camp numbered three; the magnitude of their labour is disclosed in the following tables:

TABLE 12

1942	Total out-patients	Total in-patients	Deaths
February	744	213	13
March	2,464	775	20
April	2,077	755	24
May	2,040	924	5
June	2,489	849	6
July	4,586	1,097	13
August	7,463	1,240	4
September	9,558	1,234	3

Week ending	Patients per day	
	Beriberi	Pellagra
May 29, 1942	2	1
June 5, 1942	3	2
June 12, 1942	4	1
June 19, 1942	3	3
June 26, 1942	4	4
July 3, 1942	10	6
July 10, 1942	15	15
July 17, 1942	26	9
July 24, 1942	39	27
July 31, 1942	48	46
August 7, 1942	68	60
August 14, 1942	85	46
August 21, 1942	91	29
August 28, 1942	101	23
September 4, 1942	105	19
September 11, 1942	149	16
September 18, 1942	196	14
September 25, 1942	224	15

But figures cannot depict the circumstances. It was as though stripped of all modern diagnostic aids and all therapeutic agents they had been flung back in time into the darkest of the Dark Ages when famine and pestilence stalked through the land to decimate the population and to bring to an end all community life.

Dengue occurred sporadically throughout the whole period. By August 90 per cent. of the inmates of the camp were suffering from scabies while ringworm, Singapore foot and septic sores that would not heal were almost universal.

CHANGI P.O.W. CAMP

On February 15, 1942, the survivors of the 85,000 troops of Malaya Command passed into captivity. Their experiences during the three years that followed claim a place in this history for the reason that for part of this time the Command retained its organisation with 'G', 'A' and 'Q' branches and, subject to the overriding authority of the Imperial

Japanese Army, conducted its own affairs in strict accordance with King's Regulations. H.Q. Malaya Command received and transmitted to its constituent formations such orders as were issued by the I.J.A.

On February 17 the Australian, British and Indian troops in Singapore Island moved by route march from the localities they occupied at the time of the capitulation to the barracks and camps in the Changi area. The different national groups were kept apart. The Indian units, less their British elements, in Farrar Park were paraded and exhorted by an Indian Army captain, who had been taken prisoner on December 15 when 1/14th Punjab Regt. was overrun, to join the Indian National Army (I.N.A.). Of the 45,000 Indian captives some 5,000 stoutly refused to do so; the rest, mostly because they were raw recruits, very imperfectly trained, dispirited, bewildered and leaderless, broke the oath of allegiance they had taken and changed sides to become the guards of the camps in which their erstwhile comrades

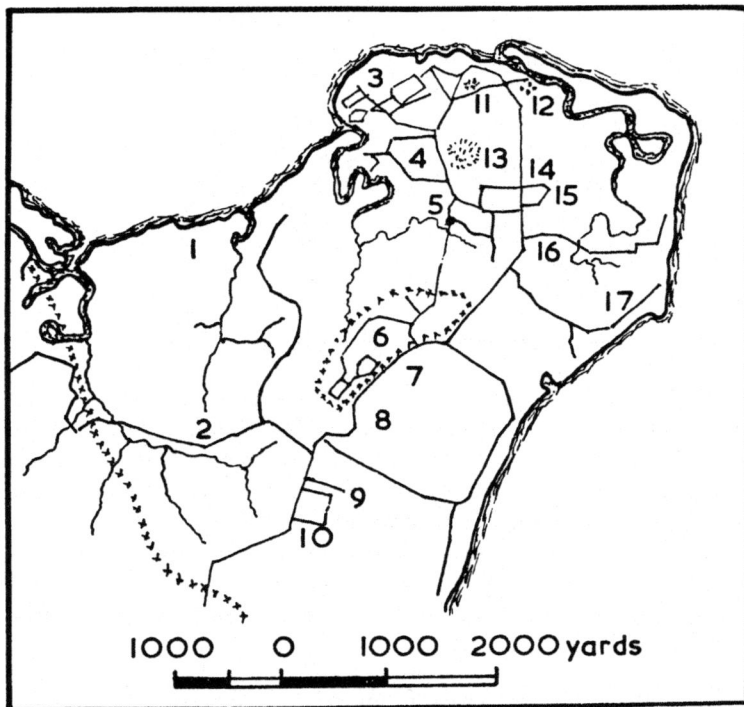

FIG. 17. The Changi Area, Singapore Island.

1. Loyang Camp.	7. Birdwood Camp.	13. Changi Hill.
2. Tampines Road.	8. Selerang Camp.	14. Wavell Camp.
3. Kitchener Barracks.	9. Liaison Office.	15. India Lines.
4. Temple Hill.	10. Changi Gaol.	16. Teloh Paku Road.
5. Robert's Barracks.	11. Battery Hill.	17. Teloh Paku Camp.
6. Selerang Barracks.	12. Changi Village.	

were now incarcerated. By their action the immediate effect of the Japanese victories on land and sea is to be measured. It is to be regretted that it is necessary to record that the behaviour of some of these Indian soldiers towards the prisoners-of-war added much humiliation to the bitterness of defeat.

The Changi area at the eastern tip of Singapore Island contained many barracks and camp sites. It measured about four miles by three and a half miles. In its centre on high ground were the Selerang Barracks which had been allotted to the A.I.F. From there the ground fell away in irregular ravines. To the east and north-west were swamps. The area generally was well grassed and in it were many trees. The soil was mostly sand and clay. The sub-soil water rose rapidly after rain.

H.Q. Malaya Command controlled the whole camp, which was divided into six areas each of which was enclosed by wire and was regarded as a separate administrative unit having its own commander and staff. Movement between these sub-areas was rigorously controlled by the guards. The troops were segregated into four formations, A.I.F., Fortress troops, 18th Division and Indian III Corps, each in its own area. The other two areas were the central hospital area (Roberts Barracks) and the garden area in which garden and wood fatigues were accommodated in huts.

It was not long before an orderly pattern of military life was restored, discipline refreshed and morale repaired. These developments were not impeded by the Japanese insistence that all rank badges should be removed and replaced by a single star worn on the left breast by all officers irrespective of rank.

Soon the Japanese military authorities began to demand that working parties should be supplied for various labour camps in the island and on the adjacent mainland. In July General Percival and all officers of the rank of colonel upwards were warned that they were shortly to be sent to Japan. Before leaving on August 16 General Percival nominated the officer commanding 1st Manchester Regt., with the approval of the Japanese, as senior officer in his place. This senior officers' party was sent from Japan to Formosa where it remained until 1944. Thereafter it was sent to North Manchuria.

On August 30 the area commanders were ordered to meet representatives of the I.J.A. There had been several attempts to escape. The Japanese now required that every P.o.W. should sign the following undertaking: 'I, the undersigned, hereby solemnly swear on my honour that I will not, under any circumstances, attempt to escape'. The area commanders unanimously, promptly and flatly refused to have anything to do with the matter. On September 1 the senior officer, H.Q. Malaya Command, was informed that all who persisted in refusing to sign would be subjected to 'measures of severity' and would be transferred to a small area. Shortly after midnight orders were received by Malaya Command for all Australian and British troops then in the Changi area to be congregated in the Selerang Barrack Square. This measured about 800 × 400 ft. and was surrounded by seven barrack blocks each of which had a floor space of 150 × 60 ft. In the barracks were 2,380 Australians. To these were now to be added some 13,350 British. Arrangements were swiftly made for the provision of adequate kitchen and sanitary facilities and for the shifting of stores.

On September 2, four P.o.W. who had escaped and had been recaptured were executed by the Japanese, the Australian and British commanders being required to attend. The troops marched to Selerang stubborn, sullen and defiant. The I.J.A. announced that unless the form was signed rations would be cut by half. Water was already rationed to a gallon per head per day. The maintenance of sanitation presented serious difficulties. Within the enclosure were many Australian sick and many grievously incapacitated—e.g. the amputees in the Australian convalescent depot. Cases of diphtheria and dysentery were presenting themselves and only these would the Japanese allow to be sent to hospital. The medical services could not do otherwise, in the circumstances, than express the opinion that the danger of serious epidemic was imminent. Malaya Command thereupon decided that the troops should be advised to sign the undertaking. On September 4 efforts were made to induce the Japanese military authorities to accept a compromise declaration admitting duress. They eventually agreed to replace the original order by one demanding signature. On the 5th the signing of the forms was completed and the troops marched back to their previous locations.

At the end of 1942 there was a great influx of Dutch P.o.W. from the Netherlands East Indies. Early in 1943 the Indian guards were replaced by Koreans, much to the relief of the captives. It had been more than irksome continually to salute these sentries and more than infuriating to endure the frequent 'face slappings' that these administered on, or even without, the slightest provocation. Many of these Indians, imitating the Japanese, had found it necessary to justify and magnify themselves by attempting to diminish those whom they wished to despise. This 'face slapping' was one of the methods used—with a complete lack of success, for captivity and its attendant deprivations had not yet destroyed in the captives an appreciation of the ridiculous. It was exceedingly difficult, if not impossible, for the captives even to begin to understand the manifest contradictions in the behaviour pattern of the Japanese. What appeared to be a display of sadism, judged by British standards, was in fact often merely the exercise of brutality. In the I.J.A. it was the accepted custom for an officer to chastise a N.C.O. and for the latter to thrash a private, this act being likened to the corrective whipping by a parent of a wayward child. Privates, in their turn, struck civilians and in war prisoners-of-war. The Japanese seemed to be totally unaware of the brutality of their actions. Undoubtedly their education and propaganda had cultivated in them the desire to avenge on individual P.o.W. the galling attitude of superiority displayed by white towards yellow. The Koreans who now took their places were a primitive, tough crowd, unreliable, brutal at times and easily corruptible. They served themselves rather than their masters and were continually on the prowl for bargains. With their eager participation a flourishing black market quickly developed.

At this time a further change of some significance took place. The I.J.A. ordained that Australian and British officers should no longer command troops, that all staff titles should be dropped and that the senior officer of H.Q. Malaya Command should henceforth be known as the senior representative officer.

In December 1943 all the working parties from the various labour camps in the island and in Johore returned to Changi camp. Between October 1942 and May 1943 a series of large parties had left Changi for various destinations, in particular Borneo, Burma, Japan and Thailand. These were designated Forces A, B, C, D, etc. By June 1943, therefore, the numbers in the Changi area had fallen to about 6,000. In December 1943 and January 1944 many of these parties—or more correctly the remains of them—returned to Changi.

In May 1944 all the P.o.W. were moved from the barracks and camps into Changi gaol in which previously British civilians including children had been interned, and the sick to a hutted camp at Kranji. The Changi and Kranji P.o.W. camps continued to be used as such until the end of the war. On September 3, 1945, representatives of the Repatriated Allied P.o.W. and Internees Organisation (R.A.P.W.I.) arrived. All Q.A.I.M.N.S. and all the I.M.D. nurses, save one, had been sent away from Singapore on February 13. The remaining one and the V.A.Ds. were transferred to Changi Gaol.

CHANGI P.O.W. CAMP. MEDICAL ASPECTS

When the troops in Singapore Island were congregated in the Changi area arrangements were made for the care of the sick by the R.M.Os. and personnel of the field medical units until such time as the hospitals with their equipment and patients could be transferred. There were 9,000 battle casualties and sick (including over 2,500 British) in the hospitals of Singapore to be transported to the Changi area, the Indians to Nee Soon, the British to Roberts Barracks, the Australians to Selerang. The Japanese staff officer controlling this move set a period of seven days for its completion and allotted only five ambulances for the transport of the lying cases. D.D.M.S. Malaya

Command protested vigorously and permission was ultimately given to use the many lorries then parked along the Changi road. No order had been issued concerning the method of transfer of the preliminary medical units but the taking of field medical equipment was forbidden. The Alexandra Hospital was required by the I.J.A. to leave behind 550 fully equipped beds, the operating room and X-ray department fully equipped, the dispensary fully stocked and the institution ready for immediate occupation. On the day the hospital moved out, February 27, it was inspected by the Japanese. Since, however, at this time the instructions of the medical services of the I.J.A. could not easily be enforced, they were not observed and the transfer of patients occupied nearly three weeks, large numbers of motor vehicles were used and the allowance of petrol greatly augmented by collection from the tanks of abandoned transport. Drugs and dressings were distributed in small lots among the troops. Instead of the 250 beds allowed to the Australians 1,120 with 1,400 mattresses were taken, as was also a complete X-ray installation. The British medical units were in their new sites by March 2, the Australians by February 23. The Indian hospital began to move on March 3.

The medical organisation was in keeping with that of the rest of Malaya Command. The titles of D.D.M.S., A.D.M.S., and A.D.H. Malaya Command and A.Ds.M.S. areas were retained. When D.D.M.S. Malaya Command, as a member of the senior officers party, left for Japan he nominated Indian Army officers for the posts of D.D.M.S., A.D.M.S. and A.D.H. Malaya Command.

Roberts Barracks Hospital became one of the six areas into which the Changi P.o.W. camps was divided. Save in respect of courts martial it was a self-contained administrative area. Its officer commanding was directly responsible to H.Q. Malaya Command for the administration of the area. Roberts Barracks consisted of eleven brick and concrete three-storeyed buildings, one two-storeyed N.A.A.F.I. building, a sergeants' mess, a cinema, a gymnasium and twenty *attap* huts. These had suffered but minor damage during the fighting. But there was no running water, no lighting and no facilities for sterilisation. The sanitary arrangements had degenerated into the primitive. On March 2 there were 986 British wounded in this hospital and more than 5,000 in unit lines. Among the medical staff were seven who held higher degrees in surgery, an anaesthetist, two radiologists besides others with experience in ophthalmology, laryngology and pathology.*

At Selerang the Australians opened fourteen sick bays each holding ten cases and their dysentery patients were concentrated in one building

---

*See 'Prisoner-of-War Surgery' in the Surgery Volume of this series.

and cared for by 2/13 A.G.H. An operating theatre and X-ray room were established in another block. All water had to be hand-carried from a source 200 yards away.

On March 6 the Japanese ordered that all the sick in the Changi area should be concentrated in one central hospital in Roberts Barracks under unified command and that this move must be completed in seven days. At a conference between D.D.M.S. Malaya Command and A.D.M.S. A.I.F. it was agreed that the policy whereby Australian patients should be treated in Australian hospitals under independent administration should be observed as far as possible and that there should be an Australian wing in the Roberts Hospital, that a R.A.M.C. officer should command the hospital area, that an Australian A.A.M.C. officer should command the Australian wing and that Malaya Command should administer hygiene in the hospital area. The officer commanding 2/13 A.G.H. was appointed to command the Australian wing which was staffed by the officers and men of the two A.G.Hs., of 2/4 (Aust.) C.C.S. and of 2/9 and 2/10 (Aust.) Fd. Ambs. 2/3 Aust. M.A.C. was attached to the wing. 2/9 (Aust.) Fd. Amb. maintained an out-patient department to which special clinics were attached.

The move was completed by March 11, 351 surgical, 283 dysentery, 80 malaria, 32 typhus and 176 general medical patients being transferred.

The conditions in the hospital were most unsatisfactory. There was gross overcrowding and each ward, designed for 60 men, was holding 144. By March 24 there were 2,600 patients in the hospital and the difficulties due to differences between the Australian and British record systems, rates of pay, ration scales and methods of maintaining discipline became magnified. A D.A.D.M.S. A.I.F. for the hospital area was appointed to link up the commander of the Australian wing with H.Q. A.I.F. but it was quickly found that this dual system of control hindered attempts to obtain outside help in matters of alteration or construction. At the end of April the question of the inter-relationship of the Australian and British medical services was reviewed. The Australians presented the view that all that was necessary was to present an appearance of conformity to the Japanese order for a single hospital under unified command and that it was possible and desirable to give to the Australian wing an independent identity with responsibility to the A.I.F. D.D.M.S. Malaya Command maintained that all matters of difference between the two services were unimportant and that it was D.D.M.S. Malaya Command that the Japanese regarded as being the one and only responsible medical authority. It was agreed that this fact should be accepted and that the cause of economy would not be served by attempting to sunder the overall control of the hospital. It was agreed too that difficulties, as they arose, should be tackled and overcome in the spirit of friendly co-operation.

In April lists were prepared for submission to the I.J.A. by H.Q. Malaya Command of such as would not be able to serve further in the war and who should therefore be repatriated. The question of the repatriation of personnel of the medical services surplus to requirements was also considered. It was decided that with the passing of time and the inevitable increase in the incidence of sickness there would be no surplus but rather a deficit. Japan had not been a signatory to the International Convention for the amelioration of the condition of the wounded and sick by armies in the field. The I.J.A. rejected all petitions for the repatriation of invalids.

When in August the senior officers were sent to Japan there were many changes among the staff of the hospital but the system of administration was in no way disturbed. It was agreed that the commander of the hospital area should allot accommodation between the Australian and British wings of the hospital and that these wings should draw their own rations and be responsible for accounting to H.Q. Malaya Command, except for supplementary items for which the officer commanding a wing was to be responsible to his own formation headquarters. The Australian wing dealt with H.Q. A.I.F. in the matter of clothing but all other 'Q' matters were adjusted through Malaya Command. The engineering services of the hospital were a British responsibility unless Australian help was required. In these ways the independence of the Australian medical services, so keenly cherished, was preserved.

In October 1942 the Australian wing had accommodation for 1,000 patients, the British wing for 2,000. There were 620 Australian beds and 1,970 British beds occupied. The hospital staff numbered about 1,500, that of the British wing 100 officers and 900 O.Rs. being top-heavy in respect of its senior officers and N.C.Os. Early in November 20 officers and 400 O.Rs. R.A.M.C. left for Thailand. 32 Coy. R.A.M.C. and 196, 197 and 198 Fd. Ambs. of 18th Division had previously been maintained separately in order to preserve the integrity of the units. They were now all brought under the control of the central office of the hospital area. The hospital and R.A.M.C. company staff consisted of an officer commanding, registrar and company officer, consulting surgeon, consulting physician (also officer i/c medical division), officer in charge surgical division, officer in charge of dysentery division, anaesthetist, pathologist, radiologist and officer in charge of the E.N.T. department, together with many G.D.Os.

The Australian wing occupied three of the barrack blocks, the N.A.A.F.I. building, the gymnasium and the sergeants' mess, together with a proportion of the *attap* huts. The operating theatre, the X-ray unit, a tuberculosis ward and a mental ward were common to both wings. All medical and ordnance stores were centralised.

The British wing was divided into surgical, medical and dysentery divisions, an infectious block and an officers' ward. In it were two dispensaries, two clinical laboratories, an E.N.T. department, a central reception room, a steward's store, a Q.M. store and a central medical store. Two kitchens served the wing. The R.A.M.C. company had its own office and Q.M. store. A sub-office served the Australian wing.

By August 1943 the number of patients in the British wing had fallen to 993. The staff was now able to leave the *attap* huts which were in poor condition and infested with vermin.

After the capitulation large quantities of medical equipment and stores found their way to Changi. These eventually had to be declared to the I.J.A. but the hospital was permitted to take them on charge. Sufficient beds and mattresses for 3,000 patients were held. Other ordnance and hospital equipment approximated to the authorised peace-time scale for a hospital of this size. The supplies of linen, blankets and hospital clothing were limited. In October the British wing possessed 800 blankets and 1,200 sheets. Towels could not be issued as the stock held was too small. By the end of 1943 only a few hundred serviceable blankets remained and sheets were used only in the surgical ward. The patient slept in his underclothes and used his own blanket. It was impossible to maintain a packstore and the patient's kit was kept under his bed; the patient, unless on the S.I. or D.I. lists, being responsible for it. The beds and mattresses were badly bug infested and no method for eliminating these pests was discovered. The bugs accompanied the troops from Roberts Barracks to Selerang and from Selerang to Kranji.

The surgical theatres and special departments were all well stocked for an ample supply of drugs and dressings were brought from the hospitals in Singapore. Replenishments in the form of Red Cross stores arrived in September 1942. The I.J.A. made infrequent and small issues of drugs and dressings.

There was no supply of water from the mains until March 3, 1943. Until then all water for drinking, cooking and washing had to be procured from a number of water points (sub-soil water) in the hospital area. Two tanks for drinking water were set up in the hospital grounds. To begin with fatigue parties took the bed linen, pyjamas, etc., to the beach daily, using a hand truck along the railway, washed them in the sea and brought them back and hung them in the hospital grounds. In August 1942 a *dhobie ghat* was constructed within the hospital wire. Operating theatre linen was washed by the staff. Linen from dysentery and other infectious cases was soaked in creosol solution for an hour before being washed.

Lavatories were flushed with sea water brought from the beach by fatigue parties. They were used only by patients who were unable to make their way outside the hospital and for the disposal of the contents of bed pans. Such as the lavatories could not accept was taken to Otway pits. For the troops slit trenches and deep trench latrines were dug in the hospital compound. For the first three months the supply of latrine facilities failed to overtake the demand, but from the middle of May steady progress was made in the provision of Otway pits for faeces and for vegetable refuse from the kitchens and swill tubs. Incinerators were built and everything that could be destroyed by fire was burnt.

No supply of electricity was available in the hospital. The only source of light was a limited number of hurricane lamps which had been brought into the area by the units. No oil for these was supplied by the I.J.A. Ultimately the R.Es. were able to provide electric light for the operating theatre and the X-ray department. On August 15, 1942, the mains were repaired and light and power became available.

Since the stores of petrol were quickly exhausted and were not replenished, motor vehicles were converted into such as could more easily be man-handled. All fuel rations and stores were transported on these 'Changi trucks'. In August 1942 it became possible to organise a regular once daily motor ambulance service for the return of patients unable to walk the distance to their unit lines and to bring others back to hospital.

To begin with all that was available for sterilisation purposes was a mobile autoclave. This was used until the fuel supply was exhausted. Primus stoves and fish kettles were used for instruments. Then the R.Es. converted the autoclave to make use of the steam from the kitchen boiler and so from May onwards the most urgent needs of the hospital were met. This steam was also used for the production of distilled water. For intravenous injection rain water, duly autoclaved, was used.

The cinema building had been severely damaged, the roof practically destroyed and the seating removed. It was repaired and on April 4, 1942, the first concert was held. The building was used also for church services. Lectures, ward concerts and reading to the patients helped them to forget their sufferings. A band and a group of entertainers from such as had been professionals before the war were formed. In 1942 and early 1943 football and hockey were played but by the end of 1943 all such strenuous exercise had to be forbidden for the rations had diminished. Up to March 1943 each area of Changi camp had its own wireless set and arrangements were made whereby all could hear the news of the outside world. Thereafter the Japanese were continually searching the camp for transmitting sets and it was decided that there should be one central reception station. Each sent its representatives to collect the day's news. But private sets still functioned in spite of every action taken by the Japanese.

In August 1943 the Japanese issued instructions to the effect that the hospital would move to Selerang Barracks, a mile and a half away, the move commencing on August 18 and being completed by the 27th.

Selerang Barracks consisted of seven blocks. Of these four were allotted to the British wing, three to the Australians. The general condition of the buildings was exceedingly poor; doors, door frames and latrine seats had been removed and the electrical system and the water flushing system badly damaged. A great deal of R.E. work had to be done before the barracks became anything like a hospital.

For the move to Selerang the I.J.A. provided one 3-ton lorry which was available for six and a half hours daily for seven days. This was used for the transport of heavy stores. Three motor ambulances were available. One was to tow loaded 'Changi trucks', the others for the transport of patients. The I.J.A. allowed 80 gallons of petrol for the complete move. When loaded a 'Changi truck' required a team of 16–20 men to haul it. Six such trucks were used by the British wing and each did between four and eight trips a day—a total journey of 10–20 miles on a rice ration.

Among the stores, etc., to be moved were 1,700 bedsteads, 1,500 mattresses, 1,000 pillows, the contents of one large hospital kitchen, one company kitchen, three officers' messes, one officer patients' kitchen, one sergeants' mess, three operating theatres, one X-ray department, a massage department, a hospital laboratory, medical stores for all the P.o.W. camps, the hospital steward's and Q.M. stores, a Red Cross store, an artificial limb factory, R.E. stores including two emergency electric lighting plants, the Palladium Theatre and its props and some 2,000 head of poultry and their pens.

Six hundred O.R. patients, 87 officer patients and 600 personnel of the hospital staff and their kits were involved in the transfer.

When the P.o.W. forces that had been sent to Thailand returned the accommodation in the hospital again became overtaxed, 140 and 150 patients being crowded into the space required by 100. Gradually, however, as these patients became restored to health the numbers lessened.

KRANJI P.O.W. CAMP

The instructions issued by the I.J.A. in May 1944 were to the effect that combatants were to move into the civil criminal gaol at Changi, hospital patients and holders of the Red Cross card to huts around the gaol and that a 1,200-bedded hospital would be opened at Kranji to accommodate the surplus. All patients requiring a month or more in hospital would be sent to Kranji. Acute surgery would be undertaken at Changi. A weekly service of ambulances or lorries would run between

Changi and Kranji. Most of these arrangements failed to materialise. Transfers took place three times monthly, then twice monthly and in July 1945 ceased altogether.

The officer commanding Kranji hospital dealt with the I.J.A. direct and not through any headquarters. The Japanese commander of the area was a N.C.O., a severe disciplinarian whose behaviour gained him a place in the list of war criminals. Under his command were 40 Koreans and 20 Indians. The latter were so embarrassed by the conflict between their old and new loyalties that ultimately they were transferred by the I.J.A. to the main I.N.A. camp. A Japanese medical officer was designated as O. i/c camp but his was an empty title and he had little or no authority. The Japanese N.C.O. demanded large working parties for labour quite unconnected with the hospital. These had to be provided under the threat of a cut or even stoppage of rations.

Kranji was a hutted camp, in rubber, at the thirteenth milestone on the main Singapore–Johore road. After the capitulation it was used as a hospital for Indian troops until May 1944. For the 1,200 beds and some 400 staff now to be accommodated fifty of the huts were allotted. These were in fairly good repair, well off the ground and with *attap* walls and roofs. The advance party, which included R.E. and hygiene personnel, repaired the huts, laid on electric lighting, extended the water points and prepared an emergency operating theatre. By June there was running water in all the wards, which were all now wired for electric light, the current being provided by an old Army field set. A main kitchen cooked for 800, a special diet kitchen for 200. Yet another cookhouse catered for sick officers. Three other kitchens were available. The whole camp was enclosed in a double wire fence.

1,600 bedsteads, some 1,300 blankets and a few sheets were brought from Changi. By the end of the year the number of serviceable blankets had fallen to 1,000 and hospital linen had joined those things that belonged to the past. Clothing and footwear were worn out and the men were in rags. In May 1945 a small quantity of Red Cross clothing became available. Individual personal equipment consisted of an enamel mug or milk tin, an enamel plate or a mess tin and a spoon.

The operating theatre and special departments were well stocked. Replenishments of drugs and dressings were obtained from the central stores at Changi quarterly. Drugs such as emetine and insulin were unobtainable.

The hospital was sub-divided, as before, into Australian and British wings.

Among the 50 officers and 425 O.Rs. of the approved hospital staff of the British wing were chaplains and welfare officers. The band and the concert party staged performances thrice weekly until July 1945 when they were forbidden. There were three camp libraries the contents of which were badly mutilated when the trick of splitting the leaves of books for the manufacture of cigarette paper was mastered.

One of the patients in hospital, a member of the S.S.V.F., happened to be a rubber planter. Under his leadership and with the consent of the Japanese a plantation of some 200 trees was taken over and a rubber factory was established. The factory supplied rubber *chaplis*, soles for boots and raw latex for repairs.

Once a month the Japanese permitted the collection of palm fronds. The fatigues also incidentally collected coconuts on their journeys. A broom factory was started. In these and similar ways occupation for the troops was provided and boredom kept in check.

RATIONS. (CHANGI AND KRANJI)

When considering that which follows it should be remembered that the Geneva Convention requires that the detaining power shall give to its prisoners the same standard diet as its own base troops receive. Japan proclaimed her adherence to the Convention after her entry into the war. But the difference between the Japanese and the European in respect of food requirements is such that a diet sufficient to satisfy Japanese base troops must, in the European, lead to slow starvation. The rations issued to the P.o.W. were certainly in some degree responsible for the progressive malnutrition among the captives. But the major factor in its causation was undoubtedly the active desire on the part of the Japanese to humiliate and to destroy their enemies.

The rations for hospital patients were derived from three sources— the Japanese basic rations, the Red Cross stores and a central mess fund. Three types of diet were prepared—'ordinary', 'dysentery' and 'extras'. The basic ration consisted of:

Rice . . . . about	450 g.
Sugar	15 g.
Salt	20 g.
Tea	4 g.
Fish	70 g.
Vegetables . . .	100 g.
Oil	25 g.
Pepper . . .	3 g.

Rice polishings, 20 grammes, was issued at intervals. The rice ration varied considerably. It was 550 g. in January, 450 in September, 300 plus maize, 50 g., in November. The bags did not always contain the stated quantity for pilfering was rife.

In January 1943 the attention of the I.J.A. was called to the unsatisfactory nature of this basic ration in a letter addressed to the headquarters of their P.o.W. administration:

'The average daily ration over a period of 20 days from January 1–20, 1943, was:

Rice	550 g.
Fish	45 g.
Salt	20 g.
Sugar	20 g.
Tea	4 g.
Ghee	14 g.
Green leaf, turnips, sweet potatoes	200 g.

'This diet is deficient in certain essentials—i.e. vitamin-B2 complex, protein and fat. The table below shows in comparison the amount of these essentials present with the standards generally accepted as a minimum necessity for the prevention of deficiency disease:

Essential Article	*Amount in Basic Ration*	*Accepted Minimum Standard*
Nicotinic acid . .	4·95 mg.	20·0 mg.
Riboflavin . .	0·94 mg.	2–3 mg.
Thiamin . . .	140 i.u.	300–600 i.u.
Fat . . .	15 g.	80 g.
Protein . . .	38 g. (3 animal)	80 g. (37 animal)

'Deficiency diseases are on the increase and will continue to be so unless the essential substances in the diet are brought up to the accepted standard. The numbers in hospital suffering from deficiency diseases on December 25, 1942, were 552; on January 21, 1943, this number had increased to 789 and is rising daily.

'Foodstuffs that could be used to bring the ration up to the standard required and which are known to be available are:

Commodity	*Amount Daily*	*Nico-tinic Acid*	*Ribo-flavin*	*Thiamin*	*Protein*	*Fat*
	g.	mg.	mg.	i.u.	g.	g.
Rice polishings	30	14	0·46	200	3	1
Towgay ⎤	100					
Soya bean ⎰ of any one or						
Peanuts ⎱ of any	2	0·9	250	27	16	
Dhall ⎦ combination						
Oil or Fat	30	—	—	—	—	22
Dried Fish	60	—	—	—	16	3
Total by this addition	220	16	1·5	450	46	41
Deficiency in present ration		15	1–2	200–400		60

'A regular special diet for hospital patients is always supplied in military hospitals of all nations. If this could be kindly considered it would be of great benefit to the patients in this hospital. The diet should include such articles as sugar, eggs, tinned milk, sago flour, tinned fish, meat extract and, for a few selected cases, fresh meat.'

Like so many other letters addressed to the I.J.A. this evoked no response. In early 1944 the Japanese introduced new ration scales and for the first time a difference was shown between workers and non-workers. All hospital staff and patients were included in the second category.

A camp conference was called and it was decided to pool all rations. The new Japanese basic rations were:

Commodity	Heavy Duty	Light Duty	Camp Issue from Pool
Rice	400 g.	265 g.	275 g.
Maize	200 g.	135 g.	130 g.
Vegetables	400 g.	200 g.	as received
Fish	50 g.	25 g.	as received
Sugar	20 g.	20 g.	20 g.
Salt	20 g.	20 g.	17 g.
Red palm oil	25 g.	25 g.	25 g.
Tea	5 g.	5 g.	4 g.
Wood	1 kg.	1 kg.	1 kg.

In September 1942 the Japanese exchange ships brought substantial quantities of Red Cross supplies of food, drugs and dressings. The food was divided into an all-round ration for the camp as a whole and a reserve for the hospital. It now became possible to provide a daily 2 oz. ration of tinned meat to all patients and ample milk for special cases. But by the middle of December 1942 the meat stocks had become greatly reduced and it became necessary to cut down the number of special diets and to reduce the issue of meat to these from 6 to 4 oz. The patients on an ordinary diet now received 1 oz. instead of 2 oz. The milk issue was likewise strictly controlled. The Japanese had supplied varying quantities of dried milk from time to time but the indications were that this source of supply would sooner or later dry up. By February 1943 the Red Cross store contained 7,050 lb. of tinned meat and 5,790 lb. of M. & V. By the end of May the meat stock was exhausted except for a small reserve for diabetics. The Japanese issued 2,345 lb. of dried milk during 1943 and another 1,000 lb. were purchased locally. Even so at the end of April 1943 it had become necessary to issue milk as a ward extra only. The milk stock was exhausted on December 31, 1943. The I.J.A. announced that there would be no further issue of this commodity to the hospital as none was available.

During 1943 the monthly milk issues (British Wing) had been:

	No. of Patients	Ordinary Diet	Special Diet	Ward Extras
February .	8,700	470 lb.	450 lb.	1,000 lb.
March .	9,300	610 lb.	170 lb.	1,010 lb.
April . .	8,400	200 lb.	120 lb.	840 lb.
May . .	7,700	90 lb.	80 lb.	570 lb.
June .	5,600			100 lb.
July . .	5,400			110 lb.
August .	4,600			100 lb.
September .	4,300			170 lb.
October .	4,600			150 lb.
November .	4,700			170 lb.
December .	5,000			45 lb.

Tinned vegetables, cocoa, biscuits, soup, nutrine, and marmite stocks were exhausted early in 1943.

In 1942 when the I.J.A. authorised the payment of allowances to officers and the O.Rs. received working pay, a central fund for the purchase of foodstuffs to augment rations was instituted. Officers received thirty dollars a month; other ranks, when working, six dollars, when not, nothing. The cost of commodities rose by leaps and bounds. An advisory committee on nutrition had been appointed and this committee controlled the expenditure of the fund. The hospital was allowed thirty cents a day for every patient. Commodities purchased with this money and issued daily were:

Towgay or beans or dhall .	3 oz.
Peanuts	1 oz.
Sago flakes	½ oz.
Palm oil	1½ oz.
Sweet potatoes . . .	3 oz.
Sago flour	1 oz.
Sugar	¼ oz.

In December 1943 to meet rising costs, the grant was increased to thirty-five cents. The cost of the supplementary diet from this fund varied from month to month:

1943	Ordinary Diets	Special Diets	Ward Extras
February . .	9·12 cents	11·56 cents	2·17 cents
March . .	6·75 ,,		3·61 ,,
April . .	7·67 ,,		4·77 ,,
May . . .	8·46 ,,		5·32 ,,
June . . .	15·45 ,,		9·87 ,,
July . . .	25·83 ,,		11·22 ,,
August . .	20·00 ,,		18·51 ,,
September .	23·06 ,,		6·25 ,,
October .	29·91 ,,		4·13 ,,
November .	26·34 ,,		4·55 ,,
December .	27·65 ,,		7·66 ,,

An officer of the A.C.C. supervised the work of the kitchens and the cooks were the pick of the trained A.C.C. and R.A.M.C. cooks.

In June 1944 the Japanese basic ration at Kranji was:

Rice . . .	500 g. (heavy work)
	400 g. (light work)
Tea . . .	5 g.
Salt . . .	20 g.
Sugar . . .	20 g.
Palm oil . .	25 g.
Dried fish . .	50 g.
Vegetables . .	100 g.
Wood . . .	1½ kg.

400 'heavy duty' rations were issued. In July, when 90 gardeners were added to the staff, 500 heavy duty rations were supplied. The rations, as before, were pooled and the monthly issues in 1944 were as follows:

June	480–430 g.
July	453–405 g.
August	460–410 g.
September	450–410 g.
October	450–410 g.
November	435–390 g.
December	435–390 g.

On January 15, 1945, the Japanese basic ration was reduced.

Commodity	Heavy Duties	Light Duties	Hospital Patients
Rice . .	500 g.	300 g.	250 g.
Oil . .	20 g.	20 g.	20 g.
Sugar .	20 g.	15 g.	15 g.
Salt . .	15 g.	15 g.	15 g.
Fish . .	26 g.	26 g.	26 g.
Vegetables .		4 to 6 oz.	
Wood . .	1 kg.	1 kg.	1 kg.

650 heavy and 250 light duty rations were allowed. The pool issued 400 g. to workers, 320 to the rest. On March 10 a drastic cut was made in the rice ration—heavy duty 300 g., light duty 250 g., remainder 200 g. The pool now issued workers 290 g., the rest 210 g. From time to time 50 g. of maize was issued in lieu of the same weight of rice. June 28 brought the final reduction. The scale remained as before but the number of heavy duty rations was reduced from 650 to 331. The camp issue became workers 270 g., remainder 230. The wood ration was cut by 50 per cent.

On August 20, 1945, the Japanese suddenly issued the I.J.A. ration to the hospital:

Rice	870 g.
Sugar . . .	30 g.
Salt	20 g.
Curry powder . .	20 g.
Vegetables . . .	690 g.
Tea	5 g.
Oil	24 g.
Meat	180 g.

Red Cross parcels and butter from cold storage and clothing of all kinds were also showered on the camp. No event could have claimed greater significance for it heralded in the most agreeable manner the end of captivity.

MEASURES TAKEN TO SUPPLEMENT THE DIETARY

The Japanese encouraged the establishment of unit and group gardens in the Changi area. They supplied the seeds and the units provided the labour. On March 5, 1942, an area of 120 acres outside the camp perimeter was allotted for this purpose. By October 1943 85 acres were in production bearing 320,000 lb. of leaf vegetables and 90,000 lb. of root vegetables. The produce was issued as rations to the camp by the Japanese. An elaborate system of urine collection for use as manure was organised. It is not to be forgotten that the gardeners were for the most part men already wearied by other occupations.

The Australians organised a yeast centre at the end of April 1942. Cultures were obtained from the Japanese. By June the centre was supplying 126 gallons per week.

Dutch P.o.W. brought with them the method of making *Tempe* prepared from soya beans by allowing a fungus to grow on the pulverised husked beans. The beans were thus partially predigested and made much more palatable.

Extracts of the coarse lalang grass and of the leaves of native vines prepared in ingenious ways provided riboflavin. As much as 50 gallons of the extract a day were made available.

When the first cut in rations was made at Kranji gardening became a major preoccupation. Within a year there was a 30 acre garden producing an average of 400 lb. of leaf daily. To reinforce the labours of the 90 officially recognised gardeners every member of the hospital staff was required to spend an hour a day working in the garden and, as at Changi, all urine was carefully collected and used for manurial purposes.

The central messing fund could provide 10 g. of black beans which were relatively cheap since they were not eaten by the Chinese population, and 25 g. of red palm oil. Red Cross stores were so low that they were issued only to a few post-operative, gastric and diabetic patients.

A camp canteen was opened by a Chinese contractor and from it tapioca root, sago flour, palm oil and a revolting fish paste, rich in protein and salt and used in normal times as manure, could be obtained. Each patient was allowed 1.50 dollars a month out of the central messing fund and the daily sugar ration was issued direct to the individual who, if he cared, could sell it to the canteen for 6–16 dollars per pound and so supplement his slender purse. The canteen then sold the sugar to the central messing fund and it was converted into alcohol for use in the operating theatre and wards.

THE PRINCIPAL DISEASES AFFECTING THE TROOPS

Changi and Kranji P.o.W. Camps

TABLE 13

Average Monthly Strength

	1942	1943	1944
January		27,135	8,498
February	51,374	26,582	8,568
March	51,344	26,380	8,561
April	50,736	18,128	8,618
May	49,187	7,311	11,500
June	46,720	5,538	
July	44,991	5,550	
August	44,775	5,372	
September	43,097	5,399	
October	45,182	7,452	
November	30,987	5,779	
December	29,047	6,718	

TABLE 14

Total Admissions to Hospital

	1942 Br.	1942 Aust.	1943 Br.	1943 Aust.	1944 Br.	1944 Aust.	Totals
All causes	26,629	9,870	6,913	5,619	2,880	3,534	55,445
Dysentery and diarrhœa	11,996	3,383	2,504	911	572	569	19,935
Beriberi	1,017	427	226	156	187	132	2,145
Diphtheria	1,361		227		49		1,637

(The Australian diphtheria figures are not included in this record. The epidemic that affected the British troops did not involve the Australians. Among the latter throughout the whole period over 100 cases of diphtheria occurred with 2 deaths.)

TABLE 15

Deaths in Hospital

	British	Australian	Dutch	Totals
1942 . .	422	79	35	536
1943 . .	44	23	21	88
1944 . .	25	36	2	63
	491	138	58	687

Malaria. Malaria was common among those who during the retreat had taken to the jungle and among those who returned to Changi after having been in one or other of the labour camps on the mainland. 6 Mal. Fd. Lab. and the field hygiene sections did everything within their powers to rid the camp area of the mosquito.

TABLE 16

Admissions on Account of Malaria

	1942		1943		1944	
	Br.	Aust.	Br.	Aust.	Br.	Aust.
January .			67	98	130	475
February .	143	206	67	58	197	304
March .	218	209	89	64	411	524
April .	155	184	45	32	133	316
May .	182	38	38	23	381	237
June .	207	47	17	14		
July .	113	22	11	16		
August .	117	71	6	16		
September .	118	39	13	19		
October .	174	36	7	12		
November .	108	94	6	17		
December .	79	114	217	216		
	1,614	1,060	583	585	1,252	1,856

Dysentery. The report of the dysentery wing of Roberts Hospital for the period February 17, 1942 to February 15, 1943, shows that admissons were 12,258 for the bacillary type and 491 for the amoebic, a total of 12,749.

A temporary hospital in a hut in India Lines and later in Changi Post Office and nearby buildings was opened by 198 Fd. Amb. on arrival in Changi and admissions began on February 19 before the dysentery wing of four blocks of the hospital proper was opened on March 15. In this wing the personnel of 196, 197 and 198 Fd. Ambs. were employed u/c O.C. 198. In the beginning the only treatment was by sea water enemata and fluid by the mouth. The climax of the epidemic was reached in March and April with a smaller peak in September and October on the arrival of the Dutch P.o.W. from Java. A sigmoidoscopy clinic was opened and many relapses of cases diagnosed as bacillary were found in fact to be entamoebic infections. Repeated stool examinations revealed an increasing number of amoebic infections. Deficiency diseases were a frequent complication of the dysenteries and in several instances were the direct cause of death.

The treatment of bacillary dysentery varied according to the availability of drugs. Ol. Ricini and Mag. Sulph. were scarce during the early months and calomel in small doses was used though not with success for it gave little relief from pain and tenesmus and the duration of the attack was prolonged. Intravenous salines were used frequently in the more severe cases during the first six months. Because of the difficulty in obtaining sterile fluids many instances of thrombo-phlebitis occurred. When sodium sulphate became available the routine saline treatment was adopted. During the early months sulphapyridine was used occasionally in attempts to eliminate pus from the faeces in sub-acute cases. The results were successful but it became necessary to prohibit the use of this drug for this purpose. When limited quantities of sulphaguanidine became available in October this was used with satisfactory effect and sulphapyridine also becoming available in limited quantities was used in the initial treatment of both acute and chronic cases.

The diagnosis of the amoebic type was made by examination of the stools for amoedae or cysts, by sigmoidoscopy and recognition of the

TABLE 17

Admissions and Deaths
(British and Dutch but excluding Australian Cases)

	Admissions	Deaths
1942: February 19 on .	243	
March . .	2,739	8
April . .	2,325	37
May . . .	1,304	32
June . . .	749	16
July . . .	847	12
August . .	854	17
September .	941	18
October .	1,145	24
November . .	520	22
December . .	329	4
1943: January . .	530	4
February 1–14 .	223	1
	12,749	195
Bacillary . . .	12,258	184
Amoebic . . .	491	11

characteristic ulceration or by both methods. Treatment was with emetine, E.B.1., K.B.1., enteriovioform, quinoxyl, stovarsol, ambraxson, carbasone and treparsol, according to which of these was available. The relapse rate was high, 35 in the 491 cases.

Diphtheria. This disease first began to manifest itself in July 1942, and thereafter assumed the proportions of an epidemic. One floor of one of the blocks was set aside for these cases and it was not long before it was full and the whole block and two *attap* huts and a marquee were in use as well as an isolation block for the segregation of the cutaneous cases occurring in considerable numbers in the skin ward. The most serious aspect of the matter was the lack of serum. Application to the Japanese G.O.C. P.o.W. Camps resulted in the arrival of 176,000 units on August 21. One medical officer and fourteen orderlies contracted the disease from their patients. The Australians supplied two M.Os. and the orderlies necessary to nurse their own cases.

TABLE 18

Admissions (British and Dutch)

	1942	1943	1944
January .		31	49
February .		17	(January–
March .	5	20	May)
April .	8	17	
May .	6	7	
June .	17	3	
July . .	46	5	
August .	186	5	
September	337	32	
October .	329	25	
November	73	33	
December	69	26	
	1,076	221	

At the peak of the epidemic there were 846 cases in the diphtheria block. In December there were still over 800 but fresh admissions had fallen to about 14 a week. By the middle of January 1943, the number had fallen to 272 and by the end of May the block was practically empty.

Dengue. Sporadic cases occurred shortly after the troops were congregated in Changi. By May an epidemic was in full force with its peak in July. During 1942 1,592 cases of this disease were hospitalised.

Pulmonary Tuberculosis. During the period February 1942–May 1944 there were 24 deaths in hospital (21 British, 3 Dutch) from this disease.

Others. The incidence of peptic ulcer rose as the period of captivity lengthened and respiratory diseases, including asthma and bronchitis, became more common. Skin diseases were exceedingly prevalent.

Deficiency Diseases. Throughout the period of captivity malnutrition remained the greatest danger to the health of the troops. It was indeed fortunate that serving with the Australian and British medical units were several officers whose knowledge of the general subject of nutrition was exceptional. It was fortunate too that there was available to them a sufficiency of scientific and medical literature on the subject. The glaringly obvious deficiencies of the ration issued by the Japanese to their P.o.W. at once attracted their attention, provoked their protestations and unleashed their energies in the search for the means of correcting the troops' dietary and combating the diseases caused wholly or partly by nutritional deficiencies.

Before D.D.M.S. Malaya Command left for Japan with the other senior officers he called into being a nutritional advisory committee compounded out of Australian and British specialists which thereafter exercised a very active supervision of the various attempts that were made to protect the troops from the hazards of malnutrition. The value of the rations issued by the I.J.A. and the effects of the efforts made to supplement these are illustrated in Table 29.

Beriberi. This disease made its appearance in April 1942 and during the next few months every clinical variety of this condition was encountered. The thiamin/non-fat ratio of the ration throughout 1942 was around 0·2, always less than 0·3. It also contained too high a proportion of carbohydrate. Notwithstanding the many and valiant attempts to improve the dietary malnutrition occurred. 2,145 admissions to hospital were on account of beriberi during the period February 1942–May 1944.

Kranji P.o.W. Camp

TABLE 19

Strength: fluctuating around 3,000 (Australian, British, Dutch)

Admissions to Hospital. All Causes

1944	Aust.	Br.	Dutch	Total in hospital at end of the months
May	540	608	43	1,191
June	57	41	4	1,140
July	91	78	34	1,138
August	104	86	32	1,156
September	92	72	13	1,044
October	79	60	32	1,049
November	56	78	23	1,026
December	104	83	30	1,039
	1,123	1,106	211	
		2,440		

TABLE 20

Admissions to Hospital on Account of Dysentery

1944	Aust.	Br.	Dutch	Total in hospital at end of the months
May	105	107	13	225
June	15	17	1	237
July	26	15	7	232
August	24	12	5	237
September	16	15	5	207
October	8	7	3	189
November	6	14	4	173
December	23	21	7	180
	223	208	45	
		476		

TABLE 21

Admissions to Hospital on Account of Beriberi

1944	Aust.	Br.	Dutch	Total in hospital at end of the months
May	55	101	2	158
June	7	6	—	146
July	16	12	3	132
August	19	6	2	118
September	12	7	3	103
October	20	15	10	135
November	15	7	6	128
December	20	18	7	139
	164	172	33	
		369		

TABLE 22

Numbers in Hospital on Last Day of Month Suffering from Deficiency Diseases

1944	Aust.	Br. and Dutch	Totals
May	179	167	346
June	175	165	340
July	266	217	483
August	249	232	481
September	260	265	525
October	248	222	470
November	201	290	491
December	203	198	401

TABLE 23

Admissions to Hospital. All Causes

1945	Aust.	Br.	Dutch	Total in hospital at end of the months
January	49	67	21	1,048
February	49	51	18	1,042
March	42	61	148	644*
April	18	16	19	660
May	13	24	19	669
June	22	26	65	743
July	21	44	91	819
August 1–18	12	18	3	811
	226	307	384	
		917		

* 400 transferred to Changi.

TABLE 24

Admissions on Account of Dysentery

1945	Aust.	Br.	Dutch	Total in hospital at end of the months
January	5	12	—	173
February	9	34	19	191
March	12	11	19	105
April	1	8	—	97
May	2	8	2	103
June	4	2	24	127
July	2	5	34	154
August 1–18	—	4	—	144
	35	84	98	
		217		

TABLE 25

Admissions on Account of Beriberi

1945	Aust.	Br.	Dutch	Total in hospital at end of the months
January	7	8	10	150
February	11	11	8	155
March	5	12	81	143
April	2	1	7	143
May	—	2	6	139
June	—	1	8	144
July	7	2	10	148
August	—	3	—	148
	32	40	130	
		202		

TABLE 26

Numbers in Hospital on Last Day of the Month on Account of Deficiency Diseases

1945	Aust.	Br.	Dutch	Totals
January	199	178	41	418
February	174	155	39	368
March	130	104	84	318
April	70	77	112	259
May	55	90	132	277
June	48	89	150	287
July	49	84	152	285
August	51	90	157	298

TABLE 27

Malaria. Fresh Infections. 1944

June	19
July	45
August	82
September	33
October	13
November	17
December	10

In August a spleen examination revealed that not less than 70 per cent. of the camp population had had malaria within the past eighteen months. *A. maculatus*, *A. sundaicus* and *A. barbirostris* were abundantly present. An anti-malaria officer was directing the hopeless efforts to control the incidence of this disease.

TABLE 28

Deaths. May 28, 1944–July 1, 1945

Australian, 27; British, 33; Dutch, 10; Total, 70

	Deaths
Beriberi, cardiac or oedematous	23
Pellagra	6
Malnutrition plus malaria plus chronic dysentery	2
Pulmonary tuberculosis	12
Cardiac infarction	1
Post-rheumatic endocarditis	1
Diphtheria	1
Bacillary dysentery	3
Amoebic dysentery	2
Liver abscess (amoebic)	1
Septicaemia	1
Otitis media	1
Carbuncle of face	1
Malaria M.T.	1
Acute appendicitis	2
Peptic ulcer (post-operative complications)	4
Carcinoma of stomach	2
Carcinoma of lung	1
Melanotic sarcoma	1
Lymphadenoma	1
Acute hepatic necrosis (C.Cl$_4$ poison)	1
Multilobular hepatic cirrhosis	1
Methanol poisoning	1

THE THAILAND–BURMA RAILWAY

'F' FORCE*

In April 1943 a party of 7,000 prisoners-of-war was sent from Changi to Thailand. By the end of August 1943, 25 per cent. of the men were dead and 90 per cent. of the remainder were seriously ill. By December 1943, 40 per cent. of the whole force were dead. The survivors were returned to Changi. This move was completed in April 1944, by which time death had claimed 3,100, or 45 per cent. of the original 7,000. (Australian contingent 28 per cent.; British contingent 61 per cent.)

The orders received from the I.J.A. concerning this force were associated with the following remarks:

(a) The food situation in Singapore was difficult; it would be better in the new place.

(b) This was not a working party.

(c) As there were not 7,000 fit men in Changi, 30 per cent. of the force were to be men unfit to march or work. The unfit would have a better chance of recovery with good food in a pleasant hilly place with good facilities for recreation.

---

*This account is based upon the 'History of "F" Force', a report compiled by the officer commanding the force and submitted by him to D.P.W. War Office. February 25, 1946.

(d) There would be no marching except for a short distance from the train to a nearby camp and transport would be provided for baggage and men unfit to march.

(e) Bands would be taken.

(f) Gramophones, blankets, clothing and mosquito nets would be issued at the new camps.

(g) All tools and cooking gear and an engine and gear for electric light were to be taken.

(h) A good canteen would be available in each camp after three weeks. Canteen supplies for the first three weeks were to be bought with prisoners' money before leaving Singapore.

(i) The force would include a medical party of about 350 with equipment for a central hospital of 400 patients and medical supplies for three months.

(j) The force was to include a H.Q.

(k) No Red Cross representative was to accompany the force nor could any Red Cross money be obtained to take with the force. Facilities would, however, be given to communicate with Singapore for this purpose if need arose.

British H.Q. Changi, with the concurrence of H.Q. A.I.F., appointed the commander of 18th Division P.o.W. Area to command 'F' Force, using 18th Division Area H.Q. as his staff. The Australian contingent was to number 3,600 and the British 3,400. The Australian contingent consisted of Aust. 27th Bde. plus detachments to bring up its strength to the required total; it included about 30 per cent. of men unfit for full duties. The British contingent included not more than 50 per cent. who were fit for marching and heavy work. It was pointed out to the Japanese authorities that the men classified as fit were all on the border-line of diseases arising from nutritional deficiencies. Indeed fitness meant nothing more than fitness to travel.

The medical component consisted of officers British, 12 R.A.M.C., 4 I.M.D., 1 F.M.S.V.F. and 1 A.D. Corps; Australian, 11 A.A.M.C., 1 A.A.D.C., a total of 30 including a S.M.O. of the Australian and a S.M.O. of the British, elements. O.Rs. British, 144 B.O.R., R.A.M.C.; Australian, 225 A.O.R. A.A.M.C., a total of 369. Among the A.A.M.C. officers were a surgical and a medical specialist and among the R.A.M.C. an entomologist.

Orders were issued by the I.J.A. for the move of the force in thirteen trains with Force H.Q. and all the heavy baggage and medical stores in the first train. Later these were altered. The first six trains carried the Australian contingent and Force H.Q. and the heavy baggage moved in the seventh.

All ranks were glass-rodded by the I.J.A. medical service and instructions were issued for re-vaccination and inoculation against typhoid, dysentery and cholera. But in the event the Australian contingent left Changi after only one cholera inoculation and part of the British contingent had no inoculation against this disease at all owing to the insufficiency of the issue of anti-cholera vaccine.

The journey to Bampong took 4–5 days. Each of the trains carried 500–600 men, one steel box car, 20 × 8 ft., for approximately 27 men. One or more medical officers and a box of medical requirements went with each train. Cooked rations of rice and vegetable stew and drinking water, generally insufficient, were supplied at various stations *en route*. Most of the train parties received neither food nor water during the last twenty-four hours of the journey. The box cars were ovens during the heat of the day, iceboxes at night. Once a day the men were allowed out of the cars, in which there were no lavatory facilities of any kind. In the intense heat thirst became an obsession.

At Bampong the train parties were marched to a staging camp a mile away from the station. It had been previously occupied by native labour gangs and was in an appallingly filthy state. The accommodation consisted of four large *attap* shelters. Latrines were merely open trenches about six feet deep. There was no water for washing and a bare sufficiency of cooking facilities. The guards were highly excitable and on several occasions P.o.W. were thrashed for no apparent reason.

It was now learnt that the rest of the journey to a destination still unknown was to be made on foot. Each train commander was given a copy of 'Instructions for Passing Coolies and P.o.W.' All heavy kit and stores, including medical stores, had to be dumped by the side of the road and no guard was allowed. When train 7 with Force H.Q. arrived all the personal kit of officers and men was likewise dumped. Following vigorous protests by the officer commanding the force the I.J.A. made the following concessions:

(*a*) A few seriously ill men were left in a Japanese hospital at Bampong.

(*b*) A few others were left in an extemporised hospital in the camp.

(*c*) Medical stores and cooking containers were sorted out from the dump for early despatch by lorry to the destination.

(*d*) The dump was guarded.

(*e*) Representatives of Force H.Q. would be sent forward by M.T. to overtake the head of the column and to take charge at Tarsu, which was understood to be the base camp of the final concentration area, and the rear party of Force H.Q., including the S.M.O. of the force, was to be sent forward by lorry when the last party left Bampong.

Permission to change Malay currency for Thai dollars was refused and so the only method of obtaining extra food, and at one camp drinking water also, was that of selling personal belongings and kit to the I.J.A. guards or to Thais.

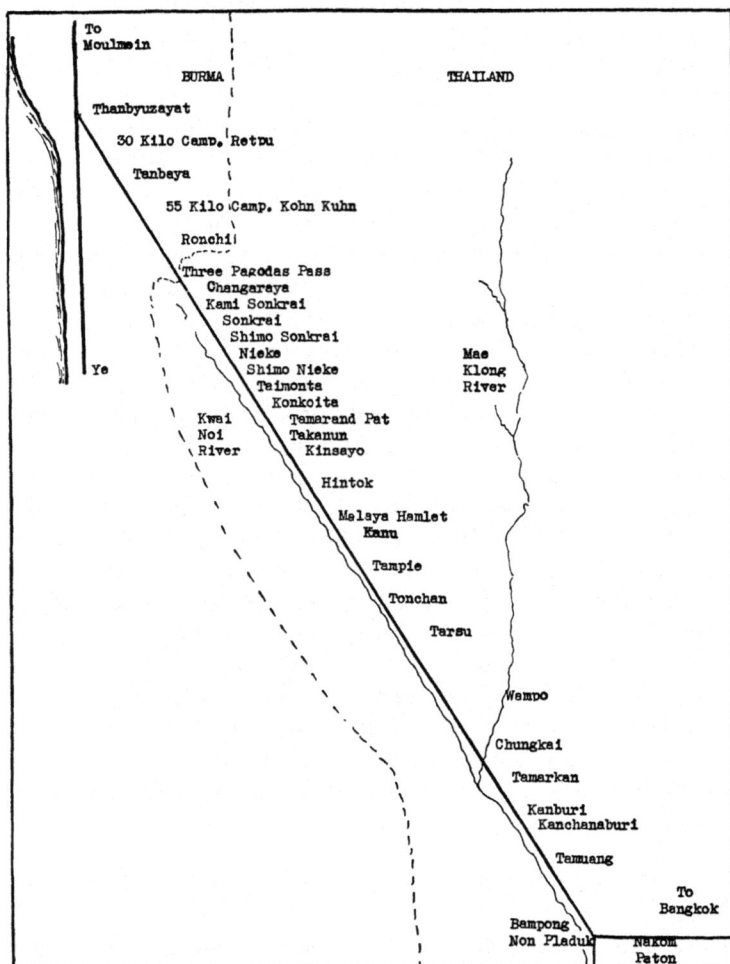

FIG. 18. The Thailand–Burma Railway. The Camps.

When the force left Changi the officers were paid up to the end of February. They did not receive pay for March, April and May until well on into June. In the meantime the only money possessed by the force was its central fund, some 12,000 dollars, all in Malayan currency, and therefore useless. In Thailand officers received 40–50 dollars monthly and 40 per cent. of this was deducted for the purchase of extra food for hospital patients.

The relegation of Force H.Q. to train number 7 was disastrous. Before its arrival the previous six parties had marched out in succession so that there was no continuity of command in the Bampong staging camp. The Japanese used twelve lorries and one ambulance to carry their own stores forward, but the monsoon rains disrupted their second run and prevented any others. After May 20 no wheeled vehicle was able to reach the final concentration area of the force. As a result all its heavy equipment, cooking gear, personal kit, Red Cross stores, reserve clothing, boots, canteen goods and three-quarters of the medical stores remained at Bampong and were not retrieved until the remnants of 'F' Force returned to Kanburi seven months later, by which time a considerable proportion had been looted.

The march lasted for about two and a half weeks over a distance of roughly three hundred kilometres, covered in fifteen stages of about twenty kms. each. The column marched by night between 2000 hours and 0800 hours. The road was a rough jungle track capable of taking wheeled traffic in dry weather only. Long stretches of it were corduroyed which made marching in the dark both difficult and dangerous. Thais lay in wait for stragglers.

On April 30 daily thunderstorms heralded the monsoon rains, which flooded long stretches of the track and lengthened the night marches to fourteen or fifteen hours. During the day's rest there was no shelter save on the sodden ground under the trees that surrounded the clearings that were the staging camps. These were usually near water. Accommodation consisted of a cookhouse and open trench latrines but of shelter there was none except in two of the fifteen camps, where there were tents for about one hundred men. The camps were under the command of junior Japanese N.C.Os. whose orders apparently were to push the columns forward as fast as possible. The greatest difficulty was encountered everywhere in obtaining permission from them to leave behind even the gravely ill. Rice and vegetable stew was supplied in quantities insufficient to maintain the strength of men engaged on such a march and water was often short. At Kanburi water had to be bought by the P.o.W. from a privately owned well. Protestation was followed by a repair of this deficiency and some weeks later when 'H' Force passed through water was obtainable. At the staging camps the P.o.W., having marched all through the night, were not permitted to rest until they had performed a variety of fatigues for the I.J.A. guards. The medical officers and orderlies who had attended the many casualties on the line of march held sick parades during the day's rest and also had to give much attention to the sick left behind by previous columns. The medical officers invariably had to dispute with the Japanese N.C.O. in charge as to the number of those who on medical grounds should be left behind, and invariably the outcome of the dispute was that men with blistered and ulcerated feet and suffering acutely from dysentery, beriberi and malaria, were driven out of the camp, often with blows, to join the column as it moved off.

Near the staging camp at Tarsu was the H.Q. of the Japanese Engineers and of the Thailand P.o.W. Administration, with a permanent P.o.W. camp and hospital as well as a Japanese military hospital. ('D' Force, which had left Changi in March, had its H.Q. here.) When O.C. 'F' Force reached Tarsu his reception by the I.J.A. H.Q. was such that he gathered that between H.Q. Thailand P.o.W. Administration and the I.J.A. H.Q. in Singapore, which retained control over 'F' Force during its sojourn in Thailand, there was much jealousy. It was from this that many of the sufferings of the P.o.W. derived.

At Konkoita staging camp, reached after a fortnight's marching, each party in turn was quartered in immediate proximity to a large coolie labour camp. The whole area was fouled and had become a vast fly-breeding quagmire. It was here that cholera added itself to the pestilences that were threatening to annihilate the force. It was here too that 700 Australians of parties 1 and 2 were handed over to the I.J.A. Engineers for slave labour locally. They did not rejoin 'F' Force until December in Nieke.

At Tarsu also the I.J.A. lieutenant-colonel who was in command of 'F' Force made his first appearance on May 8. With him were the officers of Rear H.Q. 'F' Force, including the S.M.O. On May 9 he added the O.C. 'F' Force to his party and two stages on he ordered the officers of Rear H.Q. 'F' Force to get out of the lorry in which they were travelling along with medical stores and to establish a roadside hospital for the marching columns. He then, with O.C. 'F' Force, proceeded to Nieke. This extraordinary action meant that the force was robbed of the services of its appointed S.M.O. and denied the use of its medical stores for the track almost immediately became impossible for M.T. vehicles and the Japanese did not attempt to move these stores by river.

A graphic account of this march is given in the report of the A.A.M.C. medical specialist who was in medical charge of one of the parties:

'The march was long and extremely arduous—it laid the foundation for the widespread debilitation of the force which played a major part in increasing the death rate from infectious diseases (cholera, malaria and dysentery). The march was always done at night. The average distance covered was about 23 km. and the majority of the troops covered fourteen such stages, aggregating about 300 km. "Rest nights" were given at Camps 2, 4, 7 and 9, but many men who had been left behind for a night on account of illness were unable to take advantage of these, being compelled to press on and endeavour to join their parties. After the first two marches, which were along

PLATE I. A ward in the Changkai Hospital.

(*Drawing by Chalker*)

PLATE II. Amputation ward, Changkai Hospital.

PLATE III. The cholera ward, Hintock Hospital.

(*Drawing by Chalker*)

PLATE IV. The road back from a construction camp.

a highway, the roads were bad and usually very bad; the moon gave no assistance for most of the march; rain was frequent and conditions on really wet nights were nightmarish.

'Owing to the appalling road conditions many of the marches lasted 10–14 hours with only very short halts. Little rest could be obtained at the staging camps, especially by the medical personnel, most of whose time was taken up in attending to the sick from their own and previous parties and in dressing the hundreds of blistered and ulcerated feet which were brought to them for attention. There was no shelter at any of the camps apart from improvised bivouacs and heavy rain frequently made those ineffective. Every possible endeavour was made by M.Os. to protect the sick against the weather with, however, only moderate success.

'Food was poor; it consisted almost solely of rice and onion water. At the first three staging camps it was possible to purchase supplementary foodstuffs, but thereafter these facilities ceased.

'Treatment of the troops, and in particular the sick, by the I.J.A. guards varied from march to march and from camp to camp. At some camps the M.O. of the party was allowed to leave behind, without interference, such men as he considered unfit to march. On other occasions he was subject to much interference and at several places men with active malaria or dysentery or with large infected ulcers on their feet were compelled to do a whole night's march, to the great detriment of their health.

'Thus at Camp 5 I was informed that all such had to be submitted for inspection to the I.J.A. M.O. who was stationed about half a mile away. The total of sick on this occasion, derived from my own and previous parties, was 37, 27 with infected feet and 10 with malaria or dysentery. The Japanese M.O. agreed that none of these men were fit to march but the corporal of the guard only gave permission for 10 to remain. A further interview with the I.J.A. M.O. confirmed his previous advice and produced a letter of instruction from him to the corporal.

'At the time scheduled for parade, I fell in the 37 sick men apart from the main parade and the interpreter and myself stood in front of them. The corporal approached with a large bamboo in his hand and spoke menacingly to the interpreter who answered in placatory fashion. The corporal's only reply was to hit him in the face. Another guard followed suit and as the interpreter staggered back the corporal thrust at his genitalia with his bamboo. I was left standing in front of the patients and was immediately set upon by the corporal and two other guards—one tripped me while the other two pushed me to the ground. The three then set about me with bamboos, causing extensive bruising of skull, back, hands and arms and a fractured 5th metacarpal bone. This episode took place in front of the whole parade of the troops. After I was disposed of, the corporal made the majority of the sick men march with the rest of the troops.

'At Camp 6, I was again struck and some of my patients rejected —these were the only occasions on which I personally received violence at the hands of the guards. It was the general practice of M.Os. to march in the rear of the column to succour the stragglers and to endeavour to prevent any possible molestation of these by the guards—I saw such threatened on several occasions as sick men were hurried along, but the intervention was usually successful and I never saw a blow struck under these circumstances.'

The I.J.A. Commandant arrived at Shimo Nieke on May 10 with O.C. 'F' Force. This was to be the headquarters camp of the force and at this time it consisted of two partially roofed huts and seven unroofed huts in a partially cleared hollow in the jungle. A small stream was to be the source of water for all purposes. The camp had previously been occupied by coolie labour. During the next few days some I.J.A. stores arrived from Bampong and the roofed huts were occupied by I.J.A. guards. The remains of parties 1 and 2 and party 3 arrived on May 13 and thereafter the remaining parties arrived in rapid succession. For them there was no shelter whatever, no cookhouse, no M.I. Room, no hospital. Thunderstorms by now were a daily and nightly occurrence until the monsoon proper broke in Shimo Nieke on May 17 and spread slowly northwards. Thereafter until well on into September rain was incessant and heavy. In the rain there were few breaks, one of twenty-four hours in June and another in July.

The I.J.A. Commandant now informed O.C. 'F' Force that the force would be distributed among the following camps:

Changaraya (1 km. from the Burma border)
Kami (Upper) Sonkrai
Sonkrai
Shimo (Lower) Sonkrai
Nieke
Shimo Nieke
Konkoita

Camp No.					Aust.	Br.
1	.	.	Shimo Sonkrai	. .	2,400	—
2	.	.	Sonkrai	. . .	—	2,000
3	.	.	Kami Sonkrai	. .	400	—
4	.	.	Konkoita	. . .	700	—
5	.	.	Changaraya .	. .	—	1,200
H.Q. Camp and Base Hospital (H.Q. 100, Medical 200)			Shimo Nieke	. .	100	200
					2,800	3,400

By the end of May when the move was complete the numbers in the various camps were:

Camp No.					Aust.	Br.	
1	.	.	.	.	1,000	—	
2	.	.	.	.	—	1,000	including dead
3	.	.	.	.	400	—	,, ,,
4	.	.	.	.	700	—	,, ,,
5	.	.	.	.	—	700	,, ,,
H.Q.	.	.	.	.	200	200	,, ,,
Still down the road including drivers, cooks, sick and dead					566	834	
					2,866	2,734	

A young Australian medical officer who had not previously encountered the disease diagnosed cholera among the Australian party which had marched into Shimo Nieke from Konkoita on May 15, having spent the previous day there. Over 800 Australians of this party were due to move to Shimo Nieke that night, another party moving into Konkoita from the south. There was cholera in Shimo Nieke (5 cases among 1,000 P.o.W.) and in Konkoita where there were 900 Australians and 300 British, while still to pass through these camps were 3,034 British and 766 Australians.

O.C. 'F' Force at once drew the attention of the I.J.A. Commandant to the seriousness of the danger and urged:

(a) immediate local arrangements for an isolation hospital;

(b) provision of vaccine to complete anti-cholera inoculation;

(c) no further parties to enter Konkoita or Shimo Nieke camps;

(d) cancellation of move of affected Australian party from Shimo Nieke to Shimo Sonkrai;

(e) S.M.O. 'F' Force and medical stores to be sent forward immediately from Kanu.

The Commandant agreed to (a) and (b) but did not act on (c), (d) or (e). That evening orders for the continuation of the move were issued and so the infection was spread. Fresh cases occurred in every party from Konkoita and epidemic cholera broke out in Sonkrai, Kami Sonkrai and Changaraya camps. When the news came that cholera had broken out in Shimo Sonkrai camp the I.J.A. Commandant agreed:

(a) to send the S.M.O. of the A.I.F. contingent and the A.A.M.C. medical specialist from Konkoita;

(b) to send instructions to the S.M.O. 'F' Force to move forward as soon as possible.

The S.M.O. A.I.F. contingent remained at Shimo Nieke to control the base hospital. The Australian medical specialist together with another A.A.M.C. officer, some medical orderlies and six British soldiers who were fully inoculated and who volunteered for nursing the cholera patients went forward by M.T.

The I.J.A. private in charge at Kanu refused to allow the S.M.O. 'F' Force or the medical stores to move.

A further conference found the I.J.A. Commandant very anxious. He produced out of his own private stocks six tins of milk for the patients and agreed to produce cholera vaccine, medical stores and the S.M.O. 'F' Force. All, save the medical stores, arrived.

Some 400 of the seriously ill were gradually accumulated at Shimo Nieke. Some tents were issued by the I.J.A., mostly old British tentage. The I.J.A. insisted that it should be put up on bamboo roof frames in place of *attap*. So used it did not keep out the rain. The cholera cases and suspects were segregated and in this way the hospital did much to keep the disease in check. When the hospital was cleared to Nieke at the end of June deaths from all causes had been only 2 officers and 32 O.Rs., of which 19 were due to cholera, a high tribute to the devotion of the mixed Australian and British staff.

When it was learnt that a number of sick had been left in the vicinity of Konkoita an assistant surgeon I.M.D. was sent there to do what he could.

The epidemic pursued its typical course in all the camps. In Shimo Sonkrai it ended after 110 had died (6 per cent.). At Shimo Nieke and Nieke deaths totalled only 26 out of a strength of 1,300. At Nieke the I.J.A. provided a small hut and an isolation hospital. To this the I.J.A. brought five Tamil coolies stricken with cholera; of these two survived. At Sonkrai and Kami Sonkrai camps (British troops) the state of the men and of the camps were such that medical intervention was unable to achieve the same degree of success. Cholera deaths in Sonkrai camp were 227 (14 per cent.) and in Kami Sonkrai camp 159 (23 per cent.). But by the end of June cholera north of Nieke was under control.

The total deaths from cholera in 'F' Force were approximately 650; by it nearly 10 per cent. of the whole force were destroyed.

The state of the P.o.W. was truly wretched. It was raining incessantly by day and by night. The camps consisted of roofed huts for the I.J.A. guards, huts without roofs for the P.o.W. At Kami Sonkrai and Changaraya camps part of the P.o.W. accommodation was occupied by coolies, some of whom were already down with cholera. Here the P.o.W. rations were issued to the coolies who cooked both for themselves and for the P.o.W. At Shimo Sonkrai camp a few days were allowed to set the camp in order, but at Sonkrai, Kami Sonkrai and Changaraya camps no such break was allowed. In all camps roofing to the huts was completed in the first two weeks of the march by native labour but the work was so ill done that the roofs leaked badly. In

Kami Sonkrai camp (Australian) and Changaraya camp (British) no arrangements for the segregation of cholera patients were made; all that could be done was to collect them in one portion of one of the P.o.W. huts. After about two weeks an isolation hut was provided in Kami Sonkrai camp but nothing was done in Changaraya camp until the epidemic had spent itself. Where there were 'hospitals' these were merely the usual huts with 12–15 to a bay. Everything had to be improvised—bed pans from large bamboos, cannulae for intravenous injections from bamboo tips, tables from split bamboos, water containers from long bamboos, baskets from bamboo strips, bandages and dressings from such parts of clothing as could be spared (e.g. shirt sleeves, trouser legs), mosquito nets from banana leaves, stretchers from bamboos and sacks. The only light was that from fires in the gangways of the huts and the huts were bug infested. Scabies was universal.

The columns had been allowed to bring forward from Bampong only a few food containers and medical stores. As the sick accumulated at the various staging camps the containers and stores were forcibly taken from the parties as these passed through and used for the treatment of these sick. As a result of this camps 2, 3 and 5 were practically without food containers and with very scanty medical stores. This lack of food containers created serious difficulties at camps 2 and 5 as the number of the sick multiplied because of the distances between cookhouse and water-point and the huts.

A few tools were carried by each of the parties but, as in the case of the food containers, these became accumulated in the staging camps nearer Bampong.

Two of the four interpreters with the force were arbitrarily detained by the N.C.Os. of the I.J.A. organisation controlling the march at unimportant staging camps and their services were therefore lost to the columns.

In all the camps the I.J.A. Engineers demanded maximum numbers for work. They made no allowance for any sick or convalescent not in hospital. They did not accept debility, malaria, beriberi and 'trench foot' as reasons for exclusion from working parties. The working party demanded was simply A−B.

A. Total camp strength

B. { Patients in hospital
Hospital staff
Men on camp duties

Any protest against this system was countered by threats to reduce rations. Sick and convalescent combatants were employed as wardmasters and for hospital registry work in order that they might escape the working party. In Camp 4, officers were sometimes made to work outside as labourers; in other camps they accompanied outside working parties as supervisors. A W.O. and 20 O.Rs. who had been sent from Shimo Nieke to Nieke as an advance party to form the new camp were taken off the line of march before reaching Nieke and put to pile-driving in the river. Fourteen days later a P.o.W. officer came across them and discovered that they had been forced to work from first light to 2200 hours up to their armpits in swift-running water daily with half an hour's break for a meal. Strong protests resulted in their being withdrawn from this work but it was too late and every one of them died.

The duties allowed in camp comprised cremation or burial, sanitation, cookhouse, wood cutting and collecting. These jobs demanded a considerable proficiency combined with health and strength. In no camp was it possible to organise any system of a day-to-day change-over to relieve men going out to work every day; and so the men on these duties worked on until they fell sick and went to hospital. Duties had to be performed also for the I.J.A. in the camps—ration drawing, path making, road construction, latrine digging, fence making, hut building and repairing, double bunking, basket making, wood collecting and the like. All these had to be undertaken by malaria patients and by convalescents.

EXAMPLES:

Total in Camp	Number Sick	Number Demanded for Work	Camp	Date
564	404	160	Takanun	Mid-July
1,850	1,350	345	Shimo Sonkrai	July 19
1,300	1,050	280	Sonkrai	July 28
1,670	1,075	450	Kami Sonkrai	August 16

Each morning those who could walk went out to work, to undertake heavy manual labour, under continuous blows and slashings from the incessantly screaming Japanese Engineers. At night, blood-stained, these half-naked, bare-footed, starving men returned with an astonishing range of oddments hidden in their loincloths or under their various hats, to tend their wounds and to dream of food.

The fourteen hour working day started with reveille and breakfast at about 0600–0700 hours. Breakfast consisted of three-quarters of a pint of plain rice. Parade was at first light and then the I.J.A. Engineers took over. The task of finding the men to complete the number demanded was heartbreaking. The party then marched off, drew tools and proceeded to the site of the work, 5–10 kms. away. By June, 80 per cent. of all the parties were without usable boots. The march was in pouring rain through deep mud. The work was exceedingly heavy and would have taxed the strength of a thoroughly fit labourer—the portaging of logs, pile-driving, tree hauling and the like. The Japanese O.Rs. drove the P.o.W. with blows from fists, boots, sticks and wire whips. Protesting officer P.o.W. were hit. Reluctance and resentment were regarded as mutinous and savagely punished. A very short pause was allowed for the midday meal—a pint of rice with a few beans. Long after darkness had fallen tools were collected and the march back to camp through the rain and mud began. Camp was reached about 2200 hours or later. After roll-call the party was dismissed to eat their evening meal—a pint of rice and some form of vegetable stew. Thereafter the P.o.W. sought their sleeping quarters, 6 × 2 ft. per man or less, to get what rest they could before the dawn. The sick among them had to be examined by firelight. It is not surprising therefore to learn that by the end of June the total number of men working outside the camps was no more than 700, 10 per cent. of the force.

Working pay averaged 20 cents per day per working man, or one-fifth of the rate paid to coolies.

Throughout the whole of this time the Australian and British senior officers, briefed by their senior medical officers, strove with every means in their very limited power to improve the conditions, ceaselessly demanding better food and accommodation, more medical supplies, more clothing, boots and blankets and a more humane system of employment. But the Japanese troops had been thoroughly indoctrinated. Their newspapers were full of stories of American and British atrocities. Moreover the construction of the railway in May was several weeks behind schedule and orders from Tokyo insisted that work upon it must be continued throughout the monsoon season. By May 20 the road south of Shimo Nieke had ceased to be usable by M.T. or bullock cart and there was no hope of using it again. It became essential therefore to keep open the road northwards into Burma. In May this was merely a track cleared through the jungle. It had to be corduroyed for about half its length and many bridges had to be built. For this work the P.o.W. and coolie labour gangs had therefore to be maintained in this area. It is indeed possible that the brutal treatment of the P.o.W. was partly the inevitable outcome of Japanese administrative incompetence. The actual work that had to be done could have been facilitated and accelerated in several obvious ways. For example, the six lorries that 'F' force had in the forward area were in poor condition and without non-skid chains. They could have been repaired with the greatest of ease either by the I.J.A. or by the P.o.W. themselves. Chains could have been obtained from Bampong. But nothing was done and so they continually broke down or became bogged. Clothing stores and the like could easily have been brought up by river, for by

June this was navigable for motor boats right up to Nieke. To force sick men to work was a sure method of reducing the labour force. To hold the sick in these camps meant that much man-power was absorbed in tending them. The working system that was adopted was the most certain method of ensuring that the work would not be done. Many of these points were clearly appreciated by the I.J.A. Commandant but it would appear that his views were completely disregarded by the Engineers who were the paramount authority in the 'F' Force area. Instead of tackling their problems in a commonsense way they attempted to get out of difficulty by a display of brutality.

The argument that because the surrender of Singapore had been unconditional the P.o.W. were not protected by the terms of the Hague Convention was specious. It was made at the written request of the I.J.A. G.O.C. 'in order to avoid further useless loss of life on both sides and especially the lives of civilians in the city'.

Out of the ceaseless protestations of the senior officers at long last a project did emerge. Orders were issued for the evacuation of a proportion of the patients to a hospital camp at Tanbaya in Burma. The I.J.A. gave assurance that the hospital would be provided with medical stores and good rations. This hospital was to accommodate 1,250 patients who were to be drawn from (*a*) such as could not be expected to recover from their illnesses within two months and (*b*) older men with a permanent disability or such as were unsuited for heavy work on the road. The allotment to the different camps was:

Nieke	250
Shimo Sonkrai . .	500
Sonkrai	350
Kami Sonkrai . . .	50
Changaraya . . .	100
	1,250

The move was to be carried out by M.T. in flights of 250 with nightly stages at Changaraya, Kando and Ronchi. The I.J.A. would allow a medical staff of 8 officers and 130 O.Rs., together with an administrative staff of 4 officers and 51 O.Rs. Any additional staff for the hospital would have to be found from among the convalescents. But, as was to be expected, neither the move nor the allotment of patients went according to plan.

On July 30 the advance party, consisting of the administrative staff and 8 officers and 36 O.Rs. of the medical staff, assembled at Changaraya. The remainder of the medical staff was to be spread over the flights. The advance party was supposed to drop off at Kando and Ronchi a medical officer, 3 medical orderlies and 10 administrative

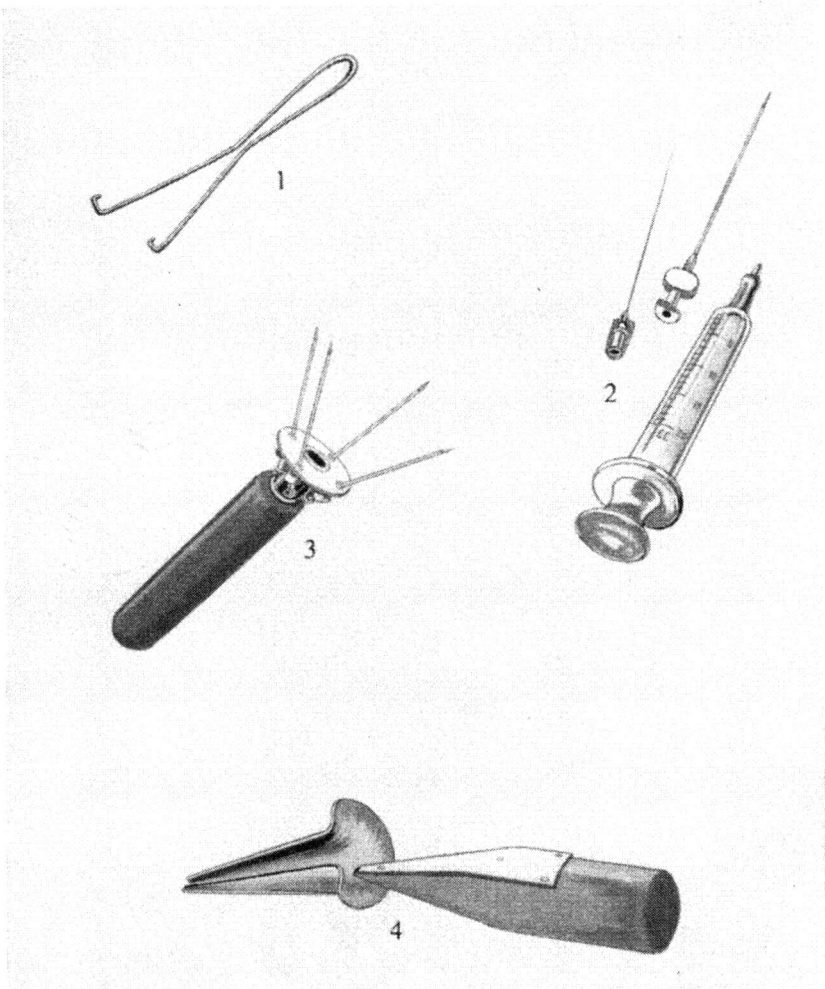

(*Drawing by Chalker*)

PLATE VA. Surgical instruments made of scrap material.

1. Abdominal retractor.

2. Improvised spinal anaesthetic needle and syringe. The 8-cm. Labat needle lacked a stilette. This was made out of fine wire. It was a perfect needle for spinal anaesthesia. The syringe tip did not fit the needle which, however, would fit an Army pattern all-metal syringe. The tip of an Army syringe was therefore sawed off and fused on by plaster-of-paris. It withstood boiling about 100 times before it had to be reset.

3. Quadruple needle used for pinch grafts of skin, enabling four bits of skin to be transplanted in one journey. It shortens the operation and greatly lessens its tedium. Over 100 large ulcers were thus skin-grafted with excellent results.

4. Proctoscopes used for injecting piles, etc.

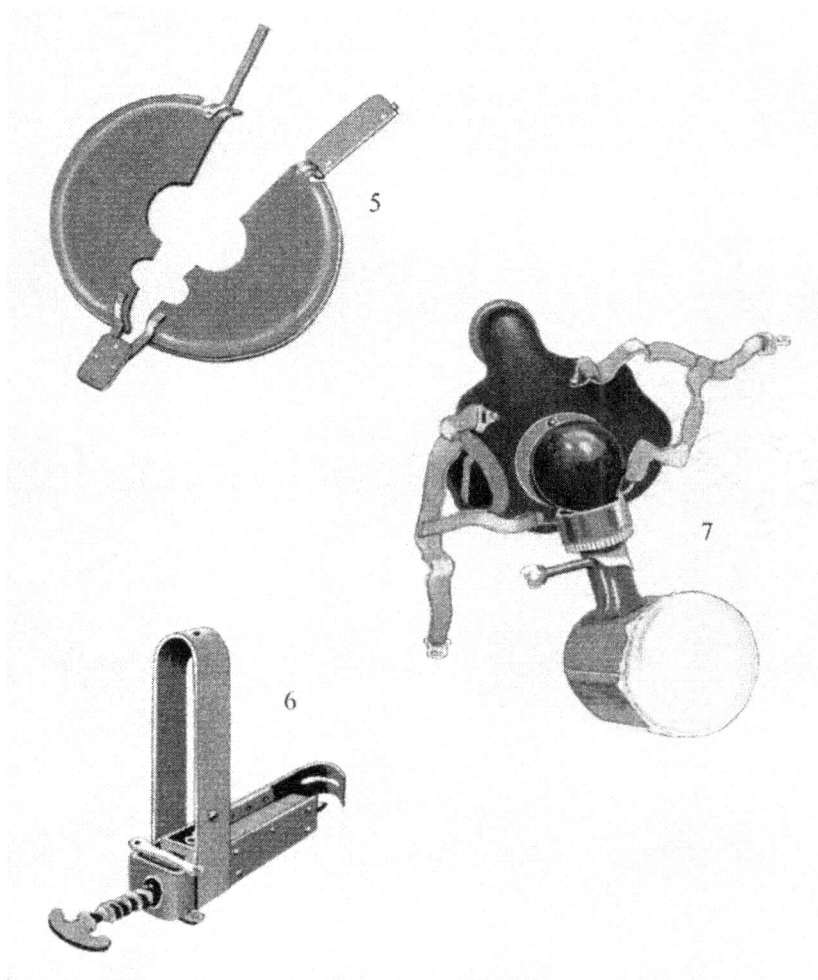

PLATE VB. Surgical instruments made of scrap material.

5. Muscle retractor made from a circular mess tin.
6. Rib cutter.
7. Anaesthetic mask, valved, improvised out of a Haldane oxygen administering apparatus and a jam tin.

personnel to look after the patients in transit. The executive order for
the advance party was delayed until the working parties had left the
camps. Consequently there was difficulty in collecting the personnel
earmarked for Tanbaya. Indeed at Sonkrai the detachment had to be
completed from among convalescents who happened to be in camp.
Two of these collapsed on arrival at Changaraya and subsequently died.

Next day the move of the advance party to Kando was made by M.T.
Here the party was housed in a hut already occupied by coolie labourers.
The move to Ronchi was carried out on foot and by M.T. The staging

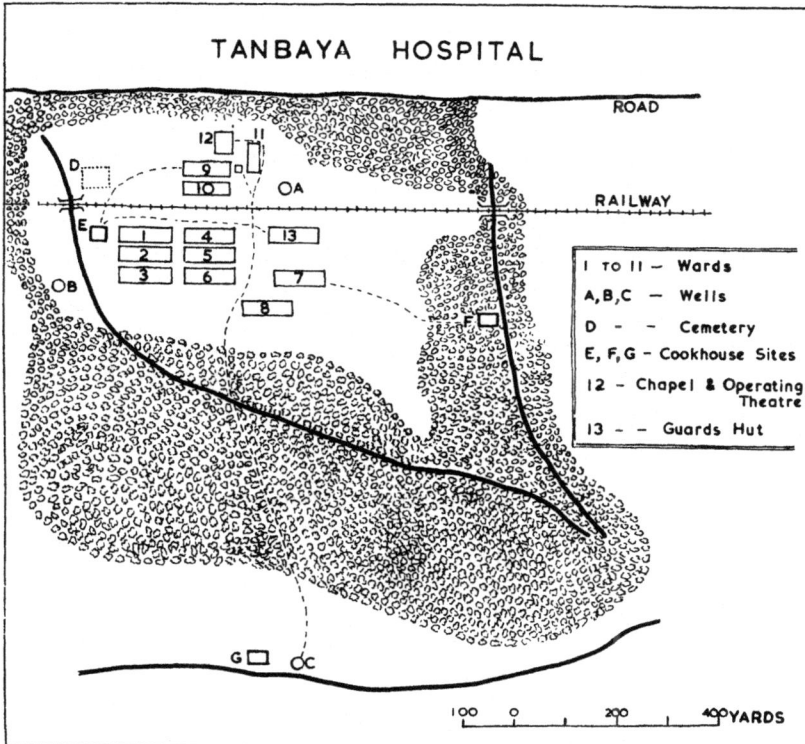

FIG. 19. Tanbaya Hospital.

party was dropped off together with six who were not fit to travel
further and the rest moved off at 0430 hours in the pouring rain and
pitch black darkness. The march was one of 14 kms. The party stayed
at Ronchi for thirty-six hours and then went on to Tanbaya on foot
and again in the pouring rain. Tanbaya was reached on August 3.

A lieutenant-colonel of the R.A. (G.S.O. 1, 18th Division) was
appointed administrative commander and the A.A.M.C. medical
specialist became officer commanding the hospital. The former was
responsible for all outside activities and for the personnel employed

13

outside the hospital and also for roll-call returns and finance. The latter's domain was inside the hospital including the discipline of the medical personnel and patients. Combatant officers were appointed to act as wardmasters. The administrative staff included the administrative commander, adjutant, quartermaster, and messing officer. The medical staff included two A.A.M.C. officers (including O.C. Hosp.), one I.M.D., one S.S.V.F., one F.M.S.V.F. and five R.A.M.C. The R.S.M. on the administrative side was a member of the S.S.V.F.; the R.S.M. of the hospital a R.S.M. R.A.M.C.

The camp was an old one, adjacent to the railway, and was in a poor state of repair. The jungle had begun to invade it. One hut and the cookhouse had roofs, the remaining huts were in the process of being repaired when the advance party arrived. The camp consisted of seven huts each 100 metres long with *attap* sides and roof and a wide platform to take two men with a gangway along one side. Each was supposed to accommodate 200 patients. In addition there was a smaller hut to hold 80 patients and this had two platforms with a gangway down the centre. Later a small camp on the opposite side of the railway line and occupied by I.J.A. railway personnel and coolies was made available. Here were two large and two small huts; the last were used as chapel and operating theatre. Latrines were of the usual open trench type. Two small streams, one of them the source of water for the camp, bounded the camp on three sides.

The organisation of the hospital became:

Ward

1	.	.	Administrative personnel
2	.	.	Malaria and beriberi
3	.	.	Dysentery
4	.	.	Malaria and beriberi
5	.	.	Malaria and beriberi
6	.	.	Dysentery
7	.	.	Medical, non-dysentery
8	.	.	H.Q. Officers. Stores. Dispensary, etc.
9	.	.	Tropical ulcer ⎫ across the railway line
10	.	.	Tropical ulcer ⎭
11	.	.	Officers' ward

Patients began to arrive on August 8. The first batch had staged at Ronchi and owing to damage to a railway bridge was forced to trek, greatly to their detriment, over two kilometres to where the trains were operating. No further patients arrived until August 21. Parties then arrived daily, the journey being made by M.T. and rail and being a serious strain on the patients. The run from Kando took anything between twelve and eighteen hours with long periods without food and long waits at the entraining and debussing points where there was no shelter. Patients, as many as 54, were herded in one closed truck. Deaths *en route* were not infrequent; as many as eight in one party were found to be dead on arrival. All that some of those who arrived had was a cloth around the waist. The last party arrived on September 7.

The numbers from the different camps, including staff, were:

	Australian	British	Totals
Ex Nieke	138	159	297
Shimo Sonkrai	320	3	323
Sonkrai	406	752	1,158
Changaraya		146	146
	864	1,060	1,924

On November 19, the work being completed, the move back to Kanburi and Singapore began. Parties, 200 strong, left on consecutive nights, the last party leaving on November 24. The journey varied from 72 to 132 hours with long halts *en route*. Closed and open trucks at a scale of 33 men to a truck were used. As usual food was insufficient and uncertain. 218 patients too ill to travel were left behind with sufficient staff to look after them.

	Australian		British		Totals	
	Officers	O.Rs.	Officers	O.Rs.	Officers	O.Rs.
Staff { Medical	1	29	2	23	3	52
{ Administrative	2	27	2	16	4	43
Patients	—	76	3	139	3	215
	3	132	7	178	10	310

This rear party moved back to Kanburi on January 31 and February 1, 1944.

The total number of deaths, including the dead on arrival, up to 1430 hours on November 24 represented about 45 per cent. of the British and 21 per cent. of the Australian populations of the camp. Deaths in the main were attributable to dysentery, amoebic and bacillary, tropical ulcers, beriberi and malaria. Malnutrition very greatly increased the mortality from these diseases.

The Tanbaya hospital project was not the success that it was hoped it would be. It could not be because of the lack of a well balanced diet and because of the complete lack of drugs. The task of the officer commanding the hospital and his staff, in spite of all their zeal, was made hopeless and agonising by the withholding of these necessities. Their work was made all the more difficult by the illnesses they shared in common with their patients. Thus on September 20 the officer commanding the hospital was convalescing from cardiac beriberi and malaria, three of his medical officers were seriously ill with typhus, two others with cardiac beriberi, one with malaria and one with dysentery, so that only two out of the total of ten were on that date capable of doing a full day's work.

When the Tanbaya hospital project was launched an order was received to close the camps at Nieke, Shimo Sonkrai and Changaraya and to regroup at Sonkrai and Kami Sonkrai. This order was received at 1400 hours on August 2. The move was to be completed on August 3 and involved marching knee-deep in mud and carrying all personal kit, cooking gear and medical equipment. There were some 1700 sick to be moved and they had to march along with the rest. One concession was obtained; the sick were permitted to stage at Shimo Sonkrai and Sonkrai on successive nights on the journey to Kami Sonkrai. In the event, however, this agreement was broken and the sick were forced to march straight through.

The I.J.A. demanded a working party 800 strong from each of the new camps. In order to balance the numbers of those who could work at the two camps it was necessary to create mixed camps of fitter Australians and less fit British. This marked difference between the Australian and British contingents is partly to be explained as follows:

(a) The Australians, officers and men, were relatively homogeneous in respect of attitude and outlook. The British relatively were a heterogeneous collection.

(b) The physical standards of the A.I.F. were incomparably higher than those of a mixed British force of regular soldiers, Territorials, militiamen, conscripts and local volunteers.

(c) The Australians had among them a far higher proportion of men who were used to looking after themselves under 'bush' conditions.

(d) The Australian contingent completed its march and reached the labour camps before the monsoon broke.

(e) It so happened that at the main Australian camp there was a Japanese officer of the P.o.W. Administration in charge. At Sonkrai and Changaraya there were only privates whom the I.J.A. Engineers overwhelmed.

The camp at Kami Sonkrai quickly developed an evil reputation which it maintained to the end. The death rate there during August, September and November was exceedingly high. The camp at Sonkrai was even worse in the beginning, but after the most seriously ill had been removed by death during August (average 10 a day) and after many transfers to Tanbaya the situation improved considerably.

About August 20, O.C. 'F' Force was informed that unless the numbers in the working parties at both camps were doubled all P.o.W., the sick as well as the fit, would be turned out into the jungle to fend for themselves in order to make room for coolie labour. This threat was not put into execution, but only for the reason that, taking into consideration the number of deaths among the P.o.W. to be expected, O.C. 'F' Force was able to offer to vacate one-third of the accommodation then occupied by 'F' Force, making this available for coolie labour.

In November 'F' Force was withdrawn to Kanburi, whence it moved back to Changi. The arrangements for the first part of this journey were disgraceful; no attempt was made to provide food or water; fourteen men died during it. Residue hospitals were left at Tanbaya and Kanburi; these returned to Changi early in 1944.

EXTRACTS FROM THE REPORT OF THE NUTRITION EXPERT
   WITH 'F' FORCE

Ready cooked food was supplied during the five day train journey from Singapore and the three weeks or so on the march. The meals consisted of boiled rice and watery vegetable stews containing a few pieces of cucumber, pumpkin or onion, and sufficed only to stave off the pangs of hunger for a few hours. The usual issue was two meals a day plus occasionally some cold pieces of dried fish as a haversack ration for the midnight halt. Those in possession of Thai currency could buy extra food from wayside hawkers during the first week of the march but even with this addition few men were able to maintain weight and strength during this period of exertion. At the fixed camps the I.J.A. supplied uncooked rations. Theoretically the ration was the same as at Changi, but in practice the amount handed over each day varied according to the stocks in hand, the state of the communications with the outside world and the mood of the Japanese quartermaster. Another cause of variation was the idea held by some officials, and at times openly expressed by them, that sickness, even though not feigned in order to avoid work, was a gross breach of discipline and an act of sabotage against the Japanese war effort. Instructions were actually issued officially from the I.J.A. H.Q. fixing a scale of 600 g. of rice daily for those working directly for the I.J.A. on the road and railway projects; 400 g. daily for those on camp duties and only 200 g. daily for those classified as unfit or sick. As sick and convalescents always outnumbered the workers, sometimes by thrice or four times to one, this order meant a marked reduction in the total amount of food issued to the camp. Although some adjustment and improvement of the sick men's ration was usually possible in the P.o.W. cookhouse, the manual workers could not be penalised too greatly for the benefit of the sick.

Items such as potatoes and boxed meat provided still another cause of variation. The Japanese quartermaster would issue a certain number of bags or boxes of these commodities regardless of their state of fitness for human consumption and this total number would be shown on his records. The preserved meat, a coarse-fibred meat probably buffalo meat, without bone was partly salted or pickled and arrived packed in boxes. It usually swarmed with blow-fly maggots and was often in such an advanced stage of decomposition that, as a grey-green fluid, it dropped through the seams of the boxes. Only one box might be salvaged of meat worth cooking from four or five issued. Sacks of potatoes suffered greatly from wet during transit and storage and many were only fit for the refuse pit. The standard of what was fit for consumption was a local one far below anything held before leaving Changi. The rice provided was a highly milled, medium grade, Burma rice; both it and the dried beans were heavily infested with weevils. Cattle which had been driven on hoof all the way from Burma provided the fresh meat; they were just as exhausted by their march as were the prisoners; they often died on the way and there was usually great anxiety to get the butchers to work before the beasts succumbed on arrival at the camps.

It was impossible to supplement the rations at all adequately by local purchases. Nieke village was the only trading centre in the neighbourhood of the camps and the one store-keeper with whom trading was permitted had a meagre selection of foodstuffs at high prices. Palm sugar cost 40 ticals (Thai dollars) per 13 oz. tin. The men received pay at the rate of ¼ tical (25 cents) when working; the sick received no pay. The camp hospital had first claim on valuable foods such as green grams which came in later. Coconut oil cost 35 ticals per 4 gallons, canned herrings 3 ticals per 15 oz. tin. At no time were the amounts available sufficient to make any appreciable difference to the food value of the camp rations as a whole, until after the return to Kanburi at the end of November where food was more plentiful and supplementary items cheaper. A supplement which may have made some difference to food in general was a leguminous plant later identified as a species of Cassia, popularly known as wild peanut. Near Sonkrai camp a large area of ground was covered with a species of wild gourd (*Cucurbitaceae*) the leaves of which made a palatable stew when cooked. At Kami Sonkrai the leaves of a certain climbing plant were similarly used. It was thought to belong to the family *Sterculiaciae*. The leaves were large and hairy but fairly soft when boiled and produced a syrupy soup. Parties of convalescents were organised to pick these various plants daily; special quantities were given to those suffering from beriberi and other deficiency diseases. The men had great faith in the value of their green stews.

Ration figures were collected for a number of the camps on the spot; others were obtained later from the 'Q' staff of the camps which had sufficient paper to keep records. The figures given are the net amounts of edible food received as rations by the P.o.W. None of the camps had weighing machines and all issues were in bulk. The amounts given in Table 29 were derived from estimate weights. These estimates were made at the time by various British and Australian 'Q' staff all of whom were experienced in handling food and estimating weights in bulk and should therefore be reasonably accurate over the period, for the daily strengths were available at each camp; these were averaged over the periods detailed in the Table.

Rations for June and early July were particularly poor. This was the time when some camps, notably those in the Konkoita and Nieke area, were almost cut off from communication with the outside world. No adequate reserve stocks were laid in before the rains came and as it was uncertain how long it would be before more supplies could get through rations were cut drastically. At Nieke in the middle of June the whole camp was receiving an issue of white rice 270 g., dried lima beans 24 g., dried green gram 15 g., fresh meat 50 mg. including bone, per head per day. This works out at an energy value of 1,200 Calories, less than that required for basal metabolism. At about the same time the Konkoita camps for eight to ten days were on a diet of 300 g. white rice daily and a little salt, varied occasionally by the omission of the salt. On this diet men were compelled to do heavy manual work on road and railway cuttings.

The later months showed an improvement in energy value except where there was a discrimination against the sick men, but only once did this food value reach a reasonable figure for the work being done.

Approximately 80 per cent. of the total energy value was supplied by carbohydrate and about 90 per cent. of this carbohydrate was derived from highly milled rice. Protein was usually small in amount and little of it was of animal origin. The amount of fat was inordinately low at all camps. There was a complete absence of green leaf vegetables and fruit, except later on return to Kanburi, and consequently a very low figure for vitamins A and C. The thiamin (vitamin B_1) values were well below the estimated normal requirements except at Tanbaya Hospital, Burma, from the last week in October onwards when rice polishings were supplied in reasonable quantities. The thiamin/non-fat caloric ratio never exceeded ·24 at any of the working camps. The amounts of vitamin B_2 complex in these components could not be assessed at the time, but those of riboflavin and nicotinic acid are approximately correct. The riboflavin values, while low, were not so far below the estimated daily requirements as were the values for nicotinic acid.

TABLE 29
P.o.W. Camp Diets. 1943

			Stand-ard	1942					
				March	April	May	June	July	August
Carbohydrate	A (g.)	.		418	428	458	460	525	525
	B (g.)	.		—	—	—	—	—	—
Protein	A (g.)	.	100	49	43	47	53	49	47
	B (g.)	.	100	—	—	—	—	—	—
Fat	A (g.)	.	100	21	16	18	22	19	18
	B (g.)	.	100	—	—	—	—	—	—
Calories:									
Total	A	. .	3,400	2,119	2,088	2,554	2,310	2,358	2,519
	B	. .	3,400	—	—	—	—	—	—
N.F.C.	A	. .		1,915	1,936	2,076	2,103	2,181	2,345
	B	. .							
Minerals:									
Calcium	A (g.)	.	·75	·236	·162	·127	·190	·156	·239
	B (g.)	.	·75	—	—	—	—	—	—
Phosphorus	A (g.)	.	·75	1·010	·850	1·002	1·103	·940	1·211
	B (g.)	.	·75	—	—	—	—	—	—
Vitamins:									
Vitamin A	A (i.us.)	.	3,000	3,785	302	231	2,324	2,330	2,402
	B (i.us.)	.	3,000	—	—	—	—	—	—
Vitamin B[1]	A (micro g.)		1,000	372·9	372·9	564·3	719·4	504·9	481·8
	B (micro g.)		1,000	—	—	—	—	—	—
Vitamin C	A (mg.)	.	30	1·2	0·2	2·5	18·7	17·6	18·7
	B (mg.)	.	30	—	—	—	—	—	—
Riboflavin	A (mg.)	.	1·5–1·8	·769	·694	·879	1·191	1·045	·924
	B (mg.)	.	1·5–1·8	—	—	—	—	—	—
Nicotinic acid	A (mg.)	.	15	6·0	5·78	7·625	8·23	7·25	6·69
	B (mg.)	.	15	—	—	—	—	—	—
Thiamin	A (N.F.C.		over ·3	·196	·194	·273	·345	·235	·205
	B Ratio)		over ·3	—	—	—	—	—	—

A.   The quantities supplied by the I.J.A. P.o.W. Ration.
B.   The quantities issued to the Troops.
—   The same as that supplied by the I.J.A. Ration. No Supplement.

	1942			1943							
Sept.	Oct.	Nov.	Dec.	Jan.	Feb.	March	April	May	June	July	Aug.
499	445	432	451	485	478	436	431	397	322	398	444
501	536	526	491	489	489	456	473	471	532	513	545
53	36	35	35	37	37	32	33	31	32	32	37
57	86	85	69	40	43	49	58	85	103	95	86
18	21	23	32	21	23	22	21	24	22	8	36
19	51	54	48	27	47	33	33	61	48	16	49
2,441	2,170	2,134	2,291	2,335	2,332	2,120	2,100	1,982	2,065	1,834	2,311
2,474	3,030	3,024	2,771	2,413	2,429	2,365	2,511	2,863	3,053	2,631	3,056
2,265	1,975	1,970	1,997	2,141	2,108	1,920	1,907	1,758	1,864	1,759	1,975
2,289	2,551	2,554	2,312	2,163	2,177	2,068	2,177	2,277	2,590	2,486	2,596
·227	·138	·112	·136	·235	·197	·135	·129	·127	·137	·109	·169
·241	·508	·518	·256	·250	·262	·422	·476	·251	·942	·645	·864
1·146	·724	·630	·783	·849	·825	·763	·687	·697	·753	·731	·934
1·296	1·740	1·751	1·074	·979	1·335	1·279	1·515	2·419	2·384	2·346	2·192
3,805	1,946	721	817	4,618	3,184	1,209	917	1,251	570	88	200
—	3,536	2,311	1,738	—	—	1,231	1,032	4,468	3,807	—	545
464	421	392	443	492	426	406	370	363	387	318	456
618	1,221	1,343	1,206	596	840	1,139	1,323	1,545	1,668	1,346	1,363
35·6	35·6	31·7	39	62	56	54	50	30	21·7	12	61
—	78	74	76	63	—	55	—	52	64	46·8	88
1·12	1·069	·981	1·092	·942	·911	·840	·837	·640	·817	·606	·994
1·164	2·096	2·036	1·693	1·078	1·131	1·298	1·718	1·860	2·354	2·276	2·620
7·75	6·54	6·08	6·19	5·11	5·12	4·74	4·48	5·150	4·607	4·470	5·816
10·27	21·33	24·37	19·27	5·82	7·423	16·50	20·01	22·748	22·652	20·698	17·486
·205	·213	·200	·22	·23	·20	·21	·19	·20	·21	·17	·23
·270	·479	·53	·52	·27	·39	·55	·61	·68	·64	·58	·53

TABLE 30

Thiamin Non-fat Ratios. 1943
'F' Force, Thailand Camps

Camp	May	June	July	Aug.	Sept.	Oct.	Nov.	Dec.
Konkoita .	·14	·16	·17	·17 to ·18	NF	·20	—	—
Nieke . .	NF	·21	·20	NF	—	—	—	—
Shimo Sonkrai	NF	·17	·18	—	—	—	—	—
Sonkrai . .	NF	NF	·19	—	—	—	—	—
Kami Sonkrai .	NF	NF	NF	·21 to ·24	·20	·23	·21	—
Tanbaya . .	—	—	—	·23	·22	·31	·61	NF
Kanburi . .	—	—	—	—	—	—	—	·27

NF, no non-fat figures available.

TABLE 31

'F' Force. The Bills of Mortality*

	Left Changi, April 1943	Died in Burma, Thailand, and on return to Changi	Escapees, fate unknown	Missing	Unconfirmed death report	Alive April 27, 1944
Aust.†	3,662	1,058	—	—	—	2,604
Br. .	3,336	2,029	5	I	I	1,300
	6,998	3,087	5	I	I	3,904

Death rate per mille per annum: Australian, 209; British, 608.

* Extracts from the report of the S.M.O. 'F' Force.
† From the *Official Australian Medical History*, p. 621:

Strength of A.I.F. ('F' Force)	3,662
Deaths up country	892
Missing up country	13
Remained up country	534
Deaths after return to Singapore	32
Returned to Singapore (December 1943–April 10, 1944)	2,223
Percentage died (approx.)	25

TABLE 32

Summary of 'F' Force Deaths. Australian and British. May 1943–April 1944

	Cholera	Dysentery and diarrhoea	Dysentery and beriberi	Dysentery and malaria	Dysentery and ulcers	Beriberi	Beriberi and malaria	Beriberi and ulcers	Malaria	Malaria and ulcers	Ulcers	Diphtheria	Smallpox	Pneumonia	Other diseases	Totals	Strength at beginning of period	Death rate per mille per annum
May	158	9	—	1	—	—	—	—	3	—	—	3	—	—	9	183	6,998	314
June	359	26	1	3	1	15	2	—	6	—	—	5	1	1	15	435	6,815	740
July	50	114	2	8	—	19	1	—	21	—	—	8	2	2	11	240	6,390	451
August	60	261	34	19	8	54	10	1	34	—	2	8	1	13	16	527	6,150	1,040
September	10	137	82	34	26	61	16	20	19	11	21	2	—	6	13	506	5,613	1,002
October	—	92	91	23	28	63	9	9	12	11	62	2	—	3	13	395	5,107	920
November	—	127	49	10	25	111	3	7	7	1	36	—	1	12	14	395	4,712	1,006
December	—	53	52	6	10	70	11	17	20	3	37	1	2	5	14	280	4,317	770
January	—	9	15	6	—	11	6	3	8	2	9	—	1	1	8	76	4,037	226
February	—	2	3	3	2	9	3	—	—	1	1	—	—	—	2	26	3,961	79
March	—	1	2	1	—	—	1	—	1	—	—	—	—	—	6	12	3,935	37
April	—	1	1	1	—	—	—	—	1	—	1	—	—	—	7	12	3,923	37
Totals	637	832	332	115	101	413	62	57	132	29	169	29	8	43	128	3,087	6,998	441
Per cent. of Totals	21	27	11	4	3	13	2	2	4	1	6	1	—	1	4	100		

TABLE 33

Distribution of Deaths (Australian and British) by Camps

	Cholera	Dysentery and diarrhoea	Dysentery and beriberi	Dysentery and malaria	Dysentery and ulcers	Beriberi	Beriberi and malaria	Beriberi and ulcers	Malaria (unspecified)	Malaria and ulcers	Ulcers	Diphtheria	Small-pox	Pneumonia	Other diseases	Totals
Changaraya . .	160	41	—	—	6	3	—	—	1	—	—	3	—	—	1	215
Kami-Sonkrai .	59	159	29	7	17	126	9	8	24	15	38	2	—	15	5	513
Sonkrai . .	232	256	16	14	1	59	7	3	35	—	23	17	4	2	9	678
Shimo-Sonkrai .	103	15	12	6	—	3	3	—	9	—	—	—	—	—	5	156
Nieke and Shimo-Nieke .	24	26	7	4	2	8	—	—	3	—	—	4	1	1	9	89
Konkoita, Tsimonia, Takanun	56	18	2	1	—	6	1	—	8	—	—	—	—	2	8	102
Tamarand Pat Transit Camps and others .	2	88	9	6	3	29	2	—	9	—	3	2	—	1	40	194
Tanbaya Hospital .	1	155	214	52	62	83	21	33	10	8	92	—	—	5	12	748
Kanburi Hospital .	—	69	42	18	10	96	16	12	26	3	13	—	2	13	24	344
Changi . .	—	5	1	7	—	—	3	1	7	3	—	1	1	4	15	48
Totals . .	637	832	332	115	101	413	62	57	132	29	169	29	8	43	128	3,087

TABLE 34

Deaths (Australian and British) Grouped in Four-monthly Periods

	Strength at beginning of period	Cholera	Dysentery and diarrhoea	Dysentery and malaria	Dysentery and beriberi	Dysentery and ulcers	Beriberi	Beriberi and malaria	Beriberi and ulcers	Malaria	Malaria and ulcers	Ulcers	Other diseases	Totals
1943 May–August	6,998	627	410	31	37	9	88	13	1	64	—	23	82	1,385
September–December	5,613	10	409	73	274	89	305	39	53	58	26	144	96	1,576
1944 January–April	4,037	—	13	11	21	3	20	10	3	10	3	2	30	126
Totals		637	832	115	332	101	413	62	57	132	29	169	208	3,087

OTHER FORCES

'*A*' *Force*. This was the first of the large parties that left Changi for employment on the Burma–Thailand railway project. It consisted of 3,000 Australians and included a medical section of 15 officers and 127 O.Rs. It sailed from Singapore on May 14, 1942. At Victoria Point in Burma a party of 1,000 men and 2 medical officers disembarked. A second party was put ashore at Mergui and the remainder of the force landed at Tavoy where it was joined by a large group of Dutch P.o.W. from Sumatra. At Tavoy the prisoners were put to work on road making and aerodrome construction.

To Mergui the Japanese had brought a party of 500 British P.o.W. and one Australian medical officer from Sumatra. These belonged to the party of key personnel that had been sent away from Singapore on February 14 and had reached Padang in Sumatra. Some of this party had been evacuated by a cruiser which called at Padang on March 1. The transport which was to take away the rest was sunk. On March 17 the Japanese arrived and six weeks later these 500 were packed aboard a filthy ship and taken to Mergui. During the voyage an epidemic of dysentery broke out.

A similar epidemic occurred during the voyage of 'A' Force and by the time Mergui and Tavoy were reached there was an urgent need for hospital accommodation. This was provided and was of the usual type with a primitive water supply and no kind of sanitation whatsoever. All that the medical section of 'A' Force had been permitted to bring away were an emergency surgical kit, a microscope and limited quantities of essential drugs. The stock of emetine was soon exhausted and the only possible treatment was with powdered charcoal from the kitchen fire.

In July a small working party left Tavoy for Ye. In August the Victoria Point and Mergui parties were transferred to Tavoy. Their arrival was followed by a flare-up of dysentery. At Mergui about 20 men had died from an acute fulminating form of amoebic dysentery which had made its appearance in Sumatra. It now appeared at Tavoy. On September 30 'A' Force, less 144 sick, 25 medical orderlies and two medical officers left at Tavoy, sailed for Moulmein and moved thence by cattle truck to Thanbyuzayat, the base camp of the working parties on the Burma section of the railway. There a base hospital was constructed. It consisted of bamboo huts with *attap* roofs. Each hut was 300 ft. long with platforms, 18 inches from the ground, on either side of a central aisle, 6 ft. wide. The space allowed was a yard a patient. At the end of 1942 the I.J.A. constructed a new hospital block with wooden floors and sound roofs and a small operating theatre was built.

As the railway probed its way into the jungle and as the distance between the base camp and the forward working camps increased, a second hospital was opened in April 1943 at 30 Kilo camp (Retpu), 18½ miles from Thanbyuzayat. In May, however, the Japanese decided that the bulk of its inmates were fit to work and so the hospital was closed, its moribund patients sent back to Thanbyuzayat and the rest distributed among the working camps.

In May cholera was discovered among the native labourers in one of the working camps. It soon was raging in several others. The monsoon rains added greatly to the discomfort of the P.o.W. The Allied air force was now bombing the line of the railway and in two of these raids on June 12 and 14, 13 Australians, 4 Dutch and 2 British P.o.W. were killed and 30 others wounded in the base hospital. The fitter patients were promptly moved to a camp five miles away and the rest carried to Retpu where on July 4 the hospital was reopened.

As the line became further extended a hospital was opened at 55 Kilo camp (Kohn Kuhn). This consisted of 8 huts and one small isolation hut. Early in July it was accommodating 1,000 patients and a little later 1,800. At first there were but two medical officers and six orderlies but later these were joined by four other medical officers. The prevalent diseases among 'A' Force were the same as those of 'F' Force. The I.J.A. issued instructions to the effect that dysentery on the death certificate was to be altered to 'hill diarrhoea'. Tropical ulcers were very numerous and severe. At Kohn Kuhn no less than 120 amputations had to be performed on account of this condition. Here, as in the hospitals elsewhere, there was much improvisation and the display of remarkable ingenuity. Bamboo provided artificial limbs, a primitive still yielded water. Japanese novocain was evaporated and distilled to give a 4 per cent. novocain for intrathecal use. Burmese brandy was distilled to provide surgical alcohol. Catgut was manufactured from the serous lining of the intestines of cattle.

As 1943 pursued its seemingly unending course the working camps crossed the Burma–Thailand border and passed through the Three Pagodas Pass and in October 'A' and 'F' Forces met. Retpu hospital was then closed and its patients transferred to Kohn Kuhn where thus far 220 men had died. At the end of November the Kohn Kuhn hospital was closed and its patients transferred to hospitals in Thailand, the more seriously ill to Nakom Paton, near Bangkok, the less to Kanburi.

Eventually, with the exception of 500 men left behind for maintenance work on the railway, 'A' Force was moved to the Kanburi area.

'*D*' *Force*. This consisted of 2,780 British and 2,220 Australian P.o.W., including a medical section, and left Changi on March 14–18, 1943 for Bampong. Thence the force moved by sections to Tarsu. One section went right on to the Three Pagodas Pass and was out of contact with the rest of the force for over a year. The other sections were distributed among the working camps between Tarsu and Kanu. The force soon lost its identity, its sections becoming absorbed into the different local groups. A hospital was opened at Kanu to serve the force and at one time was holding about 1,000 patients. The death rate in the hospital was exceedingly high and for a time the daily average number of deaths was eight. The medical history of this force was identical with that of 'F' Force. Its total mortality was estimated to have been about 18 per cent.

Gradually the remnants of this force trickled back to Kanburi.

'H' Force. This consisted of 3,000 P.o.W., mainly British but including 600 Australians and some Dutch. It included a medical section. It left Singapore on May 5, 1942 and, in similar fashion to 'F' Force, proceeded to Kanburi. There the I.J.A. carried out tests for cholera and the men were inoculated against cholera and dysentery. From Kanburi the force moved by sections to Malaya Hamlet, at the northern end of the central Thailand section of the line. One party travelled to Wanye, 40 miles beyond Bampong by train and marched thence to Tonchan South. In June cholera broke out among the coolie labourers in the Hintok area and soon was raging among the P.o.W. A hospital was opened at Malaya Hamlet and by July 3, 200 of the 400 patients therein were suffering from this disease; 111 Australians and 106 British died during this epidemic.

In August 1943 the force was moved back to Kanburi where in the nearby village of Kanchanaburi a large base hospital had been established. Eleven medical officers and 60 medical orderlies of 'L' Force (a purely medical force consisting of 15 officers and 100 orderlies, Australian and British) joined this hospital, the 28 wards of which were quickly filled with the sick of 'F' and 'H' Forces. In this hospital no less than 2,296 men of 'H' Force were treated.

'H' Force began to leave Thailand for Singapore on December 8 and reaching there was dissolved. Of its 1,057 sick, transferred from Kanchanaburi to Singapore, half died at a later date.

The privations, the starvation and the overwork to which 'H' Force was subjected are partly revealed in the following figures:

	Totals	Left Behind	Dead at 10/12/43	Percentage Dead
All officers . .	421	6	26	6·27
A.O.R. . .	627	12	165	26·83
B.O.R. . .	1,719	38	627	37·30
D.O.R. . .	503	6	33	6·64
	3,270	62	851	26·53

'L' Force was unique in that all of its members survived.

'K' Force was another purely medical party which was sent from Changi to augment the medical resources of the forces working on the railway. It consisted of 30 medical officers and 200 orderlies (Australian, 5 M.Os. and 50 O.Rs.). At Kanburi the officers were set an examination by the Japanese officer commanding the sanitary corps to test their professional competence. Failure meant employment as coolies. Everyone of them passed with distinction! The members of this party were employed in the coolie labour camps at Wanye, Nieke, Kanburi and Kanburi airport.

BASE HOSPITALS

The appalling conditions in the railway construction camps caused sickness that in its variety and incidence completely overwhelmed the meagre resources of the camp hospitals and made the provision of much larger base hospitals necessary. Tanbaya was an example of such. The I.J.A. chose sites for others as these became necessary at Tavoy, Thanbyuzayat, Retpu, Kohn Kuhn, in the Burma section, at Sonkrai and Takanun in the northern Thailand section, at Kanu and Kinsayo in the central Thailand section and at Chungkai, Tamarkan, Kanchanaburi and Non Pladuk in the southern Thailand section. As has been indicated the tendency was for the northerly base hospitals to close as new ones were opened in the more southerly sections so that when the railway was finished the sick became aggregated in hospitals at Tarsu, Chungkai, Tamuang, Non Pladuk and Nakom Paton.

A brief reference to one or two of these will serve to illustrate the conditions that obtained in all. The hospital at Kanchanaburi was opened in January 1943. By June it was holding nearly 1,000 patients. By August its stocks of drugs and dressings were almost entirely exhausted. Its wards were full of typhus, cholera, diphtheria and tropical ulcer cases. When the hospitals at Tanbaya and Sonkrai were closed, their patients were evacuated to this hospital. The hospital was closed in December 1943, its patients being evacuated to other hospitals farther down the line.

In January 1944 Nakom Paton was a working camp with a population of 1,500; 150 convalescents and the medical staff of the Tamarkan hospital were moved thereto. During the next three months, with the help of native labour, they built a hospital of 50 huts, each to hold 200 men. Cookhouses at the rate of 1 per 1,000 men and cubicled latrines, with squatting holes over concrete-lined trenches, 4 ft. deep, were constructed as was also a canteen with a concert platform. The beds were wooden platforms. There was no bedding, no towels, no washing utensils. There were separate medical and surgical blocks, an operating theatre, with a concrete floor, a resuscitation room, a dispensary and accommodation for the special departments. Nothing like this had been seen since the Changi days. Its staff included, besides the commanding officer and adjutant, a consulting surgeon, a consulting

14

physician, a consulting transfusionist, 5 S.M.Os. i/c ward groups, a pathologist, a dental surgeon, an E.N.T. specialist, an ophthalmologist, a dermatologist, an anaesthetist and a number of G.D.Os. The meetings of a very active medical society did much to maintain a high morale and to advance medical knowledge.

Though there were difficulties and deficiencies the conditions here were better than those in the more northerly camps which functioned during the period of the actual construction of the railway. The 896 surgical operations performed in this hospital included craniotomies, laminectomies, thoracoplasties, appendicostomies, ileostomies and herniotomies. Herniotomy was performed 114 times by order of the Japanese. In the medical wards emetine was made available partly by the Japanese but chiefly from the American Red Cross. Twenty-five per cent. of the whole camp strength were treated in the skin department. Post-mortem examinations were systematically carried out until the Japanese forbade them without special permission. Though the ration was much better than in the camps of the earlier period there were still important deficiencies, especially in first class protein fat and vitamins. The Calories ranged from 2,700 to 3,100, total protein from 50 to 85 g., fat from 18 to 51 g. Supplements were provided from a special fund and by the Australian and British Red Cross. Food extras also arrived from the American Red Cross. But in spite of all this there were many patients who did not respond for the reason that they had suffered irreversible changes.

In August 1944 the camp strength reached a peak of 7,353. By August 1945 the numbers had fallen to 2,868.

From March 25, 1944 to August 16, 1945 admissions and discharges were:

	British	Australian	Dutch	American	Totals
Admitted	4,363	1,868	3,190	90	9,511
Discharged	3,271	1,085	2,328	58	6,742
Died	71	21	59	2	153

This hospital, together with those at Chungkai and Tamuang, continued until the end of the war.

Tamuang base hospital was established in June 1944, that is to say when the railway was finished and the derelicts of the labour forces were moving southwards down the line towards Non Pladuk. The treatment of the P.o.W. by the I.J.A. was now far better than it had been and the rations supplied were rather better. It was now about 2,300 Calories with 50 g. of protein and 20 g. of fat. Local supplements provided another 300 Calories. Dysentery, deficiency diseases, malaria and tropical ulcer became the major causes of hospitalisation. There was no anti-malarial drug available and the malaria was of the malignant tertian type. Pellagra and beriberi, though still common, were milder, skin diseases less troublesome and septic ulcers less severe. In July some stores from the American Red Cross arrived and atebrin became available for the first time. Emetine and sulphaguanidine also became available.

Under the improved conditions the medical and surgical work reached a far higher standard. Stool examination showed that 20 per cent. of the patients were infested with Ankylostoma and 50 per cent. with Strongyloides. The principal malarial vector was shown to be *A. barbirostris*. The defibrination method and later the citrate method were employed in blood transfusion work. Inventiveness now reached new heights, irrigation apparatus, suction pumps, proctoscopes, ophthalmoscopes, pneumonia jackets, suspension gear, fly traps, fly-proof lids for latrines, disinfectors, even artificial eyes were now being made. Woodwork, cobbling, tin-smithing and the like became the instruments of rehabilitation. In this connexion an appeal made in the Chungkai hospital is of interest.

'There is a desperate shortage of such essential materials (for artificial limbs) as screws, wire, sorbo rubber, elastic and rubber bands, old braces, soft leather or webbing. Artificial eyes can be made from white mahjong pieces: more of these are required.

'The following articles are urgently needed: tins and containers of all sorts, solder, flux, nails, screws, sorbo rubber, scraps of clothing, hose tops, old socks, string, webbing, scraps of leather, rubber tubing (for transfusion purposes), glass bottles of all sorts, glass tubing, canvas, elastic or rubber bands or strips, tools of all sorts. Nothing is too old. Nothing is too small.'

In April 1945 the hospital was rebuilt and gardens made.

From September 1944 onwards the Thailand section of the railway became the target of the Allied bombers. On September 6 Non Pladuk was heavily attacked and 100 P.o.W. were killed and 400 wounded. On November 29 Tamarkan was bombed and 18 P.o.W. were killed and 68 wounded. On December 8 the whole section was attacked and 41 P.o.W. were killed and 70 wounded. Thereafter to the end the line was under constant attack. The I.J.A. would not permit the Red Cross to be flown over the hospitals and for some time would not allow slit trenches to be dug. The patients, therefore, soon began to show considerable anxiety. Most of the traumatic surgery, following the raids, was performed under spinal or local anaesthesia. Small quantities of ether and chloroform were provided by the I.J.A.

(Plates I to V illustrate the appalling conditions which prevailed in the camps and hospitals during the construction of the Thailand–Burma railway.)

OPERATION 'MASTIFF'

On August 6 and 9, 1945, atomic bombs were dropped on Hiroshima and Nagasaki. On the 10th the Japanese Government announced that it was prepared to discuss terms. On the 14th it accepted unconditional surrender.

When the war in the Far East ended there were P.o.W. and internee camps scattered widely throughout Assam, Borneo, Burma, French Indo-China, Japan, Java, Malaya, Manchuria, the Philippines, Singapore Island, Sumatra and Thailand, containing some 122,000 men, women and children in urgent need of succour. Information concerning them had been amassed from various sources and preparations for the rescue of their inmates had been made. When information was received which suggested very strongly that it was the intention of the I.J.A. to massacre its prisoners at the end of August 1945, paratroops were dropped in the vicinity of many of these camps. These kept watch and organised and armed local guerrilla bands against the time when the camps guards would be overwhelmed and the prisoners freed.

H.Q. A.L.F.S.E.A. was responsible for the rescue of the P.o.W. in the camps in its area—Assam, Indo-China, Java, Malaya and Sumatra. (Operation 'Mastiff'.) From three centres—Colombo, Calcutta and Rangoon—aircraft carrying food, clothing and medical supplies were to be despatched immediately following the cessation of hostilities. The centre at Colombo was to cover Malaya, Singapore, Sumatra and Java, with aircraft based on aerodromes in Ceylon and the Cocos Islands. That at Calcutta was to cover Eastern, Central and Southern Assam and French Indo-China with aircraft based on airfields in Jessore. From the airfield at Mingaladon, Rangoon, Western Thailand and Eastern Burma would be served.

These arrangements were essentially the same as those made by the Americans and the Australians for the relief of the P.o.W. and internee camps elsewhere.

When the I.J.A. informed its captives that the war had ended, in the majority of instances the P.o.W. assumed control of their own affairs and immediately developed their own military organisation. Operation 'Birdcage' was launched on August 28, 1945. Leaflets were dropped on the camps telling their inmates that help was on the way and advising them what to do until it arrived. The guerrillas were told that they could now move freely and were asked to make contact with the P.o.W. and internees, rendering all possible help to them. Operation 'Birdcage' was followed immediately by Operation 'Mastiff'. Supplies were dropped every day until October 15. Altogether, 950 tons of food, clothing, medical supplies, wireless sets, etc., were dropped. Medical teams, each consisting of a medical officer and a nursing orderly, were parachuted into many of the camps to provide reinforcement to the medical personnel of the camps. They were charged with the duty of making a medical appreciation of the condition of the P.o.W. and of their needs. Lists were to be prepared showing the numbers of those

(1) fit to travel by troopship and on ordinary rations.
(2) fit to travel by troopship and on convalescent rations.
(3) fit to travel by sea ambulance transport.
(4) fit to travel by hospital ship.
(5) unfit to travel for the present.
(6) dangerously ill.

The condition of the troops is revealed in the classification of the Australians in the camps awaiting repatriation.

(1) Nil
(2) 1,052
(3) 2,920
(4) 1,487
(5) 101
(6) 16 (included in (5))

The formal ceremony of surrender took place on September 2. Seaborne relieving forces, including medical detachments and representatives of R.A.P.W.I., were despatched. Of necessity in most of the Japanese controlled areas there was a time-lag between the capitulation and the rescue. In this interval the I.J.A. flooded the camps with food, clothing and Red Cross parcels. Relief reached Penang and Bangkok on September 3, Singapore on the 4th, Saigon on the 11th. To Hong Kong 3rd Commando Bde. was despatched.

The fittest among the P.o.W. were suffering from malnutrition and chronic infections in varying degree. Among these tough men who had wrestled with death and had not been defeated there were none unmarked.

(*A*) Among the nominal rolls of 2,300 Australian, British and Indian R.A.P.W.Is. who were evacuated from Singapore by hospital ship the distribution of disease was as follows:

	Per Cent.
Malnutrition and beriberi . . .	40
Nutritional amblyopia . . .	2
Amoebiasis, diarrhoea, dysentery . .	8
Malaria	8
Pulmonary tuberculosis . . .	6
Tropical ulcer	4
Psychiatric disorders	3
General medical conditions . . .	16
General surgical conditions . . .	16

(*B*) Among 6,864 R.A.P.W.Is. passing through Rangoon military hospitals during September 1945 the following conditions were encountered:

	No. of Cases
Malnutrition	52
Beriberi	20
Anaemia	88
Diarrhoea and non-amoebic dysentery	60
Amoebiasis	74
Infective hepatitis . . .	28
Malaria	215
Psychiatric disorders . . .	21
Skin diseases	85
Tuberculosis	8
General medical conditions . .	262
General surgical conditions . .	204

1,117 or 17 per cent.

(*C*) Among 1,230 R.A.P.W.Is. admitted to 47 B.G.H., Singapore, September 9–October 8, 1945, the following diseases were encountered:

		Per Cent.
Malnutrition . . .	577	46·0
Malaria	73	5·0
Dysentery and diarrhoea .	84	7·1
Surgical conditions . .	82	6·7
Other diseases . . .	163	13·3
Mild malnutrition . .	81	6·6
Unclassified . . .	167	13·6

Of the 577 cases of malnutrition further examination revealed:

	Oedematous Cases	*Non-oedematous Cases*	*Totals*	*Percentages*
Amblyopia . .	8	28	36	6·2
Riboflavin deficiency	0	3	3	0·5
Skin lesions . .	9	16	25	4·3
Tongue lesions .	51	59	110	19·1
Neurological lesions	88	64	152	25·3
Other lesions .	197	54	251	51·3
	353	224	577	

Of the 353 oedematous cases 97 (27·5 per cent.) showed signs of peripheral neuritis; of the 224 non-oedematous cases 73 (32·6 per cent.) showed such signs.

The improvement following liberation of the general condition of those who were suffering from malnutrition was so rapid that no correct estimate of the incidence of malnutrition among them can now be formed.

Details concerning the clinical aspects of the deficiency diseases among these R.A.P.W.Is., clinical and biochemical investigations of hunger oedema and clinical trials of methods of treatment of the severely undernourished, are presented in the Medical Research Volume in this series.

NURSES IN CAPTIVITY

The experience of the majority of the members of the Army Nursing Service who fell into Japanese hands was identical with that of the majority of the internees and therefore there is no compelling reason to present an account in this volume which would very largely be a repetition of that which appears in other volumes of this History. But it is desirable to refer to that which befell the Australian nurses who sailed from Singapore on February 12, 1942, in the *Vyner Brooke*. This ship was bombed and sunk off Banka Island. Many of her passengers, including 11 of the nurses, were drowned. The survivors landed on Banka Island.

On Radji Beach a party, including 22 of the nurses and about a dozen sick, collected. Japanese troops soon arrived, for the Japanese had already occupied the island, and an officer ordered the party to separate into three groups, officers, men and the nurses and the sick. The men were marched away for a short distance and shot. Then the officer group was marched to the same spot and bayoneted. The nurses were ordered to walk into the sea. When they were knee-deep in the water a machine gun mowed them down.

One did not die. Regaining consciousness she found that she had been washed up on the beach and was lying amid the corpses of her colleagues. She crawled into the jungle and hid. In the jungle she encountered a survivor of the group that had been bayoneted. These two were fed by the women of a nearby village and for ten days more remained free. But for them there was no possibility of escape and so on February 28 they gave themselves up. The nurse rejoined the 32 of her colleagues who now remained of the original 65.

On Banka Island at this time were many hundreds of internees and P.o.W. The nurses were first immured in the Customs House at Muntok, then in a cinema where they tended wounded naval and air force personnel and later were moved to coolie lines where they stayed for a fortnight. They then embarked on a ship densely packed with internees for Palembong. Arriving there they were ordered to attend the opening night of a 'club' that the I.J.A. was starting. Save for three who were too ill, the nurses obeyed this order to be told that only four of them were to remain and that non-compliance with Japanese wishes would be followed by a régime of starvation for all. Four stayed and rejoined the rest next morning safely. Thereafter all of them refused to enter the club. Stubbornly resisting further pressure the nurses managed to get a message to the Governor of Palembang through a Dutch doctor. They were transferred to another part of the town where they were housed in bungalows. Ten to a room, a cement floor for a bed, rice bags and curtains for bedclothes, mosquitoes in clouds, no fuel, mouldy rice for food, these were the conditions they endured.

They had no money and so could not buy food at the camp canteen. Some of them had to be admitted to hospital on account of beriberi. In January 1943 a high official from Singapore visited them and undertook to transmit their names by radio. This was done. In September they were moved to a desolate camp area to live in huts and to undertake manual work. A few of them, along with British and Dutch nurses were employed in the camp hospital. Their rations progressively diminished until all they had consisted of 2 oz. of rice a day with kang kong in small amounts and morsels of beans and cucumbers. Typhoid, dysentery, dengue and skin diseases were prevalent among them and all of them suffered from malnutrition. Bowing to the guards was obligatory and punishment took the form of face slapping and of standing for long periods in the blazing sun.

In October 1944 the nurses were sent back to Muntok on Banka Island. They travelled on a small river boat on which 200 women were herded together. Though diarrhoea was prevalent the only sanitary equipment provided was one bucket. Weak with exhaustion they landed to join the hospital staff. Here four of them died from a combination of beriberi and malaria.

In April 1945 they were sent back to Sumatra, to Lubuklinggau camp to be accommodated in overcrowded, verminous *attap* huts. Here four more died and the health of the rest progressively deteriorated.

On August 23 the guards of the camp were removed and on the following day the commandant announced that the war had ended. Food and drugs suddenly became plentiful and the attitude of the Japanese completely altered. Supplies dropped from the sky. Parachutists arrived and the relationship of captor and captive became reversed.

On September 16 the nurses left by train and aeroplane for Singapore where they were at once admitted to hospital.

CHAPTER 3

THE OCCUPATION OF ICELAND AND THE FAROES

BETWEEN the North-west European and the North American shores, fringing the North Atlantic Ocean, stretches a chain of islands, the stepping stones of the Vikings—Orkney and Shetland, the Faroes, Iceland, Greenland and Newfoundland.

To guard the North Atlantic passage it became imperative for Great Britain to deny every one of the links in this chain to the Germans. The United States of America, not yet at war, occupied Greenland to safeguard her own interests. In May 1940, when Denmark was over-run and Norway occupied by the Germans, Great Britain sent small forces to occupy Iceland and the Faroes. The nucleus of the force that went to the Faroes was composed of Lovat Scouts, that of the Iceland force a battalion of Royal Marines. Subsequently these islands were developed as bases for naval escort groups and long-range aircraft engaged in the protection of the convoys that crossed the ocean.

ICELAND

On May 17, 1940, 'Alabaster' Force landed at Reykjavik. It consisted of H.Q. 'Alabaster' Force (including an A.D.M.S.) and 147th Inf. Bde. (1/5th West Yorks, 1/6th D.W.R. and 1/7th D.W.R.). With it were 89th Coy. A.M.P.C., 160 Fd. Amb., 35 Fd. Hyg. Sec. and the advance party, including a number of Q.A.I.M.N.S. personnel, of 50 B.G.H. (200 beds). The main body of 50 B.G.H., including the balance of Q.A.I.M.N.S. personnel, arrived in the next convoy.

But discussions between the Canadian and British Governments had been proceeding, and out of them came an agreement that Canada should accept the responsibility of garrisoning Iceland. On June 16 the Royal Regiment of Canada disembarked at Reykjavik. On June 26, H.Q. 49th Division, units of 146th Inf. Bde., A.D.M.S., D.A.D.M.S. and D.A.D.H. 49th Division, 146 Fd. Amb. and 21 Fd. Hyg. Sec. arrived.

On July 7 the other two battalions of the Canadian 'Z' Force—the Fusiliers Mont-Royal and the Cameron Highlanders of Ottawa— disembarked. 30 B.G.H. arrived on July 12 and 20 M.B.U. on the 16th.

The mixed British and Canadian force was dispersed throughout the island, guarding vulnerable points and providing mobile columns for their reinforcement.

179

In September more British units and formations reached Iceland;
10th D.L.I. on the 16th, and on the 24th H.Q. 70th Inf. Bde. with

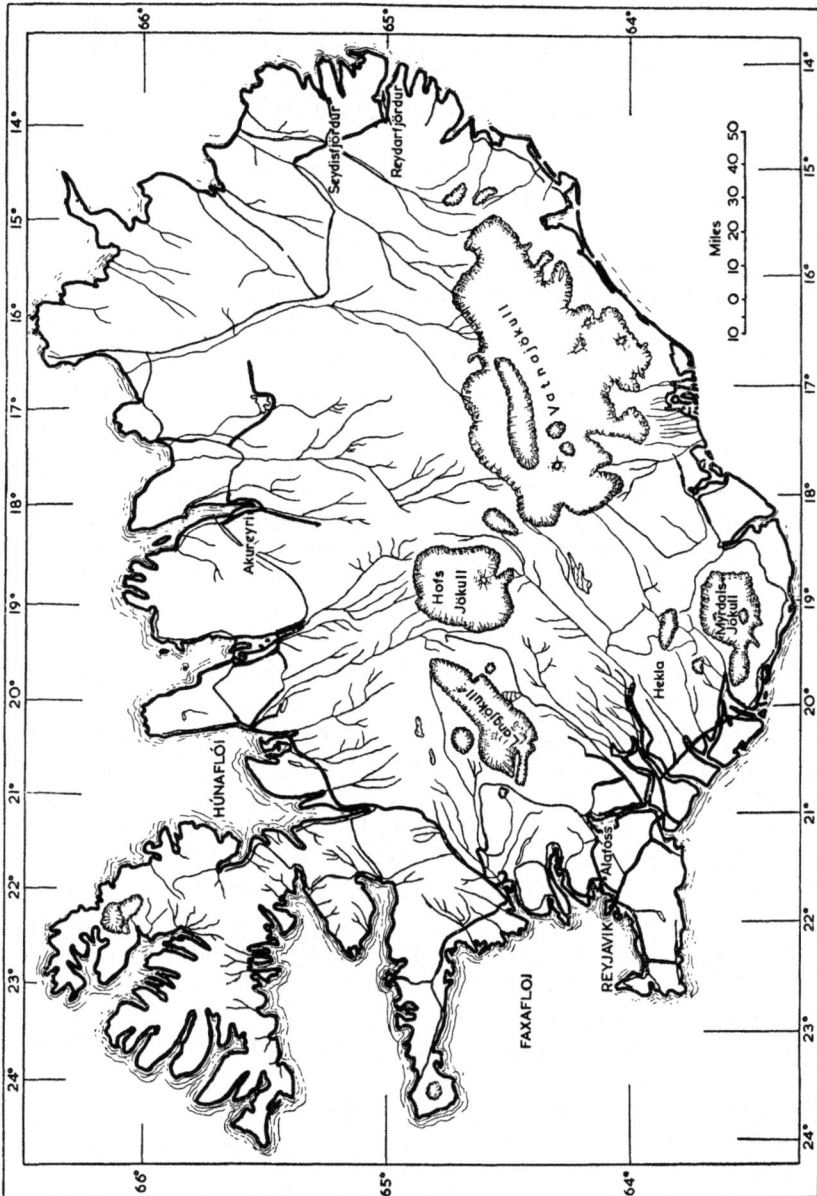

FIG. 20. Iceland.

11th D.C.I. and 12th D.L.I. (The Tyneside Highlanders), 187 Fd.
Amb., 10 Fd. Hyg. Sec., 9 and 10 M.B.Us. and two officers and ten

O.Rs., A.D.Corps (without equipment). In the ships that brought them the Fusiliers Mont-Royal and the Royal Regt. of Canada embarked for the United Kingdom, for it had now been decided that Canadian 2nd Division should not assemble in Iceland, as was previously intended, but should concentrate in southern England. The third Canadian battalion, the Camerons, remained in Iceland throughout the winter and later joined Canadian 3rd Division.

On November 27, H.S. *Leinster* reached Iceland, there to act as a 300-bedded hospital.

In the early months of 1941 R.N., R.A.F., Norwegian Naval Air Arm and Norwegian Army units reached Iceland in increasing numbers. On June 7, 12th Worcestershires arrived.

In June 1941 President Roosevelt decided to establish a U.S. base in Iceland for the protection of U.S. shipping in the Atlantic, and agreed to the replacement of the British garrison by a United States force. On July 27 the leading elements of this force, U.S. Marines, landed at Reykjavik. Thereafter the Americans, arriving in increasing numbers, progressively took over from H.Q. 49th Division. During this period, however, further British units arrived—81 B.G.H., for example, on October 4. As late as July 1, 1942, there were still some 10,000 British troops on the island. In the third week of September the main body of 146th Inf. Bde., then in the Akureyri area, embarked for the United Kingdom, shortly to be followed by the remainder of this brigade. 70th Inf. Bde. left in December and thereafter the takeover quickened until soon the last of the British garrison had departed.

MEDICAL ASPECTS OF THE OCCUPATION OF ICELAND

Iceland, one and a third times the size of Ireland, lies immediately below the Arctic Circle at the edge of the zone that is affected by the Gulf Stream. Except for an alluvial strip along the western part of the south coast the country is almost entirely mountainous, with valleys ending in fjords. Thirteen per cent. of its surface is covered perpetually with ice and snow. The mountains are commonly volcanic and there are many hot water springs and geysers with temperatures up to 100° C. The rivers and lakes are glacial in origin. The soil is thin for the most part and supports grass of relatively poor quality and stunted shrubs. Cattle, ponies and sheep are kept in large numbers and potatoes form an important part of the Icelandic diet.

The climate is temperate, the weather variable and inclement. The high winds constitute the chief source of discomfort. The summer days are very long, those of the winter exceedingly short.

The population, approximately 118,000 in 1935, is entirely restricted to the coastal areas. Reykjavik, the capital, in 1935 had a population of 34,231. The people are proud, dignified, well educated and democratic.

They are well housed, the buildings being of concrete. Sanitation tends to be somewhat primitive. Water is plentiful and of excellent quality, though pollution is not unknown.

The main occupations are fishing and its associated trades in the towns, agriculture in the countryside.

There is a well organised Government medical service under the direction of a state physician. There is an excellent medical faculty in the State University in Reykjavik.

The vital statistics of Iceland compare quite favourably with those of the northern European countries.

The principal figures for 1938 were as follows:

		(U.K. 1938)
Crude birth rate	19·7	(15·3)
Crude death rate	10·2	(12·2)
Infantile mortality rate . . .	29·2	(58·5)

Major causes of death (per 1,000 deaths):

Senility	153·1
Cancer	122·3
Heart disease	112·3
Tuberculosis	88·2
Known number of cases of gonorrhoea .	648
„ „ „ syphilis .	6
„ „ „ other forms .	o
„ „ „ leprosy .	17

THE HEALTH OF THE TROOPS

SAMPLE STATISTICS

October–December 1940
Average strength of the Force, 20,420.

The medical units serving in Iceland were as follows:

Medical Units:
50 B.G.H. (200 beds) .	Reykjavik
30 B.G.H. (300 beds) .	Laugarnes. Hutted: heating from hot springs at Alafoss
146 Fd. Amb. (60 beds).	In the Horga valley and Seydisfjördur
160 Fd. Amb. (40 beds).	Reykjavik. Hutted
187 Fd. Amb. (20 beds).	Alafoss in a village school
10 Fd. Hyg. Sec.	
35 Fd. Hyg. Sec.	
9, 10, 20 B.M.Us.	
H.S. *Leinster* (300 beds)	Off Akureyri (90–97 patients aboard)

Strength:

	Officers	Q.A.I.M.N.S.	O.Rs. R.A.M.C.
50 B.G.H. . .	11	22	99
30 B.G.H. . .	23	25	147
H.S. Leinster . .	9	22	75
146 Fd. Amb. .	11	—	190
160 Fd. Amb. .	8	—	176
187 Fd. Amb. .	11	—	199
35 Fd. Hyg. Sec. .	1	—	28
10 Fd. Hyg. Sec. .	1	—	21
Force H.Q. . .	3	—	7
R.M.Os. . .	12	—	—
	90	69	942

A perusal of the figures given in Tables 35 and 36 shows that the health of the troops during the winter of 1940–41 was exceedingly good in spite of the rigours of the climate and the conditions under which they lived; the figures call for no special comment.

TABLE 35

Principal Diseases

	Hospital admissions		
	October	November	December
Respiratory . .	60	87	54
Tonsils and pharynx	39	52	40
Digestive .	72	71	57
Bones, joints, muscles	45	73	35
Skin . . .	58	52	78
Areolar tissue . .	32	42	39
Injuries . .	58	65	77
Venereal disease .	11	16	3
Scabies . . .	54	63	14*
Infectious diseases .	3	6	13
Per 1,000 strength	432 (29·3)	527 (35·5)	410 (29·1)

* Not hospitalised after November 27.

TABLE 36

Principal Diseases

	Hospital admissions		
	January	February	March
Respiratory . .	90	144	93
Tonsils and pharynx	67	67	62
Digestive . .	76	68	64
Bones, joints, muscles	58	48	45
Skin . . .	125	86	109
Areolar tissue .	51	42	53
Injuries . . .	82	85	78
Venereal disease .	5	4	13
Scabies . . .	91	58	59
Infectious diseases .	10	12	11
Per 1,000 strength	655 (30·9)	614 (29·0)	587 (27·7)

January–March 1941

Average strength of Force, 21,191.

Number of invalids evacuated to the United Kingdom, 172.

Battle casualty. One O.R. 12th D.L.I. wounded by machine-gun fire from German aircraft.

Several shipwrecked sailors admitted.

Field ambulances set up C.R.Ss.

April–June 1941

Average strength of Force, 24,300.

H.S. *Leinster* sailed for United Kingdom May 31 leaving 4 M.Os., 6 Q.A.I.M.N.S. and 20 O.Rs. with 146 Fd. Amb. at Akureyri.

The major causes of admission to hospital remained unchanged but there were fewer cases in each category.

July–September 1941

Average strength of Force, 27,442.

30 B.G.H. moved to Helgafel to a hutted site there to prepare for the coming of a U.S. hospital unit.

October–December 1941

81 B.G.H. arrived and was sent to Hrafnagil.

January–March 1942

Average strength of Force, 22,068.

Number of invalids evacuated to the United Kingdom, 317.

50 B.G.H. was relieved by a R.A.F. medical unit and embarked for the United Kingdom on March 1.

30 B.G.H., leaving a detachment behind with 200 beds at Helgafel, sailed for the United Kingdom.

The troops were now being trained in mountain warfare during which they were required to carry a load of 80 lbs. for seven hours over very rough country and to fight at the end of the march. The immediate result was a significant rise of the sick rate. On medical advice the training was modified.

April–June 1942

Average strength of Force, 18,347.

Number of invalids evacuated to the United Kingdom, 252.

160 Fd. Amb. and 35 Fd. Hyg. Sec. left for the United Kingdom.

July–September 1942

10 Fd. Hyg. Sec. and 10 M.B.U. at Akureyri and the detachments of 9 M.B.U. at Seydisfjördur and Reydarfjördur sailed in mid-July, followed by 146 Fd. Amb., less 'B' Coy., at Seydisfjördur and Reydarfjördur ; the dental centre was evacuated in August ; 81 B.G.H. and 'B' Coy. 146 Fd. Amb. embarked during the first week of September. D.A.D.H., who had been responsible for the Force Medical H.Q. since April 22, 1942, embarked on September 20.

Before leaving, all the hutted accommodation, ordnance stores, the force medical stores and the medical stores and equipment of 146 Fd. Amb. at Akureyri, detachment 30 B.G.H., 81 B.G.H. and of the C.R.Ss. at Seydisfjördur and Reydarfjördur, were handed over to the Chief Surgeon, U.S. Army Forces, Iceland Base Command.

ACCOMMODATION

Since it was not possible to find billets for the whole of 'Alabaster' Force, a proportion of the troops were quartered in empty fish warehouses, schools and suchlike buildings, while others lived under canvas. Large store tents served as dining rooms and field-type cookers (petrol-fed) were used. The billets were not satisfactory, being poorly ventilated, and the pitching of tents was difficult; the ground was hard and rough, the winds high. The volcanic dust of which the ground was composed made drainage difficult and the frequent showers turned it quickly into mud. The surest way of keeping personal clothing dry was to place it in a waterproof bag. Ground sheets were provided and the men slept eight to a standard bell tent. During this initial period much discomfort was endured.

The construction of hutted camps was commenced forthwith and ultimately the whole garrison, with the exception of a few small detachments, moved into them. The Nissen hut was fitted with concrete ends each with two windows. The huts were banked up at the sides with rubble to a height of four feet. Bunks were arranged around the sides of the hut with their axes parallel to the axis of the hut itself. There were five double-tiered 6-foot bunks on either side.

WATER SUPPLIES

The piped supply from glacial water with reservoirs on the high ground was soft and pure. By routine order the use of well and stream water as drinking water unless chorinated or boiled was forbidden.

CONSERVANCY

The standard urinal was a soakage pit 4 ft. × 4 ft. × 4 ft. with four funnels made out of petrol tins and inset to a depth of 18 in. into the soakage pit. These funnels gave protection from the wind during the act of micturition and came to be known as 'Iceland Lilies'. Because of the wind a stout screen of flattened petrol tins was necessary. The scale was one pit per 250 men. In the hutted camps the usual concrete trough urinal came into use.

The usual box latrine was provided. The disposal of excreta presented many difficulties; the trench and the pit method could not be adopted because of the nature of the ground. To begin with disposal by tipping into the sea was the rule, but this led to much fouling of the shore. Septic tanks consisting of a concrete rectangle 3 ft. 6 in. × 12 ft. 6 in. × 5 ft. in sets of three were then tried, the effluent passing into a bed filled with loose lava rock and thence into a stream. It was found necessary to add water in considerable quantities in order to dilute the contents of the tank.

In outlying detachments a novel type of chemical closet was designed. In its original form it consisted of a cylindrical 50-gallon drum, 34 in. high and with a diameter of 22 in. A square of 18 in. was cut out and over it a wooden fly-proof seat was fitted. In one end of the drum a half-inch pipe was inserted and bent to form a siphon. When in use this siphon pipe was over a 20-gallon drum sunk into the ground. Into the 50-gallon drum two gallons of 5 per cent. sodium hydroxide were poured. The level of the contents of this drum rose until it was above the opening of the siphon pipe. A bucket of water poured quickly into the closet then initiated siphonage. The contents of the 20-gallon drum were got rid of by burial or sea-tipping.

A large central incinerator of the beehive type was built of turfs and stone and the refuse brought to it by lorry. Later all the large camps were provided with concrete incinerators of the Horsfall type.

RATIONS

The dietary was on the Northern Climates ration scale, with a total calorie value of 5,276 per day. In March 1941 it was agreed that a calorie value of 3,570 per day in summer and 3,970 in winter was adequate. Ascorbic acid tablets (25 mg.) were issued thrice weekly.

CLOTHING

Basic Scale			Icelandic Scale		
Anklets web .	. pr.	1	Coat tropal . .		1
Battle dress suits	.	2	Jerkin leather . .		1
Boots ankle .	. pr.	2	Boots field pattern and		
Cap field service	.	1	loofah socks .	. pr.	2
Greatcoat .	.	1	Sleeping bag . .		1
Overalls . .	. pr.	1	Blankets . .		2
(on special duty)			Goggles snow	. pr.	1
Shoes canvas .	. pr.	1	Stockings footless	. pr.	2
Drawers woollen long	pr.	2	Socks heavy, natural		
Vests woollen	. pr.	2	grease	. pr.	4
Gloves knitted	. pr.	1	Cap fur . . .		1
Jersey pullover	.	1	Boots rubber knee	. pr.	1
Cap comforter	.	1	Gloves: three compart-		
Shirts . .	.	3	ment . .	. pr.	1
Socks . .	. pr.	3	Overgloves .	. pr.	1
Towels . .	.	2	Trousers oilskin	. pr.	1
			Sou'westers when required		

The coat tropal was made of canvas with oiled silk interlining and sheepskin inner lining with a high collar of thick kapok. The boots F.S. were of thick chrome and of a size sufficient to allow three pairs of socks to be worn. Laundry was carried out by civilian contract.

SICK PARADE STATE

This was consistently low but showed the usual rise with the increase of time spent overseas.

Rough Averages. Number per 10,000 *Strength*

July 1940 .	. 195	January 1941	. 268
August .	. 154	February .	. 313
September .	. 179	March .	. 309
October .	. 166	April . .	. 331
November .	. 207	May . .	. 308
December .	. 246	June . .	. 332

The peak was reached in the week ending July 20, 1941, when the figure was 374 per 10,000 (37·4 per 1,000). There was no parallelism between the curve of the temperature and the curve of the Sick Parade State.

HOSPITAL BEDSTATE

The curve corresponded closely with that of the Sick Parade State. The greatest number of occupied beds was in the winter period with its peak at February 14, 1941, of 2·48 per cent. This is a remarkably low figure when it is noted that owing to the lack of facilities all cases

15

requiring treatment in bed for more than forty-eight hours were hospitalised.

PRINCIPAL DISEASES AFFECTING THE TROOPS

Respiratory. The common cold was prevalent, with peaks in August, November and January.

Tonsillitis was not as common as was expected. It was thought that the larva dust raised by the winds might yield a dust infection, but there was no evidence of this.

Tracheitis and bronchitis were common.

Intestinal. Cases of diarrhoea and enteritis were not common and nothing of the nature of an epidemic occurred.

Bones, Joints, Muscles, Areolar Tissue. Inflammatory joint conditions were of frequent occurrence. The traumatic form was to be expected among troops undertaking very heavy work on rough ground. Fibrositis, lumbago and cervical pain were common.

Integumental. Impetigo was persistently troublesome and *Tinea cruris* common. Scabies was well under control and pediculosis was rare.

Venereal Disease. The incidence of gonorrhoea was persistently and exceptionally low. The disease was notifiable in the civilian population and treatment compulsory. There was no commercialised prostitution in the country and no brothels. Syphilis in the civilian population was exceedingly rare. The few cases that occurred among the troops were men who had brought their disease with them.

Infectious Diseases. There was no *rubella* in Iceland at the time of the arrival of 'Alabaster' Force. Thereafter there was a mild epidemic, both in the troops and in the civil population.

Mental Disorders. The occasional psychotic was revealed. The conditions of service, and particularly the duration of stay, in Iceland were such that there was no obvious deterioration of the mental health of the troops.

Frostbite. No true instance of frostbite among the troops occurred in spite of the inclemency of the climate. It was possible for the troops to take good care of themselves and they were regularly well fed, well clothed and well sheltered and were not called upon to endure exposure and too great fatigue.

THE FAROES

Lovat Scouts, 637 strong, accompanied by 131 R.A. and R.E. personnel, landed at Thorshavn on the Faroes on May 25, 1940. No R.A.M.C. officer was attached to this small force but an A.D. Corps officer possessing a medical degree was, and he served in a dual capacity. He established a small hospital in a convent in Thorshavn, evacuating patients requiring attention beyond his means to the civil hospital. In November the strength of the garrison was increased by the arrival of 96 Scouts and 252 R.A. and R.E. personnel. At this time the average daily sick rate was 1·5 per cent.

In January 1941 the strength of the garrison rose to 1,600 and an additional medical officer, a corporal and 5 privates R.A.M.C. and a motor cycle for the S.M.O. arrived.

In May 1942 there occurred a disturbing outbreak of food poisoning, 47 cases; its cause was traced to a particular package of porridge oats which contained barium carbonate, 16 per cent.

In July 9 Fd. Hosp. (50 beds) arrived, to be followed in October by 4 Fd. Hosp. and a dental centre.

In February 1944 the R.A.F. took over from the Army and 9 Fd. Hosp. was disbanded and transformed into the Military Hospital, Faroes Islands. This continued to serve the garrison until June 1945.

STATISTICAL DATA RELATING TO MORBIDITY IN ICELAND AND FAROES

The relative morbidity and relative casualty rates of the troops in Iceland and the Faroes are shown in Tables 37–40.* Comparison between these and those for troops in the United Kingdom revealed that:

1. psychiatric disorders were relatively far less common both in Iceland and the Faroes than in the United Kingdom;
2. accidental injuries formed roughly the same constant proportion of all admissions to medical units in Iceland as in the United Kingdom. In the Faroes they were more common but became relatively less so as the occupation progressed, probably for the reason that in the beginning a great deal of heavy constructional work was undertaken;
3. if all cases of urethritis are regarded as gonorrhoea the relative contributions of the two principal venereal diseases in northern climates—gonorrhoea and syphilis—was 2·2 per cent., well below the 6·5 per cent. of the United Kingdom in 1943;
4. a high incidence of balanitis, associated with a high rate of operation for phimosis, was possibly attributable to climatic conditions unpropitious to punctilious personal hygiene;
5. the relative incidence of sinusitis was exceptionally high and was not associated with a conspicuously high incidence of otitis media and externa.

---

*These tables are taken from the Statistical Report on the Health of the Army 1943–45.
Relative Morbidity Rate—percentage of cases with a given diagnosis among total sick cases during a given period.
Relative Casualty Rate—percentage of casualties of a given specification among all cases in a given period, including injuries in addition to sick.

In interpreting these rates it is necessary to remember that many of the conditions that were hospitalised in Iceland were such as would have been treated in a C.R.S. in the United Kingdom.

TABLE 37

Iceland, 1940–1942; R.M.Rs. and R.C.Rs.; British O.Rs.

	1940		1941				1942	
Disease	July to Sept.	Oct. to Dec.	Jan. to Mar.	April to June	July to Sept.	Oct. to Dec.	Jan. to Mar.	April to June
(a) RELATIVE MORBIDITY RATES:								
Tonsillitis and pharyngitis .	5·8	10·1	10·8	7·0	9·0	7·8	10·6	7·0
Bronchitis . . .	9·4	9·9	7·8	6·5	5·1	7·0	6·2	4·6
Boils and carbuncles . .	8·2	7·0	8·3	8·9	10·2	7·5	6·9	5·4
Impetigo	2·8	4·9	6·0	8·0	7·1	7·9	4·8	5·0
Dyspepsia and gastritis .	4·3	4·3	2·5	4·0	3·7	5·4	5·7	3·8
Influenza	5·8	1·9	5·9	0·5	1·2	1·0	1·6	2·7
Hernia	2·4	5·2	2·3	2·5	1·0	1·3	0·7	1·4
Rheumatic conditions:								
Non-articular . .	4·3	2·5	2·4	3·6	2·3	5·7	4·0	4·5
Articular . . .	—	0·3	0·2	0·6	0·1	0·6	0·3	0·2
Appendicitis . . .	3·9	2·6	2·8	3·0	2·9	2·3	0·8	2·2
I.D.K.	3·0	2·2	2·5	2·4	2·0	1·2	1·0	2·2
Scabies	5·4	5·4	0·1	—	0·1	2·2	2·3	7·8
Peptic ulcers . . .	2·3	1·1	2·1	2·0	3·3	2·2	1·9	1·3
Urethritis—all . . .	2·1	2·1	1·4	1·5	3·8	1·6	1·5	1·1
All psychiatric disorders .	1·5	1·6	2·0	1·5	2·0	2·1	3·1	2·2
Common cold . . .	0·6	1·1	2·3	2·0	2·0	3·0	2·1	3·4
Pneumonia . . .	1·3	1·2	1·8	2·1	1·0	1·5	1·4	1·4
Otitis media and externa .	1·7	1·6	1·2	1·9	2·6	2·7	1·5	1·1
Arthritis and synovitis .	1·1	0·9	1·1	2·3	1·7	1·4	1·6	0·6
Sinusitis	1·7	0·7	1·8	1·1	2·2	1·7	1·5	1·1
Diarrhoea, enteritis and food poisoning . . .	1·1	1·0	1·4	1·6	2·4	1·3	1·1	0·8
Haemorrhoids . . .	1·1	1·0	0·7	2·3	1·0	0·7	0·6	2·1
Varicose veins . . .	0·6	1·1	0·8	1·5	1·5	3·0	2·7	2·6
Neoplasms . . .	0·9	1·0	1·1	1·0	1·3	0·7	1·1	0·8
Tuberculosis: Pulmonary .	0·2	0·7	0·9	1·3	0·5	0·8	1·3	1·0
Other .	0·4	0·4	0·2	0·1	0·2	0·1	0·1	0·2
Balanitis	0·6	0·1	1·0	0·5	0·7	0·6	0·2	—
Syphilis	0·4	0·9	0·1	0·8	0·7	—	0·5	0·3
All other diseases . .	27·2	27·5	22·8	29·3	28·4	27·0	33·2	33·0
All diseases . . .	100	100	100	100	100	100	100	100
Number of cases . .	(466)	(810)	(995)	(796)	(886)	(1,095)	(1,057)	(625)
(b) RELATIVE CASUALTY RATES:								
All diseases . . .	90·0	86·3	86·7	85·2	86·5	87·7	88·8	81·1
All injuries . . .	10·0	13·7	13·3	14·8	13·5	12·3	11·2	18·9

TABLE 38

Iceland, 1940–1942; Annual R.M.Rs. and R.C.Rs.; British O.Rs.

Disease	July 1940 to June 1941	July 1941 to June 1942
(a) RELATIVE MORBIDITY RATES:		
Tonsillitis and pharyngitis . .	8·9	8·8
Bronchitis	8·3	5·8
Boils and carbuncles . . .	8·1	7·6
Impetigo	5·8	6·3
Dyspepsia and gastritis . . .	3·6	4·8
Influenza	3·4	1·5
Hernia	3·1	1·1
Rheumatic conditions: Non-articular	3·0	4·2
Articular .	0·3	0·3
Appendicitis	3·0	2·0
I.D.K.	2·5	1·5
Scabies	2·3	2·7
Peptic ulcers	1·9	2·3
Urethritis—all	1·7	2·0
All psychiatric disorders . .	1·7	2·4
Common cold	1·7	2·6
Pneumonia	1·7	1·3
Otitis media and externa . .	1·6	2·1
Arthritis and synovitis . . .	1·3	1·4
Sinusitis	1·3	1·6
Diarrhoea, enteritis and food poisoning	1·3	1·4
Haemorrhoids	1·2	1·0
Varicose veins	1·0	2·5
Neoplasms	1·0	1·1
Tuberculosis : Pulmonary . .	0·8	0·9
Other . . .	0·3	0·1
Balanitis	0·6	0·4
Syphilis	0·5	0·4
All other diseases	28·1	29·9
All diseases	100	100
Number of cases	(3,067)	(3,663)
(b) RELATIVE CASUALTY RATES:		
All diseases	86·7	86·5
All injuries	13·3	13·5

TABLE 39

Faroes, 1941–1944; R.M.Rs. and R.C.Rs.; British O.Rs.

Disease	Oct. 1941 to Sept. 1942	Oct. 1942 to Sept. 1943	Oct. 1943 to Sept. 1944
(a) RELATIVE MORBIDITY RATES:			
Common cold	3·9	10·0	7·7
Boils and carbuncles . .	12·7	10·0	6·8
Scabies	9·4	8·4	10·8
Tonsillitis and pharyngitis . .	8·2	7·6	6·0
Bronchitis	6·4	4·3	2·3
Impetigo	1·5	3·8	4·5
Dyspepsia and gastritis . .	4·9	3·7	4·8
Rheumatism: Non-articular . .	4·2	2·7	1·7
Articular . . .	0·6	1·0	0·9
Diarrhoea, enteritis and food poisoning	2·1	2·6	2·3
All psychiatric disorders . . .	1·5	2·5	2·0
Urethritis—all . . .	2·4	2·4	2·5
Appendicitis	0·6	2·4	2·6
Hernia	2·7	2·2	2·0
Arthritis and synovitis . .	1·5	2·0	0·6
Varicose veins . . .	—	1·6	2·0
I.D.K.	0·6	1·1	2·6
Otitis media and externa . .	1·2	1·1	2·3
Haemorrhoids . . .	1·8	1·0	2·6
All other diseases . . .	33·3	29·6	32·9
All diseases	100	100	100
Number of cases . . .	(330)	(1,138)	(352)
(b) RELATIVE CASUALTY RATES:			
All diseases	79·7	84·4	85·2
All injuries	20·3	15·6	14·8

TABLE 40

All Hospital Admissions; Iceland 1940–1942 and Faroes 1942–1943; Crude M.M.Rs. per 1,000; British O.Rs.

	Iceland						Faroes			
	1940		1941		1942		1942		1943	
	All dis-eases	All in-juries	All dis-eases	All in-juries	All dis-eases	All in-juries	All dis-eases	All in-juries	All dis-eases	All in-juries
Jan.	—	—	18·1	2·8	15·0	2·1	—	—	20·1	2·7
Feb.	—	—	19·5	3·2	20·4	2·2	—	—	29·2	3·0
March	—	—	19·0	2·8	21·0	2·8	—	—	20·1	3·0
April	—	—	13·6	2·9	19·9	3·4	—	—	15·9	2·8
May	—	—	13·0	2·3	11·6	4·3	—	—	16·8	5·2
June	—	—	14·6	2·1	16·3	3·9	—	—	14·0	3·0
July	2·5	0·9	12·8	2·3	—	—	—	—	17·0	4·5
August	15·5	2·0	13·3	2·1	—	—	—	—	17·4	4·5
Sept.	17·9	1·3	11·5	1·5	—	—	—	—	20·3	3·0
Oct.	17·2	2·7	12·9	1·8	—	—	10·6	3·1	—	—
Nov.	18·4	2·4	18·8	3·0	—	—	13·6	2·8	—	—
Dec.	12·3	2·7	15·9	2·0	—	—	13·6	1·0	—	—

Crude M.M.R. = Crude Mean Monthly Rate, a rate that has not been standardised with respect to age.

CHAPTER 4

THE CAMPAIGN IN LIBYA—1940-43
C. August 1942 – January 1943
General Alexander

Précis

THE SITUATION in Russia had now become desperate. Sevastopol had fallen and the Germans were advancing rapidly on Voronezh. In order to relieve the pressure on Russia, an Anglo-American invasion of the Cherbourg peninsula was contemplated. The decision was ultimately reached that the invasion of France must be postponed and that in the place of this there should be an invasion of North-West Africa combined with an advance westward from Egypt.

In Egypt the antagonists were concerned with problems of re-equipment and reorganisation. The advantages were with Middle East Command, and so Marshal Rommel, seeing that the odds against him were increasing, decided to attack. At this time the front occupied by Eighth Army—the Alamein Line—was remarkable in that it rested on two unattackable flanks, the sea in the north and the Qattara depression in the south.

On the night of August 30–31 Marshal Rommel attacked, his aims being the annihilation of Eighth Army and the conquest of Egypt. This attack failed. After this battle of Alam el Halfa the initiative passed to General Montgomery.

By October Eighth Army was ready to strike. It was now definitely superior both in numbers and in armament, while the position occupied by the Axis force could not be held securely by the numbers available. General Montgomery decided to attack the Axis line a few miles south of the coast, for the reason that if this were successful it would cut off the enemy centre and right from the coastal road, the sole line of supply and retreat. At the same time a subsidiary attack was to be launched against the Axis right flank. XXX Corps in the north on a front of four divisions was to cut two lanes through the minefields. Along these X Corps was to pass to protect XXX Corps from the enemy's armour. Meanwhile XIII Corps in the south would launch the diversionary attack.

The attack itself was heralded by a long preliminary aerial bombardment of minefields, gun positions, dumps and depots. It opened on October 9 and lasted until the 23rd, by which time the Axis air forces in Africa were grounded. Then at 2140 hours on the 23rd nearly 1,000 guns opened fire on a six mile front and twenty minutes later, under a full moon, the infantry went in. By 0530 hours on the 24th one of the lanes on XXX Corps front was fully cleared. The first objective, Miteiriya Ridge, was partly occupied. The diversionary attack in the south by XIII Corps was not successful and 7th Armoured Division was withdrawn.

On October 24 XXX Corps consolidated its position. On the following day General von Stumme, commanding the Axis forces, was killed and on the 26th Marshal Rommel, returning hurriedly from Germany, concentrated his armour, previously disposed more or less evenly along the whole front. On the 27th the Axis armour attacked in the north but was repulsed.

General Montgomery now regrouped, XIII Corps being placed on the defensive, X Corps being withdrawn and XXX Corps used to deepen the salient.

On the 28th Marshal Rommel attacked once more, sending half his armour to relieve 164th Light Africa Division which by this time was partly cut off by Australian 9th Division in the north. Heavy fighting continued until November 1. On the following day XXX Corps advanced still further on a 4,000 yards front and at last penetrated the last of the minefields. 1st and 10th Armoured Divisions of X Corps then moved forward to engage the Axis armour and a violent armoured battle was fought about Tel el Aqqaqir on the 3rd. The Axis forces began to disengage and, abandoning the greater part of their right wing, retreated westward. Eighth Army reoccupied Mersa Matruh on the 7–8th.

In this fashion ended the battle of El Alamein, the most decisive land battle yet won by the Allies in this war. Eighth Army losses were 13,500 killed, wounded and missing and 432 tanks disabled. The Axis losses were indeed severe for in this battle four German and eight Italian divisions ceased to exist as effective fighting formations.

The retreat of the Axis forces from Mersa Matruh to the Mareth Line in Tunisia was orderly, the pace of the pursuit being dictated by the weather and by supply difficulties. Tobruk was entered by Eighth Army on December 13, Gazala on the 14th, Benghazi on the 20th, Sirte on the 25th and Tripoli on January 23. During the course of this 1,400 miles advance the Axis forces vainly attempted to stand at El Agheila, Buerat and Homs.

Below is a glossary of Arabic words used in the remaining chapters of this volume.

Abd . . . A servant of	Alam (Alem) . A directional
Abiar (Abar) . Plural of Bir	beacon. A land-
Ain . . . A fountain	mark

Bir . . . A surface water collecting point —a well

Dar . . . A house

Deir . . . A depression

Gabr . . A sepulchre

Gebel . . A mountain. A hill

Ghot (Got) . A low lying basin

Hagfet (Hazfet) . A windy place. A hill protecting from the wind

Ilwet . . A height

Maaten . . A well

Mersa . . An anchorage

Munquar . . A cliff

Nizwet (Nezuet) . A pile of rocks excavated from the Abiar, often covered with sand, to form a mound some 10 feet high

Qabr (Kabr) . A tomb

Qur, Qurat, Qaret A high piece of ground

Ras . . . A headland or cape

Sidi . . . A saint

Tel . . . A hill

Wadi . . . A dry watercourse

(i)
The Alamein Line

On August 13, 1942, General Alexander took over command of M.E.F. from General Auchinleck and General Montgomery assumed command of Eighth Army.

The Alamein Line had been constructed in 1941. Its strength lay in the fact that its southern end rested on the Qattara Depression. This stretched from the region of Siwa in the south to a point about 160 miles north-west of Cairo and 90 miles south-west of Alexandria. Its bed consisted of salt marsh and quicksand and was therefore a complete barrier to all mechanical transport and to large organised bodies of troops. Along its northern edge steep cliffs descended from an average height of 600 ft. above sea level to more than 200 ft. below sea level. Its eastern end reached to within 40 miles of the sea.

The prepared defences consisted in the main of four defended localities, at El Alamein, Deir el Shein, Qaret el Abd and on the Taga Plateau on the edge of the Qattara Depression itself. But in August 1942 all of these save the Alamein 'box' were in the possession of the Axis forces.

The Alamein position, now held by Eighth Army, was therefore not the Alamein Line. Its left flank did not rest on the Qattara Depression. The position ran from the shore to the road and railway about two miles west of the Alamein railway halt and thence southwards along the small ridges of Tel el Eisa and Tel el Makhkhad which had been captured in July. From this small salient the line then bent back to the perimeter of the Alamein box and thence to the eastern end of the Ruweisat Ridge. From this it continued southwards across flat ground, interrupted here and there by depressions, of which the Deir el Munassib was the largest. Thence it ran to a point just north-west of Qaret el Himeimat, from which the Barrel Tracks ran eastwards to Cairo. Behind the south-east portion of the Ruweisat Ridge ran a second and higher one, the Alam el Halfa Ridge on which a strong brigade position had been constructed. This position was covered by a triple minefield which extended from the coast in the north to the Taga Plateau.

XIII Corps, with 7th Armoured and N.Z. 2nd Divisions, was occupying the southern sector and XXX Corps, with Australian 9th, Indian 5th, and S.A. 1st Divisions, the northern sector of the Alamein position. Indian 5th Division now consisted of Ind. 5th, 9th and 161st Inf. Bdes. and its field ambulances were 10, 20, 26 and 75 Lt.

General Alexander, being of the opinion that Marshal Rommel would decide to attack before the Commonwealth forces in the Western Desert attained their full strength, chose to meet this attack on the Alamein position. He therefore modified the arrangements made by his predecessor for the defence of the Delta. He immediately placed Headquarters X Corps at the disposal of Eighth Army. On August 15 he also placed 44th Division u/c Eighth Army. Its divisional H.Q. with 131st and 133rd Inf. Bdes. relieved Ind. 21st Bde. on the Alam el Halfa Ridge and 132nd Bde. came u/c N.Z. 2nd Division.

10th Armoured Division (8th and 9th Armd. Bdes.) had not so far been employed; its tanks had been handed over to 1st and 7th Armd. Divisions to make good their losses. But now 8th Armd. Bde. had been re-equipped and so 10th Armd. Division, less 9th Armd. Bde., was sent up to the forward area, there to absorb 22nd Armd. Bde. of 7th Armd. Division and to take up positions at the western end of the Alam el Halfa Ridge between 44th and N.Z. 2nd Divisions. 23rd Armd. Bde., previously dispersed in support of XXX Corps, was now concentrated on the left flank of this corps so that it could serve also as a reserve for XIII Corps.

THE BATTLE OF ALAM EL HALFA

Shortly after midnight on August 30–31 the Axis forces attacked. Two diversionary attacks were made on XXX Corps front, against Australian 9th Division in the coastal sector and against Indian 5th Division positions on the Ruweisat Ridge. The first was entirely unsuccessful but the second gained ground. However, a counter-attack at first light on the 31st restored the position.

At 0100 hours on the 31st the main attack developed in the south, between Deir el Munassib and Himeimat. Strong tank columns penetrated the weakly defended minefields to come immediately under heavy

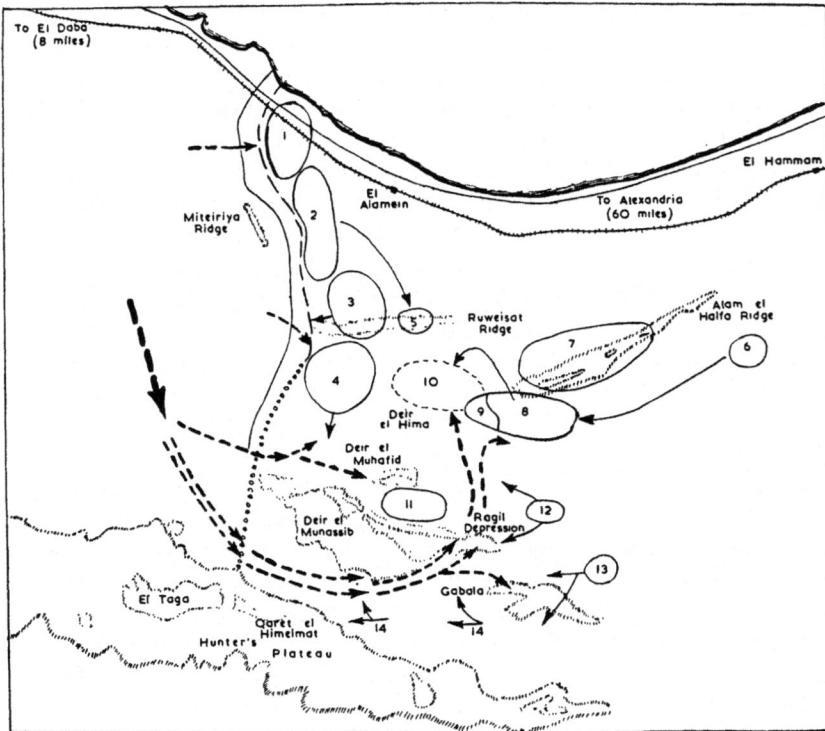

FIG. 21. The Battle of Alam el Halfa.
1. Australian 9th Division.
2. South African 1st Division.
3. Indian 5th Division.
4. New Zealand 2nd Division.
5. One Brigade of S.A. 1st Division, September 1.
6. One Brigade of 50th Division, September 2.
7. 44th Division.
8. 10th Armoured Division.
9. 22nd Armoured Brigade.
10. Second position of 10th Armoured Division.
11. 7th Armoured Division.
12. 7th Motor Brigade, August 31–September 1.
13. 4th Lt. Armoured Brigade, August 31–September 1.
14. 7th Armoured Division, September 2–5.

fire from the guns of N.Z. 2nd Division and of 7th Armoured Division.
Then at 1530 hours the Axis armour began to move from Deir er Ragil
and at 1700 hours was in contact with 22nd Armd. Bde. to the south of
the Alam el Halfa Ridge. During the night of August 31/September 1
the Royal Air Force pounded the enemy concentrations.

The enemy armour could now adopt one of two plans; it could
advance against the Alam el Halfa position or, alternately, it could skirt
this widely and then move northwards to cut the communications of

Eighth Army. General Montgomery expected Marshal Rommel to adopt the first of these plans and had made his own tactical arrangements accordingly. Marshal Rommel did as he was expected to do. As soon as this became evident, General Montgomery moved 10th Armd. Division to the area between Halfa Ridge and N.Z. 2nd Division in the Alamein Line proper. At the same time he withdrew S.A. 1st Bde. from S.A. 1st Division and sent it on to the Ruweisat Ridge, moved 151st Inf. Bde. of 50th Division from Amiriya to the position vacated by 10th Armd. Division and placed 23rd Armd. Bde., u/c XIII Corps, on the Ruweisat Ridge in the positions regained by the counter-attack of Indian 5th Division.

The Axis armour thrust against 22nd Armd. Bde. and at once became exposed to the great concentration of the guns of XIII Corps. The Axis armour withdrew but later in the day moved forward again, once more to achieve nothing. During the night XIII Corps guns and the Royal Air Force bombarded the Axis leaguers while in the north the Australians made a raid and gained ground, only to lose it again.

7th Armd. Division had, according to instructions, avoided such action as might have led to serious loss, withdrawing when strongly pressed. Nevertheless, all through the day this division had continually harassed the Axis armour on the flank and in the rear.

On September 2 Marshal Rommel changed his tactics. He ceased to attack and was preparing to withdraw. He massed his armour south of Alam el Halfa and threw a screen of A/T guns in front of it. At the same time he took care to keep clear the corridor that had been made through the minefield.

It was not General Montgomery's intention to do that which was expected of him. He preferred to attempt to close the gap in the minefield in the rear of the Axis armour. XIII Corps was set this task. Ind. 5th Inf. Bde. from XXX Corps and S.A. 2nd Inf. Bde. from reserve were placed u/c XIII Corps for this purpose and H.Q. X Corps was ordered forward in case it might prove to be possible later to make an immediate advance to El Daba.

At dawn on September 3 the Axis forces had withdrawn from contact with Eighth Army and were moving south and south-west, followed tenaciously by the armoured cars of XIII Corps. In the afternoon 7th Armd. Division moved to the area between Gabala and Himeimat. At 2230 hours N.Z. 2nd Division with 132nd Inf. Bde. of 44th Division under command attacked southwards as the first step in the closure of the gap in the minefields. Bitter fighting ensued. N.Z. 5th Bde. gained its objectives but N.Z. 6th Bde. and 132nd Inf. Bde. did not. Fighting continued during September 4, 5 and 6. It was clear that the Axis Commander meant to retain possession of this portion of the western edge of the minefield.

So on the 7th General Montgomery decided to let him have it and the fighting died down. The Axis forces had gained a thin strip of desert four or five miles in extent running from the eastern end of Deir el Munassib to include the useful high ground at Himeimat. The price paid for it included 53 tanks, 700 and more soft-skinned vehicles, 30 field guns and 40 A/T guns. The Commonwealth losses included 110 officers and 1,640 O.Rs. (Br. 984, Aust. 257, N.Z. 405, S.A. 65, Ind. 39), 67 tanks, one A.A. and 15 A/T guns. But by now replacement and reinforcement for Eighth Army were far easier and more speedy than they were for the German and Italian formations.

MEDICAL COVER

The number of casualties incurred—1,750 killed, wounded and missing—is an indication that in this battle the medical services were not taxed. No problems arose and nothing occurred that merits special description.

At Gharbaniyat, the Railhead, were:

> 14 C.C.S. (Army C.C.S.)
> 14 Fd. Amb. (dealing with minor cases and local sick)
> 20 (Ind.) Fd. Amb. (for Indian casualties)
> 6 F.S.U.
> 3 F.T.U.
> 1 Mob. Ophthal. Unit
> Mob. Dental Centre
> H.Q. 1 M.A.C. (Army M.A.C.)

From Gharbaniyat evacuation was by road, by 1 M.A.C., to hospitals in Alexandria; by rail, by ambulance train, to hospitals in the Canal Area and by air, by D.H. 86 ambulance aircraft and by empty transport planes (Bombays) returning from L.G. 28, adjacent to 14 C.C.S., to Heliopolis. Minor sick, exhaustion cases and N.Y.D.(N) cases were routed from Gharbaniyat to the Army rest station established by 200 Fd. Amb. at Ikingi Maryut. Forward filters for minor sick were established by XXX Corps using field ambulances of Australian 9th, South African 1st and Indian 5th Divisions. The forward M.D.Ss. of XXX Corps were cleared by 16 M.A.C.

The distribution of the medical units of XIII Corps and the system of evacuation are shown in Figure 22. With 7th Armd. and N.Z. 2nd Divisions at this time were Greek 1st Independent Bde. and Fighting French 2nd Bde. The M.D.Ss. of all these formations were cleared by 2 M.A.C. Twenty cars of the A.F.S. were attached to N.Z. 2nd Division.

XIII Corps had prepared an alternative maintenance axis eastwards along Grid 87 Northing to join the main Alexandria–Cairo road near Km. 136 where a company of 200 Fd. Amb. and two sections of 151

Lt. Fd. Amb. were functioning as staging units. A further staging post, provided by 15 C.C.S., was available near Km. 51 on the Alexandria–Cairo road.

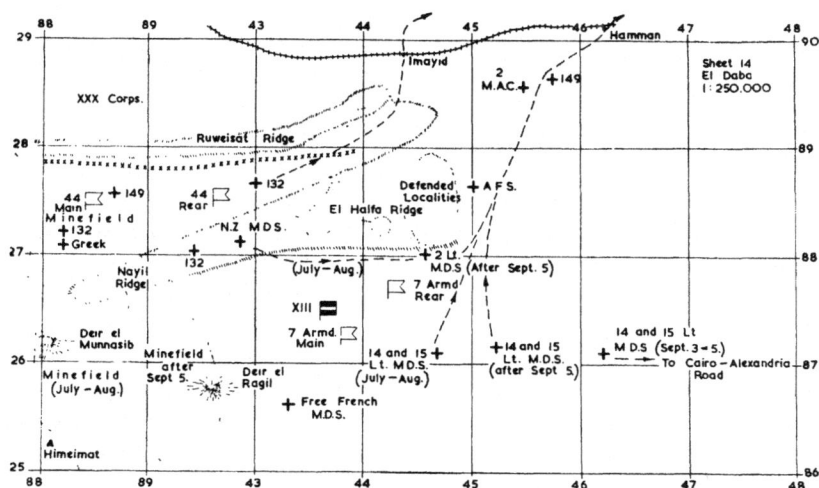

FIG. 22. XIII Corps. Medical Cover. July–September, 1942.

With the exception of a few casualties from 7th Armd. Division out on the extreme left flank of XIII Corps which were evacuated along the Grid 87 route, evacuation was through 14 Fd. Amb. and 14 C.C.S. 4 (N.Z.) Fd. Amb. dealt with 504 casualties during September 4/5.

PREPARATION FOR THE OFFENSIVE

After the battle of Alam el Halfa the German-Italian Army of Africa went at once on to the defensive while Eighth Army began to prepare for the offensive. It was decided to use XXX and XIII Corps as infantry formations and X Corps as an armoured *corps de chasse*. X Corps was therefore assembled some fifty miles in the rear of the Alamein position, there to undergo strenuous training for the rôle it was to play in the coming battle. It was now composed of 1st and 10th Armd. Divisions and N.Z. 2nd Division reorganised and strengthened by the addition to it of 9th Armd. Bde. in place of a third infantry brigade. 8th Armd. Division already lacked its infantry brigade and its 24th Armd. Bde. was now transferred to 10th Armd. Division.

On September 8, 51st (Highland) Division moved up from Cairo into reserve on the Alam el Halfa Ridge. 44th Division had been moved from the Alam el Halfa Ridge into the Alamein Line, there to relieve N.Z. 2nd Division which had been withdrawn to join X Corps.

On September 10, H.Q. Indian 4th Division with Ind. 7th Inf. Bde. relieved H.Q. Indian 5th Division and Ind. 9th Inf. Bde. on the Ruweisat Ridge. H.Q. 50th Division with 69th Inf. Bde. moved from Alexandria to join its 151st Inf. Bde. in Eighth Army Reserve. To this division was added Greek 1st Bde. Later this division relieved 44th Division in XIII Corps sector and at the same time Fighting French 1st Bde. moved up to come u/c 7th Armd. Division. 7th Motor Bde. passed from 7th to 1st Armd. Division so that 7th Armd. Division now consisted of 4th Lt. Armd. and 22nd Armd. Bdes.

Ind. 9th Inf. Bde. moved with H.Q. Indian 5th Division to the Delta. This division took no further part in the campaign in Libya. Ind. 5th Inf. Bde. joined Indian 4th Division, as did also Ind. 161st Inf. Bde. With the division to the Delta went 10 and 26 (Ind.) Fd. Ambs. The field ambulances of Indian 4th Division now were 17, 26 and 75 Lt.

It was known that, possibly owing to an inadequate medical and sanitary organisation, especially among the Italians, diseases such as dysentery and infective jaundice were extraordinarily prevalent among the Axis troops. Some units, it was gathered, had lost from these causes up to as much as 25 per cent. of their strength.

THE BATTLE OF ALAMEIN

TACTICAL PLAN

(1) XXX Corps, using Australian 9th and 51st (Highland)Divisions, would drive due west on a line roughly parallel to and below the Tel el Eisa Ridge, to form a corridor through the Axis belt of wire, mines and defended localities.

(2) At the same time XXX Corps, using N.Z. 2nd Division and S.A. 1st Division, would attack in a south-westerly direction, secure the Miteiriya Ridge and establish a second corridor through the Axis defensive belt.

(3) When these two corridors had been made through the full depth of the Axis defensive belt, X Corps, using 1st and 10th Armd. Divisions, would pass through and take up positions at the western ends of the corridors.

(4) Thus covered by X Corps, XXX Corps would then proceed methodically to destroy the enemy forces in the defensive belt and between the two corridors and on either flank, northwards from Tel el Eisa and southwards from the Miteiriya Ridge.

(5) XIII Corps with u/c 7th Armd. Division and 44th and 50th Divisions would attack in the southern sector, this attack being

synchronised with that of XXX Corps in the north. French 1st
Bde. would assault Qarat el Himeimat and 44th Division,
supported by 7th Armd. Division would attack north of

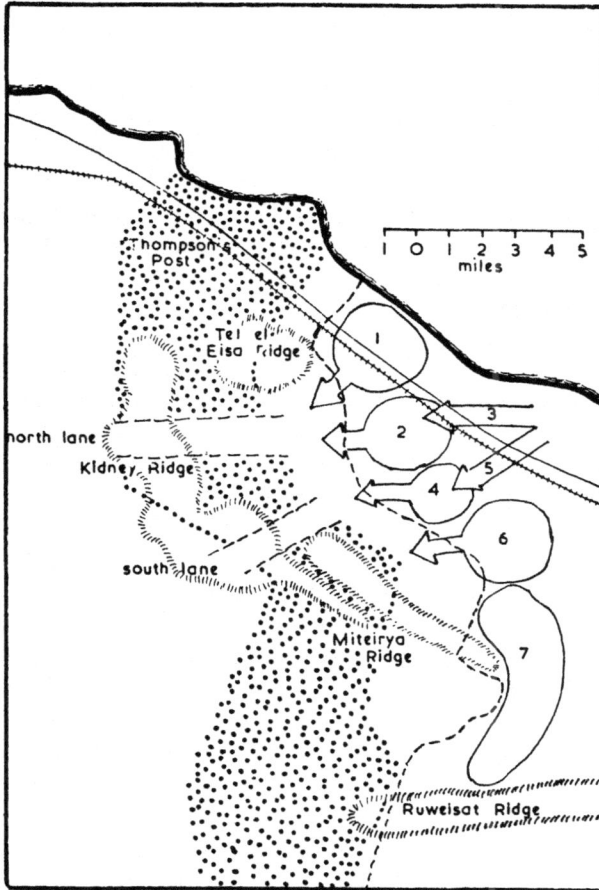

FIG. 23. The Battle of Alamein. XXX Corps Tactical Plan.
1. Australian 9th Division.
2. 51st Division.
3. 1st Armoured Division.
4. New Zealand 2nd Division.
5. 10th Armoured Division.
6. South African 1st Division.
7. Indian 4th Division.

Himeimat in an attempt to breach the Axis defensive belt and in
order to pin down as much Axis armour as possible.

(6) Should the Axis defensive belt be pierced, 4th Lt. Armd. Bde.
would pass through and move on El Daba.

16

MEDICAL TACTICAL PLAN

The Army Commander on October 18 communicated his plans for the battle to D.D.M.S. Eighth Army. He expected that the battle would last about seven days and that there would be about 10,000 casualties (excluding killed, missing and sick).

The terrain behind the Alamein Line was mostly barren rocky desert scarred with deep *wadis* and hillocks in the south and with sand dunes and low-lying soft sand in the north. Over it travel by car was difficult and rough, so that tracks were constructed with the help of bulldozers which helped both to make motor traffic easier and also to provide definite axes for the different formations. These tracks, indicated by signs such as Sun, Moon, Star, Hat, Boat, Bottle, all ran parallel to the coastal road. At intervals they were intersected at right angles by cross communications which were given such names as Springbok, Sydney and Bombay Roads.

For the evacuation of wounded in comfort the only possible way was by the coastal road and railway. The Alamein position had been stabilised for some time and it was therefore possible to make thorough preparation for the reception and treatment of casualties. An ample supply of ambulance cars together with lorries for walking wounded was made available to the field ambulances and each battalion was given an ambulance car before the battle. Moreover, there were ambulance cars and trucks available in large numbers for the further evacuation of casualties to the hospital area at Gharbaniyat and from there to Alexandria, the railhead, or to the L.Gs.

A group of M.D.Ss. had been established round Alamein's railway station and alongside the main road nearby. To these casualties would be evacuated from the forward medical units. Cases of primary injury, including abdominal wounds, were to be operated on at this level and so F.S.Us. and F.T.Us. were attached to the different M.D.Ss. for this purpose.

Three underground dressing stations had been constructed and these were staffed by British, Australian and South African units. Another Australian unit was situated nearby on the coast, while the N.Z. M.D.S. was between the railway and the road, one and a half miles from the station.

The medical tactical plan was for existing field medical units of XIII Corps and XXX Corps to deal with all casualties, X Corps opening only the essential minimum number of such units.

The arrangements that had been made for the battle of Alam el Halfa remained in force for the battle of Alamein.

The Army medical concentration area was near ambulance railhead at Gharbaniyat Station, thirty miles behind the dressing stations.

This area was under H.Q. 86 Sub-area and was near landing grounds L.G. 28 and L.G. 171.

In this area were:

10 C.C.S.
2 (Ind.) C.C.S.
1 (N.Z.) C.C.S. Hy. Sec. (Lt. Sec. with X Corps)
2/3 (Aust.) C.C.S. Hy. Sec. (Lt. Sec. with XXX Corps)
6 F.S.U.
3 F.T.U.
5 Mob. Bact. Lab.
1 Mob. Ophthal. Unit
14 Fd. Amb.
1 M.A.C.
18 M.A.S.
7 Adv. Depot Med. Stores

The units in this medical centre were required to expand: 10 C.C.S. and 2 (Ind.) C.C.S. to accommodate 425 each; 2/3 (Aust.) C.C.S. and 1 (N.Z.) C.C.S., lacking their light sections, to provide 300 and 350 beds and stretchers respectively. 14 Fd. Amb. was required to sort and to relay the serious cases to the C.C.Ss., to treat the minor cases, holding up to 400, and evacuating these continuously to 200 Fd. Amb. at Ikingi Maryut. The Indian C.C.S. was to take all the Indian cases not requiring operative treatment. 10, 2/3 (Aust.) and 1 (N.Z.) C.C.Ss. were to receive the major cases in rotation. Extra tentage would be supplied but would not be erected before the opening of the offensive. At Ikingi Maryut 200 Fd. Amb. was functioning as a convalescent centre. Though in 65 Sub-area, this unit was under the administrative control of A.D.M.S. 86 Sub-area.

Evacuation by Road:

(1) In the first phase of the battle the forward limit of Army responsibility would be the Army C.C.S. area at Gharbaniyat, where accommodation for 2,400 casualties would be provided. Evacuation of the Army C.C.Ss. would be by 6 and 18 M.A.S., 1 M.A.C. and one platoon of 3-ton lorries.

(2) All casualties from divisional field ambulances to the medical concentration centre by cars of the M.A.Cs. with X, XIII and XXX Corps.

(3) Minor cases (with the exception of those mentioned in (4) and (5) below) from 14 Fd. Amb. by 3-ton lorry to 4 Lt. Fd. Amb. at Abd el Qadir and thence by rail in ordinary passenger coaches to hospitals in the Delta, by-passing Alexandria.

(4) All Australian, Greek and Free French casualties by road by 1 M.A.C. from Gharbaniyat to their own hospitals at the base.

(5) Exhaustion cases and others suitable for retention in Army Area until returned to their units to 200 Fd. Amb. at Ikingi Maryut (Army rest station) or to divisional rest stations by the sea in divisional and corps rear areas.

Evacuation by Rail:

Lying and severe sitting cases by ambulance train from Amb. R.H. at Gharbaniyat to the Delta, the Canal Area and Palestine, under arrangements made by D.M.S., G.H.Q.

Evacuation by Air:

Selected severe cases by two D.H. 86 ambulances from L.G. 171, near the Army Medical Concentration Area, to 7 A.G.H. at Buseili (Australians), to 3 N.Z.G.H. at Helwan (New Zealanders) and to Heliopolis (others). Transport aircraft (Bombays) were also available for the flight to Heliopolis.

The M.A.Cs. were allotted as follows:

Army	1 M.A.C.
	6 and 18 M.A.S.
	'B'. Sec. 'Y'. M.A.C.
	Sec. N.Z. M.A.C.
X Corps	11 and 15 A.F.S. A.C.C.
XIII Corps . . .	2 M.A.C.
	9 M.A.S. (Indian 4th Division)
XXX Corps . . .	16 M.A.C.

In so far as XIII Corps was concerned it was arranged that:

(1) One M.D.S. for each of 7th Armd., 44th and 50th Divisions would be established.

(2) 7 F.S.U. and 25 F.T.U. would be attached to the M.D.S. of 7th Armd. Division.

(3) Both 44th and 50th Divisions would keep one M.D.S. closed in close proximity to the one that was open. The closed M.D.Ss. would be ready to reinforce the open ones or else to move forward with their divisions.

(4) If the two light field ambulances of 7th Armd. Division moved forward with their division, a M.D.S. of 44th Division would remain *in situ* and to this the F.S.U. and the F.T.U. would be transferred.

(5) 14 C.C.S., 186 Fd. Amb., 4 F.S.U. and 6 F.T.U., together with the French A.C.L., would form XIII Corps dressing station— 'Bluebeard' Dressing Station—on the Blueband Track.

(6) 2 M.A.C., supplemented by twenty-five cars of 'Y' M.A.C. from Army reserve and twenty-three 3-ton lorries from various medical units of XIII Corps, would be used for the collection and conveyance of walking wounded and would be divided into two echelons. One of these would operate between the divisional

M.D.Ss. and 'Bluebeard' Dressing Station and the other from 'Bluebeard' Dressing Station to Railhead at Gharbaniyat.

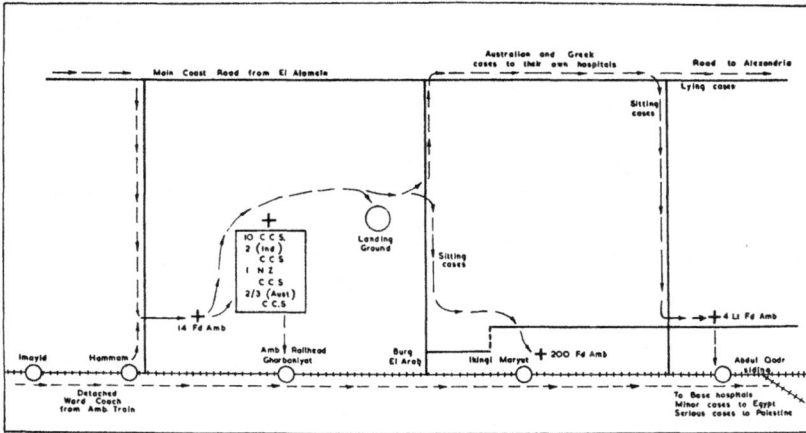

FIG. 24. The Battle of Alamein. Medical Tactical Plan.
The Evacuation Chain.

1. To 14 Fd. Amb.
2. Thence to C.C.S. Group, Amb. railhead, landing ground, or onwards by road, according to the nature of the case.
3. Of those sent by road, the less serious to 200 or to 4 Lt. Fd. Amb., the more serious to hospitals in the Alexandria area; Australian, Greek, and French cases to their own hospitals.

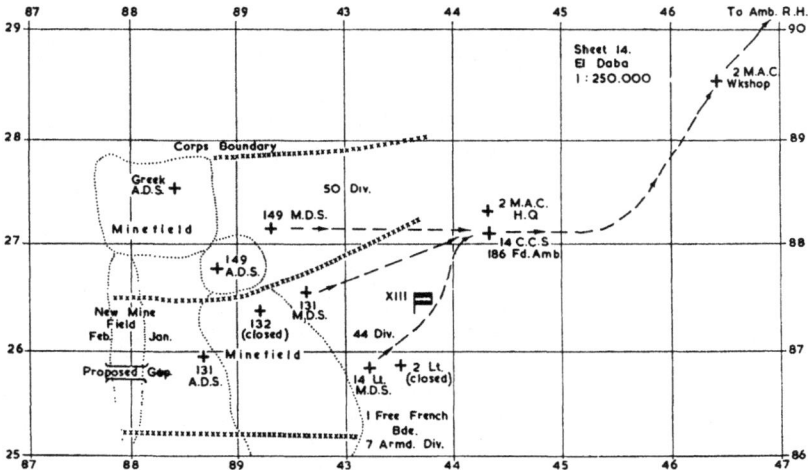

FIG. 25. XIII Corps. Medical Cover. October 1942.

44th Division, 131 and 132 Fd. Ambs.
50th Division, 149 and 186 Fd. Ambs.
  7th Armd. Division, 2 Lt. and 14 Lt. Fd. Ambs.
2 M.A.C.

'Bluebeard' Dressing Station.
14 C.C.S. French A.C.L. and
  186 Fd. Amb.

(7) When it had become possible to make use of a railway ambulance coach from Imayid Station this would be used for the evacuation of serious abdominal cases.

The distribution of the medical units of XIII Corps at this time is shown in Figure 25.

THE ASSAULT

At 2140 hours on the night of October 23–24, 1942, the thousand guns of Eighth Army opened on the Axis battery positions. At 2200 hours the bombardment was switched on to the forward Axis positions and the assaulting divisions of XXX and XIII Corps advanced to the

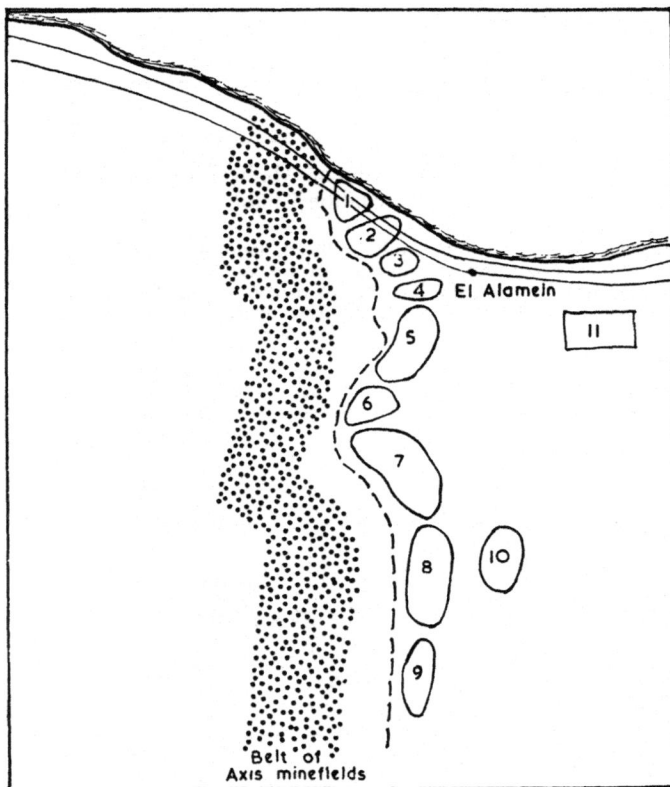

FIG. 26. The Battle of Alamein. Distribution of formations of Eighth Army before the attack, October 23, 1942.

1. Australian 9th Division.	7. 50th Division.
2. 51st Division.	8. 44th Division.
3. N.Z. 2nd Division.	9. Free French Brigade.
4. S.A. 1st Division.	10. 7th Armoured Division.
5. Indian 4th Division.	11. X Corps, 1st and 10th Armoured
6. Greek Brigade.	Divisions.

attack. All through the night heavy fighting continued and resistance stiffened. By 0530 hours on the 24th many of the objectives had been reached.

In the north Australian 9th Division had advanced some nine thousand yards from its start line. N.Z. 2nd Division had occupied the western end of the Miteiriya Ridge. In the centre 51st Division had been checked fifteen hundred yards short of its objectives and S.A. 1st Division had failed to reach the Miteiriya Ridge by about five hundred yards. The progress of X Corps had been thereby much delayed. However, the southern corridor was completed by 0630 hours and 9th Armd. Bde., u/c N.Z. 2nd Division, and 10th Armd. Division made their way to the eastern slopes of the Miteiriya Ridge. The northern corridor was not completely opened and 2nd Armd. Bde. remained within it.

At 1500 hours on the 24th the attack along the northern corridor was resumed and 51st Division and 1st Armd. Division broke through. By 1800 hours 2nd Armd. Bde. was well to the west of the Axis defensive belt.

During the night of 24–25th, 44th Division succeeded in making a small breach in the minefields in the southern sector. The French Brigade had gained the escarpment south of Himeimat but was quickly forced off it.

On the morning of October 25 General Montgomery, wishing to conserve 7th Armd. Division, ordered XIII Corps to break off action in the south. In the north XXX Corps had made a breach six miles wide and 1st and 10th Armd. Divisions had successfully withstood a number of fierce counter-attacks. So, in order to exploit these successes in the north, Australian 9th Division was ordered to attack northwards towards the sea. This attack by Australian 26th Bde. was launched during the night of October 25–26 and was completely successful. A diversionary attack by 69th Inf. Bde. of 50th Division in the Deir el Munassib was not pressed.

On the 26th, S.A. 1st and N.Z. 2nd Divisions gained a further thousand yards of ground in front of the Miteiriya Ridge and 7th Motor Bde. established itself on the much contested Kidney Ridge. During the night of 26–27th, S.A. 1st and N.Z. 2nd Divisions gained further ground and 51st Division strengthened its forward positions.

On the 27th General Montgomery proceeded to assemble a striking force to be used in the final and conclusive assault. 1st and 7th Armd. Divisions were withdrawn into reserve and to 7th Armd. Division 131st Inf. Bde. of 44th Division was added for use as lorried infantry. N.Z. 2nd Division was also withdrawn into reserve. Into its place in the line S.A. 1st Division sidestepped and into the place thus vacated by S.A. 1st Division, Indian 4th Division was inserted (Fig. 27). To N.Z.

2nd Division were added 151st Inf. Bde. of 50th Division and 152nd Inf. Bde. of 51st Division and also, for certain specific operations, 4th Lt. Armd. Bde. of 7th Armd. Division, 23rd Armd. Bde. and 133rd Inf. Bde. of 44th Division.

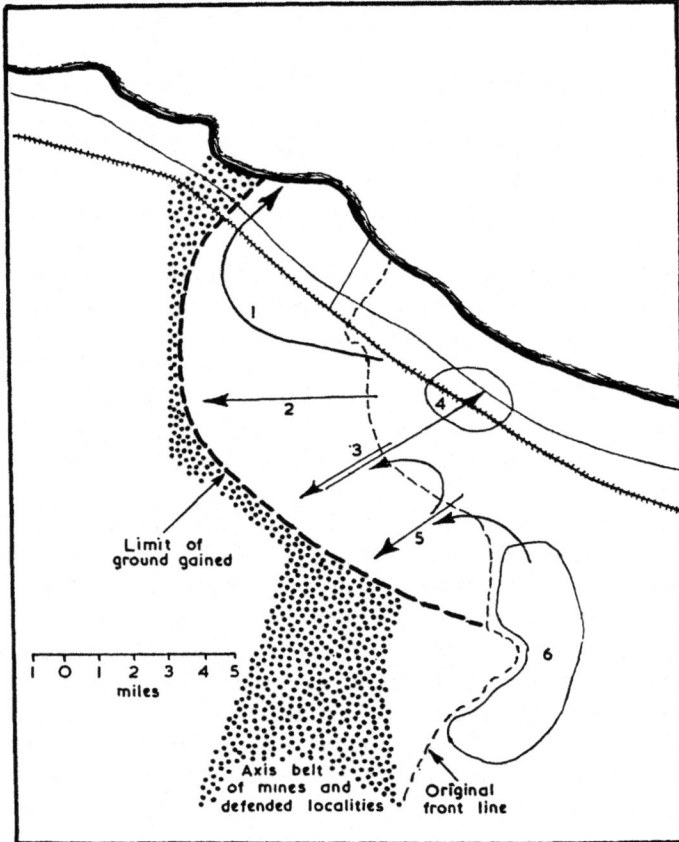

FIG. 27. The Battle of Alamein. Progress during the period October 23–31, 1942.

1. Australian 9th Division.
2. 51st Division.
3. N.Z. 2nd Division.
4. N.Z. 2nd Division, second position.
5. S.A. 1st Division.
6. Indian 4th Division.
(The New Zealand Division pulled out of the line; S.A. 1st and Indian 4th Divisions side-step to the right.)

During October 27 and 28, while Eighth Army paused to regroup, the Axis forces spent their strength in heavy but unsuccessful assaults upon Kidney Ridge.

OPERATION 'SUPERCHARGE'. TACTICAL PLAN

At 2200 hours on October 28, Aust. 20th Inf. Bde. of Australian 9th Division attacked northwards, to achieve partial success. Though checked, it held on to its gains. On the night of October 30–31, Aust. 26th Inf. Bde. struck north-east and drove towards the sea, cutting off

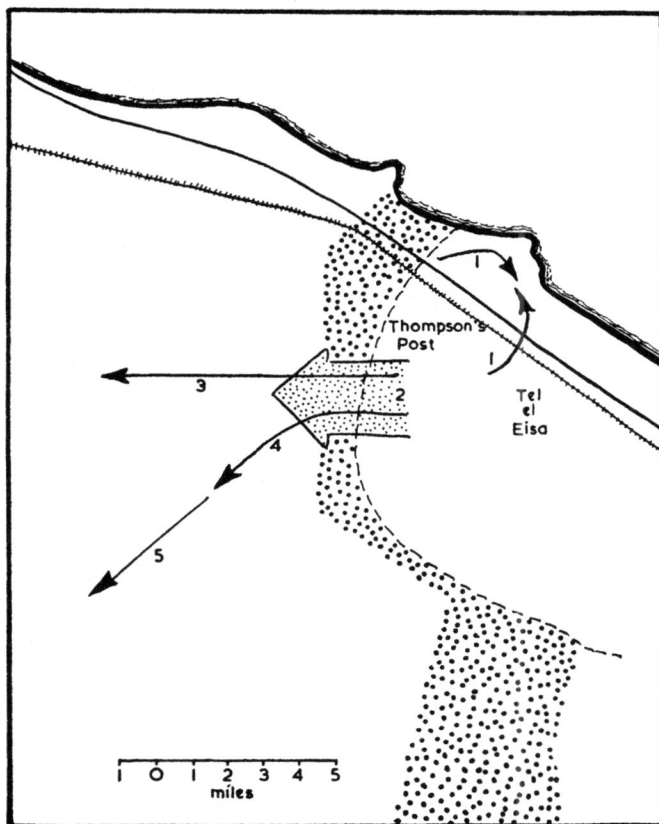

FIG. 28. The Battle of Alamein. Operation 'Supercharge'.
November 2, 1942.
1. Australian 9th Division, November 3.
2. N.Z. 2nd Division, November 2.
3. 1st and 10th Armd. Divisions, November 4.
4. 51st and 5th Bde. of Indian 4th Division, November 3.
5. N.Z. 2nd and 7th Armd. Divisions, November 4.

four Axis battalions in the coastal positions. The Germans reacted immediately and fiercely and devoted their major attention to this threat.

General Montgomery, therefore, modified his plans. He moved the main axis of the break-through farther to the south so that the blow would now fall upon the Italians.

(1) 151st and 152nd Inf. Bdes. (of 50th and 51st Divisions respectively) supported by 23rd Armd. Bde. would drive a lane through the new Axis positions, clearing the minefields as they went.

(2) N.Z. 28th Bn. (Maoris) and 133rd Inf. Bde. of 44th Division would assault and capture a number of defended localities on the flank of this advance.

(3) 9th Armd. Bde., following closely upon the infantry, would then penetrate the screen of guns along the Rahman track.

These formations would be u/c XXX Corps and their actions would be co-ordinated by N.Z. 2nd Division.

(4) X Corps would then follow up with 2nd and 8th Armd. Bdes. of 1st Armd. Division leading. These brigades would, if necessary, fight their way through.

(5) When the way was clear two armoured car regiments would move through to raid the Axis rear areas while N.Z. 5th and 6th Bdes. would concentrate in the salient thus formed and be prepared to exploit success.

(6) The attack would be supported by a strong concentration of artillery fire, first on enemy gun positions, then on enemy positions in the path of the advance and, finally, in support of 9th Armd. Bde. in its attack on the Rahman track.

THE ATTACK

At 0105 hours on November 2 the attack was launched, and by 0600 hours 151st Inf. Bde. had reached its objectives. By 0630 hours 152nd Bde. had done likewise. 9th Armd. Bde., however, had been greatly delayed by mines and gunfire and could not reach the Rahman track till dawn. For two long hours this brigade fought it out with the Axis armour and at considerable loss held open the end of the salient created by 151st and 152nd Inf. Bdes. Through it then passed on the 4th, 1st Armd. Division, ultimately to compel the Axis armour to withdraw. This was the turning-point of the battle, and indeed of the whole campaign in Libya.

During the night of November 2–3 the Axis forces began to break contact. The Royal Dragoons made their way round the Axis gun screen in the dawn mist and began at once to raid, harass and destroy. 7th Motor Bde. pressed on towards Tel el Aqqaqir and beyond and 8th Armd. Bde. succeeded in reaching the Rahman track. Then S.A. 4/6th Armd. Car Regt. slipped past the Axis gun line and raced to join the Royal Dragoons at El Daba.

To hurry the withdrawal and to turn withdrawal into headlong rout it was necessary to dislodge the Axis forces occupying the positions along the Rahman track, for only when this had been done could the armour advance. At 0230 hours on the 4th, Indian 5th Inf. Bde. attacked these

positions and by dawn had thrust the Axis gun screen back. Then X
Corps took up the chase while Australian 9th Division and 51st Division
moved forward.

Soon after first light on the 4th, 1st, 7th and 10th Armd. Divisions
crossed the Rahman track and headed for the coast road at Ghazal and
thence for Matruh. At Ghazal they were checked by an A/T gun screen.
N.Z. 2nd Division with 4th Lt. Armd. Bde. on its right flank swept
round the southern end of this screen and headed for the escarpment
at Fuka.

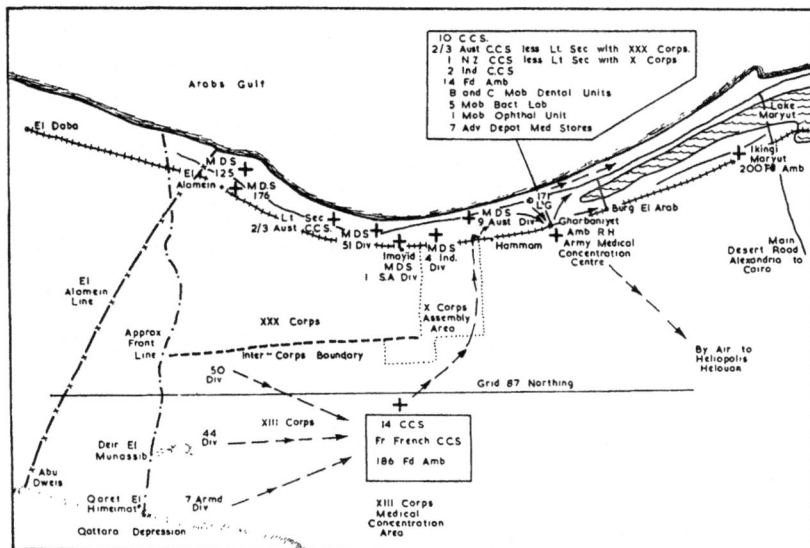

FIG. 29. The Battle of Alamein. Medical Arrangements.

On the battlefield itself the Italian formations, being without transport or, if with transport, being without fuel, waited to surrender. Less
than a third of the original Axis force at Alamein got away. Over 30,000
were taken prisoner; of these 10,000 were Germans. 450 Axis tanks had
been destroyed. Commonwealth losses were some 13,500 killed,
wounded and missing, just under 8 per cent. of the total force engaged.

THE BATTLE OF ALAMEIN—MEDICAL COVER

The arrangements made proved to be entirely satisfactory. Casualties
were less than the estimate in spite of the fierce nature of the fighting.
During the period October 24–30, 7,500 battle casualties and just over
3,000 sick passed through the Army C.C.S. group at Gharbaniyat.

Because this battle will long be studied by military historians it is
desirable to examine in some detail the experiences of the medical
units of the different formations that were involved.

X CORPS

The divisions which served in X Corps during the battle were 1st, 7th, 8th and 10th Armoured and N.Z. 2nd Divisions. The corps medical units were

12, 151 Lt. Fd. Ambs.	11, 15 A.F.S. A.C.C.
8 (S.A.) and 15 C.C.Ss.	1, 2, 5 F.S.Us.
Lt. Sec. 1 (N.Z.) C.C.S.	7 F.T.U.
6 and 8 Lt. Fd. Hyg. Secs.	

Every medical unit was holding the M.E.F. scale of transfusion materials and 7 F.T.U. was the distributing centre. All medical units were holding 14 days supplies of consumable medical stores and all had blankets and stretchers additional to the normal scale; 200 stretchers and 400 blankets per division were being maintained in each of X Corps' F.M.Cs. and could be drawn upon through D.D.M.S. All A.F.Vs. had first-aid outfits which included tubunic morphia or craquettes. Benzedrine tablets ('Pep' tablets) had been supplied to divisions and could be issued under arrangements made by A.Ds.M.S. (1st and 10th Armd. Divs. 25,000 tablets apiece; 8th Armd. Div. 2,000; N.Z. 2nd Div. 21,000; Corps tps. 1,000). Medical comforts were accumulated in the F.M.Cs. and arrangements were made with the R.A.S.C. for the supply of extra water to the medical installations (5 gal. a day to each R.A.P.; 10 gal. to each A.D.S.; up to 100 to each M.D.S. and up to 200 to each C.C.S.). The field hygiene sections were amalgamated so that their workshops could function at the highest pressure. The wireless net was completed. D.D.M.S. was linked (continuous watch) with the light field ambulances and the C.C.Ss. and (hourly 'flick') with A.Ds.M.S. 1st, 8th and 10th Armoured Divisions. Three medical officers, each with his own jeep and self sufficient for a period of three days, were appointed as liaison officers between D.D.M.S. Corps on the one hand and D.D.M.S. Eighth Army and A.Ds.M.S. divisions on the other. The value of the wireless net and of this liaison mechanism was soon to be abundantly demonstrated, for when the break through occurred they became the only means of communication between D.D.M.S. and the fast-moving units.

While the component divisions of X Corps were in their staging and assembly areas, evacuation was direct to the medical concentration centre at Gharbaniyat under arrangements made by the A.Ds.M.S. Evacuation from 24th Armd. Bde. was the responsibility of A.D.M.S. 10th Armd. Division; from H.Q. 8th Armd. Division that of A.D.M.S. 1st Armd. Division. A.F.S. cars attached to these divisions were used for this purpose. Evacuation was along Sun, Moon, Star, Barrel, Boat and Hat tracks but because these quickly became inches deep in dust the cars headed for the coast road as soon as possible.

When the divisions moved forward into battle A.Ds.M.S. divisions kept D.D.M.S. Corps informed of the location of the rearmost divisional M.D.S. D.D.M.S. then arranged for the clearance of these and interposed the corps light field ambulances in the evacuation chain as this lengthened. Initially the F.S.Us. were with the light field ambulances and the C.C.Ss. but as soon as the A.Ds.M.S. were satisfied that forward surgery was feasible in their areas D.D.M.S. sent the F.S.Us., self sufficient for three days, forward. 7 F.T.U. was attached to 15 C.C.S., by which unit small indents for medical supplies were met. It was kept closed during the battle, ready for a forward leap to El Daba. On November 3, 8 (S.A.) C.C.S. was cleared by ambulance coach from Imayid Station and prepared to move forward.

The only written instruction issued by D.D.M.S. Corps was that which dealt with the medical tactical plan. Thereafter instructions were given verbally, in person, through a liaison officer or over the wireless net.

The strength of the corps at the battle of Alamein was 46,700. The number of casualties admitted to the corps medical units from October 11–November 21 was 4,013.

Week Ending	Battle Casualties	Sick	P.o.W. Battle Casualties	Sick
October 17 .	2	811	—	—
,, 24 .	85	359	—	—
,, 31 .	384	468	9	—
November 7	406	435	33	15
,, 14	140	317	60	12
,, 21	76	390	6	5
	1,093	2,780	108	32

4,013

The nature of the wounds was as follows:

	Head and Neck	Chest	Abdomen	Limbs	Shoulders	Multiple
G.S.W. .	57	35	32	284	10	33
B.W. .	24	7	6	90	2	7
S.W. .	64	17	20	121	7	21
Bayonet and unclassified .	23	8	6	81	2	8
Burns .	13	—	—	20	—	2
Blast .	24	—	—	2	—	1
M.W. .	9	—	1	6	—	10
	214	67	65	604	21	82

AUSTRALIAN 9TH DIVISION*

It has been recounted how, when the situation in Syria had become stabilised, Australian 9th Division returned to Egypt in July 1942 to take its prominent part in the operation at Tel el Eisa.

In preparation for the coming offensive there was much movement of Australian medical units from Syria and Palestine to Egypt. Thus 2/7 A.G.H., exchanging equipment with 3 B.G.H., moved from Sidon to Buseili, there to be expanded to 1,000 beds. 2/4 (Aust.) Con. Depot moved from Sidon to Tolumbat, near Aboukir. 2/3 (Aust.) C.C.S. had returned to Egypt with the division, as had also its three field ambulances, 2/3, 2/8 and 2/11 (Aust.) Fd. Ambs. 2/6 A.G.H. at Gaza in Palestine, the A.I.F. base, was also expanded to 1,500 beds.

It was appreciated that the coming battle would be very different from any thus far fought in this campaign. The distance between the furthest objective to be taken by the division was some 20 km. from the site where the M.D.S. was to be established. Furthermore, it was recognised that when X Corps passed through there would be such congestion that evacuation would be rendered exceedingly difficult.

It was therefore arranged to attach to each regimental medical officer four field ambulance other ranks to act as guides, to allot to each R.M.O. two vehicles (ambulance cars or lorries), to have field ambulance personnel following hard upon the heels of the R.M.Os. to comb the area for casualties that might have been missed, and to maintain liaison with the R.A.Ps. by frequent visits of field ambulance officers.

Each field ambulance entering the forward area was reduced to H.Q., one company and a mobile section of the remaining company. To serve the two brigades in the line the two field ambulances concerned combined; one served its own brigade and established a M.D.S. to serve both, the other served its brigade and cleared into the common M.D.S. It was agreed that A.D.Ss. should be few and rudimentary and that as far as possible evacuation should be direct from the R.A.Ps. to the M.D.S. where surgical teams would be available. As was usual in Australian formations in this campaign, the ambulance cars of the field ambulances were pooled.

The M.D.S. of 2/8 (Aust.) Fd. Amb. was to the north-east of Alamein in E.P.I.P. tents. A group of five tents, two for operating theatres, two for resuscitation and one for sterilisation, accommodated the surgical teams. Two other brigaded tents were used for dressings. Ambulance pits were dug. Small tents and tarpaulins provided other accommodation and three marquees were kept ready for emergencies.

The M.D.S. of 2/11 (Aust.) Fd. Amb., a little nearer the front line, was sited in undulating sand dunes near the shore. A tented resuscitation

---

*For a more comprehensive account the Official Australian Medical History should be consulted.

centre was provided and an Anderson shelter formed the operating theatre. This site, it was arranged, was to be taken over by Lt. Sec. 2/3 (Aust.) C.C.S. just before the battle opened. 2/11 (Aust.) Fd. Amb. therefore prepared another M.D.S. in partly finished dug-outs north of the coast road near Abiar el Shammama. To this M.D.S. a surgical team was attached.

2/3 (Aust.) Fd. Amb. expanded the divisional rest station at El Hammam to 240 beds and prepared to hold light sick up to 14 days. One company was kept on wheels ready to move forward.

The heavy section of 2/3 (Aust.) C.C.S. was brought forward from Sidi Bisher to the medical concentration centre at Gharbaniyat where it opened at its eastern end. Nurses joined the unit on October 21. The light section of this unit was placed under Australian 9th Division for administrative purposes and to it 2/4 (Aust.) Fd. Hyg. Sec. was attached.

A check post was established on the coast road about 8 miles west of Alamein Station to ensure the smooth flow of ambulance cars and to direct the distribution of casualties among the medical units so that none of these were overtaxed. At this check post were D.A.D.M.S., one other medical officer and a N.C.O. Near to it was the car park. As each loaded car or lorry passed through the post, a replacement was sent forward. A.D.M.S. Division was in telephonic communication with the check post and the car park.

Of the 32 pooled ambulance cars 5 were allotted to Aust. 24th Bde. on the coast to evacuate casualties to the M.D.S. of 2/8 (Aust.) Fd. Amb. Two were attached to the rest station of 2/3 (Aust.) Fd. Amb. The rest were in the car park. Each field regiment and each battalion of Aust. 24th Bde. provided a 30-cwt. or a 3-ton lorry for walking wounded. These vehicles did not enter the car park. In addition each field ambulance supplied eight lorries for walking wounded, each with an orderly, two stretchers and blankets.

The first convoy of casualties reached Hy. Sec. 2/3 (Aust.) C.C.S. at 0530 hours on October 24 and was diverted to 10 C.C.S. By 1500 hours the Australian C.C.S. had admitted 354 patients and had sent on 120 to 2/7 A.G.H.

By the 28th the medical units were in danger of becoming overtaxed and transfusion supplies were running short. Personnel of 7 Lt. Fd. Amb. were attached to 2/8 (Aust.) Fd. Amb. to help in the A.D.S. and the M.D.S.

On the 29th evacuation became exceedingly difficult in the forward areas owing to the great volume of traffic and to the hanging dust. 'A' Coy. 2/3 (Aust.) Fd. Amb. was sent forward to reinforce Lt. Sec. 2/3 (Aust.) C.C.S.

On the 30th, as the Australians advanced, a German dressing station was overrun. It lay between the stations of Tel el Eisa and Sidi Rahmar and consisted of a railway hut of six rooms. It was occupied by three German medical officers, a number of orderlies and wounded. The R.M.O. of Aust. 2/32nd Bn. set up his R.A.P. in this dressing station to be replaced later by a section of 2/11 (Aust.) Fd. Amb. To this dressing station the wounded of both sides were brought. Later the German medical staff were sent back to 2/11 (Aust.) Fd. Amb's. M.D.S. to help with Axis casualties but when they showed reluctance to treat the Italians among these they were sent to the cage. This 'block-house' then became an A.D.S. until November 2 when it was heavily shelled and had to be abandoned.

On November 4 the M.D.S. of 2/8 (Aust.) Fd. Amb. was occupied with the nursing of post-operatives and with the care of the local sick. 2/8 (Aust.) Fd. Amb. and 2/4 (Aust.) Fd. Hyg. Sec. were placed u/c Aust. 20th Bde. in case this was used in the pursuit. Lt. Sec. 2/3 (Aust.) C.C.S. was moved up to Matruh and its heavy section to Gerawla. On the 29th H.Q. Australian 9th Division moved back to Palestine.

In the 'dogfight' phase it was quickly noted that exhaustion and N.Y.D.(N) cases became increasingly common. The N.Y.D.(N) cases were cleared to the divisional rest station established by 2/3 (Aust.) Fd. Amb. on the coast. They could be sent back beyond this only by permission of A.D.M.S. A psychiatric first-aid post, the first official one of its kind in the A.I.F., was instituted at the rest station of 2/3 (Aust.) Fd. Amb. and quickly proved its worth.

In the event it proved possible to evacuate casualties from difficult and most dangerous areas fairly expeditiously. The interval between the time of wounding and that of admission to Lt. Sec. 2/3 C.C.S., six miles behind the M.D.S. of 2/11 (Aust.) Fd. Amb., was six and a half hours. The experience of this battle strongly indicated that not less than fourteen ambulance cars per field ambulance were needed and that adequate flagging of the evacuation routes was an essential feature of any evacuation scheme under such conditions. It was learned too that intercommunication between the various parts of the system could be improved greatly by the exchange of written messages sent by every vehicle moving between any two component parts of it.

The total Australian casualties in this battle were 449 killed, 2,032 wounded and 222 missing.

A.A.M.C. casualties in the Battle of Alamein were:

Killed		*Wounded*		*Missing*	
Officers	*O.Rs.*	*Officers*	*O.Rs.*	*Officers*	*O.Rs.*
3	10	6	46	—	4

After this battle Australian 9th Division moved back to Palestine and thence returned to Australia.

NEW ZEALAND 2ND DIVISION*

Two A.D.Ss. in the forward area served the two brigades and attached groups. Each R.A.P. had an ambulance car attached while the divisional cavalry had two. Eight ambulance cars from the inactive 4 (N.Z.) Fd. Amb. and fifteen from the A.F.S. were attached to the N.Z. division in addition to twelve trucks from the N.Z. A.S.C. for lightly wounded. The newly formed N.Z. section of the M.A.C. with twenty-three cars loaned from the B.R.C.S. was now available for use between the M.D.S. and C.C.S. These cars were not suitable for desert work but were of considerable value on the main road. The active M.D.S. had attached to it a N.Z. surgical team and extra personnel to enable it to undertake urgent surgery and to hold and nurse serious cases.

During the battle the N.Z. F.T.U. and the light section of 1 (N.Z.) C.C.S. were called up to join the divisional medical services. The M.D.S. of 5 (N.Z.) Fd. Amb. was established between the main coast road and the railway, one and a half miles east of Alamein station and just east of Springbok Road. It was therefore favourably placed in relation to the divisional axis which was on Star track.

When N.Z. 2nd Division went into the line on October 22, 5 and 6 (N.Z.) Fd. Ambs. provided A.D.Ss. to serve the brigades. An A.D.S. for 9th Armd. Bde., which was u/c N.Z. 2nd Division, and a second one for the 3rd echelon of this armoured brigade were provided by sections of 166 Lt. Fd. Amb. 4 (N.Z.) Fd. Amb. remained with N.Z. 4th Bde. at Maadi Camp but came forward on October 26 to open a divisional rest station near Gharbaniyat. To the M.D.S. of 5 (N.Z.) Fd. Amb. were attached 2 (N.Z.) Surgical Team and a surgical team from the light section of 1 (N.Z.) C.C.S.

The R.M.Os. used their attached ambulance cars to collect all accessible cases on the battlefield. From R.A.P. back to the A.D.S. evacuation was by car sent forward from the A.D.S. The minefields through which the advance had been made rendered the collection of wounded both difficult and dangerous. The division evolved a particular system of evacuation through these minefields. Casualties at the start line were collected by an ambulance that was stationed there. The troops had been instructed before the battle that should they become casualties they should make their own way back to one of the brigade axes, of which in the attack on Miteiriya Ridge there were two. S.Bs. also made their way back to these tracks. As soon as the first gap in the minefield had been made and was open, a convoy of ambulance cars was sent forward to clear the R.A.P. which had been established just beyond the first minefield. Thereafter the tracks were patrolled by ambulance cars up to the second minefield, and when this in turn had been cleared and

---

*For a more comprehensive account the Official New Zealand Medical History should be consulted.

17

was open the same procedure was adopted. Walking wounded, according to instructions, walked back to the first gap, from which directing signs led to the A.D.S. They were guided also by the C.M.P. As soon as it was safe to do so a red light was shown at the A.D.S. Before the light was shown guidance was given by word of mouth. The ambulance cars were instructed not to leave the lighted roads and casualties between the roads were brought to them by hand-carriage. The officer commanding the A.D.S. was required to use his judgment as to the number of ambulance cars he could send forward, lest by sending too many he should find himself unable to evacuate back to the M.D.S.

During the course of the action all the medical officers attached to the British Army units then serving with N.Z. 2nd Division became casualties and N.Z. medical officers took over their work. For the attack 'A' Coy. 5 (N.Z.) Fd. Amb. was located just off Star track behind a slight escarpment, actually in front of the guns. 'A' Coy. 6 (N.Z.) Fd. Amb. moved up Bolt track and was similarly in front of the artillery line. These companies moved to these sites just before the barrage opened and then dug in and sand-bagged the dressing stations.

The first casualties were admitted to the A.D.S. of 5 (N.Z.) Fd. Amb. at 2230 hours and to the A.D.S. of 6 (N.Z.) Fd. Amb. at midnight. A steady stream poured in during the night and the next day. At 0100 hours on the 24th ambulance cars began evacuating cases from the A.D.S. of 5 (N.Z.) Fd. Amb. to the M.D.S. of the same medical unit six miles away, five of these being along the road. Evacuation from the A.D.S. of 6 (N.Z.) Fd. Amb. to the M.D.S. of 5 (N.Z.) Fd. Amb. could not commence until first light on the 24th because of the densely packed armoured columns that were moving up.

The task of the forward ambulances working between R.A.P. and A.D.S. was a most difficult one. The tracks were ill-defined and were congested with armour. Later the task became easier when the tracks had been lighted and marked.

Casualties began to arrive at the M.D.S. of 5 (N.Z.) Fd. Amb. about 0030 hours on October 24 and the surgical team thereafter worked continuously for sixteen hours. In the first twenty-four hours of the battle the A.D.S. of 5 (N.Z.) Fd. Amb. dealt with 456 battle casualties and the A.D.S. of 6 (N.Z.) Fd. Amb. with 343. On the 24th 839 cases were dealt with by the M.D.S., and of these 504 were New Zealanders. On the 25th nearly 500 passed through and on the 26th a further 300.

At this point the amount of transport that had been made available proved to be insufficient and so on the morning of October 24 four extra cars were sent forward. Each R.M.O. of N.Z. 5th Bde. took an ambulance car forward with him and the A.D.S. of 5 (N.Z.) Fd. Amb. kept a further four cars in reserve. The 3-ton lorries that were to patrol the axis through the minefields to collect walking wounded were not allowed up until after dawn and their place had to be taken by an ambulance car which ran continuously from 0100 hours until 1200 hours. 3-ton lorries were used in the evacuation of casualties from A.D.S. to M.D.S., however. The turn-round of ambulance cars at the C.C.S. thirty miles away was proving to be somewhat tardy and measures had to be taken to speed it up.

On October 24 the surgical team from the light section of 1 (N.Z.) C.C.S. was attached to the M.D.S. of 5 (N.Z.) Fd. Amb. and played its part in the treatment of 839 cases in twenty-four hours. Throughout the night of October 24–25 and on the 25th the A.D.S. of 6 (N.Z.) Fd. Amb. dealt with large numbers of casualties, mostly from the British Army units. By 1400 hours on the 25th this A.D.S. had cleared its cases. Lt. Sec. 166 Fd. Amb. arrived at 1700 hours on the 25th to assist, but by this time the heaviest work was over. The total number of cases that had been admitted to the A.D.S. of 6 (N.Z.) Fd. Amb. by 0600 hours on the 26th was 600; that admitted by the A.D.S. of 5 (N.Z.) Fd. Amb. was 94 on the 25th, 68 on the 26th and 43 on the 27th.

For the attack by N.Z. 2nd Division, together with 151st and 152nd Inf. Bdes. from 50th and 51st Divisions, south of the Australian sector, A.D.M.S. N.Z. 2nd Division was responsible for the medical arrangements of the British units under the command of the N.Z. division. These were 9th Armd. Bde., 23rd Armd. Bde. and 151st and 152nd Inf. Bdes. Each of these had a medical unit, 166 and 7 Lt. Fd. Ambs. and 149 and 175 Fd. Ambs.

On the night of the attack, November 1–2, the engineers made a special dug-in site for the A.D.S. of 6 (N.Z.) Fd. Amb. The A.D.S. of 175 Fd. Amb. was on Double Bar track, 149 Fd. Amb. and 7 Lt. Fd. Amb.'s A.D.Ss. on Diamond track, two sections of 166 Lt. Fd. Amb. provided A.D.Ss. for 9th Armd. Bde., while the M.D.Ss. of 5 (N.Z.) Fd. Amb. and of 166 Lt. Fd. Amb. were together on the main road east of Alamein station.

All evacuations from the A.D.Ss. were to be to the M.D.S. of 5 (N.Z.) and 155 Fd. Ambs., serious cases going to the former to which two surgical teams were still attached. 2 (N.Z.) F.T.U. was sent up to the M.D.S. of 5 (N.Z.) Fd. Amb. from 1 (N.Z.) C.C.S. on November 1. The surgical policy was adjusted to the possibility of a break through, when N.Z. 2nd Division would go forward through the gap along with the armoured units of X Corps. It was decided to limit the work of the surgical teams at the M.D.S. of 5 (N.Z.) Fd. Amb. to the most serious cases demanding immediate surgery.

By 0500 hours on November 2 casualties were reaching the A.D.S. of 6 (N.Z.) Fd. Amb. and during the next two days there was a steady flow. By 0900 hours 77 casualties had been admitted to the A.D.S. of

6 (N.Z.) Fd. Amb., 50 to the A.D.S. of 175 and 120 to that of 149, and by 1400 hours a total of 302 had passed through the M.D.Ss. of 5 (N.Z.) Fd. Amb. and 166 Lt. Fd. Amb. on their way to the C.C.Ss. During the day the A.D.S. of 6 (N.Z.) Fd. Amb. dealt with 268 cases while the A.D.S. of 149 Fd. Amb. dealt with over 400. On November 3 casualties were less heavy, coming in the main from the armoured units; 115 were admitted to the A.D.S. of 6 (N.Z.) Fd. Amb.

The battle of Alamein is noteworthy in that for the first time a (N.Z.) C.C.S. functioned in battle as a complete unit, and also for the reason that the newly formed N.Z. F.T.U. was used for the first time. During the battle 1 (N.Z.) C.C.S. at Gharbaniyat dealt with a total of over 1,800 battle casualties.

The large majority of the New Zealand casualties were evacuated to the N.Z. base hospitals at Helwan and El Ballah. A few were admitted to the N.Z.G.H. then functioning at Beirut. In addition many were admitted to the British general hospitals in the Canal area and in Palestine.

The main lesson that was learned from the experiences at Alamein was that when the medical services were to be called upon to handle large numbers of casualties it was most desirable to concentrate the medical units concerned, especially those responsible for forward surgery. Such concentration allowed of the even distribution of surgical intervention between the M.D.S. group and the C.C.S. group. The use of a field ambulance in front of the C.C.S. group as a sorting centre and also as a treatment centre for the minor cases proved invaluable.

The Consulting Surgeon, G.H.Q., M.E.F., in considering the work of the medical services from his own point of view, records that 'abdominal cases were treated almost exclusively by the field surgical units, the surgeons of the C.C.Ss. and the surgical teams sent forward from the base hospitals. The results appear to have been better than in any previous campaigns. This very satisfactory state of affairs is only partly due to the short lines of evacuation, for under such conditions many hopeless cases reach the operating centre alive. Credit must also be given to the high standard of technical work among the forward surgeons, to the advanced sites at which they operated, often at some risk, to the provision of beds even at the M.D.S. and to the routine use of sulphadiazine, intravenous fluids and gastric suction after operating, and to the policy of retaining abdominal cases until they had established equilibrium. Field surgical units fully justified the foresight of those who planned them as a solution to the problem of primary surgery of wounded in mechanised warfare.'

51ST DIVISION

51st Division, recreated after the disaster at St. Valéry, reached Egypt from the United Kingdom in August 1942. Like many another formation the division paid heavy toll for its halt at Freetown—sixty-five cases of malaria with two deaths. On one of the ships that carried the division there were over 5,000 souls and there was no specialist

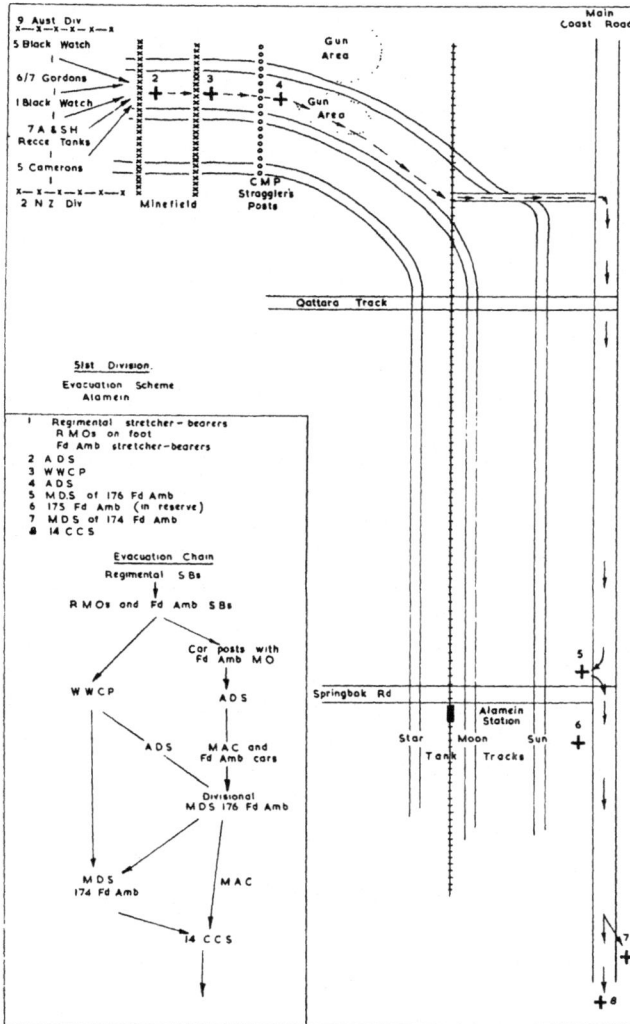

FIG. 30. The Battle of Alamein. 51st Division. Medical Cover.

surgeon aboard. A surgical team from 91 B.G.H. on another ship in the convoy had to be transhipped during the voyage to deal with three major operations.

After a period spent at Qassasin and Tahag and Mena Camp the division joined 'Deltaforce' for the defence of Cairo. Then early in

September it moved into the Alamein position. In the coming battle 51st Division's rôle was to be that of penetrating the enemy's position to a depth of six or seven miles on a three thousand yard front. This attack was to be made by 153rd and 154th Bdes., which would pass through 152nd Bde. in the Alamein Line.

It was recognized that the provision of adequate medical care would be difficult because of the conditions that would exist. The assaulting brigades were to make a rapid advance through thickly strewn minefields. Until proper vehicle gaps in the minefields had been made no ambulance cars would be able to move forward. When the armour began to move along Sun, Moon and Star tracks through the divisional sector there would surely be much interference with the evacuation of casualties. Casualties were expected to be very heavy since this was to be a frontal attack upon positions of great strength.

So it was that the scheme of evacuation depicted in Fig. 30 was devised. It is to be noted that the R.M.O. went into the battle on foot. With him went a N.C.O. and sixteen S.Bs. from the field ambulance. When possible a N.C.O. and two nursing orderlies R.A.M.C. followed up in the R.M.O's. truck. To each brigade H.Q. two medical orderlies with medical equipment were attached. Ambulance car posts, each under command of a field ambulance medical officer, moved as fast as possible along each axis, maintaining contact with the R.M.Os. The A.D.Ss. were established in the positions shown in the figure before D-day, but their existence was not made obvious until D-day itself.

To reinforce field ambulance transport, M.A.C. cars were then used to clear the A.D.Ss. and eighteen field ambulance 3-ton trucks were used to clear the walking wounded. A W.W.C.P. was established at the midpoint of the line of divisional stragglers posts and the C.M.P. aided in directing such casualties to this post.

The M.D.S. of 176 Fd. Amb., with 8 F.S.U. attached, opened in stone and concrete dug-outs near Alamein station. From this M.D.S. evacuation was by 16 M.A.C. to 14 C.C.S. at El Hammam. 174 Fd. Amb. established a M.D.S. for the lightly wounded and the exhausted on the coast just east of Bombay Road. 175 Fd. Amb. remained in reserve on wheels at Alem el Mihl.

A.D.M.S. was with main divisional H.Q. and was in telephonic communication with his field ambulances and his D.A.D.M.S. who was at rear divisional H.Q.

On the second day of the battle 175 Fd. Amb. was sent forward to join 174 Fd. Amb. which was becoming overtaxed.

These arrangements proved to be completely satisfactory. Between October 23 and November 7, 1,599 battle casualties of 51st Division and 1,086 from other formations passed through the forward medical units of 51st Division. Four officers and 22 O.Rs. of the divisional medical services were wounded and 2 O.Rs. were killed during the battle. One R.M.O. was captured but quickly escaped.

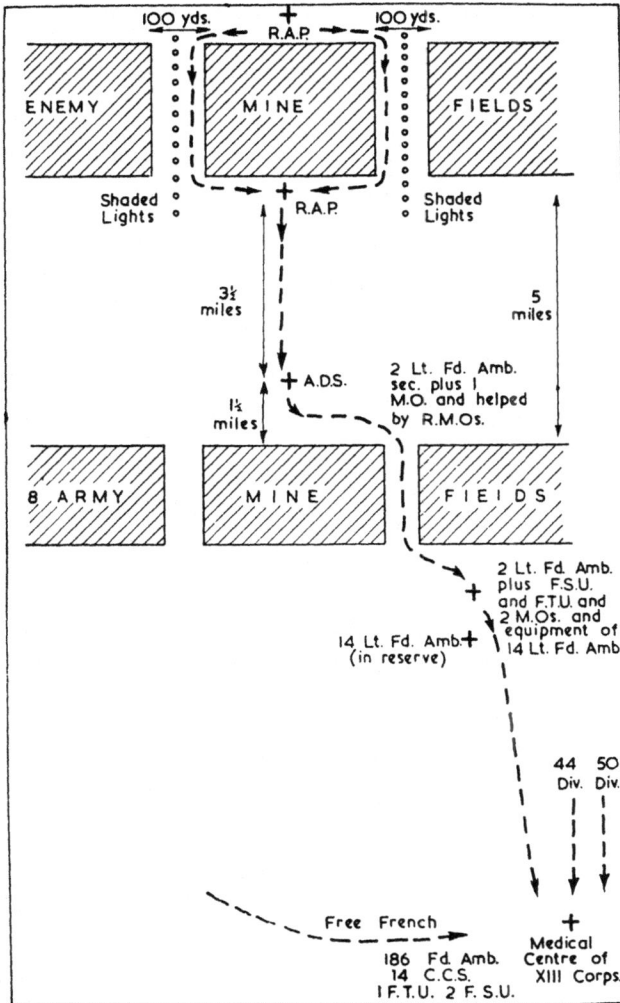

FIG. 31. The Battle of Alamein. 7th Armoured Division. Medical Cover.

7TH ARMOURED DIVISION

This division at this time was composed of 4th Lt. Armd. Bde., 22nd Armd. Bde. and Free French 1st Bde. To the British elements of this division were attached 2 and 14 Lt. Fd. Ambs.

The rôle of the division in the opening stage of the battle of Alamein was to attack in the south in order to persuade the enemy that it was in this sector that the main attack was to develop. Later it was to be pulled out to join X Corps, the *Corps de Chasse*.

The evacuation scheme of the division for the battle is shown diagrammatically in Fig. 31. Five hundred and ninety casualties passed through these medical units in the course of thirty-six hours on October 24–25.

Some details of the casualties dealt with during the battle are recorded in Table 41.

TABLE 41

Distribution of Wounds by Anatomical Region and by Arm of Service. 7th Armoured Division. October 23–November 19, 1942

Anatomical region	Armoured	Motorised infantry	Artillery	Total wounds
Head . .	42 (19·6 per cent.)	80 (14·8 per cent.)	37 (12·0 per cent.)	159 (15·0 per cent.)
Chest . .	11 (5·1 per cent.)	40 (7·4 per cent.)	24 (8·0 per cent.)	75 (7·0 per cent.)
Abdomen .	17 (7·9 per cent.)	18 (3·3 per cent.)	16 (5·0 per cent.)	51 (4·8 per cent.)
Back . .	10 (4·6 per cent.)	35 (6·5 per cent.)	21 (7·0 per cent.)	66 (6·3 per cent.)
Arms . .	32 (15·0 per cent.)	87 (16·1 per cent.)	53 (17·4 per cent.)	172 (16·0 per cent.)
Buttocks . .	16 (7·5 per cent.)	41 (7·5 per cent.)	24 (8·0 per cent.)	81 (7·6 per cent.)
Legs . .	49 (22·9 per cent.)	165 (30·7 per cent.)	89 (29·0 per cent.)	303 (28·7 per cent.)
Multiple . .	15 (7·0 per cent.)	34 (6·3 per cent.)	19 (6·5 per cent.)	68 (6·5 per cent.)
N.Y.D. (N) .	1 (0·5 per cent.)	34 (6·3 per cent.)	11 (3·5 per cent.)	46 (4·3 per cent.)
Burns . .	21 (9·8 per cent.)	7 (1·3 per cent.)	11 (3·5 per cent.)	39 (3·7 per cent.)
Total wounds .	214	541	305	1,060

INDIAN 4TH DIVISION*

Indian 4th Division had returned to Egypt from Cyprus during the first week of September 1942. It at once replaced Indian 5th Division on the Ruweisat Ridge, the latter division going back to the Delta. It now consisted of Ind. 5th, 7th, and 161st Inf. Bdes. and with it were serving 17 and 26 (Ind.) Fd. Ambs., 75 (Ind.) Lt. Fd. Amb. and 7 (Ind.) Fd. Hyg. Sec.

The rôle of Indian 4th Division in the battle of Alamein was:

(a) to hold secure the defended localities it occupied;

---

*For a more comprehensive account the Official Indian Medical History should be consulted.

(*b*) to carry out diversionary attacks by Ind. 7th and 161st Inf. Bdes. on the night of D-day/D-day+1 and to secure certain defined and limited objectives;

(*c*) to move Ind. 5th Inf. Bde. into corps reserve on the night of D-day/D-day+1.

In the battle 17 and 75 (Ind.) Lt. Fd. Ambs. established A.D.Ss. to serve Ind. 7th and 161st Inf. Bdes. and 'A' Coy. of 26 (Ind.) Fd. Amb. was attached to Ind. 5th Bde. Evacuation from these A.D.Ss. was by field ambulance cars to the M.D.S. of 26 (Ind.) Fd. Amb. to which a surgical team was attached. From thence evacuation to 17 (Ind.) Fd. Amb. was by M.A.C. in the case of lightly wounded and exhausted and to the M.D.S. of 75 (Ind.) Lt. Fd. Amb. in the case of the seriously wounded and the sick. These M.D.Ss. were cleared by M.A.C. to the C.C.S. area at Gharbaniyat. Ambulance cars of the A.F.S. were also used for this purpose.

The M.D.S. of 26 (Ind.) Fd. Amb. consisted of well dug-in elephant shelters and dug-in tentage. It had serious, non-serious and resuscitation wards. Its mobile operating theatre consisted of the usual 3-ton lorry with a trailer (an improvised Italian ambulance car).

When Indian 4th Division side-stepped into the area vacated by S.A. 1st Division, 17 (Ind.) Fd. Amb. took over the site of the South African M.D.S. and to the M.D.S. of 17 (Ind.) Fd. Amb. the surgical team with 26 (Ind.) Fd. Amb. was transferred. 75 Lt. Fd. Amb. established an A.D.S. to serve Ind. 161st Inf. Bde. about two and a half miles to the south-west of the M.D.S. of 17 (Ind.) Fd. Amb., to which its cases were evacuated.

50TH DIVISION

The composition of this division, like that of many another, underwent much change from time to time and the division itself served at one time in XIII Corps and at another under command of XXX Corps. At the beginning of the battle of Alamein the division consisted of 69th and 151st Bdes., Greek 1st Independent Bde. and Fighting French 2nd Bde. The Greeks and the French left the division on November 15. Between October 28 and November 13, 151st Bde. passed under command of N.Z. 2nd Division.

The location of the A.D.Ss. and M.D.Ss. of 149 Fd. Amb. are shown in Fig. 32, as are also those of the Greek and French field medical units. Evacuation from all these A.D.Ss. was to the M.D.S. of 149 Fd. Amb. on the divisional axis track and thence along Blueband track to 14 C.C.S. by 2 M.A.C. H.Q. 186 Fd. Amb. and one company were alongside 14 C.C.S. in XIII Corps Medical Area and were under the direct control of D.D.M.S. XIII Corps.

On November 3, 186 Fd. Amb. was released by D.D.M.S. Corps and opened its M.D.S. on the site previously occupied by 149 Fd. Amb. 'A' and 'B' Companies of 149 moved with 151st Bde. to join N.Z. 2nd Division, while H.Q. 149 remained on wheels at the M.D.S. site.

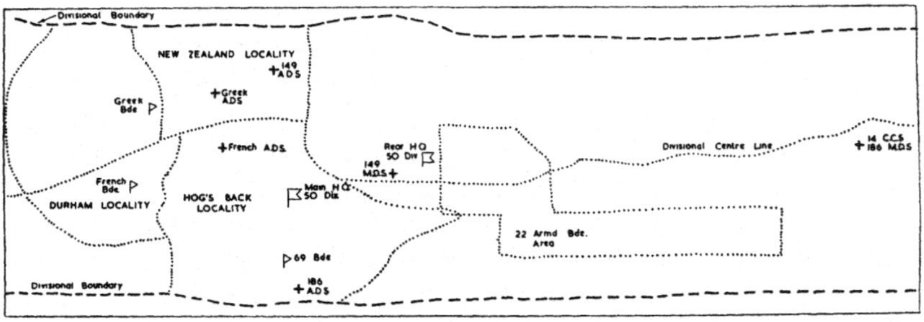

FIG. 32. The Battle of Alamein. 50th Division. Medical Cover.

Two companies of 186 Fd. Amb. and the Greek and French A.D.Ss. moved with 69th Inf. Bde. during the initial pursuit of the enemy.

44TH DIVISION

This division reached Egypt in July 1942. It consisted of 131st, 132nd and 133rd Inf. Bdes. With it were 131, 132 and 133 Fd. Ambs. and 19 Fd. Hyg. Sec. In August it joined XIII Corps. In September 133rd Inf. Bde. with 133 Fd. Amb. left the division and was replaced by 151st Inf. Bde. with 149 Fd. Amb. from 50th Division. At the same time Greek 1st Bde. with 1 (Gk.) Fd. Amb. came under command.

During the battle of Alam el Halfa casualties, few in number, were caused by aerial bombardment. 132 Inf. Bde., u/c N.Z. 2nd Division, took part in the attack on Munassib on September 1, 2 and 3. Casualties were numerous and were evacuated mainly through New Zealand medical units.

During the attack on Munassib on September 30–October 1–October 2, 131st Inf. Bde. was heavily engaged. 131 Fd. Amb. provided an A.D.S. which was evacuated by ambulance cars of the unit, reinforced by twelve from 2 M.A.C., into the M.D.S. of 132 Fd. Amb., the divisional M.D.S. On the first day 66 casualties were treated and evacuated; on the second 52 and on the third 22. To the M.D.S. of 132 were attached 6 F.T.U. and 4 F.S.U.

During the battle of Alamein 44th Division was in the southern sector. 131 Fd. Amb. furnished both A.D.S. and M.D.S. for this battle in the area of Deir el Tarfa. Their work was completely orthodox and calls for no comment. Evacuation from the M.D.S. was by M.A.C. to 14 C.C.S. 132 Fd. Amb. dealt with the daily sick.

After Alamein 44th Division was occupied in clearing the battlefield. Later, it was disbanded.

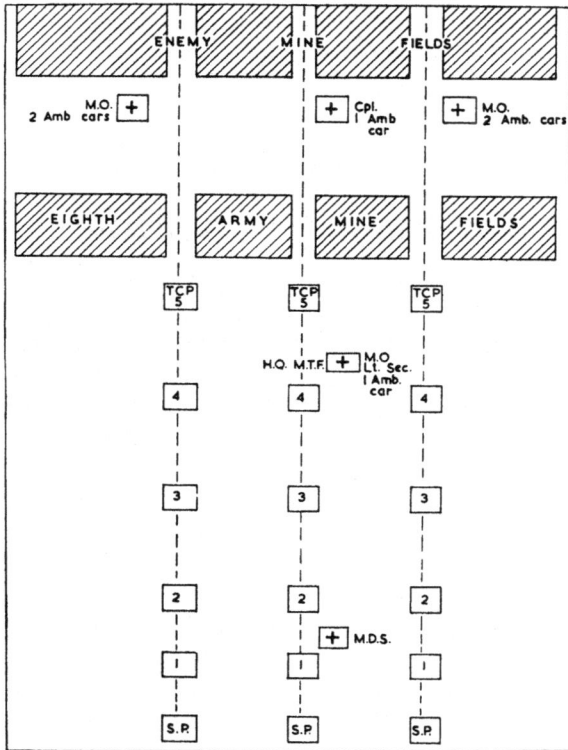

FIG. 33. The Battle of Alamein. 1st Armoured Division. Medical Cover.

1ST ARMOURED DIVISION

For the battle, the light field ambulances, 1 and 15, of the division were divided into two portions, the operative light M.D.S. and the 'Q' echelon. This arrangement proved to be most satisfactory for the reason that throughout the whole of the most strenuous phases of the battle the number of vehicles which were permitted to move forward was strictly limited to operational vehicles. The medical services, therefore, were not incommoded by this instruction since the only vehicles taken forward with the light M.D.Ss. were operational ones.

During the battle 1 Lt. Fd. Amb., less one section, served 2nd Armd. Bde. and 15 Lt. Fd. Amb. served 7 Motor Bde. The divisional field hygiene section was 1 Lt.

The total casualties evacuated were officers 61 and O.Rs. 609.

Strength of Division	*Killed*	*Wounded*	*Died of Wounds*
15,290	231	1,003	33

It was noted that the heavier the armour the higher was the ratio of killed to wounded among the crew.

(ii)

The Pursuit to Agheila

During the night of November 4–5 the Axis gun screen withdrew from its positions south of Ghazal and on the 5th the pursuit proper began. H.Q. X Corps with 6th, 7th and 10th Armd. Divisions, 4th Lt. Armd. Bde. and N.Z. 2nd Division headed west, with 1st and 10th Armd. Divisions directed on El Daba and 7th Armd. Division, 4th Lt. Armd. Bde. and N.Z. 2nd Division directed on Fuka, where the coastal road passes up a 300 ft. escarpment and so provides an excellent defensive position.

XXX Corps with Australian 9th Division and 51st Division passed into reserve. XIII Corps, with Indian 4th Division u/c, was assigned the task of clearing the battlefield.

By midday on the 5th, 1st Armd. Division was in El Daba and thence moved across the desert to cut the coastal road west of Matruh. 10th Armd. Division destroyed an armoured rearguard between El Daba and Fuka. N.Z. 2nd Division was held up for a time at the Fuka escarpment but 4th Lt. Armd. Bde. broke through and by midday on November 6 had reached Baqqush, where it was joined by N.Z. 2nd Division and 8th Armd. Bde. 7th Armd. Division struck across the desert south of the Fuka escarpment and destroyed another rearguard near Sidi Hannaish. By the evening of the 6th X Corps was within thirty miles of Matruh and S.A. 4/5th Armd. Car Regt. was already operating to the west of this place.

At this point the pursuit was halted by heavy rain. The desert became a morass in which transport was bogged and tanks could merely crawl. Movement became possible only on the coastal road and its pace was therefore determined by the stubbornness of the resistance of the Axis rearguard. Along this coastal road, on the heels of the Axis forces, 10th Armd. Division pressed, to reach the outskirts of Matruh on the evening of the 7th and to enter it next morning.

At this moment, two thousand miles to the west, U.S. and British troops were landing on the beaches at Casablanca, Oran and Algiers.

On November 8, 7th Armd. Division and N.Z. 2nd Division (N.Z. 5th Bde., 9th Armd. Bde., 4th Lt. Armd. Bde.) set out from Matruh for Tobruk. At Sidi Barrani the New Zealanders thrust aside opposition and moved on to capture Halfaya Pass. On the 11th they occupied Capuzzo, Sollum and Bardia. 7th Armd. Division, moving along the escarpment, joined the New Zealanders at Capuzzo.

On the 12th, 4th Lt. Armd. Bde. was in Gambut and El Adem and on the 13th, 131st Lorried Infantry Brigade of 7th Armd. Division entered Tobruk without opposition. Light columns pushed on to Tmimi (14th) and Martuba (15th) and in spite of acute and mounting supply difficulties 4th Lt. Armd. Bde. managed to reach Maraua on the 18th. The bulk of X Corps was obliged to wait around Tmimi until the more pressing of these supply problems had been solved.

Mobile columns provided by 11th Hussars and The Royals, u/c 7th Armd. Division, moved south-west towards Msus. They got as far as El Mechili on the 16th but rain again intervened. It was not until the 18th that they caught up with the Axis rearguards about Sceleidima and Antelat.

On the 20th, 11th Hussars once again entered Benghazi and on the 21st The Royals were in front of the Agedabia defensive position. Supplies were now reaching the forward areas and 22nd Armd. Bde. was able to move across the desert to threaten the flank of the Agedabia line. The Axis forces promptly withdrew and by November 25 they were in the much stronger Agheila position. Cyrenaica was to see them no more.

MEDICAL COVER FOR THE PURSUIT TO AGHEILA

Planning was now designed to give mobility along long lines of evacuation. Provision was therefore made for a large number of mobile corps medical units. Two mobile C.C.Ss., 8 (S.A.) and 15, the light section of 1 (N.Z.) C.C.S., three self-contained and mobile F.S.Us one., F.T.U. and 12 and 151 Lt. Fd. Ambs. were therefore attached to X Corps in addition to the New Zealand field ambulances. One hundred and sixty-six A.F.S. 4-wheel drive Dodge cars, each capable of carrying three stretcher or six sitting cases, were made available. During the advance two lines of evacuation were arranged, one along the coastal road, the other some twenty to thirty miles to the south of this coastal road over rough desert. In so far as the armoured column was concerned, to begin with only the smaller medical units could go forward. Later other corps units were brought up which leap-frogged, leaving behind sections to nurse the serious cases and at times carrying other cases forward.

In the armoured divisions there was a complete chain of wireless links, each field ambulance being in direct communication with the

A.D.M.S. and each A.D.M.S. in direct communication with D.D.M.S. X Corps. But N.Z. 2nd Division, an infantry division, had no such wireless chain. 166 Lt. Fd. Amb. of 9th Armd. Bde., u/c N.Z. 2nd Division, was the only medical unit to possess a wireless link. However, one extra set was provided and allotted to one of the N.Z. field ambulances. These two sets were on 'A' link to A.D.O.S. at rear H.Q. N.Z. 2nd Division. It was arranged also that A.D.M.S. would use the 'Q' link from rear to main H.Q. N.Z. 2nd Division.

In preparation for the advance the A.D.Ss. of 5 and 6 (N.Z.) Fd. Ambs. and the M.D.Ss. of 5 (N.Z.) and 166 Lt. Fd. Ambs. closed on November 4. A section from 4 (N.Z.) Fd. Amb. moved up to the site of the M.D.S. of 5 (N.Z.) Fd. Amb. to take over charge of the severe post-operative cases until these were fit to be moved back to a C.C.S. When, on November 4, N.Z. 2nd Division, with 4th Lt. Armd. Bde. u/c, left the Alamein position in an encircling movement on Fuka, its casualties (15) were carried forward in the A.D.S. cars.

The chase following the break-through presented nothing of any special medical interest. There were only 40 casualties during the first forty-eight hours of the pursuit. However, 6 (N.Z.) Fd. Amb. was called upon to deal with 126 battle casualties, including 33 P.o.W., on the morning of the 6th. These were evacuated by noon by 16 M.A.C. and 6 (N.Z.) Fd. Amb. thereafter moved to the south of Baqqush.

When, on November 9, N.Z. 6th Bde. occupied Matruh, 5 (N.Z.) Fd. Amb., less one company, accompanied it. The sick and the occasional battle casualty of the division during this advance to Sidi Barrani were dealt with by the M.D.S. of 6 (N.Z.) Fd. Amb., being carried along with the unit until a sufficient number had accumulated and then being sent back in convoys until they encountered a stationary medical unit.

By November 10, 1 (N.Z.) C.C.S. had moved up to the old site of 2 N.Z.G.H. at Gerawla and had opened there.

For the advance between November 8 and 11 it was necessary to carry petrol sufficient for two hundred miles and rations and water for six days. This created difficulties for the ambulance cars since it led to gross overloading. It would have been better had extra transport been provided for field ambulances for such operational purposes.

On November 12, 6 (N.Z.) Fd. Amb. established a M.D.S. south of Bardia. Evacuation therefrom was first made to 1 Mob. Mil. Hosp. and, after November 22, to 1 (N.Z.) C.C.S. which by this time had moved up to Tobruk. To 6 (N.Z.) Fd. Amb. 2 (N.Z.) F.T.U. and 2 (N.Z.) Surgical Team were still attached. On November 12, 4th Lt. Armd. Bde. and 9th Armd. Bde. passed from command of N.Z. 2nd Division and with them went 14 and 166 Lt. Fd. Ambs.

When 4 (N.Z.) Fd. Amb., 4 (N.Z.) Fd. Hyg. Sec. and 1 M.D.U. arrived in the Bardia area on November 19, 4 (N.Z.) Fd. Amb. opened a divisional rest station. On the 22nd, 5 (N.Z.) Fd. Amb. accompanied N.Z. 6th Bde. on its move forward from Matruh to Bardia to rejoin N.Z. 2nd Division, but on the 25th this medical unit moved into Tobruk to open adjacent to 1 (N.Z.) C.C.S. and to assist in holding and treating patients.

In Tobruk 4 (N.Z.) Fd. Hyg. Sec. salvaged, repaired and put into use a captured Italian mobile shower unit, thus equipping itself with a complete disinfestation plant.

MEDICAL ARRANGEMENTS DURING THE PURSUIT TO AGHEILA

On November 10, 91 Sub-area took over the local administration of the Matruh area and thereby became responsible for evacuation of casualties by ambulance train.

On November 16, H.Q., B.T.E., assumed responsibility for administration as far west as Grid 83 Easting and 86 Sub-area took over the administration of the Tobruk area. 99 Sub-area moved up to take over the Capuzzo area and 83 Sub-area went forward to administer Benghazi.

On November 18, XIII Corps passed from the command of Eighth Army to G.H.Q., as did also therefore 2/3 (Aust.) C.C.S. It was arranged, however, that 14 C.C.S., 2 M.A.C. and 7 Lt. Fd. Hyg. Sec. should remain u/c Eighth Army.

On November 28, H.Q., B.T.E., took over the administration of all territory east of the Libyan-Egyptian frontier and so 91 and 99 Sub-areas passed from under command of Eighth Army.

The forward movements of the medical units of X Corps, with dates, from the time they left Cairo are detailed below:

	Miles	151 Lt. Fd. Amb.	12 Lt. Fd. Amb.	15 C.C.S.	8 (S.A.) C.C.S.
Cairo–Alexandria road	0	—	Oct. 1	Oct. 1	Oct. 12
Burg el Arab	66	Oct. 1	Oct. 8	—	—
Hammam	76	—	Oct. 23	Oct. 23	—
Sydney Road	91	Oct. 23	Nov. 1	Nov. 3	Oct. 25
Alamein	103	Nov. 1	—	—	—
Sidi Rahmar	118	Nov. 4	Nov. 5	—	—
El Daba	136	—	—	Nov. 6	—
Fuka	169	—	Nov. 6	—	—
Gerawla	199	Nov. 7	Nov. 8	—	Nov. 9
Charing Cross	223	—	Nov. 9	—	—
Sidi Barrani	299	—	Nov. 11	Nov. 10	Nov. 11
Buq Buq	329	Nov. 10	—	—	—
Sollum	353	Nov. 12	—	—	Nov. 12
Capuzzo	365	—	Nov. 14	—	Nov. 13
Gambut	415	Nov. 15	Nov. 15	—	—
Tobruk	448	—	Nov. 19	Nov. 15	Nov. 18
Tmimi	518	Nov. 17	Nov. 24	—	—
Barce	674	—	—	—	Nov. 24
Benghazi	744	Nov. 24	—	—	—

To free the rapidly moving field medical units of X Corps, 14 Fd. Amb., with 4 F.S.U., opened at El Daba on November 6; 1 (N.Z.)

C.C.S., less Lt. Sec. with X Corps, opened at Gerawla on the 7th;
2/3 (Aust.) C.C.S., less Lt. Sec. with XXX Corps, and 7 Adv. Depot
Med. Stores moved up to Gerawla on the 9th. Thereafter other Army
units were moved westwards in relief of the field medical units of X

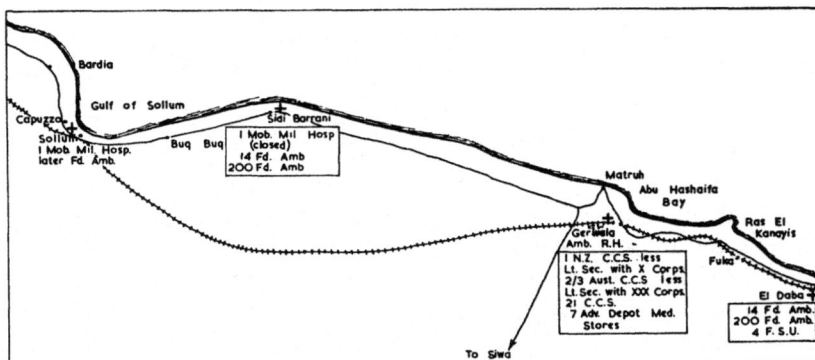

FIG. 34. The forward movements of Medical Units following the
Battle of Alamein.

Corps as these moved forward. Ambulance railhead was first at El Daba,
then Gerawla and then Tobruk itself.

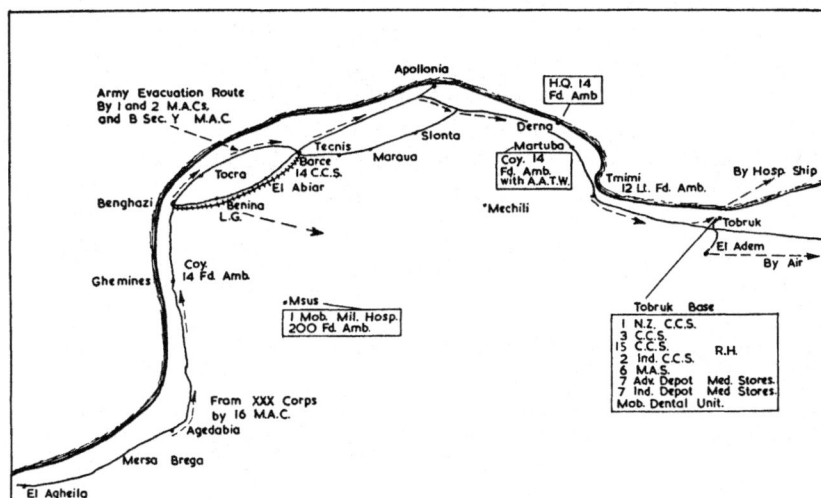

FIG. 35. Medical Arrangements before the attack on the Agheila position,
December 13, 1942.

To El Daba went 200 Fd. Amb.; to Gerawla 21 C.C.S.; to Sidi
Barrani 1 Mob. Mil. Hosp. and 14 and 200 Fd. Ambs. Then 1 Mob.
Mil. Hosp and 200 Fd. Amb. moved forward to the Capuzzo area.
Then to Tobruk went 1 (N.Z.) C.C.S., 3 C.C.S., 15 C.C.S., 2 (Ind.)

C.C.S., 6 M.A.S., 7 Adv. Depot Med. Stores, 7 (Ind.) Depot Med. Stores and a mobile dental unit; to Tmimi went 12 Lt. Fd. Amb.; to Martuba a company of 14 Fd. Amb.; to Derna H.Q. 14 Fd. Amb.; to Barce 14 C.C.S.; to Msus 1 Mob. Mil. Hosp. and 200 Fd. Amb., and to a position near Ghemines on the Benghazi–Agedabia road a company of 14 Fd. Amb.

Until November 18 evacuation in front of Gerawla was by road to Gerawla or by air to Heliopolis. After this date evacuation behind Gerawla by road ceased, for hospital ships became available at Tobruk. On November 23, H.S. *Llandovery Castle* cleared the C.C.S. group at Tobruk and thereafter a regular service was maintained.

Until Benghazi port had been opened for hospital ships it was necessary to make use of an Army evacuation line through Cyrenaica from Benghazi to Tobruk. This was provided by 1 M.A.C. to Derna and then by 2 M.A.C. to Tobruk, a total distance of three hundred miles. Overnight staging centres were Barce (14 C.C.S.), Derna (H.Q. 14 Fd. Amb. in the Princess of Piedmont Hospital). Intermediate midday halts were at Beda Littoria (coy. 14 Fd. Amb.) and at Tmimi.

By December 15 the railway line from Capuzzo westwards had been repaired and ambulance trains were running from Tobruk.

For air evacuation purposes one company of 14 Fd. Amb. was attached to the advanced air transport centre (A.A.T.C.) and one company of 131 Fd. Amb. to the casualty air evacuation centre (C.A.E.C.) to act as holding centres. These companies moved with their respective wings.

THE BATTLE OF AGHEILA

The defensive position at Agheila was a strong one. On its northern flank was the sea, while guarding its southern flank was the Wadi Fareg. In it were some 10,000 Germans and 25,000 Italians. Though Marshal Rommel was receiving much material to replace his losses, he was not receiving reinforcements, for these were even more urgently needed in Tunisia. It seemed unlikely that he could hope to do more than temporarily check the westward drive of Eighth Army, already impeded by maintenance difficulties. The railway was working as far west as Capuzzo by November 21 and as far as Tobruk by December 1. The port of Tobruk was being restored with remarkable speed. Nevertheless, General Montgomery doubted whether it would be possible to resume the advance before mid-December.

H.Q. XXX Corps assumed command of the forward area from X Corps on November 26 and, on December 3, 51st Division took over the northern sector of the front and 7th Armd. Division observed and harassed the southern flank. N.Z. 2nd Division was concentrated at El Haseiat.

18

TACTICAL PLAN

(1) 51st Division would attack along the coast road.

(2) 7th Armd. Division would operate in the centre.

(3) N.Z. 2nd Division would move wide to the south, outflank the Agheila position and then move north to cut the coast road well to the west of Aghelia.

(4) D-day would be December 14.

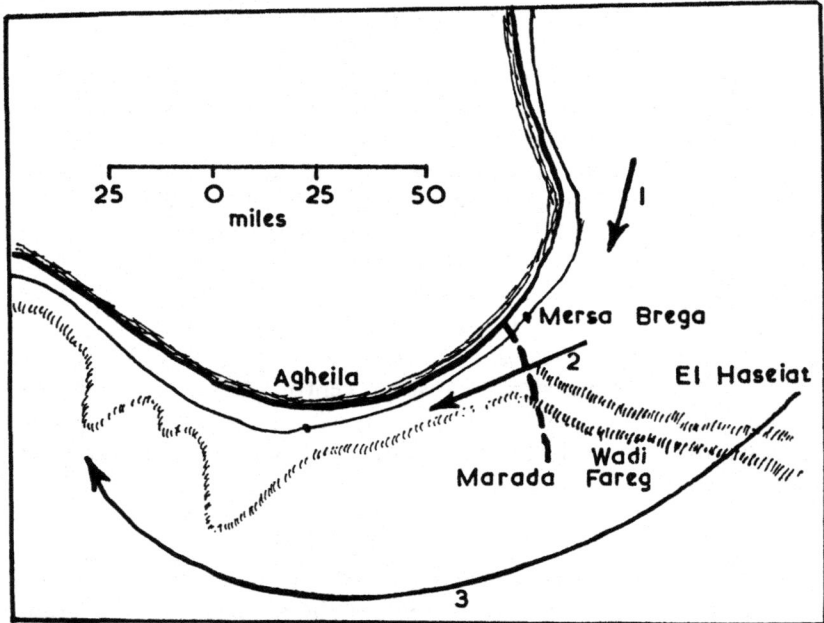

FIG. 36. The Battle of El Agheila.
1. 51st Division.   2. 7th Armoured Division.   3. N.Z. 2nd Division.

THE ASSAULT

During the night of December 12–13 it was observed that the Axis forces were vacating the Agheila position, covering the withdrawal by mine, booby-trap and demolition. These were the reasons for the slow progress of 152nd Inf. Bde. of 51st Division. 8th Armd. Bde. of 7th Armd. Division broke through, only to be checked by an anti-tank ditch on the Marada road twenty miles west of Agheila. N.Z. 2nd Division reached the Wadi Matratin, sixty miles west of Agheila, on the evening of the 15th, there to stand athwart the enemy's line of retreat. But before the New Zealanders could make adequate prepara- tions to prevent them, the Axis forces, breaking up into small groups, were able to trickle through. 4th Lt. Armd. Bde., sent in pursuit, was held up by demolition and mine. However, this brigade reached Nofilia on the evening of the 16th.

51ST DIVISION—MEDICAL COVER

The divisional M.D.S. of 51st Division was established by 175 Fd. Amb., to which 10 F.S.U. was attached, on the main road eight miles east of the front line. Two sites for A.D.Ss. were selected close up to the front line. 176 Fd. Amb. opened a M.D.S. to deal with the lightly wounded and the sick on the main road ten miles farther east. 174 remained in reserve alongside 176. Evacuation was by 16 M.A.C. to 8 (S.A.) C.C.S. north of Agedabia. For the pursuit force a modified company of 174 Fd. Amb. was provided.

Progress was slow because of the innumerable mines and booby-traps which caused many casualties. Up to December 31, 273 casualties were treated and evacuated by the medical units of 51st Division.

N.Z. 2ND DIVISION—MEDICAL COVER

At El Haseiat final preparations were made for the long three hundred mile sweep into the Desert without roads or supply lines. Petrol for four hundred miles and food and water for ten days were stowed away. Since evacuation was not practicable, enough medical personnel and ambulance cars were provided to open dressing stations and to operate wherever necessary, to hold patients or to carry them with the division as conditions demanded. It was arranged that 5 and 6 (N.Z.) Fd. Ambs., together with 144 Fd. Amb. (4th Lt. Armd. Bde.) should move with the division. With the field ambulances were two complete surgical teams equipped with hospital beds and additional equipment for brain, chest and abdominal surgery. 2 F.T.U. carried full stocks of plasma and serum and 104 pints of fresh blood in special refrigerators. In reserve at Agedabia, ready to go forward at short notice, were 4 (N.Z.) Fd. Amb., 4 (N.Z.) Fd. Hyg. Sec. and 1 M.D.U. All medical units were equipped with wireless. Twenty-three additional A.F.S. cars were attached to the division and a further ten to 14 Lt. Fd. Amb. to bring the number of ambulance cars available up to seventy-five. If necessary empty R.A.S.C. trucks would be used for the carriage of light cases. 1 (N.Z.) C.C.S. moved from Tobruk to Agedabia, where it opened on December 11 along with 8 (S.A.) C.C.S.

In the actual movement round the flank of the enemy line there were no battle casualties and the medical units were not called upon until the division deployed across the enemy's line of retreat west of Agheila on the night of December 15/16, when the M.D.S. of 6 (N.Z.) Fd. Amb., with a surgical team and a F.T.U., opened two miles west of divisional H.Q. The A.D.S. company of this medical unit proceeded with N.Z. 6th Inf. Bde. and another company went with the N.Z. 5th Bde. The M.D.S. of 14 Lt. Fd. Amb. was opened two miles south-west of divisional H.Q. In reserve ten miles east was 5 (N.Z.) Fd. Amb., but because of a threat by an enemy column 5 (N.Z.) Fd. Amb. moved back a further ten miles.

On the morning of December 16, 23 battle casualties were admitted through the A.D.S. to the M.D.S. of 6 (N.Z.) Fd. Amb. On the 17th the sick and wounded, 84 in number, were placed in charge of 'A' Company of 6 (N.Z.) Fd. Amb., which proceeded with them down the Marada track to the coast road at Agheila where the leading units of 51st Division were and the patients were handed over to 16 M.A.C. The A.D.S. then rejoined N.Z. 2nd Division.

When the division moved to the west of Nofilia on the morning of December 17, 6 (N.Z.) Fd. Amb. established its M.D.S. with 2 Surgical Team and 2 F.T.U. eight miles south-west of this town. Here 30 casualties from 4th Lt. Armd. Bde. were admitted and treated. Evacuation of the more serious cases was by two Red Cross planes from Nofilia aerodrome. On December 21 the remaining 81 patients at the M.D.S. of 6 (N.Z.) Fd. Amb. were sent back by road to 'Marble Arch', where 4 (N.Z.) Fd. Amb. was acting as a corps M.D.S. with one of its companies at the 'Marble Arch' airfield functioning as an air evacuation centre.

On December 20–21, when N.Z. 2nd Division moved to the coastal area near Nofilia, 5 (N.Z.) Fd. Amb. opened a M.D.S. while 6 (N.Z.) Fd. Amb. remained closed. Thereafter, until the end of December, this M.D.S. was called upon to treat a constant dribble of casualties caused by mines and booby-traps. The battle casualties and sick admitted to the New Zealand medical units in the battle of El Agheila from December 11 to 21 totalled 104 and 164, of whom 69 and 149 respectively were New Zealanders.

MEDICAL ARRANGEMENTS

When XXX Corps took over from X Corps, 8 (S.A.) C.C.S., 151 Lt. Fd. Amb. and 15 A.F.S. A.C.C. were transferred from X to XXX Corps. At the same time 1 (N.Z.) C.C.S. passed from Army to XXX Corps.

For the battle of Agheila ambulance cars were distributed as follows:

Army	.	. 1 M.A.C.	
		2 M.A.C.	
		18 M.A.S.	} 200 cars
		'B' Sec. 'Y' M.A.C.	
		6 M.A.S. was left in Tobruk for local duties	
X Corps	.	. 11 A.F.S. A.C.C.	66 cars

XXX Corps   . 16 M.A.C.
15 A.F.S. A.C.C. two platoons } 166 cars
N.Z. M.A.C., sec.

As the advance progressed past Agheila, H.Qs. of M.A.Cs. were moved up, H.Q. 1 M.A.C. ultimately being at Agheila and H.Q. 2 M.A.C. at Benghazi.

The evacuation arrangements worked smoothly even though the distance between Agheila and Tobruk was some five hundred and fifty miles. There were staging posts at Benghazi, Barce and Derna. 'B' Sec. 'Y' M.A.C. was made available by Army to supplement the field ambulance cars actually clearing the line.

Hospital ships became available at Benghazi from December 18. As far as possible Benghazi was cleared by hospital ship and Tobruk by ambulance train. When a full load was not taken aboard at Benghazi the ship called at Tobruk *en route* to make up the complement.

Evacuation by air was by D.H. 86 ambulance aircraft from the forward L.Gs. adjacent to the forward C.C.Ss. to Benghazi and from the L.G. at Benina to Tobruk by transport aircraft. There were also occasional transport aircraft direct to Heliopolis.

THE ADVANCE TO TRIPOLI

TACTICAL PLAN

For the advance on Tripoli it was proposed that Eighth Army should move forward in two columns: (*a*) coastal, and (*b*) inland, with an independent brigade in Army Reserve which was to operate in the area between these columns. The coastal column was to move along the Buerat–Misurata–Tripoli road and was to consist of 51st Division. The inland column was to move from the south of Buerat, Sedada, Beni Ulid, Tarhuna, Tripoli, over desert tracks for the most part. This inland column was to consist of 7th Armd. and N.Z. 2nd Divisions.

MEDICAL TACTICAL PLAN

Owing to the distances to be covered it was appreciated that control over two separate evacuation lines and two sets of C.C.Ss. by D.D.M.S. at rear corps H.Q. would be exceedingly difficult, if not impossible. Accordingly, the officer commanding 131 Fd. Amb. was instructed to co-ordinate the coastal route evacuation line and the more difficult desert route would be supervised by A.D.M.S. N.Z. 2nd Division.

Inland Column. 1st Phase up to Sedada.

(1) Evacuation from this column would be to 6 (N.Z.) Fd. Amb. at Pilastrino by 16 M.A.C., which would be attached to the N.Z. division for this purpose.

(2) N.Z. 2nd Division would open a M.D.S. in Sedada as soon as practicable. To this M.D.S. cases would be brought in A.F.S. cars attached to the field ambulances of this column. This M.D.S. would be prepared to hold cases until it was relieved by 8 (S.A.) C.C.S. Evacuation from Sedada to Pilastrino would be by 16 M.A.C. until air transport became available.

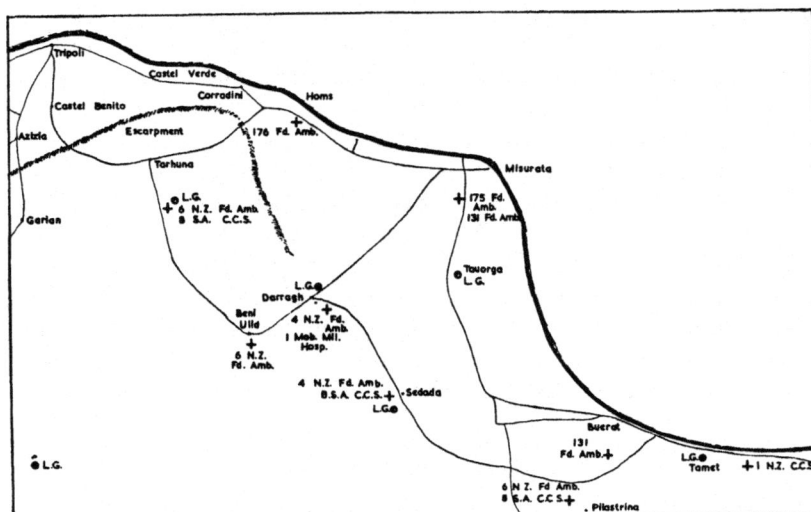

FIG. 37. The Advance to Tripoli. XXX Corps. Medical Cover.

2nd Phase. In Advance of Sedada.

N.Z. 2nd and 7th Armd. Divisions would open dressing stations on the corps axis as the situation demanded. Evacuation from these dressing stations would be by A.F.S. cars direct or, alternatively, would be staged through the dressing stations to Sedada. Suggested sites for the M.D.S. were Beni Ulid and Tarhuna areas. Evacuation from the column would be co-ordinated by A.D.M.S. N.Z. 2nd Division who would have a report centre at the main corps H.Q.

Coastal Column. 1st Phase up to Misurata–Tauorga.

(1) From the M.D.Ss. of 51st Division to 1 (N.Z.) C.C.S. at Tamet by 16 M.A.C.

(2) As the advance continued 131 Fd. Amb. would open staging sections on the route at intervals of twenty-five to thirty miles.

2nd Phase. In advance of the Misurata–Tauorga area.

(1) 131 Fd. Amb. would take over from 51st divisional M.D.S. in the Misurata–Tauorga area and would be prepared to hold cases pending evacuation. 16 M.A.C. would continue to evacuate from

the M.D.S. of 51st Division to this M.D.S. and thence to 1 (N.Z.) C.C.S.

(2) Evacuation from this column would be coordinated by O/C 131 Fd. Amb.

Centre Column. Army Reserve.

A.F.S. cars would be allotted to 2 Lt. Fd. Amb. for evacuation of cases to the M.D.Ss. of the inland and coastal columns. H.Q. and thirty cars of 15 A.F.S. would be allotted to N.Z. 2nd Division, twenty-five cars to 7th Armd. Division and ten cars to 2 Lt. Fd. Amb.

Hospitals and C.C.Ss.

1 (N.Z.) C.C.S. at Tamet would receive all cases and evacuate by air. 8 (S.A.) C.C.S., closed at Sirte, would move to Pilastrino, awaiting cars from corps or N.Z. 2nd Division to move to Sedada. 1 Mob. Mil. Hosp., closed at Sirte, would move to the area of 1 (N.Z.) C.C.S. at Tamet, there awaiting cars to move into Tripoli.

Field Ambulances.

7 Lt. Fd. Amb., less two secs., with 23rd Armd. Bde., would operate a staging post at Nofilia. 6 (N.Z.) Fd. Amb. would open at Pilastrino to receive cases from the inland column, would provide a liaison party to A.D.M.S. N.Z. 2nd Division to arrange staging posts on the Axis track for evacuation from Sedada and would close and join N.Z. 2nd Division when air evacuation from Sedada had replaced evacuation by M.A.C.

Field Surgical Units.

1 F.S.U. with 131 Fd. Amb.; 2 F.S.U. with 7th Armd. Division; 4 F.S.U. with 1 (N.Z.) C.C.S.; 6 F.S.U. with 8 (S.A.) C.C.S.; 10 F.S.U. with 51st Division; 4 Neurosurgical Unit with 1 (N.Z.) C.C.S.; 1 (N.Z.) surgical team each with 4, 5 and 6 (N.Z.) Fd. Ambs.

Field Transfusion Units.

1 F.T.U. with 1 (N.Z.) C.C.S.; the (N.Z.) F.T.U. with N.Z. 2nd Division; 7 F.T.U. with 51st Division; Adv. Blood Bank with N.Z. 2nd Division.

Field Hygiene Sections.

7 Lt. Fd. Hyg. Sec. would be ready to move at short notice with 1 (N.Z.) C.C.S. to Tripoli.

Medical Stores.

Mobile Section of 7 Adv. Depot Med. Stores with 1 (N.Z.) C.C.S.

As will be seen, quite a large number of corps medical units were employed. They were made necessary by the rapidity of the movement, by the difficulties of the terrain and because it was necessary to insure against fairly heavy casualties.

The A.F.S. ambulance cars proved to be of the greatest value. In a military operation of this kind it is necessary to attach ambulance cars to the R.M.Os.; yet if this is done from field ambulances the latter are exposed to considerable embarrassment through shortage of transport. Thus it was that these cars, with their most excellent cross-country performance, were so very useful. They were used in the later stages of the battle to the limit of their capacity. Without them satisfactory evacuation would not have been possible.

The country across which evacuation was to proceed was exceedingly difficult. There were patches of deep sand and of stone, wadis and great traffic jams, especially during the night, so that the maximum speed was of the order of five to eight miles per hour. So it was that a journey of thirty miles might take as long as six hours; the round trip, therefore, could take as long as twelve hours. Allowing for the rest and refreshment of the drivers and for the servicing of the cars, under such conditions it was not possible to use any particular car for more than one and a half journeys at the most in the course of twenty-four hours.

The distribution of the medical units of XXX Corps during the advance on Tripoli is shown in Fig. 37. 1 (N.Z.) C.C.S. was brought up to Tamet on January 14. To it was attached 4 Neurosurgical Unit, 1 F.T.U. and 131 M.D.U. Evacuation from this C.C.S. by road was by 1 M.A.C., and by air from the air ambulance unit at Tamet L.G. This C.C.S. remained in Tamet throughout the course of the operation. 1 Mob. Mil. Hosp. moved to Tamet on the 16th, remaining in reserve and assisting the C.C.S. On the 19th it was moved *via* Sedada to Darragh L.G. where it relieved 6 (N.Z.) Fd. Amb. which was holding cases pending evacuation. This hospital received both from the inland column and from the coastal column through 131 Fd. Amb. which was at Misurata. On the 24th, 1 Mob. Mil. Hosp. moved to Tripoli. During its stay at Darragh it evacuated 95 cases by air.

8 (S.A.) C.C.S. moved up to Sedada on the 18th, to Beni Ulid on the 20th and later to the south of Tarhuna where it relieved 6 (N.Z.) Fd. Amb. alongside an ambulance transport L.G. There it served as a reception centre for all casualties from N.Z. 2nd Division and 7th Armd. Division during the fighting north of Tarhuna on the 21st and 22nd. On the 24th it reached Tripoli and took over the Italian military hospital at Carnera from a section of 2 Lt. Fd. Amb.

D.D.M.S. XXX Corps observed that it was quite impossible in an operation such as this for D.D.M.S. corps to co-ordinate the evacuation from field ambulances owing to the rapidity of movement, the great distances and the ever-changing conditions.

The presence of D.D.M.S. at rear H.Q. is necessary, however, since he must be able to keep in touch with the rearward evacuation and be able to move the C.C.Ss. attached to corps. He must therefore make his H.Q. either main or else rear, and wherever he is not, there must be placed a sufficiently senior and responsible representative of himself, one who, being conversant with the D.D.M.S's. intentions, can make decisions and act on his behalf. When a town is to be occupied it is essential that the medical and hygiene staff are among the earliest to enter and they must have at hand (a) a field hygiene section and (b) a field ambulance to take over hospitals immediately pending the arrival of C.C.Ss. and to take over medical stores immediately to prevent looting.

THE BATTLE OF BUERAT

The Buerat defensive position was not naturally strong and could easily be outflanked. The main position was on the line of the Wadi Zem Zem, some twenty-five miles in length. This was held by a strong rearguard, for the bulk of the remaining Axis forces were moving west towards Tunisia.

Once again General Montgomery's chief problem was that of maintenance. The port of Benghazi could not be restored until the New Year. When he next attacked he meant to move right on to Tripoli itself. This part of the country was unknown, so that much reconnaissance was necessary. The L.R.D.G. was placed u/c Eighth Army for this purpose.

Eighth Army was leaving the Desert and entering an undulating countryside rich in vegetation, with olive, peach and apricot orchards in profusion. Its reds, purples, blues and browns mingled with the varying greens of the cultivated fields to offer relief to desert-weary eyes.

During the January–April rains the numerous wide, soft-bottomed wadis fill rapidly and the water floods the countryside. So rapidly can this flooding occur that troops bivouacked between Castel Benito and Tripoli were completely submerged before they had time to move and, indeed, one officer was swept away while asleep in his tent.

TACTICAL PLAN

(1) 51st Division would press along the coast road.

(2) 7th Armd. Division and N.Z. 2nd Division would outflank the enemy's position and thrust towards Tarhuna.

(3) 22nd Armd. Bde. would move on Bir Dufan and be prepared to switch to either flank.

(4) D-day would be January 15, 1943.

It had been intended to use 50th along with 51st Division, but a gale created such havoc at Benghazi during January 4–6 that maintenance

difficulties precluded the use of so large a force. 50th Division was therefore left in the Agheila position.

THE ASSAULT

At 0715 hours on January 15, 7th Armd. and N.Z. 2nd Divisions
attacked the Axis positions along the Wadi umm er Raml and drove
their antagonists back to the Wadi Zem Zem. 51st Division's attack

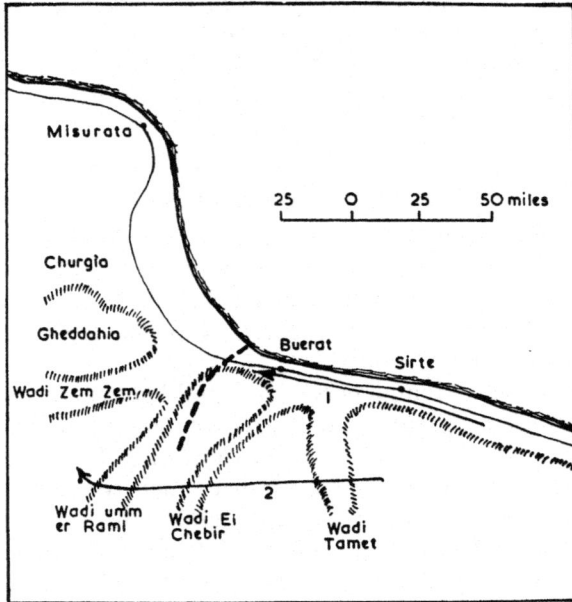

FIG. 38. The Battle of Buerat.
1. 51st Division.   2. 7th Armoured Division and N.Z. 2nd Division.

along the coast road was not strongly opposed and by the morning of
the 16th this division had reached Gheddahia and by the afternoon
Churgia was occupied.

On the 18th Misurata was entered and Eighth Army passed into
difficult hilly country in which the winding roads to Tripoli passed
through deep defiles. Demolition and mine made rapid advance impossible. 51st Division, fighting a series of sharp actions with enemy
rearguards, would not be denied and debouched into the Tripoli
plain to enter Castel Verde on the 22nd. 22nd Armd. Bde. was then
brought into the lead and headed for Tripoli, thirty miles away. A
company of 51st Division, riding on the tanks, set out in the moonlight.

7th Armd. Division entered Tarhuna on the 19th and on the 21st
thrust its way through the hills on to the Tripoli plain. So also did

N.Z. 2nd Division and after stiff fighting Castel Benito and Garian were occupied and the southern approach to Tripoli opened.

At 0500 hours on January 23, 11th Hussars from the south and 1st Gordons of 51st Division from the north entered Tripoli. By the end of the month the whole of Tripolitania had been cleared, the Fezzan by a column of Fighting French under General Le Clerc.

In three months exactly Eighth Army had traversed the whole breadth of Libya, some fourteen hundred miles, sweeping the enemy before it.

51ST DIVISION—MEDICAL COVER

In preparation for the battle of Buerat 174 Fd. Amb. established the divisional M.D.S., with 10 F.S.U. and 7 F.T.U. attached, in the Wadi Uesca. A.D.Ss. were opened by 174 and 175 Fd. Ambs. and 176 remained in reserve. It was arranged by D.D.M.S. Corps that 131 Fd. Amb. should follow up as corps field ambulance and take over 51st Divisional M.D.S. site and patients as 51st Division moved forward.

174 and 176 Fd. Ambs. each had five M.A.C. cars attached and evacuation was to be to 1 (N.Z.) C.C.S. at Tamet. 175 Fd. Amb. had ten M.A.C. cars with it for this medical unit was to move with 152nd Bde., if all went well, in the dash for Misurata.

51st Divisional casualties in this battle numbered 8 officers and 93 other ranks.

Following this battle 152nd Bde. with 175 Fd. Amb. and 154th Bde. with 176 Fd. Amb. moved forward on an axis a thousand yards west of the main road on January 17. These medical units were called upon to deal with 23 casualties during these events. On the 18th they were both in the area of Crispi and 174, having handed over to 131, was moving forward to open a M.D.S. on the main coastal road near Zliten. As the tracks were so bad it was decided that the field ambulances should hold all casualties until 131 Fd. Amb. or the corps C.C.S. moved up.

On January 20 the brigades were subjected to heavy shelling from the Homs position and 42 casualties were evacuated to the M.D.S. of 174 Fd. Amb. The Axis forces evacuated Homs but took up a strong position to the west of the town. This position was attacked by 152nd and 154th Bdes. 176 Fd. Amb., reverting to A.D.M.S., opened its M.D.S. in the military hospital in Homs and to it came 10 F.S.U. and 7 F.T.U. from 174. In this fierce engagement casualties numbered 18 officers and 158 other ranks. These were evacuated to the M.D.S. of 176. 131 Fd. Amb. had now opened in Misurata and 20 casualties from 51st Division were sent thereto.

On January 22, 174 Fd. Amb. closed and moved alongside 176 in Homs. When the break-through occurred A.D.M.S. attached six ambulance cars to the armoured brigade heading for Tripoli.

On January 23, when Tripoli was entered, 175 Fd. Amb. opened the divisional M.D.S. in the Tagiura area where it was shortly joined by the other two field ambulances, the F.S.U. and the F.T.U. Evacuation was now to 8 (S.A.) C.C.S. and later to 1 Mob. Mil. Hosp.

N.Z. 2ND DIVISION—MEDICAL COVER

The arrangements were essentially similar to those made in connexion with the battle of El Agheila. 4 and 5 (N.Z.) Fd. Ambs. moved forward with the division while 6 (N.Z.) Fd. Amb. functioned as the corps M.D.S. Twenty-five additional ambulance cars from 16 M.A.C. were attached to 4 and 5 (N.Z.) Fd. Ambs., which provided M.D.Ss. for the division. The F.T.U. and the surgical team from 1 (N.Z.) C.C.S. were attached to 5 (N.Z.) Fd. Amb., which formed a mobile open M.D.S. for the division. Attached to 5 (N.Z.) Fd. Amb. was 'B' Company 4 (N.Z.) Fd. Amb. with a C.C.S. surgical team, with provision for it to be left with any patients who required to be held for a time following operation, or alternatively, to be attached as an air evacuation unit as necessity arose. To 6 (N.Z.) Fd. Amb. was attached 2 (N.Z.) F.S.U., while 4 (N.Z.) Fd. Hyg. Sec. moved with 4 (N.Z.) Fd. Amb. It was arranged that the medical units of 7th Armd. Division would evacuate through 151 Lt. Fd. Amb. to the nearest of the N.Z. medical units. It was arranged further that N.Z. 2nd Division would post a dressing station at Sedada during the advance and others close to any L.Gs. that were functioning or likely to function on the route. From these L.Gs. air evacuation was planned to Tamet aerodrome, seven miles to the east of which 1 (N.Z.) C.C.S. opened on January 14.

On January 13, 6 (N.Z.) Fd. Amb. moved to a point near Pilastrino and established a M.D.S., being at this time some forty miles ahead of the division with only an armoured car screen between it and the enemy positions in the Wadi Zem Zem. 'B' Company 4 (N.Z.) Fd. Amb. established an air evacuation centre at Sedada when the division reached this place. When this was taken over by 8 (S.A.) C.C.S., 6 (N.Z.) Fd. Amb. moved forward along the divisional axis. In a series of leap-frogging movements the medical units maintained a chain of evacuation and air evacuation units worked from Bir Dufan and Tarhuna as well as from Sedada, and later also from Castel Benito.

The abundance of ambulance cars with short runs between staging posts and the nearness of L.Gs. made evacuation a relatively simple matter. Wireless also contributed notably to the smoothness of the operation. Casualties were extraordinarily light and the majority that were incurred were due to mine and booby-trap.

During the period January 17–24 a total of 277 battle casualties and 60 sick were evacuated from the L.Gs. at Sedada, Bir Dufan and Tarhuna. In addition a number of cases from the inland column sent from 6 (N.Z.) Fd. Amb. at Pilastrino on January 15 and 16 to 1 (N.Z.) C.C.S. were evacuated by air from Tamet. The numbers evacuated from Tamet between January 17 and 19 were 48 battle casualties and 71 sick.

1 (N.Z.) C.C.S. moved to Sirte on January 4 and to Tamet on the 14th. A British F.S.U. joined it on December 23, a British F.T.U. on January 7 and a British neurosurgical unit on January 13. To it a British mobile ophthalmic unit had been attached since October. The C.C.S. dealt with 154 battle casualties and 331 sick at Sirte and 287 battle casualties and 468 sick at Tamet. The majority of these were evacuated by road to Nofilia, staged there and then on to Marble Arch and, finally, to Benghazi, a total distance of 360 miles. In addition a number of casualties were sent back by transport plane. Ambulance planes were also used for serious cases from the forward areas.

In the divisional area on the outskirts of Tripoli on January 23, 5 (N.Z.) Fd. Amb. opened a M.D.S. and, to assist 8 (S.A.) C.C.S. in taking over one of the Italian military hospitals, 6 (N.Z.) Fd. Amb. with 2 Surgical Team and 2 F.T.U. moved into Tripoli itself. This hospital was taken over by 48 B.G.H. on February 21. On January 30, 4 (N.Z.) Fd. Amb., coming from reserve, opened a M.D.S. in the medical area and relieved 5 (N.Z.) Fd. Amb. Under command XXX Corps 1 (N.Z.) C.C.S. remained at Tamet until February 9 and then moved up to Zuara, west of Tripoli. Thereafter, following the capture of Ben Gardane on February 15, this unit was moved farther forward to a site twenty miles west of Ben Gardane on February 26.

New Zealand Casualties

	Killed	P.o.W.	Missing	Wounded
October 23, 1942– November 21, 1942. Alamein–Bardia	380	32	5	1,360
November 22, 1942– January 14, 1943. Agheila	46	9	—	162
January 15, 1942– February 2, 1942. To Tripoli	21	1	—	66

MEDICAL ARRANGEMENTS

Apart from the divisional field ambulances of 51st Division, of 7th Armd. and N.Z. 2nd Divisions and of 22nd Armd. Bde., there were with XXX Corps as corps units:

8 (S.A.) C.C.S.
1 (N.Z.) C.C.S.
1 Mob. Mil. Hosp.
131 Fd. Amb.
151 Fd. Amb.
2 Lt. Fd. Amb. (with 22nd Armd. Bde.)
16 M.A.C.
N.Z. M.A.C. sec.
15 A.F.S. A.C.C.
1, 2, 4, 6 and 10 F.S.Us.
1, 3, 7 (N.Z.) F.T.Us. (3 providing the Adv. Blood Bank)
4 Neurosurgical Unit
7 Adv. Depot Med. Stores, Mob. Sec.

D.D.M.S. XXX Corps considered that the operation about to be undertaken demanded a large number and variety of field medical units and especially of ambulance cars. The evacuation line from Tripoli to Tamet had a turn-round of over six hundred miles.

In preparation for the battle D.D.M.S. Eighth Army moved 14 C.C.S., 2 (Ind.) C.C.S. and 15 C.C.S. forward from the medical area at Tobruk to the medical area ten miles north of Agedabia. 3 C.C.S. was sent up to join 1 Mob. Mil. Hosp. and 200 Fd. Amb. in the medical area Km. 10–14 south of Benghazi. In this way a forward and a rear echelon of Army C.C.Ss. were established.

4 B.G.H. (600 beds) with a section of an I.G.H. (200 beds) took over the Italian hospital at Barce vacated by 14 C.C.S. and a convalescent depot was established at Tecnis.

On January 7, 99 Sub-area reverted to G.H.Q. and so 10 C.C.S., 3 (Ind.) C.C.S. and 131 Mob. Dental Unit passed from command of Eighth Army. On January 8, 1 Mob. Mil. Hosp. with 6 F.S.U. and 7 F.T.U. were transferred to D.D.M.S. XXX Corps, and on the 14th, 11 A.F.S. A.C.C., less a few cars for local duty, passed from X Corps to Army.

On January 23, 96 Sub-area took over the local administration of Tripoli and the medical units of XXX Corps which were in the town were placed under A.D.M.S. Tripoli for local administration. At the beginning of February 93 Sub-area under 86 Area took over the local administration of the district between Zliten and Marble Arch with H.Q. at Buerat.

On March 3 Tripolitania Base and L. of C. took over the administration of Tripoli and all L. of C. Eighth Army from Marble Arch to the Tripolitania–Tunisia border.

Until Tripoli had become available on February 20 for hospital ships, and until general hospitals could be brought forward to Tripoli, a chain of C.C.Ss. was available from Tripoli *via* Benghazi to Barce, a distance of some seven hundred and sixty miles.

The rear C.C.S. of XXX Corps was at Tamet. Thence Army cleared by 1 and 2 M.A.Cs. and by 11 A.F.S. A.C.C. (on temporary loan from X Corps) to:

Lt. Sec. 14 C.C.S.	. .	at Nofilia
3 C.C.S.	. .	Marble Arch
14 C.C.S.	. .	Mersa Brega
15 C.C.S.	. .	Agedabia
2 (Ind.) C.C.S.	.	Benghazi
200 Fd. Amb.	.	Benghazi
4 B.G.H.	. .	Barce

Eighth Army was now about to cross the border into Tunisia. As soon as it did so it passed under command of A.F.H.Q. Its story then became merged with that of First Army and U.S. II Corps, to become part of the narrative of the campaign in North-West Africa.

MEDICAL ARRANGEMENTS AT THE BASE

During the last quarter of 1942, 1 Mob. Mil. Hosp., 58 I.G.H., 10 C.C.S., 4 Lt. Fd. Amb. and 3 (Ind.) C.C.S. left B.T.E. and the following units entered it:

92 B.G.H. .	.	.	Kantara
4 Lt. Fd. Amb	.	.	Abd el Qadir
30 I.G.H. .	.	.	Buseili
10, 11 (S.A.) Fd. Amb.		.	Abd el Qadir
3 (Ind.) C.C.S. .	.	.	Gharbaniyat
21 C.C.S. .	.	.	Gerawla
10 C.C.S. .	.	.	Gharbaniyat
22 Fd. Hyg. Sec.	.	.	Matruh
32 (Ind.) Fd. Amb.	.	.	El Daba
16 C.C.S. .	.	.	Mena
150 Fd. Amb.	.	.	Km. 26, Cairo–Alexandria road

Moves within B.T.E. during this period included 30 I.G.H. (two sections) from Cairo to Suez to increase the number of embarkation beds to 400; 4 Lt. Fd. Amb. to Daba; 32 (Ind.) Fd. Amb. (one company) to Buq Buq; 3 (Ind.) C.C.S. from Gharbaniyat to Gerawla; 18 I.S.S. from Alexandria to Matruh and 11 I.S.S. from Safaja to Gerawla.

In preparation for the battle of Alamein the hospital accommodation in B.T.E. was expanded by transfers to the hospitals in Palestine and to convalescent depots. 64 B.G.H. was expanded by 200 beds, 92 B.G.H. by 300 and 2 N.Z.G.H. by 150. In these ways some 6,000 beds were made ready.

During the battle the serious cases were taken direct to the Alexandria hospitals by M.A.C. The rest were taken by ambulance train to hospitals in Cairo and in the Canal area. The walking wounded were evacuated from 4 Lt. Fd. Amb. by special trains with ward coaches attached to the Canal hospitals.

Following the battle B.T.E.'s boundary was extended first to include El Daba on November 14, and to the frontier itself on November 28.

As Eighth Army moved forward certain B.T.E. medical units began to move westwards:

10/11 (S.A.) Fd. Amb. (100 European, 300 non-European beds)	Abd el Qadir
M.I. Room	Alamein
32 (Ind.) Fd. Amb. (less one coy.) . . .	El Daba
11 Br. S.S.	El Daba
21 C.C.S. (less detach.)	Gerawla
11 I.S.S.	Gerawla
18 I.S.S.	Matruh
22 Fd. Hyg. Sec.	Matruh
32 (Ind.) Fd. Amb. (one coy.)	Buq Buq
21 C.C.S., detach.	Buq Buq

During January and February 58 B.G.H., the Hadfield Spears Unit, 16 C.G.H. and 2 B.G.H. left B.T.E. Area and 54 B.G.H. entered it. During April and May, 21 C.C.S., 54 B.G.H. and 106 S.A.G.H. left B.T.E. Area and 22 B.G.H., 1 Mob. Mil. Hosp. and 18 I.G.H. entered it. 78 Neuropathic Hospital was formed out of 1 and 2 Neuropathic Centres and opened at Geneifa on June 26.

(iii)

The Health of the Troops

During the period October 1–December 31, 1942, the health of the troops was excellent, the average daily admission rate to Army field medical units being 1·59 per 1,000, 0·63 per 1,000 less than for the previous quarter. During the quarter January 1–March 31, 1943, the daily sickness rates remained remarkably low, averaging 1·08 per 1,000. During this quarter 14,860 sick were admitted to Army field medical units and of these 6,377 came from Eighth Army Area, the majority during January and February at a time when there were less than 3,000 hospital beds in Tripoli. As this number increased the numbers evacuated fell, so that in March only 851 were admitted to Army medical units from Eighth Army Area.

PRINCIPAL DISEASES*

(a) *Infective Hepatitis* caused grave anxiety. Its incidence reached epidemic proportions and caused serious loss of man-power because of its prolonged duration. It appeared first among New Zealand troops in late September and quickly spread throughout the Army. It was noticeable that 7th Armd. Division had very few cases and that H.Q. Eighth Army remained almost free. The brigade of 44th Division with 7th Armd. Division had very few cases. It was new to the Desert and so could hardly have acquired an immunity. The formations which escaped lightly seemed to be those that were operationally relatively isolated and that were not tied to much used localities.

The incidence of infective hepatitis reached its peak in December and thereafter declined. During the quarter January–March 1943 the admission rate for this disease was 7 per 1,000 in January and 0·62 at the end of March.

(b) *Diarrhoea and Dysentery.* The admissions on account of these diseases decreased sharply in December. During the quarter January–March 1943 the admission rate for these diseases averaged 3·25 per 1,000 for the quarter.

(c) *Tonsillitis.* A mild epidemic occurred among the troops in the Alamein position.

(d) *Accidental Injuries and Burns.* These continued to exact a heavy toll and were responsible for a large proportion of the total admissions to hospital.

(e) *N.Y.D.(N) and Physical Exhaustion.* The label 'physical exhaustion' proved to be a most valuable innovation. In this phase of expanding hope the number of admissions on account of these conditions was significantly smaller than had been that associated with previous battles in the Desert.

(f) *Desert Sores.* The extent of the trouble these caused can be assessed from the following figures for November 1942:

Division	Numbers Attending R.A.Ps. for the First Time	Percentage of these with Desert Sores
50th .	680	21
51st .	1,186	40
1st Armd.	528	28
N.Z. 2nd .	1,774	35

Desert sores and septic skin conditions became less frequent as Eighth Army moved westwards. During January—March 1943 admissions on account of these conditions averaged 2·42 per 1,000 for the quarter.

---

*Reference should be made to the Volume on Medicine and Pathology in this series.

BATTLE CASUALTIES

A total of 10,766 Commonwealth battle casualties were admitted to Army field medical units during the quarter October–December 1942. Of these 10,517 were evacuated to the Delta. In addition 1,102 wounded P.o.W. were admitted and of these 980 were evacuated through medical channels.

MEDICAL SUPPLIES

Medical stores and equipment continued to be satisfactory in supply and quality. Large amounts of expendible stores (drugs and dressings) were captured, but except at Tobruk there was not any large capture of equipment. The salvage, sorting and packing of the stores in Tobruk were undertaken and carried out by 7 (Ind.) Depot Med. Stores. In view of the need of quick turn-round of all forms of transport—road, rail and sea—it was not possible to back-load any large quantity.

A mobile section of an advanced depot of medical stores was improvised and worked for the last two months of 1942. Seven $2\frac{1}{2}$-ton trucks were attached temporarily to 7 Adv. Depot Med. Stores and drivers were provided by 1 M.A.C. Four additional O.Rs. R.A.M.C. were also attached. Later, however, an amendment to W.E. III/51/1 was published authorising the addition of three corporals R.A.M.C. and three 3-ton trucks with drivers and 7 Adv. Depot Med. Stores was reorganised on these lines.

During the quarter January–March 1943 medical stores were supplied by 7 Adv. Depot Med. Stores. The officer commanding was forward with a mobile detachment. Issues to local units were made by the rear party of the stores which had a N.C.O. in charge.

Difficulties were caused by the fact that the advanced depot was not scaled to meet the demands of general hospitals. The three hospitals which were opened during this period were working at full pressure with crisis expansion. The admissions were largely battle casualties. The demands for medical stores were, in consequence, very heavy and it was necessary to send numerous urgent indents to the D.M.S. for supply.

TRANSFUSION SUPPLIES

The supply of fresh blood, and indeed all transfusion supplies, offered a new and large problem.

During the campaign such supplies were divorced from the Depot of Medical Stores and, instead, a F.T.U. was used as a main supply depot of all transfusion supplies. Although this policy meant that a trained transfusion officer was occupied almost wholly in dealing with supplies, there is no doubt that it was fully justified. At one time a second transfusion unit was used at the air transport centre to supervise the transfer of supplies between aircraft, but afterwards this was unnecessary as the R.A.F. Air Transport Wing had become accustomed to dealing with transfusion supplies. 3 F.T.U. moved with the A.A.T.W. and acted as a distributing centre for these stores. When necessary, an advanced blood bank, consisting of a refrigerator van, with a R.A.M.C. orderly and a driver, was stationed in the divisional area to supply forward units. This bank was replenished daily from the supply unit.

RATIONS AND MEDICAL COMFORTS

Troops were well fed throughout the campaign. No troops were on the battle ration for long periods, and the battle ration was favourably regarded. The M.E.F. Scale, with tinned equivalent, was on issue throughout most of the campaign. The battle ration was not tested in any way owing to units saving flour, etc., from their M.E.F. scale, overdrawing by units, and the fact that many troops on the battle ration were well forward and supplemented it with captured enemy rations or locally purchased foodstuffs. The cooking lorries for armoured formations proved eminently successful and the practice of section and individual cooking decreased. The supply of medical comforts was satisfactory and no hardship appeared to have been caused by the reduced scale.

During the second quarter, January–March 1943, the M.E.F. scale again proved adequate. Where possible it was supplemented by local produce, but fruit and vegetables were scarce up to the end of this quarter while eggs were unprocurable in quantity and could be obtained only on a barter system from the Arab population, money in whatever currency having lost its purchasing power. In Tripoli local wine was obtainable during the first six weeks of occupation.

A large fishing industry, organised and unorganised, existed in Tripoli before the occupation and by the end of March 1943 small supplies of fish were again available. Efforts were made to re-open the tunnyfish factory at Tagiura.

The supply of fresh milk presented a very difficult problem in the early stages, particularly for children and the hospitals. Fortunately sufficient tinned milk was available from Army and Red Cross sources until local supplies were forthcoming.

Supply of foodstuffs of all sorts to Giado Jewish concentration camp presented difficulties as regards transportation, man-power and cooking facilities. With an expanded L. of C., the port of Tripoli not yet open and the Army continuing its rapid advance, every vehicle and man in the Army was fully occupied, while at the same time it was evident that some weeks would elapse before the Occupied Enemy Territory

Administration would be in a position to undertake the work. Hygiene unit personnel and vehicles were therefore made available and a fourteen days' supply of meat, milk and other necessities, together with the necessary personnel and cooking apparatus, was sent to Giado.

Although fresh meat, bread and dairy produce were in short supply generally in the town of Tripoli, there was no evidence of malnutrition in the population as a whole, or of any deficiency disease. In gaols, however, and in the concentration camp at Giado those prisoners and inmates who could not afford to buy food outside had suffered great privation and many of the young and old had died of starvation. It is remarkable that in spite of the severe degrees of malnutrition among these people, particularly the very old and very young, there was little evidence of deficiency disease. No clear cases of scurvy or beriberi were seen or reported, but many had spongy gums and patchy pigmentation of the skin. These symptoms cleared rapidly when fresh meat and other food were available.

CLOTHING

Winter clothing was issued during November. In spite of transport and distribution difficulties, practically all troops received their issue.

SANITARY CONDITIONS

There was a definite improvement in sanitary discipline among troops of fighting formations who had learnt bitter lessons in the Alamein line and had seen the deplorable state of enemy troops. It is not improbable that the complete lack of sanitation among both the Germans and Italians did much to undermine their morale in the Alamein position. Unfortunately the improvement among fighting troops was not imitated by L. of C. units, the sanitary state of which remained deplorable.

On reaching Tripoli major hygiene and sanitary problems presented themselves. These were to a large extent foreseen, and before the town was occupied 13 Fd. Hyg. Sec. was sent forward to be ready to enter the town immediately behind the fighting troops. Divisional field hygiene sections were also warned as to what steps should be taken as soon as the town was occupied. Large numbers of latrine seats and tops, native and European pattern, were carried by field hygiene sections and were installed at the docks and in various villages which were taken over. Water mains had been damaged in one or two places and supplies were limited owing to lack of fuel. Electric light and power were not available for the same reason. Municipal services had completely broken down and the town was in a very dirty state, streets being littered with all kinds of rubbish and household refuse.

7, 13 and 29 Fd. Hyg. Secs. were concentrated in the town, which was divided into areas and sanitary personnel allotted to each. In this way the ground was quickly covered, control water points established, refuse disposal organised and, when labour became available, an improvised municipal service establishment working under the direction of 86 Area.

WATER SUPPLIES

Until the end of the battle of Alamein all water supplies were from the main Alexandria supply. Some of the storage tanks in the forward areas were defective, however, and chlorination was required.

After Alamein the Army existed on a series of supplies of various types. The enemy had attempted to destroy or contaminate supplies, picric acid being used for contamination purposes at one point.

In spite of these difficulties ample supplies were available except for short periods, but the amount received by troops was seldom above one gallon per day except by those in Tobruk and Cyrenaica, the limiting factors being shortage of transport and petrol required to bring water forward to widely dispersed troops.

Eighth Army had been so long on main supplies that the necessity for proper chlorination of water had been forgotten. The Royal Engineers appeared to be reluctant to use filtering and chlorination apparatus and chlorination had invariably to be carried out by hand.

In the Desert, supplies came entirely from deep wells and had to be transported anything up to one hundred and fifty miles. At this stage the ration was one gallon per man per day. One or two wells in the El Agheila area were found to be contaminated with bone oil but otherwise there was no interference with wells.

Shortage of fuel limited supplies in Tripoli during the first fortnight. This gave rise to a good deal of anxiety owing to blocking of drains and sinks and also to the fact that the intermittent nature of the supply rendered it more liable to contamination. Tripoli main supply, from deep wells, was adequate in quantity and quality, both chemically and bacteriologically, and was consistently good. Many water points in Tripolitania have a high saline and magnesium sulphate content, but on the whole water supplies were excellent. Deep artesian well water for the hospital area at Della Madia, with salinity of 90 and magnesium content of 48, was drunk without ill effects.

West and south of Zuara supplies, which were limited in amount, contained considerable quantities of sodium and magnesium salts which gave a bitter taste and an aperient action. These waters were, however, consumed in small amounts by the troops over a period of three weeks without causing any general inconvenience. Some difficulty was at first experienced in producing a good quality lime to treat these waters.

DISEASES PREVALENT AMONG THE CIVIL POPULATION

TYPHUS

Warnings of the prevalence of typhus in Tripolitania were received during the advance and were confirmed as towns and villages were occupied in succession. No epidemics were encountered but a total of 220 cases were reported. Of these 118 occurred in Tripoli, 12 at Kussabat and 7 at Suk el Giuma. Tagiura, 10 kms. west of the town, was reported to be a danger spot, but in spite of 100 per cent. louse infestation among the Arab population no outbreak occurred. When Tripoli was first occupied 25 cases were discovered in gaols, and during the succeeding weeks cases occurred in the Arab quarters of the town at the rate of one or two daily. At Giado some 50 cases were discovered and it was reported that as many had already died from the disease.

ENTERIC GROUP

For some weeks before the occupation enteric was increasing, but in spite of a breakdown in the health and municipal services no epidemic or water-borne infections occurred. The number of sporadic cases, however, did rise sharply over a period of ten days until water and sanitary services were restored.

MALARIA

Little information was available regarding the incidence of malaria among the civil population of Tripolitania. The village of Tagiura was probably heavily infected at one time, but spleen rates proved to be less than 2 per cent. East of Buerat there would appear to be little or no malaria. Misurata and Tauorga were reported free of the disease, though the latter place was said to have been dangerous some years before. Inland at Beni Ulid, Garian and Jefren, spleen rates were less than 2 per cent. and the inhabitants generally were healthy. West of Tripoli a few cases of malaria were reported to occur yearly at Sabratha and Zuara, but generally speaking there was little malaria in coastal areas up to and beyond the Tunisian border. Nor was there any evidence that malaria occurs as far inland as the foothills bordering the Gebel country.

ANTI-MALARIAL TRAINING AND ORGANISATION

With the fall of Tripoli and the rapid advance into what was reported to be malarious country, the problem of educating the officers and men became urgent. A malaria field laboratory was asked for and an advance party of this unit arrived early in February. A site for the laboratory and school had been chosen at Benito Gate and teaching was soon begun. Special malaria officers were selected and one malaria control unit mobilised per division. Mobile detachments consisting of a malaria officer, laboratory assistant and equipment from 8 Malaria Fd. Lab. were attached to corps in the forward areas to teach and to supervise training. Propaganda was instituted, pamphlets circulated and surveys carried out. The Consulting Malariologist M.E.F. toured Tripolitania and conferences were held with corps and divisional commanders.

Information had been received that U.S. II Corps and also First Army were employing suppressive mepacrine treatment with effect from April 22, and it was therefore decided to make preparations for its use in Eighth Army. These preparations were completed by the end of March and full instructions had been issued to all concerned and supplies of mepacrine arranged through S. and T. channels.

A NOTE ON AIR EVACUATION OF CASUALTIES FROM THE WESTERN DESERT*

From the onset of the battle of Alamein onwards over 2,000 casualties were evacuated to base hospitals by air. The evolution of this organisation was as follows.

Before and during the battle of Alamein a shuttle air transport service from the advanced air transport centre (A.A.T.C.), Amiriya to Heliopolis via Wadi Natrun, was operated daily. Later, when air superiority was assured, the A.A.T.C. was sited at Burg el Arab, the principle being that air transport aircraft were only allowed to operate behind the fighter aerodromes. Their movements were controlled through the operations room of No. 211 Group.

It was essential to link up the medical receiving stations with the returning transport aircraft. Therefore, for some weeks prior to the onset of the battle 24 Medical Receiving Station was located approximately one mile from the A.A.T.C. at Burg el Arab, 21 Medical Receiving Station a similar distance from the rear air transport centre at Amiriya and 22 Medical Receiving Station at Wadi Natrun. Thus the three medical receiving stations were linked by air transport with the R.A.F. hospital via Heliopolis.

Casualties which needed a long period of treatment were thus easily evacuated back to base. A few Army casualties were evacuated, i.e. head, chest and maxillo-facial injuries, to the appropriate special centre.

1 (Aust.) Air Ambulance Unit, which consisted of three D.H. 86s capable of taking six stretcher and two sitting cases each, was also located at the A.A.T.C. These aircraft were only used for very special cases such as the conveyance of very seriously ill patients and casualties being evacuated from Australian C.C.Ss. to the Australian general hospital at Buseili, where there was a L.G. adjacent to the hospital.

---

*See R.A.F. Medical Services. Vol. I, Chapter 10.

This system worked extremely well prior to the battle. When Eighth Army moved forward the A.A.T.C. and air ambulances were again linked. As the distances became greater there was an increased demand for stores to be provided by air and this demand was met by increasing the number of air transport aircraft. It was then found necessary to request D.D.M.S. Eighth Army to place a company of a field ambulance (casualty air evacuation centre) at the air transport aerodrome to act as a holding unit for casualties. It was found by bitter experience that patients had to wait for the aircraft; aircraft could in no circumstances wait for casualties. The A.A.T.C. was placed as near as possible to the road on the main Army L. of C. and was also situated as near as possible to either a medical receiving station or an Army C.C.S. The air ambulances still continued to evacuate from the forward areas provided they were allowed to land by the operational group concerned (No. 211 Fighter). An important point in the organisation was the control of the movements of air ambulance aircraft to the forward areas by the operation room of this group. This organisation increased to a considerable degree until as many as 200 patients were being evacuated to base hospitals some seven hundred miles away in a single day by returning transport aircraft alone.

Difficulty was experienced in the middle of the advance for the reason that there were two separate transport runs—one from Almaza (Heliopolis District) to rear and advanced Army and R.A.F. Headquarters, the second, 216 Air Transport Group, based on El Adem which supplied units in the forward areas. The problem which had to be solved was that of linking up these two systems. A holding medical receiving station was situated at El Adem to take the cases evacuated from the forward areas and the machines which were returning from the R.A.F. Headquarters were persuaded to land at El Adem on their return journey to pick up those casualties which had to be evacuated to base hospitals. A medical receiving station was also situated in close proximity to the L.Gs. which were the stopping places of the air transport runs, i.e.:

Benghazi for Benina .   21 Medical Receiving Station
El Adem .   .   .   22 Medical Receiving Station
Gambut   .   .   .   24 Medical Receiving Station

In this way the whole of the R.A.F. L. of C. was covered by a medical receiving station for air evacuation. As regards Army cases, these were evacuated along the road and held on the aerodrome by 14 Fd. Amb. at the A.A.T.C.

A blood bank was also formed at the A.A.T.C. Its function was to receive and store blood brought up by air transport and to distribute blood and dried plasma protein to the forward units. This unit was staffed by a specially trained transfusion officer and orderlies (R.A.M.C.) and equipped with a refrigerator truck. Some 5,200 lbs. of blood was transported by air to this centre during November 1942.

When the A.A.T.C. moved the following attached units moved with it:

> The casualty air evacuation centre (14 Fd. Amb.)
> 1 (Aust.) Air Ambulance Unit
> Blood bank

During the advance the following moves of the A.A.T.C. were made:

Burg el Arab	. .	(L.G. 171)
Daba	. .	(L.G. 104)
Matruh	. .	(L.G. 108)
Gambut	. .	Gambut Satellite (casualty evacuation centre formed)
Tmimi	. .	Tmimi Satellite
Martuba	. .	Martuba West
Benina		
Agedabia		

Types of cases. It was found by experience that the only class of case which travelled badly by air was that of perforating wounds of the abdomen. Head injuries, chests, burns, multiple injuries, all travelled well, having had prior resuscitation treatment. Speed of evacuation was of paramount importance in the case of head injuries, which were evacuated to the special centre at the 15 (Scottish) B.G.H. Owing to operational requirements, returning air transport aircraft flew back at about one hundred feet, which enabled chest cases to be carried with the minimum discomfort.

As a result of this experience the following policy became established:

(1) All returning empty air transport aircraft should evacuate casualties as a matter of duty and not courtesy, as was then the case.

(2) All transport aircraft, whether civil or R.A.F., must be fitted to take stretchers. These stretchers should be internationally standardised. There were at this time three different types: (1) American; (2) British general service; (3) Australian air ambulance.

(3) The transport machines taking stores and personnel to headquarters, stores parks, etc., should land at an aerodrome either the same as or adjacent to the aerodrome from which the air transport squadrons serving the forward areas operated.

(4) A casualty air evacuation centre, for both the R.A.F. and Army cases, should be formed and should be adjacent to both aerodromes. This centre could either be a C.C.S., a medical receiving station or a section of a field ambulance, as long as it was equipped

efficiently to feed, treat and house the casualties awaiting onward transmission by returning transport aircraft.

(5) These aerodromes should be situated as near as possible to the main road, which was the normal line of evacuation, in order that severe casualties which were being evacuated by road could be easily transferred.

(6) Telephone communication between air evacuation centre and aerodrome should be established.

(7) The competent medical authority should be consulted as to whether any proposed air transport landing ground was appropriate for the evacuation of casualties.

A NOTE ON THE ARMY SURGICAL SERVICE

In the narrative of the campaign in Libya there is to be found strong support for the generalisation that 'the surgical needs of a campaign may be deduced from the recorded geography of the terrain over which it is to be fought and from the contemporary trend of battle tactics'.* The vast emptiness of the Western Desert offered an excellent battlefield for highly mobile armies. This mobility inevitably meant frequent and rapid changes in the positions of formations and units in an almost featureless landscape. For the most part place names such as Gazala, Sidi Rezegh, El Gubi, Sidi Omar and Msus were not, as they might seem, small hamlets but merely points on a map. This mobility also meant supply lines and evacuation routes that varied continually in length and direction. Westward of Alamein there could be no front line behind which the larger medical units could function without fear of interference and no place westward of the Delta itself where a base, with its base hospitals, could be established.

The armoured fighting vehicle brought with it modified tactics, a reduction in the total numbers of the troops actually engaged in battle, an altered proportion among the lethal weapons employed, a corresponding change in the frequencies of the different kinds of wounds received by battle casualties and of the distribution of wounds according to the causal missile. The commonest were multiple lacerated wounds with retained foreign bodies and prominent among the causal agencies were H.E., the aerial bomb, the mortar and the mine. The desert was peculiar for the wide range of its diurnal temperature, for the scarcity of water and for the dust that carried with it grave risk of airborne infection. Tetanus and gas gangrene were not to be expected, but serious sepsis was.

These conditions and circumstances determined the pattern of medical strategy and influenced the organisation and functioning of

*Aird, Lt. Col. Ian, Military Surgery in Geographical Perspective, *Edin. Med. Journ.* Volume li, 4, 166. April 1944.

the Army Medical Services, since they affected (1) the time interval between the receipt of a wound and the performance of primary surgery, and (2) the time interval between the performance of primary and of secondary surgery.

The aim of military medical organisation, in so far as the surgical treatment of battle casualties is concerned, is to devise the means whereby the first interval shall not exceed eight hours and the second ten days. The length of the first interval is determined by the fact that up to about twelve hours after receipt the wound can be dealt with satisfactorily by primary excision.

In Libya the evacuation chain commonly became stretched to fantastic lengths. Evacuation by air was not developed in any systematic way until the final phase of the campaign. Ambulance railhead was as often as not far in the rear. M.D.S., C.C.S. and base hospital commonly came to be so separated in space that the available ambulance transport could not possibly cope with the demands made upon it.

It therefore became necessary to revise the whole policy of evacuation. The wounded could not be brought back smoothly and swiftly from the M.D.S. to the C.C.S. with its surgical facilities along seemingly interminable desert tracks and often through the confusion of a fluid battle. The C.C.S. was an immobile unit participating in a mobile war. Since the casualty could not be brought back to the surgeon, it became necessary to send the surgeon forward to the casualty, even up to the level of the M.D.S. The conditions demanded the provision of mobile self-contained medical units capable of opening and of closing rapidly and of moving quickly and efficiently over the open desert. These units had to be such as could be grouped and regrouped in an ever-changing pattern and as could function in association either with a field ambulance or, alternatively, farther back, with a C.C.S., according to the fluidity of the tactical situation and the elastic variation of the evacuation line. In respect of staff and equipment they had to be capable of coping by means of 'forward' surgery with wounds sustained by men who had endured long periods of water shortage and of battle rations and to protect these casualties from the hazards of sepsis during a very long and most uncomfortable journey back to hospital.

Thus it was that surgeons in the forward area were from the very beginning encouraged to improvise and to experiment, and it was not long before a valuable lore had accumulated. The theatre caravan and the tented theatre (Plates VI to IX) both came to be favoured, the former easy to open and relatively sand-proof but subject to immobilisation when most needed, the latter less easy to open and less sand-proof but always movable since it could be transferred from one truck to another in case of breakdown. Such were the experimental beginnings of developments which ultimately yielded the field surgical unit.

The same conditions and circumstances, together with the availability of the sulphonamides, determined the nature of surgical intervention in the forward medical units. Though these developments in the purely therapeutic field are dealt with in detail in the volume on surgery in this series, it is perhaps permissible to point to the interconnexion between the length and the discomfort of the long evacuation route on the one hand and the technique of immobilisation which was elaborated and which is well illustrated in the development of the Tobruk plaster, which came to be adopted in those theatres of war in which wounds of the femur had to be evacuated early after initial operation.

Libya is mainly to be distinguished from all the other campaigns that followed by differences in the extent to which the aeroplane was used for evacuation purposes. It therefore represents a set of conditions which has passed into history and for this reason commands the attention of the military medical historian.

In January 1941, at a conference called by D.M.S., M.E.F., these developments were carried further. It was agreed that the need for surgical teams with their own equipment and transport had been abundantly demonstrated. The Hartgill Committee* completely endorsed the view of this conference and gave to its recommendations definite shape. So it was that, late in 1942, the F.S.U. and the F.D.S., each with its own establishment, came into being, the former to replace the M.E. mobile surgical team and the latter to provide a light holding and nursing unit. But it was not until the time of the battle of Alamein that these new units became available to Eighth Army.

In the meantime this particular development was impeded in the Middle East by the scarcity of transport and much resort to improvisation had to be made. Surgical teams from C.C.Ss. and general hospitals were formed and provided with 3-ton lorries, but no post-operative holding was possible.

The Robin Line and the Greek Units, which were mobile surgical units, rendered truly magnificent service. But their equipment and transport were not of the usual army patterns and so they could be immobilised by the development of a mechanical fault of a part that could not readily be replaced from army stores. From their employment it became clear that the transport of such mobile surgical teams must be of a kind in common use within the Army.

A development of considerable significance was the system adopted in January 1942 at El Agheila whereby the light sections of C.C.Ss., reinforced by surgical teams and F.T.Us., functioned far forward and

---

*See Army Medical Services, Volume I, Administration, Chapter 13, in this series (H.M.S.O.).

then were replaced by their heavy sections as the light sections moved on, leap-frogging one over the other.

In the final phase of the campaign fresh tactics were adopted for the employment of the surgical facilities. Some of the C.C.Ss. were made mobile by lowering the scale of their equipment and by the provision of transport. The light section of such a C.C.S. could now move quickly and establish itself far forward. The F.S.U., completely mobile and with limited facilities for post-operative nursing, came to replace the mobile surgical team (M.E.) and the F.D.S. to satisfy the need for a light holding unit.

At El Alamein there were ten F.S.Us., half of them attached to field ambulances, the other half to static C.C.Ss. Out of this experience it was learnt that the combination of a F.S.U. and a M.D.S. was not nearly so useful as that of two F.S.Us. plus a F.T.U., since the latter constituted a really efficient advanced surgical centre.

In these ways the aim underlying the tactical employment of medical units—to achieve the most rapid restoration of the casualty and his most speedy return to duty—was consistently pursued. On the professional side accumulating experience, evolving techniques and the appearance of new therapeutic agents led to an earlier attainment of exact diagnosis and to a reduction in the duration of stay.

Historically it is of importance to note that in 1942 penicillin was used in the field for the first time in the treatment of battle casualties. This experimental work undertaken by D.D.P., M.E.F., with the very limited quantities then available was an essential preliminary to the extensive employment of this antibiotic during the course of the campaign in Sicily.

On the administrative side the creation of the mobile military hospital was an event of peculiar significance. It was another example of the reactions of the medical administration to the conditions and circumstances that obtained. It was to make its notable contribution to the solution of the difficult problem of reducing to a minimum the length of the evacuation chain and of avoiding all unnecessary transfers.

In the history of military medicine, this campaign is important in that it witnessed significant developments in medical tactical policy. It saw the siting of the general hospital far in advance of base, the provision of expert surgical facilities far in advance of the C.C.S., the endowment of the C.C.S. with mobility and the provision of holding and nursing units in corps and divisional areas.

(Plates VI to X illustrate some of the difficulties the field surgical units had to deal with in order to keep the closest possible touch with the units of the Eighth Army in action in Libya during the war of rapid movement in the Western Desert.)

A NOTE ON THE MEDICAL COMPONENT OF A MOBILE ARMY AREA HEADQUARTERS AND ITS FUNCTIONS

During the advance of Eighth Army from Alamein to Enfidaville the towns of Tobruk, Tripoli, Medenine, Gabes and Sfax were successively occupied. As H.Q. Eighth Army moved out of each of these in turn a mobile area H.Q. moved in to take over the responsibility of maintaining law and order, of restoring the essential services and of establishing a road or railhead and, if a port, of restoring dock facilities. This mobile area H.Q., commanded by a brigadier, was composed of representatives of the usual staff branches, G, A/Q, S and T, O.S. and M, together with a camp commandant's establishment. Mov. and Tn. were separate but worked in close collaboration with area H.Q.

The 'M' branch consisted of:

A.D.M.S.
D.A.D.H.
E.M.O. (also acting as D.A.D.M.S.)
Two M.Os. (in M.O. Pool)
Clerks R.A.M.C. 1 Sgt., 1 Cpl., 1 L/Cpl., 3 Ptes.
Orderlies for the two Pool M.Os. (not R.A.M.C.)
Personnel for two P.A.Cs.

The major responsibilities of the A.D.M.S. and his staff were those of organising a medical area, of restoring the sanitary services and of controlling the general sanitation of the town.

The two M.Os. in the Pool were employed in:

(*a*) a central M.I. Room for units without their own medical officer and for the staff of Area H.Q.;
(*b*) a docks M.I. Room for the labour units employed there;
(*c*) a Roadhead M.I. Room.

The mobile area H.Q. was divided into two parts, the reconnaissance party and the main body. The former, fully mobile, consisted of:

The Area Commander	Driver	Batman		
A/Q. . . .	,,	,,	1 or 2 clerks	
GII . . .	,,	,,	clerk	interpreter
A.D.S.T. . .	,,	,,	,,	,,
A.D.M.S. . .	,,	,,	,,	,,
D.A.D.H. . .	,,	,,	,,	
D.A.D.O.S. . .	,,	,,	,,	
Representative of Camp Commandant.				

This party—the 'Golden List'—followed hard upon the heels of the fighting troops and entered the town immediately following its capture. The main body (and sometimes the rear party) moved up as soon as the circumstances permitted. The main body or the rear party, when leaving a town, handed over to a static sub-area H.Q.

Prior to the forward move of the mobile area H.Q. its A.D.M.S. was informed of the general plan by D.D.M.S. Army and by D.D.M.S. of the corps that was concerned. He was told of the medical units that were to come into his area. These could be:

> *From Army Sources*
> > An Army field ambulance
> > An Army field hygiene section (sometimes two)
> > One or more C.C.Ss.
> > An advanced depot of medical stores
> > A M.A.C.
> > A bacteriological laboratory
> > An advanced blood bank (a F.T.U.)
> > One or more F.S.Us.
> > A specialist unit—e.g. a neurosurgical unit, a maxillo-facial unit or a M.D.U.
>
> *From G.H.Q.*
> > A number of general hospitals
> > A convalescent depot

Armed with this information A.D.M.S. turned to his map and town plan (if available) and noted the locations of hospitals, schools, barracks, hotels and the like and also of large open spaces outside the town and near the roads. He could assume that his plea for the allocation of medical institutions to 'M' would be granted, but since all the branches needed large areas and large buildings he could only expect that of the rest he would be given his share, usually a very generous one. Concerning these matters the area commander's ruling was final.

In the Desert the 'Golden List' usually moved about the level of rear corps H.Q. At Tripoli it moved at the level of rear divisional H.Q. and leaguered in their axis. As soon as the road was clear this advance party moved into the town to a rendezvous previously named by the area commander. An office for each of the branches was then allotted by the commander and A/Q and notice boards and direction signs were erected. The clerk of the branch was left in this office, which functioned as a report centre.

A.D.M.S. and D.A.D.H., with the interpreter, then set out in motor transport to seek and interview the 'mayor', the 'M.O.H.', the chief of police and the chief of the municipal hospital, and then to inspect the buildings and open spaces thought to be suitable for the accommodation of the medical units coming into the area and also for a transit area for medical units, separate from the medical area. The occupants of these buildings and sites were then firmly told that military units were moving in and that the premises would have to be vacated, or that the occupants would have to compress themselves into a smaller space. When stocks of medical stores and equipment were discovered, either by the medical reconnaissance party or by others, guards had to be found and placed over them without delay.

The selected medical area was, if at all possible, such as had buildings or space for tentage to accommodate the field ambulance, the C.C.Ss., the general hospitals and laboratory and for an ambulance car park. In the Desert the space available was unlimited so that wide dispersal of the units was possible.

For a medical stores area a large building with a good approach was most suitable. In it and around it were sited the advanced depot of medical stores, Red Cross stores, the stretcher and blanket dump, the blood bank and frequently the field hygiene section or its workshops.

For the M.A.C. area, preferably near the M.A.C. check post, good standing for the M.A.C. workshops was a prime necessity.

The site for the convalescent depot was always near the sea coast.

Then an area conference was held and the heads of services reported to the commander. When the accommodation had been allotted the town 'mayor' was notified in respect of buildings, 'G' in respect of land.

These matters being settled, A.D.M.S. then got in touch with the senior R.A.F. medical officer in the area, seeking information concerning R.A.F. arrangements. If a L.G. in the area was to be used, A.D.M.S. arranged for the placement of an air evacuation section (a section of a field ambulance) there. The arrangements for air evacuation were made at Army level between D.D.M.S. Army and the P.M.O., R.A.F.

The D.A.D.H. secured information concerning (1) the sources of the water supplies, the purity of the water and so forth; (2) the system of sewage disposal; (3) the organisation of refuse collection; (4) the incidence of infectious diseases; (5) the incidence of venereal disease and the control of prostitution; (6) the system of inspection of food and drink, factories, restaurants, cafés, barbers' shops.

He then made arrangements for the chlorination of the water, for the employment of labour for the cleansing of the streets (through the 'mayor') and for the employment of the personnel of the field hygiene section in supervising this and in inspecting factories, restaurants, etc.

When the mobile area H.Q. had become established in the town, medical administrative instructions were issued if the area was a large one. In a small area the detail was given in Area Orders. In general these took the following form:

(1) Instructions concerning the disposal of casualties. Local casualties went either direct or passed through the central M.I. Room to the receiving field ambulance, which acted as a sieve. There they were distributed in accordance with their needs to the open C.C.S. (surgical) or to a second C.C.S. (without a F.S.U.) or remained in the field ambulance (medical). V.D. cases were retained in the field ambulance.

PLATE VI. Caravan type of mobile operating theatre.

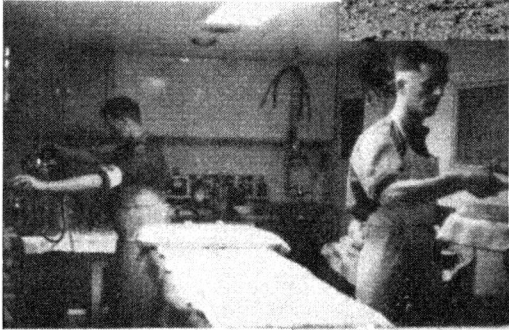

PLATE VII. Interior of caravan operating theatre.

PLATE VIII. 'Lean-to' operating truck packed.

PLATE IX. 'Lean-to' operating truck in process of erection.

PLATE X. 'A long-delayed and serious operation in a desolate scene.'

(2) Details concerning locations of and the functions allotted to the different units, the method of drawing rations and stores, the sites of the stretcher and blanket dumps, returns and records required and the means of intercommunication. (Throughout the Libyan campaign the means of intercommunication remained most inadequate; D.Rs. were very scarce, the telephone unreliable and wireless usually poor. It was not unusual for a 3-ton lorry to be used, in the absence of anything better, for the conveyance of messages.)

(3) Instructions concerning the disposal and treatment of P.o.W. and civilian sick and wounded. It was usual for the P.o.W. to include a number and variety of enemy medical personnel sufficient to deal with their own less serious cases. The more serious were admitted to British units pending the making of permanent arrangements. Similarly there were usually civil hospitals with civilian medical practitioners to which civilian sick and wounded were directed. On occasion the numbers of P.o.W. sick and wounded were such as to overwhelm the resources of the mobile area H.Q.

(4) Instructions concerning the system of evacuation by air, land and sea.

Air. The practice was for the medical unit having cases for evacuation by air to notify the air evacuation section on the L.G. and for the latter to notify the medical units of the availability of aircraft. A load of 20–30 cases was called forward to the L.G. and the officer in charge of the air evacuation section—the air evacuation officer—then got them away on returning aircraft. Such patients as remained with the air evacuation section at the end of the day were retained in the section's penthouse. The seriously ill were sent forward to the L.G. only when their despatch by air was guaranteed.

Road. The system usually adopted was as follows: Patients were brought to the medical area by M.A.C. under corps arrangements and A.D.M.S. mobile area H.Q. was responsible for their evacuation therefrom to base units by Army M.A.C. This was carried out either by the 'convoy' method or else by the 'trickle' method. In the former O.C. M.A.C. was informed by the units in the medical area how many cases there were for evacuation next morning and he then provided the requisite number of ambulance cars, which left together. In the latter, O.C. M.A.C. stationed a number of cars with the medical units in the medical area; these were loaded and despatched and as the first of these passed the M.A.C. check post a note was handed in stating the total number of cars required. As the cars left replacements were sent up to the medical area.

Owing to the long distances that had to be covered it was the rule to place a 'coffee stall' on the route, the personnel and equipment being found by some medical unit on the L. of C.

20

Train. Save at Alamein and in the base area there was no evacuation by train.

Ship. When the ship could be docked the procedure was straightforward, but if it had to be off shore it tended to be complicated. Craft, obtained by arrangement with A.Q.M.G., Mov. and Tn. and the Sea Transport officer, had to be used and of these there was a great variety —L.C.T., L.C.M., L.C.I., 'Z' craft, local tugs, launches, lighters. Hospital carriers had their own motor launches with racks for seven stretchers and were found to be most satisfactory.

A stretcher party of one officer and 30 O.Rs. was stationed on the dockside. Here tea and medical comforts were provided.

The E.M.O., who had to maintain constant touch with the officer commanding the ship, was, if possible, provided with a D.U.K.W. or a small launch. It was his responsibility to ensure that the stretchers, blankets and pyjamas going on board were returned and to come away with as many extras and as great a quantity of medical comforts as he could extract.

The mobile area H.Q. was usually followed by a sub-area H.Q., to which it handed over all the relevant files, maps, etc. Each member of the staff briefed his opposite number. When the sub-area H.Q. arrived complete this procedure was swift and the mobile area H.Q. was soon ready to move forward. But usually the sub-area H.Q. arrived in driblets so that only a partial hand-over was possible and many of the mobile area H.Q. staff had to be left behind to form a rear party, an arrangement that was found to be most unsatisfactory.

A review of the activities of a mobile area H.Q. in Libya* revealed very clearly that its efficient functioning depended very largely indeed upon the personal contacts made by the A.D.M.S. with the senior administrative medical officers of all formations in or passing through his area.

The Medical Aspects of the Occupation of Captured Enemy Towns and Ports. Colonel W. L. Spencer-Cox. *Journ. R.A.M.C.* March–April, 1944.

CHAPTER 5

THE CAMPAIGN IN NORTH-WEST AFRICA
November 1942 – May 1943

Précis

CONSEQUENT upon the entry into the war of Japan and the United States of America in December 1941, military formations of the latter country had been assembling in the United Kingdom in preparation for the intended assault upon 'Festung Europa'. Russia, deeply invaded by the German armies, was hard-pressed and was clamantly demanding that this assault should be launched without further delay. Such an operation being at this time beyond the capacity of the Allies, it was decided that in its stead the French territories of North-West Africa should be occupied by a composite United States and British force and that the Axis forces in North Africa should be eliminated by a synchronised attack from the east (Eighth Army) and from the west.

It was decided to make the landings at Casablanca (U.S. force sailing from the U.S.A.), Oran (U.S. force sailing from the United Kingdom) and at Algiers (a composite U.S. and British force—Eastern Task Force —sailing from the United Kingdom).

The landings were made on November 8, 1942, in the face of opposition, unequal in vigour at the three places, and on the 11th hostilities ceased, the French political and military authorities agreeing to collaborate with the Allies.

The Germans reacted to these events with their customary vigour. The whole of France was occupied. Troops were rushed by sea and air to Bizerta, Tunis and other ports farther south.

From Algiers Eastern Task Force despatched assault groups by land and sea to Bougie and Bône. Paratroops were dropped to secure airfields deep in Tunisia. On November 26 Medjez el Bab was occupied. But then the weather intervened to transform the roads running eastwards from Algiers into rivers of mud. The eastward rush lost its momentum and soon was halted. Eastern Task Force—British First Army with U.S. II Corps and French formations under command—had to wait for reinforcements, for better weather and for the approach of Eighth Army from the east before the Axis forces could be flung out of Africa.

Eighth Army moved forward from Tripoli to enter Tunisia and to confront the strong Mareth Line on February 13, 1943. It now came under General Eisenhower's supreme command. General Alexander became Deputy to General Eisenhower and assumed command of 18 Army Group comprising all Allied forces in Tunisia.

There were two Axis armies in Tunisia, one under von Arnim opposing First Army, the other under Rommel facing Eighth Army. The coastal passage between them was threatened by U.S. II Corps in the Sbeitla–Gafsa area. Marshal Rommel rushed a powerful force north to break through the Kasserine Pass and to threaten Thala and Tebessa. He was checked and forced to withdraw on February 23. Then on March 3 he attacked Eighth Army at Medenine and again was repulsed. The initiative now finally passed to the Allies.

On March 20 General Montgomery attacked the Mareth Line. By means of a daring and wide turning movement he forced the Axis forces out of the Mareth position on the 27th and out of the Wadi Akarit position, farther to the north, on April 6. The Axis forces facing Eighth Army then fell back to the Enfidaville position. First and Eighth Armies conjointly now enclosed the Axis forces in the north-east corner of Tunisia and the stage was set for the closing scene.

After regrouping his forces General Alexander launched the final assault on May 6. On the 7th U.S. II Corps occupied Bizerta and by the 9th all the Axis forces facing the Americans had surrendered. On the 7th also British formations gained possession of Tunis. They then cut across the base of the Cap Bon peninsula. By the 13th all resistance had ceased. An Axis force a quarter of a million strong had been destroyed. The whole length of the North African shore was now in Allied hands. The isolation of Gibraltar and Malta was ended. Russia had been indirectly aided. The Fascist régime in Italy had been severely shaken.

The difficulties attending the creation and functioning of a G.H.Q. composed of representatives of the armed forces of several nations had been recognised and largely overcome and techniques required for the most effective use of an international force had been devised and elaborated. French and British troops, enduring together, had broken down many of the barriers that initially separated them.

(i)

Operation 'Torch'

On December 7, 1941, Japan, by attacking Pearl Harbour, was instrumental in bringing the United States of America into the war. Steps were taken at once by the United States and British Governments and military staffs to determine the ways in which the armed forces of the two countries might work together to achieve the greatest degree of integrated efficiency. It was quickly decided that the weight of American military power should be directed against Germany in Europe before being hurled against Japan. In June 1942 General Dwight D. Eisenhower was appointed to the command of the European Theatre of Operations, United States Army (E.T.O.U.S.A.) and charged with the task of preparing the American contribution to the assault upon 'Festung Europa'. Shortly afterwards American military formations began to assemble in the United Kingdom.

At this time the U.S.S.R., hard-pressed, was clamantly demanding that the Americans and British should open a second front in Europe. But because of the grave insufficiencies in respect of trained men and of materials of war that then existed, the United States and British Governments and staffs were reluctantly forced to the conclusion that so ambitious a project as an invasion of the Continent could not possibly be launched in the immediate future. Seeking alternatives within their competence they considered three possibilities: (a) to seize and hold a limited bridgehead on the north-west coast of France, an operation which would pin down large numbers of enemy troops and constitute a preliminary step towards the actual invasion; (b) to intensify and expedite the campaign in the Middle East by reinforcing Eighth Army and so secure control of the central Mediterranean; or (c) to seize the French territories in North-West Africa (Morocco, Algeria and Tunisia) and, this being accomplished, to unleash a combined offensive from Tunisia and Egypt, crushing the Axis forces in Libya and opening the whole of the Mediterranean (Operation 'Torch').

After much careful consideration it was finally decided to proceed immediately with Operation 'Torch'. Since British forces, co-operating with those serving under General de Gaulle, had recently come into open conflict with the Vichy French at Oran and in Syria it was further decided that, in order to avoid any anti-British feeling among the French in North-West Africa, Operation 'Torch' should be given, initially at least, the appearance of an American military enterprise.

STRATEGIC AND OTHER CONSIDERATIONS

The occupation, by conquest if necessary, of the whole of the southern shore of the Mediterranean would (a) deny the facilities and resources of the French territories to the enemy; (b) create a nucleus around which French resistance could gather (there were many thousands of French troops and a number of air force units in these territories); (c) counter the German threat to the Russian left flank; (d) constitute a constant check to Italian military adventures; (e) go far to secure the sea passage to the Middle and Far East and abolish the isolation of

Malta and Gibraltar; and (f) free much Allied shipping for employment elsewhere.

The coastline of the three French territories is about 1,000 miles long. The natural divisions of Algeria are three, the Tell, the High Plateaux and the Desert. The Tell is a narrow strip of low-lying, swampy, malarious, fertile, cultivated land, 30–100 miles broad, between the sea and the Atlas mountain range. The ridges of the Atlas, which enclose the High Plateaux, rise to some 3,000 ft. above sea level, are uncultivated for the most part and are used for grazing. Beyond the Atlas lies the vast Sahara.

Most of Tunisia is covered by a series of rugged mountain ridges with intervening valleys running south-west to north-east. There are two low-lying areas, the Tunis plain in which nestle the towns of Tunis, Bizerta and Medjez el Bab, and the funnel-shaped Medjerda valley along which run the main road and rail connexions between Algeria and Tunis. North of this valley is a region of irregular hills clothed with cork-oak forests or thick scrub, forming an effective barrier to mechanised movement save along the coastal road Tabarka–Djebel Abiod–Sedjenane–Mateur–Bizerta. In the north of Tunisia spurs of the Algerian mountains run eastwards towards Bizerta. South of the Medjerda valley there is a mountain mass with three major massifs, Djebel Mansour, Dj. Fkirine and Dj. Kairouan. From the last of these, ranges extend to the Gulf of Tunis in the north and to the sea in the east. From Dj. Fkirine two long ranges, the Eastern and the Western Dorsales, run south and south-west. The Eastern Dorsale, two to three thousand feet high, runs southwards as far as Maknassy. It is pierced by passes—at Pichon, Fondouk, Faid and Maknassy. The Western Dorsale runs south-west to end near Gafsa and is pierced by passes at Maktar, Sbiba, Kasserine and Feriana.

The climate of the coastal belt of Algeria is temperate. January, February and March have plentiful sunshine and rain; April and May resemble an English summer; June, July, August and September are the hottest months; the first rains usually begin to fall towards the end of October; November and December are relatively cold and fresh. The climate of the interior is less damp and much hotter. Constantine, for example, is extremely cold in the winter and Biskra unbearably hot during the summer. The sirocco, the wind from the desert, blows with a fierce heat during the spring and summer but seldom for more than three days at a time. The rainfall around Algiers averages 20–30 inches and falls on 70–80 days during the year.

In Tunisia spring begins in March, summer in May, autumn in September and winter in December. During August and September storms and south winds are frequent and the countryside shimmers in the intense heat. The average temperature along the coast is 64° F. but in the interior during the summer months the thermometer often registers 120° F. in the shade.

COMMUNICATIONS

A main road ran the whole length of the territories more or less parallel to the coastline and touching the coast itself at Algiers. Branches linked this road with the coastal and inland towns. The main roads in Tunisia, leading to places of military importance, were (1) the coast road —Tabarka–Sedjenane–Mateur–Bizerta; (2) the road from Souk Ahras –Souk el Khemis–Beja–Mateur–Bizerta; (3) Beja–Oued Zarga–Medjez el Bab–Tebourba–Tunis; (4) Medjez–Massicault–Tunis; (5) Le Kef –Teboursouk–Medjez–Tunis; (6) Le Kef–Maktar–Pichon–Kairouan –Sousse; (7) Le Kef–Sbeitla–Sfax; (8) Ain Beida–Tebessa–Feriana– Gafsa–Gabes.

There were some 3,100 miles of single-track railway line in Algeria and Tunisia. One line ran from Casablanca through Rabat, Fez, Oudja, Sidi bel Abbes, Blida, Algiers, Beni Mansour, Setif, Constantine, Duvivier, Guelma, Souk Ahras, Tebourba and Medjez el Bab to Tunis. From this branches ran to Oran, Cherchell, Bougie, Philippeville and Bône. Other lines joined Bône and La Calle; Constantine and Tebessa; Constantine, El Guerrah and Biskra; Souk Ahras and Tebessa; Algiers, Blida and Djelfa; Tunis, Mateur and Bizerta; Tunis and Tabarka; Hammam Lif and Le Kef; Hammam Lif, Sousse, Sfax and Gabes; Sousse, Kairouan, Sbeitla and Feriana; Sfax and Gafsa.

MEDICAL INTELLIGENCE

The malarial season began in May, reached a peak in June, a second peak in September and receded towards the end of November. Most of the coastal belt was highly malarious, as were the valleys which stretch inland. Benign tertian and malignant tertian were the commonest forms encountered. Few protective measures were used save that the French inhabitants took quinine during the season and, when possible, moved into safer areas. Near the larger ports anti-malarial schemes were in operation, but the problem had never been seriously tackled throughout the remainder of the country. The native population took few, if any, precautions and received no treatment.

There had been three heavy epidemics of louse-borne typhus in Algeria during 1940–42, the most serious in the last of these years. The greatest incidence occurred from December to February, the peak being reached in the winter months. During 1941–42 vaccination on a large scale was carried out among the European and Arab populations and the French health authorities were of the opinion that this did much to limit the spread of the disease.

Sporadic cases of typhoid were known to occur throughout the region but there was no evidence of any recent epidemic. Bacillary dysentery was common and apparently was regarded lightly by the health authorities. Amoebic dysentery was also reported to be a common disease and liver abscess a frequent consequence.

Venereal disease was rife among the European population and it was credibly reported that 90 per cent. of the adult Arabs suffered from syphilis. Tertiary manifestations seemed to be the exception rather than the rule. Brothels were to be found in all centres of population and their supervision by the health authorities appeared to be somewhat cursory.

Sporadic cases of diphtheria, scarlet fever, smallpox, tick-borne relapsing fever, urinary schistosomiasis, plague, trachoma, dengue, helminthiasis and leishmaniasis occurred all over the region. Recent hydatid disease figures for Algeria showed that in 60 per cent. of cases the liver was attacked, in 10 per cent. the lung and in 4 per cent. the spleen.

Pulmonary tuberculosis was exceedingly rife among the native population. Surgical tuberculosis was also very common.

The distribution of poisonous snakes and scorpions was widespread, the latter being very common in the areas bordering the desert.

'110' FORCE

During the early part of 1942 this force was assembled in Scotland to form the nucleus of First Army, the British North African Expeditionary Force (B.N.A.F.).

'110' Force. Order of Battle.

> V Corps
>> 4th Division
>> 78th Division
>> 6th Armd. Division
>> 22nd A.A. Bde.
>> together with attached troops and services

On August 12 Lieut.-General K. A. N. Anderson assumed command.

ALLIED FORCE HEADQUARTERS

On August 11, 1942, A.F.H.Q., under General Eisenhower, was formed in London. The H.Q. staff, 50 per cent. American and 50 per cent. British, was organised on the American plan. The Chief Surgeon (Br. = D.M.S.) was a British officer. His main functions were to plan and to co-ordinate the activities of the medical services of the American and British forces serving in this theatre. To begin with his staff consisted of an A.D.M.S. and an A.D.H. (British) and a deputy surgeon, a supply officer and a hygiene officer (American). Later the medical section of A.F.H.Q. came to consist of:

United States Component				*British Component*				
Officers		*Enlisted Men*		*Officers*		*W.Os.*		*O.Rs.*
Major General	1	M/Sgt.	1	Major General	1	I 1	S. Sgts.	1
Colonels	9	T/Sgts.	3	Brigadier	1	II 1	Sgts.	5
Lieut. Colonels	9	S/Sgts.	2	Colonels	9		Cpls.	5
Majors	7	Tech. 3	2	Lieut. Colonels	10		L/Cpls.	7
Captains	4	Sgts.	2	Majors	3		Ptes.	17
1 Lieut.	2	Tech. 5	8	Captains	3			
2 Lieut.	1	Pfc.	4					
		Pvt.	3					
	33		25		27	2		35

In 1943 the organisation of the Medical Section, A.F.H.Q. was as under:

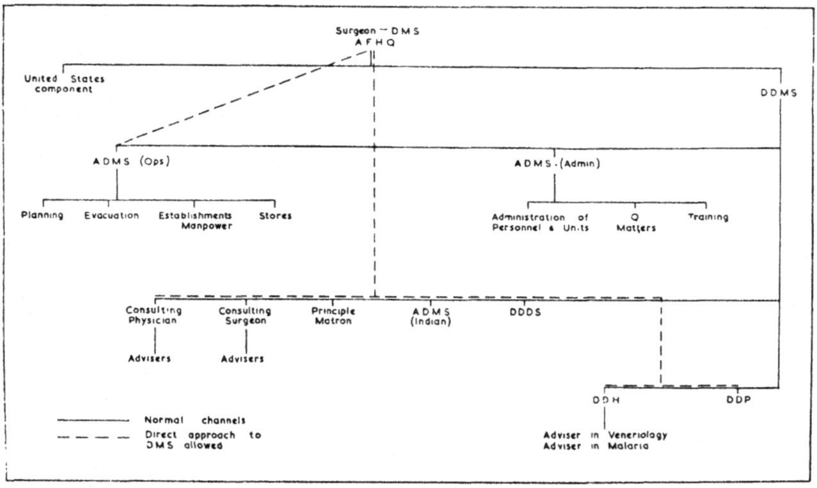

FIG. 39. The Organisation of the Medical Branch, A.F.H.Q.

Its scope and functions can perhaps best be indicated in broad outline by the following scheme:

Surgeon—D.M.S.
(Co-ordination of policy and effort)

U.S. Army Medical Services	British Army Medical Services	French Army Medical Services
U.S. Surgeon and staff	British D.D.M.S. and staff	French D.M.S. and staff

In the same building in Algiers but on different floors.

In a different building and part of French G.H.Q. and not A.F.H.Q.

PREPARATORY MEDICAL PLANNING

Medical planning was at two different levels, A.F.H.Q. and Task Force respectively. The medical planning staff of A.F.H.Q.—D.M.S. with a composite United States and British staff—was involved in the making of arrangements which would ensure that the fullest, the most harmonious and the most effective use was made of the medical services of this mixed force. It was concerned with the policies affecting the mounting of the Oran and Algiers assaults.

D.M.S. A.F.H.Q., was required to undertake a by no means easy task. The three medical services differed in respect of organisation and of the distribution of functions. He had to gain their acceptance of a common policy and to evoke from them the greatest degree of eager co-operation. To produce a truly integrated service was impossible, but under his direction a remarkable degree of harmonious collaboration was achieved.

Force '110' had been busily planning for a variety of possible operations. Thus it was that when it was decided that First Army was to take part in Operation 'Torch' preparations were well advanced. For example, the details of the phasing of the medical units, of the organisation of the light scale C.C.S., of the general hospital block loading and of the automatic maintenance block had already been worked out by D.D.M.S. Force '110'.

The planning staff of First Army was constituted as follows: with Adv. H.Q. in London were D.D.M.S., A.D.M.S., A.D.H. and a staff-captain. With rear H.Q. in Scotland were D.A.D.M.S., A.D.P., A.D.D.S. and a pool of medical officers who acted as staff-captains. The planning staffs of V Corps and H.Q. L. of C. worked in close association with these headquarters and with their own divisional and area H.Qs. D.Ds.M.S. V Corps and L. of C. were constantly in touch with D.D.M.S. First Army. The quality of this organisation is revealed in the fact that for the medical planning of Eastern Task Force only two months were required.

When First Army left for Algiers, H.Q. IX Corps took over the responsibilities of planning and of adjustment. Like First Army before it, it worked quite independently of A.F.H.Q. and directly with the War Office. When, in its turn, H.Q. IX Corps left for Africa it came under First Army. Later, when A.F.H.Q. took over, it dealt with First Army on all matters relating to First Army units and with A.F.H.Q. on matters relating to base and L. of C. units.

In so far as the control of the medical affairs of First Army was concerned the operation was divided into three phases. Before D.D.M.S. First Army landed at Algiers, A.D.M.S. 78th Division functioned as the senior administrative officer of Eastern Task Force and was assisted by A.D.M.S. 1 B.S.A. When D.D.M.S. First Army arrived, he took over from A.D.M.S. 78th Division who thereafter devoted himself entirely to the affairs of his own division. D.M.S. A.F.H.Q. was due to arrive in Algiers in January when A.F.H.Q. was scheduled to assume command. Thereafter D.D.M.S. First Army would concern himself exclusively with the affairs of First Army. It is to be noted that D.D.M.S. First Army was responsible not only for the medical planning of Eastern Task Force, but also for the utilisation of the medical services of First Army and of those of the U.S. and French formations that served under the command of First Army for the first two critical months of the campaign.

When H.Q. First Army left for Algeria it included an increment which was later to form the nucleus around which A.F.H.Q. itself would be built. In this increment was an A.D.M.S. (Liaison). This increment was progressively reinforced, beginning in January, so that after two months A.F.H.Q. was complete. The take-over was gradual in accordance with the build-up. It was not until early February that the medical section of A.F.H.Q. was in a position to assume full control. Thus during January though D.D.M.S. L. of C. was nominally under A.F.H.Q. it was found expedient for him to continue to work under D.D.M.S. First Army.

It is of interest to note that D.M.S., A.F.H.Q., arrived in Algiers at the beginning of December, a month early, in order to acquaint himself with the nature of his tasks. He at once withdrew the A.D.M.S. (Increment) from First Army to help him. Thus it came about that D.D.M.S. First Army lost the services of one who had been acting, as was planned, as A.D.M.S. Rear H.Q. First Army at a time when his burden was heaviest. It became necessary for A.D.M.S. 1 B.S.A. to deal with much of the work previously undertaken by A.D.M.S. (Increment).

The project for the capture of French North-West Africa involved a combined operation to be undertaken jointly by the forces of Great Britain and the United States under an American Commander-in-Chief with a composite British and American staff. The force was, in effect, to be divided into two parts operating simultaneously, the one, derived entirely from troops of the United States, having as its object a landing at Casablanca and Oran for the occupation of Morocco, and the other, including both British and American components, to carry out an assault upon Algiers and other ports farther to the east with the intention of capturing Eastern Algeria and Tunisia. The British component was to consist, first, of a striking force comprising one armoured division with strong reconnaissance parties from base and lines of communications units, and later, when the subsequent build-up was completed, of two armoured divisions and four infantry divisions constituting two corps under the command of First Army with base and L. of C. troops, amounting in all to a force of some 220,000, subject to the control of the Supreme Allied Commander at Allied Force Headquarters.

The outline plan of the operation prescribed that the force must be prepared to maintain itself over beaches during the first three or four weeks, by the end of which time transportation units should have succeeded in putting captured ports into working order. Moreover, the force was to be equipped on a scale which would make it sufficiently mobile to carry out an advance to a considerable depth in a country deficient in railway facilities. The general outline of the scheme from both its operational and its administrative aspects was communicated to planning branches in the War Office during the month of August 1942, and a provisional order of battle was notified shortly afterwards.

Battle casualties, including sick, were estimated, in terms of monthly rates, at 12 per cent. of the force in the first week, 10 per cent. in the second week and 8 per cent. thereafter. The total number of casualties to be incurred during the first four weeks of the campaign, including the voyage, the assault and the subsequent advance, was expected to amount to 14,000, comprising 3,250 killed and 10,750 sick or wounded. Of the latter 55 per cent. would be recoverable in the theatre of operations and many of these, being survivors from vessels sunk in convoy or at the time of the assault, would require but little medical treatment.

In planning the organisation necessary to deal with battle casualties and sick wastage it was decided that, ultimately, evacuation to the United Kingdom should be restricted to those cases whose recovery was likely to occupy three months or more. Nevertheless, during the early stage of the operations and until bases and lines of communication could be established and adequately developed for the retention of the more protracted cases, it would be necessary to evacuate direct to home ports all casualties unlikely to be fit for duty within one month. While these arrangements were operative light cases not requiring constant medical attention or active treatment were to be evacuated to the United Kingdom in returning personnel ships. The scale of hospital accommodation to be supplied was finally fixed at an over-all rate of 8 per cent. of the strength of the force. It was estimated that by the twenty-fifth day of the operation the number of troops engaged would reach 120,000, thus entailing the establishment of 9,600 hospital beds within the first four weeks. Three months from the opening of the campaign the force was to be built up to some 220,000, requiring on an 8 per cent. basis a total provision of 17,600 beds which it was proposed to concentrate in two hospital, or medical, base areas situated conveniently accessible to ports of embarkation—i.e. Algiers and, probably, Bône. Convalescent depots affording accommodation for 6,600 cases—i.e. on a scale of nearly 3 per cent. of the force—were to be established during the same time.

Although the reorganisation recommended by the Hartgill Committee* had not yet been effected, it was considered necessary to make certain modifications in the usual disposition of medical services in the field for this, the first, large-scale amphibious operation undertaken by the Army. Among these was an arrangement designed to afford surgical treatment to urgent cases as far forward as possible in the line of casualty evacuation. For this purpose each field ambulance due to land in the assault stage of the operation was to be reinforced by a surgical team detached from its parent C.C.S. and attached temporarily to the headquarters of the field ambulance for duty in the M.D.S. ; C.C.Ss. with attached F.S.Us. and F.T.Us. were to be landed early in the second day of the assault so as to augment facilities for operative surgery and resuscitation. General hospitals would follow as soon as practicable in order that field ambulances and C.C.Ss. might evacuate the casualties they had thus far been forced to retain and so become free to advance with their formations.

Included in the two armoured divisions and four infantry divisions constituting the British component of the force was the usual medical element representing a commitment of four light field ambulances, fourteen field ambulances, two light field hygiene sections and four field hygiene sections, a total of twenty-four units. All of these were already formed when the task of preparing the force was begun, although some had not yet been mobilised and some had not been finally assigned to their respective formations. To complete the medical requirements of the force in accordance with the scales prescribed by the administrative plan it was necessary to produce the following medical units for allocation to corps, army, G.H.Q. or L. of C. troops: three field ambulances, five field hygiene sections, five casualty clearing stations, five field transfusion units, twelve field surgical units, two field hospitals, twenty general hospitals, three convalescent depots and also several special surgical units, mobile laboratories and depots of medical stores. In all, British medical units included within the range of preparatory planning for the North African operation amounted to 113 in number.

For the most part, units of the force were divided into two groups, the first to be mobilised by September 1, 1942, the second by November 1, 1942. Those of the first group were to effect mobilisation according to schedule, despite the fact that the trained personnel, etc., available might not be sufficient to complete all units in all respects. Thus medical units were to mobilise without such specialists, equipment and transport as were not immediately forthcoming; they would be made up to the maximum possible and, if required for active operations before they were complete, deficiencies would be supplied from other

*Army Medical Services. Volume I. Administration. Chapter 13.

units not yet mobilised. In the case of certain units which could perform no useful function while awaiting their dispatch overseas and which could be made ready at short notice—e.g. base transfusion units and depots of medical stores—mobilisation was postponed until they were actually required, personnel and equipment being assigned to them and held in reserve pending that time.

Units were mobilised on war establishments as already existing. Revised establishments were applied only when the relative new scales of equipment had been approved, completed, and were in the hands of the units affected. As the new establishments consequent upon the adoption of the Hartgill scheme of reorganisation, although approved, had not reached the final stage, medical units remained, in function, personnel and equipment, upon the old basis subject to minor modifications required by the special circumstances of the operation. General hospitals were raised under the same arrangements as those which had sufficed to supply requirements in respect of the Middle East, African and other theatres of war. Certain suitable sites were reserved for the formation and training of hospital units and as soon as one hospital left the site another was raised and formed. Hospitals so formed were mobilised as required for active service, the process of mobilisation being completed within one month. In this way two general hospitals of 200 beds, four of 600 beds and four of 1,200 beds could be produced each month, a rate of supply sufficient to meet all demands. This gradual process of forming and mobilising eased the situation in regard to the storage of large quantities of ordnance and medical equipment.

Some difficulty, however, was experienced in finding the medical staff and technical personnel required to complete these units. Shortage of medical officers and of skilled R.A.M.C. tradesmen was already making it hard to fill drafts for the reinforcement of the armies in the Middle East and in India. The formation of hospitals for a further operational commitment was achieved only by the depletion of lower establishment formations and static units, but even after recourse to this expedient it was found impossible to advance the date of completion of several general hospitals placed low in the schedule of priority. On the contrary, it became necessary to postpone their mobilisation to a date later than originally intended. The position was made more acute by the decision that nursing sisters should not in the first instance be included in the personnel of general hospitals allocated to the force, but should follow later, probably not until two months after the hospitals had begun to function. This involved the replacement of sisters Q.A.I.M.N.S. by O.Rs. R.A.M.C., including N.Os. and O.R.As., to the extent of 14 for each hospital of 200 beds, 34 for a hospital of 600 beds, 53 for a hospital of 1,200 beds and 3 for each extension of 100 beds, amounting to a total of more than 850 additional personnel, all of them skilled tradesmen and including some 120 N.C.Os. This decision was responsible for a further complication in the process of preparing units for this project. Since nursing sisters, being part of the establishment of general hospitals, invariably accompanied their units on departure overseas to any one of the established theatres of war, an instruction to the effect that general hospitals were to be mobilised and despatched without their normal complement of Q.A.I.M.N.S. would have immediately compromised security by indicating a new field of active operations. It was therefore necessary to include Q.A.I.M.N.S. personnel in the process of mobilisation, although they were not actually required, and to retain them with their units until the last moment when the units were called forward to the ports of embarkation. Meanwhile additional R.A.M.C. personnel intended as a replacement for Q.A.I.M.N.S. were reserved and held in depots or military hospitals for posting to these general hospitals immediately before their departure.

The numbers and types of medical units for inclusion in the order of battle having been decided and specific units having been nominated and allocated to the force, it was necessary to arrange the order of priority in which these units were to be assembled, despatched and landed in accordance with the stage of the operation to which they had been assigned and the function for which they were intended. This aspect of medical planning applied more particularly to units such as C.C.Ss., general hospitals and others included as corps, army or L. of C. troops, since the disposition of divisional medical units was automatically determined by that of the formations to which they belonged and which they accompanied. In respect of units having a part to play in the assault phase of the operation there arose the vital question of equipment in relation to the circumstances in which that assault would be made. Limitations in shipping available for the transport of the numbers of troops and quantities of stores required, absence of port facilities in the early stages and difficulty in handling bulky articles over beaches, made it essential that the equipment to be taken by units landing during the first few days should be restricted to what was indispensable as distinct from that which was desirable. It was therefore necessary to reduce medical stores and equipment for landing in the first instance to an amount little in excess of what could be loaded on to unit vehicles scheduled to be put ashore during the assault phase. The personnel, transport and equipment of units was therefore divided into three categories for landing at successive stages in the course of the operations: (*a*) assault scale; (*b*) additions to complete light scale; and (*c*) further additions to complete full scale. As regards personnel and transport, steps were taken to allocate the ranks, trades and vehicles required by each unit at the outset, leaving the remainder to follow

at a later date in the programme for the build-up of the force. The
question of equipment, however, was a more complicated matter
calling for a detailed and critical review of all articles included in
the existing scales and an assessment of their intrinsic and relative
value. The objects it was sought to achieve and the results obtained
can best be illustrated by a brief description of the organisation effected
at that time in the case of the C.C.S. The total equipment of a C.C.S.
was made up as follows:

	Tons
(a) ordnance equipment	44½
(b) medical equipment and supplies	7
(c) officers' and sergeants' mess equipment	¼
(d) officers' and O.Rs.' kit	3¼
Total	55

The aim was to produce a light scale C.C.S. suitable alike for a
combined operation, including an assault landing, and for subsequent
mobile warfare. For this purpose it was desired to reduce the equipment
carried to an amount which could be moved readily by the use of a
minimum of transport but which would yet prove adequate for the
medical and surgical treatment of casualties. To meet these conditions
it was necessary that equipment for inclusion in the light scale be
restricted to what was essential rather than merely useful; that it be
apportioned for packing in panniers, cases or bundles of small size to
facilitate handling; and that the total quantity be not in excess of 35
tons dead weight and capable of being loaded into twenty 3-ton lorries.
In the first place reduction was obtained by the withdrawal of all
hospital pattern extending marquees, all hospital beds with most of
the pillows and linen, almost all stretcher-trestles, shower baths, a
proportion of anti-gas equipment, aseptic furniture for operating
theatres, certain heavy anaesthetic apparatus, a variety of splints and
dental mechanic's outfit. This equipment amounted in all to a weight of
20 tons, representing loads for nine 3-ton lorries, and on withdrawal was
sent to a base ordnance depot for storage, whence it could be called
forward at a later date as required. All other articles of equipment and
stores were retained with the unit to supply its light scale; these
amounted to 35 tons in weight and could be packed into twenty 3-ton
lorries. For C.C.Ss. taking part in combined assault operations of the
kind contemplated a scheme for the subdivision of this light scale
equipment was devised thus:

(a) equipment, consisting of surgical instruments, dressings and the
usual requirements of an operating theatre for the use of the
surgical team to be landed on the day of the assault for attachment to a field ambulance—weight ¼ ton.

(b) the lighter and more manageable equipment to be embarked in a personnel ship, to be carried from ship to shore in landing craft and handled ashore by personnel of the unit—weight 25¼ tons.

(c) equipment which, although not easily man-handled, yet required high priority in landing and which would therefore be loaded before embarkation in unit vehicles carried in transport ships and would subsequently come ashore in those vehicles—weight 3 tons.

(d) the remainder of the equipment which, having low priority in landing, would be loaded in ships allotted to the carriage of complementary stores—weight 6¼ tons.

To assist in handling it was prescribed that as far as practicable all equipment and stores were to be packed in panniers, cases or bales measuring about 24 × 18 × 15 in. All packages were to have rope handles and, in order to render them less conspicuous from the air, all light-coloured containers were to be darkened by staining. All cases and packages were to be marked with the appropriate code colours of the unit and articles for the use of the surgical team—i.e. the assault scale equipment—were to be given distinguishing marks. Things liable to suffer by immersion—e.g. tablets, dressings, etc.—were to be packed in improvised metal containers within the outer covering. Thus the weights of the various scales of equipment of a C.C.S. as reorganised for the North African campaign were as follows:

	Tons
Assault scale (surgical team only)	¼
Additional to complete light scale	34¾
Light scale (retained by unit)	35
Additional to complete full scale and held at Ordnance depot	20
Full scale	55

Light scales of equipment for field ambulances, field hygiene sections and other units were prepared on comparable lines, having regard to the particular functions of each. Steps were taken to decrease the amount of equipment pertaining to general hospitals and so reduce the demands for shipping space and transport facilities in connexion with these units. Something was accomplished in this direction by eliminating certain of the heavier or more bulky items of ordnance equipment, including a large proportion of tents and furniture. As a result of this revision it was found possible to effect reductions to the extent of 12 tons, 42 tons and 64 tons in the total weight of equipment borne by general hospitals of 200, 600 and 1,200 beds respectively. Even so, the quantity of equipment accompanying these units remained as high as 64 tons for the hospital of 200 beds, 184 tons for that of 600 beds and 270 tons for that of 1,200 beds.

21

In regard to the packing of equipment belonging to medical units it was at first intended that the special method of packing in small bundles and containers, as already described in reference to the C.C.S., should be made applicable to all units landing early in the operation. When further consideration was given to this proposal and to all that its general adoption entailed, it was found that no less than twelve general hospitals and four depots of medical stores were involved, with the consequent special packing of more than 2,000 tons of equipment. Moreover, detailed calculation showed that the numerous boxes and containers required by this method of packing would have the effect of doubling the dead weight of the equipment so packed and of increasing by 50 per cent. the shipping tonnage required to transport it. Since operational considerations entirely precluded any such increases there was no option but to abandon the idea as impracticable in reference to the larger units and to confine the process to divisional medical units, C.C.Ss. and advanced depots of medical stores.

In respect of the projected assault and the maintenance of the force during the first three months of the campaign the total weight of stores and equipment provided for medical units amounted to 2,215 tons in addition to that carried in unit vehicles.

BRITISH MEDICAL UNITS ALLOTTED TO OPERATION 'TORCH'

Type of Unit	Unit Number	Totals
B.G.Hs. (1,200 beds)	94, 95, 96, 97, 98, 99, 100, 103	8
B.G.Hs. (600 beds)	5, 31, 67, 69, 70, 71, 72, 76	8
B.G.Hs. (200 beds)	50, 83, 84	3
Fd. Hosps. 50 beds	2, 6	2
Con. Depots	8, 9, 10	3
C.C.Ss.	1, 5, 8, 12, 18, 19	6
F.S.Us.	21–32 inclusive	12
B.T.U.	4	1
F.T.Us.	1, 3, 4, 9, 10, 12, 15, 25, 26, 27, 28, 35	12
Mob. Hyg. Lab.	1	1
Base Depots Med. Stores	9, 10	2
Mob. Bact. Labs.	1, 2	2
Adv. Depots Med. Stores	3, 4	2
M.A.Cs.	45, 60, 74, 88, 112, 146, 260	7
A.C.C.	2	1
Fd. Hyg. Secs.	1, 6 Lt., 8, 25, 34, 47, and later, 20 others	26
Fd. Ambs.		18
First Army	159	
V Corps	216	
IX Corps	220	
78th Division	11, 152, 217	
1st Division	2, 3, 137	
4th Division	10, 12, 6 Lt.	
46th Division	183, 184, 185	
6th Armd. Division	1 Lt., 165 Lt.	
1st Para. Bde.	16 Para. Fd. Amb.	

Towards the end of this campaign 1st Armd. Division, 1st K.D.G. (on April 18) and Indian 4th Division, 7th Armd. Division and 201st Gds. Bde. Gp. (April 30) were transferred from Eighth to First Army.

With 1st Armd. Division were 1 and 15 Lt. Fd. Ambs.; with 201st Gds. Bde. Gp. was 5 Lt. Fd. Amb.; with Indian 4th Division came 17 and 26 (Ind.) Fd. Ambs. and Lt. Sec. 2 (Ind.) C.C.S., and with 7th Armd. Division 131 and 2 Lt. Fd. Ambs.

This transfer somewhat complicated medical arrangements for the reason that First Army had no Indian hospitals. Indian casualties had to be evacuated into the general hospitals of Eighth Army.

THE TACTICAL PLAN

Planning was made difficult by the uncertainty of the political situation in the French African territories. Loyalties were sharply divided between the policies represented by Marshal Pétain and by General de Gaulle respectively. The U.S.A. had not broken off relations with Vichy France and so it was possible for American diplomatic representatives in Algiers to glean much information concerning the possible reactions of the French in Africa to an Allied invasion. Moreover, in October 1942 an American military mission was smuggled into Algeria by submarine and was able to meet senior French officers at Cherchell in order to obtain their views. Though much that was encouraging emerged from these conversations, the projected assault remained an adventure into the unknown and the Allies were compelled to act on the assumption that the landings would be opposed, that casualties would be heavy and that their evacuation would be beset with great difficulties owing to the very limited number of medical units which could be included in the initial assault groups, the inevitable slowness of the build-up and the great length of the voyage to the United Kingdom and the U.S.A.

It was finally decided that:

(a) A Western Task Force (wholly American and sailing from the U.S.A.) would occupy Casablanca.

(b) A Centre Task Force (wholly American and sailing from the U.K.) would occupy Oran.

(c) An Eastern Task Force (composite American and British—U.S. 34th Inf. Division and Br. First Army—sailing from the U.K.) would occupy Algiers and thereafter, without delay, move on Tunis. Speed and boldness would have to compensate for paucity of numbers. Paratroops would be dropped ahead of this force to secure airfields and other important strategic points.

(d) The Navy would give protection to these task forces until land-based aircraft could provide cover.

It was regarded as impracticable to attempt to sustain a force landed farther east than Algiers. Bizerta and Tunis were far too near Axis airfields in Sicily and elsewhere.

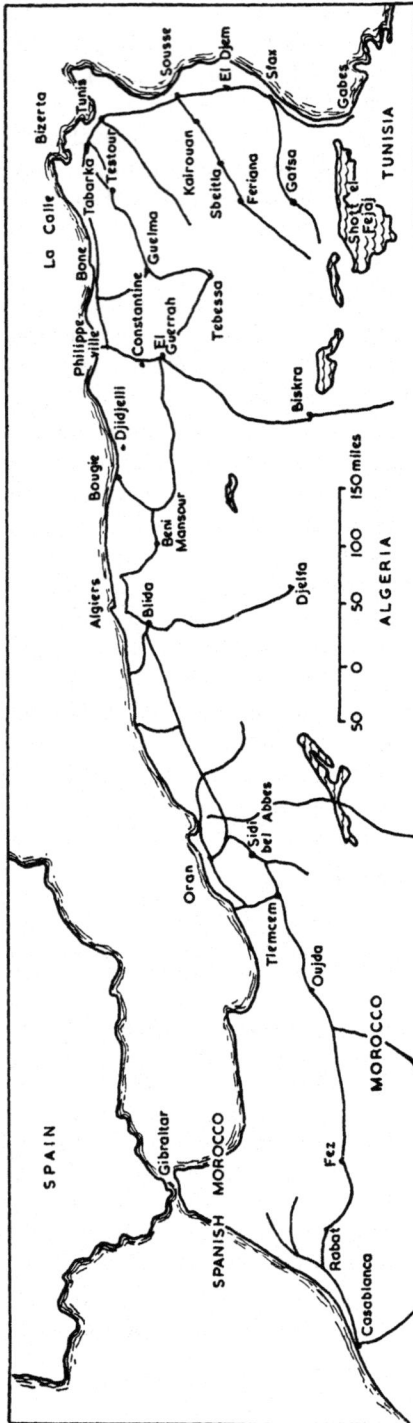

FIG. 40. North-west Africa.

MEDICAL TACTICAL PLAN, A.F.H.Q.

It was decided by A.F.H.Q. to provide hospital beds at the rate of 6 per cent., and of 5 per cent. for the American and British components respectively. G4 (Movements), A.F.H.Q., in consultation with the Medical Section, planned on the following assumptions:

(a) A grand total of 7,850 lying and 7,850 sitting cases was to be expected in the first 14 days of Operation 'Torch', with a final total of 31,600 after 6 weeks of fighting. The daily average for the first 14 days would be 1,120, for the second 1,060 and for the third 2,390.

(b) The beds available would be:

U.S.	.	.	13,143
Br.	.	.	15,200
Fr.	.	.	2,000
			30,343

(c) The available transport would be:

Hospital ships	.	2 to shuttle between Bône or Philippeville to Oran or Algiers.
Air lift .	.	200 a day from Telergma and Youks to Algiers or Oran.
Hospital trains	.	French 5; British 4; returning empty trucks to be used if necessary.
Motor amb. cars	.	to be used in forward areas only.

In so far as the British medical services were concerned the proposed build-up in respect of hospital accommodation was as follows:

By	Algiers	Bougie	Philippeville	Bône	Totals	Percentage of Force Ashore
D-day+1	1,200				1,200	4
D-day+6	1,200	900			2,100	3½
D-day+16	6,400	600	300	3,100	10,400	9½
D-day+30	6,400	600	600	2,200	9,800	6½
D-day+46	7,200	600	600	4,600	13,000	
D-day+61	7,200	600	600	5,000	13,400	
D-day+75	7,200	600	600	6,200	14,600	

Three British hospital ships (*Amarapoora* 411 cots, *Newfoundland*, 423 cots, and *Oxfordshire*, 500 cots) together with one U.S. ambulance ship would be made available immediately. By mid-February three American hospital ships would replace and relieve these. It was assumed by War Office that in the early phases no ambulance trains would be available. 54 sets of Brechot apparatus would be provided to accommodate 162 stretchers in existing rolling-stock. These would be landed at Bône. A further 428 sets would be provided at Algiers by D-day+89. 5,000 hospital beds in the United Kingdom were ear-marked in connexion with Operation 'Torch'.

It will be noted that logistic support during the earliest stages of this campaign was a responsibility of First Army. This was the reason why during these stages preference was given to the employment of British rather than of U.S. medical units.

EASTERN TASK FORCE. TACTICAL PLAN

The initial seaborne assault would be under American command. When Algiers had been taken command would then pass to G.O.C. British First Army.

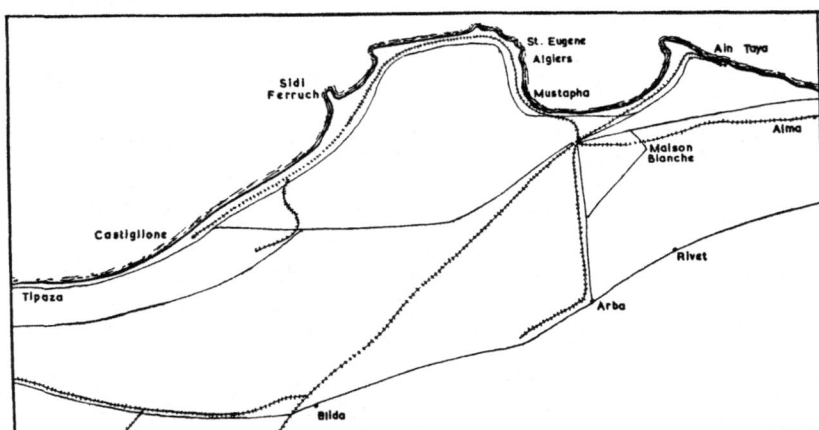

FIG. 41. Algiers and its environs.

(a) 39th Regimental Combat Team (R.C.T.) of U.S. 34th Infantry Division and 1st Commando (composite American and British) would land on both sides of Ain Taya, to the east of Algiers, seize the airfield and coast defences and thereafter move into Algiers.

168th R.C.T., U.S. 34th Infantry Division, and 6th Commando (composite American and British) would land north-east of Sidi Ferruch, to the west of Algiers, capture the forts and move into Algiers.

Terminal Force, composed of naval units, would force its way into Algiers harbour.

(b) Following closely upon the heels of the above would come the first British Landing Force. 11th Inf. Bde. (78th Division) would land north-east of Castiglione, to the west of Sidi Ferruch, secure the airfield at Blida and the nearby bridges and cross-roads. Then, with the rest of 78th Division, it would move eastwards into Tunisia. 36th Inf. Bde. (78th Division) would remain afloat in reserve during the initial stages of the assault. If all went well it would land north-east of Castiglione and north-east of Sidi Ferruch and with the rest of 78th Division move eastwards to occupy Bougie and the aerodrome at Djidjelli.

(c) On D-day + 4 the second convoy, KM.2, would arrive bringing:
    Adv. H.Q. First Army
       1st Armd. Regt. Gp. of 6th Armd. Division
       1st Para. Bde., less two companies.

(d) On D-day + 15 the third convoy, KM.3, would arrive bringing:
    Rear H.Q. First Army
    Balance of 6th Armd. Division
    1st Guards Bde. (78th Division)
    Adv. H.Q. V Corps

(e) Later convoys would bring:
    Rear H.Q. V Corps
    Balance of 78th Division
    Either 11th Armd. Division or else 46th Inf. Division
    4th Inf. Division

MEDICAL TACTICAL PLANNING IN CONNEXION WITH EASTERN TASK FORCE

It was proposed that non-divisional medical units should be despatched in the following order:

Algiers
KM.1
D-day—
D-day + 3 159 Fd. Amb.
       8 C.C.S. (200), 10 F.T.U., 21 and 23 F.S.Us.
       1 C.C.S. (200), 9 F.T.U., 31 and 32 F.S.Us.
       2 A.C.C. two platoons (33 cars)
       34 Fd. Hyg. Sec. Adv. party
       5 B.G.H. (600), two secs. 81st Pioneer Coy. attached.
       31 B.G.H. (600)
       2 A.C.C. 1 Tpn. Pln. 33 cars
KM.2
D-day + 4 34 Fd. Hyg. Sec., remainder
       50 B.G.H. (200) two secs. 194th Pioneer Coy. attached
       4 × 100 bed expansions for attachment to 5 B.G.H.
       84 B.G.H. (200) two secs. 194th Pioneer Coy. attached
       94 B.G.H. (200) plus V.D. Wing, 4 Maxillo-Facial Surgical team and two secs. 81st Pioneer Coy. attached
       8 × 100 bed expansions for attachment to 84 B.G.H.
       3 Adv. Depot Med. Stores
       2 A.C.C. 2 Tpn. Pln. 33 cars

KM.3

D-day+13 95 B.G.H. (1,200)
        96 B.G.H. (1,200)
        8 Con. Depot (2,000)
        6 Fd. Hosp. (50)
        159 Fd. Amb. up to light scale

KM.4

D-day+27 1 Mob. Bact. Lab.
        9 Base Depot Med. Stores
        46 M.B.U.
        28 M.B.U. for 78th Division

KM.5

D-day+41 99 B.G.H. (1,200)
        100 B.G.H. (1,200)

KM.6

D-day+51 150, 151 and 154 M.D.Us.
        32 M.B.U.
        10 Con. Depot (2,000)

KM.7

D-day+69 10 Base Ophthalmic Depot.

KM.1 Algiers

(a) A.D.M.S. 78th Division and A.D.M.S. 1 B.S.A. would arrive with the first convoy. With the second would come D.D.M.S. and A.D.M.S. First Army and three clerks R.A.M.C. and A.D.M.S. (Liaison) A.F.H.Q. Until the arrival of D.D.M.S. First Army, A.D.M.S. 78th Division would exercise control over the medical units and personnel, aided by A.D.M.S. 1 B.S.A.

(b) 11 Fd. Amb. (78th Division) would land with 11th Inf. Bde. on 'Apples' beach. It would evacuate its lying cases to 8 C.C.S. and its walking cases to 159 Fd. Amb. It would accompany 11th Inf. Bde. to Bône.

(c) 159 Fd. Amb. with a surgical team from 8 C.C.S. and a clearing platoon of U.S. 39th R.C.T. would land with U.S. 168th R.C.T. on 'Beer' beach. Its Lt. Sec. H.Q. would form a beach dressing station. The remainder of its H.Q. would establish a M.D.S. for lying casualties. The M.D.S. reserve company would set up a W.W.C.P. for walking cases (up to 3,000).

When the port had been secured one company would be attached to U.S. 168th R.C.T. with 8 ambulance cars. The remainder of the field ambulance plus the U.S. clearing platoon would take over accommodation in the Mustapha Civil Hospital and its environs and receive all walking wounded (approximately 1,600 by D-day+4). A surgical team or a F.S.U. would be attached if necessary.

When the port had been consolidated one company would remain with U.S. 168th R.C.T. The rest of the field ambulance plus the U.S. clearing platoon would continue to function in the Mustapha Civil Hospital and would be assisted by 70 R.A.M.C. personnel provided by 31 B.G.H.

Later the U.S. Cln. Pln. would rejoin U.S. 39th R.C.T. and the detached company with U.S. 168th R.C.T. would rejoin the field ambulance which would have been brought up to light scale by (approximately) D-day+18 and to W.E. by D-day+46 and would be prepared to move to Bône.

(d) 8 C.C.S. with 21 and 23 F.S.Us. and 10 F.T.U. attached would land on 'Beer' beach with U.S. 168th R.C.T. It would take over the lying cases from 159 Fd. Amb. and its surgical team would rejoin it. When the port had been secured 8 C.C.S. would move into the St. Eugène area as soon as 5 B.G.H. had opened and its cases transferred thereto. If it were possible to transfer these cases to a hospital ship before 5 B.G.H. had opened the C.C.S. would move to the St. Eugène area earlier. When the port had been consolidated the C.C.S. would evacuate 200 lying cases to a hospital ship and 450 lying cases to a second hospital ship to be expected on D-day+5. This second hospital ship would serve as a floating hospital pending the opening of 5 B.G.H.

8 C.C.S. would be empty by D-day+10, by which time the general hospitals would be established. The C.C.S. would then be moved forward to cover the advance to Bône.

(e) 1 C.C.S. with 31 and 32 F.S.Us. and 9 F.T.U. attached would land on 'Charlie' beach with U.S. 39th R.C.T. and take over the lying cases from the U.S. Cln. Pln. which would continue to hold walking cases.

When the port had been secured 1 C.C.S. would remain in the beachhead and hold its lying cases (approximately 300). When the port had been consolidated these cases would be transferred to a hospital ship and the C.C.S. would then move to the assistance of 159 Fd. Amb. It would be prepared to move eastward to cover the advance.

(f) 5 B.G.H. (600 beds) with two secs. 81st Pioneer Coy. attached would establish itself as quickly as possible in the St. Eugène area. It would be assisted by 50 R.A.M.C. personnel provided by 31 B.G.H. It would aim to have 100 beds available on D-day+6 and a further 100 a day thereafter until it was fully opened. It would admit lying cases only and, if necessary, all the available surgical teams. F.S.Us. and F.T.Us. from 1 and 8 C.C.Ss. would be attached to this hospital, which would be prepared for a crisis expansion up to 1,200 beds. It could call upon 31 B.G.H. for staff until 31 B.G.H. itself needed them.

5 B.G.H. could expect to remain open in this location until approximately D-day+45, when it would be replaced by 99 B.G.H. and would then close and move to Bône. The 4 × 100

bed expansions received by 5 B.G.H. on KM.2 would remain with 99 B.G.H.

(g) 31 B.G.H. (600 beds) would land with personnel only. It would provide (i) two secs. 81st Pioneer Coy. and 50 R.A.M.C. personnel to assist 5 B.G.H. (*see* (*f*) above) and (ii) 70 R.A.M.C. personnel to assist 159 Fd. Amb. (*see* (*c*) above). The remainder of the unit would select and secure a site and begin to prepare it for occupation by the unit.

When the port had been consolidated 31 B.G.H. would recall all its detachments and would aim at having 100 available beds on D-day+9, and thereafter 50 daily until fully open. It would prepare for a crisis expansion at the same rate and up to 1,200 beds.

31 B.G.H. would remain open until replaced by 100 B.G.H. It would then close and be prepared for movement to the east. Its V.D. wing would remain with 100 B.G.H.

(h) 1 Transport Platoon 2 A.C.C. would initially be under the control of A.D.M.S. 78th Division who would consult with A.D.M.S. 1 B.S.A. concerning its employment. The platoon would accompany the advance to the east.

(i) 34 Fd. Hyg. Sec. would be under A.D.M.S. 1 B.S.A. until it was required by Army. It would be brought up to light scale by D-day+5.

(j) H.S. *Tjetjalenka* would be off 'Beer' beach on D-day. Possibly evacuation might be direct from beach to hospital ship. On D-day+3 approximately the ship would be prepared to take aboard 500 casualties (300 from 1 C.C.S., 200 from 8 C.C.S.). Possibly it might be necessary to accept 800. The ship would then proceed to the U.K.

Later the ship would be required for periodic evacuation to the U.K.

(k) H.S. *Newfoundland* would be off 'Beer' beach on D-day. On D-day+4 she would be prepared to embark 450 or more casualties from 8 C.C.S. and hold them until 5 and 31 B.G.Hs. were established ashore.

Thereafter the ship would be required for coastal traffic, transporting casualties from the eastern ports to Algiers.

(l) The field medical units in the first convoy (KM.1) would carry additional dressings sufficient for the first six days in watertight tins.

KM.2. Algiers

(a) 50 B.G.H. (200) with two secs. 194th Pioneer Coy. attached would land on D-day+5 and open in the medical area. It would aim at having 100 beds available by the third day after landing and be fully open by the seventh. It would remain open until it was replaced by 99 B.G.H., when it would close and become available for movement eastwards.

(b) 84 B.G.H. (200) with two secs. of 194th Pioneer Coy. attached would land on D-day+5 and open in the medical area. It would aim at having 100 beds available by the third day and be fully open by the seventh. It would be replaced by 100 B.G.H. and would then be available for movement forward.

(c) 94 B.G.H. (1,200) with a V.D. wing and with 4 Maxillo-Facial Surgical Team and two secs. 81st Pioneer Coy. attached would land on D-day+6. It would aim to have 100 beds available by the third day and 2,000 by the nineteenth. This hospital would remain in the Algiers base area.

(d) 2 Transport Platoon 2 A.C.C. would land on D-day+5 and proceed forthwith to Bône. It would detach 12 cars at Algiers, 6 at Bougie, 6 at Philippeville and 12 at Bône. It would join up with 1 Tpt. Pln.

(e) 3 Adv. Depot Med. Stores would land on D-day+5 and open as quickly as possible for the supply of local units. A 'brick' of 10 tons of expendible stores would arrive in KM.3 for the replenishment of medical supplies of medical units.

It would remain open in Algiers until 9 Base Depot Medical Stores arrived (approximately D-day+45). It would then be available for movement to Bône.

THE ASSAULT

On November 5, 1942, General Eisenhower, together with certain members of A.F.H.Q., flew to Gibraltar, there to set up his advanced headquarters. The three convoys sailed. The enemy was encouraged to conclude that what he saw was but another Malta convoy. During the night of November 7–8 the ships altered course and turned towards their respective objectives. The troops, transferred from transports to small landing craft, touched shore in the early morning of November 8.

Western Task Force encountered fierce opposition and endured some 2,000 casualties. Rough seas developed to make reinforcement difficult. Fierce fighting continued until November 10, when an armistice was signed in Algiers between the Allies and the French in North Africa and all hostilities ceased.

Central Task Force likewise met with stubborn resistance, there being over 1,000 American casualties, including 200 killed. This resistance was overwhelmed within forty-eight hours and Oran was taken.

Eastern Task Force met with but little opposition and Algiers was quickly occupied. Battle casualties totalled 12 killed and 60 wounded.

11 and 159 Fd. Ambs. landed according to plan, but rough weather developed to prevent the C.C.Ss. getting ashore until two days later, when the signing of the armistice at once reduced the demands made upon the medical services. The landing of medical units and stores was therefore relegated to a low priority and all effort was concentrated

upon the despatch of 78th Division on its rush to Tunisia. 159 Fd.
Amb. opened in the Mustapha Civil Hospital in Algiers and functioned
as a C.C.S. Casualties among the American R.C.Ts. were received
since at this time only British medical units were available.

On November 9 the Germans reacted strongly and, with the approval
of the Vichy Government, began to pour large numbers of aircraft and
troop-carrying planes into Tunisia. On this day General Anderson
reached Algiers from Gibraltar and took over command.

On November 10 hostilities between the Allies and the French
ceased. First Army began to establish a base at Algiers. 'Hartforce',
a mobile column built around a company of 5th Northamptons to act as
the spearhead of the eastward dash towards Tunis 560 miles away, was
formed and sent on its way by road.

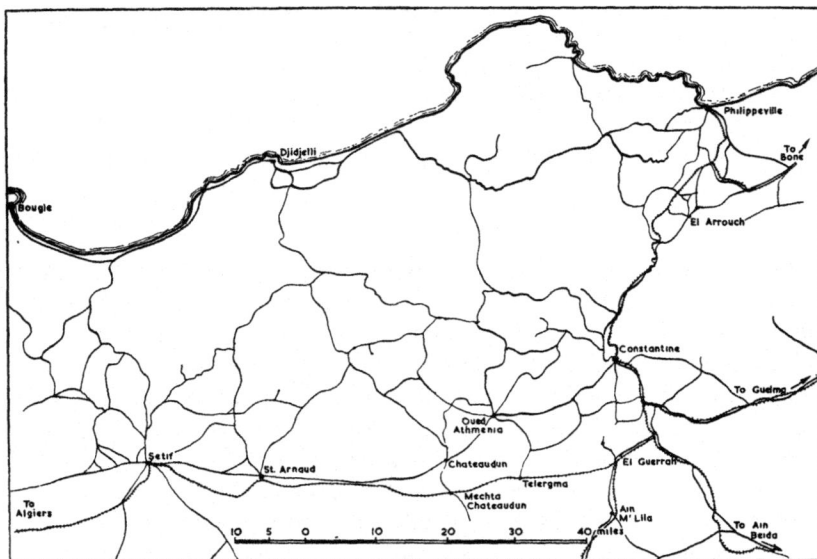

FIG. 42. Algeria. Bougie–Philippeville.

On November 11, 36th Inf. Bde. was despatched by sea from Algiers
to Bougie. This brigade consisted of 5th Buffs, 6th R.W.K. and 8th
A. and S.H. with attached troops and services. Accompanying it and in
order to provide medical cover for the advance beyond Bougie went:

217 Fd. Amb.
220 Fd. Amb.
1 Fd. Hyg. Sec.
12 C.C.S. with 22 and 24 F.S.Us., 11 F.T.U. and two secs. 129th
    Pioneer Coy. attached.
69 B.G.H. with two secs. 129th Pioneer Coy. attached.

The medical tactical plan for this operation was as follows:

(a) 217 Fd. Amb. (78th Division), with a surgical team from 12 C.C.S. attached, would serve 36th Inf. Bde.

(b) 220 Fd. Amb., with a surgical team from 12 C.C.S. attached, would, if the landing was unopposed or if 'Hartforce' had secured the port, establish a dressing station to cater for local air-raid casualties. If, on the other hand, an assault landing had to be made, then the light section H.Q. would form a beach dressing station while the M.D.S. would open to receive lying cases. The reserve company would establish an A.D.S. for walking wounded.

This field ambulance would continue to collect casualties and transport them to 12 C.C.S. and to 69 B.G.H. when these were opened. If casualties were numerous the field ambulance would deal with the walking wounded, sending to the C.C.S. only the lying cases.

The field ambulance would be brought up to light scale in KM.3 and would then be prepared to move to Bône, where it would be brought up to W.E. by D-day+45.

(c) 1 Fd. Hyg. Sec. would come under A.D.M.S. Base or L. of C. Sub-area for duty. It would remain in Bône and would be brought up to light scale in KM.11.

(d) 12 C.C.S., with 22 and 24 F.S.Us., 11 F.T.U. and two secs. 129th Pioneer Coy. attached, would land on D-day+1 and take over casualties from 220 Fd. Amb. The surgical team with this field ambulance would then rejoin its parent unit. If casualties were numerous the C.C.S. would accept lying cases only. The C.C.S. would hold its cases until these could be accepted by 69 B.G.H. As soon as it became empty the C.C.S. would be moved eastwards.

(e) 69 B.G.H. (600 beds), with a V.D. wing and two secs. 129th Pioneer Coy. attached, would land on D-day+2/D-day+3, less its G.1098 but with full I.1248 plus 600 stretchers and 1,800 blankets, and establish itself in buildings. It would aim to have 100 beds available by the third day after landing and 600 by the ninth. It would remain in Bougie and on receipt of its equipment in KM.11 would build up to its normal capacity.

(f) H.S. *Amarapoora* or H.S. *Newfoundland* would be available to embark casualties when the port had been secured. The ship might have to hold these casualties until the hospitals in the Algiers base were open. Later the hospital ship would be required for evacuation from Bône, Philippeville and Bougie to Algiers.

Bougie and the aerodrome at Djidjelli were occupied in the face of German opposition from the air. The medical units were unfortunate in that half of the total personnel lost their kits, 220 Fd. Amb. its entire equipment, 12 C.C.S. most of its stores, and 69 B.G.H. a fifth of its sheets and blankets, while the F.S.Us. had two of their lorries put out of action by enemy bombing. These misfortunes, however, did not prevent these medical units from discharging their functions. A portion of the French hospital at Bougie was taken over, while a company of 220 Fd. Amb. with 24 F.S.U. attached opened at Djidjelli.

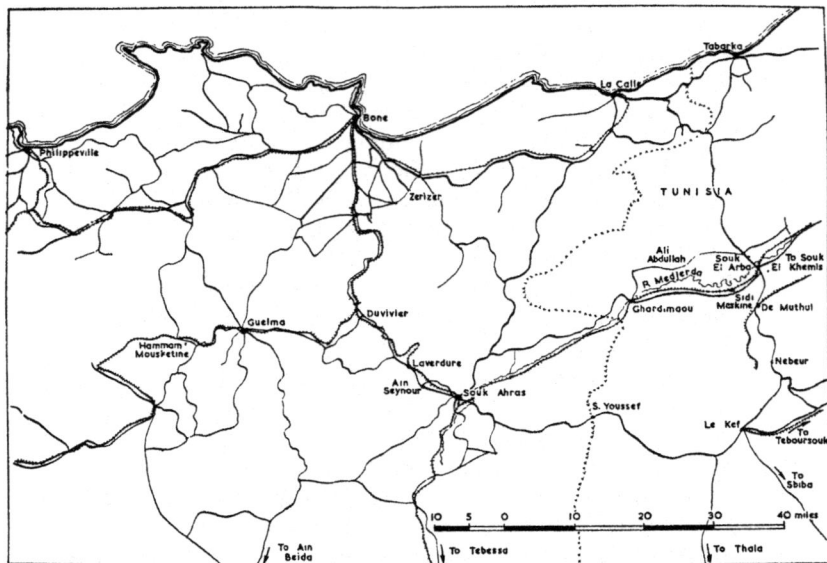

FIG. 43. North-west Tunisia.

6th Commando left Algiers by sea for Bône and on November 12 two companies of 3rd Parachute Bn. of 1st Para. Bde. were dropped near Bône. The port and the airfield were seized. 6th R.W.K., with a light section of 217 Fd. Amb., left Bougie for Bône by sea. 8th A. and S.H., with a light section of 217 Fd. Amb. left Bougie by rail and road for Setif. 5th Buffs, with a light section of 217 Fd. Amb. remained in Bougie and Djidjelli. H.Q. 36th Inf. Bde., with 217 Fd. Amb. less three light sections, set out from Bougie by road for Bône.

On this day in Algiers 159 Fd. Amb., now in the Stadium St. Eugène, was holding some 200 patients, most of them being injured Royal Navy and Merchant Navy personnel. The second convoy, KM.2, arrived at Algiers.

On November 13 D.D.M.S. and A.D.M.S. First Army, with three clerks R.A.M.C. and A.D.M.S. (Liaison) A.F.H.Q., landed. The equipment of 1 and 8 C.C.Ss. was disembarked.

8 C.C.S. opened on the 14th in the Stadium St. Eugène and admitted some 30 patients. Sixty were expected from Bougie by train. The

equipment of 5 B.G.H. was landed. D.D.M.S. First Army placed 31 and 32 F.S.Us. and 9 F.T.U. at the disposal of A.D.M.S. 78th Division to reinforce the medical cover of the forward troops. D.D.M.S. found abundant reason for criticising the sanitary arrangements that had been provided in the Botanic Gardens transit camp.

On the 15th the equipment of 94 B.G.H. was landed. To this unit D.D.M.S. attached 4 Maxillo-Facial Surgical team.

First Army was now about to cross the Algerian–Tunisian border in its attempt to seize Bizerta and Tunis before the Germans had found it possible to build up a sufficient force to deny these objectives to the Allies. Axis troops were in Bizerta, Tunis, Sfax and Gabes and were being rapidly and strongly reinforced. French troops in Tunisia were not resisting but were withdrawing towards the Tunisian–Algerian border. The Allies had secured the use of the principal ports and airfields in Morocco and Algeria. British bases had been established at Algiers and Bougie and the port of Bône had been occupied. With the Allies there were now some 100,000 French troops, mainly colonial and of good quality, but as yet unorganised and ill equipped.

The battle of Alamein had been fought and won and Eighth Army was in Tobruk and Gazala.

In Algeria First Army was stretched between Algiers and Bône.

At the end of this, the amphibious phase of Operation 'Torch', the distribution of British troops was as follows:

Algiers	Adv. H.Q. First Army
	Adv. H.Q. 78th Division
	11th Inf. Bde., less 'Hartforce'
	1st Para. Bde.
	1st Commando
	H.Q. 22nd A.A. Bde.
	Recce Party Adv. H.Q. V Corps
	Rear H.Q. 64th A/T Bty., 64th A/T Regt. R.A.
	Armd. Regt. Gp., 6th Armd. Division.
Medical . .	D.D.M.S. First Army
	A.D.M.S. 1 B.S.A.
	A.D.M.S. A.F.H.Q.
	A.D.M.S. 78th Division
	5, 31, 50, 94 B.G.Hs.
	1 and 8 C.C.Ss.
	159 Fd. Amb.
	165 Fd. Amb. (two secs.)
	31 and 32 F.S.Us.
	9 F.T.U.
	3 Adv. Depot Med. Stores
	two platoons 2 A.C.C.

Bougie	5th Buffs, two coys.
	H.Q. 52nd A.A. Bde.
	218th H.A.A. Bty. R.A.
	45th Lt. A.A. Bty. R.A.
	Tp. 135th Lt. A.A. Bty. R.A.
Medical .	. 69 B.G.H.
	12 C.C.S.
	220 Fd. Amb., less one coy.
	22 F.S.U.
	11 F.T.U.
Djidjelli	5th Buffs, less two coys.
	359th Fd. Bty. R.A.
	35th L.A.A. Bty. R.A. (two troops)
	256th Fd. Coy. R.E. sec.
Medical .	. Lt. Sec. 217 Fd. Amb.
	one coy. 220 Fd. Amb.
	24 F.S.U.
Setif	8th A. and S.H.
	502nd Fd. Bty. R.A.
	256th Fd. Coy. R.E. sec.
Medical .	. Lt. Sec. 217 Fd. Amb.
Bône	6th R.W.K.
	6th Commando
	5th Northants A/Tk. Pln. (two secs.)
	3rd Para. Bn. A.A.C. (two coys.)
Medical .	. Lt. Sec. 217 Fd. Amb.
On the road Algiers–Bône .	'Hartforce'
	56th Recce Regt. 'C' sqn.
Bougie–Bône	H.Q. 36th Inf. Bde.
	138th Fd. Regt. R.A.
Medical	. 217 Fd. Amb. (less 3 lt. secs.)
At sea	R.A. units and maintenance brick.

THE ADVANCE INTO TUNISIA

On November 15, 36th Inf. Bde. moved from Bône into Tunisia along the road through La Calle and Tabarka. U.S. paratroops dropped at Youks-les-Bains and moved at once to Tebessa and Gafsa. The British 1st Para. Bn. was dropped on the airfield at Souk el Arba on the following day and at once moved forward to Beja and Sidi N'sir.

11th Inf. Bde.—2nd L.F., 1st Surreys and 5th Northamptons with 11 Fd. Amb.—together with 'Bladeforce' (formed out of elements of 6th Armoured Division around 17/21st Lancers and with 165 Fd. Amb.) moved up from Algiers through Souk el Arba to join up with 1st Para. Bn. and the French garrison of Medjez el Bab.

On the 17th, 36th Inf. Bde. clashed with German troops at Djebel Abiod. 'Hartforce' was cut off but, taking to the hills, it fought its way back to join the brigade on the 21st. The brigade then pushed on to Jefna but was there checked.

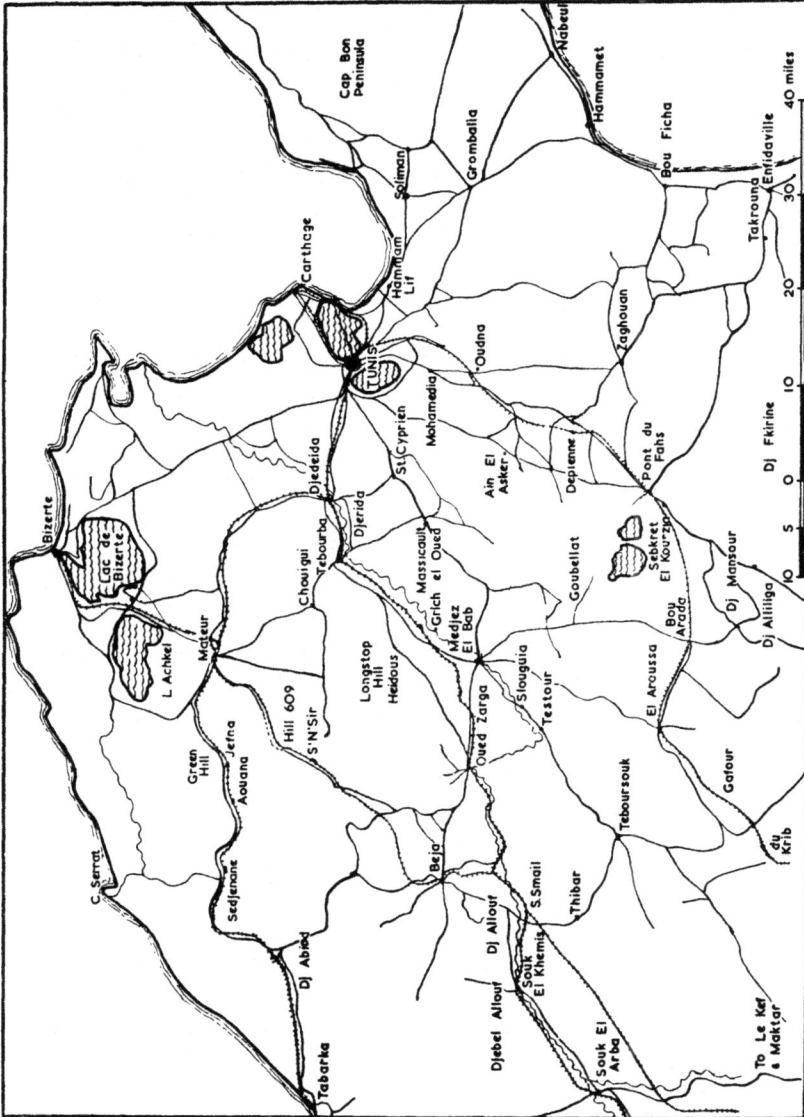

FIG. 44. North Tunisia.

On November 19 the French garrison at Medjez repulsed two German attacks but was finally obliged to withdraw from the town, the key to the road route to Tunis. 'Bladeforce' was holding Oued Zarga and 1st

22

Para. Bn. was in Beja. 11th Inf. Bde. and the main body of 'Bladeforce' were concentrating at Beja and Souk el Arba respectively.

The opposition which 11th and 36th Inf. Bdes. and 'Bladeforce' was now meeting grew in strength and stubbornness daily. They pushed forward, however, though suffering serious loss to regain Medjez, to occupy Tebourba and finally to reach Djedeida, only 12 miles short of Tunis itself, and to get within 15 miles of Mateur. But to hold these positions until adequately reinforced was far beyond their power. 11th Inf. Bde. was driven out of Tebourba and off Dj. Ahmera ('Longstop') immediately to the north of Medjez el Bab, and were obliged to fall back on Medjez itself. 1st Guards Bde., arriving with the third convoy, was promptly sent forward to take over the Medjez area while 11th Inf. Bde. was pulled back to the area of Testour and Slouguia. 'Bladeforce', with 1st Para. Bn. under command, took up a position about 10 miles south of Mateur, there to remain unitl December 12 and in the meantime to engage in offensive patrolling. 6th Commando moved to Tabarka on November 21 and on the 26th, with 8th A. and S.H. of 86th Inf. Bde., took part in the unsuccessful attack on the German positions on 'Green Hill', near Sedjenane and dominating the road and rail routes from Tabarka to Mateur. In this area both 36th Inf. Bde. and 6th Commando remained until Green Hill was attacked again, and again unsuccessfully, on January 5. 1st Commando sailed from Bône on November 26 for Tabarka, there to be attached to 36th Inf. Bde. On November 30, six British and four U.S. troops of this commando embarked and were landed 60 miles east of Tabarka to seize and hold certain road junctions. This was accomplished and the positions were held, one for 24 hours the other for 72. The troops actually got within 4 miles of Bizerta. But the advance of 11th and 36th Inf. Bdes. had been checked and the losses of the commando were heavy—British, 4 officers and 56 O.Rs.; U.S., 2 officers and 72 O.Rs.—and so after three days the troops withdrew down the coast road to rejoin 36th Inf. Bde. and to be used as infantry of the line.

On November 28, Eighth Army was facing the El Agheila position.

Advanced Headquarters A.F.H.Q. moved from Gibraltar to Algiers.

On the 29th 2nd Para. Bn. was flown from Algiers and dropped on the Depienne airfield. It moved forward straightway to Oudna, there to seize the airfield. It was attacked by German armour and aircraft and, losing 16 officers and 250 O.Rs. killed, wounded and missing, was forced back to Medjez el Bab, whence it moved to Souk el Khemis to rest and refit. 3rd Para. Bn. was sent by rail from Algiers to a position north of Beja where it was employed in an infantry rôle.

On December 2 General Anderson informed A.F.H.Q. that he considered that it was highly improbable that he would be able to

complete the task of denying Tunisia to the enemy. His ground forces
were stretched to the limit, his communications had become precarious,
there was no adequate reserve of supplies for the forward zone and
heavy scale enemy attacks had developed and were still mounting. In
his opinion, unless Bizerta and Tunis could be captured quickly, he

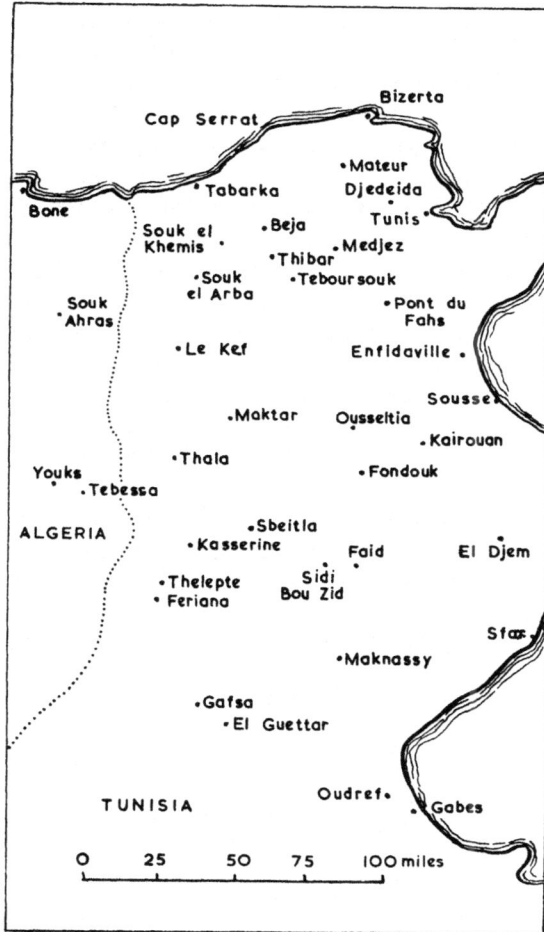

FIG. 45. Tunisia.

would be forced to withdraw in order that his troops might be given
adequate air cover. He asked that 46th Division should be sent to
North-West Africa together with an armoured brigade.

Under the conditions that then existed all the advantages were with
the enemy. He was able to reinforce his front in Tunisia far more
quickly than could First Army. The proximity of his airfields in Sicily

and southern Italy permitted him to launch continuous raids upon Algiers, Bougie, Bône and other Allied bases. The distance from Algiers to Medjez el Bab by road was 522 miles, by air 359 miles. The distance from the enemy base at Tunis to the battle front at Medjez el Bab was 35 miles by road and 32 by air. The single-track railway from Algiers to the front could not cope with the demands of an army in the field. The rolling-stock was in poor condition and there was an acute shortage of fuel. The roads were not built for continuous heavy traffic. The weather was exceptionally wet and the roads were deep in mud and the airfields, having no concrete strips, were unusable. The civil telephone and telegraph systems, which to begin with were the only ones available to First Army, were in a poor state of repair.

Nevertheless, strenuous attempts to thrust towards Tunis were continued. 2nd Coldstream Gds. attacked and took Djebel el Ahmera (Longstop Hill), to the north of Medjez el Bab and dominating the exits therefrom. On December 22 they were relieved by an American unit. On the following day this was heavily attacked and driven back. 2nd Coldstream Gds. were then sent in to retake the hill. On Christmas Day they in their turn were forced back and it was finally accepted that the eastward rush had lost its momentum and that the advance on Tunis must be postponed indefinitely until the weather improved and the forward troops had been reinforced.

The battlefield, drenched in torrential rain, now became stabilised on the general line Pichon, Bou Arada, Medjez el Bab, Sidi N'sir, El Aouana, with scattered units farther south covering the forward airfields at Thelepte, Youks and Souk el Arba.

The distribution of the components of the Eastern Task Force and of the base and L. of C. areas and sub-areas at the end of December 1942 was as follows:

Distribution of Eastern Task Force

Tebessa	. .	H.Q., U.S. II Corps
		U.S. 1st Armd. Division
Sbeitla	.	French units
Bou Arada	.	6th Armd. Division
Medjez el Bab	.	1st Gds. Bde. Gp. of 78th Division
Munchar	.	11th Inf. Bde. Gp. of 78th Division
		U.S. 18 R.C.T.
Beja–Sidi N'Sir	.	Miscellaneous force u/c 78th Division
Sidi Askeur	.	1st Para. Bde.
Sedjenane	.	36th Inf. Bde. Gp. of 78th Division
Souk el Khemis	.	H.Q. V Corps
		U.S. Combat Command B. of U.S. 1st Armd. Division.

Base and L. of C. Areas and Sub-areas.

	H.Q.				*Date Established*
1 L. of C. area	.	Algiers	.	.	. November 17
		Setif	.	.	. November 29
1 L. of C. sub-area		Constantine	.	.	. November 17
2 L. of C. sub-area		Souk Ahras	.	.	. November 28
1 B.S.A.	. .	Algiers	.	.	. November 10
2 B.S.A.	. .	Bougie	.	.	. November 12
3 B.S.A.	. .	Philippeville	.	.	. November 16
4 B.S.A.	. .	Bône	.	.	. November 18

The Order of Battle of the First Army at this time is given below:

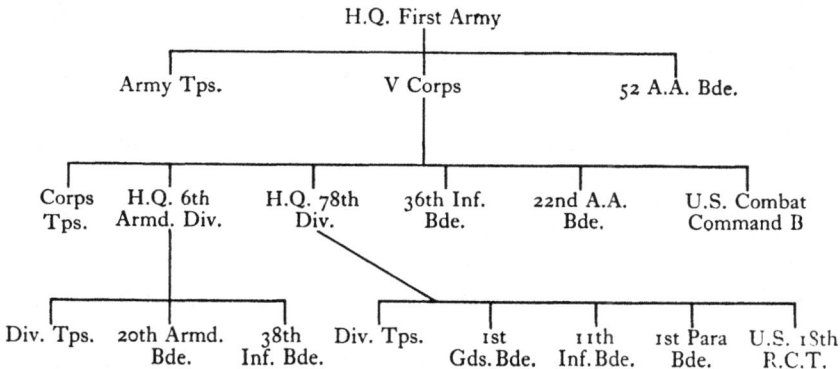

H.Q. First Army

Army Tps. — V Corps — 52 A.A. Bde.

Corps Tps. — H.Q. 6th Armd. Div. — H.Q. 78th Div. — 36th Inf. Bde. — 22nd A.A. Bde. — U.S. Combat Command B

Div. Tps. — 20th Armd. Bde. — 38th Inf. Bde. — Div. Tps. — 1st Gds. Bde. — 11th Inf. Bde. — 1st Para Bde. — U.S. 18th R.C.T.

MEDICAL ARRANGEMENTS DURING THIS ADVANCE

On his arrival at Algiers in KM.2, D.D.M.S. First Army took over the control of medical personnel and units from A.D.M.S. 78th Division. He inherited two problems of considerable complexity. One was that of finding suitable accommodation for the larger medical units in Algiers and its environs. The city was greatly overcrowded with British, United States and French units of various kinds, all needing and demanding room. The French were allies. Bids on behalf of medical units were given low priority for the reason that the tasks of the most immediate urgency were those of establishing a base and of getting the combatant formations away to the east as rapidly as possible. The other problem was that of getting adequate medical cover for the units heading for Tunisia. Transport sufficient to move eastward all that was desirable was not available. Bids for it had to be assessed by the relative importance of units to the tasks in hand. Higher authority decided that in so far as medical cover was concerned risks would have to be run. All that D.D.M.S. could do, therefore, was to reiterate his warning that the medical cover in Bône and beyond was grossly inadequate and to repeat his requests for transport.

He meant to move 159 Fd. Amb. and 1 and 8 C.C.Ss. forward just as soon as transport could be obtained. Casualties incurred in front of Bougie would be sent back to 69 B.G.H. at Bougie or else held until 1 and 8 C.C.Ss. arrived in the forward zone.

It was quickly appreciated that Bône could not be used as a forward medical base for it was receiving far too much attention from the Luftwaffe. It was decided therefore that one 600-bedded hospital should be sent to Bône and that a medical area should be provided somewhere farther back on the main railway line.

On November 16, 50 B.G.H. opened 50 beds in Algiers for infectious disease cases.

On November 17, 1 C.C.S. moved by rail from Algiers to La Calle, on the 18th 5 B.G.H. from Algiers to Bône and on the 19th 8 C.C.S. from Algiers to Souk Ahras and 159 Fd. Amb. from Algiers to Souk el Khemis. On the 21st 8 Con. Depot opened in a preventorium in Algiers.

With KM.3 no less than 2,700 medical personnel arrived at Algiers. The stores of many of the medical units were taken on by sea to ports farther east and so the dreaded dissociation of personnel and equipment occurred to lead inevitably to serious trouble.

On November 23, Adv. H.Q. First Army moved from Algiers to Constantine and permission was obtained for D.D.M.S., A.D.M.S. and A.D.H. to move with it. On the 26th, 2 Fd. Hosp. left Algiers for Setif and the personnel of 84 B.G.H. for Bône by sea, exchanging their equipment which was in accordance with scale G.1098 for that of 83 B.G.H. (the personnel of 83 were not available for this move). On the 27th, 31 B.G.H. left Algiers for Oued Athmenia, there to open in the Arab sanatorium, taking over from 220 Fd. Amb. which was holding some 70 casualties. Within twelve hours of opening 31 B.G.H. had admitted 120 cases straight from the front line.

The French authorities placed three improvised ambulance trains at the disposal of the British medical services. At first only one of these was available and this made its first clearance of 200 patients on November 27 from 8 C.C.S. which was rapidly filling at Souk Ahras. The train had a mixed staff of French and British personnel.

On December 1, 95 B.G.H. was provided with accommodation in Beni Achnoun. The distribution of the senior administrative medical officers was now as follows:

A.D.M.S. 78th Division
    Adv. H.Q. 78th Division .   Oued Zarga
    Rear H.Q. 78th Division .   Souk el Arba
D.D.M.S. V. Corps
    Adv. H.Q. V Corps   .   Souk el Khemis
    Rear H.Q. V Corps   .   Souk Ahras

```
A.D.M.S. 6th Armd. Division
      H.Q. 6th Armd. Division .    Le Kef
      Command Post First Army     Ain Seynour
A.D.M.S. First Army
      Adv. H.Q. First Army    .    Constantine
D.D.M.S.  First Army
      Rear H.Q. First Army    .    Algiers
D.D.M.S. L. of C. area
      H.Q. L. of C. area  .   .    Setif
A.D.M.S. 1 L. of C. S.A.
      H.Q. 1 L. of C. S.A.    .    Constantine
A.D.M.S. 2 L. of C. S.A.
      H.Q. 2 L. of C. S.A.    .    Souk Ahras
A.D.M.S. 1 B.S.A.
      H.Q. 1 B.S.A.      .    .    Algiers
A.D.M.S. 2 B.S.A.
      H.Q. 2 B.S.A.      .    .    Bougie
A.D.M.S. 3 B.S.A.
      H.Q. 3 B.S.A.      .    .    Philippeville
A.D.M.S. 4 B.S.A.
      H.Q. 4 B.S.A.      .    .    Bône
```

D.D.M.S. V Corps, organising evacuation in front of Souk Ahras, augmented his resources by acquiring six Michelin Diesel railcars from the French. Each of these carried 21 lying and 24 sitting cases. Though one of them was destroyed by enemy action the rest were adequate for evacuation between Souk el Arba and Souk Ahras and, on occasion, between Souk el Arba and Oued Athmenia. In this way motor ambulance transport was freed and could be used almost exclusively for evacuation in front of Souk el Arba.

A.D.M.S. 78th Division was making use of supply aircraft, returning empty, for the evacuation of casualties and this arrangement was regularised.

D.D.M.S. First Army found reason to criticise in the strongest terms the sanitary arrangements on troop trains and initiated action for their improvement.

On December 3, 8 C.C.S. at Souk Ahras was full and 170 cases were evacuated direct from the front by Michelin railcar to 31 B.G.H. at Oued Athmenia.

On December 6 the forward medical units were in danger of being overtaxed:

31 B.G.H. at Oued Zarga was holding 300 patients
5 B.G.H. at Bône was holding 300 patients
8 C.C.S. at Souk Ahras was holding 306 patients
220 Fd. Amb. at Guelma (W.W.C.P.) was holding 150 patients.

All the ambulance trains were in transit with casualties. In Algiers there were 1,069 patients in the hospitals and only 346 vacant beds. Casualties were reaching Algiers at the rate of 150 a day. A hospital ship was expected. Seventy-three patients had been evacuated by air to Gibraltar by A.D.M.S. (Liaison) A.F.H.G.

The situation was critical both tactically and administratively. 11th Inf. Bde. was now only about 800 strong and 36th Bde. was checked and had endured serious losses. The stream of reinforcements was sluggish. Plans were made to build up a defensive position in the area Ghardimaou–Souk el Arba with all speed. D.D.M.S. V Corps asked that 84 B.G.H. should be moved to Souk Ahras, that 19 C.C.S., then moving up, should join 1 C.C.S. at Djebel Allouf, that 8 C.C.S. should remain u/c V Corps but should be administered by A.D.M.S. 2 L. of C. S.A. while at Souk Ahras, that another general hospital should be sent to Bône and that 159 Fd. Amb. (Army) should be attached to 1st Guards Bde. which was not accompanied by its own field ambulance (152).

D.D.M.S. First Army then rearranged the distribution of Army forward medical units.

6 Fd. Hosp. was to be sent from Constantine to Ouled Rahmon
220 Fd. Amb's. M.D.S. from Guelma to Constantine
71 B.G.H. from St. Armand to Guelma
70 B.G.H. from St. Armand to Bône
72 B.G.H. was to remain at St. Armand

70, 71 and 72 B.G.Hs. at this time were at St. Armand waiting for their equipment which was trickling in to Bône by sea. 18 C.C.S. had arrived complete at Bône by sea and 6 B.G.H. at Constantine. The personnel of 19 C.C.S. were ferried forward to Bône from Algiers by a platoon of 2 A.C.C. and thus were brought to their equipment. 18 and 19 C.C.Ss. were then placed under orders of D.D.M.S. V Corps and were sent forward by him to open at Ali Abdullah. 84 B.G.H. was at Bône, closed, for its equipment in accordance with scale I.1248 had not yet arrived. When it did arrive the unit was ferried forward by the transport of 8 C.C.S. and of the attached F.S.Us. to Souk Ahras. This move took seven days to complete. 1 C.C.S. had been ferried forward from La Calle in relays by its own transport and that of the attached F.S.Us. and opened at Djebel Allouf, six miles north-east of Souk el Khemis. It was dealing with minor cases likely to return to their units within fourteen days.

The Michelin railcars were now not running farther west than Souk Ahras, for it had been found that if they did go as far back as 5 B.G.H. at Bône or 31 B.G.H. at Oued Athmenia, they were lost to the forward zone for as long as 24–48 hours. Ambulance R.H. was Sidi Meskine for the reason that Souk el Khemis and Souk el Arba were required exclusively for supplies.

D.M.S., A.F.H.Q., arrived in Algiers on December 6.

On December 11, V Corps began to reorganise on a shorter defensive line and in conformation there was a slight modification of the medical arrangements.

Before the regrouping of V Corps the medical cover for 6th Armoured and 78th Divisions was as follows: D.D.M.S. V Corps had placed 159 Fd. Amb. at Beja where it was acting as a forward surgical centre. To it were attached three F.S.Us., including the surgical team of 16 Para. Fd. Amb., and one F.T.U. The average number of operations performed daily at this time was 80.

It was receiving casualties from 11 Fd. Amb. (78th Division) on the Medjez–Beja road, from 217 Fd. Amb. (78th Division) at Sedjenane and from the three sections of 165 Lt. Fd. Amb. (6th Armd. Division) with 'Bladeforce' at Sidi N'sir.

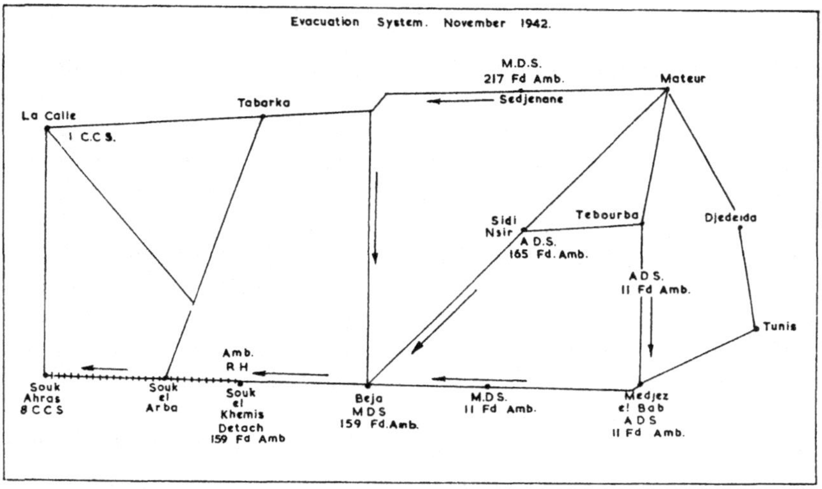

FIG. 46. Evacuation system as at November 29, 1942.

From A.D.S. of 11 Fd. Amb. through M.D.S. of 11 Fd. Amb. to M.D.S. of 159 Fd. Amb. at Beja by Amb. Car.

From M.D.S. 217 Fd. Amb. to M.D.S. 159 Fd. Amb. by Amb. Car.

From M.D.S. 159 Fd. Amb. to detach. 159 Fd. Amb. for entrainment at Souk el Khemis.

With the regrouping 217 Fd. Amb., with 32 F.S.U. attached and serving 36th Inf. Bde. remained at Sedjenane, but since the road to Beja was now too near the front line to be used for such a purpose, evacuation was by M.A.C. to 5 B.G.H. at Bône through a staging post established by a section of 216 Fd. Amb. (V Corps).

159 Fd. Amb. (First Army) remained at Beja and served 11th Inf. Bde. Most of the surgery hitherto undertaken by 159 Fd. Amb. was now

undertaken by 1 C.C.S. at Djebel Allouf (six miles north-east of Souk el Khemis).

11 Fd. Amb. (78th Division) was with 1st Guards Bde. and 152 (78th Division) was in Medjez el Bab. 165 Lt. Fd. Amb. was with 6th Armoured Division in the neighbourhood of Teboursouk monastery at Thibar and a company of this unit was at ambulance railhead at Sidi Meskine.

A little later 152 Fd. Amb. rejoined 1st Guards Bde. and 159 Fd. Amb. then went into Army Reserve at Le Kef and F.S.Us. and F.T.Us. were moved up to 11 and 165 Fd. Ambs., so that along the whole of the front surgical facilities were available.

Arrangements were made to move 83 B.G.H. forward to La Calle and 4 Adv. Depot Med. Stores from Bône to Ali Abdullah.

In the L. of C. and at the base the hospital situation was more satis-factory than it had been. 31 B.G.H. at Oued Athmenia, 5 B.G.H. at Bône, 67 at Philippeville, 69 at Bougie and 94 at Algiers were all well established, but 95 and 96 at Algiers were still not fully open although they had been ashore for a month. 50 B.G.H. was closed at Guelma in reserve, 2 Fd. Hosp. at Setif, 71 B.G.H. at Guelma was seeking a new site for the reason that alongside the one that the hospital was occupying an airfield was being constructed. 5 Neurosurgical Team, arriving, was attached to 31 B.G.H. and 1 Mob. Hyg. Lab. to 6 Fd. Hosp. at Constantine. Preparations were being made for a 2,000-bedded convalescent depot at Philippeville. 72 B.G.H. was to be ferried forward from St. Armand in troop carriers of 2 A.C.C. and take over the accom-modation occupied by 84 B.G.H. and 8 C.C.S. at Souk Ahras. 84 B.G.H. and 8 C.C.S. were to close and go into reserve at Souk Ahras.

5 C.C.S., having lost most of its I.1248 and G.1098, was at Philippe-ville being re-equipped. 12 C.C.S., which had also fared badly by losing equipment, was now re-equipped and functioning at Tebessa with two F.S.Us. and a F.T.U. attached. It was serving U.S. 12th Airforce at Biskra, R.A.F. and various administrative units. Evacuation from it was by air direct to Algiers.

Three ambulance trains were in service with their stables at Souk Ahras, Constantine and near Setif. Arrangements were so made that there was always one of them at Souk Ahras. The journey from Souk Ahras to Algiers took 22 hours. The trains were staffed with British personnel and British equipment was being substituted for French.

9 Base Depot Med. Stores was at Algiers ; 10 Base Depot at Bône ; 3 Adv. Depot was in process of being moved to Constantine and 4 Adv. Depot was closed, as was 10 Base Depot, at Bône. The advanced depots held ten tons of additional stores for day to day needs. Stores in lots of 3–4 cwts. were being regularly sent forward to Souk Ahras by air whenever transport was available.

The functioning of the medical services was efficient and smooth. The siting by D.D.M.S. First Army of hospitals well forward more than compensated for the unsatisfactory hospital situation in Algiers and for the bare sufficiency of ambulance transport in the forward zone.

On December 22, the situation generally was such that D.D.M.S. sent in bids for KM.9 for 150 Q.A.I.M.N.S. personnel for service with 5, 31 and 67 B.G.Hs. The first party of Q.A.I.M.N.S. had reached Algiers at the end of December. One ship with two hundred of them aboard was torpedoed when nearing the Algerian coast. Five were drowned; the rest got ashore, having lost all their belongings. They were issued with battledress, and so a new fashion was set. Q.A.I.M.N.S. personnel were serving in the hospitals in Algiers, Bougie, Philippeville and Constantine and on the ambulance trains, and were to be sent to the hospitals further forward as soon as accommodation could be made ready for them. Elsewhere the hospitals and C.C.Ss. were to remain without them until, in the opinion of the local commanders, the conditions were sufficiently safe.

(ii)

Stalemate

On January 1, Eastern Task Force was dissolved and A.F.H.Q., with its H.Q. at Algiers, assumed control of all operations in North Africa. Rear H.Q. First Army moved forward to Constantine, there to join its Adv. H.Q. L. of C. and base sub-areas passed from First Army to H.Q., A.F.H.Q., with the exception of 2 L. of C. S.A. at Souk Ahras and 1 L. of C. S.A. at Constantine.

On January 3, 139th Inf. Bde. of 46th Division reached Algiers. On the 15th A.F.H.Q. Command Post opened at Constantine and on the 17th the balance of 46th Division arrived. The composition of this division is given below:

46th Division
    128th Inf. Bde.
        1/4th Hampshire Regt.
        2/4th Hampshire Regt.
        5th Hampshire Regt.
           attached troops and services including
        185 Fd. Amb.
    138th Inf. Bde.
        6th Lincolnshire Regt.
        6th York and Lancaster Regt.
        2/4th Kings Own Yorkshire Light Infantry
           attached troops including

184 Fd. Amb.
139th Inf. Bde.
  2/5th Leicestershire Regt.
  2/5th Sherwood Foresters
  16th Durham Light Infantry
  attached troops including
  183 Fd. Amb.
15 Fd. Hyg. Sec.
26, 28, 32 F.S.Us.

During January the Germans launched a series of localised attacks on the Eastern Dorsale line. The accumulated results of these were sufficiently serious to bring about an event of great significance. General Eisenhower placed U.S. II Corps and French XIX Corps under the command of General Anderson, commanding First Army. From the beginning of the campaign the French, although actively co-operating with the British, had been unwilling to serve under British command. Thus it was that often the tactical control of the Allied forces in battle had been imperfect. General Eisenhower now felt justified in over-riding the objections of the French.

The distribution of troops in the forward zone in January 1943 was as follows:

Southern Sector	U.S. II Corps
Sbeitla – Gafsa – Feriana – Tebessa	
French Sector	Division de Tunis
Pichon – Ousseltia – Djebel Bargou – Robaa – Bou Arada	
6th Armd. Division Sector	6th Armd. Division
Slouguia – Goubellat – Bou Arada – El Aroussa	
	38th Inf. Bde.
	6th Inniskilling Fusiliers
	2nd London Irish Rifles
	1st Royal Irish Fusiliers
	1st Derbyshire Yeomanry
	1 Lt. Fd. Amb.
	165 Lt. Fd. Amb.
Medjez el Bab Sector	1st Guards Bde. Gp. (less 2nd Hampshire Regt.)
	3rd Grenadier Gds.
	2nd Coldstream Gds.
	8th Argyll and Sutherland Highlanders (36th Inf. Bde.)
	Four French battalions
	11 Fd. Amb. (78th Division)
78th Division Sector	78th Division (less 1st Gds. Bde. and
Mine de Khanguet –	36th Inf. Bde.)
Sidi N'sir –	1st Para. Bde.
Oued Zarga –	1st Commando
Beja	U.S. Artillery units

On the right:

    11th Inf. Bde. (less one bn.)
        1st East Surrey Regt.
        5th Northamptonshire Regt.
        159 Fd. Amb. (First Army)

Northern Sector
    Jefna –
    El Arouana –
    Sedjenane

On the left:

    1st Para. Bde. (1st, 2nd and 3rd Para. Bn.)
    16 Para. Fd. Amb. (1st Para. Bde.)

    36th Inf. Bde. (less 8th A. and S.H.)
    6th Commando
    217 Fd. Amb. (78th Div.) with 32 F.S.U. attached.

36th Inf. Bde. was about to be relieved by 139th Inf. Bde. of 46th Division and 217 Fd. Amb. by 183.

H.Q. 46th Division and 138th Inf. Bde. moved from Algiers to Bône. On January 30, the Germans attacked the French positions at the Faid Pass and breached the Eastern Dorsale line. They dug in and resisted all attempts to dislodge them. U.S. II Corps withdrew to Sidi Bou Zid. (Fig. 49.)

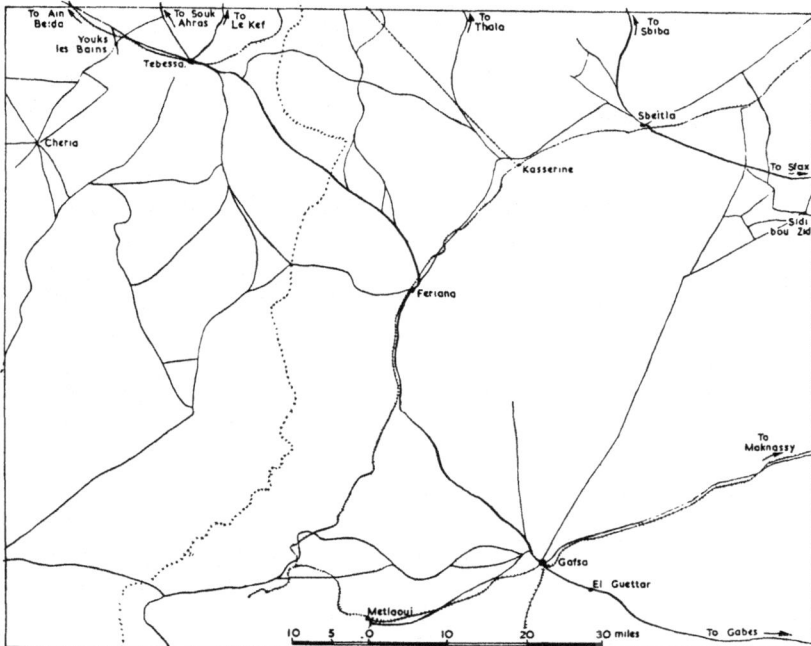

FIG. 47. Tunisia. Tebessa – Sbeitla – Gafsa.

By the end of January it had become quite clear that the opposing forces, though enduring very different circumstances, were too evenly matched to make a quick decision possible. There had been much fierce fighting locally at 'Green' and 'Bald' Hills, outside Sedjenane; at Medjez el Bab and 'Longstop' Hill, on the main road to Tunis; at El Aroussa, in the valley leading to Pont du Fahs, and in the American sector about Sbeitla and Gafsa. Tactically the stalemate was complete. The four main passes into the Tunis plain were strongly held by the enemy. The Allies were pressing continuously and hard but were waiting for Eighth Army to move up from the south before unleashing their full strength for the final throw.

On February 1–5, 25th Army Tk. Bde., and on February 14, 3rd W.G. (1st Gds. Bde.) arrived. On February 3, 46th Division was in the forward zone on the left of 78th Division and therefore on the extreme left of the line. 1st Para. Bn., with the aid of French units, captured Djebel Mansour in the centre sector, losing 35 killed, 132 wounded and 16 missing. 3rd Gren. Gds. attacked Djebel Alliliga, losing 6 officers and 72 O.Rs. On February 9 Main H.Q., First Army, moved to Laverdure.

All Axis forces had been driven out of Tripoli across the Tunisian frontier by Eighth Army by February 4.

They had fallen back on the Mareth Line with strong forward positions at Ben Gardane and Medenine. Eighth Army flung them out of the first of these places on February 16, and out of the second on the following day.

According to the agreement reached at the Casablanca conference in January 1943, on entering Tunisia Eighth Army came under command of A.F.H.Q. There were now two groups of Axis forces in Tunisia, those in the north under Generals von Arnim and Messe opposing British First Army, U.S. II Corps and French XIX Corps, and those in the south under Marshal Rommel which had been beaten, pursued and beaten again by Eighth Army. For the present the passage between the two along the coast was clear. In order to keep it clear Marshal Rommel on February 14 dealt a swift and hard blow at the U.S. forces in the plain west of Faid. The American positions at Sidi Bou Zid, on the Djebel Lessondo to the north of this village, at Sbeitla and south of Hadjeb el Aioun on the Sbeitla–Pichon road were encircled. A counter-attack by U.S. 1st Armoured Division was repulsed with heavy loss. General Anderson thereupon ordered a withdrawal to the Western Dorsale. The gateway through the Western Dorsale was the Kasserine Pass. Its defences were brushed aside and the German armour swiftly advanced to occupy Kasserine and Feriana and to press towards the Thala–Tebessa road. The airfield at Thelepte was lost.

On the 18th the Germans regrouped and replenished, and on the following day began to probe along the Sbeitla–Sbiba, the Kasserine–Thala and the Feriana–Tebessa roads.

On the 15th General Alexander, Deputy to General Eisenhower, arrived in Algiers from Tripoli. After discussions with General Eisenhower he flew to Telergma and toured the battle front. He found the situation so critical that he decided not to wait until February 20, the date when 18 Army Group would officially be formed, but to assume command at once. On the 18th he took over control of the battle and returned to his H.Q. at Constantine.

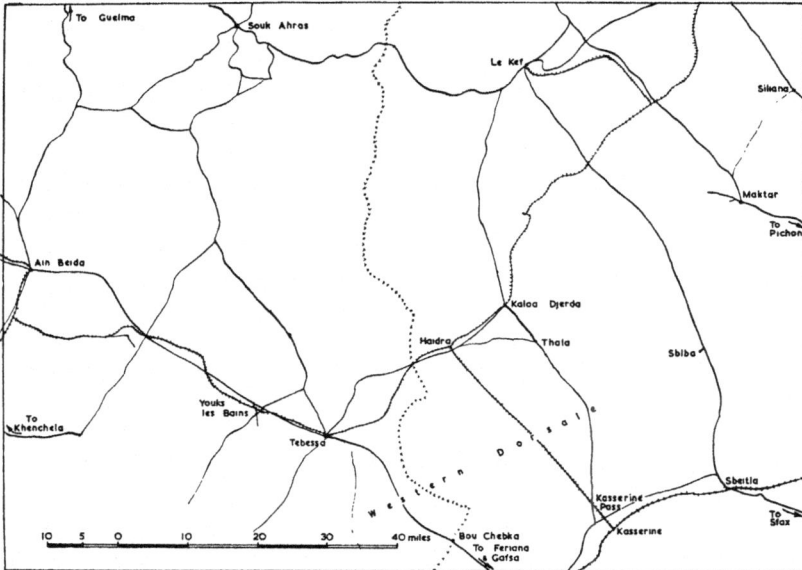

FIG. 48. Tunisia. The Kasserine Pass.

On the 19th the German thrust along the Kasserine–Thala road was the most successful, and on the 20th it was strongly reinforced and the advances along the Sbeitla–Sbiba and Feriana–Tebessa roads abandoned. The German armour pressed northward towards Thala and Le Kef. General Alexander instructed General Anderson to concentrate his armour for the defence of Thala. 'Nickforce', based on 26th Armd. Bde. Gp. of 6th Armoured Division and reinforced by 2/5th Leicesters, 2nd Hamps. and two U.S. field artillery battalions of 9th U.S. Division and with 165 Lt. Fd. Amb. less three sections, set out by forced marches to the scene of action. The German attack was held ten miles from Thala, near the Tebessa–Le Kef road, on the evening of February 21.

By midday on the 22nd it had become clear that the opportunity for the exploitation of the Kasserine victory had passed, and on the 23rd the Germans began to withdraw along the Kasserine Pass. By the 25th this pass was again in Allied hands and by the 28th Sbeitla, Kasserine and Feriana were reoccupied. The Axis forces had withdrawn to the Eastern Dorsale and retained Gafsa.

On February 21, General Alexander called upon General Montgomery to exert all possible pressure upon the Axis forces in the Mareth position in order to compel Marshal Rommel to weaken his thrust along the Kasserine Pass. This was done, although Eighth Army preparations for an engagement of this magnitude were administratively not yet mature.

On February 20, U.S. II Corps, French XIX Corps, British First and Eighth Armies and the French 'L' Force under General Leclerc, moving northwards from Lake Chad, were formally amalgamated to form 18 Army Group. (18=the combined numbers of the two British armies.)

As the rearguards of Marshal Rommel were withdrawing to the Eastern Dorsale General von Arnim struck with all his strength all along the front of V Corps from the sea to Djebel Mansour at Goubellat, Medjez, Sidi N'sir and Jefna. On February 26, the attack on Medjez was repulsed, as was that at Bou Arada, by 38th Inf. Bde. At Sidi N'sir, the 5th Hamps. of 128th Inf. Bde. were overwhelmed, but not before 46th Division, with 128th Inf. Bde., was able to occupy 'Hunt's Gap', the pass that led to Beja. Very heavy fighting continued here for a week in terrible weather. Losses were heavy but the defence held firm.

General Anderson created 'Y' Division to control the right sector of V Corps in the area of Goubellat and Bou Arada. It consisted of 1st Para. Bde. and 38th Inf. Bde. The medical units associated with this improvised formation were 1 Fd. Amb. (1st Division), 165 Lt. Fd. Amb., three sections, 16 Para. Fd. Amb., 26 and 32 F.S.Us. and 36 F.T.U.

On March 2, the attack west of Jefna was resumed. On the 3rd Sedjenane was lost and 46th Division was obliged to withdraw to a fresh position at Djebel Tamera, eight miles farther west. 46th Division was reinforced with 1st Para. Bde. and the French Corps Franc d'Afrique, a volunteer unit. Nevertheless, Djebel Tamera was lost on the 17th and by the 21st the division had been forced back to Djebel Abiod. The fighting in this sector had been exceedingly bitter and the weather atrocious. Von Arnim had gained important ground but had failed to secure his chief objectives, Medjez and Beja.

H.Q. IX Corps and 1st Division had now arrived in North Africa. H.Q. 1st Division and two brigades took over the Medjez sector and 3rd Inf. Bde. replaced 'Y' Division; 6th Armoured Division and 1st Gds. Bde. went into reserve.

U.S. II Corps of four divisions was now concentrated in the Tebessa area to be used when necessary as a mobile reserve and to form a bastion between the Allied forces in northern Tunisia and the approaching Eighth Army. Vast numbers of vehicles arrived from the U.S.A. to give complete mobility to the Allied formations. The decrepit railway was now in excellent condition as the result of the labours of the U.S. Engineers and could deal with a daily tonnage of 3,000.

Finally, the Allied air strength now greatly exceeded that of the enemy.

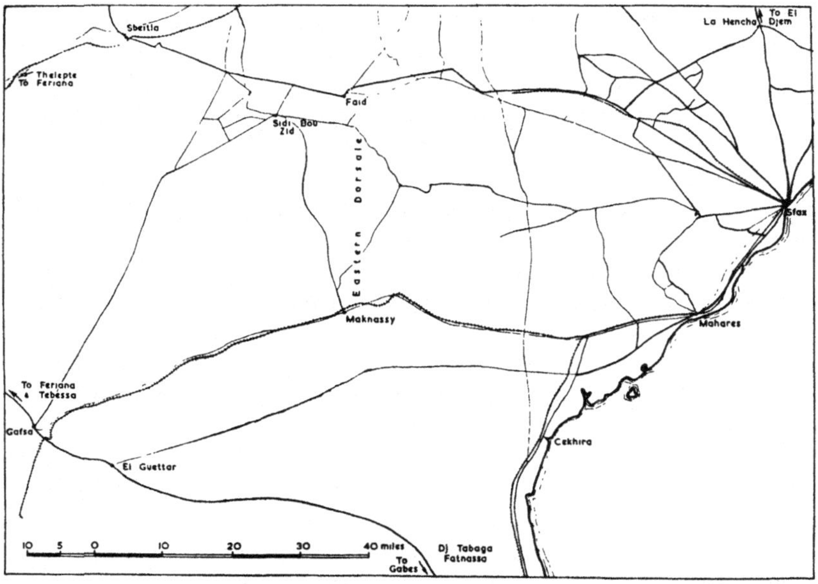

FIG. 49. The Southern part of the Eastern Dorsale.

To attract Axis troops away from the Mareth Line, now about to be attacked by Eighth Army, General Alexander directed U.S. II Corps to make a diversionary attack to secure the Eastern Dorsale and to threaten the coastal plain beyond. Accordingly, II Corps planned to thrust towards Gafsa, El Guettar and Maknassy and to demonstrate towards Faid and Fondouk. On March 16–17, U.S. 1st Division entered Gafsa unopposed. On the 20th the battle of Mareth opened. U.S. 1st Division pushed on beyond Gafsa to meet fierce opposition in the mountainous country beyond El Guettar. With U.S. 1st Division on the left of the Gabes road and U.S. 9th Division on the right the Americans attempted to thrust the Axis force back from the high ground. On the 23rd, the Axis force, reinforced with armour drawn from the Mareth position, counter-attacked but was repulsed with heavy loss. In this way U.S. II Corps made a very solid contribution to the success of Eighth Army.

23

MEDICAL ARRANGEMENTS DURING THIS PERIOD OF STALEMATE

During January nothing of particular interest occurred. An anti-malaria school was opened in Sidi Meskine and 8 Fd. Hyg. Sec. arranged a malaria class for N.C.Os. of field hygiene sections at Hammam Mouskoutine. On the 16th, 84 B.G.H. and 8 C.C.S. at Souk Ahras were full and special arrangements had to be made to clear them. From 12 C.C.S. at Youks les Bains most of the patients requiring general hospital care were sent to Algiers by air.

U.S.A.A.F. units at Biskra were suffering severe casualties from nightly bombing raids. D.M.S., A.F.H.Q., was asked to send a small hospital unit to this isolated place, nearly 250 miles from Algiers. As no suitable U.S. medical unit was then available, 50 B.G.H. (200 beds) was warned for this duty by D.D.M.S. First Army. Transport Command provided 40 Dakotas and in two lifts, on January 17, the entire unit, personnel and equipment (save for one lorry load of the heaviest stores) was moved to its new site.

On the 18th a small epidemic of typhus broke out in Constantine. There were 191 cases, including 9 Europeans, and immediate steps were taken to protect the troops in and around the town.

The problems relating to medical cover to be dealt with at this time by D.D.M.S. First Army were by no means simple. There were three corps to be served, British V, French XIX and U.S. II. The first was north of the line Le Kef–Gafour–Bou Arada; the second between this and the line Thala–Kairouan–Sousse; south of this was the U.S. II Corps. Behind each corps was a L. of C. sub-area. 2 L. of C. S.A. in the north centred on Souk Ahras, the French L. of C. S.A. centred on Le Kef and the U.S. L. of C. S.A. centred on Tebessa.

In the British sector evacuation was either to 83 B.G.H. at La Calle or else to 72 B.G.H. at Souk Ahras. These were cleared under L. of C. arrangements to the base. The French sector included two French divisions and U.S. 1st Division. The French evacuation was by road or rail to the French military hospitals in Le Kef (676 beds) or to Tebessa (242 beds). Other French military hospitals which were used were at Souk Ahras (325), Ain Beida (200), Guelma (237) and Constantine (1,208). U.S. 1st Division cleared as far as the second line U.S. medical units, whence evacuation was to 18 and 19 C.C.Ss. at Ali Abdullah or to 72 B.G.H. at Souk Ahras. The controlling centre for the evacuation of American casualties was 159 Fd. Amb. at Le Kef.

In the southern U.S. sector U.S. II Corps had U.S. 9 Evac. Hosp. (750) in the Bou Chebka area. Thence head, thoracic and abdominal cases were flown to Telergma for 31 B.G.H. at Oued Athmenia and the others direct to Algiers. U.S. 48 Surg. Hosp. was close by the aerodrome at Thelepte, near Feriana, and 12 C.C.S. at Youks les Bains acted as a staging centre in connexion with 31 B.G.H.

The French military hospitals were being supplied by 4 Adv. Depot Med. Stores at Constantine and were holding 30 days supplies for

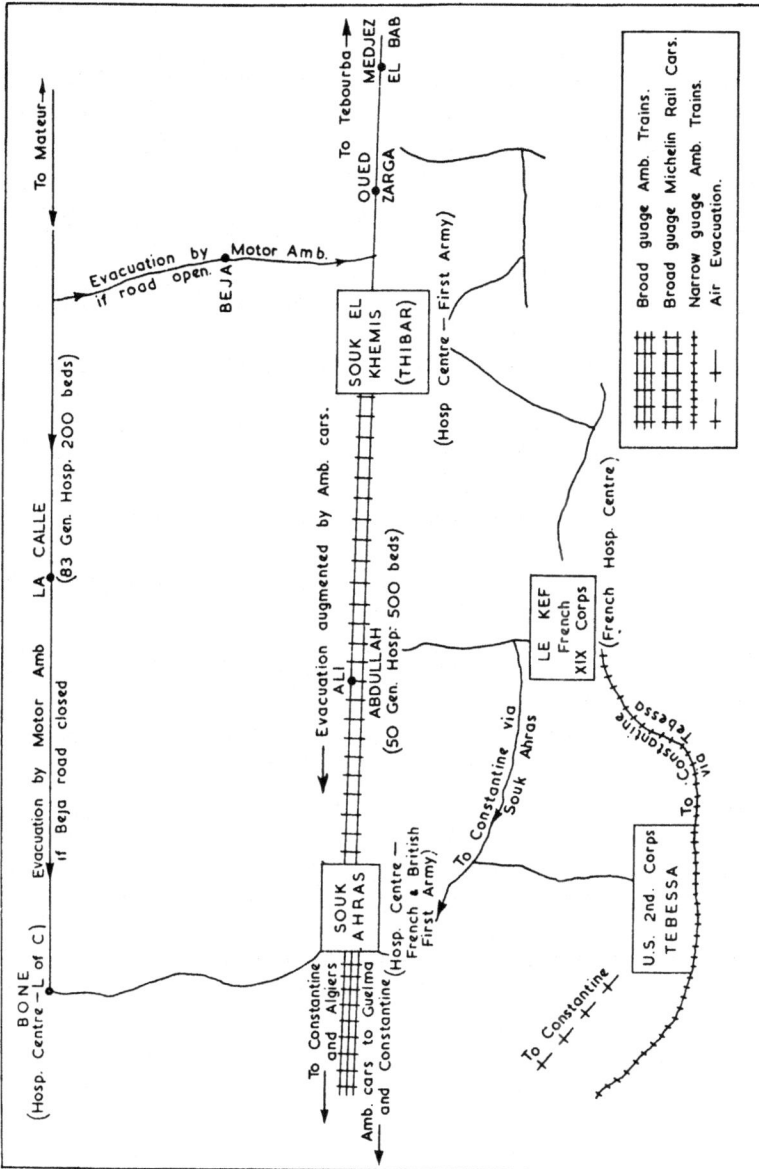

FIG. 50. The evacuation system, January–April 1943.

30,000 men at Le Kef, Ain Beida and at Guelma. The French were very short of ambulance cars, as was also V Corps. V Corps, roughly 80,000 strong, had two platoons of 8 M.A.C., 19 motor ambulances and

18 troop carriers of 2 A.C.C. French XIX Corps, about 20,000 strong, had one platoon (33 cars) of 6 M.A.C.; 6 cars of 6 M.A.C. were with U.S. II Corps (45,000) and the rest of the cars of 6 M.A.C. were in Army reserve.

On February 23, 170 casualties were admitted to 72 B.G.H. at Souk Ahras which now had 550 occupied beds. Evacuation therefrom was to 71 B.G.H. in Guelma by 2 A.C.C. 84 B.G.H. at Souk Ahras had enlarged and had 200 beds available.

When the Axis forces withdrew from the Kasserine area 159 Fd. Amb. was moved from Thala to Le Kef and 165 Lt. Fd. Amb. with 25 F.S.U. placed at the disposal of D.D.M.S. V Corps. The attack on V Corps front that followed closely upon the Kasserine battle was associated with an increased inflow of casualties into the forward hospitals. M.A.Cs. and ambulance trains proved to be inadequate to deal with the problems of evacuation and the experience yielded strong support for the demands of D.D.M.S. First Army for additional transport.

On March 5, 220 Fd. Amb. opened in La Calle to relieve the pressure on 83 B.G.H. which was functioning as a C.C.S. 156 and 157 M.D.Us., arriving, were attached to 83 and 84 B.G.Hs. respectively.

On the 8th, to reinforce the facilities of V Corps, 30 F.S.U. from 5 C.C.S. at Philippeville was sent to 83 B.G.H. ; U.S. II Corps passed from the command of First Army to 18 Army Group on this date. The 28 motor ambulance cars that had been serving U.S. II Corps were posted to XIX Corps.

4 B.T.U. at Bône was u/c A.F.H.Q. It supplied all the medical units from Algiers to the front line. Because of the great distance separating it from the Algiers base and because so many of the units it supplied were far forward, D.M.S. A.F.H.Q. agreed that it should be placed u/c First Army.

On March 13, the medical branch of First Army moved from Ain Seynour to Laverdure. Orders were issued for 71 B.G.H. and the advance party of 97 B.G.H. at Guelma to move to Souk Ahras and for 5 Neuro-Surg. Unit to join 31 B.G.H. at Oued Athmenia.

On the 26th, 10 M.A.C., arriving, was posted to French XIX Corps and 5 M.A.C. to the new IX Corps area. 4 Adv. Depot Med. Stores opened in Ali Abdullah.

At the end of this phase the distribution of medical units, excluding the divisional, was as follows:

BASE HOSPITALS

The four 1,200 bedded hospitals (94, 95, 96, and 99) had grown by 100 bed expansions to become 1,600 bedded. Later still they were to undergo further 500 bed expansion. 94, at Beni Messous in buildings and tents, with a separate wing for infectious diseases in a school some distance away, was a general purpose hospital, receiving naval casualties, having a V.D. wing and, later, a wired-in P.o.W. compound. It accommodated the maxillo-facial unit. 95 B.G.H. at Beni Achnoun was in a school with tentage in the extensive grounds. A compound of Arab-style cement huts was used for the psychiatric wing. The ophthalmic centre was with 95, which ultimately was to grow to 2,500 beds. 96 B.G.H. was near Maison Blanche airfield and received the U.S. casualties evacuated by air from U.S. II Corps sector. At this hospital eight surgical teams, including three American, were available. U.S. casualties were cleared by air to the U.S. hospital base at Oran, which in turn cleared to Casablanca. 99 B.G.H. had its surgical section in a new sanatorium at Rivet, 20 km. outside Algiers and 1,500 ft. above sea level. Orthopaedic and chest cases were here received and treated. The medical section was under canvas at Alma. Later 99 had a large P.o.W. section.

8 Con. Depot never got its site in Algiers. A.D.M.S., B.S.A., finally found an ideal site at Sidi Ferruch, 20 km. to the west. To this unit the personnel of 9 Con. Depot was attached. Accommodation for 3,000 was provided. An officers' convalescent wing was established at Tipaza, 60 km. to the west of Algiers, capable of holding 200. A number of villas were taken over as sleeping quarters and an excellent mess was provided in a local hotel. A convalescent home for Army nurses was opened in a villa east of Algiers. The American Red Cross and the B.R.C.S. were doing magnificent work. The former body had established centres at Casablanca, Oran and Algiers and had extended its organisation into the forward areas. The B.R.C.S. had its main depot in Algiers with advanced depots in the forward zone. A fleet of B.R.C.S. ambulance cars was operating in Algiers and 'visitors' (welfare officers) were posted for duty at the larger hospitals.

Bougie. 69 B.G.H. in tents to begin with, but hutted later, was in a highly malarious area and in somewhat of a backwater. It was used for 'cold' surgery.

Philippeville. 67 and 100 B.G.Hs., in buildings, huts and tents on the shore well away from the port, ultimately expanded so that they provided 2,500 beds.

Bône. 5 and 76 B.G.Hs. were under canvas at Zerizer, 20 km. outside Bône. This was another malarious site but control measures were taken and the personnel remained healthy. Associated with these units was 4 B.T.U.

L. OF C. HOSPITALS

Oued Athmenia. 31 B.G.H., expanding up to 1,000 beds, was well established near Oued Athmenia. It was used as a clearing hospital for air evacuation, being near the Telergma airfield. The area was notorious for the prevalence and virulence of malaria. Strict control measures were taken and the staff remained healthy.

Setif. 2 Fd. Hosp. of 50 beds was dealing with local sick and the many accidental injuries.

Constantine. 6 Fd. Hosp. was being used for surgical emergencies. 1 Mob. Fd. Hyg. Lab. was attached.

Mechta Chateaudun. 98 and 103 B.G.Hs. were sited a few km. off the main Setif–Constantine road on the main railway line. They provided 2,400 beds with expansions of another 600.

Nearby, at Ain M'Lila, 10 Con. Depot was in tents and with a recreation hut seating 800. To this unit was attached a surgical team so that if necessary it could be used as a W.W.C.P.

Guelma. 97 B.G.H., in tents in an olive grove, was receiving its patients by long distance M.A.C. cars. This unit was under orders to move to Souk Ahras.

FIRST ARMY HOSPITALS

Biskra. 50 B.G.H.

Thibar. 70 B.G.H.

Souk Ahras. 72 B.G.H. in buildings and 84 B.G.H. under canvas. To 84 B.G.H. 4 Maxillo-facial Surgical Unit was attached.

Guelma. 71 B.G.H.

La Calle. 83 B.G.H.

Three U.S. hospital bases had been established, the Atlantic Base Section (A.B.S.) at Casablanca, the Mediterranean Base Section (M.B.S.) at Oran and the Eastern Base Section (E.B.S.) with its H.Q. at Constantine.

Excluding forward and corps medical units, there were 35,590 beds available by the end of March and some 3,000 men were being discharged from medical units and returned to duty each week. When it seemed likely that there might be a temporary shortage of hospital beds the Directeur du Service de Santé offered to find 5,000 and plans were drawn up by A.F.H.Q. for admitting American and British personnel to selected French hospitals.

U.S.			British		
A.B.S.	.	. 3,000	Algiers	.	. 6,000
M.B.S.	.	. 5,343	Bougie	.	. 800
E.B.S.	.	. 1,250	Philippeville	.	. 1,800
			Bône	.	. 1,400
			L. of C.	.	. 3,600
			First Army	.	. 2,400
		9,593			16,000

+ 2,000 French   beds

Con. Hosps . 3,000   Con. Depots . 5,000
Strength: 3/4/43   U.S. . . 341,686
                   British . 248,174
_____

Total . . 589,860

Though everything was done to ensure that American casualties were delivered to U.S. medical units and British casualties to British, it was but inevitable that quite commonly an American casualty found himself in the strange atmosphere of a British hospital and a British in the magnificence of an American medical unit. So it was that a man could become separated from his letters from home. The American missed his peculiar brand of cigarette, his candy and his coffee, and came to dislike the red tie that goes with the British blue hospital suiting. The British guest of an American unit longed for his tea and his own variety of tobacco. The American Red Cross and the B.R.C.S. came to their rescue. American liaison officers and sergeants were posted to British hospitals. The wounded American had, however, earned his Purple Heart Medal and since it was at times exceedingly difficult for D.M.S., A.F.H.Q., to make the appropriate arrangements whereby a high-ranking American corps or divisional officer could make the award to a dangerously wounded man lying in a British medical unit, the presentation was, in many cases, made by a senior American medical officer on the staff of A.F.H.Q.

C.C.Ss.
    5 at Philippeville
    8   Souk Ahras
  12   Youks les Bains moving to Sekret Youssef
  18   Ali Abdullah
  19   Ali Abdullah
Fd. Ambs.
  159 (Army) Le Kef
  220 (V Corps) La Calle
M.A.Cs.

Unit Number			
Original	*New*	*Allotment*	*Location*
3	60	D.D.M.S., L. of C.	Constantine
4	45	D.D.M.S., L. of C.	Algiers
5	74	D.D.M.S., IX Corps	Corps Area
6	88	D.D.M.S., First Army	Army Area
8	112	D.D.M.S., V Corps	Corps Area
10	260	D.D.M.S., First Army	Army Area—to French XIX Corps
15	146		
2 A.C.C.		A.F.H.Q.	Algiers

There were now nine ambulance trains, five French and four British. The service was administered by A.D.M.S., Constantine B.S.A. A Fleet Medical Officer (R.N.) attached to A.F.H.Q. was responsible for the medical aspects of the hospital ship service.

MEDICAL SUPPLIES

As for medical supplies, each convoy brought a standard 'brick' which not only replaced such as had been expended but also provided reserves for the future. 9 Base Depot Med. Stores was well established at Algiers and 10 was in reserve at Bône. 3 Adv. Depot Med. Stores was open in Constantine and 4 in Ali Abdullah. All resources were pooled and interchange between the Americans and British was a frequent occurrence. The French were exceedingly deficient in almost everything and every effort was made to satisfy their needs.

(iii)

The Advance of Eighth Army into Tunisia

Following the occupation of Tripoli on January 23, 7th Armd. Division continued to advance westwards along the coast road with 4th Lt. Armd. Bde., moving parallel with the division but farther inland. A delaying action was fought to the east of Ben Gardane but 7th Armd. Division moved round the flank of the position and the Axis forces thereupon fell back to the Mareth Line.

51st Division moved up to take over the coastal sector facing Mareth. 201st Guards Bde. took up its position between 51st and 7th Armd. Divisions. Finally N.Z. 2nd Division came up to form a perimeter around Medenine.

MEDICAL ARRANGEMENTS—EIGHTH ARMY

Until Tripoli became available as a port on February 20, and until general hospitals could be brought up thereto, a chain of C.C.Ss. had been provided between Tripoli via Benghazi to Barce:

Nofilia . . .	14 C.C.S. Lt. Sec.
Marble Arch . .	3 C.C.S.
Mersa Brega .	14 C.C.S. Hy. Sec.
Agedabia . .	15 C.C.S.
Benghazi . . .	2 (Ind.) C.C.S.
.	200 Fd. Amb.
Barce . . .	4 B.G.H.
	16 I.G.H., one sec.

At Tobruk (99 Sub-area) were 10 C.C.S. and 3 (Ind.) C.C.S.

Evacuation from Ben Gardane was by 43 M.A.C. and 'B' Sec. 'Y' M.A.C. (100 cars in all) to Tripoli via Zuara. Returning empty lorries were also used. By air, evacuation was from the forward L.Gs. to 3 C.C.S. at Marble Arch by D.H. 86 ambulance aircraft or by transport planes from Castel Benito to Marble Arch, Benina, El Adem, or to L.G. 224 near Mena for the base hospitals in the Delta. At Zuara, a staging post was established by 8 (S.A.) C.C.S. and H.Q. 43 M.A.C.

MEDICAL ARRANGEMENTS IN 'TRIPBASE'

On March 3 Tripolitania Base and L. of C. took over the administration of Tripoli and all L. of C. Eighth Army from Marble Arch to the Tunisian frontier, thus freeing Eighth Army itself from the burden of detail. 86 Area was at first under 'Tripbase' but was replaced by 83 Area on March 8. 86 Area was thus made available for employment farther forward. At the end of March the composition of the medical section of Tripolitania Base and L. of C. was as under:

D.D.M.S. 'Tripbase' and L. of C.

General Hospitals and Con. Depots	Pool of medical reinforcements for Eighth Army	L. of C. E	O.E.T.A.	L. of C. W	Med. Stores	83 86 Area
48 B.G.H. (500) at Canava 2 B.G.H. (1,400) Azzizia Bks. and hospital 16 C.G.H. (500) less one sec. Azzizia 3 N.Z.G.H. (900) H.Q. 14 Fd. Amb. Maxillo-facial Unit 7 Adv. Depot Med. Stores 1 B.T.U. detach. N.Z. M.A.C.		Medical Embarkation	Tripoli Town Medical Arrangements			Tripoli Town Hygiene Arrangements

Rear H.Q. Eighth Army was on the outskirts of Tripoli until March 10. On March 6, D.D.M.S. moved up to join Main H.Q. at Km. 39, west of Ben Gardane. On March 12, Rear H.Q. merged with Main H.Q.

As XXX Corps approached the Mareth Line, Lt. Sec. 1 (N.Z.) C.C.S. was brought up from Tamet to Sabratha where it opened in the hospital buildings on February 10. Next the heavy section of this C.C.S. moved forward to open in the hospital at Zuara Marina on February 11. The hospital buildings thus taken over were found to be so very insanitary that the decision was reached never again to make use of Italian hospital accommodation.

As the line of communications further lengthened, 15 C.C.S. was brought up to a site six miles to the east of Ben Gardane. When the Mareth Line was reached, Army assumed responsibility for evacuation from Ben Gardane. 1 (N.Z.) C.C.S. moved to a position fourteen miles east of Medenine where 151 Lt. Fd. Amb. was already open.

THE BATTLE OF MEDENINE

7th Armd. Division and 22nd Armd. Bde. took Ben Gardane on February 16 and, together with 51st Division, occupied Medenine on February 17 and Foum Tatahouine on the following day. Meanwhile General Leclerc's force, reaching the battle zone and placing itself under General Montgomery's command, was given the task of moving

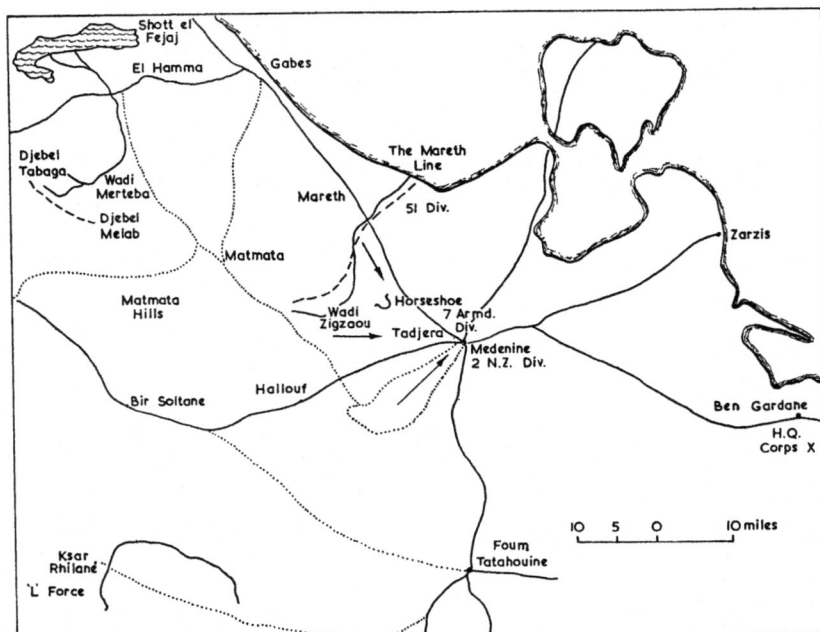

FIG. 51. The Battle of Medenine.

from Nalut to Ksar Rhilane, thence to operate eastwards and thus to screen the concentration of N.Z. 2nd Division in preparation for the Mareth battle and to threaten the Axis' western flank. 1st Armd. Division, Indian 4th Division, 50th Division and N.Z. 2nd Division were at this time concentrating in the area of Tripoli.

During the course of the Axis thrust towards Tebessa on February 15, on U.S. II Corps front, 7th Armd. Division pressed hard along the coastal road and 51st Division along the main Gabes road towards the main Mareth position. With the cessation of the Tebessa thrust it became manifest that the Axis forces were concentrating for an assault upon Eighth Army positions at Medenine. N.Z. 2nd Division was therefore moved forward from 'Tripbase' to Medenine together with 201st Guards Bde. and 8th Armd. Bde. By March 3, Eighth Army was ready and looked forward with quiet confidence to the coming battle. 51st Division and 201st Guards Bde. were on the right, the latter on Tadjera Hill, 7th Armd. Division was in the centre about Tadjera Hill and N.Z. 2nd Division in Medenine, while to the rear, at Ben Gardane, there was a detachment of H.Q. X Corps together with local defence elements. The position was not protected by wire or minefields but the force was well supplied with A/T guns and had strong reserves of armour.

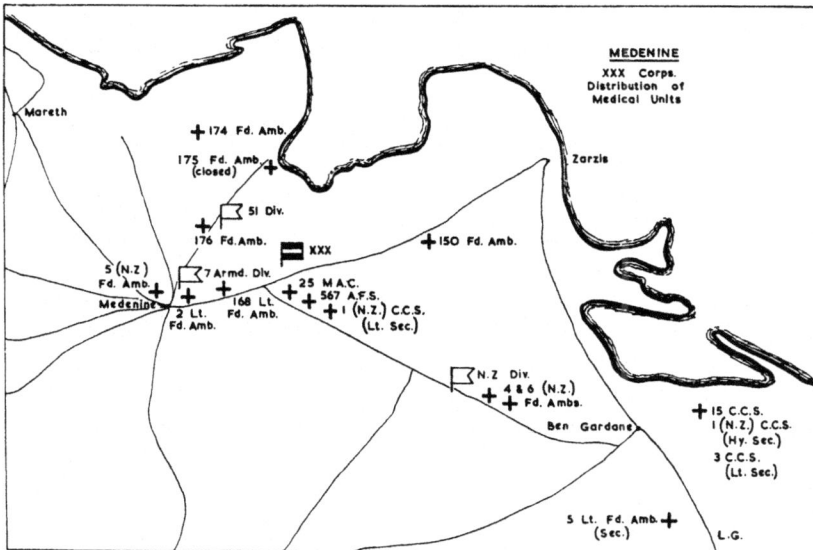

FIG. 52. The Battle of Medenine. Medical Cover.

On March 6, 15th, 21st and part of 10th Panzer Divisions, aided by lorry-borne infantry, thrust towards Tadjera on the front of 7th Armd. Division on no less than four occasions. They were repulsed by the A/T gun line supported by massed artillery and during the night of March 6–7 withdrew, leaving on the field 52 tanks destroyed by gun-fire.

This was Marshal Rommel's last battle in Africa. He left for Germany and was succeeded by General von Arnim.

MEDICAL COVER

On February 28 the distribution of the medical units of XXX Corps was as follows:

1 (N.Z.) C.C.S. was in the forward area with 151 Lt. Fd. Amb. in close proximity. This forward area was on the Medenine–Ben Gardane road a few miles east of the Zarzis road junction. In view of the possibility that the Axis forces might attempt an outflanking movement in the south, the heavy section and the nursing sisters of 1 (N.Z.) C.C.S. were sent back to Ben Gardane, there to join 15 C.C.S., so forming a XXX Corps rear medical area. In the forward area associated with the light section of 1 (N.Z.) C.C.S. were the M.D.Ss. of 5 and 151 Lt. Fd. Ambs.

By March 4 it was evident that the impending attack was to be a serious attempt by the Axis forces to inflict a decisive defeat on Eighth Army. Thus the danger of a heavy thrust from the south became greater. It was in anticipation of this possibility that, as mentioned above, the heavy section and the nursing sisters of 1 (N.Z.) C.C.S. were moved back to Ben Gardane, to which place a light section of 3 C.C.S. had been moved.

The final arrangements were as follows:

5 Lt. Fd. Amb., less three sections, and 151 Lt. Fd. Amb. were grouped with the Lt. Sec. of 1 (N.Z.) C.C.S. as a forward corps medical area. 2 F.S.U. and 1 F.T.U., which had been attached to 151 Lt. Fd. Amb., joined the Lt. Sec. of 1 (N.Z.) C.C.S. to form an advanced surgical centre. The officer commanding 1 (N.Z.) C.C.S. was appointed S.M.O. of this forward corps medical area. A control post was established at the western end of this forward medical area to admit cases firstly to 151 Lt. Fd. Amb. until this was either full or working to capacity and thereafter to 5 Lt. Fd. Amb., all of these patients being recorded as direct corps admissions. All cases requiring surgery or major resuscitation were to be transferred at once to the Lt. Sec. of 1 (N.Z.) C.C.S.

In view of the increasing threat of an outflanking movement from the south, 150 Lt. Fd. Amb. opened a M.D.S. on the Medenine–Zarzis road as an alternative evacuation route. A track was marked from the forward area to the Zarzis road. The plan was that, if this threat developed, a sentry would be posted by the officer commanding 25 M.A.C. at this road junction to divert ambulance cars from the Medenine–Ben Gardane road to the Zarzis road. Similarly a sentry at Ben Gardane would divert returning traffic on the same route. Casualties would then be dealt with by 150 Lt. Fd. Amb. while units of the forward medical area packed up and moved over the marked track. In this way it was hoped that a continuous line of evacuation would be ensured.

In view of what happened at Sidi Rezegh in November 1941, it was laid down as a direction that should enemy armour occupy a medical area the minimum staff necessary adequately to attend the wounded, together with adequate food and medical supplies, would be left and that all senior officers and all others who could be spared would move and all vehicles be taken away. In the event this threat did not materialise.

When N.Z. 2nd Division moved up to Medenine 5 (N.Z.) Fd. Amb. went inside this perimeter, 4 and 6 (N.Z.) Fd. Ambs. being in reserve on the Medenine–Ben Gardane road.

Of the field ambulances of 51st Division, 176 established its M.D.S. on the Bou Grara–Medenine road; 174 was with its brigade; 175 remained on wheels. When 23rd Armd. Bde. came u/c 51st Division 150 Lt. Fd. Amb. was released to Corps and was sent to reinforce the corps medical centre. Divisional casualties numbered 3 officers and 72 O.Rs.

During the actual battle the enemy forces were unable to reach the defensive positions of XXX Corps save at two points. Since there was no penetration of the defensive position battle casualties were exceedingly few, indeed the total number of wounded for the period 1800 hours March 5–1800 hours March 7 was 10 officers and 177 other ranks. It was noted that in this comparatively small number of casualties the total of penetrating abdominal wounds was 10.

The conditions of the battle did not constitute a real test of the medical arrangements that had been made. It became clear, however, that the provision of a forward corps medical area, with its facilities for major surgery, was most useful in that it saved for serious cases a long run back to Ben Gardane. In retrospect it seemed that had the casualties been as numerous as had been estimated—3,000 during the course of four or five days—the arrangements made would have dealt with them satisfactorily.

Air evacuation was only on a very light scale. Over a period of four days 28–30 cases were thus evacuated.

THE BATTLE OF THE MARETH LINE

The Mareth Line, originally constructed by the French to protect Tunisia from an Italian attack from Libya, stretched for some 22 miles from the sea near Zarat to the Matmata Hills in the west. About Zarat the defences were based upon the Wadi Zigzaou which had been widened and deepened and also strengthened by a complicated system of concrete emplacements. The line was everywhere protected by wire and minefield. A switch line had been constructed along the Wadi Merteba between Djebel Melab and Djebel Tebaga to the south-west of El Hamma, with the result that the Mareth position could not be turned save by a wide detour of some 150 miles over waterless desert to the Tabaga gap. The L.R.D.G. had reconnoitred possible routes round the western edge of this switch line in the previous January.

TACTICAL PLAN. OPERATION 'PUGILIST'

    (a) XXX Corps, now consisting of 50th, 51st and Indian 4th Divisions, 201st Gds. Bde. and 23rd Armd. Bde. and using 50th

Division and 23rd Armd. Bde., these to pass through 51st
Division, would attack along the coast route.

(b) N.Z. 2nd Division, heavily reinforced, would pass round the
western flank to break in behind the Matmata Hills and
establish itself across the Gabes–Matmata road.

(c) X Corps with 1st and 7th Armd. Divisions and 4th Lt. Armd.
Bde. would be held in reserve ready to exploit success.

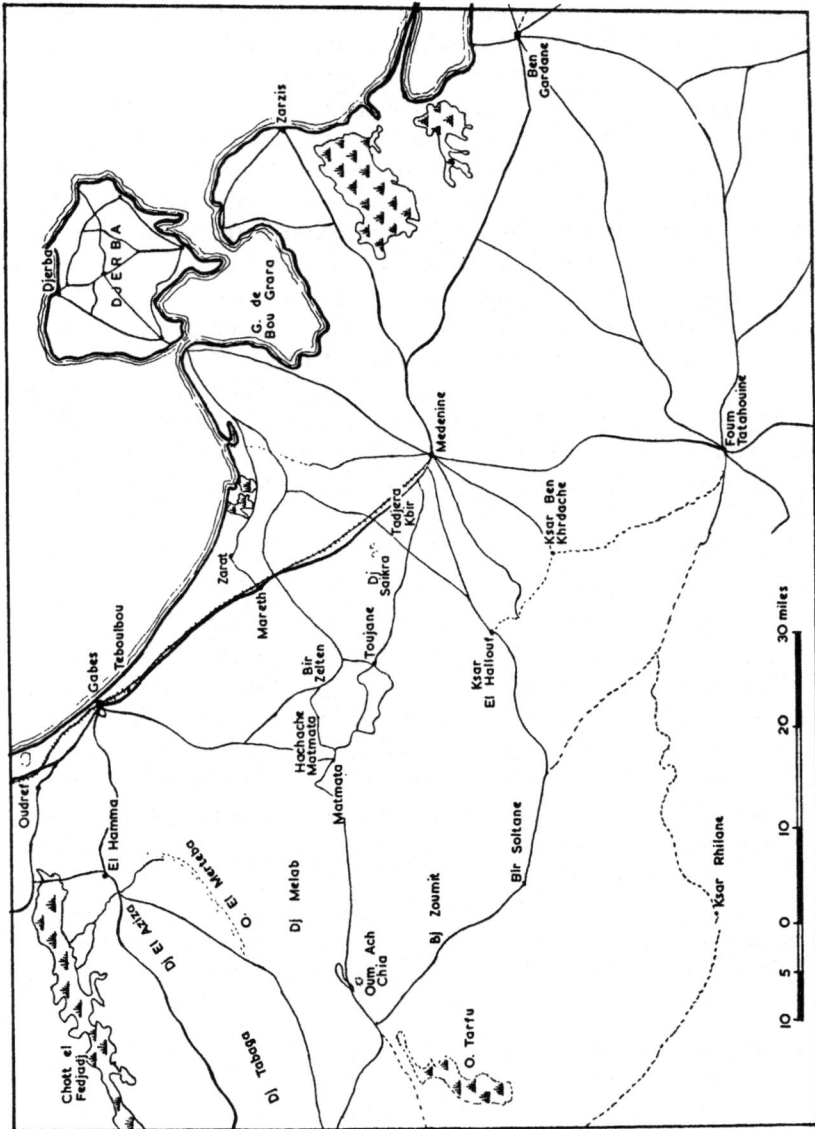

FIG. 53. South-east Tunisia.

In a preliminary operation on March 16–17, 201st Gds. Bde. attacked the 'Horseshoe Feature' at the south-west end of the Mareth Line. It encountered every conceivable sort of mine sown in apparently unlimited numbers and endured very severe casualties and made no headway.

Preceded by a terrific artillery bombardment, 50th Division, with the Seaforth and Camerons of 152nd Bde. of 51st Division, went in at 2330 hours on March 20. The troops crossed the Wadi Zigzaou, captured their immediate objectives and held on. During the night of March 21–22 the bridgehead so gained was expanded both laterally and in depth. But heavy rain fell to prevent rapid reinforcement and to preclude air support being given. During the afternoon of March 22 Axis armour with infantry support recaptured most of the ground. General Montgomery thereupon promptly changed his plan. He decided to halt the thrust of 50th Division, to press against the Mareth Line on the right in order to pin down as much Axis strength as possible and to make his major assault on the extreme left about El Hamma.

50th Division was withdrawn from the northern bank of the Wadi Zigzaou on the night of March 23–24 and XXX Corps, regrouped with 7th Armd. Division on the right, 50th Division in the centre and 51st Division on the left, began to press against the centre of the Mareth Line while Indian 4th Division launched an attack round the western end of this line to open up the road Medenine–Hallouf–Bir Soltane through the hills.

Meanwhile N.Z. 2nd Division, with 8th Armd. Bde., 1st K.D.G., 1st Buffs, a medium artillery regiment, General Leclerc's force and the Greek Sacred Squadron (the whole being designated for the time being N.Z. Corps, of 27,000 men, 6,000 vehicles, 120 tanks and 120 guns) had moved off on March 11 and had passed through 'Wilder's Gap' to reach the defile between Djebel Melab and Djebel Tabaga (known to Eighth Army as 'The Plum') late on the 20th. On the 23rd, General Montgomery despatched H.Q. X Corps and 1st Armd. Division to join N.Z. Corps moving by the same route.

At the Plum Defile the advance of N.Z. Corps was checked. The Desert Air Force thereupon intervened. For two and a half hours during the afternoon of March 26 bombers and fighter-bombers continuously attacked the Axis forces and caused such destruction and disorder that N.Z. Division with 8th Armd. Bde., under cover of an artillery barrage, were able to break into the defences. Then 1st Armd. Division passed through to penetrate to a depth of some 6,000 yards before darkness fell. As soon as the moon rose the advance was continued, and by dawn of March 27 the British armour was nearing El Hamma.

Meanwhile, on the main Mareth position, Indian 4th Division u/c XXX Corps had successfully attacked toward Hallouf and by midday on March 27 had opened the lateral road to Hallouf and Bir Soltane.

On March 29 the Axis forces, under pressure, withdrew from El Hamma, which was then occupied by 1st Armd. Division. On the same day Gabes and Oudref fell to the New Zealanders.

MEDICAL COVER

The arrangements made for medical cover for the battle of Medenine continued in operation for and during the battle for the Mareth Line.

N.Z. Corps

An A.D.S. accompanied each New Zealand brigade. 168 Lt. Fd. Amb. accompanied 8th Armd. Bde. The main body of 6 (N.Z.) Fd.

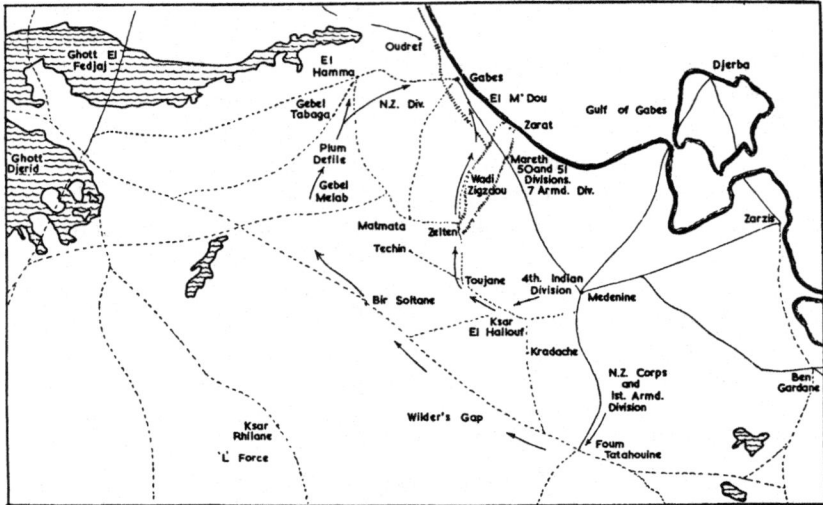

FIG. 54. The Battle of Mareth.

Amb. was with the reserve group with rear divisional H.Q. Those of 4 and 5 (N.Z.) Fd. Ambs. and 4 (N.Z.) Fd. Hyg. Sec. were with rear divisional H.Q.

On March 21, 6 (N.Z.) Fd. Amb. was ordered forward to Oum Ach Chia, there to establish its M.D.S. to serve an improvised air-strip that was about to be constructed. Here this unit remained to form the nucleus of a medical centre for the remainder of the battle. Because of the roughness of the road back to the Lt. Sec. of 14 C.C.S., which had been moved up to 'Wilder's Gap', the M.D.S. of 6 (N.Z.) Fd. Amb. was required to hold its cases until they could be evacuated by air. To it was attached the Mob. Surg. Unit of 1 (N.Z.) C.C.S. The New Zealand Consulting Surgeon was with the (N.Z.) C.C.S. and not at the base.

On March 22, 4 (N.Z.) Fd. Amb. and 2 F.T.U. joined 6 (N.Z.) Fd. Amb. at Oum Ach Chia. On the following day a company of 5 (N.Z.)

Fd. Amb. also moved there and established an air evacuation centre to hold thirty cases awaiting emplaning. From March 24 to the end of the month 402 out of a total of 1,190 sick and wounded admitted to the medical units of New Zealand Corps were evacuated by air to Senem L.G. near Medenine.

On March 24 a convoy of lightly wounded was sent back to 14 C.C.S. by road. The Bir Soltane–Hallouf track was open by this time and 14 C.C.S. had moved to Bir Soltane.

When on March 26 the attack on the Plum Defile began, it was arranged that N.Z. Corps should collect and hold its own wounded. 6 (N.Z.) Fd. Amb. was designated as the holding unit. 4 (N.Z.) Fd. Amb. was to accept all 8th Armd. Bde. casualties, hold all light cases and send all serious cases to 4 (N.Z.) Fd. Amb. 5 (N.Z.) Fd. Amb. was to move with Corps and so was to remain on wheels. Its company at the air evacuation centre handed over to 4 (N.Z.) Fd. Hyg. Sec. and joined its parent unit.

The assault upon the Plum Defile was a daylight affair and so the ratio of killed to wounded was higher than that of most of the previous battles of Eighth Army (1 : 4). During the first thirty-six hours of the engagement the A.D.S. of 5 (N.Z.) Fd. Amb. dealt with 224 casualties, including 44 P.o.W. Between 1600 hours on March 26 and 0800 hours on the 27th, 168 Lt. Fd. Amb., 4 (N.Z.) Fd. Amb. and the two surgical teams from 1 N.Z.G.H. and 1 (N.Z.) C.C.S. dealt with 240 casualties. 127 were evacuated by air; nevertheless, by the end of the day on the 27th, there were 400 cases with 4 (N.Z.) Fd. Amb.

On March 27, 5 (N.Z.) Fd. Amb., moving with N.Z. 2nd Division, was nearing El Hamma. On the 29th it opened on the Gabes–Hamma road, evacuating its cases to 1 (N.Z.) C.C.S. which had moved up to Teboulbou, five miles south of Gabes. 4 (N.Z.) Fd. Hyg. Sec. at this time was fully occupied in delousing some 5,000–6,000 P.o.W.

During the course of this operation the sick rate in the New Zealand Corps had been remarkably low, 1 in 2,000 per day.

X Corps

The composition of this corps, like that of the others, underwent frequent changes. For the battle of Mareth it came to consist of:

	Field Ambulances	*Field Hygiene Section*
1st Armd. Division	1 and 15 Lt.	1 Lt.
7th Armd. Division	2 and 151 Lt.	7 Lt.
4th Lt. Armd. Bde.	14 Lt.	
Corps Tps. . .	12 Lt.	
Leclerc Force .	Gp. Sanitaire	

During the attack on the Plum Defile a difficulty arose. At this time there was with X Corps one, and only one, F.S.U. D.D.M.S. Corps allocated it to 12 Lt. Fd. Amb., the corps field ambulance, which was close upon the heels of the field ambulances of 1st Armd. Division. But A.D.M.S. 1st Armd. Division maintained that for the efficient discharge of his responsibilities it was essential that a F.S.U. should be with a medical unit of his division. The matter was referred to the G.O.C. who agreed with the A.D.M.S. As things turned out, the F.S.U. would have been able to render better service had it remained with the corps field ambulance. D.D.M.S. remained of the opinion that the distribution of such units as the F.S.U. within the formation to which they are allotted should remain the responsibility of the administrative medical officer of that formation and of none other. This is a matter of importance to the medical services since it must be maintained that the prime responsibility of such an officer is that of ensuring that the medical facilities at his disposal shall be used to the best advantage. This surely is a professional matter rather than one that is to be decided by any military considerations.

In this phase of the campaign, with its rapid movement and ever-expanding distances between units, the need for wireless intercommunication between the elements of the medical services was clearly displayed. So also was the great promise of the developing system of air evacuation. Between March 26 and 31 no less than 284 patients were thus evacuated from one of the forward field ambulances of the Corps. Had aircraft been available in adequate numbers for this purpose there need not have been any evacuation by road, a truly terrible journey through the Matmata Hills *via* Hallouf to Medenine.

XXX Corps

Since 50th Division was likely to endure the greatest number of casualties, 25 F.T.U. from 51st Division and a surgical team from 14 C.C.S. were placed at its disposal. 51st Division, since it was not to be involved until later in the battle, was temporarily left without either F.S.U. or F.T.U. It was arranged that the A.D.Ss. of all the divisions concerned would be evacuated into a local area in which all the divisional M.D.Ss. that were open would be congregated. In this way the most advantageous use could be made of the ambulance car pool which was located immediately behind these combined M.D.Ss.

Because of the complete superiority in the air that was now being enjoyed, it was thought to be quite safe to group all the corps medical units into one large medical area. Since all tracks and roads radiated from the town of Medenine toward the battle line it was here that this medical area was situated. In it were 1 (N.Z.) C.C.S., the heavy section of 14 C.C.S., the light section accompanying N.Z. Corps, 3 C.C.S. and a light section of 2 (Ind.) C.C.S. 5 and 151 Lt. Fd. Ambs. had now rejoined their formations and so 150 Lt. Fd. Amb., on loan from

23rd Armd. Bde., took their place along with 3 Sec. of 151 Lt. Fd. Amb. attached to 150 Lt. Fd. Amb. These medical units in combination provided a total capacity of about 1,000 lying cases.

It was arranged that ambulance cars from the M.D.S. should be directed by the C.M.P. into the checking post of 25 M.A.C. and thence to 150 Lt. Fd. Amb. Here they were directed to one of five shelters, in each of which a medical officer was available. These medical officers removed any light sitting and walking cases and then redirected the ambulance cars to the C.C.S. The ambulance drivers, being so informed, knew exactly to which C.C.S. they were to deliver the patients. They did so along the specially graded track parallel to the road. On arrival at

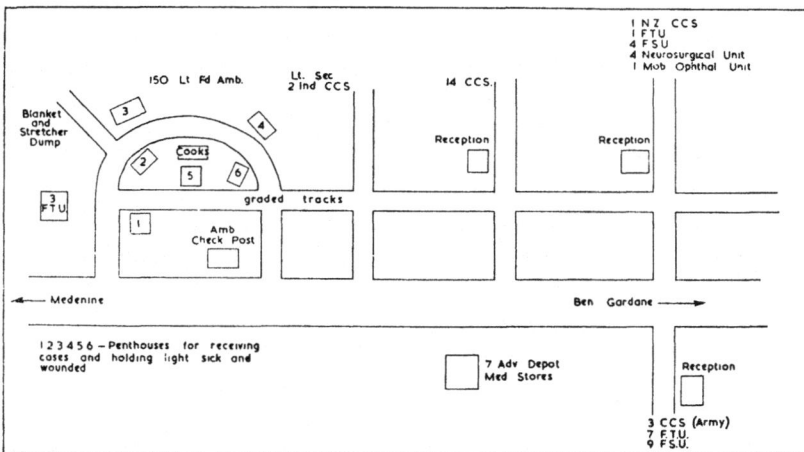

FIG. 55. The Battle of Mareth. XXX Corps Medical Area.

the C.C.S. the stretchers were unloaded and taken into the reception tent. The ambulance cars were then free to return to the forward area without delay. A small dump of stretchers and blankets was maintained by each C.C.S. to replace those unloaded from the ambulance cars. A large dump was kept at 150 Lt. Fd. Amb. with blankets, stretchers, splints and hot water bottles in case of shortages. A further dump was kept in the ambulance car pool of 25 M.A.C. A car pool was maintained by 25 M.A.C. and 576 A.F.S. directly behind the divisional M.D.Ss. and a shuttle service was organised so that as soon as one car left the M.D.S. another one from the pool went forward to take its place. The Adv. Blood Bank was sited by the officer commanding 3 F.T.U. with the M.A.C. car pool so that blood was immediately available to forward units. All Indian cases were admitted direct to the Lt. Sec. of 2 (Ind.) C.C.S.

The advantages of this system were that the light cases never got to the C.C.Ss. but were adequately treated at the field ambulances. Medical officers at the field ambulances did not comprehensively examine lying cases but simply classified them according to their A.F.W. 3118 (field medical card). Thus brain injuries and eye cases were directed to 1 (N.Z.) C.C.S., to which the neurosurgical and ophthalmic units were attached. The heavy section of 14 C.C.S. was reserved for medical cases only. Its surgical team was therefore loaned to 50th Division as a surgical unit for its M.D.S. On admission to the C.C.S. reception tent cases were ferried to their appropriate wards by ambulance cars kept by the C.C.S. for such internal duties. Each C.C.S. had two cars for this purpose.

All walking and light sitting wounded and light sick were thus collected by 150 Lt. Fd. Amb. which evacuated them by returning second and third line transport to the Army C.C.S. area. The provision of C.M.P. personnel by A.P.M. XXX Corps to act as traffic sentries and also to direct returning empty transport enabled this evacuation to work very smoothly, and of 1,617 cases dealt with by 150 Lt. Fd. Amb. no less than 1,434 were sent back by empty transport. The quick turn-around by the ambulance cars ensured the most rapid evacuation from the divisional M.D.Ss. With 150 Lt. Fd. Amb. thus controlling the distribution of cases, C.C.Ss. were able to work in eight hour shifts or else to capacity, thus giving a respite to the surgical staff, time to evacuate and clear, time during which the theatres could be cleaned and stocks renewed and opportunity to supervise the after treatment of the patients.

These arrangements worked exceedingly well and during the action 1,137 battle casualties and 770 sick passed through the C.C.Ss.

Air evacuation for the more serious cases was available from Senem L.G. about five miles away from the C.C.S. area, but this was mainly reserved for use by N.Z. Corps which at this time was out of touch with the ordinary evacuation chain.

On March 28, in accordance with arrangements made by D.D.M.S. XXX Corps, the officer commanding 25 M.A.C. led a convoy of thirty ambulance cars, two load carriers and two cook's trucks *via* Hallouf Pass to the N.Z. M.D.S. at Bir Soltane, whence 216 cases were evacuated, those left behind being 23 abdominal cases together with some 50 serious cases of other kinds for whom air evacuation was available under Army arrangement.

March 29 saw the end of the battle. The Axis force withdrew, followed closely by 51st Division and immediately thereafter by 150 Lt. Fd. Amb. and 1 (N.Z.) C.C.S. to form the nucleus of a new C.C.S. area just east of Gabes.

The medical cover for 50th Division is shown in Fig. 56.

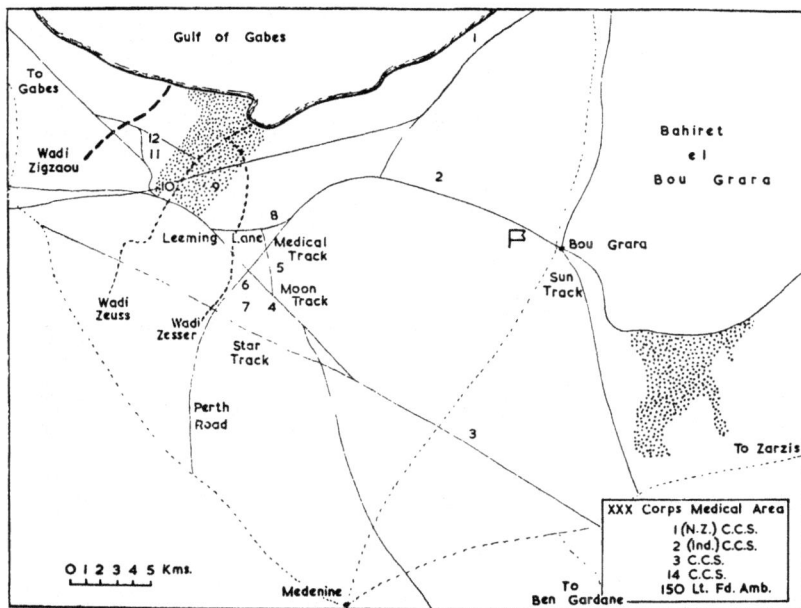

FIG. 56. The Battle of Mareth. Medical Cover. 50th Division.

```
 1. 149 Fd. Amb. H.Q.      March 15–18
 2. 186  ,,      ,, M.D.S.    ,,   13–21
 3.  ,,   ,,     ,, Staging   ,,   24–25
 4. 26 (Ind.) Fd. Amb.
 5. 567 A.F.S.
    7 F.S.U.
    25 F.T.U.
    Amb. car pool
 6. 149 Fd. Amb. M.D.S.       March 18–27
 7. 186  ,,      ,, H.Q.        ,,   21–24
 8. 186  ,,      ,, 'A' Coy. A.D.S.   ,,   13–17
 9. 186  ,,      ,, 'B' Coy. A.D.S.   ,,   16–19
                  'A' Coy. A.D.S.   ,,   17–20
10. 186  ,,      ,, 'A' Coy.        ,,   22–26
11. 149  ,,      ,, A.D.S.          ,,   21–23
12. 186  ,,      ,, A.D.S.          ,,   20–22
```

Of the field ambulances of 51st Division, 174 established the divisional M.D.S. on the main divisional axis four miles south of Makrelouf; 175 was in reserve alongside 174; 176 remained on wheels ready to move with 154th Inf. Bde. to Gabes. The A.D.Ss. of 175 and 176 Fd. Ambs. moved forward and dug in.

When 51st Division attacked on March 22, since it seemed impossible for evacuation to be carried out by day, arrangements were made whereby 175 Fd. Amb. attached to 5th Camerons:

1 Sgt. and 5 N.C.Os.

2 Sgts., 2 cpls., 2 L/cpls. and 26 ptes. to furnish stretcher squads

and 176 Fd. Amb. moved its M.D.S. ten miles forward to a site five miles beyond Makrelouf.

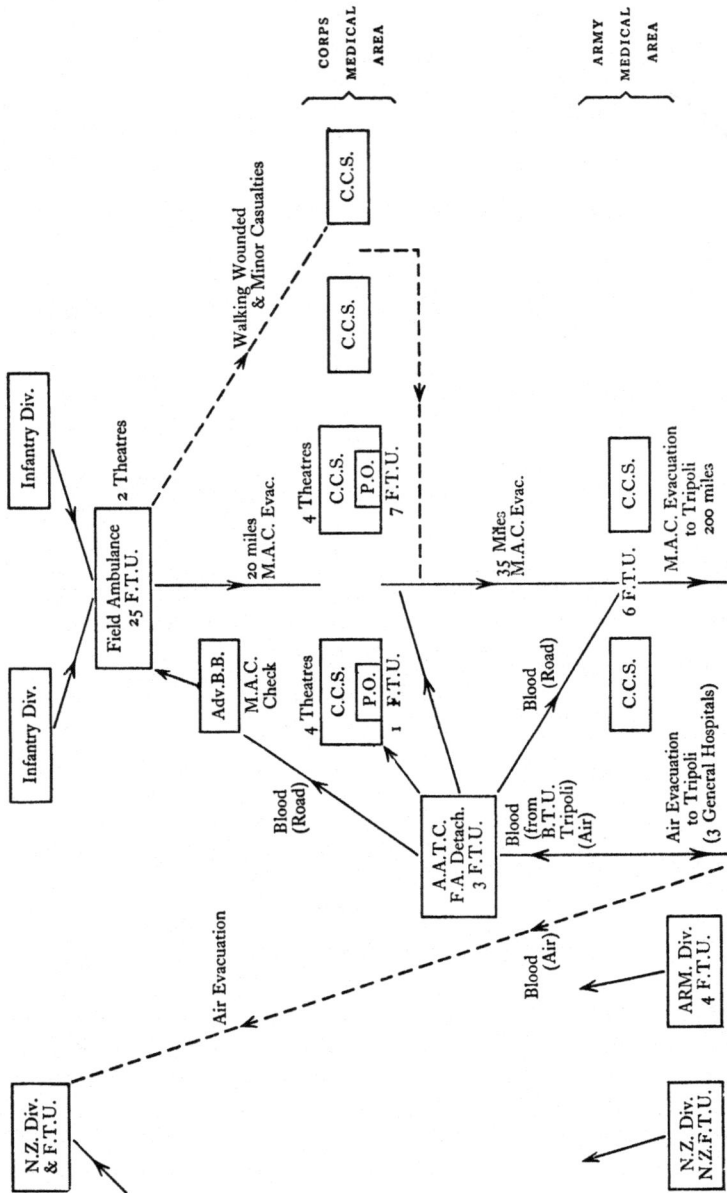

FIG. 57. The Battle of Mareth. The scheme for the provision of transfusion supplies.

During the course of this action 107 casualties were evacuated. On the 24th, 4 officers and 106 O.Rs. of 51st Division and 20 O.Rs. of other divisions passed through the M.D.S.

After the battle 174 Fd. Amb. moved to a site five miles north of Makrelouf, 175 established the divisional M.D.S. at Teboulbou and 176 went into reserve on the coast, just south of Gabes.

With Indian 4th Division into Tunisia went Ind. 5th and 7th Inf. Bdes. and with these 17 and 26 (Ind.) Fd. Ambs. and 15 (Ind.) Fd. Hyg. Sec. For the battle of Mareth one company of each of these field ambulances was brigaded and 26 (Ind.) Fd. Amb. selected to provide the divisional M.D.S., 17 (Ind.) Fd. Amb. being held in reserve. The M.D.S. was established about fifteen miles north of Medenine in dug-outs.

When the division was assigned the task of clearing the roads from Medenine to Hallouf, Khrdache and Toujane and of operating in mountainous country, 18 S.B. squads were provided by divisional H.Q. A company of 17 (Ind.) Fd. Amb. accompanied Ind. 17th Inf. Bde. and a company of 26 went with Ind. 7th Inf. Bde. to provide A.D.Ss. 26 (Ind.) Fd. Amb. established the divisional M.D.S. and to this a surgical team was attached.

MEDICAL ARRANGEMENTS

To obviate unnecessary delay in the departure of aircraft, holding parties from 200 and 14 Fd. Ambs. were stationed near the L.Gs. in Army zone to shelter, feed and attend patients awaiting emplaning or disemplaning. 'A' Company of 14 Fd. Amb., with the Adv. Blood Bank attached, moved with the air transport centre and the air ambulance unit throughout the operations. Later two companies of 14 Fd. Amb. were used exclusively for forming air evacuation centres for duty on L.Gs., to hold cases until returning transport planes were available.

A L.G. was constructed at Ben Gardane and was much used. Here, and also at Senem aerodrome, where there was a section of an air evacuation company, empty transport planes returning to Castel Benito were used to capacity. On March 26, 1 (Aust.) Air Ambulance Unit moved from Castel Benito to Senem. There was a fairly continuous stream of evacuation from the forward L.Gs. to Senem and thence to Castel Benito, while from this latter place a considerable number of serious casualties were flown back to El Adem and to the Delta.

As Eighth Army had advanced, under arrangement with D.M.S., G.H.Q., M.E.F., hospital ships were called forward in succession to Tobruk, Benghazi and Tripoli as required, and when 'Tripbase' was formed the responsibility for calling for these ships was delegated to D.D.M.S. 'Tripbase'.

There was only a metre-gauge railway line from Tripoli to Zuara, and this was found to be useless for the evacuation of casualties.

The distribution of the transfusion units during the battle of Mareth is shown in Fig. 57. At this time the war establishment of a B.T.U.

included no forward distributing section. To repair this deficiency it was necessary to misappropriate a F.T.U. 3 F.T.U., attached to the A.A.T.C., functioned as the forward distributing section of the B.T.U. with its H.Q. at Tripoli. An advanced blood bank was established at the forward M.A.C. check post point. (The letters P.O in the figure and within the C.C.S. stand for 'pre-operative' and indicate that here there was an organised resuscitation ward.)

THE BATTLE OF WADI AKARIT

Following upon the battle of the Mareth Line the Axis forces retreated to the Wadi Akarit position north of the Gabes plain. This position extended for some 12–15 miles from the coast to the Ghott (Shott) el

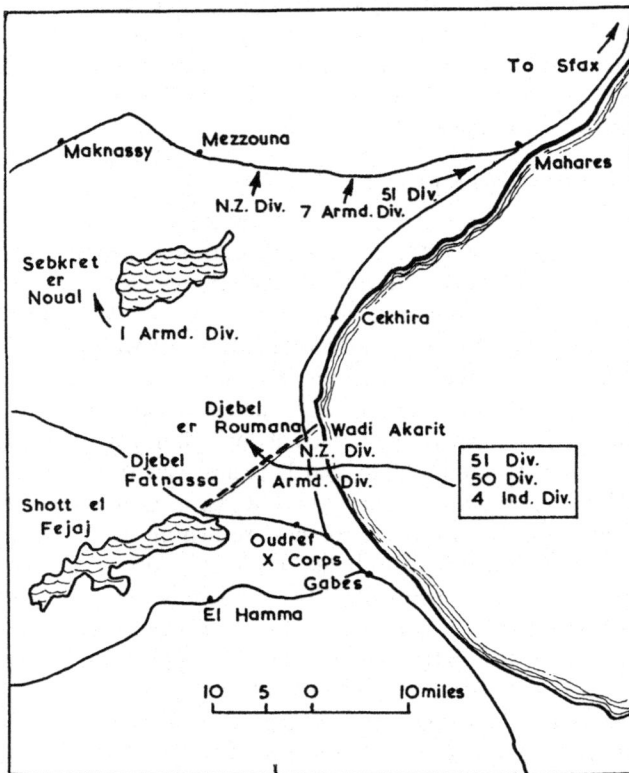

FIG. 58. The Battle of Wadi Akarit.

Fejaj, a system of lakes and salt marshes. From the coast for a distance of about ten miles inland there was a deep and wide watercourse—the Wadi Akarit—and this had been extended for some 3,000 yards to the east by a ditch. The north bank of the wadi was dominated by a range of steep-sided hills with two main groups of peaks, Roumana to the north and Fatnassa to the south, the two being joined by a hogsback of rolling hills in front of which a deep anti-tank ditch had been constructed.

Contact with the Axis forces was made on this line of the Wadi Akarit on March 29 by N.Z. 2nd Division and 1st Armd. Division of X Corps. It was quickly revealed that this position was extremely strong naturally, was firmly held and could not be turned by any outflanking movement.

On April 6 at 0400 hours, in the dark and not on a moonlight night as had been the habit of Eighth Army, XXX Corps attacked. 51st Division gained its objective, the Roumana group of peaks, but failed to hold it. Indian 4th Division took and held the Fatnassa group while 50th Division in the centre made but little progress. Then X Corps, now including N.Z. 2nd Division and 8th Armd. Bde., was unleashed against the line, but encountered fierce and stubborn opposition. However, during the night of April 6–7, the Axis forces disengaged and withdrew to the north. Eighth Army at once took up the pursuit with XXX Corps, moving along the coast road, and X Corps along the inland tracks.

MEDICAL COVER

On March 30 the forward medical units of Indian 4th Division (17 and 26 (Ind.) Fd. Amb., 15 (Ind.) Fd. Hyg. Sec.) moved into the concentration area south of Gabes. 17 (Ind.) Fd. Amb. at once opened a M.D.S. to function as the forward M.D.S. and to clear P.o.W. and Br. O.Rs. The former were to be evacuated to 1 (N.Z.) C.C.S. on the Mareth–Gabes road. Indian casualties were to be sent to 2 (Ind.) C.C.S. at Medenine.

For the actual battle it was arranged that 26 (Ind.) Fd. Amb. should open the divisional M.D.S. at Oudref, about ten miles north of Gabes, while 17 (Ind.) Fd. Amb. would be held in reserve. One company from each of 17 and 26 would be brigaded with Ind. 5th and 7th Inf. Bdes. respectively and would each open A.D.Ss. Since the terrain was such as to preclude the use of motor ambulances, seventeen stretcher squads would be formed out of personnel of 17 (Ind.) Fd. Amb. and 15 (Ind.) Fd. Hyg. Sec., each squad to consist of 2 I.O.Rs. with one stretcher and two blankets. The surgical team of 17 (Ind.) Fd. Amb. would join 26 (Ind.) Fd. Amb. when this unit had opened its M.D.S. with its reception ward, serious ward, resuscitation centre, mobile surgical operating theatre and its main operating theatre. During the course of the battle this M.D.S. admitted 342 casualties.

When, on April 7, N.Z. 2nd Division advanced, 5 (N.Z.) Fd. Amb. was left behind to deal with the casualties of the earlier stages and then to follow the division to the north. 6 (N.Z.) Fd. Amb., with main divisional H.Q., acted as the receiving M.D.S. This unit dealt with some

50 cases on the 8th. To care for these the unit left a company behind with instructions to clear them to 1 (N.Z.) C.C.S. when this reached La Skhirra. 4 (N.Z.) Fd. Amb. then moved up to join the reserve group and on the 12th reached El Djem. 6 (N.Z.) Fd. Amb. reached La Hencha. On the 13th, 4 (N.Z.) Fd. Amb. left one company and the attached surgical team from 1 (N.Z.) C.C.S. behind to tend its patients and moved forward to Sidi Bou Ali. On the 14th the two N.Z. surgical teams joined 4 (N.Z.) Fd. Amb. and 1 (N.Z.) C.C.S. moved up to a site eight miles north of El Djem.

186 Fd. Amb. of 50th Division established its M.D.S. in the village of Oudref, calling upon the Royal Engineers with their bulldozers to help make the roads and to sink their tentage. To this M.D.S. 6 F.S.U. was attached. In front of the M.D.S. were a rear A.D.S. and a forward Lt. A.D.S. close up to the R.A.Ps. and in the open in front of the gun-line. Though shells were falling all around none came near the A.D.Ss. It was concluded that their well displayed Red Cross flags and markings were seen and respected. During the course of the battle some 400 casualties passed through these units and there was some duplication of admission since some casualties were evacuated forward from A.D.S. to rear A.D.S. and thence to the M.D.S. This was unavoidable in the circumstances, for it was the brigade staff captain who gave permission only for a light section of the A.D.S. to go forward at the beginning of the battle. The heavy section was never free enough thereafter to go forward and join up with the light section. The absence of a F.T.U. at the M.D.S. was felt.

MEDICAL ARRANGEMENTS AT THE TIME OF THE BATTLE OF WADI AKARIT

At Gabes . .	1 (N.Z.) C.C.S.
	14 C.C.S.
	15 C.C.S.
	2 (Ind.) C.C.S.
	151 Lt. Fd. Amb., less one sec.
	4 Neurosurgical Unit, attached to 1 (N.Z.) C.C.S.
	1 Mob. Ophthal. Unit, attached to 1 (N.Z.) C.C.S.
Medenine . .	3 C.C.S.
	151 Lt. Fd. Amb., one sec.
	H.Q. 18 M.A.C.
At Ben Gardane .	1 Mob. Mil. Hosp.
Zuara . . .	8 (S.A.) C.C.S.
	H.Q. 43 M.A.C.
In 'Tripbase' .	2 and 48 B.G.Hs.
	3 N.Z.G.H.
	14 Fd. Amb. H.Q.

PLATE XI. A Regimental Aid Post in the Wadi Zigzaou. The Battle of Mareth.

PLATE XII. A Regimental Aid Post in the Gabes Gap.

PLATE XIII. An advanced dressing station, Tunisia.

PLATE XIV. The plasma drip in use between the Regimental Aid Post and the Advanced Dressing Station, Tunisia.

PLATE XV. An ambulance convoy on the Gabes–Sfax road.

PLATE XVI. A Lockheed Lodestar air ambulance in Tunisia.

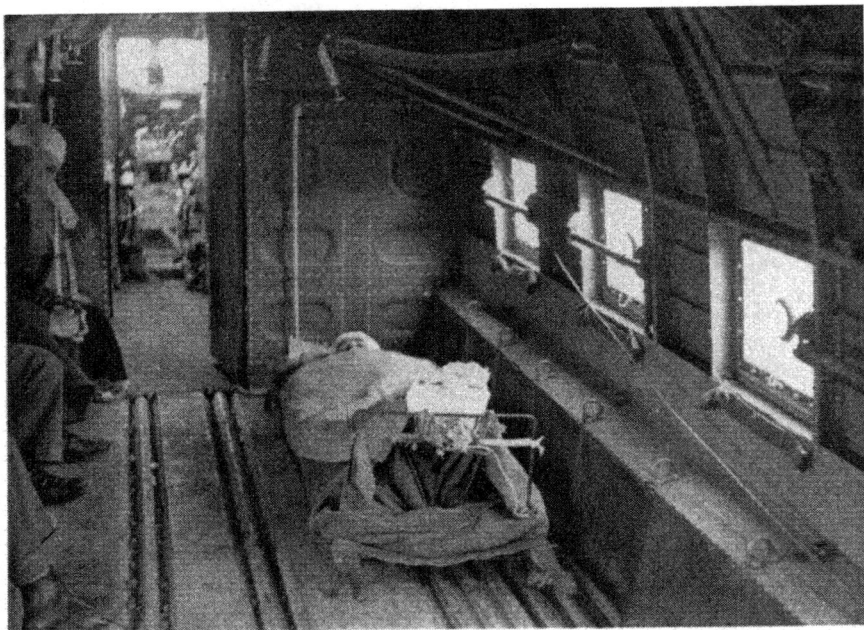

PLATE XVII. Air evacuation in Tunisia.

PLATE XVIII. Chiropody in The Field, Tunisia.

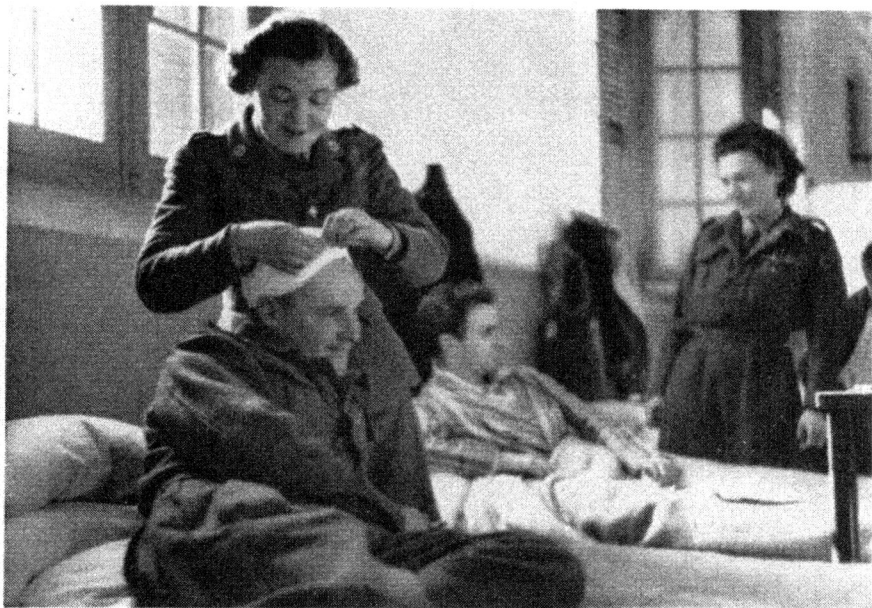

PLATE XIX. 94 British General Hospital, Algiers. Battledress for Q.A.I.M.N.S.

PLATE XX. Physical medicine in Tunisia.

In 'Tripbase' . N.Z. M.A.C.
      7 Adv. Depot Med. Stores
      Maxillo-facial Unit
      a U.S. Base Hosp.
      1 and 2 S.D.F. Secs.
      1 Basuto Sec.
      1 Swazi Sec.
      7 Con. Depot
      N.Z. Con. Depot
      7 Dental Lab.
      11 Dental Lab.
      52 Fd. Hyg. Sec.

During the week following this battle admissions to the general hospitals in 'Tripbase' numbered 3,517. Between April 7 and 10, 2,808 were admitted. The total admissions during the period January 1–March 31 were 22,905, of which 6,230 were battle casualties.

(Plates XI to XV illustrate some aspects of the work of the advanced medical units during and after the Battles of the Mareth Line and Wadi Akarit.)

(Plates XVI and XVII illustrate the air evacuation of casualties, and Plates XVIII to XX medical work at units at the bases.)

(iv)
The Final Offensive

PRELIMINARIES TO THE FINAL BATTLE

On March 30, 138th Inf. Bde. of 46th Division, 36th Inf. Bde. of 78th Divison and 1st Para. Bde., assisted by the French Corps Franc d'Afrique and a Tabor of Moroccan Goumiers, reoccupied Sedjenane and on the 31st captured El Aouana and occupied Cap Serrat, an advance of eighteen miles being made in four days in mountainous country covered with dense scrub while all the time rain fell in torrents.

On April 5, 4th Division assumed command in the sector north-east of Beja. On the 7th, 78th Division attacked north of Oued Zarga to capture Djebel el Ang and Djebel Tanngouche, ridges over 3,000 ft. high eight miles north of Medjez. Next day both ridges were lost again, but a second attack by 78th Division recaptured the whole of the first and part of the second. At the same time 4th Division attacked north of 'Hunt's Gap' and by April 14 had reached the hills south-west of Sidi N'sir. Medjez was now completely freed and positions gained from which the final assault could be launched.

Following their defeat at Wadi Akarit the Germans and Italians withdrew northwards towards their next defensive position about

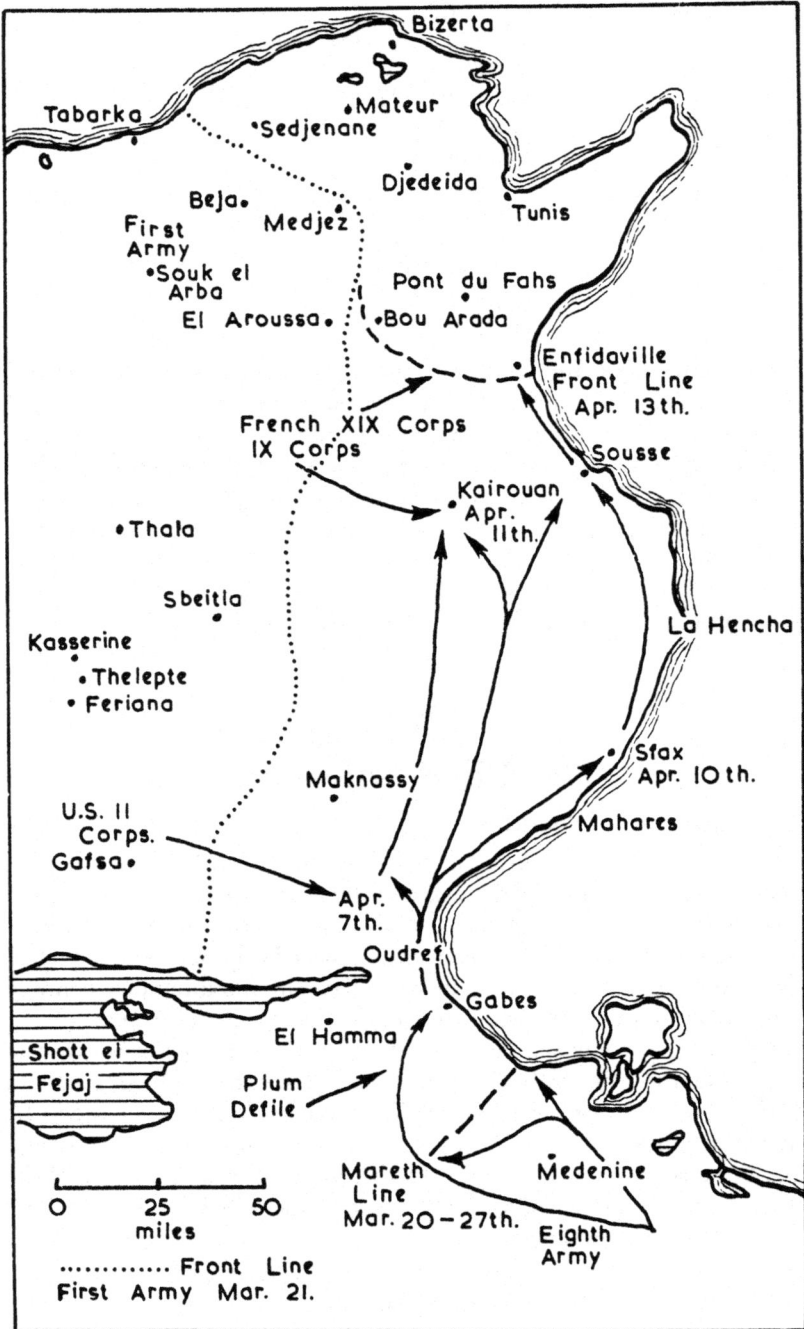

Fig. 59. Operations preparatory to the Final Offensive.

Enfidaville. At the same time, during the night of April 6–7, the two armoured divisions which had been used to restrain U.S. II Corps around El Guettar, also withdrew. At once U.S. 1st Armoured Division plunged toward the coast, and by 1610 hours that afternoon its patrols had met patrols of Indian 4th Division of Eighth Army probing westwards. The front was now a continuous one and the Axis forces were cooped up in the shrinking north-east corner of Tunisia.

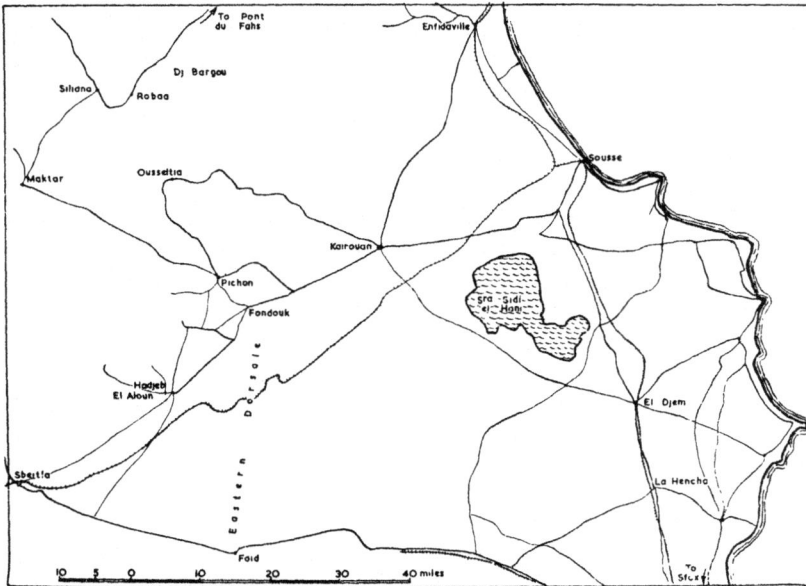

FIG. 60. Tunisia. The northern part of the Eastern Dorsale.

In anticipation of the retreat of the Axis forces from Wadi Akarit to the Enfidaville position, General Alexander prepared to strike north-east from the Fondouk area towards Kairouan and beyond. For this purpose H.Q. IX Corps was placed in command of 6th Armoured Division, 128th Inf. Bde. of 46th Division and U.S. 34th Division. The Corps was assembled east of Maktar. On April 8, U.S. 34th Division made a frontal attack on the Axis positions south of the strongly defended Fondouk Pass and was repulsed with heavy loss. 128th Bde. had better fortune to the north of the pass and entered Pichon. On the 9th, 6th Armoured Division was launched straight at the pass and plunged through.

On April 10, 6th Armoured Division fought a successful engagement with Axis armour south of Kairouan and entered this holy city next morning.

Meanwhile Eighth Army was pressing northward and XXX Corps entered Sfax on April 10. X Corps, farther inland, was keeping abreast. On the 12th, while XXX Corps halted round Sfax, X Corps resumed the advance to enter Sousse and to press against the Enfidaville position on the 13th. French XIX Corps, working in close harmony with IX Corps, having driven the Axis forces from the Eastern Dorsale as far as ten miles north of Pichon, moved forward and patrols of IX Corps and Eighth Army joined hands on April 11.

The Axis positions now consisted of two fronts at right angles facing west and south, the salient angle being protected by Djebel Mansour and Djebel Fkirine. General Alexander decided to make his main attack on the western face of this perimeter, while on the southern face Eighth Army exerted the maximum pressure. General Montgomery was asked to send to First Army an armoured division and an armoured car regiment. On April 18, 1st Armoured Division and 1st K.D.G. of Eighth Army joined IX Corps of First Army.

At the same time U.S. II Corps was transferred from the Gafsa–Maknassy area in the south to the extreme north facing Bizerta, from the sea to a point about ten miles north of Medjez. This secret move of some 110,000 troops and 30,000 vehicles for 200 miles straight across the lines of communication of First Army was an amazing triumph of co-ordinated staff work. This transfer meant that the front of First Army became correspondingly shortened. On the right of First Army French XIX Corps wheeled to occupy a line running from a point about twenty miles from the sea at Enfidaville to Bou Arada. On its right was XXX Corps of Eighth Army.

The tactical plan for the final battle was as follows:

(1) Eighth Army would attack on the night of April 19–20 with 50th Division on the coast, N.Z. 2nd Division just west of Enfidaville and Indian 4th Division, with French 'L' Force under command, west of Takrouna.

(2) 7th Armoured Division would guard the western flank, make contact with French XIX Corps and be available to exploit any success achieved.

(3) French XIX Corps would attack the three mountain positions commanding Pont du Fahs when, in the opinion of First Army, these positions had become sufficiently weakened by the attacks on either flank.

(4) First Army would begin to attack on the morning of April 22, using IX Corps with 46th Division and 1st and 6th Armoured Divisions. The infantry would destroy the enemy positions west of the salt marshes of Sebkret el Kourzia and the armour would then pass through and assault Djebel Mengoub, fifteen miles from Tunis.

(5) V Corps would attack on the evening of April 22 with 1st and 4th Divisions south of the river Medjerda directed on Massicault and with 78th Division north of the river with Djebel Ahmera (Longstop) as the first objective.

(6) U.S. II Corps would attack on April 23 with U.S. 1st Division, moving along the Sidi N'Sir road with the pass above Chouigui as its objective and with U.S. 9th Division on the axis Sedjenane—Mateur.

MEDICAL ARRANGEMENTS FOR THE FINAL OFFENSIVE

In association with the formation of IX Corps the following arrangements were made by D.D.M.S. First Army on April 1:

8 C.C.S. at Le Kef u/c IX Corps would accept its casualties.

12 and 19 C.C.Ss., with attached F.S.Us., F.T.U. and M.D.U., would pass u/c IX Corps forthwith.

5 M.A.C. would be allotted to IX Corps.

60 wagon orderlies for 5 M.A.C. would be provided by 6 M.A.C.

A dump of 300 stretchers, 900 blankets, 100 water bottles, two 1-ton battle bricks of medical supplies, would be held at 8 C.C.S. for IX Corps.

20 Fd. Hyg. Sec. u/c XIX Corps at Maktar, which was in the middle of IX Corps concentration area, would provide D.Rs. and motor cycles for use by D.D.M.S. IX Corps.

The estimate of casualties in V and IX Corps in the forthcoming operation was 900 a day (50 per cent. lying, 50 per cent. sitting). D.D.M.S. First Army made the following arrangements for their reception and treatment:

50 B.G.H. (now at Guelma) and 70 B.G.H. to be moved to Ali Abdullah prior to opening in Thibar. 76 B.G.H. to be moved to Ali Abdullah if A.F.H.Q. placed this hospital under First Army.

72 B.G.H. to remain at Souk Ahras u/c Area.

71 B.G.H. to be prepared to move to area of Djerida, south-west of Tebourba. Djerida would be the ambulance railhead.

84 B.G.H. to be prepared to move to Mateur.

3 Adv. Depot Med. Stores to move from Constantine to Souk Ahras.

D.A.D.M.S., L. of C., to be in charge of evacuation from First Army and U.S. II Corps. He would be prepared to clear 850 casualties daily.

5 C.C.S. to move from Ali Abdullah to Thibar.

19 C.C.S. (IX Corps) to move from Ali Abdullah to Le Kef *en route* for Maktar.

6 M.A.C. to move from Ain Seynour to Le Kef.

4 Maxillo-facial Surgical team to be attached to 84 B.G.H. at Souk Ahras.

By April 16 there were 1,400 beds available at Thibar and Souk Ahras, the hospitals there having been cleared to L. of C. hospitals. The following moves were now arranged:

70 B.G.H. to open in Thibar at once.

50 B.G.H. to move from Ali Abdullah to the monastery in Thibar, April 18–19.

71 B.G.H. to move from Souk Ahras to Thibar, April 22–24.

83 B.G.H. to move from La Calle to near Le Krib, April 20–21.

3 Adv. Depot Med. Stores to move from Souk Ahras to Thibar, April 18–19.

D.D.M.S. office would move from Laverdure to a point on the Souk el Arba–Nebeur road, south of De Muthul station on April 21.

159 Fd. Amb., less two coys., to move from Le Kef to Ali Abdullah (one coy. of this unit was with 25th Tk. Bde., another provided sections at R.H. Souk el Khemis, R.H. Sidi Smail, relieving 216 Fd. Amb., and one section was with 51st R. Tks.).

1 Mob. Hyg. Lab. from 84 B.H.G. to 50 B.G.H. at Thibar.

1 Mob. Bact. Lab. from 8 C.C.S. to 70 B.G.H. at Thibar.

He also issued the following general instructions:

(a) Fd. Ambs. and U.S. Med. Bns. would collect the wounded from brigades and regiments and transport them to the dressing stations. There resuscitation would be carried out with the ample supplies of plasma and whole blood that would be available. As far as possible triage would be exercised in these field medical units, which would move forward as the troops advanced.

(b) Evacuation from the divisional units would be by M.A.C. or U.S. Amb. Bn. cars to C.C.Ss. or U.S. Evac. Hosps., which would be grouped as far as possible and all of them reinforced by F.S.Us.

(c) C.C.Ss. initially would be located as under:

V Corps	. Oued Zarga	. 1, 5 and 18 C.C.Ss.
		four F.S.Us.
		three F.T.Us.
		one Fd. Hyg. Sec.
IX Corps	. Gafour .	. 8 and 12 C.C.Ss.
		three F.S.Us.
		two F.T.Us.
	Bou Arada	. 19 C.C.S.
		two F.S.Us.
		one F.T.U.

(d) Adv. Operating Centres would be formed in 1st and 4th Divisions and 6th Armd. Division by the remaining F.S.Us., these being attached to the divisional field ambulances.

(e) Field medical units would be kept clear. Steps would be taken to ensure that adequate transport would be available. Accommodation would be prepared in Army and Base hospitals.

The Allied force was exceptionally well equipped with surgical aid. In addition to the intrinsic surgical facilities of the base and other hospitals and of the C.C.Ss. there were no less than twelve F.S.Us. and the U.S. Auxiliary Surgical Groups, which consisted of a variety of specialist teams. 3 Gp. for example, was composed of 26 teams:

Surgical	.	12	Chest	. . .	2
Orthopaedic	.	3	Shock	. . .	3
Neurosurgical	.	2	Gas	. . .	2
Mixed	. .	2			

These resources were pooled, and on March 24 the suggestion was made to the effect that U.S. teams of this latter group should be posted as follows:

To D.D.M.S. First Army	24 teams to Army hospitals
D.D.M.S., L. of C. .	26 teams to hospital centres
B.S.A. Algiers . .	10 teams to base hospitals and convalescent depots.

In First Army the teams (U.S. and Br.) to be distributed as follows:

To V Corps . . .	30 teams, including 19 in reserve
IX Corps . . .	8 teams, including 5 in reserve

On April 15 D.D.M.S. First Army was visited by Principal Matron, A.F.H.Q., who discussed with him the policy relating to the employment of Q.A.I.M.N.S. personnel in First Army medical units. Thus far D.D.M.S. had adhered to the policy of not having Q.A.I.M.N.S. personnel with the C.C.Ss. Tentage could not be provided for them. He was now prepared to take Q.A.I.M.N.S. personnel in Army general hospitals up to 50 per cent. of the W.E. and the full quota when the fighting in Tunisia was finished.

THE FINAL BATTLE

EIGHTH ARMY—THE BATTLE OF ENFIDAVILLE

The Enfidaville position was exceedingly strong, consisting of a series of precipitous ridges and spurs overlooking Enfidaville. Of these, Takrouna Hill, a bald outcrop of limestone rising abruptly from the plain and with a village on its summit, dominated the area. These positions were strongly held. In front of them were minefields covered by M.G., mortar and artillery fire. X Corps (7th Armd., N.Z. 2nd, Indian 4th and 50th Divisions) attempted to push the Axis forces out of it before they had had time to settle in. But the effort was fruitless, and so on April 19–20 a heavy attack was launched by 50th Division along the coast, by N.Z. 2nd Division on Takrouna Hill to the west of

25

Enfidaville, by Indian 4th Division on the Garci Massif and by 7th Armd. Division on the left flank. 50th Division took Enfidaville; Indian 4th Division secured Djebel Garci and N.Z. 2nd Division, after what was possibly the hardest fight of all in its eventful history, took Takrouna and a series of heavy counter-attacks were repulsed on April 20 and 21. General Montgomery then decided to force the coastal defile. On 24–25 April, N.Z. 2nd Division and 201st Gds. Bde. captured Gebel Terhouna, five miles north of Enfidaville and commanding the coastal road, but the attack of 56th Division along this road on the 29th failed. It became manifest during these operations that any further success on this front would be dearly bought. So on April 30, Generals Alexander and Montgomery decided that while Eighth Army held on to its gains First Army should be reinforced by the transference to it of 7th Armd. and Indian 4th Divisions and 201st Gds. Bde. Remaining with Eighth Army were now N.Z. 2nd Division, 51st and 56th Divisions, French 12th Division and two armoured brigades. 50th Division went back to Egypt to prepare for the invasion of Sicily. The front line was held by 56th and French 12th Divisions with 51st Division in reserve, while N.Z. 2nd Division with an armoured brigade thrust towards Saouaf.

On the night of May 9–10, 56th Division bombarded the enemy in the Enfidaville position as 6th Armd. Division closed in from Bou Ficha. Thus trapped, the enemy surrendered. Eighth Army's long march—1,800 miles in six months—was ended.

MEDICAL COVER

Immediately after the battle of Wadi Akarit, Indian 4th Division moved to a concentration area just south of the wadi. Its medical units moved to a medical concentration area near Bir Guezah. For the attack on Djebel Garci the division moved to a concentration area near Lamench. Leclerc's force and 23rd Armd. Bde. came u/c Indian 4th Division and with the latter formation came 150 Lt. Fd. Amb. On April 19, 17 (Ind.) Fd. Amb. established the divisional M.D.S. about fifteen miles to the south-west of Enfidaville and to it was attached a section of 150 Lt. Fd. Amb. to deal with the casualties of 23rd Armd. Bde. u/c Indian 4th Division. To this unit also were attached Lt. Sec. 2 (Ind.) C.C.S., a mobile surgical team from 26 (Ind.) Fd. Amb., ten ambulance cars of 18 M.A.S. with eleven cars of the American Friends Service Unit and 25 F.T.U. The country was mountainous and ambulance cars could not be used to clear the R.A.Ps. The officer commanding 26 (Ind.) Fd. Amb. was therefore made responsible for the evacuation from the R.A.Ps. through A.D.Ss. to the divisional M.D.S. and all available medical personnel were placed under him for this purpose. Three squads of stretcher-bearers were allotted to each

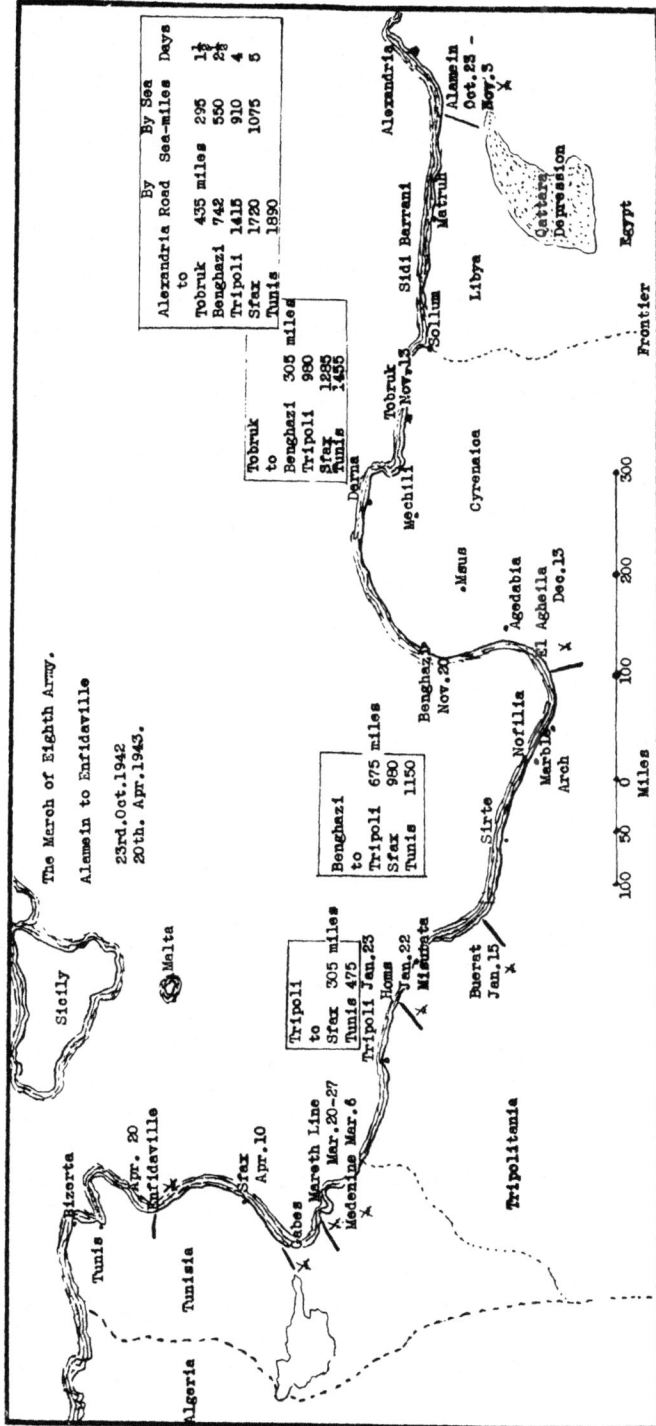

FIG. 61. The March of Eighth Army. Alamein to Enfidaville.

battalion of Ind. 5th Inf. Bde.; the A.D.S. was established near tactical headquarters of the brigade. British casualties were evacuated to 14 C.C.S. at Kairouan, Indian casualties to Hy. Sec. 2 (Ind.) C.C.S. at Sfax. At 14 C.C.S. a staging squad provided by 26 (Ind.) Fd. Amb. was stationed to deal with Indian casualties. Two hundred casualties were admitted to the M.D.S. on April 20. 25 F.T.U. was sent up to the M.D.S. on April 21.

Evacuation from the New Zealand R.A.Ps. on Takrouna Hill was possible only during the night since they were under fire almost continuously. They were sited in wadis and slit trenches. Behind them there was a hand-carry of a mile and a quarter. The time soon came when the R.A.Ps. served by the A.D.S. of 5 (N.Z.) Fd. Amb. were over-full. Three ambulance cars and six 3-ton lorries, together with six more lorries from the divisional M.D.S., were sent forward.

On April 20, 276 casualties were evacuated by this A.D.S. to the M.D.S. of 4 (N.Z.) Fd. Amb. with its two attached surgical teams at Sidi Bou Ali. This M.D.S. dealt with 334 casualties on this day. Evacuation was to 1 (N.Z.) C.C.S., six miles north of El Djem, by 21 cars of the A.F.S. and 5 cars from 5 (N.Z.) Fd. Amb.

On the 29th the M.D.S. of 4 (N.Z.) Fd. Amb. was busy again dealing with 151 casualties from 56th Division.

With 1 (N.Z.) C.C.S. were:

1 Mob. Ophthal. Unit
4 Neurosurgical Unit
4 F.S.U.
1 F.T.U.

Evacuation therefrom was to 3 N.Z.G.H. at Suari Ben Adem, fifteen miles south of Tripoli, by road or by air from the L.G. near El Djem.

On May 4, N.Z. 2nd Division moved up to support the French in their advance in front of Pont du Fahs. 4 (N.Z.) Fd. Amb. at Sidi Bou Ali was joined by 1 (N.Z.) C.C.S. When N.Z. 2nd Division moved back to Egypt 1 (N.Z.) C.C.S. remained behind at El Djem and later moved back to Suari Ben Adem, near 3 N.Z.G.H. and 1 (N.Z.) Con. Depot.

After Wadi Akarit 50th Division moved forward and a medical centre was selected near Sfax. 201st Gds. Bde. and 5 Lt. Fd. Amb. came under command. The M.D.S. (5 Lt. Fd. Amb.) was opened alongside the M.D.S. of 4 (N.Z.) Fd. Amb. and the A.D.S. (5 Lt. Fd. Amb.) opened some 6–7 km. south-east of Enfidaville on the main Sfax–Enfidaville road. To the M.D.S. 6 F.S.U. and 25 F.T.U. were attached.

Then 56th Division (two brigades) relieved 69th and 151st Bdes. of 50th Division and took over command of 201st Gds. Bde. 50th Division then returned to the Delta, 149 Fd. Amb. with 151st Bde., 140 Fd. Amb. with 168th Bde. and 186 Fd. Amb. with 69th Bde., together with

22 Fd. Hyg. Sec., 15 C.C.S., 1 and 2 F.S.Us., 3 F.T.U. and two M.C.Us.

On the L. of C. and at Tripoli, Eighth Army Base, medical units were now distributed as under:

At Kairouan	.	14 C.C.S.
El Djem	. .	1 (N.Z.) C.C.S.
		2 (Ind.) C.C.S. (Lt. Sec.)
		4 Neurosurg. Unit
		H.Q. 25 M.A.C.
Sfax	. .	3 C.C.S.
		2 (Ind.) C.C.S. (Hy. Sec.)
		15 C.C.S.
		H.Q. 151 Lt. Fd. Amb.
		1 Mob. Ophthal. Unit
Gabes	. .	1 Mob. Mil. Hosp. with detach. 2 (Ind.) C.C.S.
		H.Q. 18 M.A.C.
		43 M.A.C., sec.
Medenine .	.	151 Lt. Fd. Amb., two secs.
Ben Gardane	.	8 (S.A.) C.C.S.
In 'Tripbase'	.	as on April 5 plus
		11 B.G.H.
		93 B.G.H.

During the advance of Eighth Army in Tunisia 14 Fd. Amb. provided parties to work with the advanced air casualty evacuation units as these moved forward from Tripoli (L.G. at Castel Benito) in succession to the L.Gs. at Ben Gardane, Senem (Medenine), Gabes, Sfax, El Djem and, finally, Kairouan. At the base air casualty evacuation centre at Cairo West there was also a detachment of 14 (Ind.) Fd. Amb.*

---

*It is of considerable interest to note the mode of development of the system of air evacuation during the campaigns in North Africa. At first, though asked for, no aircraft could possibly be spared for such a purpose. Then, as the demands for medical officers in the forward areas became more insistent and more clamant, pressure came to be exerted in the proper places and special cases were carried back by returning aircraft, as an act of grace. Next, as air-supply to forward areas became a routine affair, empty returning aircraft were increasingly used for the evacuation of selected casualties. Finally, special ambulance aircraft, with special crews and with a special ground organisation, were made available for the transport of medical supplies forward and for the evacuation of casualties to the rear.

Synchronously, to deal with casualty receipt and despatch, casualty evacuation units came into being. To begin with these were detachments or sections of existing medical units such as field ambulances, field hospitals or casualty clearing stations. These were posted at or near L.Gs. and airfields. Gradually these were replaced by improvised and separate units until these in their turn became officially recognised and authorised as air casualty evacuation units. Indeed, supply and evacuation by air became the system of choice, especially in those theatres where land and sea communications were long and difficult. Since one of the main aims of the Medical Services is that of reducing to a minimum the time between the receipt of a wound and the delivery of the casualty into the hands of the surgeon, it follows that air evacuation must indubitably have been the means of saving much life and of preventing much serious disability. (*See also* R.A.F. Vol. I. Chapter 10, pp. 483–485.)

On April 20 and 21 the Axis Commander, in an attempt to retard the inevitable, attacked between Medjez and Goubellat, but was repulsed. Then, on the 22nd, 46th Division attacked north of Bou Arada and 6th Armd. Division passed through, followed by 1st Armd. Division on the 23–24th. The armour was quickly checked, however, about Sebkret el Kourzia and Djebel Kournine. On April 25 the Axis forces in the salient south of the Bou Arada–Pont du Fahs road withdrew and French XIX Corps advanced some eighteen miles to reach the general line Djebel Derhalfa—the road Enfidaville to Pont du Fahs station. Between April 22 and 30, 1st, 4th and 78th Divisions captured the main features in front of Medjez, including Longstop Hill. In the north U.S. II Corps cleared Djebel Tahent–Hill 609–near Sidi N'sir, which dominated the approaches to Mateur.

On May 3 and 4, the Axis forces withdrew all along the front to the line of hills west of Bizerta, east of Mateur and east of the Oued Tine valley, and U.S. 1st Armd. Division occupied Mateur.

By May 5 the Allied forces were regrouped and ready for the final assault.

First Army Front. Order of Battle. May 4, 1943.

    H.Q. First Army
        1st Armoured Division (from Eighth Army)
        139th Inf. Bde. Gp.
        1st K.D.G. (from Eighth Army)
        51st R. Tks.
    V Corps
        1st Division
        46th Division, less 139th Inf. Bde. Gp.
        78th Division
    IX Corps
        6th Armoured Division
        7th Armoured Division (from Eighth Army)
        4th Division
        Indian 4th Division (from Eighth Army)
        25th Tk. Bde., less 51st R. Tks.
        201st Gds. Bde. (from Eighth Army)
    U.S. II Corps
    French XIX Corps

THE TACTICAL PLAN

    (1) V Corps would attack and capture Djebel Bou Aoukaz, near Medjez, so as to cover the left flank of IX Corps when this attacked.

    (2) IX Corps would break into the enemy's position on a narrow front with 4th Division and Indian 4th Division.

(3) This being done, 6th and 7th Armd. Divisions would pass through, press on and seize the high ground six miles due west of Tunis so as to breach the inner defences of Tunis.

(4) V Corps would thereafter keep the corridor so made open and be ready to use its infantry divisions to sustain the attack of IX Corps.

(5) 1st Armd. Division would remain on the Sebkret el Kourzia sector.

(6) Meanwhile French XIX Corps would capture the Djebel Zaghouan.

(7) U.S. II Corps, with the Corps Franc d'Afrique under command, would move on Bizerta.

THE ASSAULT

V Corps with 1st Division successfully attacked Bou Aoukaz on the afternoon of May 5 and held it against counter-attack. At 0330 hours on the 6th, 4th Division and Indian 4th Division attacked and had taken all their objectives by 1100 hours. A very heavy concentration of artillery fire and an intense air bombardment had prepared the way. The two armoured divisions passed through and by nightfall had cleared Furna and reached Massicault, half-way to Tunis. At first light on the 7th, 6th and 7th Armoured Divisions moved forward from Massicault, brushed aside opposition at St. Cyprian and at the junction of the Medjez and Bizerta roads and, in the late afternoon of May 7, 11th Hussars and 1st Derbyshire Yeomanry entered Tunis. On the U.S. front events had moved with equal and equally dramatic suddenness. Bizerta was entered on May 7 and the enemy in this area surrendered unconditionally on the 9th.

On May 8, 7th Armd. Division moved northwards up the Bizerta road towards Protville to join up with U.S. 1st Armoured Division while 6th Armd. Division turned south-east towards Hamman Lif, there to encounter fierce resistance. On the 10th, 6th Armd. Division overcame this, captured Soliman, entered Hammamet and at once pushed on towards Bou Ficha.

4th Division, u/c IX Corps, moved up to Soliman and swept round the Cap Bon peninsula while 1st Armd. Division, u/c IX Corps, moved northwards through Ain el Asker, Mohammedia, Crateville and on to Grombalia.

V Corps moved eastwards with Indian 4th and 1st Divisions to complete, with French XIX Corps, the encirclement of the Axis armies.

On May 12, 6th Armd. Division attacked southwards from Bou Ficha while 56th Division of Eighth Army shelled the trapped Axis forces from the Enfidaville position. Mass surrenders occurred and by the 13th all resistance had ceased. Disaster had completely overwhelmed the German and Italian formations.

MEDICAL COVER

The collapse of the enemy was so immediate and so complete that Allied casualties were few and the medical services never extended.

The movements of a few of the divisional medical units are representative of all.

On April 21 a company of 10 Fd. Amb. of 4th Division was overrun in the Medjez area and the commanding officer and the quartermaster

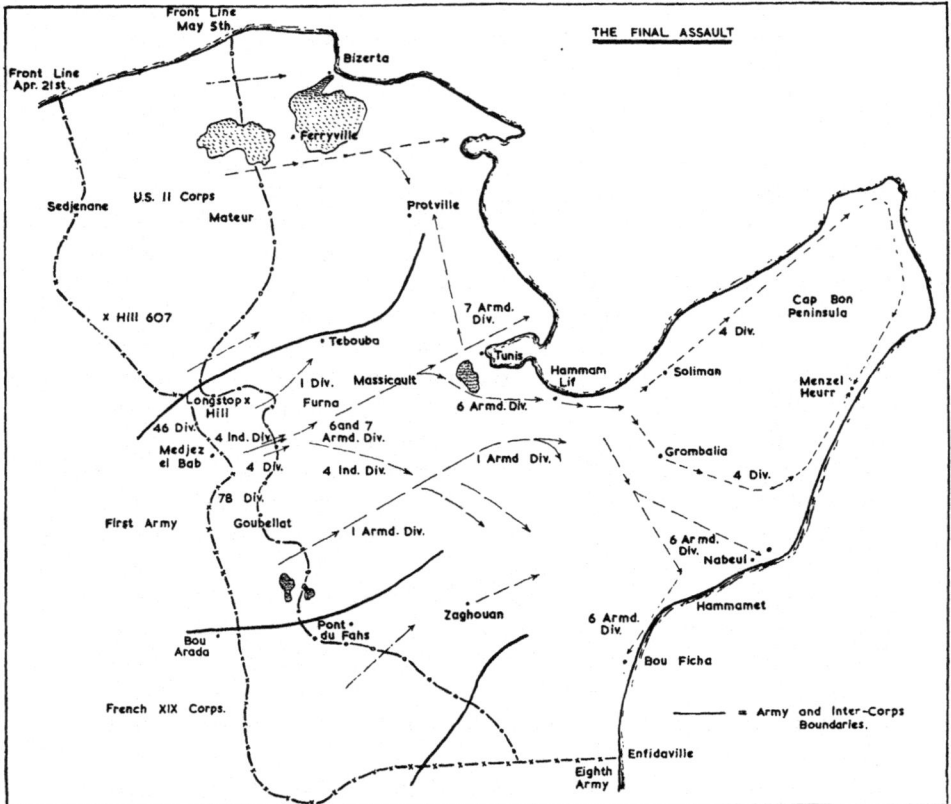

FIG. 62. The Final Battle in Tunisia.

of 12 Fd. Amb. of 4th Division were captured when looking for a site for their unit.

1 Fd. Amb. moved with 1st Gds. Bde. of 1st Armd. Division. On May 7 it opened a M.D.S. at Furna. On the 8th this moved to El Attar, there to deal with some fifty casualties. On the 9th the unit moved into Tunis to open in a school. Then on the 10th, it moved to Grombalia and on the following day to Hammamet. On the 14th it took over a German

hospital in Nabeul and opened a C.R.S. On June 5 it handed over to 5 Lt. Fd. Amb. and left for Mateur.

With Indian 4th Division from Eighth Army to IX Corps went 17 and 26 (Ind.) Fd. Ambs. and Lt. Sec. 2 (Ind.) C.C.S. On May 4 the division reached Medjez, when a company of 17 (Ind.) Fd. Amb. established a M.D.S. and Lt. Sec. 2 (Ind.) C.C.S. with surgical team attached opened. H.Q. 26 (Ind.) Fd. Amb. established a divisional M.D.S. while H.Q. 17 (Ind.) Fd. Amb. and one company remained closed and in reserve. O.C. 17 (Ind.) Fd. Amb. was made responsible for organising and co-ordinating all evacuation in front of the divisional M.D.S. and under his command were placed all medical personnel not otherwise engaged.

For the final assault one company of 26 (Ind.) Fd. Amb. was brigaded with Ind. 5th Inf. Bde., one company of 17 (Ind.) Fd. Amb. with Ind. 7th Inf. Bde., H.Q. and one company of 17 and a company of 26 were held in reserve and H.Q. 26 opened the divisional M.D.S. near Grich el Oued to the north-east of Medjez. The companies with the brigades established their A.D.Ss. alongside the tactical H.Q. of their respective brigades and a car post was staffed with one officer and 4 O.Rs. When later Indian 4th Division moved to Ain el Askar, eighteen miles south-west of Tunis, 17 (Ind.) Fd. Amb. opened a M.D.S. in this area and Lt. Sec. 2 (Ind.) C.C.S. moved to Bir Merherga. 220 Fd. Amb. (IX Corps) and 8 and 12 C.C.Ss. followed 4th Division and Indian 4th Division of IX Corps moving on Tunis and on the night of May 6 opened just north of Furna on the Tunis road, some fifteen miles from Medjez el Bab. On the next day the unit moved forward to Mohammedia, south of Tunis. H.Q. 152 Fd. Amb. took over a German hospital in Tunis itself on May 8.

V Corps' C.C.Ss. did not open in Oued Zarga in the initial stages of the battle lest their presence should disclose information of value to the enemy. Casualties went direct to the general hospitals which functioned as C.C.Ss. In Thibar, on April 23, 50, 70 and 71 B.G.Hs. were open. There were some 900 casualties on this day; 450 were sent back by ambulance train to Souk Ahras, 300 to the W.W.C.P. at Ali Abdullah and the remainder were admitted to the Thibar group of hospitals.

On the 27th D.D.M.S. First Army found reason to advise D.D.M.S. IX Corps that the F.S.Us. working with his field ambulances in accordance with the recommendation of D.M.S., A.F.H.Q., should be attached to IX Corps' C.C.S. as surgical reinforcements. The C.C.Ss. were well forward and evacuation was swift. There was no reason in the circumstances to provide expert surgical facilities in front of the C.C.S.

On May 1 the ambulance R.H. moved from Souk el Khemis to Sidi Smail. On the 3rd, 76 B.G.H. at Bône was at long last transferred from A.F.H.Q. to First Army. Arrangements were made with Eighth Army for the evacuation of Indian 4th Division casualties to 'Tripbase'. During the final battle there were about 80 Indian casualties altogether. They were either evacuated by road *via* Sfax or else from Sidi Smail to Sfax by air.

At Medjez el Bab .	Lt. Sec. 2 (Ind.) C.C.S.
Teboursouk .	14 C.C.S. with an Indian staging squad from 26 (Ind.) Fd. Amb.
Sbeitla . .	18 M.A.C., one sec. 176 Fd. Amb. coy. 567 A.F.S. pln. an Indian staging squad from Hy. Sec. 2 (Ind.) C.C.S.
Sfax . .	Hy. Sec. 2 (Ind.) C.C.S.

Air evacuation from Thibar to Sfax started on May 7. The aircraft also transported blood from Sfax to Hergha L.G. for Eighth Army and Eighth Army patients being sent back to the United Kingdom from Hergha to Sidi Smail.

From Enfidaville to Tripoli is 450 miles by road. 'Tripbase' was responsible for evacuation from Pisada on the Tunisia–Tripolitania border. A staging post was placed at Zuara, about half-way between Tripoli and Pisada, and staffed by 8 (S.A.) C.C.S., as was also a small post at Pisada itself. At this C.C.S. the wounded were fed and rested. Convoys arriving in the evening stayed at the C.C.S. for the night. Evacuation was by 43 M.A.C. at Zuara. 'Coffee stall' posts were established at Medenine and Ben Gardane. In the closing phases D.D.M.S. 'Tripbase' with Adv. H.Q. joined Rear H.Q. Eighth Army at Sfax.

From Tripoli evacuation was by sea and air. Hospital ships were called forward from Alexandria and, having loaded, returned to Alexandria. During the battle of Wadi Akarit, when casualties were very numerous and the base hospitals in the Delta full, the hospital ships off-loaded at Benghazi. During this period 7,226 cases were evacuated by sea; 470 cases were evacuated to the Delta by air, a distance of some 1,700 miles. The average time taken was about nine hours.

On the eve of the final attack 1, 5 and 18 C.C.Ss. with surgical teams and Lt. Sec. 2 (Ind.) C.C.S. were at Oued Zarga, 8 C.C.S. at Slouguia, 14 C.C.S. at Teboursouk and 19 at Bou Arada. On May 5, 76 B.G.H. moved from Bône to Oued Zarga preparatory to opening in Medjez el Bab when the front had moved forward sufficiently. When this happened 72 B.G.H. at Souk Ahras was to pass to L. of C. control.

On May 7, 1 C.C.S. was earmarked for Tunis and 18 C.C.S. for Bizerta, both of these to clear to 5 C.C.S. at Oued Zarga. On the 9th, 12 C.C.S. was west of Massicault and 8 C.C.S. closed and in reserve at Massicault. 50 B.G.H. at Thibar was closed and prepared to move forward and an A.D.M.S. Tunis was nominated. There were no further changes in the distribution of medical units until after the final surrender.

(v)
The Specialist Services

P.o.W. MEDICAL SERVICE

D.M.S., A.F.H.Q., had been warned to prepare for 50,000 P.o.W. In the event there were more than a quarter of a million, large numbers suffering from malaria and dysentery, following the final battle for Tunisia. All the German and Italian senior administrative medical officers sailed on the last hospital ship to leave Tunis. A P.o.W. medical service was organised and placed under the control of a medical staff officer of A.F.H.Q. and under the supervision of the Hygiene Officer A.F.H.Q. This service was required to prepare hospital accommodation as under:

U.S.   P.o.W. camps, 75,000 for 3 months increasing to 125,000
Br.   P.o.W. camps, 100,000
        on the basis of 5 per cent. or 5,000 beds.

Hospitals of two classes were established: (*a*) enemy hospitals taken over, and (*b*) reception hospitals in P.o.W. camps, these being affiliated to the nearest U.S. or British general hospital to which cases requiring more than seven days hospitalisation were sent. For the enemy minor sick C.R.Ss. were created. The medical staff for all these was found from among captured enemy personnel augmented as required by U.S. or British medical officers and O.Rs. P.o.W. hospitals were distributed as follows:

TABLE 42

	Class A			Class B		
	German	Italian	Totals	German	Italian	Totals
Tunis	300 beds	300 beds	600	100	100	200
Thibar	1,500 beds	—	1,500	400	—	400
Bône	800 beds	—	800	200	—	200
Constantine	—	300 beds	300	—	100	100
Algiers	400 beds	400 beds	800	100	100	200
	3,000 beds	1,000 beds	4,000	800	300	1,100

Grand total, 5,100 beds

D.M.S., A.F.H.Q., records that all American and British wounded found in German medical units had invariably been skilfully treated and well cared for.

THE ARMY DENTAL SERVICE

D.D.D.S., A.F.H.Q., in his report at the end of the campaign refers to the following matters of general interest:

1. It was found expedient to establish an Allied Force Dental Centre in Algiers to meet the needs of officers, particularly of U.S. and British officers.

2. The existence of special maxillo-facial units made it no longer necessary to carry as many as four dental mechanics on the establishment of the 1,200 bedded general hospital. Two were thought to be enough.

3. Because the C.C.Ss. taking part in the assault landings were reduced to light scale their dental teams were deprived of much of their equipment. Thus it was that before the arrival of the F.D.Us. a denture requiring a simple repair had to be sent back not less than fifty miles to the nearest general hospital, there to be processed. D.D.D.S. suggests that the following alternatives deserve consideration:

   (*a*) that the mechanical equipment of a C.C.S. on light scale should be sent up to the C.C.S. by D-day+7 to D-day+14;

   (*b*) that from the establishment of a C.C.S. on light scale two dental mechanics and mechanical equipment should be deleted and that one extra F.D.U. should be added to each C.C.S. on light scale in corps or Army;

   (*c*) that there should be an assault scale for all field dental equipment;

   (*d*) that to lessen the weight all vulcanite should be replaced with acrylic material in units on assault scale.

4. D.Os. attached to field ambulances, in the considered opinion of D.D.D.S., were called upon far too commonly and frequently to undertake non-dental duties. He suggests that they would be far more usefully employed if they and their 30 cwt. vehicles were placed directly under corps operational and locational control on a scale of one per brigade.

5. D.Os. attached to parachute field ambulances could not be fully employed in their professional capacity owing to the facts that training and operational commitments interfered with and interrupted their work and most of their equipment remained unavailable. Thus it came about that the record of a month's work showed that a D.O. with a parachute field ambulance was doing no more than what could be done in one or two days in other circumstances.

May 1943	*Completions*	*Attendances*	*Extractions*	*Conservations*
133 Para. Fd. Amb.	47	106	28	55
16 Para. Fd. Amb.	9	21	—	15
127 Para. Fd. Amb.	43	113	27	—

In D.D.D.S's. opinion these D.Os. should be replaced by F.D.Us. under G.H.Q. control and a sufficient number of A.D.Corps personnel should be trained in parachute jumping and in parachute field ambulance work and should be attached to parachute field ambulances for operational purposes.

6. Experience strongly suggested that there should be not less than three F.D.Us. per corps, one per division and one per L. of C. sub-area; that these F.D.Us. should be made available early in the operation and that their usefulness would be increased greatly by adding one additional mechanic to their establishment.

7. When a maxillo-facial unit is attached to a general hospital at the base and there evolves into what in fact is a small special hospital accommodating some 150–190 patients of which some 90–100 are jaw cases, its A.D.Corps establishment becomes totally inadequate. It needs to be augmented by one additional D.O., not less than one additional dental mechanic and an additional clerk. It should have a complete field dental outfit, a field dental mechanics outfit and a casting outfit. When a maxillo-facial unit is attached to a C.C.S. or to some other medical unit at C.C.S. level, then to its I.1248 equipment there should be added an emergency kit, portable in a shell dressing haversack. Experience proved that such a unit did its best work when attached to a base general hospital. The quality of the work done by surgeons and D.Os. in the forward zone was such that there was no need for the maxillo-facial units to be placed far forward.

8. At the end of the campaign the ratio of D.Os. to British troops had become 1 per 3,000. There were nineteen stationary F.D.Cs. and seven F.D. Labs. in base and L. of C. areas and no less than twenty-eight M.D.Us. in the forward zone.

9. Dental condition of British troops in North Africa, June, 1943:

TABLE 43

Inspection of Men Not Recently Dentally Treated

Number of men inspected	5,000
Number of men dentally fit (War) on inspection . . .	1,900 (38 per cent.)
Number of men requiring one extraction	
one conservation	
scaling	
all three	
(one visit)	1,910 (39 per cent.)
Number of men requiring a moderate amount of treatment	
(2 or 3 visits)	235 (4·7 per cent.)
Number of men requiring new dentures . . .	215 (4·3 per cent.)
Number of men requiring renewal of dentures . .	125 (2·5 per cent.)
Number of men requiring repair of dentures . .	140 (2·8 per cent.)

THE ARMY OPHTHALMIC SERVICE

In the spring of 1943 the Consulting Ophthalmologist to the Army visited Algiers. On his advice mobile ophthalmic teams were organised in the forward surgical centres for the treatment of eye injuries and in divisional areas for the testing of vision and the provision and repair of spectacles. Thus it came about that a soldier whose glasses were broken could be provided with a new pair and be back to duty within twenty-four hours. Large supplies of lenses were held in the depots of medical stores and prescriptions could be dispensed without delay.

THE ARMY PSYCHIATRIC SERVICE

Some months before First Army proceeded to North Africa the Directorate of Army Psychiatry had urged that an adequate number of psychiatrists should go with the force and should be given suitable opportunity to carry out prophylactic work and deal with psychiatric casualties as they arose and so maintain the efficiency of the combatant units. This request was not accepted, however, and only two R.A.M.C. psychiatrists were sent out in December 1942.

It was necessary for D.A.P. to protest, in May 1943, at the lack of information which he received concerning prospective military operations and at the consequent lack of psychiatric arrangements for these operations. He stressed the fact that it had been necessary to appoint two psychiatrists to First Army after that force had sailed and that the force still lacked an adviser in psychiatry who should have been sent out simultaneously with other consultants to the force in January. The adviser in psychiatry was not, in fact, sent out until the end of May 1943. In the meantime the psychiatric service in that theatre was supervised by the Consulting Physician.

One of the two psychiatrists sent out to the force in December 1942 spent the next six weeks in the forward area with V Corps and made contact with unit and field ambulance medical officers and instructed them in the treatment of psychiatric casualties. He was able to work at a R.A.P., see psychiatric casualties as they came off the battlefield and, as a result, devise methods of dealing with such casualties in forward areas.

In February 1943, partly owing to pressure of work at the base, it was unfortunately necessary to remove this psychiatrist from the forward area to assist the second psychiatrist with the force who was working at the base at 95 B.G.H. Here a large number of cases had accumulated prior to the psychiatrists' arrival in North Africa. At one time the psychiatric unit in this hospital contained over 500 patients and the assistance, for part of the time, of the psychiatric consultant to the U.S. Army Air Force and of two other American psychiatrists was obtained. Only a small number of men were returned from this unit to full combatant duty, but over 80 per cent. were returned to limited service in L. of C. or base areas. The small percentage returned to full combatant duty was due to the relatively late stage in the illness before treatment was commenced and to the absence of suitable facilities for treatment in more forward areas. Many should never have been evacuated to the base at all and would not have been so evacuated had an organisation existed for dealing with this type of casualty in forward areas. The large number of psychiatric cases reaching 95 B.G.H. and the absence of sufficient trained staff to cope with the rush meant that treatment was in some cases less thorough than it should have been and, in consequence, a number of rather shaky 'bomb-shy' men were to be found later awaiting disposal in the base depots.

The Consulting Physician to the force who, in the absence of an adviser in psychiatry, carried all the responsibility for instigating action with regard to the management and treatment of psychiatric casualties, and did everything in his power towards this end, made arrangements during the fighting for a rest centre, which was run by 159 Fd. Amb. at Ali Abdullah. About 800 men went through this centre, of whom 500 were sent back to their units. This wise and necessary step must have saved quite a number of men who would otherwise have broken down more completely and have had to be sent back to the base.

Referring to the psychiatric situation in North Africa prior to the arrival of the Adviser in Psychiatry in May 1943, the Consulting Psychiatrist to the Army stated in a report to D.G.A.M.S. after a visit to the force: 'Some excellent work has been done forward and some equally good work at the base, but the absence of psychiatric personnel and the attitude taken towards their work was hampering. The failure to realise that psychiatric casualties must occur after certain stresses and fatigue under enemy action in the best selected and trained forces, and still more among those who are neither well selected nor perfectly trained, had led to some unfortunate situations which could have been avoided and which have resulted in wastage of man-power and hospital bed accommodation. In modern warfare approximately 10–15 per cent. of all casualties are psychiatric and as such demand special management and treatment which it is not always possible for medical specialists or G.D.Os. to give.' He also referred to the 'unsatisfactory situation and man-power wastage which occurs where the idea is that psychiatric breakdown can be avoided by administrative instructions or disciplinary action', and pointed out that the experience in North Africa showed beyond doubt that it was essential that adequate psychiatric staff should in future accompany every expeditionary force if there was to be no repetition of the situation.

The arrival in North Africa of the Adviser in Psychiatry in May 1943 coincided with the appointment of an Officer i/c Personnel Selection and an effective re-allocation of down-graded personnel was made possible. The Adviser initiated the formation of two official base psychiatric centres of 200 beds each (capable of being expanded to 300 beds). The centre at Algiers, which was completed in June 1943, was known as 6 Base Psychiatric Centre. It was an independent unit although it was attached to 95 B.G.H. for purposes of accommodation and administration. The second centre, known as 'B' Base Psychiatric Centre, was attached to 104 B.G.H. at El Arrouch, south of Philippeville.

The following observations are taken from a report made by D.M.S., A.F.H.Q., based on the work of the Adviser in Psychiatry, A.F.H.Q., and of the psychiatrist i/c the psychiatric wing of 95 B.G.H.:

In corps areas exhausted, anxious and unstable men sent down from divisions and forward areas were admitted to the corps hospital centre with the label 'E' (exhaustion). Of these 45 per cent. were returned to duty and the remainder evacuated to the advanced psychiatric wing (A.P.W.) of a general hospital.

The A.P.W. received the following types of case:

(a) In battle such cases as would be sent to the corps centre in quiet periods. The reason for this was that the centre had to be kept clear during battle.

(b) Acute anxiety states, mild and already improving under forward psychiatric treatment.

(c) Acute anxiety states from other hospitals not having received specialist treatment.

(d) Relapses, hysterias, repressive states, psychotics and mental deficiency.

Relapses were fairly common; hysteria was rare. Repressive states were common in personnel with long service overseas. Mental deficiency was rare for the reason that most cases of such had been eliminated from the force by earlier selection. As the campaign proceeded, it was found that the mental symptoms became milder, the treatment less hampered by hostility reactions, fresh symptom formation less common and the general morale raised with success in battle. The attitude to further service in a fresh category improved and there were fewer relapses.

The following factors were observed to affect the incidence and severity of mental disturbances:

(a) Air attack, and particularly dive-bombing, was one of the principal causes of exhaustion.

(b) Air superiority, air cover and freedom from air attack diminished the number of cases.

(c) Victory, which shattered the myth of German invincibility, resulted in a raised morale.

(*d*) Regularity in the delivery of mail contributed notably to the maintenance of morale.

(*e*) Formations with previous battle experience produced fewer exhaustion cases than did raw ones. This may have been due to the action of a continuous weeding-out process.

(*f*) Fatigue was an important factor. Units fighting for long periods without relief and suffering from all the hardships of life in forward areas showed a high rate.

(*g*) Good leadership was important. When officer and N.C.O. casualty rates were high the number of exhaustion cases increased. Good M.Os. and chaplains could, by their example, do much to conserve and augment the morale and mental health of troops in their care.

The functions of the A.P.W. were:

(1) The establishment of out-patient clinics for the treatment of early and mild cases. Court-martial and disciplinary cases were also examined.

(2) As soon as possible after admission it was decided whether or not the patient would be likely to be fit within fourteen days. If not, he was evacuated to the base.

(3) The treatment consisted of rest, mild sedation and one or more lengthy interviews. The early interview relieved anxiety, hostility and doubt on the part of the patient and prevented the formation of new symptoms. Thereafter followed a week of P.T., occupational and diversional therapy and group activities and then consideration was given to the re-posting of the man.

The results obtained are illustrated by the following figures relating to a sample which included instances of the most severe neuroses occurring in this theatre:

Cases admitted	600
Evacuated to United Kingdom	5 per cent.
Returned to some form of duty	95 per cent.

At the base psychiatric wing the patients, after a term of treatment, were passed on to a non-medical rehabilitation centre from which, after a further period, some were sent to a convalescent depot, others to the Personnel Disposal Board which dealt with some 200 cases a week. Of these the ultimate classification was as follows:

Tradesmen	. 16 per cent.	For training	26 per cent.
Non-tradesmen	. 18 per cent.	For base units	40 per cent.

THE ARMY SURGICAL SERVICE

It was found that the best results were obtained when special surgical centres were formed in selected hospitals. To these specialist surgeons with teams of specially trained nurses and orderlies were posted. Such centres were:

Maxillo-facial . Algiers
Orthopaedic . Algiers and Philippeville
Chest . . Algiers and Army hospitals
Neurosurgical . Souk Ahras and C.C.Ss.

A 'Penicillin' research team, working under the auspices of the M.R.C. and administered by D.M.R., was attached to the surgical wing of 95 B.G.H. at Algiers.

During the period November 1942–May 1943 the twelve British F.S.Us. performed 6,062 operations with 348 deaths, a mortality rate of 5·7 per cent.

TABLE 44

Type of wound	Number of operations	Mortality rate
Head	161	14·9
Chest	202	4·4
Abdomen	270	24·8
Abdomino-thoracic	54	31·4
Fractures (G.S.W.)	1,350	1·9
G.S.W. Femur	215	7·4
Multiple	934	3·5

It is of interest to recall the mortality rates of certain of these injuries during the War of 1914–18 :

1914 Abdominal . 95 per cent. G.S.W. Femur 70–80 per cent.
1917 Abdominal . 50 per cent. G.S.W. Femur 30 per cent.

In 1914 abdominal operations were not allowed. In 1917 Thomas's splint was applied in the R.A.P. In 1943 the more serious cases were treated in advanced operating centres and there were many more surgeons.

THE ARMY TRANSFUSION SERVICE

This was now thoroughly organised and staffed with experienced officers, being regarded as an essential feature of the field medical services. To it much of the success of the surgeons in this campaign must be ascribed. The twelve F.T.Us. drew their supplies from the B.T.U., which in its turn was supplied by the B.T.S.D. at Bristol. The amounts supplied totalled 6 pints of blood, 30 pints of plasma and 30 pints of crystalloids per 100 wounded. According to A.Tr.S. records, of the 16,674 wounded admitted to medical units in the forward zone 1,604 were transfused (10 per cent.); 1,084 pints of blood and 4,000 pints of plasma were used, an average of 0·7 pint of blood, 2·5 pints of plasma and 3·2 pints of protein per case.

THE ARMY PHYSICAL MEDICINE SERVICE

D.M.S., A.F.H.Q., asked for the appointment of an adviser in physical medicine. One was appointed in November 1942 and arrived in North Africa early in 1943. In August 1943 he submitted a report to D.M.S. and from this the following excerpts are quoted:

'It was found that at the end of May 1943, 80 per cent. of all cases in the convalescent depots were surgical cases and that accidental injuries were more numerous than battle casualties. Morale was found to be high and most of the men were keen to get fit. It was discovered that convalescent depots were not suitable for the treatment of psychoneurotic persons.

'A seaside location is preferable for the organisation of a rehabilitation centre provided that it is safe from bombardment, is near a hospital centre, is non-malarious and is on a good camp site.

'It is important to have permanent buildings available for indoor recreational activities in the evenings.

'To begin with masseuses were concentrated in the Algiers base. As their numbers increased the forward hospitals were staffed to provide remedial exercises in the early stages and the period of convalescence was soon reduced.

'During battle a modified type of depot is required to cater for minor sick, lightly wounded and exhaustion cases. This need may be met by sending forward a detachment to deal with 500–1,000 men, this sub-unit being made available to D.Ds.M.S. corps.

'A small physical medicine department was established in each hospital where the masseuses worked under the supervision of an appointed officer.

'In addition a system of exercises for bed patients, both individual and in groups, has been successfully started. A.P.T.C. instructors were found to be of great value in restoring and maintaining the physical fitness of the convalescents; one should be attached to every general hospital. Occupational therapy should take an important place in the rehabilitation programme.

'In the convalescent depot training was divided into four grades and the following scheme adopted:

(1) C.Os. parade of the whole depot; previous day's intake inspected separately and personally by the C.O.

(2) One period of general P.T.; classes arranged in grades.

(3) One period of road work or purposeful P.T., also by grades.

(4) Two periods of remedial P.T. in the following classes:
   (a) Foot and ankle;
   (b) Knee and thigh;
   (c) Backs and abdominal conditions;
   (d) Shoulder girdle and elbow.

(5) One period to company disposal, camp fatigues, etc., the remainder to lectures on current affairs by the N.C.O., A.E.C.

(6) After 3 o'clock bathing for all and games on the beach.

(7) In the top grade, obstacle training and route marches.
'A nightly entertainment is important; music, card games, debates, etc., were all popular. A cinema is highly desirable.'

The volume of the work and its value can perhaps be assessed by reference to the following figures:

Unit	Period	Admitted	Discharged
8 Con. Depot	January 18–May 31	3,963	2,296
9 Con. Depot	April 4–May 31	2,409	1,203
10 Con. Depot	April 26–May 31	1,826	626

Convalescents were disposed as follows:

Returned to United Kingdom, Category C	.	4·6 per cent.
Discharged to duty	.	84 per cent.
Down-graded	.	4 per cent.
Returned to hospital	.	7·4 per cent.

The percentage of cases returned to hospital was high; of those so returned the majority fell into one or other of the following categories: intercurrent disease, relapse or recurrence of the medical or surgical condition, unsuitability.

In order to cope with the 10 per cent. of men who need more personal supervision D.M.S. recommended that a special rehabilitation wing be formed with a staff consisting of:

(1) a graded specialist in physical medicine
(2) 2 remedial-trained A.P.T.C. instructors
(3) 6 masseuses, one trained in occupational therapy
(4) the necessary administrative personnel, cooks, etc.

THE ARMY RADIOLOGICAL SERVICE

Towards the end of the campaign there were 45 X-ray units in the field. The work done by them can be illustrated by the following figures, which relate to May 1943:

Beds Occupied	Total X-ray Examinations	Average No. of Films per Case	Total Films	Films per Hospital
10,445	7,095	1·63	11,450	962

(vi)
The Health of the Troops

DISEASES OF SPECIAL MILITARY IMPORTANCE

VENEREAL DISEASE

On January 12, 1943, a small working party under the chairmanship of C.A.O. and consisting of G.O.C. U.S. Base Troops, D.M.S. and Deputy Surgeon, was set up to receive information concerning the incidence of venereal disease and to consider measures for its control. The rate was found to be 25–30 per 1,000 per annum; it was lowest among the forward troops (8 per 1,000 per annum) and highest among U.S. coloured troops (400 per 1,000 per annum).

On March 5, D.M.S., A.F.H.Q., issued a directive to all senior administrative medical officers, with copies to administrative officers of A.G.1 and 4.

(1) Reference was made to the order of February 11, issued by General Eisenhower, which stressed the responsibilities of all formation commanders for ensuring the health of the troops under their command.

(2) It was laid down that co-operation with the provost-marshal and the civil police was to be maintained and that clandestine prostitutes were to be arrested.

(3) In the towns and in troop quarters P.A.Cs. were to be established and properly controlled.

(4) The provision of organised recreation was recommended—e.g. Red Cross canteens with women helpers in the coffee bars.

(5) The treatment of prostitutes was to be carried out by the French medical authorities in consultation with Army venereologists.

MALARIA

In January 1943, D.M.S. made an aerial survey of Algiers and issued a memorandum on the diagnosis and treatment of malaria, especially of the malignant form occurring in the non-malarious season, which had been prepared by the Consulting Physician. On February 23, a conference on malaria was convened in Algiers under the chairmanship of the American Base Commander and was attended by G.1, Deputy Surgeon, Consulting Physician and Hygiene Officer (U.S.), by D.M.S., A.F.H.Q., and his D.D.H., D.D.P. and G.I. (Br.) and by the senior officers of the French military and medical services. Representatives of the Pasteur Institute in Algiers and of Civil Affairs, together with a number of eminent malariologists, also attended. The problem was defined, methods of control discussed and a small working party appointed.

As the malarial season began in April and lasted for six months, a campaign was launched to remind base and sub-area commanders of the importance of carrying out control measures. D.M.S. visited them to reinforce the advocacy of this working party. By the beginning of March much control work had been carried out. In A.B.S. Paris green was sprayed from the air. By April mosquito nets, repellent cream and protective clothing for night duty had been issued. Instructions had been given to the troops that as far as possible all parts of the body should be covered after sundown. Officers were advised never to halt or camp after sundown on low-lying ground where there were trees. By April 5 a directive had been issued concerning the control of malaria by:

(a) the maintenance of discipline;
(b) suppressive medication;
(c) personal protection;
(d) site selection;
(e) carrier control;
(f) the killing of adult mosquitoes;
(g) the destruction of larvae;
(h) the management of malaria cases.

Bulk supplies of mepacrine had arrived in March and tablets were issued to units with their rations. As from April 22, four tablets were taken by every man each week, two on Monday and two on Thursday. After the third dose there were widespread complaints of diarrhoea and vomiting. Much anxiety was evoked and much criticism levelled at the medical services. It was decided to alter the method of administration so that one tablet was given four times a week. This being done, the untoward sequelae disappeared and tolerance was quickly acquired.

In spite of all the measures that were taken the malaria rate began to rise as the season advanced. By June the admission rate was from 17–25 per 1,000 per annum. By July it had risen to 225·9. The worst areas, as was foreseen, were Philippeville (588·1) and Bône (778·4). The campaign was intensified and at last the incidence began to fall. By the end of August it had become 162·7 per 1,000 per annum, in Philippeville 380 and in Bône 319·7. At the end of September these rates had fallen still further to 116, 151 and 146 respectively.

It had been learnt that all ranks, without exception, had to be educated to the importance of malaria and trained in the methods of self-protection, that one tablet of mepacrine a day was necessary, that every unit must have its malaria squad and that this should be under the control of a divisional officer.*

ENTERIC GROUP

The entire U.S. force had been compulsorily inoculated and practically all British troops had consented to be so protected. Water discipline was

---

*It is worth comparing these findings with those of other campaigns of this war—the Australian and American campaigns in the East Indies and Philippines and the Burma campaign. In every case the process was the same, formations, units and individuals would only learn the hard way by bitter experience. It was not until senior commanders and formation staffs became 'malaria-conscious' that any real progress in prevention could be achieved; it was not until universal preventive medication became possible that real control of the disease was established under field service conditions. Anti-mosquito measures formed a valuable step in protection, but universal dosage with the best available preventive drug, mepacrine, was necessary for success.

good and all supplies used for drinking or cooking were chlorinated either in bulk or else by individual methods.

In the first twelve months there was a total of 272 cases. Those who did contract the disease suffered from a severe type and 47 died. The following comparative figures are informative:

	Strength	Number of Cases	Number of Deaths
S. African War .	208,000	58,000 (28 per cent.)	8,000
1914–18 War .	6,100,000	31,000 (0·5 per cent.)	750
Operation 'Torch'	1,420,000	272 (U.S. 62) (Br. 210) (0·2 per cent.)	47 (U.S. 6) (Br. 41)

DYSENTERY

Bacillary dysentery became a problem in the hot weather, causing much sickness until the troops became better trained and flies were controlled by the use of D.D.T. The admission rate was from 1–5 per 1,000 per annum. Very few cases of amoebic dysentery occurred.

TYPHUS

The U.S. troops were fully protected on arrival. In the case of First Army only 30,000 doses of vaccine were available before embarkation and it was decided to give priority to medical personnel. At a later date supplies sufficient to give protection to all the troops reached Algiers. So great was the dread of this disease that all save a few of the troops consented to be inoculated. Orders were issued forbidding troops to sleep in native dwellings or to give lifts to Arabs in army vehicles. The troops were strongly advised to avoid intimate contact with the natives.

	Protection	Number of Cases	Number of Deaths
U.S. Troops .	. 100 per cent.	15	0
Br. (before inoculation) .	0 per cent.	50	14
Br. (after inoculation) .	100 per cent.	4	0

It is to be noted that the strength of First Army when protection was practically 100 per cent. was at least five times greater than it was in the period when protection was nil.

In some of the native villages in the battle area typhus raged, and it became a matter of the greatest urgency that an epidemic in such a village should be brought under control. In one instance volunteers from 11 Fd. Amb. were called for to deal with such an outbreak. All offered themselves. A small party was selected from among them. It marched into the village, cleansed the dwellings, bathed the occupants—

men, women and children—and disinfested the whole place. The epidemic subsided. In the same area a French doctor and his wife, supported by a soldier with a 'Tommy-gun', inoculated several thousands of Arabs with excellent results.

Research on typhus was carried out by members of the Rockefeller Institute's Typhus Commission with the co-operation of the Director of the Algerian Health Service. A specialist entomologist provided by D. of H., War Office, was at work on insecticides, including D.D.T.

OTHER DISEASES

Smallpox. U.S. troops were protected by universal vaccination. All save a very few British troops were likewise protected.

U.S.	.	.	.	9 cases	0 deaths
Br.	.	.	.	146 cases	7 deaths

Of the 7 who died 5 had objected to vaccination on conscientious grounds while the remaining 2 had no discernible vaccination scars.

Supplies of fresh calf-lymph were readily obtainable from the Pasteur Institute in Algiers.

Tetanus. Both U.S. and British troops were completely protected by previous toxoid injections and boosting doses. In the whole force there were but 3 cases (one a German prisoner) with one death.

Scabies and Pediculosis. Sickness from these causes was minimal. The mobile bath and laundry units together, or organised bathing, all contributed to this satisfactory state of affairs.

Schistosomiasis. No case was reported. Troops were expressly forbidden to bathe in fresh water.

Hydatid Disease. No case was reported. The troops lived on their rations, always well cooked.

Tuberculosis. The incidence of tuberculosis among the troops was in no way different from that of the Army at home.

GENERAL SICK RATES

D.M.S. kept a careful watch on the sick returns of formations. It soon became clear that in any formation in which the senior administrative medical officer was not in close touch with his G.O.C. and the 'A' Staff the sick rate was invariably higher than in others in which the commander was paying serious and continuous attention to the advice of his senior medical officers. In the case of U.S. formations, battalion commanders whose units showed persistently high sick rates exposed themselves to the risk of disciplinary action.

FIELD HYGIENE

Field hygiene sections at assault scale took part in the initial landings at Algiers and Bougie. Each consisted of 1 officer and 4 O.Rs. with M.T.

Their first duty was to supervise sanitation in the port area. The scope of their duties increased as the military population of these places increased. At the end of 1942 there were field hygiene sections in each B.S.A.—Algiers, Bougie, Philippeville and Bône—and one in L. of C. S.A. at Guelma and one in V Corps area at Souk el Arba. They were supervising the sanitation in the port areas, in the port transit camps and in the staging camps along the main routes to the front. They sought the help of, and co-operated with, the French Service de Santé and the local medical practitioners.

In each of the French territories there was a well organised public health and preventive medicine service headed by a director. The service was responsible for all matters relating to public health, including marine sanitation, the control of sera and vaccine, the control of epidemic outbreaks and campaigns of disease prevention. The director was the technical counsellor to the government. He was assisted by a colonial physician and by the head of the anti-malarial service. Each territory was divided for public health administration purposes into a number of zones, each of which was in charge of a colonisation doctor who visited native communities, supervised local hospitals and other medical institutions, vaccinated the children and gave consultations. Each colonisation doctor was assisted by a number of 'native technical adjuncts' trained in a special three year course and by a number of colonial visiting nurses. In addition to possessing this elaborate and progressive sanitary organisation Algeria was the site of one of the world's great medical research centres, the Pasteur Institute, which systematically had attacked all the principal problems of contagious disease as encountered in North Africa.

In February 1943, D.M.S. called the attention of A.F.H.Q. to the insanitary conditions and habits of the native peoples and to the dangers to the troops that lurked therein. He requested authority to clean all areas surrounding places occupied by the troops. This was given and an order was signed for General Eisenhower by the Adjutant-General and issued to all formations, both American and British, stressing the responsibility of commanders for doing everything within their power to conserve the health of the troops, advising co-operation with the local authorities and authorising the expenditure of public funds. This health charter, which proved to be of the greatest value, was amended later to include Sicily, Italy and all the countries in the province of C.M.F.

The greatly enlarged use of the ports created deficiencies in respect of sanitary arrangements. Large numbers of troops were being dis-embarked and large labour forces were employed in the unloading of ships. Transit camps had to be improvised in dock and camp areas and the standard of hygiene in these was low. Staging camps on the L. of C.

and at railway halts were, in the early days of the campaign, quickly fouled. The field hygiene sections were instructed to post sanitary assistants to these areas and native labour was employed. By the end of 1942 a marked improvement had been achieved.

D.A.Ds.H. were on the staffs of the four port areas and on the two L. of C. S.As. at Constantine and Souk Ahras.

Five mobile bath units were functioning by late December, though not to full capacity since three of them were deficient in respect of G.1098 equipment. These units were distributed thus: one at Bougie, Philippeville, and Bône, respectively, and two in V Corps area.

RATIONS

For the first three months of the campaign the whole of First Army, including base and L. of C. troops, was issued with 'compo' rations. This ration, well designed, well balanced and well packed, included everything a man needed for the day—food, a 'Tommy cooker', boiled sweets, cigarettes, matches, laxative chocolate, even lavatory paper. Army biscuits took the place of bread until the field bakeries arrived. It was possible to supplement the ration with large quantities of citrus fruit. The American ration, with a higher carbohydrate content, was preferred by U.S. troops.

CLOTHING

The British troops wore battledress with heavy underclothing in the winter. Forward troops were issued with two blankets per man. In the spring, tropical clothing was issued consisting of khaki drill shorts, bush shirts worn outside the shorts, and trousers for wear after nightfall. D.M.S. strongly advised against the wearing of shorts, pointing out that trousers gave greater protection against injuries, scratches and insect bites. However, it was left to formation commanders to decide whether or not shorts should be worn. U.S. troops wore trousers and long-sleeved shirts with collars and ties. In the hot weather the men wore the minimum of clothing—extremely abbreviated shorts, socks and boots. Their fine bodies soon became beautifully bronzed but suffered much from desert sores.

A stock of 10,000 topees was held in reserve. Only a few were ever issued and these to men on special duties such as C.M.P. personnel on point duty. Dark glasses were available and were issued only on medical authority.

WATER

Because of soil and stream pollution all water supplies were regarded as presumably contaminated. It was therefore laid down as a general rule that all supplies should be treated accordingly. Very few of the hospitals were on a full allowance of 50 gallons. They were forced, therefore, to exercise strict economy in the use of water.

SAMPLE STATISTICS (D.M.S., A.F.H.Q.)

D.M.S., in giving unstinted praise to all those who served with him, consultant and stretcher-bearer alike, gives the following sample figures (compiled at the time) and makes the following observations:

The problem of handling battle casualties was never so arduous as that of dealing with the vast numbers of sick.

TABLE 45

Examples of the Daily Hospital Admission Rate per 1,000 Troops

	British		Totals
	Sick	Wounded	
November 8–December 11, 1942 .	0·8	0·42	1·2
December 12, 1942–January 1, 1943	1·1	0·30	1·4

British casualties from November 8, 1942–January 30, 1943, were:

Killed	. . . .	765
Wounded	. . . .	2,381
Missing	. . . .	2,459

During the closing stages of the campaign the medical units of divisions were handling and evacuating from 400–600 casualties daily.

TABLE 46

Total United Kingdom Losses of First Army throughout the Whole Campaign

	Killed	Wounded	Missing	Totals
Officers . .	382	833	307	1,522
Other Ranks . .	4,061	11,792	6,235	22,088
Totals . .	4,443	12,625	6,542	23,610

TABLE 47

Total Number of Casualties Passing Through the Medical Services from November 8, 1942–May 31, 1943

Force	Officers	Enlisted Men	O.Rs.	Totals
U.S. . .	1,800	18,881		20,681
Br. . .	1,508		23,969	25,477
Fr. . .	327		12,594	12,921
	3,635	55,444		59,079

TABLE 48

First Army Records of Numbers evacuated from April 9, 1943–May 15, 1943

	Road and rail		Totals	Air	Grand totals
April 9–15	. British and U.S.	. 3,809 ⎫			
	French . .	. 233 ⎬	4,141	1,821	5,962
	P.o.W. . .	. 99 ⎭			
April 16–23	. British and U.S.	. 4,149 ⎫			
	French . .	. 210 ⎬	4,485	1,053	5,538
	P.o.W. . .	. 126 ⎭			
	British and U.S.	. 7,958 ⎫			
	French . .	. 443 ⎬	8,626	2,874	11,500
	P.o.W. . .	. 225 ⎭			

From April 18–May 15, 1943, the total numbers of those evacuated were :

$$\left.\begin{array}{ll} \text{U.S.} & 10,388 \\ \text{Br.} & 31,775 \\ \text{P.o.W.} & 1,773 \end{array}\right\} = 43,936$$

TABLE 49

Excerpts from Weekly Operational Summary Number 2 Dated May 29, 1943

Paragraph 2. Total Strength of Forces:

	Officers	Enlisted Men and O.Rs.
U.S. . .	30,405	415,806
British . .	11,247	227,128
French . .	9,200	246,000

Paragraph 3. Hospital Situation:

	Wounded	Sick	Totals
U.S. . .	3,457	8,075	11,532
British . .	6,867	4,849	11,716
French . .	4,900	6,300	11,200

Casualty Rates per 1,000 of Strength

	U.S.	Br.	Fr.
Wounded . . .	8	29	19
Sick . . .	18	20	24

Paragraph 4. Total Casualties to date:

	Officers	Enlisted Men and O.Rs.
U.S. . .	1,800	18,881
British . .	1,508	23,969
French . .	327	12,594

Paragraph 9. Enemy Casualties:

(a) P.o.W. captured since May 5, 1943:

First Army . .	. 133,002
U.S. II Corps front .	. 39,064
French XIX Corps front	. 34,619
X Corps front . .	. 31,558
	238,243

(b) Total Casualties since November 8, 1942:

Killed	30,000
Wounded . . .	26,400
P.o.W.	266,600

TABLE 50

First Army Sick Rates per 1,000 per Week

Period . .	January 1	8	15	22	29
Strength .	62,148	66,164	64,105	62,546	69,634
Sick rate .	14·1	11·1	10·9	10·5	7·3
Period . .	February 5	12	19	26	
Strength .	75,259	80,770	78,815	74,477	
Sick rate .	8·5	7·7	7·6	10·5	

TABLE 51

Monthly Health Returns. Rate per 1,000 per Annum

	U.S.		British	
	January	February	January	February
Total admission rate .	733·00	727·00	427·98	384·12
Respiratory . .	224·48	180·98	—	34·12
Gastro-intestinal . .	21·32	19·15	13·48	37·80
V.D. (white tps.) .	30·47	36·65	25·41	17·46
(coloured tps.) .	498·24	404·50	—	—
Enteric . . .	—	—	—	—
Typhus . . .	—	0·11	0·45	0·54
Smallpox . . .	—	—	—	0·12
Hepatitis . . .	—	6·31	12·57	5·94
Scabies . . .	—	—	—	56·20
Pediculosis . . .	—	—	—	109·38
Deaths . . .	—	2·17	—	1·38

TABLE 52

Evacuation by Hospital Ship

Between December 1942 and April 1943, the following numbers of patients were
evacuated to the United Kingdom:

H.S. *Newfoundland*:	December .	.	.	373
	March .	.	.	355
	April .	.	.	380
H.S. *Amarapoora*:	January	.	.	376
	March	.	.	397
H.S. *Oxfordshire*:	February .	.	.	310
	March	.	.	373
				2,564

H.S. *Oxfordshire* also cleared some 400 cases from Algiers to Oran on December 9, 1942, an operation which greatly eased the congested bed situation in the British base. In the final stage of the campaign the naval authorities allowed hospital ships to clear casualties from Bône to Philippeville and from Algiers to Oran, thus providing a most welcome and useful alternative evacuation route.

TABLE 53

Evacuation by Air. December 1942–June 1943

From	To	Cases
Telergma	Oran	5,500
Tebessa	Oran	3,000
Feriana	Oran	400
Bône	Oran	1,000
Algiers	Oran	1,400
Telergma	Algiers	3,500
Souk el Arba	Algiers	1,100
Bône	Algiers	500
Various	Algiers or United Kingdom	100
		16,500

Exceptionally, special cases were flown direct to the U.K. and to the U.S.A.

TABLE 54

Numbers Evacuated from Tunisia to Tripoli
April 1–June 30, 1943

	Battle casualties	Sick	Totals
Road	5,791	9,145	14,936
Air	1,910	783	2,693
Totals	7,701	9,928	17,629

OFFICERS CONVALESCENT WING

It was found that the best results were obtained when the O.C. was a R.A.M.C. officer and the adjutant and P.M.C. (President Mess Committee) combatants. Opened at Chenoua, near Tirpaza, on April 23 the wing received between this date and May 31, 198 officers, of whom 82 were discharged to duty and 10 were returned to hospital.

ARMY SELECTION CENTRES

These centres were established in order that everyone should be occupied in such a way that their attributes should be most suitably and most efficiently employed. To them were referred men who for medical reasons had been down-graded. An analysis of 2,000 down-gradings showed that the causal disabilities were distributed as follows:

TABLE 55

Per cent.

Psychiatric	.	.	32
Locomotor	.	.	26
Upper limb	.	.	14
General medical	.	.	10
Ear	.	.	6
Eye	.	.	3
General surgical	.	.	3
Skin	.	.	2
Other conditions	.	.	4

REINFORCEMENT CENTRES

Commandants reported that 1–2 per cent. of men coming to these centres from hospital required further remedial treatment.

SAMPLE STATISTICS—EIGHTH ARMY. ARMY MEDICAL UNITS

TABLE 56

Admissions. Sick. January–March 1943

Month	U.K.	U.D.F.	N.Z.E.F.	Indian	Fr.	Grk.	U.S.A.	S.D.F.	P.o.W.	Others	Totals
Jan.	4,723	169	440	327	84	5	7	61	1	324	6,141
Feb.	3,884	196	396	250	16	5	9	30	6	388	5,180
Mar.	4,167	269	509	273	11	—	2	8	11	290	5,540
	12,774	634	1,345	850	111	10	18	99	18	1,002	16,861

TABLE 57

Evacuations. Sick. January–March 1943

Month	U.K.	U.D.F.	N.Z.E.F.	Indian	Fr.	Grk.	U.S.A.	S.D.F.	P.o.W.	Others	Totals
Jan.	2,720	101	348	221	72	15	3	44	2	155	3,681
Feb.	1,371	75	200	70	5	3	5	10	—	106	1,845
Mar.	553	30	200	13	6	2	—	2	1	44	851
	4,644	206	748	304	83	20	8	56	3	305	6,377

TABLE 58

Ratio per 1,000 *Admissions. All Causes (other than Battle Casualties)*

Month	Strength (approx.)	Admissions per 1,000	
		per month	per day
January	170,000	36·12	1·16
February	170,000	30·47	1·08
March	179,000	30·94	0·99
Average strength for quarter	173,000	32·46	1·08

TABLE 59

Principal Causes of Admission to C.C.Ss., Army Field Ambulances and Tripoli Base Hospitals. January–March 1943

Disease	Admissions per 1,000 per month		
	January	February	March
Injuries, Accidental . . .	3·18	3·62	4·58
Burns	0·57	0·62	0·37
Infective hepatitis	7·05	2·37	0·62
Digestive disorders	3·30	2·84	3·70
Diseases of the skin . . .	2·83	2·71	2·73
Inflammation of the areolar tissue .	2·42	2·02	2·42
Diseases of bones, joints and muscles	1·93	2·11	1·76
Tonsillitis	1·47	1·60	1·43
Diseases of respiratory system . .	1·21	1·22	1·32
Diarrhoea and dysentery . .	1·82	0·78	0·87
Physical exhaustion . . .	0·12	0·03	0·08
N.Y.D.(N.)	0·43	0·43	1·25

TABLE 60

Admissions. Battle Casualties. January–March 1943

Month	U.K.	U.D.F.	N.Z.E.F.	Indian	Fr.	Grk.	U.S.A.	S.D.F.	Others	P.o.W.	Totals
Jan.	856	31	105	27	1	1	1	7	28	10	1,067
Feb.	443	13	26	11	11	1	—	4	11	9	529
Mar.	2,368	40	345	28	8	2	—	5	21	124	2,941
	3,667	84	476	66	20	4	1	16	60	143	4,537

TABLE 61

Evacuations. Battle Casualties. January–March 1943

Month	U.K.	U.D.F.	N.Z.E.F.	Indian	Fr.	Grk.	U.S.A.	S.D.F.	Others	P.o.W.	Totals
Jan.	705	29	99	19	3	8	—	6	15	9	893
Feb.	293	7	22	5	11	1	—	4	4	9	356
Mar.	183	2	7	—	4	2	—	—	2	—	200
	1,181	38	128	24	18	11	—	10	21	18	1,449

TABLE 62

Hospitalised Injuries Caused by Enemy Action and not so caused*

M.E.F. and B.N.A.F. (A two-months sample)

Injuries:	M.E.F. May–June 1942	M.E.F. October– November 1942	B.N.A.F. December 1942– January 1943
Number in sample	2,637	4,859	2,511
Enemy action	59·2 per cent.	65·4 per cent.	48·2 per cent.
Not enemy action	40·8 ,, ,,	34·6 ,, ,,	51·8 ,, ,,
Injuries by Type:			
Number of cases	2,637	4,859	2,511
Fractures	22·1 per cent.	18·4 per cent.	27·7 per cent.
Burns	12·7 ,, ,,	10·4 ,, ,,	5·3 ,, ,,
Others	65·2 ,, ,,	71·2 ,, ,,	66·9 ,, ,,
Injuries by Anatomical Region:			
Number of cases	2,637	4,859	2,511
Head	5·3 per cent.	4·9 per cent.	9·5 per cent.
Maxillo-facial	4·3 ,, ,,	7·0 ,, ,,	5·5 ,, ,,
Eyes	2·2 ,, ,,	2·7 ,, ,,	1·6 ,, ,,
Thorax	4·2 ,, ,,	5·2 ,, ,,	4·3 ,, ,,
Abdomen, etc.	2·1 ,, ,,	2·2 ,, ,,	2·6 ,, ,,
Limbs	68·7 ,, ,,	67·4 ,, ,,	67·2 ,, ,,
Others	13·1 ,, ,,	10·6 ,, ,,	9·4 ,, ,,
Injuries Disposal:			
Fractures:			
Number of cases	583	893	696
Duty	79·8 per cent.	77·9 per cent.	71·6 per cent.
To United Kingdom	18·3 ,, ,,	18·3 ,, ,,	26·4 ,, ,,
Died	1·9 ,, ,,	3·8 ,, ,,	2·0 ,, ,,
Burns:			
Number of cases	336	505	134
Duty	93·8 per cent.	94·4 per cent.	93·7 per cent.
To United Kingdom	3·6 ,, ,,	2·5 ,, ,,	5·6 ,, ,,
Died	2·7 ,, ,,	3·2 ,, ,,	0·8 ,, ,,
Other Forms of Injury:			
Number of cases	1,718	3,461	1,681
Duty	89·9 per cent.	90·5 per cent.	86·9 per cent.
To United Kingdom	8·3 ,, ,,	6·1 ,, ,,	12·4 ,, ,,
Died	1·9 ,, ,,	3·4 ,, ,,	0·7 ,, ,,

* From the Statistical Report on the Health of the Army, 1943–45, p. 215.

As the control of preventable disease becomes more powerful the loss of man-power due to injury not caused by enemy action is thrown into greater relief. In M.E.F. and B.N.A.F. such injuries accounted for some 30–50 per cent. of the total. It is reasonable to assume that a high proportion of accidental injuries are preventable. If they were avoided the pressure upon the field surgical units would be considerably eased and much man-power conserved.

TABLE 63

United Kingdom Troops. Deaths in Hospitals M.E.F. 1943
Relative Rates

	Statis-tical* report	Holler-ith tabula-tion	N.Z.E.F. 1940–45		M.E.F.† report	Holler-ith tabula-tion
Nervous system	8·3	6·3	12·6	Nervous diseases	11·2	6·3
Appendicitis	2·6	1·9	8·0			
Pneumonia	6·2	2·9	7·4	Pneumonia	4·8	2·9
Neoplasms	10·0	8·2	4·2			
Poliomyelitis	9·3	9·6	4·2			
Dysentery	4·6	1·9	4·2	Dysentery	1·6	1·9
Typhoid	10·9	13·9	4·2	Enteric gp. of fevers	8·2	13·9
Typhus	10·4	9·6	3·2	Typhus	7·5	9·6
Infective hepatitis	4·1	1·4	3·2	Infective hepatitis	2·1	1·4
Nephritis	2·0	0·5	3·2			
Diphtheria	4·7	1·4	2·1	Diphtheria	3·7	1·4
Tuberculosis pul-monary	4·1	1·4	2·1	Tuberculosis	5·0	1·4
Otitis media	1·0	0·5	2·6			
Peptic ulcer	1·0	1·0	1·6			
Smallpox	7·0	8·7	1·0	Smallpox	4·3	8·7
Malaria	4·7	1·4	1·0	Malaria	2·4	1·4
Heart		4·8	9·5	V.D.H.	1·1 ⎫	
Septicaemia		1·0	6·3	Other diseases of the circulatory system	4·8 ⎭	4·8
Haemorrhage, cerebral, etc.		3·9	5·3			
Anaemia		3·9	3·2	Meningococcal infection	1·6	4·8
Acute abdominal			4·2	P.U.O.	0·3	
				Rheumatic fever	0·5	1·0
				Effects of heat	0·3	0·5
				Psychosis	1·1	0·5
				Psychoneurosis	1·1	
				Inflammation of the bronchi	0·5	0·5
				Other respiratory diseases	5·3	1·9
				Other digestive diseases	10·9	11·5
				Diseases of ear and nose	2·4	1·0
				Skin and I.A.T.	0·5	0·5
Others	10·1	15·8	6·7	Others	18·8	24·1
	101·0	100·0	100·0		100·0	100·0

*From The Statistical Report on the Health of the Army 1943–45. H.M.S.O.
†From the Statistical Report produced by M.E.C.
Hollerith Tabulation prepared by A.M.D. Stats., 1953.
N.Z.E.F. From the New Zealand Official Medical History (provisional narrative).

(vii)
Reflections upon the Campaign by D.D.M.S., First Army

PLANNING

During the planning stage of operations there are a number of vital lessons which must be appreciated if the medical services are to be placed on a sound basis from the outset.

The major considerations to be borne in mind are:

(i) in an opposed landing the bulk of casualties occur at the outset.

(ii) there is no medical base on which to rely and this has to be built up in the reverse of the orthodox order—i.e. from the front line (highwater mark) backwards.

The practical applications drawn from the above are as under:

(a) Medical units earmarked for the initial landing must on no account have personnel separated from their equipment. This applies particularly to field ambulances, C.C.Ss., F.S.Us. and general hospitals. A medical unit without equipment is like an infantry battalion without weapons—an encumbrance.

(b) Medical units destined for an assault and those required for future rapid development and follow-up must have received adequate training and be familiar with their equipment. This point may be considered self-evident, but nevertheless it was not fully appreciated. Thus

(i) only two out of the six C.C.Ss. were under First Army for training and organisation prior to embarking;

(ii) there was a general cross-posting of C.Os. just prior to embarkation;

(iii) there were no general hospitals under First Army for training, nor did these hospitals see their equipment until they landed in the theatre of operations—in some cases equipment and personnel were landed at different ports. The need for tactical packing of general hospitals and C.C.Ss. is emphasised.

(c) The medical cover available varies according to the 'G' estimates and other factors such as shipping space, but it is considered that one field ambulance plus two field surgical units should be the minimum for a brigade group for the first forty-eight hours. Extra items such as additional sterilised dressings and pentothal will be required.

(d) The large number of initial casualties coupled with the scarcity of medical units in the early stages requires a definite division of wounded into lying and sitting. The sitting to be catered for on a grand scale until such time as better facilities occur, while lying cases get the best facilities available.

MEDICAL INSTALLATIONS AND UNITS

FIELD AMBULANCES

These units were found excellent for all tasks and abundantly proved their worth.

The Hartgill Committee's recommendations for reorganisation of the Medical Services would have had some slight advantages in divisions but would not have worked in corps and Army. For instance First Army field ambulance was at one time carrying out the following tasks at the same time:

(1) H.Q. running a 150 bedded hospital for local sick and N.Y.D. (N) cases—a surgical unit was attached, also a 1,000 bedded rest centre for nervous exhaustion and light cases.

(2) One Coy. with 25th Tank Bde. which had arrived from the U.K. without its light field ambulance.

(3) The remaining company was manning Michelin Auto-rail ambulance cars, producing ambulance railhead detachments and running a 50 bedded holding hospital for lying cases at railhead.

The Hartgill Committee's suggested organisation has the following disadvantages in a very mobile campaign:

(a) Head and chest cases after operation cannot be moved for 7–10 days. An army may have five divisions in the line extending over 50–100 miles of front. This means 5–10 pockets of anything up to 20 immovable cases scattered over this frontage.

(b) The above situation recurs after each battle. Battles may occur every 5–6 days after the army has advanced 50–100 miles.

(c) Serious cases are not assisted to recover if retained after operation in situations subjected to shelling or bombing.

It is doubtful whether the F.D.S. proposed by the Hartgill Committee could cope with these difficulties.

In modern mobile warfare it is essential that the army in the field should be self-contained. This new conception is vital so that the Army is able always to keep the field ambulances and C.C.Ss. empty while the L. of C. is extending forward. The requirement in this campaign with two British corps of seven British divisions was an allotment of four 600 bedded general hospitals and three 200 bedded general hospitals.

CASUALTY CLEARING STATIONS

The light C.C.S. devised for the assault landing was retained during the entire operations without reverting to the normal type. This was made necessary by the scarcity of transport. The light C.C.S. requires 22 additional lorries to move it as against 55 for a full C.C.S.

These light C.C.Ss. did very excellent work and it is considered that the idea of a light, easily moved C.C.S. should be retained.

Each C.C.S. should have a water cart.

GENERAL HOSPITALS

Two hundred and 600 bedded general hospitals as allotted to First Army had to be completely reorganised in order to suit the operational conditions. The salient feature of this reorganisation was that the hospital was designed to move and set up in tactical blocks. These blocks were self-contained and functioned immediately on opening. In this way it was found possible to move an open 600 bedded general hospital and have it open and full at the other end in three days.

This new mobility of Army general hospitals requires the allotment of domestic load carriers and water trucks on the unit G.1098.

M.A.CS. AND A.C.CS.

The scale on which M.A.Cs. should be allotted is one M.A.C. per corps and one A.C.C. per army. The reason for recommending an A.C.C. for Army is the fact that it possesses a platoon of troop carrying vehicles.

During the campaign 18 T.C.Vs. were allotted to First Army from L. of C. With these vehicles, apart from the collection of stores and the evacuation of casualties, the following tasks were performed during the battle period:

(1) Complete move of 600 bedded general hospital . . 8
(2) Complete move of 200 bedded general hospital . . 5
(3) Move of Adv. Depot Med. Stores 2
(4) Move of field hospital 1
(5) Move of C.C.S. 9

This platoon of T.C.Vs. enabled 'Medical' to be self-contained and less of a drag on a hard pressed 'Q'. Moves would never have been completed in time if transport had had to be obtained from 'A'.

As all M.A.Cs. in this campaign were of the new R.A.S.C. type, it is recorded that they worked very well. The method of 'Medical' having complete and direct control and R.A.S.C. exercising technical supervision was employed throughout the campaign and should be a clearly accepted principle.

FIELD SURGICAL UNITS

This campaign with its active and passive periods provided a certain amount of information on the successful handling of these units.

(a) During the static phases when brigades were holding fronts of 12 or more miles and when lateral communications were poor, the method of allotting F.S.Us. to divisional field ambulances was adopted and worked well.

(b) During active phases the principle, not a new one, was employed of allotting two F.S.Us. to each C.C.S. and the dispersal of F.S.Us. to divisions should normally be unnecessary.

(c) The normal grouping employed was 3 C.C.Ss. accepting 100 cases each in rotation, each with a F.T.U. and two F.S.Us. attached.

(d) In an advance, when transport was tight, IX Corps, which had the mobile rôle, utilised the corps field ambulance to go forward early with two F.S.Us. attached pending the arrival of a C.C.S. later. This was a successful method.

FIELD TRANSFUSION UNITS

It is considered that an additional unit is necessary for the effective working of the transfusion service. This unit can be commanded by a non-medical officer and called an Army transfusion unit. Its task would be to deliver blood from B.T.U. to medical units within the army. It should have a semi-mobile section located near the rearmost Army general hospitals and an advanced section located at a central forward point—e.g. group of C.C.Ss.

EVACUATION

AMBULANCE PLANES

The salient feature of this campaign was the failure of air evacuation from First Army, although it is reported to have worked well on the L. of C. The main difficulty was to induce planes to be flown sufficiently far forward.

The reason for the failure of this valuable method of evacuation was that whereas Eighth Army British planes were marked with the Red Cross and were accustomed to use very far forward landing grounds, U.S. planes were not.

The conclusions drawn from this campaign are:

(1) that Army should be allotted a flight of Red Cross planes.

(2) that these planes must be controlled by Army through its air group.

(3) that planes must be stabled well forward to be of maximum use.

(4) that air evacuation from Army area should be placed in its proper perspective—useful adjunct to other normal means—on account of its dependence on weather.

(5) that a small holding unit of the nature of a field hospital should always be allotted to Army. This unit would hold casualties at

ambulance air head and move forward in accordance with the situation.

MOTOR AMBULANCES

The Austin motor ambulance was a more popular vehicle than the Humber F.W.D. 2-stretcher ambulance.

There is need for roomier four-wheel drive motor ambulances for field ambulance work.

Over the distances traversed and the roads encountered there was great need for a waggon orderly per motor ambulance. At first a company from each of First Army and IX Corps field ambulances provided the additional waggon orderlies and later these were provided from the reinforcement pool. The simplest method of providing for this very definite need would seem to be to employ A.T.S. in lieu of nursing officers batmen and to utilise the nursing orderlies thus freed for waggon orderlies.

It was necessary to mark all motor ambulances with large visible Red Crosses (3 foot) on back, sides and top and a smaller one on the driver's hood. These proved most effective and should be a standard feature at all times.

There is also a definite need for the proper equipping of all motor ambulances if a normal exchange is to be maintained and patients properly looked after. It is recommended that the G.1098 and I.1248 of field ambulances and M.A.Cs. be adjusted so that every motor ambulance is equipped on a standard pattern as under:

4 stretchers	1 bedpan E.I.
4 warmers, stomach	1 feeder E.I.
1 urinal E.I.	1 vomiting bowl (improvised)
12 blankets	4 pairs pyjamas

Considerable difficulty was experienced in making motor ambulances run singly and not in convoy. It is estimated that motor ambulances running independently and filtering gives a 33 per cent. larger clearance capacity as well as allowing more rest for the driver and bringing a steady, easily handled flow of patients into general hospitals and C.C.Ss. It also prevents receiving hospitals being swamped, which occurs when motor ambulances run in convoys.

Each Q.L. (T.C.V.) will lift 20 walking wounded casualties plus kits. The normal equipment should be 40 blankets G.S. and one urinal E.I.

Finally, all anti-tank rifles and Bren guns and mines should be removed from all M.A.Cs. and A.C.Cs. These do not accord with the Geneva Convention. When the unit moves, if these are distributed throughout the column the enemy concludes they are fighting vehicles sneaking along under cover of the Red Cross motor ambulances. He thereafter shoots up all motor ambulances and medical units.

The provision of ambulance trains with Brechet apparatus brought out one definite defect. The British pattern was found to be inferior to the French equipment. The springing of British Brechet is such that at normal speeds the 'play' is sufficient to cause discomfort and with even war express speeds the play is up to one foot up and down with a lateral motion as well. Under these conditions patients had to be tied in to keep them on the stretcher. An improvised adjustment was made by 'Tn' (Transportation).

Regarding the running of ambulance trains, it is recommended that they should be worked by Army from before backwards and stabled well forward. It is realised that the control of trains is the prerogative of G.H.Q. and when controlling several armies it may be necessary to hold them centrally. Nevertheless, it is considered that the principle of making Army self-contained should be constantly remembered.

In this theatre a number of Michelin Diesel Auto-rail cars were obtained from the French and staffed from First Army and V Corps field ambulances. The finding of these trains, with an average daily lift of 160 equal lying and sitting, was of immense value throughout and especially so in the early stages.

MULE EVACUATION

During this campaign a great deal of country, especially north of the road Oued Zarga–Medjez el Bab, was mountainous and unfit for motor transport. The methods used were mule cacolets and litters and also hand-carriage. 78th Division used Bren gun carriers with success in the Heidous area north of Medjez el Bab.

In most cases motor ambulances could reach the R.A.P. but collection forward of this was by long and difficult hand-carriage. In such circumstances regimental stretcher-bearers must be augmented by field ambulance stretcher-bearers.

HYGIENE

Although the incidence of sickness was relatively low yet more men were admitted to hospital on account of sickness than as a result of enemy action. It was only during the last battle that the admissions of wounded exceeded those for sickness.

Over-emphasis of the dangers of special diseases such as malaria, typhus and venereal disease, led to neglect of the common diseases, with the result that diarrhoea and dysentery due to neglect of sanitation occurred at the close of the battle.

The retention of battle dress for a period of a month after the issue of K.D. was fully justified as the risk of chill from the cold nights was great, especially on high ground.

The lack of instruction in the best use of the 14-man compo box was evident—for example much more variety could have been achieved if the fat from stews had been collected and used for frying.

The acceptance of vendors and cafés without any control was far too frequent. If the policy is to place cafés 'in bounds' then a selection should be made and these cafés kept under strict supervision by a medical officer. No vendor should be permitted.

Water from a tap was too readily regarded as safe. An adequate pure drinking water supply well signposted must be provided at once when a concentration of troops occurs.

The responsibility for the sanitary control of docks, railway stations, transit camps and staging areas must be defined at once and clearly understood by all concerned. The early provision of pure drinking water supply, adequate latrines, ablution facilities and places set aside for cooking is essential. All these must be clearly indicated by notice boards.

The policy with regard to brothels must be laid down beforehand and communicated to all formation commanders. It was quickly shown that the brothel cannot be regarded as safe and if put 'in bounds' only leads to a false sense of security. If the time spent in this campaign in trying to decide whether brothels should or should not be recognised had been spent on the early provision of welfare centres it is probable that the incidence of venereal disease would have been lower.

Rest camps provided well forward are a vital necessity if man-power is to be conserved. A convalescent depot in Army area must be provided to prevent unnecessary evacuation. Many cases diagnosed as N.Y.D. (N.) are just cases of exhaustion, and if treated as such at once recover.

Bathing and laundry facilities must be provided early. The simple expedient of a petrol tin shower did not seem to be widely known, yet baths of this kind would have helped considerably to tide over the period before M.B.Us. arrived.

The provision of soap is absolutely essential; the possibility of providing soap with the compo ration might with advantage be explored. The shortage of soap was acutely felt in the early stages of the campaign.

Troops likely to work in contact with native populations must be protected beforehand against endemic diseases such as typhus. The rigid supervision of sanitation among native workers is absolutely essential and proved to be not such a hopeless task as had been imagined.

The care and maintenance of unit water trucks was not good in many cases. A careful inspection of all water trucks is absolutely essential before a unit embarks.

A 100 per cent. reserve of sanitary and water duty personnel must be maintained. Time and time again units were found without trained personnel on the job.

Units must be prepared to carry out their own R.E. work in regard to camp sanitary appliances. Material was short and the R.E. were fully occupied with other tasks.

Camp areas must be occupied before sanitary fixtures can be installed. The first unit in must understand the necessity of allotting sites for latrines, ablution, cookhouse and incinerators since otherwise later arrivals are faced with a wilderness of fouled ground.

DISEMBARKATION

The following points must be borne in mind:

(1) Troops are undoubtedly softened by a sea voyage; they cannot therefore carry heavy loads and march long distances to transit camps unless they are trained as assault troops. This applies particularly to L. of C. troops. Intermediate rest points must always be established.

(2) Provision must be made for inclement weather and if rain is expected dry sites for camps must be selected.

(3) Troops arriving overseas for the first time at once forget all they have been taught regarding sanitation. Rigid discipline must be maintained for the first few days after disembarkation while the men accustom themselves to their new surroundings.

Units become interested in hygiene when they come face to face with the problems overseas. It is important, therefore, that schools of instruction in sanitation for officers and O.Rs. should be opened at the earliest opportunity by hygiene sections.

RETURNS

Simplified methods of rendering returns in First Army worked well. The modification of the system of notification of infectious diseases was implemented too late, however, to be of any value. The method is a step in the right direction but further modification is still necessary if it is to be really satisfactory.

A.F.A. 35 (Infectious Disease Notification Form) should only be rendered by medical officers to their respective formations *via* D.D.M.S. army in the case of army troops, D.D.M.S. corps or L. of C. in the case of corps or L. of C. troops and A.D.M.S. division or area in the case of divisional or area troops, a copy being sent to the O.C. of the unit in each case.

The lack of information regarding the number of casualties admitted from day to day to forward medical units was felt at First Army. Early information of the state of field ambulances would allow Army to arrange for evacuation in good time; a daily wire from corps would fill this gap.

It was clearly brought out that if returns are to be accurate and promptly rendered a close liaison must be maintained between those who render them and those who receive them. The War Office must be asked early what they want and then returns arranged accordingly. An explanation by an Army staff officer should be given to all formation administrative medical officers and also to all hospital registrars. Once it is understood for what purpose a return is required it is probable that more care will be taken with regard to accuracy and promptness.

The rendering of A.F.I. 1220 (Personal Medical Record) by forward general hospitals was found to be impracticable except for men discharged to duty. As full notes as possible were therefore entered on A.F.W. 3118. The A.F.I. 1220 should only be prepared by the general hospital which discharges men to duty or transfers them to convalescent depot or hospital ship.

PRISONER-OF-WAR CAMPS

The health of the prisoners was good, but a large percentage were lousy and quite a number were suffering from dysentery.

The extremely large numbers encountered caused great difficulties in accommodation and the following points were brought out:

(a) If a large P.o.W. cage holding up to 15,000 is contemplated then a piped pure water supply near at hand must be available.

(b) Arrangements must be made to bathe and delouse every prisoner and thereafter keep them free from lice.

(c) Special areas in each cage must be set aside for sleeping, latrines, cooking, ablution and bathing, water point and incinerator— in other words the basic principles of organisation are required. This was lacking in the early days.

(d) Until deep trench latrines with fly-proof covers can be provided, and as long as an open trench is used, petrol must be used to scorch the faeces.

(e) The commandant and staff of the cages must not be changed every few days as occurred in North Africa.

EQUIPMENT

Many lessons were learned regarding equipment necessary in mobile warfare and for the speedy clearing, moving and setting up of 200 and 600 bedded general hospitals.

The chief among them were:

CASUALTY CLEARING STATIONS

(a) The light C.C.S. can be kept right up with the battle and there is usually no labour or time for R.E. work.

(*b*) C.C.Ss. therefore definitely require one water truck, six *chagluls* for keeping water cool and a quota of collapsible deep trench latrine structures added to their standard equipment.

GENERAL HOSPITALS

(*a*) 200 and 600 bedded general hospitals which have passed from static to a mobile rôle with Army, require some adjustment in their standard equipment.

(*b*) Water is the most important item and for this 200 bedded hospitals require one water truck or water tank lorry and 600 bedded hospitals three on their G.1098. Similarly, owing to moves and to the difficulty of obtaining transport for domestic duties such as collection of rations, the conveyance of laundry, etc., one 3-ton lorry is required by a 200 bedded general hospital and two 3-ton lorries for a 600 bedded hospital.

(*c*) Deep trench latrine superstructures are also required as for C.C.Ss. and also six and twelve *chagluls* respectively.

(*d*) A.C. generators must be included in the G.1098. At present such are an R.E. supply and were not available for working the X-ray sets for several months after the assault.

ADVANCED DEPOTS, MEDICAL STORES

Advanced depots of medical stores proved most unsatisfactory for the work they were called upon to perform in this campaign, and it was only due to the devotion of the Os.C. and personnel that they have been reasonably efficient. They had to provide the needs of mobile general hospitals while not equipped or staffed to do so.

Their I.1248 was found to be deficient in many respects, e.g. pentothal, sulphanilamide, etc., for surgical purposes. Nor was their I.1248 adjusted to meet the demands of F.S.Us. Some difficulty was encountered in identifying dental equipment and also with the supply of common optical lenses.

The outstanding needs are:

(*a*) The unit should have a cook and adequate cooking facilities.

(*b*) An increment should be added to handle general hospital supplies and a dental clerk orderly to deal with dental equipment.

(*c*) Eight additional store tents are required to house battle reserves and general hospital supplies.

(*d*) The lighting facilities are totally inadequate and require the addition of one Kw. lighting set or a minimum of one pressure lamp per tent and one for the office.

(*e*) A mobile section is required, as used in the Middle East. In the present campaign units were travelling over 100 miles on congested roads to obtain supplies, and the move of an advanced depot of medical stores forward would have delayed the collection of supplies by Army from the base depot of medical stores. In order to keep up with the battle a light section comprising: one sergeant, two privates, two drivers R.A.S.C., one 3-ton penthouse lorry (as a store) and one 15-cwt. truck (for collection and holding), is necessary. This addition is necessary if medical supplies are to be maintained over long distances—in this instance medical supplies were stretched to the limit.

It is noted that delays occurred in despatches from the base depot of medical stores for want of a vehicle, and in the end collection was arranged by Army in medical T.C.Vs.

RESERVES AND BATTLE 'BRICKS' OF EQUIPMENT

It was found necessary in the assault phase to add a 10-ton 'brick' of expendible items of medical equipment to advanced depots of medical stores. Later a 1-ton standard battle 'brick' was maintained for replenishment of field ambulances. It was also found necessary to equip all R.M.Os. and units up to a definite scale in the essential surgical supplies and to allot blood plasma and solution in a similar manner.

Reserves of stretchers and blankets should be held by medical units on a scale determined when planning, together with a very substantial dump for Army and corps. This latter is necessary if expansion of installations is envisaged since general hospitals are only capable of crisis double expansion if the necessary equipment is available.

ENEMY MEDICAL EQUIPMENT

The large amount of valuable enemy medical equipment captured required the assistance of a definite medical depot staff to handle it and to supervise the work of P.o.W. medical storemen. This depot has also to provide for replenishments to captured enemy hospitals treating P.o.W. sick and wounded. In this campaign a Q.M. and staff were taken from a general hospital, to its detriment, for this important task. It is considered that there should be at least one experienced Q.M. held at G.B.D. for replacement and for such important tasks as this.

NURSING OFFICERS' CLOTHING

Certain difficulties were experienced with nursing officers' clothing and in future arrangements should be made early for the provision of this. The most effective method would seem to be to allot a quota to each general hospital on repayment.

For forward work with its attendant laundry difficulties it is strongly recommended that white should not be used and khaki substituted.

PERSONNEL

ADMINISTRATIVE MEDICAL OFFICERS AND Os.C.

One point that emerged very clearly was the need for high calibre senior officers. The A.Ds.M.S. of L. of C. and base areas require the most careful selection as the whole Army is based upon them. The apparently prevalent idea that these appointments are medical administrative backwaters should be discarded at once.

Similarly with Os.C. general hospitals employed with Army. These are new units requiring vigorous administration coupled with extreme adaptability and are no place for the aged in mind or body. These units should be considered as field units and Os.C. and Os.C. divisions specially selected.

MEDICAL OFFICERS

A marked deficiency in the military training of medical officers was noted. The following are examples of this:

(1) The need for a battle R.A.P. equipment produced from the normal items held by the R.M.O. when going into battle was commonly not recognised. Much valuable equipment was lost through lack of observance of this elementary principle.

(2) R.M.Os. were hazy as to how to obtain replenishments of supplies, nor were they in many cases aware of what was medical and what was ordnance equipment. They did not know how to obtain items such as cresol and medical comforts.

(3) There was a singular lack of knowledge of R.M.Os'. duties in regard to their responsibilities in advising C.Os. on hygiene and in inspection of troops.

A radical change in depot training and in post depot field ambulance training would seem to be required.

STAFF DUTIES

There was great difficulty in obtaining sufficiently knowledgeable junior officers to fill posts as D.A.D.M.S. The need for some sort of medical staff course for officers recommended for promotion to major is evident. It is considered that this should last a month at least and be given by officers with administrative and operational experience.

It is further considered that this course should be open to Os.C. medical units and should include the basic principles of unit internal administration and of tactics.

Since there is no standard course of instruction units are administered and controlled in different ways by different A.Ds.M.S. and unit commanders and so it is that officers posted from one unit to another take a considerable time to learn the particular unit's fads and methods and to become efficient members of the team.

This question of basic training cannot be over-emphasised. It merits urgent attention, for in North Africa not even the necessity of passing back information was appreciated.

NURSING OFFICERS

There is no doubt whatsoever that the attachment of suitable nursing officers to forward medical units is beneficial to the welfare of patients. The lessons learnt from this campaign were:

(1) That with Army C.C.Ss. and general hospitals the quota of nursing officers is too high. The ideal would be: 50 per cent. W.E. plus matron and home sister for 600 bedded and 200 bedded general hospitals and 6 nursing officers for a light C.C.S., the difference to be made up at the rate of 2 N.C.Os. to 3 nursing officers.

(2) That nursing officers must be volunteers who have been told that they will get little comfort and must be prepared to rough it without complaint.

N.C.OS. AND O.RS.

A lack of basic training among the rank and file was evident. There was difficulty in obtaining really sound R.S.Ms., and clerks of good calibre were at a premium.

It is considered that the category of Pte. clerks should be as under:

> Clerks—shorthand typist
> Clerks—typist

The former is invaluable and tends to have all the work thrown at him without any commensurate rise in status. This should be adjusted by making shorthand typist clerks class II after testing and six months' service.

It was noticed that the scarcity of good clerks made the establishment of clerks on medical administration H.Qs. inadequate.

During this campaign A.M.P.C. personnel were attached to medical installations as under:

200 bedded general hospitals	1 section
1,200 and 600 bedded general hospitals . . .	2 sections
C.C.Ss.	1 section
Adv. Depots Med. Stores	½ section

The work of the A.M.P.C. cannot be too highly praised and the mobility of units and their speed in opening must, in large measure, be attributed to them.

DENTAL*

The following recommendations are made as a result of the nine months' field experience in North Africa with First Army:

(*a*) All dental personnel at present attached to field ambulances, C.C.Ss. and Army general hospitals—i.e. 200 and 600 bedded hospitals and 50 bedded field hospitals—should be transformed into mobile dental units. A mobile dental unit should then be attached to each of the above-mentioned medical units. This would greatly increase the amount of dental work since, when C.C.Ss. and general hospitals are concentrated into groups of three, one M.D.U. could be left with the group and the remaining ones could be sent wherever they were most urgently required. This would also save an enormous amount of petrol, as the M.D.U. could proceed to unit after unit and remain there until all work was completed. At present units are conveyed to dental centres. An economy would also be effected in dental personnel and equipment as the present M.D.Us. would then be unnecessary.

(*b*) These M.D.Us. should consist of one dental officer, one dental clerk orderly (corporal) and two mechanics (one of whom should be a corporal). Transport should be one 3-ton lorry complete with double penthouse. No car is required. One extra vulcaniser should be provided with each M.D.U. The Beatrice stove should be replaced by a 4-burner primus stove.

---

*See Administration Volume II. Chapter 5. The Army Dental Service.

CHAPTER 6

A REVIEW OF THE HEALTH OF MIDDLE EAST FORCE. 1942–1943*

(i)

The Constitution, Environment and Activities of Middle East Force

IT IS DOUBTFUL if military history has previously shown, or will ever exhibit again, the complex that characterised Middle East Force during 1942 and 1943. Its soldiers came from three-quarters of the globe. There were men from the temperate climates of the United Kingdom, France, Belgium, Poland, Yugoslavia, Greece, Australia, New Zealand and South Africa. There were Africans from every part of the Continent—east, west, and the High Commission Territories of the south. There were Indians of all types, and men from such Indian Ocean islands as Mauritius, Ceylon and Seychelles. Finally there were the groups recruited locally—Palestinians, Maltese, Cypriots, Syrians, Arabs, Iraqis and Sudanese. The soldiers of all these races were compounded into a mighty army which numbered nearly a million men distributed among Eighth Army in the Western Desert of Egypt and Libya, Ninth Army in the Lebanon and Syria, and the garrisons and base installations of Cyprus, Malta, Palestine, Egypt, Aden, Sudan and Eritrea. Their campaigns were conducted among equally heterogeneous civilian communities, where colour, religion, customs and state of urban and rural development were infinitely varied. Arabs, Syrians, Lebanese, Negroes, Ethiopians, Europeans, Copts, Jews, Moslems and Christians were all represented. From these civilian communities came over a quarter of a million men to move the stores and to build the warehouses, workshops, roads, railways, docks, barracks, hospitals and fortresses demanded by Middle East Force.

The physical and climatic environment containing these armies and communities showed extremes. In the west, south, and east were the immense sandy and gravel deserts of the Sahara, Sinai and Arabia.

*As acknowledged in the Preface this chapter derives from the paper by Richmond, Colonel A. E. and Gear, Lt.-Col. H. S. *The Health of the Middle East Force*, 1942–43. *Journ. R.A.M.C.* Vol. 85. July 1945.

Here days and nights were hot and dry in summer, but in winter tolerable days too frequently were succeeded by bitterly cold nights. In the mountains of the Lebanon and Palestine, snow and sleet created arctic conditions in winter. The Delta of Egypt, the Nile Valley and the coastal plains of Palestine and Syria are green with vegetation and foliage. However, except for some patches in Palestine, Syria and Cyprus, forests are lacking in the Middle East scene. This geographical setting was immense. It covered half the Mediterranean, the eastern half including the islands of Malta and Cyprus. In it there were half-a-dozen States with their own national systems—Syria, Palestine, Egypt, Sudan, Eritrea and Libya. It possessed thousands of miles of water-ways in the Nile and its Delta, along which moved hundreds of barges and tugs carrying warlike stores. The common railway system, extending a thousand miles from Tobruk in the west, through Egypt, Palestine and Syria to link with the Turkish railways and so with Europe, owed its completion to army engineers from South Africa, Australia and New Zealand. A vast telephone system produced a clear voice in Cairo from Baghdad as easily as it did from Benghazi. The region possessed in Cairo, Alexandria, Beirut, Tel Aviv, Haifa, Jerusalem and Damascus, mighty oriental cities from which came manufactured products and other supplies, and to which soldiers streamed in thousands on leave.

The constitution of Middle East Force and its environment provide some of the background of the story of its health. A further important factor lay in its activities during 1942 and 1943. The spectacular rôle was played by Eighth Army in the Western Desert. This was in three stages—the static first stage when Eighth Army faced the enemy at Gazala, the second in the unhappy retreat in May and June 1942, back through Tobruk, Mersa Matruh to El Alamein, and then the final stage in the victorious advance from there to Tunisia, reached in March 1943, and culminating in the combined operation against Sicily. In the Sicilian Campaign Eighth Army remained a Middle East responsibility for administrative purposes until August 1943, after which it passed under the control of Allied Forces Headquarters in North Africa. Thereafter, only the unhappy incident of the Dodecanese Islands, when Leros, Cos and Lemnos changed hands twice, was to be classified as an operation. The shift of the war to Italy changed the nature of Middle East Force so that, at the end of 1943, its importance lay not in actual fighting but in guarding the vital communications through the Suez Canal, acting as an insurance for peace in the important group of countries in the Eastern Mediterranean, and in developing its workshops and warehouses to match the needs of armies elsewhere.

This aspect of the importance of Middle East Force has been naturally overshadowed by the desert campaigns, but should not be minimised. The force went a long way to becoming self-supporting. It obtained much of its food locally, it achieved miracles of manufacture and improvisation in meeting the immense demand for every conceivable article used by an army—mines, clothing, machinery, vehicles, weapons, hardware and medical apparatus. Its repair shops kept vast numbers of both ordinary and armed vehicles going, and guns and apparatus of all kinds ready for use. As well, therefore, as the special problems of war, Middle East Force had also to concern itself with many health and medical aspects of an industrial community.

THE HEALTH AND MEDICAL ORGANISATION

Following the usual system of decentralisation, Middle East Command had a number of local area and sub-area commands, apart from its operational forces of Eighth and Ninth Armies, etc. These subsidiary headquarters possessed senior medical officers administering the local medical functions. In each headquarters, a hygiene officer acted as a technical adviser in his field. Some of these local commands were immense, with correspondingly large and varied medical responsibilities. The most prominent operational command—Eighth Army—was completely self-contained in having a headquarters medical branch, and medical staffs at the headquarters of the corps and divisions. Field ambulances, field hygiene sections, casualty clearing stations, and such special units as hygiene, malaria and pathological laboratories, dental, blood transfusion, surgical and other special units were lavishly provided.

In the static or area commands, the most complex and largest was that responsible for Egypt. In its executive function of providing medical services it held large numbers of both general and special hospitals containing thousands of beds. Not only were these for local troops but were also the main hospital provision for Eighth Army and such other areas as Cyrenaica and Tripolitania. Other medical functions were involved in the care of convalescents in various depots, in the examination and regrading of thousands of men returned to depots or discharged from hospital, in the ordinary everyday medical treatment and examination of men in units and depots. The health organisation in M.E.C. consisted of a hygiene specialist at command headquarters and at each area and sub-area, a total of eight in all. Field hygiene sections under the area hygiene officers maintained a supervisory and advisory rôle over the troops, camps, barracks, factories, workshops, and depots, in their areas. The hygiene officers and field hygiene sections whose area contained large urban communities, such as Cairo, Alexandria, Port Said, etc., had, in addition, large responsibilities in supervising premises used by the troops on leave or for recreation—hostels, hotels, leave camps, cafés, etc.

All routine provision of medical supervision, care and treatment, and of the machinery to maintain the troops' health, to protect them from infectious disease and suitably clothe, feed and house them, was thus met by this system of decentralised medical authorities. All major problems of direction, policy and co-ordination were left for handling by the Medical Branch of G.H.Q.

These various medical staffs supervising, advising and directing, from G.H.Q. down through army, corps and divisional headquarters on the one hand, and command, area and sub-area headquarters on the other, ultimately depended for the successful execution of their duties on the various medical units and on the regimental medical officers. In the Middle East, as elsewhere, the unit medical officer watched over the health of the soldier, treated him when ill, sending him to hospital when his condition put him out of action, supervising his environment, his food, exercise, clothing, recreation and, in fact, all his activities. The unit medical officer had the help, in major problems, of hygiene personnel and of field malaria units. However, his success depended always on the willingness, interest and enthusiasm of the commanding officer who has the ultimate responsibility for the health of his troops, whether he be army, divisional, brigade or battalion commander.

HYGIENE TRAINING AND EDUCATION

The heterogeneous army of the Middle East included many disciplined self-reliant troops accustomed to hot climates and tropical diseases but, on the other hand, there were large groups who either entered it as local raw recruits or arrived from other countries and climes unprepared for the special hazards of the Desert and Delta and the Mediterranean littoral. Attitudes to the importance of disease and to the need for high standards of health and cleanliness consequently varied considerably. There were units with a high degree of discipline, actuated by the belief that their sick rate could be controlled, and others still accepting dirt, defect, disease and death fatalistically. A mixed problem of training, education and propaganda was thus presented. Many units and individuals were guided by the right principles but had not sufficient practice to safeguard themselves fully or to achieve the maximum of physical and mental well-being. Others were simply contemptuous of real soldiers bothering themselves with anything so childish or mundane as killing flies, avoiding mosquitoes or being particular as to the state of cleanliness of their camps, kitchens or their persons.

As far as possible, British principle and method were used, partly because the vast bulk of Middle East Force was of British origin, partly to secure the advantages of uniformity and partly because these were known by previous experience to be suited to the local problems. Conversion of the potential and actual leaders of the Army to the importance of hygiene led to special emphasis on its principles being given in courses for staff officers and in the programme of officer training units. Formal training was undertaken by one specially established institution—The Middle East School of Hygiene—and by hygiene officers and field hygiene sections in each force and area. The School of Hygiene accomplished an enormous programme.* There were formal courses of lectures and demonstrations held each month for groups of medical officers, regimental officers and non-commissioned officers, and rank and file. The subjects taught covered hygiene in all its aspects, field sanitation and water control. Drawn from Eighth and Ninth Armies and from each base and other area, nearly 200 individuals a month passed through these formal courses, to return to their units, it was hoped, as disciples of the gospel of hygiene. This was important work and enabled modern hygiene method and knowledge to be quickly disseminated throughout the Middle East. But over and above such set programmes the school was continually filled to capacity with groups gathered together informally. These were of all kinds. There were medical and hygiene officers newly arrived, others standing by for new appointments, combatant officers, sanitary and water duty personnel from local units and many others. The school also helped in the initiation of non-British formations into local hygiene methods. Cadres from Polish, Belgian and other Allied groups were trained for this purpose and these, in their turn, established hygiene training units in their own forces. The teaching was naturally severely practical but kept dynamic and up to date. This was achieved by the constant contact the school maintained with field problems and by a programme of research and investigation. Many outworn practices and principles were revealed and discarded and more rational methods substituted. For example, in the case of excremental disease, a major cause of wastage of man-power, methods of prevention were rigorously reviewed. As a result fly control was scientifically planned and proper methods taught, such as the destruction of breeding material in improvised incinerators and by the harmless disposal of human faeces in the famous incinerator petrol-tin latrine. This converted a previously difficult problem of latrines in the desert to a simple one. Fly traps were evolved which when placed away from cookhouses and mess-tents and baited with moist material did reduce fly populations and divert flies from contaminating food.

Considerable ingenuity was achieved in improvisation without which field units especially could scarcely have carried out their sanitary functions. The four-gallon petrol tin and the 44-gallon oil drum were

---

*See A.M.S. Administration, Vol. II, Chapter 2 in this series.

transformed into incinerators, grease traps, cookers, fly traps, disinfectors, shower baths, food containers, refuse receptacles and many other useful pieces of apparatus. The school played a major part in inventing, standardising, and popularising these useful devices. On a smaller and less formal scale, instruction in field sanitation was included in the programme of all field hygiene sections. For the purpose these units prepared demonstration grounds in which were shown full-scale models of all types of sanitary apparatus.

Full use was naturally made of all hygiene and medical officers in educating units in the importance of hygiene. Thus it was obligatory for these officers to give lectures on such subjects as malaria control and venereal disease prevention, and many others.

In the general distribution of knowledge, and in securing the adoption of uniform methods, all the usual channels were used by medical headquarters. Precise instructions and orders covering food, general sanitation, infectious disease control, such specific diseases as typhus, malaria, venereal diseases, etc., appeared at intervals both in the *Middle East Standing Orders for War* and in regular General Orders.

However, health achievement is so essentially dependent upon individual co-operation that modern methods of propaganda were adopted in educating the officers and the men in the principles of health and disease control. For this purpose use was made of the public press, pamphlets, leaflets, posters, etc. In the early stage of the campaign leaflets of a formal type were issued dealing with such subjects as fly control, typhus, malaria and venereal diseases. Later, fortunately, the publication called '*Army Illustrated Magazine*' ('A.I.M.') appeared. Its presentation of material followed lines suggested by psychologists. All army subjects were reviewed in it, such as armoured fighting vehicles, mountain warfare, combined operations, supply systems, etc. These were treated in a simple, bright, concise way and were profusely illustrated. This magazine was eagerly included in the machinery for Army health education. Articles, cartoons, quizzes, covering general health training, physical fitness, fly and mosquito control, and first aid, were published during 1943 and gained much popularity. Posters had only a limited success, due to the spate which flowed from all Army departments. The hoardings of the Middle East were covered with brightly coloured symbols of various aspects of national savings, salvage, careful driving, health protection, etc. This profusion made it impossible to catch the eye with any particular poster. However, several health designs covering typhus, flies, mosquitoes, camp cleanliness, were distributed. In their development much was learned from a study of the many excellent American hygiene posters. Hygiene education films were disappointingly poor. With the exception of the Walt Disney colour film on 'Mosquitoes and

Malaria', and the South African venereal diseases film 'Two Brothers', the films in the Middle East were dull and often out of date.

There was much competition, naturally, in the Army for the more useful but limited channel of education available in special C. in C's. orders or letters, leaflet inclusions in the soldier's pay-book, and in such popular Army papers as '*Parade*'. Health education managed to secure a fair share of these.

Letters were sent to senior Army commanders requesting their special support for anti-malarial and anti-V.D. measures. The conversion of senior Army and formation commanders to the importance to their operations of preventing disease and enhancing health had probably the best of all propaganda results. Several enthusiasts were enrolled among these exalted people—in certain cases their accretion to the cause being helped by visual demonstrations of the destructive power of disease, as for example by malaria in Sicily. Arresting facts which convinced many senior combatant officers of the importance of health in developing an effective army were the statistics of previous campaigns as well as those of the Middle East, demonstrating that loss of man-power caused by disease and defect exceeded by many times that due to battle weapons. This information was included therefore in several articles and circulars. One group which were perhaps not as successfully converted to preventive medicine and positive health as might have been possible were the medical officers themselves. An inertia in this class, or possibly a mental orientation inclined too much towards clinical practice, resulted in it not always being a very positive agent in dispersing health knowledge. Many medical officers were too easily satisfied with a prescription or an incision as the beginning and end of their functions.

MAN-MANAGEMENT—MORALE—WELFARE—REHABILITATION

It was not fully appreciated either by lay or medical opinion how comprehensive Army hygiene has become. Gone are the days when it was solely pre-occupied with infectious disease, sanitation and water supplies. It now accepts responsibility for studying all influences likely to enhance or undermine the vigour, fitness, well-being and efficiency of the soldier. In a phrase, man-management is now included in the province of modern military medical services. In this section, therefore, some of these factors as affecting the individual in the Middle East will be discussed, but others, such as food, deserving fuller treatment, will be treated later.

ACCLIMATISATION

The Middle East, as already mentioned, provides a variety of physical conditions. Nevertheless, its tropical features were the most prominent of the factors affecting the health of the troops during 1942 and 1943. However fit physically and mentally men may have been on leaving such home territories as the United Kingdom, they were not accepted as ready for immediate battle on arrival in the Middle East. Accordingly a period of acclimatisation was arranged, usually four to six weeks, in the Canal Area of Egypt, before formations were passed on to any active rôle. This allowed physiological and, frequently, though not by design, an immunological adaptation. On the first count, the body and mind became attuned to heat, glare, dust and the harsh environment of vast desert landscapes. Secondly, in spite of care, many newly arrived units suffered from enteritis, sandfly fever and sunburn. Occurring in the settled conditions of base camps, not much harm resulted. If, however, troops had suffered these disabilities in action, serious consequences to the strategy and tactics of the forces concerned might have followed. A 'salting' process occurring in base camps was, therefore, not altogether a disadvantage.

Though heat was the influence affecting most troops, many groups required care in winter. These were the large numbers from such tropical and semi-tropical environments as Central and West Africa, Southern India and Ceylon, the Islands of the Indian Ocean and the deserts of North Africa. It would have exposed such personnel to serious risks to have drafted them direct on arrival in winter to areas with almost Arctic conditions of rain, snow and cold, such as are found in the mountains and plains of the Lebanon and Syria, or even in some parts of Palestine. A medical classification was therefore given to the General Staff as to the regions in which these tropical troops could be employed. This took into account not only their tropical or semi-tropical origins but also whether such troops came from rural and primitive conditions or from sophisticated urbanised communities. That rural people take less kindly to changes of social circumstances and, if from the Tropics, are usually chronically infected with such diseases as malaria, hookworm and schistosomiasis, were factors not overlooked. The classification was roughly as follows:

(a) Indians from hilly provinces, Syrians and Lebanese could be employed in the same areas as European troops.

(b) Basutos, as they came from a plateau with a cold winter, after a winter of acclimatisation in the Middle East, could also be employed anywhere, but should always be kept under medical observation.

(c) Mauritians and Seychellois after winter acclimatisation could be utilised in any location.

(d) Africans from East Africa, the High Commission Territories, the Congo and West Africa, and Indians from the tropical areas should have careful acclimatisation in Egypt or the plains of Palestine before exposure to winter in Europe or in Syria. In addition, these troops were not to be used in areas with a prolonged winter of rain, snow and frost.

That this medical concern in acclimatisation was justified had proof in summer and winter incidents. The crisis of the retreat to El Alamein in the middle of the summer of 1942 brought reinforcements rushing to the Middle East. The S.S. *Queen Mary* arrived at Suez jammed with troops. Their disembarkation and move to transit camps took place in extremely hot trying conditions resulting in a large number of heat-stroke cases. Then in the winter of 1943 several Pioneer companies of West Africans were employed in wet winter conditions on port duties at Benghazi and Tobruk. There was a consequent high incidence of lobar pneumonia, but the exhibition of sulphonamides prevented fatalities. With the exception of these two minor incidents, the vast bulk of the force during 1942 and 1943 had an uneventful phase of acclimatisation. This adaptation, assisted by the measures to be described in the next two sections, gave protection in a high degree from the deleterious summer and winter physical effects.

HEAT AND LIGHT EFFECTS

Heat was most dangerous when troops were newly arrived in the Middle East. The journey up the Red Sea followed by a slow tedious disembarkation into landing barges and a journey of some distance to the camping areas strained new troops to breaking point on occasions, as in the case of the S.S. *Queen Mary* already referred to. Liners of the North Atlantic route were particularly unsuitable for use in the Tropics, and so aggravated the hot conditions of the Red Sea. That overcrowding of troopships, owing to the serious shipping state, could not be avoided, was recognised. However, to minimise heat effects, every endeavour was made to increase ventilation, to allow the full use of decks, to reduce physical exertion on the day of landing, to provide full drinking water supplies and to arrange for the early detection and treatment of symptoms of heat exhaustion, both on the ship and at the landing stage.

In so far as general service in the Middle East during 1942 and 1943 was concerned, no special heat problem arose. General instructions were issued to all units, giving, in simple language, the part played by high air temperature, high humidity and still air in causing a strain on the body-cooling mechanism. Attention was directed to the need for avoiding the sun as far as possible in very hot areas in the heat of the day and for wearing head-dress. Strenuous work was, during this period, to be reduced to essentials. Regular bathing and the wearing of loose open-necked clothing were recommended. Generous amounts of drinking water to which salt was added in the proportion of $\frac{1}{4}$ tea-spoonful to 1 pint of water were to be taken. Allowance was also made in the ration scale for the amount of salt per man per day to be raised in summer from $\frac{1}{2}$ to $\frac{3}{4}$ ounce in areas where heat was excessive. Anxiety as to heat exhaustion occurring in crews of armoured vehicles was not unnatural. Surprisingly enough this was not a major hazard. The absence of cases of heatstroke or heat exhaustion in tank crews from the summer battles of the Western Desert was practical proof of the experimental work done on the subject by 1 Medical Research Section. This had shown that, though katathermometer readings reached alarming heights inside a stationary tank in the open, the starting of the engine, thus operating the tank's ventilating system, drew sufficient air through the vehicle to maintain an adequate cooling action on the bodies of the crew. That armoured vehicles would not provide problems in other conditions, say, in jungle warfare, was not to be deduced from Middle East experience. It was the low relative humidity of the desert air which protected the body's cooling mechanism. Other problems of heat arose in workshops, factories and such installations as base laundries. During the heat waves (*khamseens*) of early summer, conditions were often almost intolerable, especially at night under 'blackout' restrictions. Only general measures of improving ventilation, providing ample drinking water, etc., could be applied in these instances. Air-conditioning would gladly have been used if the machinery had been available, but only one or two plants could be obtained. These were installed in such essential premises as the G.H.Q. telephone exchange, and the hospital at Massawa, probably the hottest station in the Middle East. The excessive sunlight, as judged by Western European standards, produced a demand for general issues of tinted spectacles. This was resisted on the principle that the average human eye is capable of an enormous range of adaptation and could meet most conditions of the Middle East. Naturally such units as A.A. with a special need to overcome direct glare were given tinted eye-shields. Sunlight almost certainly seemed a strong aetiological factor in the causation of desert sores.

CLOTHING

A soldier's clothing has many aspects which concern his health and protection from harmful agencies. The troops of the Middle East had summer and winter outfits. That of summer consisted initially of a drill open-necked shirt, shorts and slacks, while in winter the dress was the well-known battledress. Head-dress early in 1942 consisted of either the *topee* or forage cap. Various modifications were made during the two years. A steady medical campaign for the abolition of shorts had only a partial success, when late in 1943 the ratio of 2 pairs of shorts to 1 pair of slacks was reversed. The use of slacks was made obligatory only in operational areas. The medical case in favour of slacks and long-sleeved shirts only was based on the following arguments:

(i) The larger the skin area covered the greater the protection against insects including such vectors of disease as the anopheline mosquito and the sandfly.

(ii) Exposed skin showed a much higher incidence of the so-called desert sore—the vague heterogeneous group of skin ulcerations arising out of the combination of such agencies as slight skin injury, fly contact, dirt and sand impregnation, and sunlight.

(iii) Burns always affected exposed areas such as face, hands, forearms and knees most severely. Ordinary clothing was found, in tank fires, to afford a high degree of protection against flash burns.

(iv) If gas warfare developed, the more skin covered by clothing the better.

As the war progressed, sources of clothing changed and materials had to be examined before accepting new contracts. Thus the summer issue was changed to include bush shirts. Both the design and material of these, in early issues, were objectionable. The soldier disliked the untidy shapelessness of this garment and medically its loose thin texture was criticised, as it allowed mosquitoes to pierce through to the skin. Head-dress underwent changes too. The *topee*, except for small specially exposed groups in the hotter areas, was abandoned without any harmful sequelae.

EQUIPMENT

A large proportion of equipment used was of standardised British Army types. Modifications were required in but few instances to meet Middle East conditions. The chief medical interest was associated, therefore, in locally-made equipment. Local production eventually became an important Middle East function, and many matters were referred for technical medical advice and opinion. Water containers, which were the solution of the problem of supplying rapidly advancing troops in the desert, were obtained by the use of 2-gallon and 4-gallon petrol tins and initially also of the captured 2-gallon 'jerricans'. In the case of the petrol tins, confirmation had to be obtained of their freedom from soluble lead. Later when petrol came to be transported in terne-plate, i.e. lead plated sheets, containers, special attention was drawn to the dangers of using these for storing food or water or of converting them into cooking utensils. Local equipment such as food plates, cutlery, hair and shaving brushes, blankets, tentage, camp furniture, required medical opinion as to its suitability or influence on the health and welfare of the troops. Wherever possible, trials of new or modified equipment were made. In this way useful information was collected on the design of helmets, web equipment, and anti-mosquito clothing.

MORALE AND WELFARE

In the Army in this war, 'Hygiene' accepted a watching brief over the morale and welfare of the troops. It is an extremely large and important subject deserving a report to itself, but here only its salient features and certain illustrative examples can be given from Middle East experience. Fundamental to morale and welfare are freedom from disease, good varied food, satisfactory clothing and housing. These general aspects are described in separate sections of this account. However, over and above this minimum, much was done with the special object of enhancing morale. In the sphere of amenities, hygiene authorities added their support to the demand for sport and recreation for the troops. Swimming was encouraged. Many units had the benefit of proximity to the Mediterranean. For others inland baths were constructed. Chlorination of these was undertaken under the supervision of local hygiene personnel. Sports grounds were developed as quickly as possible. Football had the widest appeal, being played by Europeans, Africans and Asiatics. Apart from amenities provided by voluntary agencies, canteens, rest huts, etc., were an official feature appearing early in all permanent or semi-permanent camps. Many of these competed in originality of layout, brightness of decoration, and in comfort and cosiness with any peace-time restaurant or 'local'. In order to maintain scrupulous cleanliness of kitchens, dining halls, ablutions, etc., all such institutions received regular scrutiny from local hygiene officers. In the leave camps that were established in Tripolitania, Egypt, Palestine and Syria, every care, too, was taken to enable the residents to escape from the Army atmosphere. Apart from such physical provision, facilities for mental relaxation were developed as time went on. There were mobile cinemas, libraries and concert parties, which, reaching forward areas and remote isolated detachments, were a direct fillip to morale.

In the normal course of their duties, hygiene officers took note of any such factors as delay in receiving home mail, lack of equipment, food, cooking apparatus, etc. Such defects were then brought to the notice of the appropriate authorities.

REHABILITATION AND OPTIMUM USE OF MAN-POWER

Where every man-hour was important, the responsibility of the Army hygiene authorities did not stop at keeping personnel fit and free from disease. It extended its functions to reducing to a minimum the period after hospital discharge before a soldier returned to duty and, secondly, to placing every man, especially those not fully fit, in the most productive employment. In regard to the first aspect all long-term patients from hospitals went to convalescent depots. These institutions were not places where a soldier followed an aimless, lazy life for a few days or weeks. Each patient was guided into a carefully planned existence of feeding, occupation, exercise and, in a few instances, special medical treatment, designed to restore his health, vigour, and function as rapidly as possible. The Middle East was fortunately possessed of several excellent convalescent depots caring for various categories of troops. Situated mostly in excellent seaside spots, an ideal environment was provided. Each had the advice, too, of a specialist in physical medicine and a team of physical instructors and masseurs to carry out remedial exercise, restoration of muscular and joint function, hardening of physique, etc. The physical hardening process continued when the ex-patient, leaving the convalescent depot, passed to his base depot awaiting return to an active useful life. The senior medical officers of these depots, advised by the staff of physical medicine experts and psychologists, ensured that each soldier was brought to the highest pitch of fitness, and received any final medical treatment or such apparatus as dentures, glasses, special boots. In addition, any soldier examined here by a medical board and classified as lower than A.1 came under the system distributing personnel into categories of employment most suited to their particular standards of fitness.

The Army possesses a comprehensive system for the continual check-ing of fitness of all those classified, at some time or another, because of eye, foot, muscular, dental or general medical condition, as temporarily below par. In the Middle East all men in medical categories B and lower were reviewed regularly. Thus it was possible to comb out fit men from base and L. of C. jobs for meeting the insatiable demand of operational units. Medical advice was necessary also in using the regrettably large group of personnel with permanent physical or mental inadequacies. The medical categorisation adopted for the British Army as a whole required certain sub-classifications to meet Middle East conditions. Thus a class of so-called 'restricted posting' was intro-duced, composed of individuals whose defects necessitated their use in limited kinds of work only. Specialists and boards handling these cases indicated in their findings the work or employment considered suitable. The personnel authorities then made postings accordingly.

WATER SUPPLIES

The excellence of the supplies developed and maintained by the Engineers in base and L. of C. areas, and the adequacy of equipment for purifying and transporting water to troops during the various moves in the Libyan and Tripolitanian desert, relieved considerably the anxiety of the medical authorities in connexion with water.

In Egypt, a most comprehensive system was quickly extended along the vast camps up and down the Suez Canal, and along the desert area to the north of the Sweet Water Canal. The other noteworthy engineering feat was the coastal military supply, by which water was carried across miles of desert from Alexandria for Eighth Army in its various phases of advance and retreat during 1942 and 1943. This vast system was a monument to the energy and capacity of the Engineers. At suitable points along the Sweet Water Canal water filtration and purification units were erected. Into these, water from the Canal was pumped. Passing through rapid sand filters after alum treatment, sediment and gross impurities were removed. Chloronomes then discharged chlorine into the emerging flow sufficient to raise the free concentration of the gas to 0·2 part per million. An extensive reticulation system with various booster pumps and holding reservoirs conveyed the water over the enormous area of the Army camps in the region of the canals. In Cairo, water was obtained from the civilian supply. Thus for base units in Egypt, medical supervision was reduced to a minimum. Throughout the two years no breakdown in this system occurred, and so literally hundreds of thousands of men received drinking, cooking and ablutionary supplies in a satisfactory manner.

Eighth Army supplies called for more medical concern. As the distance westward into the desert from Alexandria increased, so sweet water in adequate quantities became more difficult to provide. The pipe-line was pushed after the advancing elements as rapidly as possible on both occasions that the enemy was pressed back into Libya. In spite of the size of this system the quantity of water could not be raised above approximately one and a half gallons per man per day. To relieve the pipe-line therefore, and to seek additional means for increasing the supply, every local well and other source was investigated and, if at all acceptable, exploited to the maximum. Ancient Roman subterranean aqueducts at places like Mersa Matruh and other coastal sites were opened and made to contribute. For these isolated supplies from wells and aqueducts much hygiene supervision was demanded. Initially the purity, salinity and other factors were assessed, and means of purification defined. These almost invariably were superchlorination using Army water sterilising powder (bleaching powder) followed by detasting with sodium thiosulphate. At many sources units had to rely on their own treatment of water. Here a hygiene assistant gave instructions as to the proportion of the sterilising powder to be added. This practice was inefficient in that the addition of the sterilising agent to small variable collections of water was difficult to regulate. On seeking a solution to this problem the Middle East School of Hygiene evolved a chlorine dosing tap which will be mentioned later.

There were two annoying aspects of the water problem in Eighth Army which concerned hygiene officers. The first was the excessive salinity of desert wells. Many such supplies gave readings of over 200 parts per 100,000. It was surprising, therefore, that many tolerated water with up to 250 parts for even weeks without untoward effects. However, excessive salinity was reduced wherever possible by mixing such waters with sweeter supplies from other wells or with water transported from the pipe-line. The second problem was that of water sources damaged by the retreating enemy. Apart from physical destruction of wells and their equipment, the enemy polluted them with human and animal bodies, dieseline oil, kerosene and filth of all descriptions. In addition to the clearance of gross materials these supplies were rendered fit by continuous pumping and sterilisation with excess of bleaching powder. No instance of deliberate specific poisoning by the enemy using arsenic or other agents was discovered in the desert campaigns.

The mobility of certain of the phases of modern warfare evoked a miscellany of water apparatus for use in the field. From the simple water-cart there evolved a series of mobile water purification plants. Units such as battalions were self-contained when possessed of the standard Army water-truck. Equipped with the modern metal filters of the Stellar or Meta type such trucks were capable of supplying up to 200 gallons at a filling. Each truck was supplied with a testing box and the necessary chemicals of kieselguhr, water sterilising powder and taste remover tablets. A dangerous tendency of units when at the base, and therefore drawing on command supplies, was to allow the maintenance of their water-trucks and the training of personnel in the use of such apparatus to lapse. Early in 1942, inspections showed that many units, if suddenly thrown into action, and therefore possibly on to their own resources for securing water, would have been seriously handicapped through their water-trucks being out of working order and with no one trained to deal with water apparatus. This unhappy discovery led to all water apparatus being brought into good repair and a direction to all medical officers to discharge their responsibility of having their units prepared with efficient apparatus and trained personnel. Another item of water apparatus which was available, but in this particular theatre not much used, was a portable filtering apparatus consisting of a standard metal filter and hand-pump mounted on a tripod. A few of these units were carried by Eighth Army and were available for supplying small detachments as they could deliver water at the rate of 100 gallons per hour. For the mass handling of water supply in the field the Engineers fortunately possessed several large units capable of handling quantities of water up to 3,000 gallons per hour. One such type was mounted as a trailer but others were self-contained mobile units. In these large-scale water purifiers filtration was done through a series of metal filters in the usual way but purification depended not on chlorination but on chloramination.

In discussing the difficulties of dealing with small quantities of water at isolated water points, it was mentioned that the M.E. School of Hygiene had evolved a simple method of regulating chlorination. This consisted of an ebonite dosing tap attached to a suitable receptacle at the water point. In this receptacle was placed water sterilising fluid made up to the necessary concentration. By turning the water tap an exact quantity of water sterilising fluid was trapped in the tap and then discharged into the water container to be treated. Depending on the size of the water container one or more turns of the ebonite tap were made to provide sufficient water sterilising fluid to purify the contents.

One further aspect of water apparatus requires mention. This refers to the colossal scale on which water containers improvised from petrol cans, 'Jerricans' and 'Ammericans', were used to carry water forward during the advances of Eighth Army in the Western Desert. As petrol containers were the source of the majority it was necessary for the medical authorities to ensure that no harmful contamination would arise by carrying water in them. It was known that one type of these containers was made from terne-plate. Also the majority of containers had been used to transport petrol of a high octane. Various experiments were therefore carried out to determine whether water in such containers would take up lead in dangerous quantities. The terne-plate containers were rejected *in toto* for, being lead covered, they gave off dangerous quantities of lead in solution. The other containers, however, unless badly soldered, were accepted for water purposes, provided they had been thoroughly washed out so as to remove all traces of high octane petrol. Bituminising the interiors was later adopted. It was fortunate that at no time was there any anxiety about stocks of chemicals required for the various water supplies. Chlorine gas, water sterilising powder, alum, kieselguhr and de-tasting tablets were always available in quantity. In addition, large stocks were held of 'halazone' tablets for use by any formation having to depend on its water-bottles for collection and purification. On behalf of the War Office M.E.C. carried out several series of tests of the new halazone tablet and confirmed that it retained its strength of liberating up to 8 parts per million of available chlorine after storage for two to three months in the M.E.

That the water supply to the forces using the above methods was not harmful is demonstrated by the fact that no outbreak of water-borne disease occurred. However, on one occasion, the Army was concerned in protecting itself against water-borne enteric in Malta in May, June and July, 1943. This was an extremely interesting example of water-borne disease. Enemy bombing had fractured a water main, a fact, however, which was not known at the time. No harm resulted, until some months later when, in the process of clearing an aerodrome, a 'bulldozer' broke a sewer alongside the previously damaged water main. This allowed crude sewage to enter one of the principal water mains supplying certain villages and a section of Valletta. From this combination of accidents there resulted an exceedingly severe civilian outbreak of typhoid with several hundreds of cases. With the exception of a few cases among Maltese soldiers the Army escaped. This remarkable fact is attributed not only to the protection given by T.A.B. vaccine but also to the arrangements made, immediately the contamination of the supply was known, to purify at distribution the water used by the Army. This, with direct control and discipline, was more easily and expeditiously done in the Army than in the civilian population.

FOOD SUPPLIES

GENERAL POLICY

To achieve proper feeding of an army is one of the most complex problems perplexing military administrators. The basic difficulties were increased many times in the case of Middle East Force, especially in the years 1942 and 1943. All those factors of race, climate, religion, etc., already mentioned, influenced the subject of food. But there were others. As shipping became the crucial consideration in the general war economy in 1942, the method of stocking the Middle East larder had to be reviewed. Then, in addition, the Japanese successes in capturing Malaya and the Dutch East Indies, and their direct threat to India and Australia, shook the whole supply system of the Middle East. Not only had imported supplies in general to be reduced drastically, but India and Australia in the dark early months of 1942 had to be discounted to a large extent as a continuing source of such important supplies as rice, flour, meat, oil and canned goods.

Though it was the policy of Middle East Command from the outset to become as self-supporting as possible, the events of 1942 lent extreme urgency to the process. The quantities of flour, frozen meat, oatmeal, rice and the large range of canned goods, which the Army previously had obtained from overseas, had to be replaced by local products. This was not easy, for the whole Middle East agricultural and industrial production, already taxed by civilian demands, was also denied access to normal peacetime supplies. It was necessary, therefore, as a first step, to expand existing and create new local sources. This in turn called for more agricultural seed and machinery, industrial plant, and such items as tin-plate, nearly all of which had to come from overseas. However, through the stimulus and co-ordination provided by the Middle East Supply Centre under the Minister of State, Mr. Casey, this immense and complicated task was accomplished. Thus, with but little friction or dislocation, the Army adapted itself to a new system of food supplies, where imported products of meat, oil, cereals and canned goods were replaced with similar or allied products coaxed out of expanding or new local ventures. Though much manipulation of types of foodstuffs was demanded, and a slight reduction in quantities was unavoidable, the soldier did not go hungry, nor did his health in any way suffer.

The complexity of Army food problems led to the creation of the Middle East Ration Committee. Consisting of representatives from the Supply, Catering and Financial Services, it handled the continuous stream of questions on ration scales, food preparation methods, substitution of imported items by local products, seasonal changes of supply, etc. Charged with adapting the Army feeding to the change in sources of supply following strategical developments all over the world, the Ration Committee bore the heavy responsibility of reducing ration scales and introducing new and frequently untried local foods to replace those unobtainable from overseas. With the constant change in the composition and function of the Middle East forces, the fluctuation in the fortunes of its campaigns, the varying supply situation and the shifting scene of operations from the desert to Sicily and the Mediterranean Islands, the work of the committee never reached finality. The measure of its success is not to be found solely in the health and vigour of the troops, but also in the fact that the soldier himself, with negligible exceptions, did not complain.

SOME MEDICAL FACTORS REGARDING FOOD

That the modern army administrator grasps the importance of the medical aspects of feeding troops was amply shown in the Middle East. In the creation of the various ration scales fundamental to the whole system and organisation of obtaining, distributing and consuming food, the medical opinion was supreme. If a certain type or a fixed quantity of food was requested by the medical representatives, these demands were met. Only complete impossibility of getting any item was advanced by the supply authorities for not adopting any given medical recommendation.

In the construction of ration scales, an early difficulty lay in the lack of authoritative calorie, vitamin and salt values for the majority of foods. In 1943, a useful work was therefore performed by the War Office nutrition advisers in issuing a comprehensive table of generally accepted values for all the commoner food items. It became possible then to determine the value of the scales with considerably more confidence. These scales in number and variety are scarcely credible. During 1942 and 1943, over thirty-five scales were in use. They, as will have been deduced from the remarks above on the changing supply situation, rarely remained fixed for long. Ceaseless labour was therefore entailed in checking their calorie and vitamin values, quite apart from the stupendous task the fluctuation of such a large number of scales imposed on the supply services. It is only possible to give here some of the salient features of the medical aspects of the Army feeding in the two years. The scale which was used by the majority of troops, and which it was the policy of the Ration Committee to apply to as many categories as possible, was the Middle East Field Service Ration Scale. Originally, it had a value of 4,000 Calories per man per day, but the 'tightening of the belt', referred to above, brought it down to 3,700 for a short time in 1942. Nevertheless, it was soon increased to an approximate value of 3,800 in 1943. Its vitamin value when fresh items were supplied was, on a conservative basis:

Vitamin A . . .	4,000 i.u.
Vitamin B_1 . . .	550 i.u.
Vitamin B_2 . . .	1·5 mg.
Nicotinic acid . .	24 mg.
Ascorbic acid . .	75 mg.

Occasionally, on active operations or in areas where fresh supplies were difficult to get, certain so-called dry equivalents were issued. These were biscuits in lieu of bread, pressed meat, tinned fruit, tinned milk and tinned vegetables. Under such conditions, accessory quantities of vitamins were supplied. At first these took the form of marmite or yeast tablets and ascorbic acid tablets, but later a compound vitamin tablet containing:

Vitamin B_1	400 i.u.
Vitamin B_2	1 mg.
Nicotinic acid . . .	10 mg.
Ascorbic acid . . .	25 mg.

was available in large quantities. In the scale, proteins were provided in the form mainly of meat, bacon, fish, eggs, cheese and milk. Fat was not made prominent as local conditions obviously did not favour a high fatty diet. The chief fat item was margarine, but cooking oil was also provided. Bread, flour, oatmeal, potatoes and pulses were the main sources of carbohydrates. It was the austerity policy of 1942 and 1943 which reduced the quantity of frozen meat (imported from Australia), potatoes, oatmeal, rice and tinned food. Compensation was obtained by increasing bread, local fresh meat and cooking oil, as well as introducing ground nuts into the scale. The field service scale was gradually adopted by the majority of groups, including the U.K., Dominion, Free French, Maltese, Mauritian, Cypriot, Greek, Polish and Yugoslav troops. Contrary to expectation, little difficulty was experienced by these troops in changing over to a scale basically designed for the taste of British troops. However, there were many other groups whose religious or racial dietetic customs could not be ignored. Indians were provided with a scale including *atta* as its bulk item, and such items as *dhalls*, *ghi* and Indian condiments. Africans from the High Commission Territories of South Africa and from East and West Africa were eventually placed on a single African scale allowing for the special desire for the bulkiness of mealie meal and bread. Ground nuts were a useful item in these scales in giving high calorie and vitamin B values. Sudanese, Libyans and Arabs were given a scale with a high content of local bread and cooking oil.

Incompatibilities were involved in producing the various so-called 'battle assault' and special operational ration scales. Raiding and reconnaissance parties in the desert had to travel light and could not get water; assault troops in the opening stages of battle had to be self-contained for several days until the normal supply lines could be established; parachute troops could not expect supplies to get through to them for several days; and finally, tank crews in battle could not always depend on getting back to supply areas. These special ration scales created conflicting requirements. The need for mobility, freedom for fighting, the least bulk and weight in transport, for non-perishable readily-prepared foods on the one hand, clashed with providing high calorific, palatable, sustaining and refreshing meals. Modern food developments eased considerably the problem of constructing ration scales which had high calorie value, small weight and bulk, were non-perishable, and needed little or no cooking. Nevertheless, field experience corrected the view that troops will subsist for any length of time on a purely concentrated artificial 'tablet' diet. In time, various operational scales were evolved. The battle ration used, for example, by Eighth Army in its attack at El Alamein had a calorie value of 3,100 and, besides the basic items of biscuits and pressed meat, included cheese, jam, tinned milk, vegetables and fish, and the ingredients for tea. The extremely efficient follow-up of supplies behind the advance, however, saved the troops from any long spells on the battle ration. The limit of ten days laid down was never exceeded. Another scale of the type which met rather peculiar conditions was that used by the commandos. In it, sugar, ground nuts, cheese, dried fruit, raisins, chocolate and tinned fish were very acceptable items, and proved satisfactory in many raids. In the Sicilian campaign occurred the first opportunity of trying out the pack type of ration. A composite 14-man pack ration had been prepared by the War Office to meet the needs of 14 men for one day, or 1 man for fourteen days. It contained a variety of items, all canned, which gave an energy value of 3,000 Calories per man per day. There were dishes of sausage, steak and kidney puddings, meat and vegetables, fish and cheese. Experience in the Middle East of these various operational rations showed the value of such items as dried fruits, ground nuts, boiled sweets, chocolate and tinned fish. These items are palatable for troops living strenuous, exciting lives for a few days, they are of high calorie value, and easily carried. No cooking is required. Ingredients for a hot drink, tea in the case of British troops, should always be included in scales such as these.

In all routine scales special care was taken to ensure adequate vitamin values. Wherever possible, this was done through the inclusion of sufficient quantities of 'protective foods'—meat, milk, fruit and vegetables. The vitamin A content was maintained by using fortified margarine, cheese, milk, and fixing a minimum quantity of fresh or dried carrots and of first class green types in the vegetable issue. Dried apricots were also specified in the dried-fruit issue. Red palm oil, which could only be got in small quantities, was added to African and prisoners-of-war scales as an invaluable means of enhancing vitamin A values. The vitamin B series were the most difficult to provide. For this purpose, a proportion of either wholemeal flour or imported fortified B_1 Canadian flour in the Middle East flour mixture was fixed. Oatmeal, meat, milk, pulses and potatoes were depended upon, too, as sources of the B series. The ground nut was a very welcome Middle East dietetic item as it had not inconsiderable quantities of vitamin B_1, riboflavin and nicotinic acid. The local market was accordingly exploited to its limit and ground nuts added to most scales. Vitamin C did not create any difficulties. Usually, fresh fruit and vegetables were available. The supply authorities, co-operating fully, enabled local contracts to be drawn up so that fresh vegetables of high vitamin A and C content were always selected in preference to such types as marrows, squashes, etc.

Both to add variety to the rations and to balance their vitamin content, such locally available items as eggs, fresh and smoked fish, kidney and liver were used wherever possible. When ordinary methods of supplying vitamins failed, the combined vitamin tablet mentioned above was a stand-by to ensure the adequacy of rations. Fortunately in the Middle East there was rarely any difficulty in maintaining satisfactory fresh supplies.

Experience of supervising the nutrition of an army revealed that having a properly balanced ration scale with sufficient protein, carbohydrate, fat, mineral salts and vitamins is but half the story. In the Middle East, medical supervision was as much concerned in other aspects of nutrition as in calculating calorie and vitamin values. These included defining conditions for the preservation of the value of fresh items, and for cooking and preparing food to protect its nutritional and hygienic qualities.

To get the Army to safeguard foodstuffs in transport from depots to units and to cook properly was a very thorny problem indeed. Fresh supplies suffer rapid deterioration in the field, intensified in the conditions of heat, dust and flies typical of a Middle East summer. A gigantic civilian army, too, can scarcely be supplied in a few months with sufficient trained conscientious cooks—cooks, too, who have to prepare food with few of the devices and apparatus available in an ordinary peace-time modern kitchen.

These various problems were tackled vigorously and not without success through the co-operation of the supply, medical and catering authorities. The supply authorities for their part built up a system of clean, efficient depots, refrigerator vehicles and stores, mobile bakeries and butcheries, which brought food in a clean, fresh, wholesome condition right up to the doorstep of field units. Units, by education, example and occasionally coercion, were brought to a high standard in methods of collecting food from depots, transporting it forward and storing it in unit areas. Improvised food containers to carry and store fresh meat, vegetables, cereals, etc., were soon in the possession of most. Kitchens and food preparation quarters were eventually accorded proper hygiene respect and rigorous standards of cleanliness and orderliness applied.

In demonstrating the importance of the kitchen and the cooks in the economy of the Army, immense help was received from the Army Catering Corps. Its schools of cookery and its system of local catering advisers and inspectors produced in a very brief time a long-needed improvement in the type of man selected as cook, in his training and in his work. The Corps undertook, too, continual experiments and research with excellent results in the way of making field kitchens, ovens and other apparatus, and in methods of dealing with such items as rice, 'bully', ground nuts, etc., so as to make them palatable to troops previously unaccustomed to these foods. In all its methods, the Corps gave full emphasis to medical recommendations for the preservation of vitamins in the storage and preparation of food supplies and to cleanliness in handling food.

The feeding of patients in hospital had many exasperating features. The wide dispersal of wards, frequently over sandy desert country, made the transport of food from central kitchens a major problem. No completely suitable hot trolley or container could be devised. The hospital kitchens, as all others, had to depend on oil as a heating medium. Lack of engineering supplies and personnel and the complicated control of oil burners left a largely unsolved problem of dealing with soot in these large-scale kitchens. However, by the end of 1943, the high place of cooks and kitchens in helping the Army to be fit and vigorous had been secured, and the handling of food at all stages from the depot to the mouths of the soldiers was efficient and cleanly. Food waste was so reduced that even an oriental swill collector found little to extract from disposal receptacles.

The peculiar food problems of A.F.V. crews operating in the Desert demanded special attention.*

'The construction and supply of a ration scale is only part of the procedure of feeding an army. As the Middle East campaigns have shown, however satisfactorily a well-balanced and adequate ration emerges from Details Issue Depots, much can happen to destroy its value before consumption by the troops. Apart from the time taken to train cooks in a large civilian army, the dispersal of units resulted in the disappearance of organised company cooking in the field. There grew up the practice of each small group, usually each vehicle crew, fending for its meals. Such vehicle or section cooking is very unsatisfactory. Well-cooked complete meals, at regular intervals, are replaced by casual feeding out of a tin. This results in waste of rations, and the débris from cooking and feeding is scattered far and wide over camping areas. A corollary to this problem arose in the case of A.F.Vs. Fighting all day, leaguered in strict blackout conditions at night, too tired to look after themselves, the crews of tanks and armoured cars were too often unable to get more than an occasional bite of a biscuit. To counter these unsatisfactory methods company cooking was reintroduced, and, except in actual highly mobile phases, most units used it during operations. For armoured units, a mobile cooking lorry was evolved by fitting a No. 2 petrol cooker and food-containers to a three-ton lorry. This simple improvised vehicle carried hot meals forward to the fighting crews and, in general, proved most valuable during the El Alamein operations.

'A further special ration problem which received some attention prior to the operations was the provision of a pack ration for A.F.Vs. Tanks and armoured cars have to face occasional periods of isolation. They must be self-contained to meet such emergencies, and the provision of food, including liquids, led to the trial of the packs produced in the United Kingdom of two-men and three-men one-day rations and, on a smaller scale, of an American pack ration. In addition, most A.F.Vs. were supplied with special half-gallon vacuum-flasks for hot drinks. This was a valuable measure. However, experience under desert conditions suggests that pack rations have a limited value for A.F.Vs.'

DISEASES ASSOCIATED WITH FOOD

Food deficiency diseases were rarely encountered. This was a mark of the success achieved in constructing balanced ration scales and in getting food supplies properly distributed and prepared for the forces scattered throughout the Middle East. The only group in which avitaminosis occurred was that of Libyan prisoners-of-war. Through certain circumstances, outside local control, their ration scale had to

---

* See 'Hygiene Aspects of the El Alamein Victory' by Lt. Col. H. S. Gear, *B.M.J.*, 18.3.44, page 384.

be changed. A theoretical sufficiency of riboflavin was allowed in the diet but, in practice, owing to a mixture of factors, including the racial method of food preparation, a deficiency apparently occurred. This resulted in widespread minor manifestations of ariboflavinosis, especially in the form of stomatitis and glossitis. The careful medical supervision continuously maintained soon detected the incipient condition. Treatment with milk and yeast produced early cure. Except for quite abnormal isolated instances, scurvy, pellagra and beriberi did not occur anywhere in the Middle East forces. As the present day medical practitioner is conscious almost to a fault of the possibility of food deficiency, it can be accepted that any cases in the Middle East would have been detected. Several surveys by heads of hospital medical divisions and by the Consulting Physician also failed to discover any food-deficiency disease. On the contrary, the men of the Middle East Forces were amazingly fit. They filled out, put on weight, showed bronzed glowing skins and indeed exhibited all the signs of well-nourished healthy beings.

Food poisoning inevitably made some appearances. Typically, the cause in most cases could only be surmised on circumstantial evidence. In most cases, the evidence led back to rehashed food kept overnight. The comprehensive system of food inspection in depots and in the field served as an efficient screen against damaged food getting into kitchens. Intrinsically sound though the Army food was proved to be, it was nevertheless, in spite of all precautions, on occasions a vehicle of intestinal disease, e.g. dysentery, enteritis and, to a smaller degree, typhoid. As will be elaborated in a later section, food, water and fly-borne disease were major causes of sickness. Yet in the Middle East campaigns, owing both to general sanitary improvement, and to the better protection of food, these diseases took much less toll than in previous wars.

CARE OF PHYSICAL ENVIRONMENT

In the section on man-management, the efforts to provide physiological adaptation of the soldier to his new environment were broadly described. Some of the attempts to modify and control some at least of the components of this oriental and sub-tropical setting are dealt with under this heading.

SITING OF MILITARY COMMUNITIES

The three insects, fly, mosquito, and sandfly, had much to do with the placing of military communities, whether in camp, barrack or workshop. In having the large base, transit and L. of C. camps situated, for example, in desert areas such as Quassasin, Tahag and Amiriya in Egypt, and in country districts in other territories, the main uncontrollable sources of fly breeding, viz. native villages and towns, were largely avoided. However, the segregation of military populations as far as possible had other objects. It reduced contact with vendors of doubtful food and drink, and with such infections as typhus, smallpox, plague and venereal disease. These diseases in the military in the Middle East had a close interconnexion with civil urban communities, e.g. plague in Suez and Port Said, typhus and smallpox in Cairo, Alexandria and the Canal ports.

To revert to the influence of insects, the major rôle played by the anopheline mosquito was not unexpected. As an initial guide to the staff, the whole Middle East was surveyed by the various malaria field laboratories. This showed areas broadly classified as highly malarious, malarious, and non-malarious. Wherever possible, military installations were naturally limited to the non-malarious regions. If for some strategic or operational need this could not be so, local malaria surveys secured the best site within the selected area and indicated the measures required to reduce the risk of infection. Amazing though it may be, the inclusion of medical representatives in discussions on such fundamental hygiene problems as camp siting was by no means accepted as automatic by Army staffs in the early months. However, steady propaganda eventually achieved this essential measure. One of the mental fixations that had to be removed was that the hazards of an area were static. Thus, staff officers were inclined to think if they were supplied with a map showing areas classified broadly as highly malarious, malarious, and non-malarious, that these constituted a permanent fixed guide for all time in the future. They only slowly came to realise the peculiar local features of malaria, for example, and its characteristic fluctuations due to season, weather conditions, etc.

The sandfly produced some serious geographical problems. 'Unsalted' groups suffered exceedingly when quartered in sandfly areas. Such an important institution as the officers' training unit, conducting intensive short term courses, was at one time almost crippled by sandfly fever. Its transfer to a new site was seriously considered, but vigorous local control measures fortunately were sufficiently successful to avoid this. The coastal plains of Palestine and Syria, in addition to the areas around Cairo, had the most unenviable reputation in producing sandfly fever outbreaks.

Especially difficult problems in placing troop sites developed with the withdrawal of Eighth Army to El Alamein in June and July 1942. Forces were hastily gathered together for the defence of the Nile Delta, Alexandria and Cairo. There was no avoidance for them of the populated irrigated regions. They were subject consequently to the hygiene hazards already mentioned—flies, mosquitoes and too close contiguity to native communities. In addition the canals were dangerous because of schistosomiasis and general excremental pollution. Urgent

orders and vigorous hygiene supervision were arranged to bring home
to these troops the hazards of the Delta environment.

SANITARY SERVICES

Having obtained as clean and as disease-free areas as possible,
emphasis had then to be placed on their maintenance. This led to
standards of camp and barrack cleanliness being made very strict and
to efficient services of disposal for waste products being provided. By
a combination of propaganda and discipline, camp and barrack cleanliness came, in time, to be excellent. This was no mean accomplish-
ment, as the average urban-bred civilian soldier is by nature extremely
careless of his physical environment. He has become accustomed to
having litter, waste paper and night soil disappear effectively without
any effort on his part. He has to have habits instilled in him so that,
first, he himself does not add to the litter and filth of his environment
and, second, personally feels a responsibility for cleaning it, even if
someone else has made the mess.

In the Middle East, sanitation was ever an important part of hygiene
work and, in keeping with British Army practice, much ingenuity went
in improvising apparatus and structures for burning refuse, treating
waste waters and rendering human excreta innocuous. The general
methods employed were those described in the current textbooks of
field sanitation.

BATHING FACILITIES

As personal cleanliness is an important routine in promoting general
bodily health, as well as in preventing skin diseases, persistent pressure
was applied by the medical authorities in seeking adequate bathing
facilities in all areas. In base and L. of C. areas the matter was relatively
simple. Here standard bath-houses supplying hot and cold showers
were erected. The forward units, especially in the deserts, had too
frequently no chance of general baths. Near the coast the sea was
enjoyed by all and its usefulness increased by the issue of sea-soap.
Much experiment and trial produced several improvised bath sets
approaching the ideal, viz. light, easily transported and erected, sturdy
and using little water. These were also an advantage in temporary
camps and for such special tasks as dealing with refugees infested with
lice. A large scale improvised bathing centre, formed from several of
these special portable sets, overcame the difficulty of cleaning and
disinfesting the scores of thousands of Italian and German prisoners
taken in the El Alamein advance.

REFUSE DISPOSAL

Middle East experience amply confirmed the advantage of incineration of garbage, refuse, etc. Mere burying is rarely done sufficiently

well to prevent fly breeding. However, in forward areas, incineration on occasions could not be employed because of attracting enemy attention. In operation areas the general problem of waste disposal was much intensified by the enforced dispersal of men and vehicles. Early on, this had produced so-called vehicle cooking. Each group of men in a vehicle, troop-carrying lorry, armoured-car, gun or tank, being isolated from their fellows, came to fend for its own food. Apart from its evils of improperly prepared meals, dispersed vehicle camping also scattered refuse and waste products in an uncontrolled fashion over all camping areas in the desert. A policy was defined therefore in 1942 to return to company cooking, arguments securing this being both those in favour of preventing scattering of refuse and equally, if not more important, those emphasising careful preparation of real meals instead of 'feeding out of a tin'. This eased the problem of refuse disposal in forward areas considerably and contributed much to lessening the fly nuisance.

In more stable base and L. of C. areas the handling of refuse approached civilian conditions. Wherever the size and siting of camps allowed, the controlled tipping method of disposing of refuse was adopted. The general recommendations of the Ministry of Health were followed, e.g. deposits made in layers of not more than 6 ft. in depth with each layer covered by at least 9 inches of earth and the whole process kept under the most rigid hygiene supervision. Following experience elsewhere, the method proved successful in the M.E. provided supervision was never relaxed.

WASTE WATER DISPOSAL

One of the fortunate features of handling waste water in most areas of the M.E. is that the dryness of the climate and the strong sunlight results in evaporation methods being particularly successful. Wherever possible, therefore, waste water was run into a series of pans to allow this process of evaporation to take place under the optimum conditions. Each pan had a hard, smooth, level floor and was provided with a containing border of approximately 2 ft.

In certain areas waste water was disposed of through irrigation channels by which quantities of excellent vegetables were obtained. It was remarkable to see, for instance, in the desert areas, how enthusiastic officers commanding hospitals were able to obtain most excellent additional vegetable supplies by careful distribution of their waste water into desert vegetable gardens. This method was stimulated wherever possible. 'The nigger in the wood-pile' of waste water disposal seems always to be the grease trap. In spite of much education, local engineering services frequently neglected this most important apparatus by constructing traps without the essential principles of adequate capacity and properly placed baffles and inlet and outlet pipes. This weakness too frequently was responsible for improper waste water disposal and serious insanitary conditions.

NIGHT SOIL DISPOSAL

The Middle East campaign saw the vindication of a policy of using deep pit latrines wherever possible. All permanent and semi-permanent camps were converted to this system with obvious improvement over the previous bucket removal system. There were no particular novel features in the deep pits used but, as always in sanitary control, direct adherence was necessary to the principles of construction and maintenance, e.g. adequate depth with an absolute minimum of 8 ft., the provision of fly-proof superstructure, and constant inspection to remedy any wear and tear or carelessness in their use. A special problem in the maintenance of deep pit latrines, as with other camp structures, arose when large camps were temporarily unoccupied as it was quite impossible to provide sufficient guards to hold off marauding thieves. Latrine structures were damaged and contents exposed to fly breeding. In these circumstances deep pits were sprayed with a mixture of boiler oil and tar oil to prevent fly breeding. In the forward areas, especially in the Western Desert where the subsoil was of rock, making the construction of deep pits impossible, the problem of innocuous disposal of night soil was solved by the introduction of the incinerator latrine. For this, petrol tins were used as receptacles and twice daily incineration of contents was obtained by ignition of a small quantity of petrol and some oil. With careful maintenance one of these latrines was shown to last 15 men for a fortnight. The bore-hole latrine had little application in the M.E. as troops were rarely sited in areas where such structures could be provided.

FLY CONTROL

The fly was one of the most irritating features of the M.E. environment. It was confirmed over and over again that, except where a unit was placed amid some civilian community, camps depended for freedom from flies on their own efforts. Camps with properly supervised refuse, waste water and latrine disposal could be as free from flies as any civil local authority equipped with full sanitary services. Therefore, in the campaign to eliminate the fly, emphasis was continually placed on these essentials. The results were completely satisfactory, as in the summer of 1943 the vast majority of Army communities were relatively free from flies and the average soldier had learned the lesson that camp cleanliness paid. The main problem arising in connexion with flies, and one which threatened the fitness of Eighth Army, was that associated with the retreat and the holding of the El Alamein line in the period from July to September, 1942. The disorganisation following the retreat from Gazala to El Alamein had produced a lowering of hygiene standards, disruption of hygiene supervision of camps and lines of communication, and a crowding together into the area between El Alamein and Amiriya of vast numbers of small units as well as hordes of Bedouin and native refugees. Literally appalling conditions of fly infestation developed. Flies were present in such incredible numbers that during daylight the men of Eighth Army had no respite. For the fighting units in the forward lines this was an exceedingly serious matter as men, who during the night were awake on either guard or patrol duties, could get no rest during the day. General Auchinleck himself, therefore, backed up directly medical recommendations, which resulted in the refugees being cleared back from the camping areas and a special fly control unit being organised to clear the whole area in and about the El Alamein defence line of fly-breeding materials such as dead bodies, litter, refuse, etc. In addition, a vast quantity of mosquito netting was distributed among the men so that they could obtain peace for sleeping and resting during the day. These special measures fortunately were successful and by the end of September the problem had abated considerably with the result that excremental diseases never seriously weakened the strength of Eighth Army. This was in no way due to sulphaguanidine which was later to be of such advantage in dealing with dysentery. At the time of the battle of Alamein, this antibiotic was available only for the treatment of cases in hospitals and casualty clearing stations, and then on a limited scale. It was not available for early treatment at unit level.

As for the Germans and Italians in the same area, indescribably filthy conditions produced such a serious fly menace that the incidence of dysentery, diarrhoea and enteritis materially sapped both the man-power and vigour of the enemy forces.

One technical point of some interest and importance that M.E. experience revealed was the necessity of subscribing to certain principles in using fly traps. These are: that the traps must be placed away from cookhouses, dining halls, messes and latrines; they must be truly counter-attractions for flies to the above type of premises. Then traps must be of the proper size with full play allowed for light attraction and always properly baited with moist bait. Used in this way, it was shown that fly traps literally did attract flies away from cookhouses, etc., and did catch such enormous numbers as to lessen appreciably the fly population in the camp locality.

TYPE OF ACCOMMODATION

In the early stages of the campaign, providing troops with accommodation was a difficult problem for the same reason that all problems were difficult, namely, lack of supplies and the necessity for improvising as much as possible. On the other hand the generally warm, sunny climate throughout most of the M.E. reduced the necessity for shelter. Initially, therefore, the majority of camps consisted merely of tents with fixed structures to serve as cookhouses and ablution and latrine blocks. This primitive provision, however, was improved with the increased availability of such materials as wood and cement so that gradually the more permanent camps came to have huts for all central services including cookhouses, messes and canteens, while gradually a policy of replacement of tents with huts for sleeping accommodation was pursued. Nevertheless, at no time was either labour or material sufficiently generous to allow of optimum standards being secured; therefore, as a compromise, a minimum space standard of 45 square feet per man had to be accepted for sleeping accommodation in huts. Similarly, the numbers in tents had to be increased above those allowed in peace-time. The situation was carefully watched but no untoward effects in the form of a rising incidence of respiratory disease occurred.

There were three types of accommodation provided, governed by the two main factors—the permanency of the camp and the availability of supplies. These types were known as tented, partially hutted, and fully hutted camps. Partially hutted camps were on a scale which supplied tents for sleeping accommodation and for messes, but huts for cookhouses, canteens, latrines and ablution blocks. Medical concern in the hutted camps lay largely in securing the adoption of standard designs covering billets, cookhouses, latrine blocks, and in the proper distribution and layout of buildings within the camp area. Wherever possible, hospitals were naturally put on to a fully hutted scale. Air-conditioned accommodation would have been a very welcome advantage, especially in Egypt during the summer months, but the extremely limited number of air-conditioning plants available prevented any general use of this principle. It was, therefore, limited to certain operating theatres and to the hospital at Massawa.

Though not entirely eliminated from Middle East military accommodation the notorious bug was thrown back on the defensive even in its historic haunts in Cairo, the Kasr-el-Nil Barracks and the Citadel. This was not the result of any such magical insecticide as D.D.T., but of a rigid comprehensive régime followed by every unit itself dealing with bug harbourages such as wall cracks, regularly turning out into the sun all bedding and movable fittings, and regularly cleansing premises with paraffin emulsion.

(ii)

Problems with Racial and Civilian Features

ALLIED FORCES

The heterogeneity of Middle East Force did not simplify hygiene administration. In most continental armies hygiene is scarcely recognised so that a considerable inertia and even opposition had to be overcome before most Allied formations would accept the necessity of having a hygiene organisation or of following sanitary principles in laying out camps, taking preventive measures against disease, etc. A frequent argument was that the Army in question had to fight, that it was tough, and quite impervious to such minor afflictions as dirt, flies and disease. If the British were queer enough to worry about these things they should employ native labour to clean up camps and not submit real soldiers to the indignity of picking up litter! Some groups were never really converted. Their camps, bivouacs, etc., remained filthy, and the incidence of preventable disease confirmed their disdain of hygiene. A notable exception was the Polish Corps. Composed of soldiers evacuated in 1942 from Russian Turkestan, *via* the Caspian and Iran, it was at first disinterested, but by the time it went into action in Italy, its practice in sanitation, fly control, and malaria prevention, was an example even to British regular units.

In most continental Allied armies the status, or rather lack of it, accorded to unit medical officers was not helpful in effecting hygiene control. In certain Services such an appointment did not even carry commissioned rank. This lack of authority, combined with the absence of any direction giving commanding officers responsibility for maintaining the health and sanitary conditions of their units, raised almost insuperable obstacles to proper hygiene practice. On several occasions a unit medical officer, fired with hygienic zeal, correctly giving an adverse report on camp conditions, and calling for vigorous action, was threatened with disciplinary action for his impudence! Only continuous, tactful propaganda, countered such unsatisfactory attitudes to Army hygiene. In the two years, however, steady but slow progress was achieved in most units, and so reduced their danger to themselves and their neighbours.

Initially each Allied force claimed its own ration scale, incorporating items to its national taste. With few exceptions, however, the Middle East Field Service Scale was eventually adopted in place of national ration issues. The practice of insisting on central kitchen and messing areas, even in the field, was new to some Allied formations. These too frequently cooked and fed as individuals in their own bivouacs, tents and huts. Insanitary conditions arising from such a practice were deplorable and resulted in it being expressly forbidden.

AFRICAN PERSONNEL

The emphasis on acclimatisation in the case of African personnel has already been mentioned, as has also the inclusion of bulky cereals in their ration scales. Their inborn physical pride, love of cleanliness and discipline assisted in their rapid acceptance of hygiene practices. Camps occupied by such units as African Pioneer Corps companies were usually conspicuous by their orderliness and cleanliness. Their mimicry of the European, and not actual necessity, led to their insistent demand for headgear and footwear. The characteristically broad African foot was conveniently accommodated by the broad fittings of the standard British Army boot, so that only a limited demand for special African fittings arose. In winter, special care, as already mentioned, was taken to protect them by securing hut accommodation, extra blankets and such additional items of clothing as pullovers and cap-comforters. No serious incidence of respiratory disease arose. The occurrence of pneumonia in West Africans in Cyrenaica has been discussed in an earlier section (p. 403). No serious developments occurred as a result of large bodies of tropical Africans, and therefore including carriers of such conditions as malaria or schistosomiasis, arriving in the Middle East. Some Congo Africans, where initial selection had not been strict enough, showed an undue incidence of sickness, but on the whole Africans arrived and remained fit. The medical problem giving most concern with all Africans was venereal disease. The African with his undeveloped sense of responsibility and with little inclination to control physical urges is not touched by the usual appeals of education and propaganda made to Europeans. His resultant promiscuity and unconcern in its consequences produced a heavier incidence in gonorrhoea, syphilis and soft sore than in any other group. A comprehensive campaign of discipline, treatment, welfare, and tribal and racial pleas at the most only kept the problem within fair limits.

OCCUPIED ENEMY TERRITORIES

The medical and health supervision of the three occupied enemy territories, Eritrea, Cyrenaica and Tripolitania, was an interesting variation to the usual military routine. To fulfil the Geneva Convention stipulations generously and yet to convert the previous showy, ill-balanced, extravagant Italian medical services into an efficient organisation, giving due weight to preventive medicine and public health, was not a simple task. Initially, the intolerable insanitation of such key places as Asmara and Massawa in Eritrea, Derna, Benghazi and

Barce in Cyrenaica, and Tripoli had to be eliminated so as to make these areas safe for British forces as well as for their own inhabitants. The drive of the British principal medical officers and their local British health inspectors had, within a year, got the gross filth of generations removed, efficient sanitary and water services functioning, and basic hospitals, dispensaries and clinics providing essential medical care for the civil population.

When the medical stores left by the Italians were consumed, Army stocks were drawn upon to supply all essential pharmaceutical and disinfectant items. Hospital equipment was maintained so that the large hospitals in Asmara and Tripoli, for instance, continued to function as fully as ever. In keeping with British practice two main lines of development were followed. First, the improvement of sanitation and health of all urban communities as mentioned above. For this purpose a British health inspector was appointed to supervise each large community, and an Italian and native staff appointed to remove refuse, clean up war-shattered areas, disinfest lousy populations and control malarious areas. Secondly, a system of dispensaries providing simple first aid and preventive care, e.g. for eye conditions, was evolved in each territory. This, for the first time in most cases, gave such modern public health facilities as child, school, and maternal care to the territories. The fortunate freedom of the occupied countries from any large-scale epidemics, mass ill-health or malnutrition is in a large part the outcome of the more efficient and comprehensive medical and health services brought in by the British. This help was given too without any large demand on the British taxpayer. The British staffs consisted of a principal medical officer, less than six assistant medical officers, less than a dozen health inspectors and a small group of stores and office personnel. Each staff controlled a fairly large number of Italian and native medical officers, technicians, and nurses. In Eritrea and Tripolitania medical institutions were only slightly damaged, but in Cyrenaica damage and disappearance of equipment and stores meant a new beginning in every respect.

ALLIED CIVILIAN WAR ORGANISATION

The Middle East for strategic and economic reasons, as has been stated, became self-contained to a considerable degree. The chief organisation in achieving this on the civil side was the Middle East Supply Centre under the jurisdiction of Mr. Casey, the Minister of State. In its functions of controlling the distribution and import of food and medical supplies it had much in common with the Army. A liaison was therefore provided by officers of the medical branch of G.H.Q. serving on the relevant standing committees. The available shipping space and medical supplies were thus allocated between the Army and the various local civilian communities to the best advantage of the war effort.

RELATIONS WITH MIDDLE EAST CIVIL GOVERNMENTS

Apart from their co-operation in the work of such bodies as the M.E. Supply Centre and the M.E. Relief and Rehabilitation Administration, the Army hygiene authorities had direct concern in the general health conditions of the various civil communities. Each local medical authority was therefore charged with maintaining the closest liaison with civil medical officials, and observing such facts as disease incidence, food and water supply, malaria and typhus control. The need for this interest is obvious, both for protecting the Army and the civil tranquillity on which the ease of military planning and operations depended so much. A civil State disorganised by an epidemic would have been a serious encumbrance to Middle East Force.

In earlier sections food problems of the various territories were discussed. In their civil aspects military medical opinion was frequently required. The Egyptian cooking oil problem became acute, and groundnut oil was selected as being a suitable substitute for the native cottonseed oil. Palestinian citrus, with strong military medical backing, was eventually admitted into Egypt so that the troops could enjoy a higher fruit ration. Sudan meat and Syrian meat and Syrian dates were further local food products in which the Army was interested.

As a further example of joint military and civil interest the huge civilian labour forces employed by the Army may be instanced. From lowly road labourers up to skilled technicians a watch was kept over their health. Civilian practitioners and hospitals assisted the Army in giving medical care, while the Army provided, in many cases, rations, camp accommodation, facilities for bathing, etc. Trained industrial Army medical officers watched carefully over the needs of thousands of civilians working at lathes, work-benches and factory machines in Palestine, Syria and Egypt. Lousiness in all civilian labour was reduced to a minimum and so the threat of typhus removed. Loss of manhours from accidents and minor illness was under continuous investigation and thus the output of clothing factories, accumulator works, tank and vehicle repair shops was maintained. Such steady health and welfare work was an important field of military and civil co-operation, but a more spectacular one was dealing with communicable disease. Though friction might easily have developed here, with civilian States anxious lest the military traffic introduce and spread disease, and the Army nervous of its man-power and labour forces being crippled by endemic disease, there was a general happy co-operation throughout the year. Yellow fever was the threat from outside most feared by local civilian governments, especially that of Egypt. Middle East Force did everything in its power to conform to the various precautionary measures such as the vaccination of personnel travelling through the endemic African areas, and the disinsectisation of aircraft and shipping arriving in Egypt from infected areas. Smallpox cases arrived in shipping, on occasions, but vigorous vaccination and isolation of sick controlled the disease.

As far as endemic Middle East conditions were met the three provoking crises for both military and civil interests were plague, typhus and malaria spread by *A. gambiae*. Plague at various times appeared in Haifa and Jaffa in Palestine and in the Canal ports of Egypt. Some of the outbreaks in the latter areas reached serious proportions. The Army assisted the civilian efforts energetically by protecting its own personnel in the areas by anti-rodent measures and by vaccination. Typhus was a serious source of anxiety in the winters of both 1941-42 and 1942-43. In the latter season a major epidemic raged, especially in Egypt, though fortunately the mortality rate was not typical. A fair number of cases occurred in the civilian labour force of the Army. Military cases were isolated and scattered, though with some concentration in the urban areas. The usual high mortality in individuals over thirty was again noted. The winter of 1943-44 was fortunately fairly free from typhus.

(iii)
The Incidence of Disease and Injury

There is, unfortunately, no direct way of assessing the magnitude of the contribution which measures directed to the maintenance and augmentation of the health of the troops make to such an event as the victory at Alamein. Their effects cannot be isolated and weighed.

There is ordinary clinical opinion which confirmed that the average soldier in the M.E. looked at the optimum of his physical powers in his possession of a healthy skin, a clear eye, a brisk movement and a generally contented mind. There is the proof of achievement, for the forces of the Middle East were not overwhelmed by reverse, maintained morale for years, and in the end achieved complete victory. Only a fit and healthy army could have accomplished these things against a strong enemy.

Though the positive instrument for accurate measurement of the health efficiency of an army is lacking, the negative index lies in the incidence of disease. Disease incidence is both a criterion of wastage of man-power as a whole and, in the case of certain specific conditions, also of the degree of failure of preventive medicine. This index for

Middle East Force in 1942 and 1943 was based on hospital admissions
which are given as ratios in the following table:

TABLE 64

Admissions to Hospital in Various Campaigns

Campaign	Battle casualties ratio per 1,000 strength	Non-battle casualties ratio per 1,000 strength	Total ratio per 1,000 strength
Middle East, 1942 . .	31·1	553·6	584·7
Middle East, 1943 . .	22·5	490·5	513·0
France and Flanders, 1914–18	364·3	646·6	1,010·9
Macedonia, 1915–18 . .	43·1	1,195·1	1,238·2
Egypt and Palestine, 1915–18	59·0	741·0	800·0
Mesopotamia, 1914–18 . .	89·0	1,164·0	1,253·0
South Africa, 1899–1902 .	38·0	728·0	766·0
East Africa, 1914–18 . .	32·0	2,244·0	2,276·0

These Middle East rates of hospital admissions are excellent, bettering
the records of the War of 1914–18, though it is admitted that direct
comparisons cannot be made. This table also shows that the campaign
followed the general rule that disease is more damaging to the human
strength of an army than enemy weapons. This was even true of Middle
East Force during its hectic periods of activity in 1942.

The detailed study of the hospital statistics of the Middle East Force
deserves a report to itself. Here only a few salient features can be
described. An interesting chart is that of the seasonal ratios of hospital
admissions shown in Fig. 63. This gives striking visual confirmation
of the importance of the summer conditions in causing hospital admissions. These were the intestinal diseases, malaria, many skin
conditions, sandfly fever and infective hepatitis.

Fig. 64 lists the principal causes of admission in per cent. of total
admissions and as a ratio per thousand strength. The parallelism
between the two years is clear, the only major exception being the
change-over to skin conditions and other diseases of the digestive
system as the most important cause of admissions. The second
important fact made clear by Fig. 64 is that the first six most important
causes of hospital admissions are largely preventable—skin diseases,
digestive conditions, accidental injuries, dysentery, malaria and venereal
diseases. Even in 1942, the year of maximum operational activity,
injuries in action occupied only seventh place. The chart then is a
decided confirmation of the importance of preventable disease in the
causation of human wastage in a theatre such as the Middle East.

The following specific conditions warrant special notice :

INTESTINAL DISEASES

Though there is a largely common epidemiological background to dysentery, enteritis and gastro-enteritis, yet their bacteriological and clinical differences make classification difficult. It has not therefore been possible to give the exact incidence of this group, but if to dysentery is added a proportion of the group included under Other Diseases

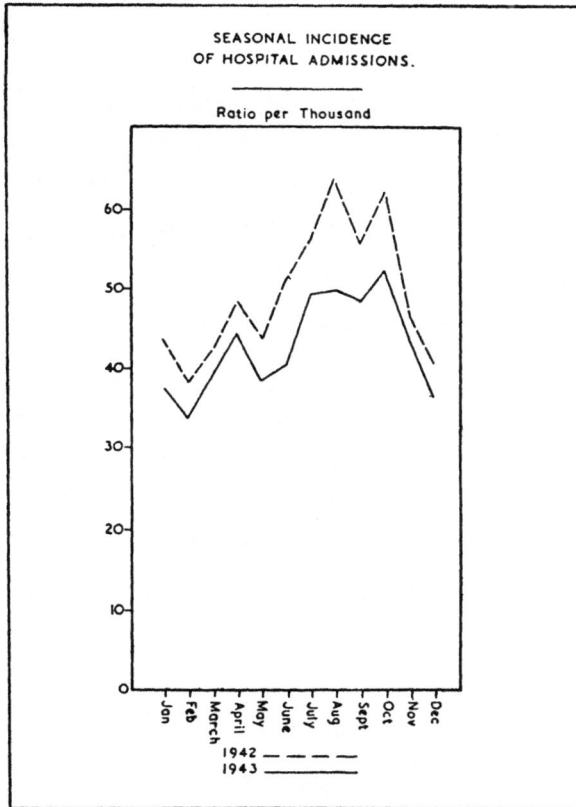

FIG. 63. Seasonal incidence of hospital admissions, Middle East, 1942 and 1943. (From the *'Journal of the R.A.M.C.'*)

of the Digestive System to cover cases of enteritis, etc., then there is no doubt of the predominant position of intestinal diseases in the Middle East disease record. The efforts to control them are all mentioned in various sections of this chapter—education in personal and camp cleanliness, control of flies, food, food-handlers, water supplies, and sanitary services. This many-sided attack was fairly successful, but it is a campaign which is endless. Depending so much upon the individual and unit sense of responsibility, it is difficult to maintain efficient control. Much thought had, therefore, to go into devising new propaganda methods to attract fresh enthusiasm each year for such

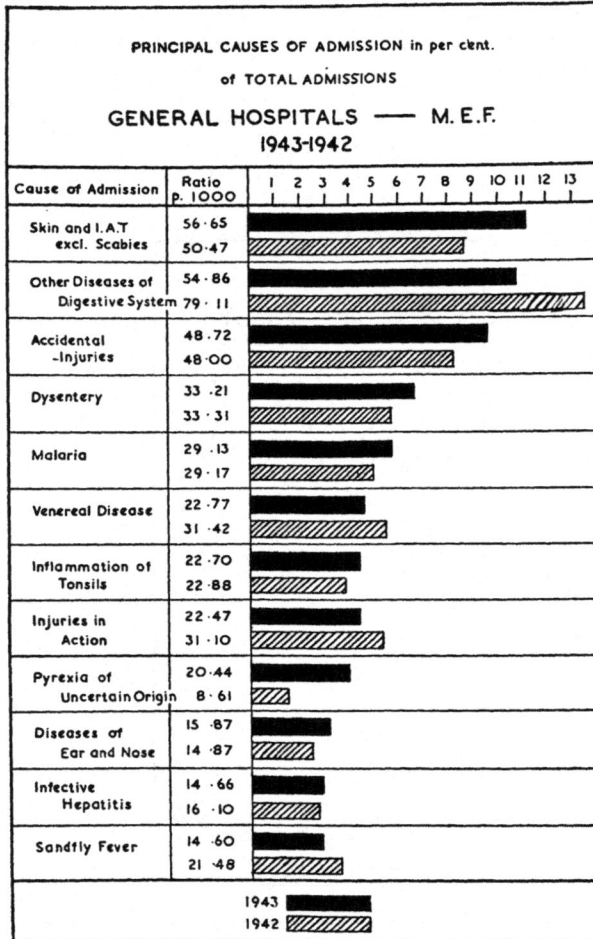

PRINCIPAL CAUSES OF ADMISSION in per cent. of TOTAL ADMISSIONS GENERAL HOSPITALS — M. E.F. 1943-1942		
Cause of Admission	Ratio p. 1000	1 2 3 4 5 6 7 8 9 10 11 12 13
Skin and I.A.T excl. Scabies	56·65 / 50·47	
Other Diseases of Digestive System	54·86 / 79·11	
Accidental -Injuries	48·72 / 48·00	
Dysentery	33·21 / 33·31	
Malaria	29·13 / 29·17	
Venereal Disease	22·77 / 31·42	
Inflammation of Tonsils	22·70 / 22·88	
Injuries in Action	22·47 / 31·10	
Pyrexia of Uncertain Origin	20·44 / 8·61	
Diseases of Ear and Nose	15·87 / 14·87	
Infective Hepatitis	14·66 / 16·10	
Sandfly Fever	14·60 / 21·48	
	1943 / 1942	

FIG. 64. Principal causes of admissions to the General Hospitals, M.E.F., 1942 and 1943. (From the 'Journal of the R.A.M.C.')
Column 1. Principal causes of admission.
Column 2. Ratio per 1,000 strength.
Column 3. Principal causes of admission in percentage of total admissions.

unspectacular work as clearing up refuse, protecting cookhouses, maintaining latrines in good order, etc. Then, obviously, much more education is required before every individual is fastidious about the origin and protection of his food, and the automatic cleansing of his hands before eating, etc.

SKIN CONDITIONS

The glaringly obvious effects of weapons, malaria, typhus, dysentery, venereal diseases cloud any appreciation of, and even lead to neglect of more common and, in many circumstances, more important causes of man-power wastage. Two of these ordinary very serious causes in the Middle East were skin conditions and accidents. Skin and areolar tissue conditions resulted in hospital admissions to the extent of 56·65 per 1,000 strength in 1943 and 50·47 in 1942.

Under the heading of Diseases of the Skin and Areolar Tissue are included such items as boils, abscesses, epidermophytosis, desert sores, impetigo, septic dermatitis, etc. The lack of interest of the medical services was reflected in the vague diagnoses and uncertain treatments common in this group of diseases. Investigation and its consequential suggestions for control were thus hampered. A steady insistence in orders, hygiene and medical memoranda and in propaganda was part of the programme to reduce skin conditions, while on hygiene recommendations the Army administration set about providing ablution facilities, supplies of foot powder, and arranging for regular foot and skin inspections. Especial attention was paid to desert sores and epidermophytosis.

Tinea pedis was extremely common and, as usual, was most troublesome in summer. The following general preventive measures were instituted: regular foot inspections, regular use of Army foot powder, disinfecting vats of 1 per cent. sodium hypochlorite solution in ablution rooms and bathing pools, regular washing of changing-room floors, etc., with cresol, prohibition of sharing of towels, etc.

ACCIDENTAL INJURIES

The lack of interest in accidents is regrettable, as they constitute a most serious detrimental influence on both the human and material resources of any army. Vehicles and other equipment are damaged and destroyed and human lives are cut short or their usefulness decreased. In both 1942 and 1943 accidental injuries led to 48 men per 1,000 of Middle East Force being admitted to hospital. The record of deaths in hospital, which of course does not include deaths of individuals dying outside medical units, confirms the seriousness of accidents, for in 1942 and 1943 they were responsible for 31 and 30 per cent. respectively of all hospital deaths. Even in such an active operational year in the Middle East as 1942 accidental injuries led to more hospital deaths than battle casualties.

As accidents caused such a large number of deaths it is not surprising that the proportion of serious injury was also high. This is borne out by the fact that orthopaedic centres in the period July 1, 1942, to June 30, 1943, handled only just over 3,000 cases due to battle casualties and yet nearly 6,000 cases of major bone and joint injuries due to accidents. This is a further disturbing index of the part played by accidents in causing serious damage to human material in an army. Major bone and joint injuries require considerable and specialised (and hence expensive) surgical care and time to treat. A large number of such patients also suffer a permanent loss of efficiency. All these conditions are theoretically preventable, and by bringing these extremely important facts to the notice of the administrative authorities, a stimulus was provided for a general campaign to reduce road accidents, accidental fires, industrial mishaps, etc. However, the problem is an extremely complex one branching out into all army activity and but slow progress is achieved. As with so many problems of public health administration, educating the individual to an awareness of the importance of his part is fundamental to improvement.

MALARIA

A curious coincidence is that in both 1942 and 1943 the annual ratio per 1,000 strength of hospital admissions due to malaria was 29. Such a ratio is admittedly not alarming by comparison with calamities due to malaria in such campaigns as that of Salonika in the War of 1914–18. Nevertheless, when it is borne in mind that on the whole the Middle East is only mildly malarious, a ratio of 29 is not completely satisfactory. Broadly speaking the whole of the Middle East, excluding the true deserts, is malarious. Within this general malarious region certain areas are particularly dangerous such as the Jordan valley and certain places along the Palestine and Lebanon coastal plains. The primary function undertaken by the Army malarial organisation was therefore to determine accurately the geographical variation of the malarial hazard. Initially three, but latterly two, malaria field laboratories were available for this work. Within a few months the main malaria surveys were completed. For such areas as a large part of the Lebanon and Syria these were pioneer studies. The malaria season was taken as covering the period from the beginning of April to approximately the middle of November, except in the Sudan and Eritrea where it continues throughout the year. The common vectors were: *Anopheles pharoensis* in Egypt, *A. gambiae* in Upper Egypt, the Sudan and Eritrea, *A. superpictus* and *sacharovi* (*elutus*) in Palestine, the Lebanon, Syria and Cyprus. *A. claviger* is common in Palestine and the Levant and was a frequent cause of sharp, local outbreaks sometimes mysterious in origin. Other vectors of not such general importance are *A. sergenti* and *A. multicolor*.

The comprehensive malaria control organisation was designed to maintain constant observation on the ecology of the various anopheline vectors, develop new methods of control, undertake general anti-larval measures through special malaria control units, and train and supervise units and camp staffs in anti-larval, anti-adult and personal protection measures. Advisers at each command headquarters, local hygiene officers and sections, two malaria field laboratories and nearly thirty special malaria control units, employing large gangs of labourers, composed the special Middle East control organisation.

The lessons learnt were not really new. The chief one was that the work of special units in dealing with mosquito breeding and adult destruction, though frequently adequate in permanent camps, must be supported by unit and personal effort in the field if malaria incidence is to be reduced to manageable proportions. Usually it is only a forceful example of an outbreak which drives this need home. There was only gradual acceptance of medical insistence that, as no single simple drug, device or measure is a safeguard, all measures, including siting of camps, oiling or 'Paris greening' of breeding places, spraying insecticides into sleeping and living quarters, wearing clothing (long sleeves and slacks) to cover arms and legs, supplying insect repellent to exposed skin areas, sleeping under netting, and when necessary taking mepacrine as a suppressant, must be used. As with so many preventive medical measures dependent upon the individual, malaria control is much simpler to plan than to execute. Only vigorous education, training and discipline secure success. This was exemplified several times. A battalion on dispersed guard duty along a Syrian border, in spite of over a year's experience in the Middle East, neglected such precautions as checking that all men were wearing slacks, applying mosquito cream, and using sleeping mats, with the result that scores of cases occurred in a few weeks. Rigid application of these protective measures, with mepacrine suppression, abruptly ended the outbreak. In Syria, a brigade moved into a semi-permanent camp, and, discipline again being lax in supervising the adequacy of both local mosquito control and personal precautions, suffered serious sickness. These local instances, complementary to the losses due to malaria in the Sicilian campaign, converted completely the Army administrative authorities to the importance of malaria prevention. It is almost a psychological law that no amount of propaganda, exhortation or training will, in the actual absence of the hazard, persuade an army to take adequate precautions. Actual experience and direct knowledge were the most potent influences in the Middle East in such conversion.

VENEREAL DISEASE

Hospital admissions due to venereal diseases were 31·4 per 1,000 in 1942 and 22·8 per 1,000 in 1943. The proportion of types was approximately, syphilis 8 per cent., gonorrhoea 28 per cent., venereal sore

32 per cent., other forms 32 per cent. The significant figure here is the high proportion of venereal sore. It had been expected that this venereal problem would present itself. A large heterogeneous mass of soldiers in war-time, in the circumstances to be found in the Middle East, seemed destined for much venereal infection. The usual preventive and treatment measures which were taken to meet this eventuality do not need special description. These were education and propaganda mainly through unit medical officers, provision of personal prophylaxis and unit early treatment centres—in the case of large urban areas centrally situated prophylactic ablutionary centres—special hospital treatment, and finally a vigorous and comprehensive programme of sports, recreation and welfare.

However, a short reference to the special problem of brothels is justified. In practically all urban areas in the Middle East brothels were flourishing and were the preponderating potential source of infection. A strong medical demand for placing such premises in the Middle East out of bounds to troops was based on the following arguments:

(i) They were far and away the most likely source of venereal diseases both from their nature and their easy accessibility. No such volume of contacts as occurred in brothels could be visualised as being possible through street or secret prostitution.

(ii) Such premises were almost invariably insanitary themselves and situated in most insanitary, sordid and degrading environments. Venereal diseases thus were but one of several health hazards to be met with in brothels. Typhus and scabies were distinct examples of infections, and doubtful drink and food were only too frequently consumed by patrons. Correctly, too, the medical authorities pointed out the influence of such conditions on morale, though perhaps such other factors as prestige and political repercussions of a policy of toleration of brothels lay outside medical judgment.

After some considerable discussion, where fears of the proposed policy were raised, brothels were placed out of bounds during 1942. The results were watched closely. None of the expressed fears, such as intolerable conditions of street prostitution, or an increase in crimes of violence, or a deterioration in discipline, were confirmed. Generally the behaviour of troops improved materially during the period after brothels were placed out of bounds, while venereal disease incidence significantly declined. Thus the early anxiety of venereal diseases becoming a burdensome problem fortunately was not justified. This was a result due to the same general form of attack, employing all possible preventive, curative and associated welfare and disciplinary measures, as is required in dealing with so many problems of either military or civilian public health.

INDUSTRIAL HAZARDS

The elaboration of the Middle East into a vast war workshop made industrial medicine no mean function of the Army Medical Services. It is probably difficult for those who did not tour the Middle East in war-time to visualise the variety and size of the industrial hazards of such military installations as tank and vehicle repair depots, mine-filling factories, car battery and accumulator works, petrol tin factories, food factories, etc. The protection of the working population in these installations so as to maintain and even to boost production was, throughout, an urgent duty. Special industrial medical officers were appointed to each area, and in each factory and depot were placed first-aid orderlies or nurses. These latter were usually locally employed civilians. Industrial plant was designed or modified to eliminate noxious fumes or dust. Working hours were watched so that the maximum compatible with optimum production was not exceeded. Refreshments on site and full facilities for ablution, etc., were arranged.

OTHER CONDITIONS

Typhus was throughout each winter a challenge to the force more through its potential capacity for disorganising civil government and services than as a direct threat. The main features of the measures against it have been sketched above. Infective hepatitis struck one serious blow in the latter stages of the advance from El Alamein when hundreds of cases occurred in New Zealand, Australian and United Kingdom divisions. Intensive research had not elucidated its epidemiological puzzles by the end of 1943. In 1942 its incidence was 16 per 1,000 strength and in 1943, 14·6 per 1,000 strength. The menace of sandfly in crippling large numbers of new arrivals in August and September has been indicated. Scabies was a nuisance only in Malta, where frequent direct contact of Maltese troops with their families produced many reinfections. Diphtheria was prevalent in only a few units, but at no time was sufficiently serious to call for universal immunisation of the force. Schistosomiasis, in spite of Egypt being one of the notorious endemic foci, claimed only isolated cases, a result to be ascribed to the placing of few troops in the irrigated areas and to the general knowledge of the origin of this disease in canals and streams. Tuberculosis, as residence in the Middle East lengthened, became more obvious. Typically it took the progressive infantile form in rural Africans, in whom it had most serious prevalence.

Summary

The diversity and size of the Middle East in its geographical, racial, and political features added to the extreme complexity of health problems in the mixed heterogeneous formations composing Middle East Force. These difficulties were intensified by the years 1942 and 1943 finding the Allies on the defensive resulting therefore in restricted supplies. The care of the force was undertaken on orthodox lines with medical and hygiene administrative officers and units in each command and formation. The weakness of this orthodoxy lies in the tendency of the Army (and civil national services, too, it may be said) to concentrate on the executive care of medical units and casualties and to neglect to some extent less spectacular preventive and public health needs.

In the purely health sphere, accepting the fundamental principle that the individual soldier and unit must be self-reliant, considerable emphasis was given to health education and propaganda, using all the usual media of schools, lectures, demonstrations, leaflets, posters and films. The hazards of heat, light and local infections were met by such measures as careful attention to pure water and food. Adequate balanced ration scales were not always easy to compose when lack of shipping reduced imports of certain types of food. Local supplies were then exploited. Repeatedly, Middle East experience has shown the importance of protecting food from depot to the soldier's mouth to ensure its purity and its adequacy. The Army cook at last came into his own. No food-deficiency disease occurred. The menace of the fly, the mosquito and the sandfly was met by camp siting, control of breeding places and intensive training of all troops in personal protection. Camp cleanliness was shown to pay. Special measures were needed to meet the quite phenomenal fly plague after the retreat from Gazala to El Alamein.

Sanitation and preventive medicine were novel ideas to most Allied formations in Middle East Force. Conversion of these groups was slow, though the Poles eventually were most praiseworthy practitioners of military hygiene. Especial care had to be given to the African, a newcomer to conditions of modern warfare and largely rural tropical in origin, therefore susceptible to crowd diseases. Captured enemy territories of Eritrea, Cyrenaica and Tripolitania were quickly cleared of long-standing insanitation and given better-balanced medical and health services for their native populations.

The Middle East hygiene authorities were also involved in various advisory and co-operational capacities with Middle East States in civilian problems of food supplies, epidemic diseases and medical stores. Typhus, plague, smallpox in several States, and malaria in Upper Egypt carried by *A. gambiae*, were acute civil problems affecting the Army. The success of the principles and application of military hygiene in the Middle East campaigns of 1942 and 1943 is partially measured by the low incidence of hospital admissions which were for the two years 553·6 and 490·5 per thousand strength. These rates are a distinct improvement on those of any previous wars. However, it is rather in the positive picture of health and vigour shown by the soldiers and in their successful achievements in adversity and final victory that it is revealed that hygiene did not fail to make its contribution.

CHAPTER 7

THE ARMY PSYCHIATRIC SERVICE.
MIDDLE EAST FORCE. 1940–1943*

A CONSULTANT in Psychiatry (termed Psychological Medicine to begin with) was appointed to Medical Headquarters, M.E.F., on June 20, 1940. He at once set himself the task of designing a service that would be capable of dealing with the psychiatric problems of M.E.F. and which would reduce to a minimum the evacuation of psychiatric casualties to the United Kingdom. His services were made available to the Royal Navy, the Royal Air Force and to the Dominion and Allied contingents in Middle East Command. The Army Medical Services provided hospital accommodation for psychiatric casualties for the Navy, the Army and the Air Force, for the numerous Allied contingents and, partly, for the Dominion Forces.

(i)

The Growth of the Psychiatric Service

A consultant is an adviser to his D.M.S. for the speciality he represents. The consultants appointed to M.E.F. formed a panel of the organisation of the D.M.S. at General Headquarters and possessed no administrative powers. When recommendations made involved administrative action, it was essential to consult with all the medical and other officers involved so that memoranda could be presented in such a form to the D.M.S. (*via* his principal administrative officers) that simple assent on his part would be all that was required to make the recommendation effective. If agreement to a memorandum was given it could then form part of a Medical Administrative Instruction which would be sent out to the medical administrators involved. This meant that after considerable experience and tuition a consultant did become to some extent responsible. To make the work of a consultant effective, the understanding, sympathy and assistance of many branches of G.H.Q. as well as of organisations outside the Army, such as the British Red

---

*As acknowledged in the Preface this chapter derives from a personal record maintained by Brigadier G. W. B. James, who served as Consulting Psychiatrist, G.H.Q., M.E.F.

Cross Society, must be enlisted, and also frequently the government departments of the countries in which the force is operating. Extensive liaison is essential.

By Christmas 1940, the consultant had visited all the base hospitals and many of the medical and combatant units both in the Western Desert and on the borders of the Sudan and Abyssinia. A general

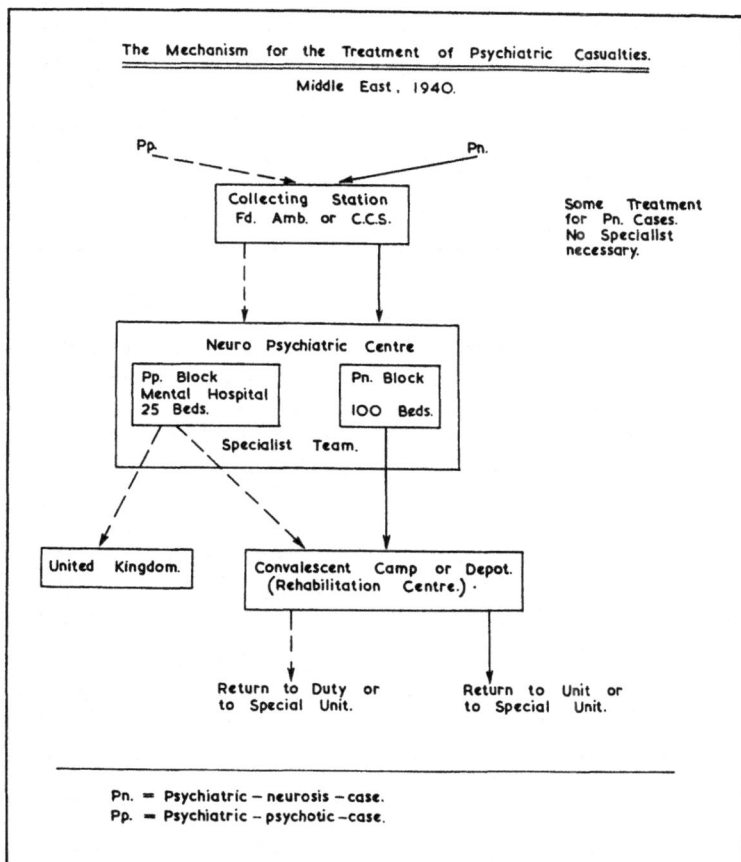

The Mechanism for the Treatment of Psychiatric Casualties.

Middle East, 1940.

FIG. 65. The mechanism for the treatment of psychiatric casualties, Middle East, 1940.

policy was laid down and provision made for casualties occurring in the fighting that was to be expected. At 64 B.G.H. in Alexandria a psychiatric centre was instituted at which psychiatric first aid and early treatment could be carried out. In October 1940, a specialist in psychiatry was attached to this hospital. From this centre, cases, being sorted, were passed on to general hospitals in the base areas. Men presenting difficulty in the matter of disposal were retained in hospital pending a visit of the consultant. From hospital the psychiatric cases were evacuated to 2, 3, 5 and 7 Convalescent Depots.

Very quickly the following accommodation for psychiatric cases was made available:

64 B.G.H. Alexandria .	Observation ward. Psychiatric centre. Specialist in psychiatry.
63 B.G.H. Cairo .	. Observation block 120 beds. Accommodation for officers.
25 B.G.H. Cairo .	. Out-patient clinic visited by consultant twice weekly. Officer accommodation.
27 B.G.H. Tel el Kebir .	A large hut provided for psychiatric cases.
23 B.G.H. Jerusalem .	A small observation block.
60 B.G.H. Nazareth .	A small observation block.

On the appointment of an area psychiatrist in 1942, a second out-patient clinic was opened at 63 B.G.H.

Arrangements were made with the officer in charge of 2nd Echelon whereby men regraded on psychiatric grounds, and concerning whom a medical recommendation concerning future employment had been made, could be suitably posted. It was arranged that those psychiatric casualties who were being evacuated to the United Kingdom would travel thereto *via* the Union of South Africa.

In October 1940, the consultant recommended that two psychiatric centres of 170–200 beds should be created and attached to two general hospitals at the base. In July 1941, 1 Psychiatric Centre was attached to 19 B.G.H. near the Great Bitter Lake on the Suez Canal and 2 Psychiatric Centre was attached to 23 B.G.H. on the plain between Jerusalem and Jaffa. These developments were made in accordance with the policy that Middle East Command must be prepared to deal with its own psychiatric casualties. It was recognised that too easy evacuation would soon yield a problem of unmanageable proportions.

In the early reports addressed to D.M.S. the preventive aspect of psychiatric work was underlined. The importance of treatment centres and of the careful organisation of facilities for convalescence and rehabilitation was emphasised and the necessity for welfare and other preventive work on a large scale was stressed. A special note was made of the importance of an improvement in the postal service since lack of news from home in those early days, when the bombing of Britain was in the mind of every soldier serving in the Middle East, appeared constantly as a causal factor in breakdown. Other amenities recommended were residential clubs or hostels for officers and men on leave, concert parties and travelling cinemas, the dissemination of accurate news, the distribution of books and periodicals, and the great advantages likely to accrue from having women's units in Middle East Force. A suggestion was early put forward that contact with some social welfare organisation in the United Kingdom was urgently required. The object of this was to establish a link by social visits or other means with those homes which either from bombing, financial, domestic or marital circumstances were causing distress and even neurosis to soldiers in the force. It was hoped that written or cabled reports would relieve the anxieties created by absence of news from home or, at the worst, would put an end to wearing and harassing uncertainties. The Director of Personal Services to the Middle East Force set up in 1941 a branch of the Soldiers', Sailors' and Airmen's Families Association and branches were eventually extended to every command in the force. By June 1943, the Association had dealt with 18,500 enquiries, the subjects varying from news of bombed families, missing or sick relatives or children, to financial and other domestic difficulties, among which marital infidelities became increasingly prominent. In 1941, the Deputy Adjutant-General set up a free legal aid department.

Soon after the opening of the two psychiatric centres the pressure on their beds was such that it became necessary to recommend to D.M.S. (September 1941) that a 600 bedded psychiatric hospital would be necessary at an early date. It is worth while noting that the pressure on the beds in the two psychiatric centres was in great part caused by the length of the waiting list of those soldiers who were to be evacuated to the United Kingdom. A period of many weeks usually ensued before the psychiatric cases could be evacuated and their management while waiting gave rise to considerable disturbance and difficulty. 41 B.G.H., a psychiatric hospital of 600 beds, arrived in January 1942 and opened on March 2, 1942. It was not possible to plan and build special hospital buildings in time for the arrival of the personnel and its equipment. By a wise decision the hospital was housed in a 1,200 bedded site vacated by an Australian general hospital which was leaving the force. This enabled room to be allowed for the many different classes of patients admitted to this unit, which from this date onwards bore the brunt of the rapidly increasing psychiatric work. Eighteen days after its opening there were already ten different classes of patients, and a request had been made for six interpreters—the languages at that time required being Italian, Afrikaans, modern Greek, French, Arabic, Hebrew and Swahili. Later many more nationalities required care, and at the end of 1942 no less than twenty-eight nationalities, not counting the non-European personnel of the Union Defence Force, were represented among the patients of this hospital.

At all times the staffs of the psychiatric centres and 41 B.G.H. overcame their many difficulties with cheerful efficiency. By reason of the various nationalities and customs, differences in race, religion, colour, sex, and rank, many separate kitchens, dining rooms and recreation rooms were required. For example, Hindu and Mohammedan diets for Indian soldiers necessitated separate kitchens, while separate dining rooms were obviously required for German and Italian prisoners, for their officers, for coloured troops, for British officers of both sexes, for N.C.Os. and other ranks. In addition, there was the usual need to classify patients according to their mental condition.

In its first quarter of full work, 1,000 cases were admitted to 41 B.G.H. and extensions by 200 beds were required at intervals until in 1943, 1,000 beds were made available. As the force increased in size and the demands made by so great a mixture of nationalities increased, it became evident that a second psychiatric hospital would eventually be required. There was another reason for this recommendation, made to D.M.S. in June 1942. It was hoped that such a victory would be gained eventually over enemy forces that an advanced unit of some sort would become necessary, and it was proposed to make the second psychiatric hospital provide an establishment which would enable 200 beds to be split off from the parent body and act as an advanced psychiatric treatment centre.

During 1942, efforts were made to build a specially designed psychiatric hospital on the west bank of the Great Bitter Lake about half-way down the Suez Canal. It was designed to be partly a permanent brick building and partly tented. The staff was to be obtained by fusing the two psychiatric centres and obtaining the balance required from the United Kingdom. The hospital was planned with a large hall serving as theatre, cinema, concert hall and church. Two large bays for occupational work were set aside in the building used for stores built by the 'Stonehenge' type of construction. The new hospital had an out-patient department, its own operating block and wards devised so that a minimum of staff could look after two wards of 24 patients, a total of 48. An adequate supply of single rooms for disturbed patients was also planned. This second hospital, 78 General Neuropathic Hospital, opened in June 1943.

As the territory of M.E.F increased—for example by the conquest of Syria—it was recommended that all general hospital sites be given a hut or huts in which psychiatric casualties could be received and treated for a few days or which, if specially constructed, could hold and treat cases until they were well enough to be moved on to a convalescent depot. For example, in Syria on a beautiful site overlooking the sea, 3 and 22 B.G.Hs. were built and each had a good stone hut with 20 beds specially constructed for the reception of psychiatric cases. The hospitals were built side by side and one specialist was appointed to look after both huts and to act at the same time as an area psychiatrist to Ninth Army.

PRISONERS-OF-WAR

Early in 1941, one of the results of the capture of so many Italian soldiers as prisoners-of-war was a sudden and urgent need to provide accommodation for those among them who were suffering from psychosis. It was laid down that neurotic prisoners-of-war must be handled in their own camps. The problem of psychotic breakdown was solved by enlisting the help of the Minister of Health in the Egyptian Government. Accommodation was granted for mentally disordered prisoners-of-war in one of the Egyptian state hospitals at Abbassia. The accommodation allowed for officers, non-commissioned officers and white and coloured other ranks. Prisoners were treated and nursed by Egyptian medical colleagues and their staff. A British military medical officer paid frequent visits to the hospital and the consultant saw every prisoner each month and furnished a report to D.M.S. on each visit. The International Red Cross visited the hospital and approved this temporary arrangement, and on the opening of a military 600-bedded psychiatric hospital, the prisoners were transferred to British hospital care.

THE DOMINION, INDIAN AND ALLIED FORCES

The Consultant to Middle East Force was in constant touch with the Ds.M.S. of the Australian Imperial Force, the New Zealand Expeditionary Force and, on its arrival from East Africa in 1941, the Union Defence Force of South Africa. In addition, the A.D.M.S. acting as liasion officer for the Indian Medical Service was situated at G.H.Q. and the Indian hospitals and divisions in the field were visited by the consultant as frequently as was possible. He was also in touch with the Ds.M.S. of the Polish Army, the Royal Greek Forces and, later, with the Chief Surgeon of the American Expeditionary Force. All these forces were given the freedom of the psychiatric services of the British Army.

THE AUSTRALIAN IMPERIAL FORCE

The A.I.F. had no psychiatric specialist available at first, but appointed a consultant in 1941 and developed accommodation in their general hospitals together with a special treatment centre in a convalescent depot situated in Palestine. The work at this depot was carried out by an Australian medical specialist with great understanding and skill in psychotherapeutic methods, but the arrangement was not entirely satisfactory. The presence of acute or sub-acute cases in a convalescent depot is always undesirable and a separate camp of 500 beds was finally established under the command of a specialist in psychiatry. The camp was divided into two companies, each being commanded by a combatant officer, thus relieving the psychiatrist and his medical officers of most administrative duties. This was the first purely psychiatric convalescent camp and accepted not only men who were in need of treatment for neurosis but also men with mild psychotic manifestations. The work done at this camp was of a very high standard and developed good therapy on practical psychotherapeutic lines, together with occupational work, physical and athletic training.

A visit was paid to Tobruk during the historic defence of the little North African port. The town was completely surrounded and isolated. Supplies and reinforcements arrived by sea and casualties were evacuated also by sea, often by destroyers, so that the invalids shared the hazards of the dangerous journey back to Alexandria and the medical bases. The Australian A.D.M.S., the general hospital in the town and the field ambulances, all of the Australian Army Medical Corps, had between them evolved within the Tobruk perimeter (where any sort of rest and quiet was next to impossible) practical and effective methods of handling psychiatric casualties. It must be recalled that the siege began during the first disappointing and arduous retreat from the Tunisian border and that a number of Australian units, freshly arrived, had taken part in this most exacting and fatiguing type of military operation as their first experience of battle. At this time it was vital to retain for some form of duty every possible soldier, and therefore to evacuate psychiatric casualties sparingly. Regimental medical officers were instructed to pay special attention to the early signs of potential breakdown in the soldiers under their charge. Further, they were encouraged to deal quietly and confidently with badly rattled 'bomb happy' individuals who inevitably descend on a busy regimental medical officer during action, producing an over-powering temptation to decide on evacuation. One of the field ambulances acted as a screen for all such soldiers evacuated from the front and carried out treatment on the lines of rest, sedation, feeding and occupation so successfully that 56 per cent. of psychiatric casualties were returned to their units after a few days' rest and treatment, some of them admittedly still in a somewhat unstable condition but anxious to try again; 44 per cent. were sent on from the field ambulance to the general hospital in Tobruk town. There they were treated in what became known as 'Z' ward, a deep concrete dug-out in a hillside on the summit of which was a heavy A.A. gun post. This dug-out shelter was reasonably quiet and quite safe and here more lengthy treatment was possible and enabled a further 50 per cent. of the remainder to return to their units. During the latter part of the siege a tented annexe to the general hospital was constructed on the open beach north of the town, and soon after it was opened it received the nervous casualties.

A serious disadvantage attaches to nursing psychiatric casualties in very safe dug-outs or caves, consisting of a very natural reluctance to leave the safety of their shelter. This tendency is known to afflict normal people, and in nervous casualties may become greatly exaggerated. Nursing in the open was found to be a great deal better and the tented wards enabled good rest and change to be given to the more seriously shaken soldiers. Examination and assessment of each case, however, must be undertaken in surroundings which are as safe and quiet as possible. For this reason 'Z' ward continued to be used for examination and some treatment right up to the time of relief.

When the bulk of the Australian Force left the Middle East, Australian 9th Division remained. It developed the plan of using a psychiatric specialist or graded specialist at the level of the C.C.S. to deal with psychiatric casualties. Soldiers arriving at the C.C.S. were examined and asked almost at once to contribute a pint or so of their blood for the blood bank. Liberal fluid was then given and the patient was fed and put to bed with a generous sedative. As soon as he was rested and the symptoms relieved the soldier was got up and took part forthwith in the work of the desert station. At one C.C.S. the patients (invariably referred to as 'bomb happy' among the A.I.F.) were given the task of washing the linen from the operating tents. This was much relished by patients and the washing was well done, dried in the sun, ironed and packed ready for sterilisation. The contribution of whole blood by psychiatric casualties was found to be a sound psychological aid to treatment. It gave the soldier the feeling that he was doing something for his comrades, that by his voluntary sacrifice of blood he 'atoned' for his breakdown and was made to feel that he remained a useful member of the group by which he feared he might be regarded as an outcast. The medical base of the A.I.F. remained in south Palestine, where at a general hospital specially constructed wards housed cases of psychosis, while men suffering from neurosis were looked after in a general ward of the hospital under a specialist in psychiatry.

THE NEW ZEALAND EXPEDITIONARY FORCE

Contact was first made with the N.Z.E.F. in the Western Desert in the autumn of 1940. In due course the force had its full share of fighting and experienced the psychiatric difficulties which are common to all fighting units. The New Zealand base was a few miles from G.H.Q., M.E.F., and a New Zealand general hospital nearby, with a specialist attached, received nervous casualties. A small psychiatric block was ultimately built in the grounds of this hospital. After treatment soldiers were moved on to a seaside New Zealand convalescent depot and then returned to a reinforcement unit. The final disposal of all psychiatric cases in the N.Z.E.F. was in the hands of A.D.M.S. G.H.Q., N.Z.E.F., a psychiatrist of experience. This arrangement was most valuable. It meant that one officer made the recommendations regarding the final disposal of difficult clinical cases and was the only authority to decide on final evacuation to the home country. Such an arrangement is only possible in a comparatively small force and it is not every D.M.S. who will find a skilled psychiatrist in the person of his A.D.M.S.

The consultant remarks that it is impossible to write of the New Zealand Force without recalling the Maori. The Maori battalion took immense pride in its fighting efficiency and was very sensitive to anything which might be construed as a failure in courage or endurance. At the same time officers and N.C.Os. understood the nervous new-comer or the man who showed anxiety symptoms during or after action. In this Maori battalion it was the custom to appoint two trained and experienced soldiers as 'battle friends' who lived and fought with the stranger or the weakling until he could be reported as fully trained or as fit and healthy once more. This is an instance of the many practical devices put into action by several of the fighting units in Middle East Force in attempts, often very skilful, to assist 'green', 'browned off' or 'war-worn' comrades.

THE UNION DEFENCE FORCE OF SOUTH AFRICA

The force arrived in the Middle East during 1941, after the successful termination of the East African campaign. In October 1941, the D.M.S. of this force was advised by the consultant to set up 50 beds for psychoses and 250 for neuroses, with some further accommodation for non-European personnel. No specialist psychiatrist accompanied the force and there had been no sort of selection or psychiatric screening at the time of enlistment; officers and men were volunteers. A base general hospital was established near Cairo and a specialist obtained from the Union, the first woman specialist in psychiatry to work with a field force. She arrived from the Union in 1942 and worked at the centre established at 5 S.A.G.H. at Helmieh for which a very small psychiatric annexe was constructed. At the end of the African campaign most of the Union Defence Force returned to South Africa.

The psychiatric services of the British Army were always available to the Dominion troops and it was a great interest and pleasure to the medical and nursing staff of the centres and hospitals to receive Dominion soldiers. At one time, during the very heavy fighting of 1942, hospital ships landed casualties directly at a Palestinian port. A number of Dominion troops were thus transferred in a few days from desert battles to 2 Psychiatric Centre in Palestine. These men won the affection of the whole staff and set a great example of cheerful spirits and high morale for all other patients under treatment.

THE INDIAN ARMY

The consultant observes that like other troops the Indian divisions had hard and bitter periods of service. But in addition to his great qualities in action, the Indian soldier compels admiration by his consistently smart appearance and his dignified conduct out of action, whether during periods of recreation or on leave. The Indian fighting soldier takes up arms as a profession, often having a proud family or village tradition of service, sometimes in a particular unit. It is true that the soldier does not necessarily appreciate the geographical position and size of his country or its place in the British Commonwealth; he will probably know little of the causes of the war or of abstractions like democracy and freedom; but when trained he makes a wonderful soldier. Indian troops were not in any way selected in India, but their morale, training and leadership were of the highest quality. As would be expected, therefore, psychiatric casualties in the Indian Army were few among front line troops.

Nevertheless, as the Middle East campaign lengthened, it was found that in a number of good Indian soldiers with excellent records at the end of two or more years' service overseas, a wound was a serious mental as well as physical trauma. The soldier began to think of his home, his relatives and, in some cases, of religious rites possibly left undone by reason of his absence. The result was not infrequently an obstinate hysterical addition to his wound, usually necessitating his return to India.

It was quite otherwise with the followers of the Indian Army. These men, recruited from lower castes, the sweepers, water-carriers, laundry-men, cooks—unselected men often of low intellectual calibre—were full of psychiatric troubles, the commonest being conversion hysteria. The language difficulty placed obstacles in the way of the British psychiatric specialist and application was made to D.M.S., India, for an Indian Medical Service officer with psychiatric experience and possessing the knowledge of the necessary languages.

The care of psychiatric casualties among Indian troops was undertaken by three base hospitals which developed three small centres within their establishments. A detachment of an Indian hospital in Cairo (15 I.G.H.) was situated on a desert strip bordering the new road from Mena to Alexandria. Here a stone hut was designed and built containing two wards, bathing annexes and single rooms for the more disturbed patients. Wooden huts provided dining and occupational rooms and wards for nervous cases. The whole was enclosed by a fence and formed a compound. D.M.S. India kindly despatched to the Middle East an I.M.S. officer with psychiatry as his speciality and speaking the necessary languages. His devoted energy was of great value and the Indian psychiatric centre at Mena became widely known for its somewhat peculiar solid stone hut, its flower gardens and the unusual games played by the patients. Two other Indian hospitals received Indian psychiatric casualties. One (10 I.G.H.), situated in the Canal area developed a series of small tented wards, each containing four patients. These wards were dug down in the sand to protect against blast and had a wooden support to the canvas roof maintained by the sand bag blast walls. The other Indian hospital (22 I.G.H.), situated in Palestine, evolved a very successful compound within a wire fence with tents along three sides looking on to a centre court. This compound was ultimately placed in the charge of Indian nursing sisters who had received training and experience at the British psychiatric hospital (41 B.G.H.) in the Middle East. This was in the nature of an innovation in the nursing of Indian psychiatric casualties, who at one time were watched over by an armed guard and if restless restrained by various rough and ready methods. The hospital in Cairo and its detachment was visited by the Consultant to the British Army and also by the area psychiatrist. The Indian hospital on the Canal was visited by a specialist from the neighbouring British psychiatric hospital (41 B.G.H.) and the Indian hospital in Palestine could call on the services of the nearby British 2 Psychiatric Centre.

During the period in which Tenth Army (afterwards 'Paiforce') was part of Middle East Force, wards at a combined British and Indian hospital were used for psychiatric casualties. A separate consultant was appointed to this Army. The Consultant to Tenth Army visited Middle East Force and was shown most of the installations and arrangements existing in the Force in a series of brief tours. At all times close contact was kept with the consultants in 'Paiforce', India and North Africa. Indeed it may be said that Middle East Force was ultimately able to accept considerable convoys of patients from both 'Paiforce' and India, being enabled to do so as a result of its growing accommodation.

THE ALLIED FORCES

The Royal Greek Army, based in Palestine for a long period, used the British services for psychiatric casualties. During the summer of 1942 an increasing stream of Greek refugees was finding its way into Syria, in many cases complete with their families. The fit male refugees became soldiers in the Royal Greek Army and rejects for the Army were sent to a camp in the Lebanon. The Greeks, like other members of the Eastern Mediterranean nationals, were frequently illiterate, especially if coming from the Greek islands in the Aegean. On the other hand, they were in no way defective mentally. These Greek peasants seemed constitutionally unable to learn the handling of machines. This put them at some disadvantage in a mechanised army as they never made good drivers of mechanical vehicles, gunners or engineers and seemed to be peculiarly destructive to machinery. A New Zealand medical officer speaking fluent modern Greek was appointed medical liaison officer to the Headquarters, Royal Greek Forces. A hospital was designed and built in Palestine, at Hadera, in the hope that the Greek medical service would be able to care for their own casualties and sick. D.M.S. was advised that a psychiatric block should be attached to this hospital and in due course it was designed, built and opened, after which psychiatric casualties of the Royal Greek Army were largely cared for by their own medical services.

Polish, Free French, Czech, Yugoslav, Chinese and, later, American forces all required help of a psychiatric kind and casualties were received into the British centres and hospitals. British out-patient facilities were used by them and the British area psychiatrists consulted. Purely Allied figures for 1941 are not available, but in 1942, 550 Allied cases of all ranks were treated and for the first quarter of 1943 Allied soldiers were seen at the rate of 1,160 per annum.

THE WOMEN'S SERVICES

Psychiatric casualties among the Women's Services also required special accommodation, which at first was not available. Such cases had to be admitted into the wards receiving women at various general hospitals in the Middle East. With the arrival of 41 B.G.H. a hut was set aside for women. By the use of single rooms some separation of officers and other ranks was made possible. With the building of 78 B.G.H., the second psychiatric hospital, more generous accommodation became available and officers and other ranks were separated. In 1943, it was recommended that a hut for women be built in Palestine in the grounds of 2 Psychiatric Centre. The clinical cases requiring hospital care met with among women were most frequently cases of psychosis, some of considerable severity. Considerable numbers of A.T.S. personnel were local enlistments—Palestinian A.T.S. (P.A.T.S.), Cypriots (C.A.T.S.) and Polish A.T.S.—and during late 1942 and early 1943 local enlistments were being enrolled in the W.A.A.F. Unfortunately, until a late date would-be recruits were not submitted to a psychiatric interview such as was available to many male local recruits and there was a demand for beds for an increasing annual number of women auxiliaries. Up to June 1943 there had been no psychiatric casualties from the British companies of A.T.S. requiring in-patient treatment.

THE EVACUATION OF PSYCHIATRIC CASUALTIES

It has already been mentioned that the atmosphere at the psychiatric centres was disturbed by the presence of any considerable number of men known to be awaiting passage out of a command to the United Kingdom. This was equally true of officers. Most psychotic officers had to be retained in centre or hospital, but a few of the neurotic evacuees were able to live in the officers' mess of 2 Convalescent Depot on the Canal. From time to time warning was received that so many psychiatric cases would be leaving for South Africa *en route* for the United Kingdom. It is worth recording for future use some very important points with regard to the evacuation of psychiatric casualties.

(1) The hospital ship concerned must be inspected with a view to any minor alterations enabling psychiatric cases to travel in reasonable safety with a minimum of nursing staff. The establishment in a hospital ship of mental nursing orderlies is normally one per hospital ship. Certain hospital ships should have extra mental nursing orderlies attached to them and safe accommodation for, say, 50–100 cases of a psychiatric kind. The points to which attention must be given are:

(a) the exits to the deck from wards (there must obviously be only one exit from the ward to the deck);

(b) the question of portholes must be gone into, especially in places like lavatories and bathrooms;

(c) if precipitation into the sea is an easy matter, an extension to the bulwarks is easily put up, consisting of rope netting made fast to metal uprights. Netting is recommended, as if canvas is used the men resent not being able to see across the sea;

(d) airing space must be chosen with a view to seeing that there are no possible means of precipitation from the airing space to a lower deck or into the holds of the ship. In the event of men who travel in an actively suicidal state (to be avoided whenever possible), the presence of an entirely enclosed space for use on an airing deck should be considered. Sometimes it is quite possible to rope off a small space and see that it is secured by netting, but it must always be remembered that the crew require free access to all parts of the ship, which may make roping off an entire part of the deck very difficult. Experience in the Middle East showed that psychiatric cases did not resent being kept in a species of rope cage on the airing deck provided one or more nurses were in the cage with them.

(2) A nurse should always be with psychiatric cases and the patients should be occupied with simple games or occupational work of a diversional nature. Hospital ships carrying psychiatric casualties should be provided with enough material to give occupation on the voyage. Games and books should be plentiful, a point that tends to be overlooked. If it is intended to show films on the voyages of hospital ships (and they are very much enjoyed by the men), it is important to see that those films are good and show suitable subjects.

(3) An embarkation hospital was essential in the Middle East for both arriving and out-going personnel. 13 B.G.H. at Suez was selected, the hospital being situated on a desert site just to the north-east of the Suez–Cairo road under the Attica Hills. One of the early convoys of psychiatric cases created such disturbances at this

hospital, having to wait there three or four nights instead of only one, that a wired-in compound was erected around two large huts which at one time had been used for medical stores and which were situated just outside the hospital perimeter. Separate latrine and ablution facilities were also provided and this compound could be used for a period of several days if necessary. The departure of a convoy from hospitals was an event which created a good deal of bustle and excitement among both patients and staff. Kit and clothing had to be made up, labels prepared, escort parties arranged—a very great drain on psychiatric hospitals—and, last but not by any means least, eleven copies of nominal rolls of the party had to be provided together with all essential medical documents.

During the three years, September 1940 to August 1943, there were only two calamities among psychiatric casualties being transferred to the Union of South Africa, both by precipitation into the water. This speaks volumes for the care and attention these cases received on board the hospital ships.

Towards the end of 1942 and in early 1943, large numbers of psychiatric casualties had accumulated in the hospitals and the accommodation at 41 B.G.H. especially was severely taxed by the necessity for holding large numbers of psychotic individuals from many nationalities. For some there was no possibility of evacuation. It was impossible to return to their homes Greeks, Free French, Belgians, Poles, Yugoslavs, Czechoslovakians, Malayans, an occasional inhabitant of Indo-China and, also, German and Italian prisoners-of-war. It was very difficult to return others such as Seychellois, Mauritians, an occasional Turk, West Indians and West Africans, Cypriots and Maltese.

Another problem arose in connexion with local enlistments. For example, if a Palestinian, either Arab or Jew, was discharged from the Army on mental grounds and was unfit to be received into the civilian population, it was found early on that there were not sufficient civilian mental hospitals in Palestine to receive them. A considerable number of unbalanced Jewish and Polish personnel were unfortunately accepted for service in the A.T.S., and while it is not claimed that the number of women who required care as a result of chronic mental illness was high, it meant that a number of the limited beds provided for the Women's Services were continuously occupied by women for whom no civilian mental hospital in the countries of the five seas was available. As may be imagined, the atmosphere of the centres or hospitals required to hold chronic mental cases as free patients was subjected to a demoralising influence.

The evacuation of officers was slowed by the infrequency of hospital ship accommodation, and here again the long period of waiting, either in the convalescent depot, psychiatric centre or hospital, led in many instances to deterioration of morale in those centres where such officers were detained.

A point worthy of mention in respect of transportation by sea of psychiatric casualties is the labelling of these cases. They must be so labelled that the officers on the ships realise when they are dealing with a possible suicidal or dangerous patient. There is always a tendency to send patients home under a neurotic rather than a psychotic label, and this is especially marked with officers. It should be recorded that for many neurotic cases, passage by ordinary transport is quite possible, but here again the notes sent should be sufficiently clear to enable the medical officer on the transport to realise the nature of the case.

Movement of psychiatric casualties by air was quite frequent in the later stages of the desert campaign and will no doubt be the method of moving all casualties in the future. Over short distances it presents no difficulties, but for long journeys requiring staging at night, hospital accommodation at each stop, safely enclosed and adequately staffed is necessary. Actively suicidal patients should not be moved by air over great distances.

It was not until early October 1942 that the consultant was able to visit the hospitals built for the Imperial Forces in the Union of South Africa, and at this time a careful study of evacuations was made with the officer in charge of the medical division at the Oribi Imperial Military Hospital, Pietermaritzburg.

The psychiatric cases were disembarked at Durban and then usually transferred to the care of the South African Medical Corps at Oribi Imperial Hospital on the outskirts of Pietermaritzburg, where 250 cases could be accommodated. Wards for 60 psychotic patients were available but difficult and anti-social psychotic soldiers were placed under the care of the civilian mental hygiene service in the Pietermaritzburg Mental Hospital (known as Townhill). Approximately 200 soldiers had been dealt with in this way between November 1940 and October 1942. At the time of the consultant's visit to South Africa only 10 psychotic soldiers remained at Townhill. The men were for the most part deteriorated schizophrenics or general paralytics whose treatment had not been successful. Two severe depressions were seen and one case of chronic excitement. At this hospital both the officers and other ranks wore civilian clothing and meals were all taken in the same dining room. Pocket money at the rate of 5/- per week was provided and the patients had daily papers, access to the hospital libraries and wireless programmes. Church services were held on Sundays and chaplains visited the men during the week. Two guineas weekly was paid at Townhill for an officer and £1/8/- weekly for a N.C.O. or other rank. Daily rates were thus 6/- and 4/- a day respectively. All the accommodation for psychiatric casualties both at Oribi and at Townhill Hospital was excellent and the Townhill Hospital provided an 'open' convalescent villa from which parole was granted freely. It was hoped that when the Imperial Convalescent Hospital at Howick was ready it would serve as a convalescent centre for neurotic cases not requiring further treatment, and 150 or 200 beds were envisaged for this work. Occupational work was at a high level in both hospitals and was being planned on an extensive scale at Howick.

From May 1, 1941 to October 1, 1942, a period of seventeen months, a total of 1,456 psychiatric cases were evacuated from the Middle East, of which 1,188 were drawn from the British Army, 121 from the Royal Navy and 152 from the Royal Air Force. Taking all these Services together, the diagnoses were as follows:

TABLE 65

Psychoses	Numbers	Per cent.	Neuroses	Numbers	Per cent.
Manic depressive states and psychotic depressions	73	(5·07)	Anxiety neuroses, including effort syndromes	266	(18·28)
Schizophrenia	422	(29·0)	Hysteria, all forms	97	(6·666)
Toxic and organic psychoses	27	(1·856)	Neurasthenia, obsessional states and neurotic depressions	127	(8·727)
Mental deficiency	140	(9·62)			
Other psychoses	8	(0·548)			
Epilepsy	151	(10·38)			
Psychopathic or temperamentally unstable individuals	145	(9·965)			
	966	(66·439)		490	(33·67)

The psychiatric wing at Oribi Imperial Military Hospital was part of the medical division and Canadian sisters with psychiatric experience formed most of the nursing staff.

Officers for the most part were dealt with in the usual officers' quarters at the Oribi Imperial Military Hospital. A few officers had been allowed to live in quarters in Durban or elsewhere. Officers had the great advantage of being allowed to use the club at Pietermaritzburg and their amenities were on a very generous scale. There was, nevertheless, in spite of the comfort and kindness with which these invalids were surrounded, a general desire to return to the United Kingdom and it was evident that cases once evacuated from Middle East Force were seldom likely to return to the force as useful members of the Army.

Hospital ships to the United Kingdom were very scarce and during 1942 only one ship had been able to clear the centres in the Union of South Africa.

THE GROWTH OF OUT-PATIENT WORK

Establishments for area psychiatrists to the Cairo and Alexandria districts were obtained early in 1942 and specialists appointed to these areas began their work on April 1. The consultant had run an out-patient centre in Cairo since 1940, but it had become impossible to attend very regularly on account of other duties. Nevertheless, a great number of soldiers had been referred for opinion and it became obvious that whole-time out-patient officers were required. The Area Psychiatrist to Cairo Area was attached to 15 B.G.H. in Cairo (Agouza) and was responsible for out-patient consultations at this hospital and also for opinions and recommendations regarding officers requiring psychiatric help. In addition, this specialist was put in charge of the observation centre at 63 B.G.H. at Helmieh where a separate out-patient centre was established. The specialist also visited other hospitals, detention barracks and the base depots of New Zealand and South African troops. The psychiatrist in Alexandria performed similar duties and was responsible for the wards at 64 B.G.H. and maintained a close liaison with the specialist to the Royal Navy. In Palestine, area work was done at first by an experienced psychiatrist who became officer in charge of the medical division of 62 B.G.H. in Jerusalem. When this hospital proceeded to Tobruk, the officer commanding 2 Psychiatric Centre took over as much of this work as he was able to manage in addition to his hospital duties.

Soon after the capture of Tripoli, a specialist officer was sent up to the town to organise an advanced psychiatric wing. He became the Area Psychiatrist, Tripoli (1943), visited neighbouring units as required and had, in addition, the duty of visiting Malta. The work of these area psychiatrists was most valuable. They acted principally as out-patient consultants and they all had access to beds so that there was no delay in the admission of the soldier when that was required. The area psychiatrists were able to help materially with local problems, with instruction and reports to unit medical officers and with disciplinary cases. They were also able to take some part in selection procedure, especially in the examination of local recruits and of the special selection boards later instituted for the examination of certain units like the parachute troops or those about to be transformed, for example, from yeomanry to armoured units or yeomanry to signals.

An illustration of the work of the Area Psychiatrist at Cairo for a quarter in 1942 is given on the next page.

			Officers	Other Ranks
British Army	⎫ Including Women's	⎧	3	301
Royal Air Force	⎬ Services	⎨	1	12
Dominion Troops	⎭	⎩	—	197
Coloured Troops	. . . .		—	102
Indian Army .	. . . .		—	4
			4	616

One result of the appointment of area psychiatrists was the realisation of a long cherished desire to see out-patients exceed in-patients in Middle East Force. This occurred in the first two quarters of 1943 with a good margin.

THE FOLLOW-UP SYSTEM

A follow-up system for all psychiatric casualties was established from January 1, 1941. A card printed in the Middle East was filled in by medical officers at observation centres, psychiatric centres or psychiatric hospitals for each patient admitted. The cards were forwarded at intervals to the office of the consultant at G.H.Q., where a register was compiled and the cards filed alphabetically. Follow-up letters were sent out three and nine months after discharge from the medical unit concerned. The letters were sent to the officer in charge of 2nd Echelon who forwarded them to the location of the unit concerned, a heavy piece of work. With troops undergoing such wide dispersal and frequent moves over extensive areas and their engagement in such varied operations, it was not expected that anything approaching 100 per cent. of answers would be obtained; in fact 30 per cent. were returned during 1941, a figure which slowly increased to over 60 per cent. by 1943, so that fair samples were obtained of the ultimate disposal of psychiatric casualties and a great number of cards became available for further analysis. The card was designed with a view to being of further use after discharge from the Army, each containing clinical information useful in the after-care of soldiers who might require it on return to civil life.

THERAPY

As soon as specialists were collected in sufficient numbers and the psychiatric centres were built, staffed and opened (July 1941), special methods of therapy were introduced, e.g. prolonged narcosis, psychotherapy, electric convulsive therapy and occupational therapy with some emphasis on outside work and games, physical training, swimming, basket ball, football and the like, which were comparatively easy to start and required little equipment. As instructors and equipment were obtained (equipment such as sports garments, apparatus for physical training and the necessities for various sports), team contests of all kinds

were promoted and encouraged. The apparatus for E.C.T. was manufactured locally by an electrical engineer to a factory manufacturing
artificial teeth in the outskirts of Tel Aviv. There were certain special
complications encountered in therapy. Continuous narcosis even for
short periods requires a very considerable consumption of sedative
drugs, and with the rapid growth of the Army suitable drugs were at
times in short supply. Even when despatched, there were losses *en
route* so that improvisation was often necessary on the part of medical
officers. Thus, if intravenous barbiturates or paraldehyde were not
available, barbitone, phenobarbitone, chloral-hydrate or bromides, or
a combination of such alternatives, were used. A list of drugs was
prepared for the Committee on Drugs in December 1941.

One feature of continuous narcosis in hot climates became early
evident. The nursing of cases undergoing this treatment required
special care, as the temperature regulation of the body became easily
disordered during treatment and very high temperatures were sometimes recorded, a point which required constant watching. In hot
climates the sudden rises of temperature experienced during narcosis or
hypoglycaemic states easily get out of hand.

REHABILITATION

The potentialities of the convalescent depot as a rehabilitation unit
became more and more a matter for investigation. In 1942 the experiment was made of handing over 200 beds to a specialist in psychiatry at
a convalescent depot situated at El Arish, a mud town of some size and
long history situated on the coast of the Sinai peninsula. The results
of this experiment, made on somewhat unpromising material, were
impressive. After three or four weeks' training with open-air games,
bathing and swimming, lectures, entertainments and any necessary
minor treatment, usually for the very common complaint of sleep
disturbed by battle dreams, soldiers became bronzed and fit and actively
cheerful, losing the look of dispirited apathy, indifference or depression
with which many were admitted, even after a period of hospital treatment. A similar block of beds was later set up in connexion with an
advanced psychiatric wing at Tripoli during 1943. The convalescence
and rehabilitation of psychiatric casualties are matters which require
detailed study. A convalescent depot for psychiatric casualties alone,
commanded and staffed by medical officers with special experience
both in psychiatry and the principles of rehabilitation, would probably
prove an economical and effective method of dealing with breakdown,
especially among troops affected by battle conditions. Among such
soldiers morale and spirits are quickly restored. Their successful
rehabilitation is partly medical, partly educational, partly social and
partly administrative in character.

OCCUPATIONAL THERAPY

In 1940 this important subject had already received consideration. A woman who was a fully qualified occupational therapist had been marooned in the Middle East by the entry of Italy into the war. In September 1940 she had already begun work at 64 B.G.H. at Alexandria. A woman in Cairo with the British Red Cross Society had evolved a small box of materials containing certain simple occupational equipment, a box which was made available by the B.R.C.S. for matrons at general hospitals. The work at the hospital in Alexandria was of a high standard, although materials were scanty. An exhibition of occupational work done by psychiatric casualties in the centre established at this hospital was given at G.H.Q. in March 1941. A great many people attended this exhibition and the consultants concerned with occupational therapy, D.A.G. and the B.R.C.S. subsequently held conferences from time to time with a view to developing occupational therapy for all patients in hospital in the Middle East.

The result was that by 1942 a complete policy concerning the subject was defined in a detailed memorandum concerning occupational work and was issued by D.M.S. Appendices to this memorandum gave a list of articles that could be obtained from various sources, including Army services, for such occupational work. This memorandum envisaged occupational therapy being practised at general hospitals, convalescent depots, psychiatric centres and orthopaedic centres and included in the list basket making, bookbinding, fretwork, leatherwork, painting and sign-writing, rug making, weaving, tapestry, carpentry and tin-smith work. Also included was equipment for remedial therapy. The B.R.C.S. provided a yearly grant of 2/6d. a bed towards the purchase of materials not provided by their issues or by W.D. issues. The psychiatric centres and hospitals developed occupational work in many directions. Thus, in spite of the fact that many of the wards were situated in desert sand, gardens were started. 2 Psychiatric Centre, which was situated in Palestine, not only developed remarkable flower gardens begun by the enthusiasm of the matron, but also started a large kitchen garden which grew much produce such as beans, peas, potatoes, tomatoes, cucumbers, cabbages and lettuce. The season for the vegetables was short, but patients in the centre were able to enjoy fresh vegetables for a period and were credited with the material consumed so that it was possible to purchase seed, etc., to carry on the kitchen garden established. The difficulty with regard to garden and farm work was the question of water, the early arrival of hot weather and, in desert areas, the constant shifting of the sand. Animals were also kept at hospitals and centres—fowls, rabbits, budgerigars and pigeons were especially popular.

Apart altogether from the curative and remedial aspect of occupational therapy of almost any kind, it has a special place in a force separated so far from home and family in giving soldiers a therapeutic distraction from constant thoughts about home during hospital periods. The psychiatric hospitals naturally developed many more outlets of an occupational kind than the general hospitals. As instances of this, the concert parties proved a constant source of work and occupation at the psychiatric hospitals and centres; not only were band instruments purchased for patients but they made all the clothing for costumes, and the carpentry for the stage, the electrical work and the painting of scenery were done by them. On the works side, shops were opened for the repair of hospital furniture, for repairs to clothing, for the cobbling of boots and shoes and for the manufacture of articles such as office furniture which were frequently sold to units requiring stationery boxes, in and out trays and the necessary signs and notices required in all hospital grounds.

D.Ds.M.S. made administrative arrangements for the teaching and distribution of occupational therapy in the various commands. Many women resident in the Middle East or who were there before the outbreak of war, rendered invaluable help. The early assistance of the commissioners and the deputy commissioners of the British Red Cross Society and the Order of St. John of Jerusalem enabled occupational therapy in the psychiatric wards to be got under way at an early date. In Palestine the Commissioner of the Order of St. John of Jerusalem gave most valuable assistance and by her aid, occupational work at 2 Psychiatric Centre was commenced almost as soon as this was opened. As the occupational work proceeded another woman undertook the organisation of supplies and did a great deal herself in the hospitals of Jerusalem (48 and 60 B.G.Hs.), devoting much time to teaching and helping in the departments. Interesting exhibitions were held in Jerusalem and in Haifa and Tel Aviv and by means of sales a good deal was done to promote the purchase of materials and make occupational therapy self-supporting.

The shortage of trained occupational therapists was a great difficulty. The M.N.Os., N.Os., and sisters who were anxious to learn something of the work were attached to psychiatric centres as soon as their occupational departments were opened. In this way an occupational therapist was trained for 2 Psychiatric Centre and the woman concerned was taken on the staff of this centre and was allowed to live in the sisters' mess of 23 B.G.H. The demand for occupational therapists grew steadily during the campaign and eventually it was decided to establish a school at 63 B.G.H., Helmieh. D.D.M.S., B.T.E., arranged for the development of occupational therapy in the hospitals of his command.

The B.R.C.S. gave an exhibition of occupational therapy at Shepheard's Hotel, Cairo, on June 30, 1943, which was opened by the American Ambassador. The great scope of the work in all the hospitals serving British troops in Egypt was very evident and of great interest. One of the unusual exhibits was a stand of beautifully coloured artificial flowers made from odd bits of bread and salvaged coloured strips of paper. Models of battleships, complete with guns, were made out of all sorts of salvaged materials, and interesting leather-work such as pocket books, purses and photograph frames were very attractive. Some hospitals evolved toys as a speciality. The toys made by 2 N.Z.G.H. at Helwan had always been one of their great specialities. The psychiatric hospital (41 B.G.H.) and the two psychiatric centres exhibited a collection of toys specially made for the children of Malta. This exhibition was held at G.H.Q. on March 27 and 28, 1943, and three large boxes containing nearly 300 toys were sent to the island. One administrative difficulty concerning occupational work is the tendency hospitals must almost necessarily develop to retain in hospital certain experts for an unduly long period. For example, it is difficult to part with a patient who is an expert tailor or tin-smith, or who makes a first-class female impersonator in the concert party. In order to minimise this danger a rule was made by which a term was put to hospital residence without special permission and reference to the consultant. In order to acquire funds for occupational work in hospitals sales were held from time to time and, in fact, the centres and hospitals were usually able to become self-supporting.

THE MENTAL HEALTH OF UNITS IN THE DESERT AND IN THE SUDAN

The consultant first visited troops in the Western Desert in October 1940. At this time the railhead was at Daba and the Army of the Nile, afterwards Western Desert Force, and, from November 1941, Eighth Army, was busily preparing a series of defences in the nearer portions of the Western Desert. It was comparatively easy to visit individual battalions and units, to make contact with regimental medical officers and the administrative medical officers of divisions.

The medical officers of units referred a number of men on these early visits who had already become problems to their company officers. A number of unstable, mentally dull and backward men were interviewed with their regimental medical officers and sent down to one of the established observation wards in the medical base area. The medical officers could be divided into three main groups—(*a*) those fully aware of psychiatric problems and anxious to learn how such problems could be handled; (*b*) those who insisted that their units presented no psychiatric problems and would not do so when any action began ;

and (c) those frankly impatient of all psychiatric patients and insistent on immediate evacuation without any attempt at treatment. This last group were inclined to describe themselves as 'simple soldiers'—forgetting apparently that they were doctors. This type of attitude was not so common among regimental medical officers as among those of field ambulances, where it was frequently widespread. Fortunately the majority of regimental medical officers met in these early days were fully cognisant of the importance of psychiatric breakdown, as it was already occurring in 1940 before any fighting of a serious kind had taken place.

Some fourteen days spent in the Western Desert in October and November 1940 showed clearly that certain welfare and other matters were of great importance at that time. Men were impatient of inaction. Dominion troops especially were getting restive. In the more forward areas one found that news was so scanty that rumour formation was common. The morale of the units was often well illustrated by the type of rumour that passed round. Thus at one unit the consultant was asked whether it was true that the Germans had landed in Kent, while at another he was asked whether it was true that Mussolini had committed suicide! It was obvious that units were not sufficiently supplied with news, with wireless receivers or with local papers, and that British troops were more than a little anxious and concerned about the bombing at home. Here and there one met men who had already lost relatives in the early bombing raids on Britain. The Corps Commander very kindly gave the consultant an interview at the end of the first tour and asked for recommendations. The consultant made the suggestion that offensive operations, even if on a small scale, would be a very good tonic to the men. It was not, of course, known to him that operations against Sidi Barrani had already been planned.

In December 1940 D.M.S. despatched the consultant to the Sudan with special instructions to investigate the breakdown of a British battalion in action. The study of the battalion which had broken down was of great importance, illustrating as it did most of the factors which make for poor morale in a fighting unit.

The battalion had been heavily bombed from the air. The obsolescent R.A.F. aircraft had been driven off and no A.A. guns were available. The ground was rocky. An ammunition truck blew up. In the ensuing confusion it was rumoured that the order to retire had been issued. Men began to drift away from the battlefield. The rumour reached the R.M.O., having in its passage gained the semblance of an authoritative instruction, and he moved to the rear, taking his wounded with him. Calling upon the A.D.S. he passed on the information and the A.D.S. packed up and moved back. Some of the troops went back as far as twenty-five miles. Others encountered the commander of the brigade to which their battalion belonged and at once acted upon his order to return whence they had come.

Following the action there were 26 cases of either panic reaction or of true anxiety states. Among them were some with conversion symptoms such as deaf mutism or hysterical paraplegia. There were two suicides.

On interviewing officers and men it became evident that all the factors conducive to poor morale with resultant failure in action were present in this case. The battalion had been overseas for over two years and there had been a long history of unhappiness in the officers' mess for various causes.

The men had been doing a lot of defensive digging in the region of Atbara in very high temperatures for nearly eight months and had lost a very large number of non-commissioned officers (76) on promotion to other units.

This episode is recorded in some detail as it provides useful lessons. Breakdown in battle was almost invited by the conditions under which this unit went into action. The men were tired by long tropical service; they were moved rapidly and without rest and the nature of the operation was not clearly understood by all ranks. The officers had been in an unhappy state as a group and leadership was therefore at a low level, with certain quite outstanding exceptions among the junior officers. A.A. guns were absent and the men saw the aged R.A.F. machines driven from the scene of action. One particular factor which seems to have upset the men was the sight of wounded of another battalion streaming back with unpleasant looking wounds. These wounds had been caused by mine injuries and resulted in a good deal of facial disfigurement.

A report was written for D.M.S. for transmission to the C. in C. and a copy was sent to the *Qaid*. The recommendations made suggested that the battalion should have a wholesale reposting of officers, that it should be moved to a more temperate climate and be occupied in strict military training and that the physique of the men be carefully checked over and regradings made where necessary. It was also recommended that prominence should not be given to this episode. It falls to be recorded that this battalion did exceedingly well in the heavy desert fighting of the next two years.

One point of medical interest was the use of repeated sedatives on the psychiatric cases arriving at the base hospital (32 B.G.H.), situated at Gordon's College in Khartoum. Generous sedatives were given to the men on their arrival and the doses were repeated until the men were well enough to be up and about. Very favourable reports were made upon the results of this sedation.

The policy underlying the treatment of psychiatric casualties in M.E.F. was a constant one, undergoing such modifications as were rendered necessary as the campaign lengthened. This policy is shewn in graphic form in Fig. 65.

Many soldiers sent out to the Middle East were of poor quality, often unstable mentally, and had received a minimum of good training. These men easily broke in battle and would come streaming back as frightened, unhappy individuals, and the combatant officers were very anxious that these men should not be returned to their units. This attitude was often a very prominent feature of the combatant officer's outlook on psychiatric casualties, and in some cases when men were sent back to their original units re-evacuation took place by a fresh channel in the hope that a second evacuation would succeed in ridding the unit of the particular undesirables.

Experience brought forcibly to the fore the wide areas over which actions took place and their remarkable speed. It is not always remembered that the Egyptian Western Desert and the Libyan Desert are large enough to contain India. The constant movements of medical units and the long distances between medical posts in the early days made static treatment even for a few days a matter of difficulty. The policy, therefore, was to get men back into general hospitals and, as soon as they were built, into special centres in the Delta or Palestine, there to be treated and afterwards rehabilitated by a period at a convalescent depot.

In the battles of 1940, beginning with Sidi Barrani and ending with the remarkable march of 7th Armoured Division and the *coup de grâce* administered at Beda Fomm, the absence of psychiatric casualties was striking. In a quarterly report to D.M.S. for the period January 1 to March 31, 1941, the consultant was able to report that the figure of 200 would be overstating the total from all three Services. The clinical features were nearly all of the anxiety type and certain hysterical features were not uncommon. Most usual was a limited amnesia or 'blackout'. Gross conversion hysterical lesions were very few in number and such hysterical symptoms were mainly headaches, loss of memory, hysterical deaf-mutism and an occasional case of amblyopia.

The absence of nervous casualties in the first battles of the Army was remarkable. Some of the actions fought had been quite severe and the final march of the column which cut off the Italian retreat from Benghazi was a fine military feat carried out with comparatively scanty supplies in abominable weather, and must have been a very great strain on all taking part. The very low figures of psychiatric casualties resulting from this early phase were explained at the time as being due to a number of factors, among which the most important were the speed and success of the actions. There were no 'slogging matches' as yet in the desert; battles were brief in time and hold-ups did not occur; the morale of the troops was tremendously high, partly owing to the fact that a period of inactivity and comparative boredom had been ended. The Royal Air Force rendered invaluable assistance and almost prevented the bombing of troops by the Italian Air Force, and the supply services were extremely successful over the hundreds of miles of desert in front of the railhead or improvised port. Also, it may be mentioned, much unstable human material, having manifested itself, had been removed from units before action commenced. The consultant noted the close relationship between the state of training and the evidence of neurosis. Thus, an experienced and highly competent armoured division with its infantry and gunners provided only one moderately severe anxiety case requiring hospital care throughout the whole period from Sidi Barrani to Beda Fomm.

During this campaign the question of concussion and its effects became prominent. Of special interest were cases resulting from direct hits on armoured fighting vehicles and the too frequent accidents, such as collisions. The consultant was frequently asked by medical officers how best to treat patients during the period of illness and how to deal with after-effects, which were mainly headache, vertigo, loss of concentration and a pronounced intolerance to sunlight. A special recommendation was made to D.M.S. that reinforcements should not be despatched to the Middle East who presented a clear history of concussion, on account of the sensitivity to sunlight that many soldiers presented after quite mild head injuries. One clinical feature which was perhaps unexpected was the great frequency of profound depression met with among the anxiety cases.

In December 1940 and later, many senior officers asked questions about the diagnosis 'anxiety neurosis' and a memorandum was written on the matter for D.M.S. The diagnosis, so readily understood and accepted by a psychiatrist, struck combatant officers as being a medical justification for fear, enabling men to escape from action with medical approval. The mechanisation of the Army made disappearance quite easy; not only were troops dispersed widely but a great many vehicles were available and a badly frightened man possesses a certain psychopathic courage and will take himself rapidly from the scene of action. It was for this reason that in the booklet on psychiatric casualties it was stressed that no simply frightened men should leave their units and no men should report to medical officers or medical posts of any kind without being accompanied either by stretcher-bearer or non-commissioned officer, or possessing written authority from officer or N.C.O.

The British forces were not to remain long with any possibility of rest after Beda Fomm had been fought and won by February 8, 1941. There was need for troops in Greece and in the Sudan. The battle of Keren, after some ten days' fighting, was won by Indian 4th and 5th

Divisions on March 27, while on March 5, British troops landed at Piraeus and contact was made with the Germans on April 8. The hard-won positions on the Tunisian border were attacked on March 31 and the fighting withdrawal back to the Egyptian frontier was commenced. In June the attack on Capuzzo was launched, a failure with rather bitter losses. From April to June, Iraq was a source of anxiety; troops were sent to Basra from India and, in June, to Baghdad. In June, British and Free French troops advanced on Syria and very hard fighting took place until the French troops asked for an armistice on July 11. The campaigns in Greece and Crete were fought and altogether it may be fairly said that the year 1941 was a hard one for Middle East Force. Fortunately, on the Libyan frontier there was a static period from June to November 1941, when the British troops once more took the offensive.

Notes and diaries of the early months of 1941 show the constant preoccupation on the part of the consultant with clinical cases. Not only was the out-patient department at 15 B.G.H. well attended but problems arose with civilians, officers and other ranks of other Services in addition to the Army. Officers' wives and children also required assistance. In the early part of the year the small observation centres at 63 B.G.H. in Cairo, at 64 B.G.H. in Alexandria, at the New Zealand General Hospital at Helwan and at the Australian General Hospital at El Kantara all showed an unexpected press of psychiatric work. The same story came from Palestine, 60 and 62 B.G.Hs. in Jerusalem and 61 B.G.H. in Nazareth. There followed for the consultant a good many months of constant travelling and clinical work.

A quick visit to Alexandria during the evacuation from Greece showed that the men were arriving tired but looking astonishingly fit and sunburnt and full of the expedition, talking very freely about the retreat and the evacuation with universal admiration and praise for the Royal Navy which had brought them over and, in some miraculous way, had fed everybody on the journey. The men were very insistent that they could have beaten the Germans if only they had had air cover and better weapons. Many men spoke of the skill of the German leadership, the fanaticism of the German troops and their tremendous weight of equipment and especially of the dive-bombing, which had been incessant. Some of the men had been immersed and a few such men of both Navy and Army were seen in the psychiatric centre at 64 B.G.H. The stress of these times was beginning to be shown in the psychiatric cases seen at Alexandria on April 26, of which 32 were Royal Navy, 14 Army and 1 R.A.F.—a total of 47; 21 of the naval cases were associated with battle conditions, 6 were epileptics and 4 schizophrenics. A number of other men had been distributed in the hospitals in the Canal area.

Almost immediately Crete was heavily attacked by German aircraft and it looked as if the German Luftwaffe would be attacking Alexandria, as indeed happened very shortly afterwards. D.M.S. at this time discussed briefly with the consultant the possibility that Alexandria might become a most unsuitable place for retaining and treating psychiatric casualties. Nevertheless, it was felt that the centre at 64 B.G.H. should remain. It was sufficiently far out of Alexandria to be well away from the docks, where the Fleet was an obvious target, and it was hoped that air attacks would not be on a sufficiently heavy scale to make the removal of this very important centre necessary.

By June 1, 14,967 British Imperial Troops had been evacuated from Crete out of a total of 28,614. Once again Alexandria was visited by the consultant and once again the astonishing morale of the British and Imperial troops was quite remarkable to observe. There was a sharp rise in naval psychiatric casualties, and little wonder. The amazing thing during these very anxious days was to find that so few psychiatric casualties presented themselves. The men were tired, distressed at the loss of comrades, inclined to be annoyed with the entirely blameless R.A.F., but quite certain that given adequate arms and air cover they would be more than a match for the German Army.

In early May the consultant wrote a memorandum for the Fleet Medical Officer pointing out the rise in naval casualties, the principal reason for the rise and making certain suggestions which were accepted by the Fleet Medical Officer and carried out in due course.

During these months of 1941 it began to be clear that not only were psychiatric casualties quite numerous in all the contingents composing Middle East Force, but that a great many of them could have been prevented by an adequate selection procedure or examination of a psychiatric kind previous to embarkation, and some stringent comments can be found in the correspondence and reports of the consultant during 1941.

Over and over again during these months the well-known absorption of the neurotic or the psychotic in his own difficulties and troubles was impressed upon the psychiatrist observer. Here were forces from all parts of the British Empire going through tremendous events in the Desert, Greece and Crete, in Abyssinia and the Sudan, but on many of the officers and men seen these historic events created no impression. The individual, whether officer or man, became absorbed in his anxiety or difficulty, in his supposed wrongful treatment by others, in his domestic worries, which sometimes proved quite imaginary, or his hypochondriacal aches and pains. An impression during these days was given of the urgent necessity not only for some closer links with home but also for the better dissemination of news and a wider education on world affairs.

Urgent requests for expert psychiatric screening before drafts were despatched to the Middle East began to be written by the consultant to the United Kingdom as early as February 1941.

In November 1941, fighting again flared up in the Western Desert and at first the British attack appeared to go according to plan and rapid movement looked likely once more to be the order of the day. Operations were seriously held up, however, at Sidi Rezegh. The sortie from Tobruk also was held up and the result was a heavy series of attacks and counter-attacks and a three-week battle which ended in the defeat of the enemy and the occupation of Benghazi and El Agheila. Then the Axis counter-attack swept the Western Desert Force back from the El Agheila position half-way across Cyrenaica to the Gazala line. In the desert from this time onwards until May 1942 there was a lull, although a lot of minor skirmishing and patrolling took place. During this time the psychiatric arrangements were as hitherto. Cases were treated where possible in forward units by their medical officers and those needing evacuation came back the very long journey to the Delta or to Palestine. At a medical conference held at 15 B.G.H. in Cairo in April 1942 the need for more forward psychiatric work was expressed by several field ambulance officers. The most that could be done at this time, however, was to set aside a field ambulance during quiet periods to act as a rest station.

The fighting around Tobruk late in May 1941 and the long tank battles around Sidi Rezegh increased psychiatric casualties and special attention was paid about this time to the problem of armoured units as regards food and sleep in particular. The consultant carried out a long tour of the Western Desert area in July 1941, staying with field ambulances and divisions. One impression gained from the tour suggested that more offenders than hitherto were being seen; that is to say the consultant was being asked to see men who were on charges of absence without leave or for other delinquent behaviour. During this tour cases were seen of coal miners who had learned that expert miners had become exempt from military service. These men who felt they had got into the Army 'too soon', not unnaturally felt they had been unlucky and rather resented their position. The consultant was asked to see men nearly everywhere and it was obvious that there were still some units who were carrying round mentally dull and backward individuals. Another strong impression gained on this tour was the tendency for R.A.S.C., Signals, R.A.M.C. and other units to express themselves as sick of the desert and resentful at having to remain so long there, feeling that 'anyone who wanted it could have it', as they expressed it. 7th Armoured Division was visited, among others. The A.D.M.S. of this division had always been insistent that the removal of what he expressed as 'queer' men or mentally retarded men from units did not create an impression on the unit that the man had 'got away with it'. He always maintained that the morale of a company went up when it had no longer to carry round a man who was a source of difficulty and even peril to others, especially if his behaviour was bad in action. This observation was amply confirmed on many occasions. Even where men were known to be 'swinging it', although troops would resent such soldiers 'getting away with it', yet all were agreed they were better away if they possessed no stomach for the fight. The evidence of battle nerves among forward troops could be seen on this visit more frequently than before. Here and there the men would show tremors or a stammer and comrades would tell of disturbed nights, of shouting during sleep and sometimes even of attacks on others in a somnambulistic state. Yet as a rule men would object to leaving their own units and going into hospital.

The sick and wounded were seen in advanced dressing stations or regimental aid posts and it was clear that there was some general and widespread fatigue with desert living. Officers and men were met during this tour who had had bad news from the United Kingdom of homes destroyed or damaged, of relatives killed or wounded, and these tidings were very hard to bear, affecting not only the recipient but having a depressing influence upon his comrades. There was much depression at this time about the condition of things in the United Kingdom; men wondered whether there was enough food to go round, what the damage caused by enemy bombing was really like and how extensive it really was. Some men would say they believed that England was in ruins and others had the feeling that relatives were grossly short of proper food. Wherever possible men were reassured with such details as were available, but these were very meagre. In future campaigns it should be regarded as imperative that men who are far away are given really adequate news of what is going on in the United Kingdom. The life of the country was obviously changing and men were inclined to resent women relatives being compelled to do work of a varied nature. The Middle East was not just a few days away from home; the men there felt it was 16,000 miles away and they were starving for really authentic news of home conditions. The consultant wrote about this and asked that documentary films showing bomb damage and the daily life of workers at home should be sent out to the Middle East.

In general it may be said that life was hard during these days for men in the desert. There was very little beyond a bench or table even in the divisional and Army messes. All units had to move in the shortest time possible and medical units accustomed themselves to pack and be gone in fifteen minutes. For the individual the sudden arrival of darkness meant that a man could only wrap himself in his blankets and settle for sleep. A few men made very ingenious candle lamps with old

biscuit or petrol tins. The candle within was effectively shaded from
the enemy and the enterprising owners were able to read a novel or,
what was treasured perhaps beyond everything else, the local paper
from home. Men did not want to read *The Times* or the well-known
weekly or monthly journals; what they all craved for was the local
Gazette, Star or Post describing events in their home town. Many
fighting units carried round a small box of tattered papers and books,
referred to as 'the library'.

Medical equipment seemed remarkably adequate and the opportunity
was taken of going through the panniers of field ambulances with a view
to putting in extra sedatives. Owing to supply difficulties it was necessary
to concentrate on one sedative, and phenobarbitone was chosen as
being portable and manufactured locally. Many medical officers interviewed on this tour noted that sick parades had increased in number and
it was pointed out everywhere that the men reporting sick were often
those back from Greece or Crete and that reassurance and mild sedation
at night would help them through a period of war nerves. On the way
back to Army Headquarters the desert reserve column was visited and
some Territorial Hussars who had been turned into anti-tank gunners
(Northumberland Hussars) impressed the observer with the feeling
of psychological solidity almost universally met with in good Territorial
units.

The suggestion had been frequently made that isolation in the desert
for long periods would inevitably lead to homosexuality. There was no
evidence whatsoever that this was true, but during the year 1941 and
after there were instances of determined passive homosexuals arriving
in the Middle East and giving a good deal of trouble at the base depots.

Units in the desert were at that time getting leave with fair regularity,
a week every three or four months. A good many complaints were
received from men of the long journey to Alexandria or Cairo, but of
course this could not be otherwise and the time occupied by the journey
did not count, so that a week's leave might mean that a man was away
from his unit for a fortnight or even more.

One medical point that was observed during the tour was the great
improvement in desert consciousness of all troops. Nearly all units had
a system by which cuts and abrasions were immediately dressed by a
medical orderly so that healing took place more quickly and the danger
of desert sore was minimised. From the psychiatric point of view it
was clear first that psychiatric breakdown was remarkably small and
that medical officers had learned something of the first-aid treatment
by sedation and rest, wherever possible, and were finding the method
useful. On the other hand, several commanding officers discussed
with the consultant the increase in their units of absence without
leave.

One very striking feature was the scarcity of psychiatric casualties among fighting troops. By far the most common units at this time producing psychiatric casualties were the supply services who had tremendous distances to cover, frequently by rough navigational methods and the use of a sun compass. They were often interfered with by enemy aircraft.

Nearly everywhere welfare problems seemed much more prominent than definite psychiatric problems. Men were often unable to obtain access to the N.A.A.F.I., and N.A.A.F.I. supplies were always short. Things like shaving soap and toothpaste were the items which men often spoke about, and the supply of news and mail was also a constant problem.

In May 1942, the enemy offensive against the Gazala positions began and the severest tank battle of the war, the siege of Bir Hacheim, and the final withdrawal to the Egyptian frontier took place as from June 14. By July 1 the withdrawal to the Alamein line had taken place. D.D.M.S. Eighth Army asked the consultant to visit the Army during July. This was done and the units visited comprised Rear Army H.Q., Headquarters, XIII and XXX Corps, units of 7th Armoured Division, 1st Armoured, 50th Division, New Zealand 2nd Expeditionary Force, South African 1st Division, Australian 9th Division and Indian 5th Division. The consultant for the most part stayed at the main dressing station of the Army run by 14 (British) Field Ambulance. All the sick came through this M.D.S. and the consultant was able to examine some 50 cases sent back with labels varying from N.Y.D.(N.) to battle stress, bomb blast, shock, concussion, eye-strain, myalgia and fibrositis. The majority had little disability that could not be corrected by encouragement, rest and sleep. Careful investigation was made at the South African M.D.S. (18 S.A. Field Ambulance) as well as at the A.D.Ss. of the South Africans and the New Zealanders and the New Zealand M.D.S. run by 4 N.Z. Field Ambulance.

The conclusion was reached that the proportion of psychiatric cases to total sick and battle cases of the Army was everywhere from 7 to 10 per cent. But the great majority of this percentage consisted of exhausted soldiers who were restored to full vigour by rest and sleep. From July 1–23, 1942, the centre at 64 B.G.H. in Alexandria, as in the days of 1940, once more acted as a psychiatric C.C.S., and during this period nearly 500 men were treated at this centre, the great majority of them being restored in a few days with sleep, feeding and rest and able to pass on to their base depots or to convalescent depots. Many soldiers on arriving at the centre would fall asleep in full equipment before they could be undressed and put to bed. When these cases of simple physical exhaustion were taken out of the 7–10 per cent. of all battle and sick cases from Eighth Army the proportion of true psychiatric casualties requiring further treatment for their nervous condition was approximately 2 per cent. of total battle casualties and sick. Once more it was noted that among British units the infantry showed a low incidence of exhaustion and of psychiatric casualties. Thus, out of 171 psychiatric casualties seen among British troops on this tour, 39 were R.A., 31 R.A.C., 70 came from the R.A.S.C., R.C.S., R.E., R.A.M.C. or R.A.F. and only 31 came from infantry units, most of them being instances of quite severe breakdown.

During the tour briefly described, the consultant was able to meet hundreds of officers, N.C.Os. and men in the Army and could feel that their spirit was unbroken. There was disappointment, and sometimes hostility, at finding themselves still with inadequate weapons (e.g. two-pounder A/T guns) and an insufficient supply of heavy tanks. There was also a most complete and utter exhaustion which recalled some of the days in the War of 1914–18, when men coming out of the line would look wrinkled, yellow and apathetic. Sometimes one found whole units which had become apathetic, while many soldiers presented a curious dried up yellow appearance not infrequently seen after long desert service. But there was never any realisation or acceptance of defeat, and officers and men were determined to stand on the El Alamein line, a determination which was splendidly reinforced by the arduous work of the C. in C., who seemed to be everywhere, cheering and encouraging his troops. While it is true to say that some fighting units were perhaps utterly weary and even dispirited, it was impossible to find any that did not regard their long retreat as a phase in the campaign, and the question of defeat was, in the consultant's experience, never entertained at this or any other time. Through all the gloom and disappointment the steadiness, courage and faith in themselves of the men in Middle East Force burned with a steady light, even if it were temporarily dimmed by hard knocks, fatigue and disappointment. One administrative aspect of Eighth Army was perhaps noticeable and unsatisfactory; that was the way in which units had got mixed. Divisions had strange units among them and composite battalions had here and there been formed.

It may be noted that visits to base units at this time were not so satisfactory. Men were talking more of defeat in certain base installations than anywhere in the fighting units.

Expressions such as 'We've been let down' and 'Rommel is too good for us' were commonly heard.

As a result of this rapid tour the consultant framed certain recommendations to D.M.S. on July 28, 1942, and suggested that an army or divisional rest station or camp should be set up on the coastal strip between El Alamein and Alexandria, where exhausted men could be treated and rested without going into hospital. It was also urged that the diagnosis 'physical exhaustion' should be permitted as a diagnosis for a week or ten days in suitable cases and only changed when soldiers were obviously suffering from neurosis requiring more lengthy treatment. It was also recommended that a more satisfactory method of getting men back to their units should be established. Great difficulty was being experienced in returning men to their units owing to rapid movement of the units of Eighth Army. The diagnosis 'physical exhaustion' was immediately introduced and an army rest centre was set up by the 200 Field Ambulance at Ikingi Maryut, west of Amiriya. All cases of physical exhaustion who were sent to this unit were fed, rested, bathed and provided with clean garments, their own being sent to be laundered in Alexandria, only a few miles away. Hairdressing and chiropody were also available to the men. Besides sea-bathing, active games were arranged and the number of all admissions restored in a week to physical and mental well-being was high (60 per cent.).

An account of the work of this field ambulance at this time is given by its officer commanding.

'The period over which the ambulance worked at Ikingi Maryut was from July to November 2, 1942, when the ambulance moved back to the desert. For accommodation the ambulance had blocks of four or six E.P.I.P. tents put up together on concrete bases ; each block was capable of holding from 50–60 men without overcrowding. In all, the ambulance could accommodate 300 patients. On admission the men got bed boards, palliasses and clean blankets. For patients who were not ambulant and who required more nursing for a few days we had a small house with a room for 20 patients on stretchers. There we kept patients with pyrexia until they were either fit to be in camp or had to be evacuated to a general hospital. Feeding was as good as we could make it on the rations provided and with small buildings for cook-houses, good ranges and a liberal ration issue the cooks were able to provide patients with well-cooked and appetising meals. Baths were in the form of showers, outdoors, and as the weather was warm hot water was unnecessary. The dirty clothing of patients was exchanged for clean clothing on admission and the dirty clothing washed in Alexandria for re-issue. Much of this clothing, however, was unserviceable after long and hard desert service.

'The unit hairdresser was kept busy; a chiropodist was available. Among other amenities provided there was a large recreation tent, a canteen furnished with comfortable basket chairs, small tables and a bar where N.A.A.F.I. goods—cigarettes, chocolate, soap and soft drinks—were obtainable and beer when issued. The recreation tent was well provided with table games such as cards, draughts, etc., and a good table-tennis table. Many of these amenities were provided by Welfare, Eighth Army.

'The field ambulance dance band used to play in the canteen several evenings in the week; unfortunately, there was no cinema sufficiently near for patients to visit and only a few mobile cinemas came our way in those times, but several shows were given by E.N.S.A. parties.

'Welfare provided equipment for outdoor games and we had cricket, soccer, hockey, basket ball and base ball. All patients, after their first few days of rest, were encouraged to join in games with the staff, and those who were not fit enough or did not feel like it got a lot of fun out of watching the games.

'In the matter of discipline, there was the minimum of interference with the patients so long as they kept within the camp bounds and behaved themselves. There was only one parade in the day; men formed up after breakfast to see the medical officer, and for the rest of the day they could do as they pleased; for example, they could sleep all day if they so desired. The medical officers in charge were two experienced general practitioners in civil life, and a patient began and ended his treatment with the same medical officer who first saw him on admission. Many of the patients admitted during this period required dressings for desert sores and minor septic conditions from which a high proportion of the men suffered. Mild diarrhoea was also common and cleared up rapidly. Men with any suggestion of dysentery were evacuated to 64 B.G.H. No psychotherapeutic treatment was attempted beyond advice and encouragement from the medical officer; all severe cases of psychosis or neurosis were speedily evacuated to a psychiatric centre as were a proportion of those "exhaustion" cases who did not respond to rest and good feeding. Hypnotics were available for cases with insomnia, but their use was discontinued before discharge. The average stay in the unit for pure exhaustion was 5–10 days, but a number of men whose exhausted condition was complicated by I.A.T., coryza, diarrhoea and other minor ailments had their stay prolonged to 14 or 21 days.

'Every attempt was made to give men as easy and comfortable a time as we could, with a minimum of disciplinary interference.

'On several occasions bombs were dropped nearby, and two bombs fell in the camp itself, but without casualties or damage. These incidents retarded the progress of some men quite markedly. During the opening phases of the battle of El Alamein there was a primary high proportion of severe neurosis cases who had to be evacuated, after which as the battle continued the simple physical exhaustion cases became more numerous.'

A summary of the work of the psychiatric service in 1942 is given in Table 66.

TABLE 66

The Work of the Psychiatric Service, 1942

	In-patients	Out-patients	In-patients	Out-patients	Officers	Other Ranks
	Officers		Other Ranks		Totals	
British:						
Royal Navy . .	73	76	375	526	149	901
Royal Marines . .	2	—	16	10	2	26
Merchant Navy . .	4	2	3	—	6	3
Army . . .	359	290	5,046	2,910	649	7,956
Royal Air Force . .	26	12	444	187	38	631
Dominion Troops . .	22	21	1,066	746	43	1,812
Commonwealth Troops:						
U.D.F. (non-European)	3	—	196	42	3	238
Indian Army . .	20	14	26	30	34	56
Sudan Defence Force .	—	—	1	—	—	1
Trans-Jordan Frontier Force . . .	—	—	3	1	—	4
Maltese . . .	1	—	5	—	1	5
Mauritian . . .	—	—	136	—	—	136
Palestinian . . .	—	—	495	237	—	732
Cypriot . . .	—	—	88	5	—	93
Seychellois . . .	—	—	7	—	—	7
Cingalese . . .	—	—	9	—	—	9
Women's Services . .	20	3	11	36	23	47
Allies:						
U.S.A. . . .	1	3	11	4	4	15
Fighting French . .	1	3	27	11	4	38
Poles	8	5	152	57	13	209
Royal Greek Army .	5	2	110	78	7	188
Yugoslav . . .	1	1	11	5	2	16
Czechs . . .	—	—	34	28	—	62
Chinese . . .	—	—	1	—	—	1
Others:						
Egyptian . . .	—	—	8	—	—	8
Turks . . .	2	—	—	—	2	—
P.o.W.:						
Italian . . .	10	12	24	28	22	52
German . . .	—	—	1	—	—	1
Libyan . . .	—	—	3	—	—	3
Civilians . . .	—	2	2	2	2	4
	558	446	8,311	4,943	1,004	13,254

Officers:	In-patients . . .	558	
	Out-patients . .	446	
Other Ranks:	In-patients . . .	8,311	
	Out-patients . .	4,943	
Total		14,258	

* Dominion = Australian, Canadian, South African (excluding non-European) Army, Navy and Air Force personnel.

33

(ii)
Psychiatry in Eighth Army, 1942–1943

In 1942, a plan was tried of exchanging graded psychiatrists with the medical officers of units in the two corps of Eighth Army. The idea was to supply a graded psychiatrist to each corps who could be called on to advise where necessary and at the same time to train at one of the psychiatric units a medical officer who had experience of regimental work. These officers proved themselves excellent regimental officers while serving with units and became much more valuable as psychiatrists as a result of their experience with fighting units in action. For the battle of El Alamein, however, it was thought that the Army would benefit by having a psychiatric specialist in one of the mobile medical units, and one was posted to 1 Mobile General Hospital, and with the exception of one brief period when he worked at a C.C.S. he remained with 1 Mobile General Hospital until the end of the campaign. The hospital was the first non-divisional medical unit to enter Tunis.

During the months of October, November and December the psychotic cases of Eighth Army totalled 16. The psychoneurotic cases are expressed as numbers per thousand of the force and the table below sets out psychotics, true nervous cases and cases of physical exhaustion as a ratio per thousand:

TABLE 67

Month	Mental Cases	Nervous Cases	Physical Exhaustion
October .	8	0·52 per 1,000	0·61 per 1,000
November .	7	0·57 per 1,000	1·04 per 1,000
December .	1	0·29 per 1,000	0·15 per 1,000
Total . .	16	—	—

The Army reached the El Agheila line in December 1942 and halted there for the preparation of the attack on Tripoli. From December 29 to January 23 operations were successfully carried out, and Tripoli fell on January 23, 1943. The Army went on to what became known as the Mareth line, where it again halted. During the El Agheila and subsequent battles to the fall of Tripoli 100 psychiatric cases were examined by the Army psychiatrist and 50 per cent. of them could be ascribed to some form of enemy action.

After the fall of Tripoli it became obvious that with the Army so far away a fresh organisation would be necessary, and a psychiatric specialist was sent up, as soon as Tripoli was organised as an advanced medical base, with instructions to establish an advanced psychiatric unit with hospital beds, convalescent depot beds and other arrangements that he could work out with the Army authorities with a view to evacuating as few psychiatric casualties as possible to the now far distant Delta. He organised a psychiatric wing first at 48 C.G.H. and, ultimately, at 2 B.G.H., to which he was attached for the purpose.

The psychiatric specialist with Eighth Army from January to March saw 170 psychiatric casualties, but from March to the end of the campaign on May 13 he saw 456 soldiers with the Army and was able to dispose of 17·7 per cent. in the field; 82·3 per cent. were evacuated for treatment at the advanced psychiatric wing. It is interesting to notice that of these 456 cases dealt with in the rapidly moving Eighth Army 23 per cent. gave a history of neurosis in civilian life, 5 per cent. gave a history of breakdown prior to arrival in the Middle East as a result of earlier operations, 23 per cent. gave a history of previous breakdown and treatment in the Middle East, 6 per cent. gave a history of out-patient psychiatric treatment in the Middle East and 40 per cent. of the total cases seen gave evidence of some demoralisation prior to breakdown.

THE MECHANISM OF FILTRATION, INVESTIGATION, TREATMENT, EVACUATION AND REHABILITATION

The specialist i/c advanced psychiatric wing was made the area psychiatrist at Tripoli and was given the task of organising the diagnosis, treatment, rehabilitation and redistribution of psychiatric casualties coming through the advanced psychiatric wing. The cases were collected at 2 B.G.H. where a ward of 100 beds was set aside for psychiatric cases. Accommodation was good and consisted of a large ward with five small annexes. The far end of the ward was screened off and used for sleep treatment, and the number of beds in this section varied, seldom being below ten and rarely over thirty. At the near end of the ward new arrivals were kept as far as possible on the left side, and patients completing treatment on the right side. Throughout treatment the patient was given the conception of something active being done for him and the atmosphere of the ward was excellent from the point of view of psychiatric treatment. The staff consisted of one psychiatrist, one G.D.O., one nursing officer, a chaplain and six M.N.Os. Ordinary hospital routine was maintained with the difference that a military atmosphere was always present. The healthy atmosphere of the ward resulted from the fact that the patient felt that a team of individuals was co-operating to cure him, and that his troubles were considered in the most sympathetic manner.

After admission cases were sorted and classified as follows:
(1) *Filtration.* Those fit for almost immediate transfer to the re-habilitation centre, simple mild cases of physical exhaustion.

Of cases passing through the filtration centre 33 per cent. were sufficiently restored to go straight to the reinforcement unit on the way back to their units or for distribution on lines of communication for a further period of convalescence. Of cases in the filtration centre 65 per cent. proceeded to the convalescent depot for rehabilitation and only 2 per cent. required evacuation to the base hospitals in the Delta.

(2) *Investigation.* Mainly cases of psycho-somatic syndromes.

(3) *Treatment.* (a) Those requiring narcosis therapy, particularly those with anxiety, tension and insomnia;

(b) Those needing abreaction and complaining of 'blackouts' or headaches;

(c) Mild psychotics who would benefit by convulsion therapy.

(4) *Evacuation.* A small number (2 per cent.) who required base hospital treatment and who were eventually evacuated to the hospitals in the Delta.

These methods of therapy need not be described, but an abreaction technique with the use of ether was developed. After having had the process explained to him, the soldier lay down and was instructed to recall as much of his battle experience as he could remember. Ether was then dropped slowly on an open mask and it was found that the soldier would relive his battle experiences. When this situation was established the ether was stopped and the patient allowed to recover and encouraged to talk about his battle experience. Strong suggestion was then made that the patient's symptoms would disappear and he was sent back to the ward to sleep, with sedatives, for a varying period up to 24 hours.

REHABILITATION

The rehabilitation centre consisted of 200 beds at 7 Convalescent Depot and occupied buildings previously used as garages. The depot was situated close to the sea where excellent bathing was available. The patients had access to all the depot facilities, which included a gymnasium, football pitch and a good occupational therapy department. The work in this department was real military work, such as the overhaul of cars and the manufacture of articles with lathes or carpenter's tools, and diversional handicrafts were avoided. The stay in the depot averaged fourteen days. Of the cases admitted to the rehabilitation centre 95 per cent. went to the reinforcement unit and 5 per cent. went to a special rehabilitation unit which consisted of a farm run by the British military administration (B.M.A.) and which before the war had been an Italian experimental agricultural station. All the men worked on the farm and were visited twice weekly by the area psychiatrist. When men were fit they were sent to the advanced reinforcement control unit where they were received into what was termed the convalescent wing which was for psychiatric casualties only. The wing was run by a sergeant, two corporals and a sergeant instructor P.T. The average number of patients in the convalescent wing was 70 and the stay did not exceed fourteen days. These men were divided into three categories:

(*a*) Those fit for immediate return to unit;

(*b*) Those in need of special posting;

(*c*) Those in need of further rehabilitation and even treatment.

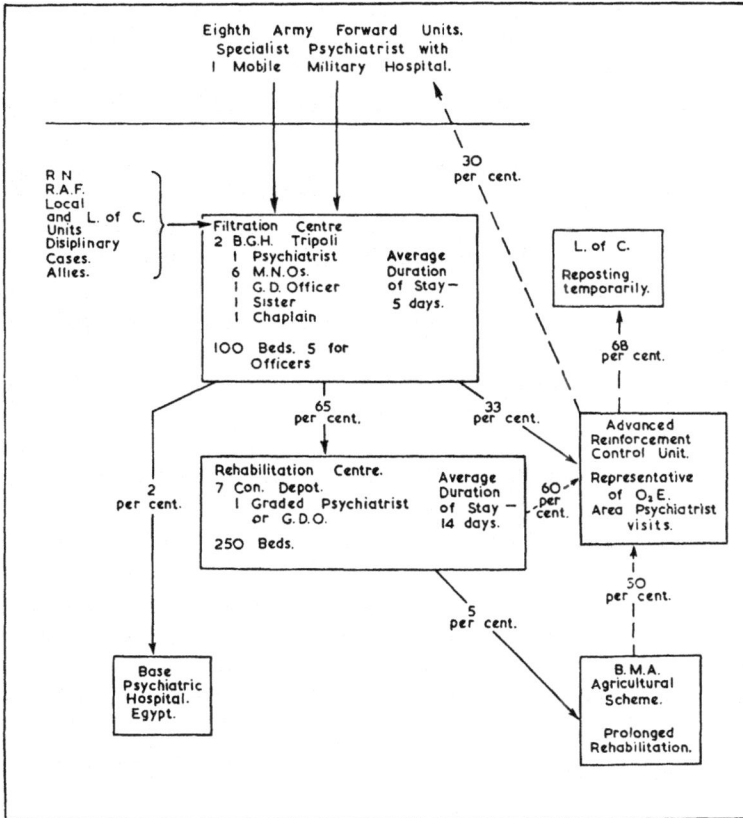

FIG. 66. The organisation of the Advanced Psychiatric Wing, Eighth Army.

The men who were fit to return to their units were sent direct to their own unit lines. Those requiring special posting were men symptom-free, but considered by the psychiatrist to be unfitted for their present jobs. A recommendation for the best type of work was suggested by the psychiatrist and by arrangement with O.2.E.* a

---

*Officer in charge, 2nd Echelon—office to which all field records are sent.

suitable posting was obtained according to the recommendation made, thus following out the procedure developed in 1940. This advanced psychiatric wing proved of great use to Eighth Army and relieved the L. of C. of a very considerable load. Figure 66 sets out in graphic form the constitution of the advanced psychiatric wing, and Table 68 shows the figures from March 15 to May 15, 1943, and the work done up to the conclusion of the African campaign.

PSYCHIATRIC CASUALTIES. ALAMEIN—ENFIDAVILLE

Certain observations may here be made concerning the phase which began with the last battle of Alamein and ended with the destruction of the enemy forces in Tunisia. During the first part of the battle psychiatric casualties remained at a low figure. On the other hand, the consultant saw some of the worst cases of acute anxiety resulting from battle conditions that he had ever encountered since the work commenced in September 1940. The incidence of these severe battle cases fell most heavily on the R.Es., whose task it was to clear passages through enemy minefields so that the infantry and tanks could pass safely through. These men had a very dangerous and arduous job. They were not only clearing mines but they were subjected also to barrage fire and to frequent mortar fire. They lived in minefields and sleep was hardly possible over stretches of days. Those cases seen by the consultant at base hospital were men of very high morale and were all anxious to return as quickly as possible to their units. As soon as they were more or less symptom free it was recommended that they spend a long period at a convalescent depot.

As the campaign progressed, however, and especially when the troops got into the rocky, wooded and more built over areas of Tunisia, the neurosis rate rose very considerably. This was partly due to the long series of battles (campaign neurosis) and partly due to the country and severe weather experienced. Compared with the small figures of breakdown in the early phases of the final campaign quoted in the table given below, the quarter January to March showed a figure of over 5 per 1,000 for troops in Eighth Army. It had been noted before that psychiatric breakdown was least in desert fighting and that directly a change of terrain was experienced battle 'nerves' tended to rise.

TABLE 68

The Advanced Psychiatric Wing. Tripoli

March 15–May 15, 1943

Admissions:			Disposals:		
As result of battle .	977	69 per cent.	To duty . . .	98 per cent.	
Others . . .	94	24 ,, ,,	Within 28 days of evacu-ation . . .	93 ,, ,,	
Out-patients .	343	6 ,, ,,	Within 90 days . .	5 ,, ,,	
	1,414		To base psychiatric hospital	2 ,, ,,	

DRAFTS AND THE SELECTION OF PERSONNEL

As early as February 1941, letters were written to the Consultant in Psychiatry at the War Office pointing out that drafts arriving in the Middle East were not always of a very satisfactory type. This became more marked during 1941 and was at its worst in 1942. Admissions to psychiatric centres or hospitals showed an unduly high proportion of men who had previous psychiatric illness or who were mentally subnormal. It was the consultant's considered opinion that 40 per cent. of psychiatric casualties in the Middle East could have been foreseen by a careful psychiatric survey or even a reasonably careful medical history. Many of these patients received in psychiatry centres showed evidence of psychopathic traits in their previous history which would have been readily recognised if any accurate case history had been taken.

In a report written in 1941 the consultant noted that these dull and backward men were able to escape accurate ascertainment during peace-time soldiering, but when faced with the stresses of embarkation, a long voyage overseas and arrival in a strange country with strange languages and peoples, with the necessity of maintaining themselves in the heat and sand of the desert with its accompanying discomforts and the absence of customary supports, such as aids to personal cleanliness and the serving of regular meals, such men began to show up in their proper light. The process of breakdown was exaggerated by action, proving once more that it cannot be too frequently and emphatically stated that modern war provides no place for the retarded and backward man among troops required to engage in active combat with the enemy. An important lesson can be learnt from the fact that, taking as a sample over 6,000 cases of psychiatric illness in Middle East Force, less than 40 per cent. were related in any way to war stress and over 60 per cent. were cases of breakdown in men who had no experience of battle conditions. In one quarter over 80 men were admitted to psychiatric centres or hospitals more or less direct from transports, or within a week of arrival in the Middle East, while in another quarter 74 men were admitted direct from transports or broke down within four weeks of arrival in the Middle East. An analysis of this last figure is available from rough notes made by the consultant in 1942 (*see* Table 69). This shows a total of 30 psychiatric (psychotic) (Pp) casualties and 44 psychiatric (psychoneurotic) (Pn) casualties.

It was indeed difficult to see how any medical man could have passed such individuals for military service. A hard driven area psychiatrist in 1942 wrote in a quarterly report: 'It is obvious that it is the policy at some depots in the United Kingdom to export the most useless and ill-trained men when drafts are sent overseas'.

Experience has shown beyond all doubt that such men can influence to a grave extent the morale of the unit to which they are posted. They create problems and disturb the efficiency of others, sometimes very gravely. It is because so many officers, sometimes highly placed, fail to realise the gravity of the problems that such individuals are often posted from one unit to another in the hope that eventually one will be found in which they will become more efficient or, at any rate, less tiresome. Proper disposal is hospital care and evacuation, yet even medical officers would be found who regard the evacuation of dullards and psychopaths as 'soft' or even as an 'injustice'.

TABLE 69

Psychoses:
Severe depression	4	
Maniacal states	2	
Schizophrenia	4	
Psychopathic personalities leading to conduct disorders	9	
Total .	—	19

Mentally Deficient:
Grossly feeble-minded	2	
Dull and backward	9	
Total .	—	11

Neuroses:
Chronic anxiety states	20	
Chronic hysteria	20	
Obsessional neuroses	4	
Total .	—	44
		74

It is not claimed that all the drafts were of this material. Happily most of the drafts contained excellent material and gave a good account of themselves. Of the evacuation for psychiatric reasons of all British Services (Army, Navy and Air Force) to the Union of South Africa for the seventeen months May 1, 1941 to October 1, 1942, 10 per cent. were psychopathic and temperamentally unstable individuals, 10 per cent. were epileptics, 10 per cent. were mental defectives and nearly 30 per cent. were labelled schizophrenics. It is unfortunately true, however, that some drafts consisted of a lot of individuals who had no common aim or morale and who arrived frequently in a somewhat resentful spirit. This was exaggerated enormously if a man felt he had been sent overseas as a punishment or if he had been sent overseas, for example, without having seen some specialist he had been advised was necessary for his case.

The consultant presents the view that if wars are to be won against first-class troops, reinforcements to fighting forces should preferably consist of drafts of organised companies or squadrons with their own officers, which have their own group morale and which have rid themselves of undesirables during the process of training. The trouble given by the undesirables is out of all proportion to their numbers. They occupy hospital beds for lengthy periods and they serve as centres of disaffection and create difficulty for everyone concerned.

On August 6, 1942, a most satisfactory interview was granted by the Adjutant-General who was visiting Middle East Force. He gave instructions that instances of men arriving with psychiatric difficulties in the Middle East should be reported direct, together with the name of the depot from which they were despatched. While tremendous improvement took place with the arrival of fresh and well trained divisions and plenty of equipment in the later part of 1942, it must not be thought that the problem ceased entirely. In 1941, 27 feeble-minded men were included in a draft of 80 for a searchlight unit; in 1942, a draft of 200 contained 4 per cent. illiterates, some of whom were untrained and untrainable for infantry, and even in 1943 four illiterates arrived in a small draft of Guardsmen. Externally they appeared admirable soldiers, but they were discovered after leaving the depot to be emotionally too unstable for battle. Infantry training depots were seldom able to identify soldiers suffering from the milder forms of mental defect; they revealed themselves in their true colours only in the desert and in fighting conditions.

SELECTION PROCEDURE IN THE MIDDLE EAST

It is of some interest to record the problems that obliged psychiatrists and others in the Middle East to evolve some method of selection. Early in 1942 two battalions of yeomanry were to be transformed—one into signals and the other to an armoured unit. These were the North Somerset Yeomanry and the Cheshire Yeomanry. All men were required to do the matrix test and had an interview with officers (who were briefly instructed) of the battalion not their own. Thus the officers of the Cheshire Yeomanry examined the men of the Somerset Yeomanry and *vice versa*. A psychiatric interview was also given to each individual. Towards the end of 1941 parachute training seemed to indicate some method of screening volunteers for the airborne brigade that was being formed and trained. The examination of the Yeomanry units showed that the men in them gave a very high intelligence rating and contained a high proportion of officer material. The selection board set up for the parachute volunteers consisted of the Officer Commanding, Parachute Regiment, President; the medical officer of the battalion and a psychiatric specialist. The board rejected a very large number of volunteers and some interesting facts were elicited during the process. Thus it was found that many men volunteered for parachute training because they were 'browned off' with their present units. Others volunteered for the sake of extra pay and others again volunteered for a more active part in the work on account of some guilty feeling at occupying an office chair at headquarters; in this way a number of clerks volunteered and many of them were unsuitable.

In January 1941, a War Office Selection Board reached the Middle East and was attached to G.H.Q. (Southern) situated at Maadi.

During the whole of the period in the Middle East considerable anxiety was created by the quality of some of the local enlistments of men and women, and in May 1943, it was suggested to D.M.S. that there should be established a centre in Jerusalem or Sarafand where both men and women recruits would be received for a period of ten days, during which time they would draw Army pay and rations, be examined physically and an estimation made of their intelligence and aptitudes, each one being seen by a psychiatrist. If, at the end of ten days, they were not considered suitable for Army service the recruits were to be returned to civil life. It was suggested that hospital buildings recently vacated by 42 B.G.H. in Jerusalem would be suitable for this work. Eventually some sort of selection centre was set up in the training camp for Palestinians at Sarafand, where it had long been badly needed. The custom had been, from July 1941, for recruits showing evidence of unsuitability or lack of the necessary intelligence to be reviewed by a psychiatrist at 2 Psychiatric Centre which was quite close to the depot at Sarafand, and in this way a considerable number of Palestinian recruits had been refused admission to the Army on psychiatric grounds.

Another source from which problems of selection frequently arose was the Middle East O.C.T.U. As this was for a long time situated in Cairo, it was easy for the consultant to see doubtful cadets. An experiment was tried by the consultant and the commandant in which the consultant saw a sample of intakes and gave a written opinion as to the suitability of the cadets for a commission and their probable place in the course. The forecasts given were surprisingly accurate. The commandant of the O.C.T.U. started his course by interviewing every cadet, and his forecasts were also remarkably accurate as regards the ability of the cadet to complete the course and obtain recommendation for a commission.

The small number of expert psychiatrists in the Middle East did not allow any early selection procedures to be carried out on a large scale, but with the arrival of the W.O.S.B. the general interest in selection procedure was stimulated and soon there were two boards functioning, one of them travelling. The psychiatrists at these War Office Selection Boards which were set up in the Middle East in early 1943 were a great stimulus to their colleagues who had been in the Middle East a long time and gave to them an idea of the great development of psychiatric procedures that had taken place in the United Kingdom.

It was realised that to establish any adequate selection centre for recruits, both male and female, in Palestine a Middle East job analysis would be necessary. The great difficulty in connexion with the selection of local recruits was the question of languages. It meant that the tests used would have to be translated into Arabic, Hebrew, German and modern Greek, a task which quite literally appalled 'M' Branch. For this and other reasons it was suggested to D.M.S. in the quarterly report for the last quarter of 1942 that the Director of Selection of Personnel should be represented at G.H.Q., Middle East Force, by a deputy director with a specialised staff. It was pointed out that a method of sifting men no longer fit for battle was also much needed, and that D.D.S.P. and staff could assist in recommending fresh postings for these men by an intelligent, scientific method.

WAR-WORN AND OTHER CLASSES OF SOLDIERS UNABLE TO CONTINUE IN COMBATANT DUTIES

The rather vexed question of what was variously called the 'war-worn' or 'burnt out' soldier, or alternatively 'campaign neurosis', deserves consideration. In ordinary language all these terms suggest that there is an end to the endurance and courage of men constantly in action. The consultant formed the impression that the average soldier presented what might be regarded as a remarkably constant level of mental health, and that in times of great difficulty and stress it was often the leaders who became 'burnt out' and whose condition was reflected in the men they led. The practical outcome of such an opinion is not to look so much for soldiers who had 'had their war' but to look for leaders who have had theirs. It may perhaps be useful to record the fact that on many occasions the consultant found that certain medical and medico-legal difficulties, such as high 'absence' rate, increased neurosis rate and high V.D. rate, seemed to be associated, at any rate in part, with the mental health not of troops alone but also with that of deputy commanders. Thus, the second in command of a battalion was not infrequently found to be the cause of such disabilities among the men. Among N.C.Os., sometimes the battalion sergeant major, sergeant or corporal, by driving and pursuing relentlessly the men under his charge, could be the cause of similar disabilities among the men of their units.

Early in 1942, the increasing difficulty in finding work for men whose category had been lowered for psychiatric reasons was becoming somewhat formidable. After a good deal of thought a memorandum was presented to D.M.S. in April 1942 which suggested the formation of a special pioneer battalion in an attempt to solve this problem. The battalions suggested were to be labelled 'non-combatant services battalions of the Pioneer Corps' and would consist of headquarters company and three companies, 'A', 'B', and 'C'. The headquarters company was to be a large one and capable of dealing with more than three companies without change as the campaign progressed. For example, it was thought there might be enough soldiers who were unable to endure further combatant service, at any rate for a period, to require 6, 9 or even 15 of such companies, the headquarters company serving to administer the whole. The headquarters company was to have an officer commanding, a specialist in psychiatry and one other medical officer and a specially instructed staff with some skill in the examination of the soldiers. The men would be downgraded by medical boards in the usual way, but on reception to the headquarters company were to be physically and mentally examined and a careful study made of their employment record. The facts discovered were to be card-indexed and the soldier who claimed knowledge of any skilled trade was to be attached to the appropriate corps for a period of trial. If a soldier proved that he was a useful tradesman he would then be transferred to the corps (i.e. R.E. or R.A.S.C.) where he could be most usefully employed in non-combatant duties. If, however, his period of trial was unfavourably reported on, the soldier would then go into one of the three companies, 'A', 'B' and 'C', divided as follows:

> *'A' Company.* This would receive war-worn soldiers of good morale and they would be armed and employed on guards and similar duties at base installations of various kinds. Part of their days would be spent in training.
>
> *'B' Company.* This would consist of the constitutionally neurotic and the psychosomatic sick.
>
> *'C' Company.* This was to consist of the dull and backward group of defective men.

It was intended that the companies should be divided into not less than five platoons and they should move about as required within the command, and a great many occupations were suggested. Thus the armed men of one platoon could be resting in the headquarters camp, one of the platoons could be doing hospital guard, another could be unloading or loading barges on river or canal, while yet another platoon could be working and doing guards at the very large base ammunition depots. A number of indoor occupations were suggested for 'B' Company, composed of the constitutionally neurotic and the psychosomatic sick. 'C' Company, containing the dull and backward group, it was recommended should be on constructional work in the open air and it was suggested that work on roads or buildings would be suitable for these men.

One of the difficulties about absorbing white soldiers into the Pioneers was the fear that the white man would 'lose face' if he was seen by natives to be doing labouring work. This general attitude was very marked among the Union Defence Force. In May 1942, the proposal was put to a conference with D.M.S., the C. in C. and the army commanders, and after considerable discussion the proposal was turned down. It is not known on what grounds the scheme was rejected, but it was suggested that one or two of the army commanders had a fear that the battalion might be considered a somewhat punitive measure operating against soldiers who had given good service and through no fault of their own had come to an end of their nervous resources. At a later stage, however, armed and unarmed Pioneer units were instituted in accordance with the practice in the United Kingdom.

The war-worn soldier did become a very considerable anxiety throughout 1942. Some battalions had been continuously engaged in forward areas for months or years. The withdrawal to the Alamein line in 1942 was accompanied by very hard fighting, especially in the 'Knightsbridge' Box. The worst period of the campaign for fatigue was undoubtedly May, June and July 1942. During the long retreat units had become very mixed and a lot of straightening out was necessary after the halt had been called successfully at the Alamein line. It was the consultant's opinion that the state of exhaustion of Eighth Army after the summer fighting in 1942 was partly due to the fact that so little organised rest and change was possible for units engaged in the Western Desert. The men got tired of fighting, became somewhat apprehensive of the German power and leadership and were 'fed up' with the desert, the rough conditions of living, the flies, the sand storms, the disappointing movement in the wrong direction and the chronic shortage of effective arms and equipment. The brief periods of rest in the desert during continuous operations, while essential and successful in relieving physical fatigue, did very little to restore the cumulative effects of constant mental strain. Men went back to battle willingly enough, but unless arrangements had been made for whole battalions or large formations to get away from fighting for a generous period of rest and training in fresh surroundings, the incidence of war-worn soldiers almost invariably rose to a high level. It was noticed by the consultant that fatigue was often evident in staff officers before battles began. During battles the loss of sleep told most severely on these tired staff officers and the young officers under 25 years of age. On the other hand, as would be expected, the younger officers became much more quickly restored to full health and vigour by rest than the older officers. Another point that is worth recording is the effect of change of terrain. Thus psychiatric cases tended to rise every time the troops went through Cyrenaica with the appearance of hidden danger in the hills, buildings and trees. This rise in psychiatric cases was well marked also when troops arrived among the rocks and much closer country with buildings, olive groves and trees in Tunisia.

Throughout the period of 1942 much consideration was given to the question of fatigue and what may be termed the exhaustion of nervous capital. As has been recorded, the diagnosis 'physical exhaustion' was introduced in the summer of 1942 after one of the consultant's periodic tours of Eighth Army.

A note may be added concerning the very hard worked staff officers at G.H.Q. Naturally, and perhaps properly, G.H.Q. becomes the butt of the fighting man. Expressions like the 'Gaberdine swine' were coined to describe the quite imaginary luxurious staff officer living in Cairo. Certain war correspondents who arrived in the Middle East late in 1942 wrote in rather disparaging terms of the luxury and ease presumably enjoyed by the staff of G.H.Q. There were many staff officers at G.H.Q. who seldom, if ever, had the time to visit the resorts apparently frequented by correspondents. Cairo was the capital of a country not at war; many of the inhabitants were making a great deal of money out of the war and it was perhaps inevitable that a good deal of display and luxury was concentrated in Cairo. Cairo was also a great centre for leave, not only for officers and men from the Desert but also from other parts of Middle East Command, and a close examination of the crowds at Gezira watching cricket or football, tennis or bowls would reveal to any skilled observer that many were fresh comers with the sand still in their garments. It was also essential to give leave to a somewhat cooler climate to men from the Sudan, from Eritrea and Abyssinia and from Palestine and Syria and the hot lands of Iraq and Iran.

People fresh from home in 1942 forgot only too readily that Middle East Force had then been fighting desperately with very little respite since the anxious days of June 1940. It is unfortunate that such impressions about G.H.Q. got about. A much truer picture could and should have been given of a group of very hard-working officers who seldom took part in the gaieties of the great capital.

Throughout the period of the Middle East campaign D.M.S. wisely insisted that officers on the staff of G.H.Q. should take a half day a week and should get local leave whenever it was possible, but there were times when a half-day holiday was frankly impossible for many officers and it was frequently stated that if local leave was taken the pile of work awaiting the officer on his return spoiled the enjoyment of local leave in advance.

(iii)

The Incidence of Psychiatric Casualties in the Middle East

On arrival in the Middle East an attempt was made to forecast for D.M.S. the probable expectation of psychiatric casualties. It was assumed, over-optimistically, that the men between 20 and 40 years of age composing the force would be a selected group.

In writing of psychosis, by which is meant the conditions legally termed insanity, the consultant estimated that the annual expectation of psychosis in the Army should not exceed 52 cases per 100,000 men, so that the yearly incidence of insanity in a force of half a million would be 260 cases annually. It was possible to obtain figures provided in the annual reports over a five-year pre-war period compiled by D.D.H. in the Middle East. These figures showed that over a quinquennial period the cases evacuated for all mental causes had been 134 per annum per 100,000. On enquiry these figures were found to include cases of 'nerves', of chronic delinquency and of mental deficiency as well as psychosis. It was not possible to abstract the cases of pure psychosis from these figures.

With regard to neurosis, it was pointed out to D.M.S. that any accurate forecast in figures was difficult, if not impossible. The general factors that would govern the incidence of nervous casualties were indicated, the chief of them being the quality of the personnel of the Army, its training level and the severity and nature of the combatant actions to be experienced.

With regard to the actions, the incidence of neurosis would depend upon whether such actions were sporadic, continuous and prolonged, successful or otherwise. It was further pointed out that climatic conditions and the incidence of special diseases, such as tropical diseases, would have their due effect. Experience in France showed that up to 20 per cent. of the sick were cases of anxiety or other neurosis, and a visit to the E.M.S. Centre at Ewell in Surrey just before sailing for the Middle East showed that 5 per cent. of convoys from France, including sick and battle casualties, during the last battles and evacuation were cases of neurosis, while cases of neurosis received from the Norway campaign formed 8 per cent. of all casualties and sick. It was recalled that during the War of 1914–18 nearly 9,000 cases of neurosis left France in 1916 alone.

A firm suggestion was made that 5 per cent. of those arriving for treatment in the Middle East hospitals would prove to be cases of neurosis, and it was estimated that this figure would be exceeded in battle periods and would diminish during periods of comparative peace. It was also pointed out that successful actions would decrease the incidence; unsuccessful or lengthy defensive actions would increase the incidence of neurosis. These estimated figures prove to have been too optimistic. The estimate was based upon a consideration of British troops alone, and it was not then (1940) appreciated that Middle East Force would become such a mixture of nationalities and that the psychiatric services of the British Army would have to provide accommodation and treatment for all comers.

In general, it may be stated that during the early campaigns of Middle East Force convoys coming into the Delta showed that from 10–20 per cent. of all sick proved to be cases of neurosis or psychosis. This figure held up to 1942, when there was a steady fall, so that before, during and after the battle of Alamein the incidence of neurosis in convoys fell to a remarkably low figure, roughly 1–2 per cent. of sick. With the establishment of the advanced psychiatric centre in Tripoli cases arriving in the Delta fell almost to vanishing point and only 2 per cent. of cases admitted to the advanced psychiatric wing required evacuation to the Delta, and these were mostly cases of psychosis requiring evacuation.

RETURNS

Figures proved difficult to collect with accuracy. Returns were asked for by the consultant and kept at G.H.Q. In 1942, however, extra returns required of medical units had reached such a formidable figure that a committee was formed to examine them, and some of the psychiatric returns were abolished.

In December 1941, a recommendation was made that the Army Form A.31, a return of all diseases, should be used for psychiatric cases, and that all psychiatric casualties should be returned as 'mental diseases' and the column for the figures divided by a diagonal stroke, Pp figures being placed above the dividing line and Pn casualties below it. Pp casualties were defined as cases of insanity, mental deficiency and psychopathic states and temperamental instability. Pn casualties were all the others. In this way a rough conception was obtained of psychiatric casualties by monthly returns from commands on A.31, which were circulated quarterly.

The figures here submitted, therefore, are not considered satisfactory or accurate, but they do give some idea of the actual numbers of psychiatric casualties, which include in-patients and out-patients for all Services and all forces in M.E. Command.

TABLE 70

Annual Incidence of Psychiatric Casualties, 1940–43

1940: October–December (552)
Annual incidence (based on three months' experience) .   .   .   2,200
1941: Figures for this year do not include Allies, Indian troops or the
Tenth Army, but do include Imperial troops—i.e. New Zealand,
Australian and South African—admitted to British Centres   .   7,429
1942: Including Allies and Indian troops   14,259
Out-patients—5,388
1943: All troops (annual incidence based on six months January 1–June 30)   11,442
Out-patients—6,224

Whatever the value of these figures may be they are an accurate representation of the growth of psychiatric casualties during the fighting years. The annual rates (based on three months) begin at 2,200 in 1940 and go up to 14,259 for 1942, falling slightly in 1943 to 11,442, an estimated annual rate from the actual figures of six months.

There is another set of figures which is very important, and that is the ratio of psychiatric breakdown to the total strength of Middle East Force. These work out as follows:

TABLE 71

Psychiatric Casualties Expressed as Incidence per 1,000 of M.E.F.

	Psychiatric casualties	Battle casualties	For comparison	
			Malaria	Dysentery
1940 (based on 3 months) .	8·5	Not Available		
1941 (all troops) . .	24·0	36·7	19·5	28·9
1942 (all troops) . .	21·2	31·1	29·1	33·3
1943 (based on 6 months January to June. All troops)	15·2	22·5	29·1	33·2

These figures, though not finally checked, are given in this account for the reason that they were those collected by the consultant and appear in returns rendered to the War Office during the course of the war. They can be so broken down as to disclose the incidence of psychiatric casualties among United Kingdom personnel. The figures given in Table 72 refer to in-patients only.

TABLE 72

British Services Only. Annual Admissions to Psychiatric Centres or Hospitals

	Royal Navy		Royal Air Force		British Army		Totals	
	Officers	O.Rs.	Officers	O.Rs.	Officers	O.Rs.	Officers	O.Rs.
1940 (based on 3 months)	8	72	32	196	96	1,212	136	1,480
1941 . .	43	290	112	638	162	2,338	317	3,266
1942 . .	73	375	26	444	459	5,046	558	5,865
1943 (based on 6 months)	186	282	30	466	328	5,218	544	5,966
Totals—4 years .	310	1,019	200	1,744	1,045	13,814	1,555	16,577

When these cases are related to battle experience a somewhat surprising result emerges. Whereas in the Royal Naval figures nearly 90 per cent. of cases were directly due to battle conditions, the Army and Royal Air Force casualties show that only a minority were associated with such conditions. In one analysis of a sample of cases, only 34 per cent. had relation to battle conditions. Among a sample of 2,500 admissions to 41 B.G.H. only 33·3 per cent. had any relation to battle conditions. A sample of 1,080 patients treated in hospitals in the Middle East was examined by the consultant in June 1943 and it was found that 36 per cent. might be considered to have been precipitated by battle conditions, including bombing on lines of communication. If these figures are averaged it will be seen that battle conditions precipitated at most only 35 per cent. of psychiatric casualties. The comparatively low incidence of battle conditions as a cause of psychiatric breakdown is confirmed by an analysis of the units from which psychiatric casualties were drawn. Thus from a sample of 3,724 British Army casualties the distribution among units was as follows:

TABLE 73

Percentage Incidence by Units of a Sample of 3,724 Psychiatric Casualties among British Troops in M.E.F. occurring between 1942 and 1943

	Casualties	Average strength
	per cent.	per cent.
Services, including R.A.S.C., R.A.M.C., R.E.M.E., R.A.P.C., R.A.O.C., A.D.C., C.M.P., R.A.Ch.D., Pioneers, A.C.C., etc.	32	37
Infantry	22	17
R.A. (including R.H.A. and A.A.)	20	22
R.A.C., R.T.R. and Recce units	12	9
R.E.	9	9
Royal Corps of Signals	5	6
	100	100

The table shows that in spite of their numerical incidence the psychiatric casualties in the services were less than their expectation when related to average strength by arms, while in infantry and R.A.C., though smaller in total numbers than that in the services, were in excess of their expectation when related to average strength in the force. The R.A. and R.C.S. showed an incidence less than that which might be anticipated by their average strengths, while only the R.E. showed an incidence which corresponded exactly to their average strength.

It was not surprising to find that the incidence of psychiatric casualties fell relatively more heavily on the fighting men. All men serving in the desert in 1940, 1941 and 1942 suffered great physical and mental strain. Supply services had long distances of desert to cross, with the ever present risk of attacks from the Italian or German air forces. Men suffered constant loss of sleep and rest, the glare of the sun and the sandy fog churned up by their vehicles. Such conditions, even when cheerfully endured by drivers and gunners, R.A.S.C., R.A.M.C., R.E. and other similar units, inevitably took their toll. Infantry and gunners had particularly severe trials to endure. Guns often presented open targets and could be fired upon or bombed and were subjected to intense dive-bombing or low level attacks by machine guns or cannon. Gunners complained bitterly of the German 50 mm. and 88 mm. guns. Infantry had a particular hatred for mortars, though they too put dive-bombing high on the list of disliked enemy weapons. The uninterrupted dive-bombing in the Desert, Greece and Crete and in the Eastern Mediterranean during 1940 and 1941 had its effect on men who experienced it right up to the end of the African campaign. The majority of casualties among forward troops seemed to be actually precipitated by the important physical factors of fatigue, shortage of sleep, exposure and the imperative necessity for constant fighting in dreary surroundings without adequate recuperative periods for rest and training away from the eternal sand and rock of the desert country. Individual leave was generous; but this is not enough. Whole units require recuperative and training periods and the more unpleasant the terrain in which they fight the more necessary such periods become.

A sample of 1,033 psychiatric casualties examined by the consultant in November 1942 showed that 38 per cent. of them were related to battle conditions. It can safely be concluded that about 37 per cent. of all psychiatric casualties occurring in the Middle East campaigns were precipitated by the conditions of battle.

TABLE 74

Analysis of 200 Officer Patients—British Services only

	per cent.
Psychotic group	25
Anxiety states (including obsessional)	40
Hysteria	12
Organic conditions resulting in psychosis or neurosis	3
Reactive depressions or neurasthenia	17
No appreciable psychiatric disorder	3

Types of Commission—200 British Officers, all Services

Regular Commissions	23
Territorials	10
Reserve of Officers	3
Emergency Commissions	64

One feature was unexpectedly prominent in the series of 200 officer cases here considered ; 38 per cent. of the sample showed unwise consumption of alcohol as one of the principal factors causing breakdown. This finding was not only unexpected but somewhat startling. A close examination of the cases showed that they fell into two main groups. The lesser group consisted of men of confirmed alcoholic habits, sometimes of many years standing, while a larger group used alcohol for two purposes—(1) to obtain sleep and as an aid to the assuagement of manifest anxiety symptoms, and (2) as a stimulant to get through very heavy periods of work, often administrative in character. It was found repeatedly that officers during periods of a rush of work would use alcohol to 'ginger themselves up', as they put it, and thus get through an extra spell. The inevitable breakdown occurred in most cases. In this table there is a significant increase of anxiety states and of states of depression as compared with other rank figures and a slight diminution in psychoses. Nearly 60 per cent. of the officer casualties were associated in some way with battle conditions.

DIAGNOSES

Figures, to be of value, require among other things a uniform method of collection; further, they imply a uniformity in diagnosis that among so many clinicians was very difficult to obtain. Psychiatrists do not always mean the same thing by the use of the same diagnostic label— e.g. hebephrenia, anxiety hysteria, schizophrenia, psychopathic personality, paranoid states.

TABLE 75

5,000 Psychiatric Cases (all ranks) seen in M.E.F.
British Services only

Diagnoses	No. of cases	Percentage
Psychotic group, which includes psychosis, mental deficiency and cases of psychopathic personality and temperamental instability	1,483	29·7
Anxiety states (including obsessional) . . .	1,878	37·6
Hysteria, which includes anxiety hysteria and conversion hysteria	782	15·6
Reactive depression and neurasthenia . . .	407	8·1
Organic conditions giving rise to psychosis or neurosis	370	7·4
Medico-legal cases	63	1·3
No apparent disease	17	0·3
Totals	5,000	100·0

Tables 75 and 76 deal with the distribution of diagnoses among samples of Middle East Force taken at various periods. Table 75 is derived from follow-up cards at G.H.Q. examined late in 1942. This analysis provides a fairly large group of cases and a word or two may be said about the results. The psychotic group, for administrative purposes and especially for evacuation purposes, was made to include cases of mental deficiency, psychopathic personality and the diagnosis temperamental instability. While this was unfortunate from the point of view of the clinician it was a practical method of dividing the casualties. The psychotic group amounted to nearly 30 per cent., a high figure of comparatively useless personnel. It will also be noted that nearly 40 per cent. were diagnosed as anxiety states and only 15 per cent. as hysteria. Conversion hysteria would be considerably beneath this figure as some clinicians would give the diagnosis of anxiety hysteria on the follow-up card, which usually meant that the case was primarily an anxiety state with hysterical features.

Table 76 deals with a sample analysis of 6,364 casualties in Middle East Force and includes Dominion, Colonial and Allied Troops and all Services. It was made in May 1943. The clinical groups were divided as follows:

TABLE 76

Diagnostic Analysis of 6,364 Psychiatric Casualties in M.E.F. (May 1943)

Diagnoses	No. of cases	Percentage
Psychotic group, which includes psychosis, mental deficiency and cases of psychopathic personality and temperamental instability	1,904	30·0
Anxiety states (including obsessional)	2,289	36·0
Hysteria, which includes anxiety hysteria and conversion hysteria	1,203	18·5
Reactive depression and neurasthenia	307	5·0
Organic conditions giving rise to psychosis or neurosis	507	8·0
Medico-legal	122	2·0
No apparent disease	32	0·5
Totals	6,364	100·0

A further sample may be given in a third table drawn from 1,080 patients of the British Army only, treated in hospital in Middle East Force, January to March 1943. Diagnoses were distributed as follows:

TABLE 77

British Army only. 1,080 *Cases* (*January–March,* 1943)

Diagnoses	No. of cases	Percentage
Psychotic group, which includes psychosis, mental deficiency and cases of psychopathic personality and temperamental instability	238	22·0
Anxiety states (including obsessional) . . .	420	39·0
Hysteria, which includes anxiety hysteria and conversion hysteria	226	20·9
Reactive depression and neurasthenia . . .	46	4·3
Organic conditions giving rise to psychosis or neurosis	105	9·7
Medico-legal cases	35	3·2
No apparent psychiatric diseases	10	0·9
Totals	1,080	100·0

This table shows a drop in the psychotic group of diagnoses and a rise in the conditions labelled hysteria, which is rather surprising.

This sample of 1,080 patients, treated in hospital in the early months of 1943, was examined with regard to the age distribution, which was as follows:

TABLE 78

Age	No. of cases	Percentage
20 and under . .	58	5·4
21–25 . . .	383	35·5
26–30 . . .	290	26·9
31–35 . . .	150	13·9
36–40 . .	103	9·5
41 and over . .	62	5·7
Not known . .	34	3·1
Totals . . .	1,080	100·0

It will be noted in Table 78 that the age group 21–30 constitutes 62·4 per cent. of the total, which is exactly what would be expected in view of the mean age of the forces as a whole. It will be noted that the incidence of breakdown in the age group 26–30 is considerably less than in the group 21–25. It was constantly noted during the three years under review that many of the battle anxiety states were reactions of moderate severity in the younger soldiers.

This sample was submitted to an analysis in order to discover the incidence of various employments in peace-time. In this example of

1,080 soldiers the most common civil employments are shown in Table 79.

TABLE 79

Peace-time Employments of 1,080 Cases of Psychiatric Breakdown

Civil employment	No. of soldiers	Percentage
1. Skilled workers	278	25·6
2. Unskilled workers	219	20·2
3. Employed in business and commerce .	156	14·4
4. Regular Army	140	12·9
5. Motor drivers	71	6·6
6. Professional class, civil servants, etc. .	54	5·0
7. Engineers	26	2·4
8. Railway workers	17	1·6
9. Not known	119	11·3
Totals	1,080	100·0

TABLE 80

Diagnoses	Skilled workers	Un- skilled workers	Motor drivers	Engin- eers	Rail- way workers	Busi- ness and Com- merce	Pro- fes- sions, Civil Ser- vice, etc.	Regular Army, R.N. and R.A.F.
Distribution in sample	26·5	19·3	6·6	2·4	1·6	14·4	10·0	12·0
Anxiety neurosis	47·2	26·3	42·2	46·2	35·3	44·0	15·7	50·7
Psychosis, etc.	20·8	38·4	18·3	19·2	5·9	23·6	25·8	20·0
Hysteria	20·5	23·9	19·7	19·2	35·3	17·8	41·4	20·7
Organic conditions	7·3	10·5	9·9	11·6	17·6	11·4	11·4	5·7
Depression	4·2	0·9	9·9	3·8	5·9	3·2	5·7	2·9
Totals	100·0	100·0	100·0	100·0	100·0	100·0	100·0	100·0
Anxiety neurosis	31·0	12·6	6·9	2·7	1·4	15·7	2·5	16·2
Psychosis, etc.	21·4	28·6	4·6	1·8	0·4	13·2	6·4	10·0
Hysteria	27·4	23·2	6·5	2·3	2·8	12·9	4·6	13·4
Organic conditions	20·4	21·3	6·8	2·9	2·9	17·5	6·8	7·8
Depression	26·1	4·3	15·2	2·2	2·2	8·6	17·5	8·7

Breaking down the sample still further with regard to civil employment, the next table shows diagnoses as a percentage of each employment and employments as a percentage of each diagnosis of the sample of 1,080 cases. This table, derived from a study of employments as samples of 1,080 psychiatric cases all ranks British Army only, possesses considerable interest. It was found that the employments were distributed according to the figures under the top columns of the tables.

In Table 80 the employment was unknown in 11 per cent. of cases of anxiety neurosis, 13·6 per cent. of psychosis, etc., 6·9 per cent. of hysteria, 13·6 per cent. of organic conditions and 15·2 per cent. of cases of depression.

The conjugal status of 1,080 psychiatric casualties in the British Army is shown in Table 81.

TABLE 81

Conjugal Status of 1,080 Psychiatric Casualties, British Army

33·6 per cent. were married
35·7 per cent. were single
30·7 per cent.—not recorded

Total   100·0

Diagnosis expressed as a percentage of conjugal status and status as a percentage of each diagnosis are shown in Tables 82 and 83.

TABLE 82

Diagnosis as a Percentage of Conjugal Status in 1,080 Psychiatric Casualties

Diagnosis	Married	Single
Anxiety neurosis .	40·8	35·6
Psychosis, etc. .	20·4	29·4
Hysteria . .	23·4	23·1
Organic conditions .	8·5	9·9
Depression . .	6·9	2·0
Totals . . .	100·0	100·0

TABLE 83

Status as a Percentage of Each Diagnosis

Diagnosis	Married	Single	Not known	Totals
Anxiety neurosis . .	35·2	41·7	23·1	100·0
Psychosis, etc. . .	26·6	51·2	22·2	100·0
Hysteria . . .	37·6	50·4	12·0	100·0
Organic conditions .	29·5	46·7	23·8	100·0
Depression . . .	53·0	21·7	25·3	100·0

A sample of 2,275 record cards was examined in late 1942 with a view to determining the period of overseas service in the Middle East before breakdown occurred. The sample was drawn from all services and all troops in the Middle East. Table 84 is a dramatic answer to the statement that is frequently made that psychiatric cases give no adequate service.

TABLE 84

Period of service overseas	No. of cases	Percentage
Less than three months . . .	204	9·0
Over three months but less than six .	328	14·0
Over six but under twelve months .	477	21·0
Over one year but under two years .	771	34·0
Over two years	495	22·0
Totals	2,275	100·0

The tables so far given have attempted to record by means of samples the incidence of psychiatric casualties in M.E.F. over a period of two years and more. It remains to consider the results of 6,364 follow-up letters which, it will be remembered, were managed from the Medical Branch of G.H.Q. with the help of the O. i/c 2nd Echelon, G.H.Q. These are given in Table 85.

RELAPSE RATE

In reviewing the follow-up cards collected at G.H.Qs. from January 1, 1941, to March 31, 1943, it was found that there were 494 (7·76 per cent.) relapses. Over 4 per cent. relapsed on two or more occasions. All these relapses required fresh hospital treatment, but the service given between discharge and relapse was usually nine months or more. The shortest period between discharge and relapse was five weeks, the longest eighteen months.

Of the 6,364 cards examined 5,870 were direct admissions. Of these primary admissions the British Army accounted for 3,724 (63 per cent.). The other 37 per cent. came from the Royal Navy, the Royal Air Force, the Merchant Navy, the Women's Services, Dominion, Indian, Colonial and Allied troops and civilians working in the M.E.F. area, and prisoners-of-war. Table 85 shows the disposal on discharge from hospital of these 5,870 psychiatric casualties of all ranks and all Services. It shows in brief that about 75 per cent. of all psychiatric casualties were retained in M.E.F. for some form of duty.

FOLLOW-UP

Table 86 shows the results of the follow-up letters in the 3,724 replies received. The information collected was the condition of soldiers nine

TABLE 85

Disposal on Discharge from Hospital of 5,870 Psychiatric Casualties of All Ranks and All Services

Disposals	Totals	Psychosis, mental defect and psychopathies	Anxiety state	Hysteria	Psychoneurotic depression and neurasthenia	Organic states	Medico-legal cases	No appreciable psychiatric disorder
	5,870 100%	1,711 29·15%	2,124 36·18%	1,119 19·06%	287 4·90%	482 8·21%	118 2·01%	29 0·49%
Returned to full duty	2,152 36·66%	381 22·26%	792 37·29%	536 47·90%	125 43·55%	207 42·95%	101 85·59%	10 34·40%
To convalescent depots	545 9·30%	78 4·56%	297 13·98%	100 8·94%	27 9·42%	41 8·51%	—	2 6·90%
To base depots	442 7·53%	72 4·21%	209 9·84%	89 7·95%	24 8·36%	38 7·88%	8 6·78%	2 6·90%
To duty. Regraded category B	766 13·05%	175 10·23%	406 19·11%	151 13·49%	18 6·27%	11 2·28%	2 1·69%	3 10·34%
To duty. Regraded category C. Local enlistments	90 1·53%	47 2·75%	20 0·94%	16 1·43%	5 1·74%	2 0·41%	—	—
Discharged. Category E. Local enlistments	478 8·14%	310 18·12%	63 2·97%	65 5·81%	16 5·57%	24 4·98%	—	—
Transfer to other corps or units	40 0·68%	24 1·40%	11 0·52%	3 0·27%	1 0·35%	1 0·21%	—	—
Transferred to other hospitals	364 6·20%	152 8·89%	74 3·48%	67 5·99%	14 4·88%	47 9·75%	1 0·85%	9 31·03%
Evacuated from M.E.F.	656 11·17%	390 22·79%	123 5·80%	40 3·57%	34 11·85%	69 14·31%	—	—
Died	18 0·31%	13 0·76%	—	—	—	5 1·04%	—	—
Not known	40 0·68%	10 0·58%	16 0·75%	6 0·54%	1 0·35%	5 1·04%	1 0·85%	1 3·45%
Other—includes pending decision	279 4·75%	59 3·45%	113 5·32%	46 4·11%	22 7·66%	32 6·64%	5 4·24%	2 6·90%
Totals	5,870 100%	1,711 100%	2,124 100%	1,119 100%	287 100%	482 100%	118 100%	29 100%
Remaining in M.E.F. for some form of duty	4,399 74·94%	929 54·29%	1,809 85·07%	962 85·97%	214 74·56%	347 71·99%	112 94·91%	26 89·65%

TABLE 86

Analysis of Follow-up of All Replies (3,724) Showing Condition of Soldiers Nine Months after Discharge from Hospital or Psychiatric Centre

	Totals	Psychosis, mental defect and psychopathy	Anxiety states	Hysteria	Psychoneurotic depression and neurasthenia	Organic conditions	Medico-legal cases	N.A.D.
	3,724 100%	1,110 29·81%	1,396 27·49%	669 17·96%	196 5·26%	304 8·16%	38 1·02%	11 0·30%
Full duty	1,415 38·0%	230 20·6%	649 46·6%	334 49·8%	75 38·3%	98 32·2%	25 65·7%	4 36·4%
Light duty	635 17·1%	105 9·5%	321 22·9%	139 20·8%	24 12·2%	37 12·2%	6 15·9%	3 27·2%
Died, missing, P.o.W., killed in action	336 9·0%	108 9·8%	104 7·5%	58 8·7%	20 10·2%	39 12·8%	5 13·2%	2 18·2%
Total serving or missing while serving	2,386 64·1%	443 39·9%	1,074 77·0%	531 79·3%	119 60·7%	174 57·2%	36 94·7%	9 81·8%
Transferred or evacuated from command	1,338 35·9%	667 60·1%	322 23·0%	138 20·7%	77 39·3%	130 42·8%	2 5·3%	2 18·2%
Total replies received	3,724 100%	1,110 100%	1,396 100%	669 100%	196 100%	304 100%	38 100%	11 100%

months after discharge from a hospital or centre. It shows that 64 per cent. of soldiers discharged from hospital or centre nine months previously were (if a reply to the follow-up were received) still serving in the Middle East, or had died, were killed, missing or taken prisoner while so serving.

In greater detail the follow-up figures show that considerable casualties had occurred in the psychosis group of cases while the anxiety group and hysteria group had done remarkably well. Thus among the anxiety states 77 per cent. were giving good service nine months after discharge, and of hysterics 79 per cent. were continuing in some form of duty. The expression 'Full Duty' means a return to the original unit.

EFFORT SYNDROME

The incidence of effort syndrome during the Middle East campaigns was unexpectedly low and the majority of men were properly regarded as instances of an anxiety state. Their histories, general appearance and symptomatology supported this view and it is interesting in passing to note that the effort syndrome cases were mainly drawn from the services of the Army rather than the fighting troops, among which its occurrence was very low. The civil occupations most prominent among effort syndrome cases were the same as those most prominent among the men suffering from neurosis. At one time quite a large group of men in one training depot developed effort syndrome. On investigation it was found that most belonged to a group of reinforcements which had arrived in the Middle East after a long voyage (ten weeks) on a crowded transport. In soft condition the men entered on a strenuous course of exercise and training which resulted in the precipitation of the well-known symptoms in a few days. Adjustment of the training programme in respect of newly arrived drafts was all that was necessary to stop the incidence of effort syndrome from training depots.

An effort syndrome centre was opened at 23 B.G.H. in Palestine on July 1, 1941, and was closed at the end of February 1943, cases occurring after that date being admitted direct to psychiatric hospitals or centres. A follow-up of the results of treatment of these effort syndrome cases produced 77 per cent. of answers and showed that nine months after discharge from hospital the following distribution was obtained:

TABLE 87

Result of Follow-up of a Sample of 254 Soldiers Suffering from Effort Syndrome Nine Months after Discharge from Hospital

	No. of cases	Percentage
Full duty at original units . .	132	51·96 ⎫
Lighter or changed duties . .	61	24·03 ⎬ 80·79
Killed, died, missing or P.o.W. .	12	4·80 ⎭
Evacuated from the Command .	27	10·63
Discharged from Army (local enlistment)	19	7·48
Relapsed and requiring hospital treatment	3	1·10
Totals	254	100·0

Soldiers were reported on as 'very efficient', 'efficient', 'satisfactory', 'fair', or suffering from 'recurrence of symptoms not requiring hospital treatment'. Replies were as follows:

Of 132 men on Full Duty

Very efficient	.	4 (Promotion had been given to 2)
Efficient	. .	102
Satisfactory	. .	23
Fair	. . .	3

60 had had recurrence of symptoms not requiring hospital treatment.

Of 61 men on Light or Changed Duties

Very efficient	.	0
Efficient	. .	46
Satisfactory	. .	8
Fair	. . .	2
Inefficient	. .	5

46 had had recurrence of symptoms not requiring hospital treatment.

DEATHS

During the period under review there were 44 deaths in psychiatric hospitals and centres, including observation centres, all over the M.E. This excluded Tenth Army, Malta and the Sudan.

Of these deaths it is interesting to note the high mortality in all states of excitement in M.E.F. 23 of the hospital deaths were due to excitement, whether due to confusional toxic states, to acute 'schizophrenic' excitement or to manic depressive excitement. In addition 4 of these deaths were due to acute alcoholic states with excitement and restlessness as in delirium tremens. So far as can be ascertained from the notes and records of the consultant, only 10 of the deaths were in the British Army, the remainder being in the R.N. (2), R.A.F. (3), A.I.F., U.D.F., N.Z.E.F., Allies, coloured troops and local enlistments.

TABLE 88

Causes of Deaths in Psychiatric Hospitals and Centres

Acute toxic confusional excitement (including alcoholic, enteric, septicaemia and unknown causes) . . .	9
Manic depression: Excitement	7
Depression	2
Schizophrenia with excitement	5
Suicides	10
G.P.I.	1
Cerebral tumour	1
Epilepsy (with status)	1
Tetanus	1
Cerebral abscess	2
Amoebic liver abscess with confusion	2
Broncho-pneumonia	1
Subdural haematomata (one due to injury) . . .	2
	44

The death from tetanus was in a Maori soldier who was admitted to a psychiatric centre with a tentative diagnosis of hysteria. He had a G.S.W. of the upper arm, had become mildly confused and had localised twitchings of the muscles of the upper arm.

SUICIDES

It is worth while recording the method of the hospital suicides:

Precipitation under road traffic . . .	1
Precipitation under rail traffic	2
Hanging	5
Cut throat	2
	10

Of the ten suicides five were soldiers in the British Army, two were Royal Air Force other ranks, two were Palestinian pioneers and one was in the Royal Greek Force.

One of the psychiatric hospitals of M.E.F. had a road running through it which carried considerable traffic. This road made it possible for a suicidal patient to throw himself in front of a lorry or other vehicle, and it is remarkable that more such deaths did not occur. Special precautions were taken to slow the speed of vehicles, and gates were built at either end of the hospital area to ensure that vehicles were authorised and proceeded very slowly.

While it is highly unlikely that a note was made of all suicides in this large area, an attempt was made to keep a tally on the suicide rate, for it is an important indication of morale. The numbers known are here recorded year by year:

Suicides in M.E.F. outside Hospitals or Centres

1940 (based on 3 months actual figures) . .	8
1941	12
1942	9
1943 (based on 6 months)	6

Out of these figures four were known to be officers. These suicides were not fully documented. They occurred in several sets of circumstances—(1) as a result of unrecognised mental illness; (2) as a depressive sequence of physical illness (malaria, sandfly fever, infective hepatitis and dysentery were prominent); (3) in impulsive psychopathic individuals several occurred either just before action or soon after the end of action. In some of these instances a history of impulsive violent behaviour in the past could be traced, and at least two had made previous attempts, probably indicating the presence of periodic mental disorder; (4) it must also be recorded that several of these suicides might not have occurred if prompt action on the part of a medical officer had insisted on the removal of the patient to hospital. In two examples officers died by their own hands because of a well-meaning but most foolish determination to 'cheer him up, occupy and distract him and keep him out of one of those places'. One officer was clearly retarded and depressed after an attack of epidemic hepatitis and eventually shot himself while his kindly but unwise host believed he was dressing to go out to an E.N.S.A. party. The other case followed sandfly fever, the officer having been given leave 'so that he could recover from a state of depression'.

It was rumoured that a considerable number of suicides occurred during the evacuation of Crete, but very conflicting reports were received, some eye witnesses describing 'hundreds' and others two or three. It is probable that some men shot themselves in the mountains which had to be crossed to reach the southern shores and that some pioneers (locally enlisted) of German origin jumped from the cliffs rather than fall into the hands of their persecutors.

With regard to suicide associated with action, several occurred before action, probably in men who had come to the end of their battle endurance and who felt they were going to crack. There was personal knowledge of three such cases but probably there were more. Others occurred after action, sometimes taking place after a first action or a few hours after the end of a particularly unpleasant and bloody clash with the enemy. It seemed often that one or more comrades or officers had been lost and the suicide shot himself with a view to joining them, no doubt partly under the influence of that common and irrational feeling among soldiers after battle of culpable responsibility for the death of comrades in action.

Attempted Suicides. These were not uncommon in some of the Allied Forces. They were staged with a view to drama rather than reality, but there were some attempts which were meant and which, as so often happens, terminated at once an attack of depression.

OUT-PATIENTS

There are no accurate figures for out-patient consultations during 1940 and 1941, but in 1942 the actual numbers of out-patients seen by the psychiatric services in the Middle East were 445 officers and 4,943 other ranks, a total of 5,388. In 1943, based on actual figures for six months, the total annual rate (all ranks) was 6,224, a figure which actually exceeded the in-patients for the first time. Of these about 560 were officer consultations. The ratio of officers to other ranks varied in an interesting manner. Thus, in the Royal Navy the proportion of officer and other ranks in-patients was roughly 1 to 3; in the Royal Air Force 1 to 9 and in the British Army 1 to 14; or, taking all Services together the in-patient officer/man ratio was 1 to 10. The out-patient ratio over all the Services was remarkably constant at 1 officer to 11 other ranks. The ratio varied during the campaign; thus at times in the British Army the officer/man ratio for in-patient treatment was 1 officer to 15 other ranks and at other times this ratio was 1 to 12. No particular causes seemed responsible for this variation in the in-patient admission ratio between officers and other ranks, but the psychiatrists working in the Middle East would frequently say that the proportion was lowered by the arrival of a large officer convoy to Middle East Force.

FACTORS INFLUENCING BREAKDOWN

(a) *Constitutional Factors.* The examination of many samples of breakdown revealed that constitutional factors were present in a great number of individuals, and it was a matter of constant surprise that so many officers and men had managed to get into the Army or other Services in the face of so many obvious danger signals in their personal and family histories. It was repeatedly found among case material that men had suffered previous breakdown of a neurotic or psychotic character in civilian life, that employment records were poor, indicating defect or instability or a mixture of both, that far too many men had been unable to manage their lives in a social sense and had experienced financial, marital and other troubles as a chronic accompaniment to living as civilians. Childhood and adolescence were often loaded with undesirable personal traits, the most frequent being somnambulism, enuresis, anxieties and phobias, truancy at school, delinquencies of various types, broken homes and the story of having been 'under the doctor' or 'delicate as a child'.

(b) *Family History*. A sample of 500 examined in 1942 showed that a family history of psychotic, neurotic or social and behaviour disorders was evident in 20 per cent. of case histories. One interesting point should be recorded. Many soldiers gave the story that their fathers or uncles were in the War of 1914–18 and had broken down with 'shell shock', and in quite a number of cases men were examined whose fathers were still in receipt of pensions for psychiatric disabilities as a result of the War of 1914–18. This would surely indicate a family atmosphere of a most undesirable kind, and it might well form the basis of a question to be put to recruits.

(c) *National Outlook and Morale*. In a citizen army drawn from all sections of the nation of which the army is composed, it is obvious that the individuals joining the armed forces carry into the Army an attitude of mind taken from their civilian outlook on life in general. In this way the morale of the soldier finds its roots deep in national life, in the education that he will have received, the economic conditions in which he has grown up, the training that he has received for his avocation and his place in the industrial life of his country. There can be no doubt that the period between the two wars had not prepared the manhood of Britain for another outbreak of war in which the very utmost would be demanded of every individual. There was one feature of national life which became evident repeatedly; this was the bitterness with which many men of the War of 1914–18 looked back upon their army career in that war. The attitude of the fathers was clearly reflected in the attitude of their sons. There was a general expectation among men in Middle East Force that they would suffer much the same fate as their fathers, who had been glibly promised 'a country fit for heroes to live in' and had subsequently spent many years drawing unemployment benefits. The results of this type of treatment of British soldiers were very forcibly impressed on a psychiatric observer on many occasions. Men worried about their pay and the pay of their dependants; they had no confidence in the help dependants would receive in the event of their own death in the service of their country, and they frequently pointed to the vastly superior amenities enjoyed by soldiers from other parts of the British Empire and of American soldiers. War always gives rise to inequalities of every kind, but it was sometimes very hard to cheer men who were sweating away in the Sudan and who learned of the pay of, for example, American soldiers. This is equally true of underpaid services like the nursing service of the Army.

It is impossible to stress too much the importance of education where morale is concerned. It was quite terrifying to learn how little education most of the men seemed to have received.

As well as national morale the question of individual morale with its many implications was of considerable importance. It is a question

35

which is so bound up with leadership, training and competence as a unit in fighting battalions or divisions that it cannot be discussed in all its aspects. The campaigns in the Middle East convinced the consultant that the presence of half-trained, militarily incompetent and irresolute men with a poor individual morale was a menace to the military competence of the Force as a whole. As in the War of 1914–18, it was observed repeatedly that the highest number of psychiatric casualties occurred in units with poor physique, low intelligence, poor training, discipline and leadership. The reverse was true also and units with good leadership, a high state of military training and military competence seldom produced more than a few cases of true psychiatric breakdown.

Few medical men possessed the gift of leadership. When it was possible to place a doctor with this gift in charge of a psychiatric unit it was quite amazing to note how the unit changed. Several times it was possible to observe quite remarkable morale in units like the R.A.O.C. with, on the whole, second-rate material, physically and often mentally. Unusual leadership was usually associated with successful military groups, were they in the forward areas, on lines of communication or base.

FACTORS PRECIPITATING BREAKDOWN

(a) *Separation from Home.* A great deal has been written about what has been described as 'separation anxiety'. There is no doubt that the disrupting of domestic and family ties is a serious matter for individuals. The Army was never in a position to say when this separation from home was to be terminated. In the Middle East members of the Royal Navy knew they would serve two years on the station and then receive repatriation. The Royal Air Force served two or three years and were then posted to a home station. The Army was told that it might do seven years overseas and that there was no certain repatriation before that period. To young men this period of time appears to resemble infinity, and it is fortunate that it was cut down.

During 1940 and 1941 there was a great deal of anxiety among members of Middle East Force concerning the bombing in the United Kingdom. Unfortunately it must be recorded that at a time when news from home was desperately important to the soldier his mail proved scarce and irregular. Nearly every report written by the consultant during his term of service in the Middle East referred to this question of mail. It was not until 1943 that some slight improvement took place and mails arrived with a certain regularity and speed. During most of the time under review mails were slow and irregular in arrival. Loss or delay in the arrival of mail was a potent cause for anxiety and depression which at times was very widespread even among perfectly normal officers and men. It came to be realised that this one emotional link with home has an importance to the soldier and to his country which cannot be over-estimated.

(*b*) *Climate*. In the wide area of the Middle East nearly every sort of climate was encountered. Fighting took place in mountains, as in Greece or Abyssinia, in hilly and mountainous countries such as Syria and in arid waterless deserts such as the Libyan Desert where temperatures could range between tropical heat and arctic cold within twenty-four hours and where the dust storms or driving rain were at times exceedingly trying. The shortage of water in desert conditions was constant and led to an inability to keep garments clean and changed at sufficiently frequent intervals. The flies were a great irritant, especially at certain periods when they were almost overwhelming. Troops in the Alamein line in the summer of 1942 had a great deal to put up with from flies, as they did in the Mersa Matruh box in 1940. Some of the worst experiences with flies resulted from the taking of enemy positions, for the sanitation of Italian and German troops seemed, as in the War of 1914–18, to be most unsatisfactory. Indeed in some respects it was almost absent in both Italian and German armies, and it must regretfully be recorded that strict hygiene and sanitation was equally absent from some of the Allied troops who did, however, learn its vital importance in the later stages of the campaign.

In the early days of the campaign the effects of sun on individuals were sometimes prominent. By far the most common hysterical manifestation complained of by men in the Middle East was the headache for which no adequate cause could be found. On enquiry it would be found that the headache had commenced on the transport at Freetown and the consultant was asked by many medical officers how this complaint could best be relieved. Many placebos were tried and one of the most effective was to give the sufferer a few tablets of sodium chloride to take when the sun was felt to be causing the headache. Another placebo advised by the consultant was the administration of sodium or magnesium sulphate morning and evening. What was important was to teach medical officers that they must make up their own minds as to whether the headache had any organic basis and avoid sending the sufferer from one specialist to another.

These headaches were often a reflection of the personality of soldiers. The officer or man coming out to the Middle East grudgingly and unwillingly would seize on any somatic disorder and was assisted in this way by the widespread opinion that the rays of the sun in Africa possessed a special virulence from which troops had to be protected. Most of the so-called tropical neurasthenic conditions are primarily due to the personality of the individuals who suffer from them and the attitude taken to any form of service in hot climates.

(c) *Battle Stress*. During the early days of 1940 and 1941 by far the commonest factor creating breakdown was bombing, either high-level or dive-bombing. Nearly all troops who experienced dive-bombing complained bitterly of the effect upon their morale, especially when such dive-bombing was unopposed and when soldiers on the ground had no weapons with which to retaliate. Later in the campaign men became astonishingly acclimatised to attacks by dive bombers, but in the early days it was very different, and in a report to D.M.S. in 1941 the effects of dive-bombing were stated by the consultant to be an important cause of battle nerves.

In 1942 an investigation into the effects of enemy weapons was made by 1 Medical Research Section of the Directorate of Medical Research and the consultant, and a report despatched to the War Office. This report attempted to distinguish between psychological effects and physiological effects, and the report concluded that in November 1942, enemy mortar held the first place among British troops, especially infantry. Among Italian prisoners, the British mortar also headed the list and was followed by low-level attacks from the air. Among German prisoners captured in the Alamein battles shelling by artillery was said to produce the greatest effect, followed by low-level air attacks. An experienced German medical officer who was captured recorded his opinion that the British weapon with the greatest morale effect used at Alamein was the Beaufighter with cannon and that next to this came the Hurri-bomber.

In the choice of the most disliked enemy weapon there was no noticeable difference between officers, N.C.Os. and other ranks. On the other hand, there was a noticeable difference of choice among the different arms of the Army. Thus, mortars were the choice of the infantryman, dive-bombing and machine-gunning the choice of motorised infantry and drivers of the R.A.S.C., while shelling and dive-bombing were the usual choice of gunners, who included, in company with the R.A.C., anti-tank shells, particularly the 88 mm. shell. The most disliked enemy weapon seemed to be determined in some men by factors other than the effects of the weapons themselves. Thus some weapons had for some greater effects by night than by day. Many of the examinees stated that the effects of enemy weapons in battle were felt more readily and severely when the men were suffering from the effects of fatigue, and especially from loss of sleep, while others stated that the sight of comrades being killed or injured by any particular weapon resulted in their fearing that weapon more than others. No very accurate conclusions could be drawn from the investigation made, but it was obvious that the enemy weapons most disliked did tend to alter during the campaign. Coloured tracer at night was very effective as a morale breaker on both sides; it gave men the same sense of being picked out personally as did the Stuka dive-bomber of the earlier days.

The conditions of battle most likely to produce nervous reactions in healthy men, apart from the sights of battle and the death of comrades or leaders, are loss of rest and sleep and proper food. In desert fighting the long continued slogging matches of Italy and North-west Europe were for the most part absent. This is one of the reasons why battle casualties were at such a low figure. But there were special features of battle in the desert which called for attention; constant sweating was one, with the consequent loss of fluids. There were days, especially among armoured units, when the intake of fluid was quite seriously restricted. The very short hours for rest was another important factor and led to great scarcity or loss of sleep. If this went on for long enough men lost weight and developed a mild confusion or clouding of consciousness which rendered them unable to remember orders and therefore to carry them out.

Irregularity of food was in some battles quite a potent factor in producing breakdown. Infantry and armoured units were frequently on the move before 'first light', which might be 3·30 a.m. or much later in the winter. A hasty meal was snatched, and too often this meal would prove to be bully and biscuits and probably without hot tea on account of the danger of lighting fires. The day might be quite far advanced before men were able to 'brew up' and have something hot, if it were only the infantryman's comfort in the desert, the 'mug o' char'. On the move there was almost a universal tendency to brew up tea in the halts that took place. Sometimes the halts were just not long enough to enable the soldier to bring his water to the boil and this caused a sense of irritation and frustration well-known to the consultant.

Long continued fighting with the factors sketched above at work for two or three weeks would render physical exhaustion, with or without confusion, a not uncommon type of casualty in all but the very strong. Such men would fall solidly asleep every time they sat down and they frequently arrived at a base psychiatric hospital or unit remarkably refreshed by the journey.

In discussing battle stress it is important to take note of the condition of mind in which men went into battle. It is of the utmost importance that officers and men are thoroughly briefed, right down to the lowest ranks, in the task that is ahead of them and exactly how it is to be done. A man who goes into battle without any clear idea of the purpose behind the engagement and the method by which his commanders intend to carry it out is not unnaturally in a state of tension, nervousness and apprehension. Here again it cannot be too strongly insisted that soldiers require extensive education. For example, dispirited, tired and exhausted men would often say to the consultant that they could see no use in defending the desert and 'anyone who wanted it could have it'. This attitude was a defect in educational methods among troops and a reflection upon junior leaders, who sometimes seemed little more informed than their men.

One more point concerning mails. This has nothing to do with their lack or irregularity, though that in itself was an irritating and depressing feature of life in Middle East Force, but concerns the contents of the mails. A great many letters from home were shown to the consultant by unhappy and miserable soldiers, who might receive such letters on the eve of an engagement. Letters from wives were too often full of complaints, a recital of the difficulties of life, of the miseries of separation, of the illnesses of children, and of the food difficulties, etc., and these recitals are bound to have a very depressing effect upon the morale of a soldier who has no chance of getting back to his home. Towards the end of the three years under review another type of letter began to arrive. This was the letter from a mother-in-law, an aunt or a well-wisher among the soldier's friends, detailing the way in which his wife was 'carrying on'.   In fact it may fairly be said that as the campaign lengthened anxieties about the bombing, which were so prominent in 1940 and 1941, were replaced by anxieties concerning marital infidelity among too large a proportion of the troops. Letters of this kind in the pocket of a soldier going into battle bring him half-way toward becoming a nervous casualty. It is only right to record that the opposite was also true, however, and that many heroic women at home kept all their difficulties and troubles out of their letters to their men-folk overseas.

(d) *Cumulative Effects of Battle.* There can be no doubt to any impartial observer that on active service there is a gradual wastage in nervous capital, a loss of vigour and freshness, of interest in the work in hand, all of which are induced by the repeated impact of battle experiences as well as those factors which have already been discussed. The result is what has been termed 'campaign neurosis', the 'burnt out' soldier, described by the soldier himself as a condition which means 'he has had his war'. The condition is particularly dangerous among leaders, and it must always be kept in mind that no rank is immune from this condition. When it occurs among leaders the condition is readily reflected among the led. It must be distinguished from other types of breakdown, and its symptoms in a first-class fighting unit are rises in the sick rate, including neurosis, a rise in delinquency and a falling off in the fighting efficiency of a hitherto keen and accomplished battalion or even division. The practical question involved is the length of combat service which is the optimum for a fighting man or a fighting unit. M.E.F. was highly tried in this respect; not only were units and individuals constantly exposed to battle conditions over a long period but their service entailed much hardship in the way of constant travel. Thus, an Indian division and British gunners, after taking part in the Libyan campaign in the winter of 1940-41, were pulled out and despatched to the Sudan, arriving in time for the severe and lengthy action at Keren which decided the fate of the Duke of Aosta's Italian armies. The troops were then returned some 1,600 miles to the Western Desert, arriving just in time to aid in halting the German advance to the Egyptian frontier in the spring of 1941. The same was true in the case of units that fought in Greece and Crete. The survivors of these campaigns got little respite; they were quickly involved in fresh fighting in the Western Desert or in Syria, having travelled great distances and having suffered heavy defeats as well as having won resounding victories.

The answer to the question how long a man will endure is not easy. The consultant wrote a report for D.M.S. in 1941 which drew attention to the severity of certain single actions and expressed the view that any troops subjected to dive-bombing or other disliked enemy action preventing sleep and rest would crack in five days. Later experience led this opinion to be altered to four days. In single actions of great severity a man in continuous action begins to look over his shoulder and wonder if he is adequately supported, if comrades, especially trusted comrades, are behind him. It is hardly necessary to record that the soldier must have air cover, and his psychological comfort and sense of security are enormously increased if he can see the R.A.F. overhead, if he knows there are guns and tanks and fresh infantry behind him. Uninterrupted and unhindered dive-bombing by Stukas was only too often the fate of the infantryman in the early days of M.E.F. and it left its mark on men, hastening the onset of nervous bankruptcy which characterises the 'burnt out' soldier. Continuous fighting will exact its price, and in the opinion of the consultant an officer should not be more than a year in unrelieved operational work, for the sake of his men. The same is true of N.C.Os. Men can probably do two years, after which there is an increasing risk of nervous breakdown or of loss of interest, with an increased risk of delinquency and consequent failure in morale and fighting efficiency.

The physical condition of the soldier is of prime importance in the prevention of combat exhaustion. A soldier who has undergone good pre-combat training and who is at the peak of his physical efficiency is far less liable to these breakdowns than his less well-trained fellow. The state of the health of the soldier is of the utmost importance. If he is convalescing from a physical illness, such as diarrhoea or upper respiratory infection, and has not fully recovered from such physical disorders when he is committed to battle, he is more likely than the next man to develop combat exhaustion. Soldiers who are not fully recovered from intercurrent illness should not be sent into battle.

Fear will affect the physical well-being of a soldier by impairing his digestion and he will lose weight. A soldier who has been fearful and apprehensive over a period of weeks becomes physically run down and thereby leaves himself open to the development of a neurosis. This factor was emphasised by reports from the British Army in the Middle East. Hunger is another physical factor in producing such breakdowns. A soldier who has gone along for many days without proper rations becomes more susceptible to the development of combat exhaustion. The same may be said of thirst.

The physical status of the tactical situation is another important aetiological factor in the production of these neuroses. Situations in which retreat is necessary heighten the percentage of combat exhaustion cases. For example, during the long retreat at Kasserine Pass, the percentage of neuropsychiatric disabilities rose to 50 per cent. of the total. It was noted, furthermore, that tactical situations in which troops were pinned down caused an increase in such casualties.

REFLECTIONS OF A CONSULTANT IN PSYCHIATRY

It is highly desirable that all regular R.A.M.C. officers shall have received training in psychiatry. In planning for an expeditionary force allowance should be made for 2 beds per 1,000 strength for psychiatric casualties.

A separate convalescent depot for psychiatric casualties is most desirable.

For forward psychiatric work, each division should have its own psychiatric specialist and one of the divisional field ambulances should be so trained that it can handle and treat psychiatric casualties.

It is imperative that the Army shall not receive or retain men whose I.Q., temperament or character are such as to render them incapable of becoming useful soldiers.

It is desirable to review the traditional system by which the youngest and least experienced medical officers serve as regimental medical officers.

CHAPTER 8

THE ARMY PATHOLOGY
AND TRANSFUSION SERVICES
IN THE MIDDLE EAST

THE PATHOLOGY SERVICE

THE BASIS of the pathology organisation in M.E.C. was the central hospital laboratory, grouped where possible, but usually (except in Cairo and the Canal Zone) unavoidably dispersed. D.D.P. was at headquarters with one A.D.P. (who in addition was O.C., Central Pathology Laboratory) and a second A.D.P. was in Palestine. When the Persia-Iraq Command was transferred to M.E. in 1944, there was a third A.D.P.

By March 1941, a strong team of pathologists had become available, capable of dealing with most if not all of the problems that were likely to arise. There were 26 British general hospitals in the M.E., most of them open. The twenty-four 1,200 and 600 bedded hospitals had fully equipped laboratories and specialist pathologists. Four smaller hospitals of 200 beds were provided with laboratories staffed by graded pathologists. In addition there were three mobile bacteriological laboratories. The Australians and New Zealanders had provided their own hospitals—eight Australian and three New Zealand—and their own pathologists. With the Indian contingent were five general hospitals. These differed from the British in that they did not have a laboratory as an integral part of the unit. They depended upon the Indian field laboratories which were transportable and designed to work in association with a general hospital or with a C.C.S. Their resources were similar to those of the British mobile bacteriological laboratory.

The C.P.L. in Cairo was accommodated in the hospital building that had been taken over by 15 B.G.H. Here, too, were 1 B.T.U. and a biochemical laboratory. Associated with the C.P.L. was a virus laboratory in which investigational work on infective hepatitis, anterior poliomyelitis and typhus was undertaken.

In order to ensure that medical officers were familiar with the clinical and laboratory aspects of malaria, courses of instruction were arranged at the medical school of the Kasr-el-Aini Hospital in Cairo. Other courses were offered by the instructional section of 1 Mob. Mal. Fd. Lab.

The completed organisation in M.E.F. consisted of D.D.P. and three A.Ds.P. One A.D.P. was with D.D.P. at Medical H.Q., G.H.Q., M.E.F. Among his duties was that of training candidates for the post of graded pathologist. The second A.D.P. was pathologist to 16 B.G.H. in Jerusalem and adviser to D.D.M.S. Palestine. He also had control of the laboratories in Syria, the Lebanon and Cyprus. The main laboratories in his area were at Sarafand, Haifa and Beirut. He, it was, who arranged for the supply of calf-lymph and anti-rabic vaccine from the Government laboratories in Jerusalem.

In the Sudan the medical services were dependent for their pathological work upon the Lee Stack Medical Research Laboratories in Khartoum.

The third A.D.P. was adviser to D.D.M.S. Persia-Iraq Force with headquarters in Baghdad.

As the activities and responsibilities of M.E.C. spread throughout the Middle East the dispersal of the general hospital pathological laboratories correspondingly increased. They were scattered from Tripoli, Benghazi and Tobruk in the west, to Athens, Salonika, Cyprus, Asmara, Palestine, Teheran and Baghdad in the east. The central reference laboratory in Cairo served them all.

THE TRANSFUSION SERVICE

The Transfusion Service was the responsibility of D.D.P., G.H.Q., and consisted of a base transfusion unit (B.T.U.) and a number of field transfusion units (F.T.Us.) operating with Eighth Army. In addition, each general hospital had a small transfusion section which was staffed by the hospital itself.

BASE TRANSFUSION UNITS

The B.T.U. prepared and issued apparatus and all transfusion fluids, including blood, plasma, salines, sulphanilamide preparations and blood grouping serum. The forward units received all supplies, including blood, from the base, but general hospitals obtained blood from local donors while all other supplies were sent from the Base.

Volunteer blood donors were obtained from troops stationed either temporarily or permanently in base areas. At first these men were bled entirely at the B.T.U., but as demands increased at the time of the El Alamein battle it became necessary to create a mobile bleeding section consisting of 1 officer and 17 O.Rs. This was situated near the Infantry Base Depot at 19 B.G.H., Geneifa, where some 70,000 troops were stationed. About 7,000 of these men were bled during the El Alamein period and up to December 1942. Only group 'O' blood was used as it was found impracticable to use other groups for the provision of whole blood.

Small quantities of blood plasma were always prepared by the B.T.U. for issue to forward medical units. Owing to the difficulty in obtaining transport from the United Kingdom all the plasma had to be prepared at the B.T.U. for the invasion of Sicily in July 1943. This involved bleeding some 20,000 men of all groups and processing the blood to obtain plasma; for this work a temporary increase in the establishment of the unit was obtained.

1 B.T.U. remained at Cairo from August 1940 to April 1944, when it returned to the United Kingdom to be attached to the Army Blood Supply Depot, Bristol, prior to joining 21 Army Group. Very soon after its arrival in Egypt it was quartered with 15 (Scottish) B.G.H., where it remained throughout its stay. At first it occupied only a very small space (about 1,000 sq. ft.), but later, owing to the large increase in work, 10,000 sq. ft. of working space was acquired; this was provided partly by hospital premises and partly by hutments erected specially.

It was not practicable to move the B.T.U. from the Cairo area since this unit required so much in the way of services—water, gas and electricity—and no situation existed between Cairo and Tripoli where it could be housed. The B.T.U. therefore remained in Cairo throughout the campaign, and with the varying fortunes of battle which took the British forces to Benghazi, back to the frontier, then to Tobruk, Gazala, and back to Alamein, there were great differences in the length of the line of communications between the base and field units.

Soon after the arrival of the unit a small detachment of two O.Rs. was sent to Alexandria (64 B.G.H.) to undertake the preparation of plasma and saline for issue in that area. This detachment worked under the transfusion officer of the hospital and remained in existence throughout the unit's stay in M.E.F.

During this time the unit had a number of officers and O.Rs. attached for instructional courses. The aim was to provide instruction in transfusion to 1 officer and 2 O.Rs. from each general hospital in the command and also to give instruction when required to personnel of forward units. At first these instructional courses comprised only small numbers; later 6 officers and 20 O.Rs. were taken on each course, which lasted approximately 1 week.

In the earlier part of the campaign in the Western Desert casualties were light, and owing to lack of transport only small quantities of transfusion supplies were used. But the work of the B.T.U. was continuous throughout the whole campaign, for while blood was only required in battle periods, at other times it was necessary to prepare plasma and salines and to carry out courses of instruction.

Table 89 shows the issue of transfusion fluids in comparison with the number of casualties in the forces employed. It will be observed that

TABLE 89

Blood, Plasma and Saline Issues

Table showing the number of bottles of Blood, Plasma and Saline issued by No. 1 Base Transfusion Unit per 100 wounded in M.E.F. during the campaigns of 1940–1943

Period	Battles	Total wounded	Issues (bottles)			Per 100 wounded (bottles)		
			Blood	Plasma	Saline	Blood	Plasma	Saline
Nov. 1940–Sept. 1941	Sidi Barrani–Benghazi	5,641	165	850	3,300	2	15	59
Oct. 1941–Mar. 1942	Sidi Rezegh, Tobruk, Benghazi, Bardia	9,201	1,725	1,340	3,265	18	15	35
April 1942–Sept. 1942	Gazala, Cauldron, Bir Hacheim, Fall of Tobruk	14,069	3,170	6,290	5,995	23	45	42
Oct. 1942–March 1943	Alamein, Agheila, Buerat, Mareth, Wadi Akarit	16,405	8,240	8,210	15,070	50	50	91
April 1943–Aug. 1943	Enfidaville, Tunisia, Sicily	11,689	5,710	4,315	9,650	48	37	83
		57,005	19,010	21,005	37,280			

In addition to these figures, which represent only casualties in the Western Desert, 6,024 were wounded in the Sudan and Abyssinia, 3,406 in Syria and 2,170 in Greece and Crete. All these campaigns were provided for by 1 B.T.U. The quantities of stores issued to these Forces were, however, quite small.

the amount issued increased progressively throughout the campaign. This was partly due to the increase in the number of wounded, and even more to the increased use of transfusion.

A large number of group 'O' donors had to be bled before and during the Alamein battle, and this was done at the Infantry Base Depot at Geneifa. All the apparatus both for bleeding and for forward units was prepared in Cairo. The small resources of the unit were taxed to the utmost during this time although large reserves of plasma and saline had been accumulated previously in readiness for the battle.

The Alamein battle led to a great increase in the use of transfusion fluids. This was in part due to the number of casualties, but even more to the increase in the knowledge of what transfusion would accomplish for severely wounded men. The stationary character of the fighting, where a well defended position had to be assaulted, enabled the medical services to look after the casualties better than when mobile fighting was in progress over large areas of the Desert. It became obvious that the B.T.U. was too remote from the Army to allow it to undertake detailed distribution to the five F.T.Us. involved in the action, and these F.T.Us. were themselves too occupied with their own transfusion work to allow them to undertake supplies to other medical units. A unit whose sole duty was the supply of blood and apparatus to F.T.Us. and to all other units was clearly required and this duty was allocated to 3 F.T.U. which was augmented by 5 men and 4 vehicles and was stationed in the medical concentration area just behind the Alamein line. During the subsequent advance the unit moved forward with the adv. air transport centre so that blood coming by plane could be stored in the unit's refrigerators on arrival. 3 F.T.U. in turn sent out a forward truck with orderly and driver (designated the Adv. Blood Bank) to supply the more advanced medical units; thus the chain of supply from base to forward units was complete. All stores, including blood, were issued through these channels and used apparatus was at the same time returned to the base. This distribution system worked admirably and continued to function throughout the advance through the Desert to Tunisia. At the time of the Mareth battle and subsequent fighting it was impossible to arrange a regular supply of blood from Cairo owing to the distance involved and a detachment from 1 B.T.U. was established at Tripoli which at first undertook only bleeding, all the apparatus being supplied from Cairo. Subsequently this forward detachment was replaced by 5 B.T.U. and all work was performed there.

The large production of plasma in April 1944, before the invasion of Sicily, caused another peak period of transfusion work—12,000 bottles of plasma were prepared in three months and at one time 500 were produced in one day.

In all 19,000 bottles of group 'O' blood were issued and 97,000 donors were bled. The difference between these two figures is due mainly to the number of bleedings which were taken for the production of serum and plasma. In 1941, 3,250 bleedings were taken for plasma production and 1,350 for group 'O' blood; in 1942 the figures were 24,000 and 8,000, and in 1943, 52,000 and 9,000. The largest number of bleedings in any one month was 13,000 in April 1943. Throughout the campaign there was little difficulty in obtaining the necessary donors. All blood had to be taken from military personnel, but everyone realised that the blood was an important life-saving factor and troops proved very willing to act as donors during periods of rest. All the grouping serum required was provided for by local bleedings and a large number of tests for titre and bleeding for serum were performed for this purpose.

Great difficulties were experienced in obtaining the necessary number of trained men for the unit's work. The original establishment was completely inadequate and at times the unit had 100 men over the authorised numbers. These extra men were obtained from the R.A.M.C. Base Depot, M.E.F., and were without training in transfusion work.

Up to 1943 most of the transfusion equipment, except for needles which could be sent by air, was obtained from local resources. The supply from the United Kingdom was small and sporadic owing to the distance round the Cape. Improvised equipment was made locally—

TABLE 90

Transfusion Units M.E.F. December 1942

	B.T.U. Cairo	Bleeding Detachment Geneifa	Eighth Army F.T.Us.	Totals
Officers	2	1	6	9
O.Rs., R.A.M.C., or F.A.U. .	54	16	13	83*
Drivers, R.A.S.C., or F.A.U. .	7	1	13	21
R.E. Refrigerator Technician .	1	—	—	1
Native cleaners, labourers, etc. .	23	—	—	23
Totals	87	18	32	137

* This number of men was employed during the El Alamein period. The numbers are in excess of official establishments at the time.

Vehicles (refrigerator) . .	2	—	7	9
(load carriers) . .	7	1	6	14
Totals	9	1	13	23

Total Officers and O.Rs. (excluding locally enlisted labour)   .   .   .   114
Vehicles   23

for instance, beer bottles were used for blood plasma with rubber corks specially made locally to accommodate the standard Army blood-giving needles. Saline was always issued in beer and whisky bottles. The Cairo Rubber Company made all rubber tubing and corks which were required for this purpose.

The requirement of distilled water was between 1,000 and 2,000 litres per day. For this purpose the unit's two Mannesty stills were run continuously. Previous to the arrival of these stills in 1942, all the distilled water had been obtained from the Egyptian hospital at Kasr el Aini.

Table 90 shows the number and distribution of men and vehicles employed in the base and field units in December 1942, just after the Alamein battle. Six members of the Friends Ambulance Unit who joined the unit in 1941 are included in these numbers.

FIELD TRANSFUSION UNITS

The number of F.T.Us. functioning at any one time depended upon the operations in progress; this number varied from one to six (*see* Table 91). These units were attached to C.C.Ss. and field ambulances under the direction of D.D.M.S., Eighth Army. They gave transfusions of blood, etc., as required, and commanding officers paid

TABLE 91

Field Transfusion Units with Eighth Army—December 1942

Unit	Officers	O.Rs. R.A.M.C. or F.A.U.	Drivers or F.A.U.	Vehicles	
				Refrigerators	Load carriers
1 F.T.U. . . .	1	2	2	1	1
3 F.T.U. (Supply Unit) .	1	3	5	3	3
6 F.T.U. . . .	1	2	1	1	—
7 F.T.U. . . .	1	2	2	1	1
25 F.T.U. . . .	1	2	1	1	—
N.Z. F.T.U. . . .	1	2	2	1	1
	6	13	13	8	6

frequent visits to other units in their respective areas to ensure that they were adequately supplied with equipment and that they understood its use. Each of these F.T.Us. had a refrigerator truck with a capacity for storing 100 bottles of blood.

Previous to June 1942, each F.T.U. made a separate demand on the base for blood and transfusion supplies; after this time all the distribution was undertaken by 3 F.T.U.

The first field unit to leave the base was 1 F.T.U., which joined Western Desert Force on January 8, 1941, and returned on February 22,

1941. During this time it travelled as far as Derna and undertook 16 transfusions.

F.T.Us. were demanded by D.D.M.S. Eighth Army when they were required for operations. When they were not required forward they were attached to the base and assisted with the work there. In the intervals between battles these units had little to do, but in battle they had more work than they could well deal with. In general the battles lasted only three to five days so that it was possible for the units concerned to work almost continuously during such periods. During the El Alamein battle, six units—1, 3, 6, 7, 25, and the N.Z. F.T.U.—were attached to Eighth Army. Of these, two, 3 and 1, were concerned mainly with distribution; the others were attached to C.C.Ss. and field ambulances in various parts of the line.

All these units took part in the subsequent advance. After the collapse of resistance in Tunisia they were withdrawn for refit either to Cairo or to Tripoli. After the mounting of the Sicilian operation all these units left M.E.F. and were supplied by 5 B.T.U. from Tripoli.

A F.T.U. was always attached to the C.C.S. which dealt with the casualties coming from forward field ambulances and the main bulk of the resuscitation work was usually done at this level. But in the Desert, where the forward lines of communication were so extended, it was often necessary to send F.T.Us. with F.S.Us. to the M.D.S. of field ambulances and occasionally even to the A.D.S. The bulk of the transfusion work was always required at the place where the first surgical treatment was given. This was often the C.C.S., but sometimes more work was done at the M.D.S. than at the C.C.S. In the Mareth battle, for instance, where the first C.C.S. was 20 miles behind the M.D.Ss., the bulk of the work was done at the M.D.Ss. If the line of communication from C.C.S. to base was very long it was occasionally advisable to have a F.T.U. attached to a C.C.S. on the rear lines of communication.

It was found that one F.T.U. could cope with the resuscitation problems of two or three F.S.Us. It was therefore economical to group units in this manner. On the other hand, in many circumstances, such a large number of surgeons would not be necessary in one place and often a F.T.U. would only have to deal with the work of one F.S.U.

Before October 1942 there was usually only one F.T.U. with Western Desert Force. Two or three of these units, however, were despatched for short times for particular operations. At this time three F.T.Us. undertook distribution and instructional duties in addition to giving transfusions. This arrangement worked satisfactorily at first but became impracticable when the work increased.

The maximum number of new cases treated by any F.T.U. in 24 hours during battle periods was about 35. This maximum was seldom reached and a more normal number would be 10 to 15. In addition to this pre-operative work there were always a varying number of post-operative saline transfusion cases to look after and it became clear that some extra provision was necessary for these patients. It was never possible to arrange for extra transfusion orderlies for this work, and this made the work very difficult where a large number of abdominal cases were being treated.

STATISTICS OF TRANSFUSION

Table 92 shows the number of transfusions recorded in forward units and in general hospitals between October 1942 and May 1943.

TABLE 92

Period	Number of transfusions	
	Forward Units	General Hospitals
Alamein Battle, October 1942 .	941	328
Alamein to Tripoli, November 1942– January 1943	400	1,206
Tripoli to Cape Bon, January–May 1943	635	848
	1,976	2,382
Total	4,358	

The wounded during this period totalled 19,000; thus 10 per cent. of wounded (1,976) were transfused in forward units. The 2,000 transfusions in general hospitals were in the majority of instances (but not always) given to the same men who were transfused forward. In general hospitals two or more transfusions might be given to the same patient, but in forward units each transfusion was given to a different patient.

The figure of 10 per cent. of wounded requiring transfusions was an average for the whole campaign. Transfusions were more numerous and of greater volume where mine casualties were common, as at Mareth. The following table shows the transfusions given and fluids used at Mareth compared with those at Enfidaville. At Mareth mines were numerous and there was no cover in the open desert; at Enfidaville the country was well wooded and there were very few mines.

The amount of protein fluid given to the average case in the forward area was three pints. Some cases had very large amounts, in some instances seven to nine pints. A number of cases who had been transfused by F.T.Us. were followed up through 2nd Echelon and it was found that 70 per cent. were alive several months after wounding. Of the 30 per cent. who died the great majority died in the forward

36

medical units and no correlation could be established between the amount of fluid given and the result.

For transfusions at surgical levels blood was always available, as well as plasma, and in severely wounded men blood was preferred to plasma for pre-operative resuscitation except in the case of burns. For transfusions forward of surgical level, i.e. at A.D.Ss. and at M.D.Ss.

TABLE 93

	Wounded in one corps area	Percentage transfused	Transfused blood and plasma per 100 casualties		
		per cent.	Blood	Plasma	Totals
Mareth March 16–25, 1943 .	1,393	18	46	20	66
Enfidaville April 29–May 5, 1943	820	12	23	9	32

The total volume of blood and plasma per 100 casualties was twice as great at the battle of Mareth as at that of Enfidaville.

where no F.T.U. was attached, plasma alone was usually available and transfusions were only given to severe cases where the blood loss had been so great that it appeared the patients would not be able to survive the journey to surgical level without previous transfusion. Field ambulances were supplied with this plasma at first by the F.T.Us. and later by the Adv. Blood Bank (or advanced truck of 3 F.T.U.) which was situated at the ambulance check point. In exceptional cases blood was supplied to these units in refrigerator boxes, but as it could not be stored for more than 24 hours this was only possible in battle periods.

MATERIALS USED

It is not possible to give any accurate estimate of the total quantity of materials used as no records were kept by forward units other than by F.T.Us. Table 89 shows the amounts of fluids issued. A proportion of these materials will have been discarded or lost, so that the actual amounts used are probably at least 25 per cent. less than the amounts shown. About 25 per cent. of the blood issued over the whole campaign was returned unused.

The blood and plasma issued caused very little trouble. About one per cent. of patients transfused in forward units had reactions but they were invariably mild in character. When the blood was three weeks old, or when its appearance suggested that it was not suitable for use, it was returned to the B.T.U. On arrival at the unit it was usually between two and three months old and had often been roughly handled in transit. The returned bottles were all sterility tested (except when the quantity of work in hand rendered this impossible).

Of 1,675 bottles so tested, 216 or 13 per cent. showed contaminations. This contamination rate in the returned blood fell from 15 per cent. in 1941 to 3½ per cent. in 1943. When blood was taken in tents in the desert the returns showed fewer contaminations than when the blood was taken at the B.T.U. in Cairo, where in spite of all the usual precautions the aerial contamination of exposed plates was always very high.

Eighty-three bottles of plasma returned owing to suspected contamination were similarly tested and nine were found to be contaminated. Dried plasma, which all came from the A.B.S.D. at Bristol, caused no difficulties except for occasional transient rigors which occurred when the administration was rapid.

Saline was all produced at the B.T.U. and there was no difficulty with this except during the early months of 1941 before rubber bungs were obtained for the bottles.

LESSONS OF THE CAMPAIGN

TACTICAL AND ADMINISTRATIVE

At the start of the campaign the usefulness of transfusions was not fully realised and the arrangements made to deal with the problem were on a small scale. As soon as the importance was realised it became evident that a B.T.U. of between 50 and 100 men was necessary. The size and equipment of such a unit would vary according to whether it would merely have to distribute blood and plasma and to manufacture glucose-saline or whether it would also be responsible for the production of blood and possibly plasma. The requirements of such a unit were laid down in the war establishment of a B.T.U. in 1944.

When the volume of work increased it became evident that the B.T.U. could not maintain sufficiently close contact with the Army to ensure efficient distribution and that a forward distributing section was required.

In order to make adequate provision of transfusion materials some information as to the expected number of casualties in forthcoming operations was necessary and care had to be taken to maintain a high standard of security. As blood would only keep for twenty-one days, large quantities of group 'O' blood were taken during the two or three days preceding each battle, but this presented no difficulty from the security point of view as blood of other groups was being taken at all times for the production of plasma.

In M.E.F. there was no definite allocation of F.T.Us. to army and corps, and with fighting of such a sporadic type as occurred in the Desert this would hardly have been an advantage, for the F.T.Us. which remained with G.H.Q. troops were sent forward when required and withdrawn to the base as soon as the forward work permitted.

It was evident, however, that if continuous fighting were to take place, as happened after the Alamein battle, such allocations to corps and Army would be an advantage from the administrative point of view. The war establishment of 1944 allowed for this modification.

The requirements of post-operative work were never allowed for apart from the F.T.U. establishment, and where abdominal cases accumulated it was difficult to deal with both pre- and post-operative duties together. This difficulty would be met by the incorporation of two transfusion orderlies in a C.C.S. establishment to deal with most of the post-operative problems.

Difficulties were encountered owing to the impossibility of maintaining trained officers and men in the transfusion departments of general hospitals. Soon after these men were trained, particularly in the case of the officers, they were often posted to forward units and new men without training were allocated to these duties. It was noticeable that hospitals which were able to maintain their staffs intact over long periods had much better results than those who could not do so. It was suggested that the transfusion officer in a general hospital should be a permanent appointment, but owing to the scarcity of medical man-power it did not prove possible to do this.

MEDICAL AND TECHNICAL

The final work of forward resuscitation must be done at the level where the patient receives his first surgical treatment. Usually this is the first C.C.S. at which he arrives, but in the Desert it was not uncommonly the M.D.S. or even the A.D.S. of a field ambulance. Any transfusion which is done forward of this level has only the purpose of ensuring that the patient shall arrive at the surgical level in a fit state for operation and only patients who have suffered such a severe loss of blood as to be incapable of travelling without transfusion should be resuscitated at this level. It is necessary to emphasise that the immobilisation of a fractured femur at the earliest possible time after wounding is even more important for the survival of the patient than is the giving of a transfusion.

With long and rough journeys in ambulances between the A.D.S. or M.D.S. and the C.C.S. it was not uncommonly found that a seriously wounded patient would be transfused and would leave the forward unit in good shape but nevertheless would be in a profound state of shock through loss of circulating fluid during the journey by the time he arrived at the rear unit. From this state it was difficult to revive him a second time. A system of giving plasma transfusions in ambulance cars was developed and proved of great benefit to these severely wounded men. About 200 of such transfusions were given during 1943. Such transfusions could only be given if a medical orderly was sent with the man in the ambulance, and this of necessity made it a difficult procedure, for forward units could not easily spare orderlies during battle times. In cases where the man was sent down without an orderly the transfusion either stopped altogether or found its way into the tissues of the arm rather than into the vein.

In addition to the forward transfusion work there was a considerable amount of transfusion in general hospitals and this proved one of the most difficult parts of the service. Owing to the wide distribution of these hospitals very little assistance could be given by the B.T.U. apart from giving all officers and O.Rs. an initial course of training. Patients in general hospitals were often in a septic condition. Transfusions were given to combat the secondary anaemia due to prolonged sepsis and reactions to transfusion at these hospitals were much more common than in forward units. Each hospital sent a monthly return of transfusions and reactions and an effort was made to give as much help as possible. The most common avoidable cause of these reactions was the failure to clean apparatus, including glass vessels and stills, with sufficient thoroughness. Mismatch transfusions were very rare, although two were reported in general hospitals, one due to keeping group 'A' blood in a refrigerator where it was mistaken for 'O' blood, and another due to an inadequate time being spent in performing a direct matching test with donors' cells and patient's serum.

THE TYPE OF CASE

Cases of severe limb injury and of multiple wounds with large blood loss required more blood than any others. Bleeding in these cases was frequently from large vessels and 5 to 7 pints of blood were not uncommonly required before they could be operated on. Where these large quantities of fluid were needed blood was found to be greatly superior to plasma and patients were said to tolerate operations much better if blood could be used for all except the first pint or two given in the forward unit. When tissue damage was extensive early removal of damaged tissue was found to be of great importance.

Abdominal cases required less blood (2 to 4 pints) except in the rare cases of gross intra-abdominal bleeding. In the average abdominal case the superiority of blood over plasma was not so marked as in the limb cases. The post-operative treatment of these cases demanded much care both in the administration of saline and in the gastric suction and this treatment usually occupied the transfusion units for six or seven days after the end of a battle. This was always the time when the demand for saline was greatest. A quantity of 6 pints of glucose-saline— a solution of 4 per cent. glucose with 0·3 per cent. sodium chloride— per day for the four to five days after operation, until the patient could take fluid by mouth, was found to be ideal, but in practice the quantities given were usually somewhat less than this and 37 abdominal cases during the Mareth battle received an average amount of 13 bottles of saline each, or, excluding the 10 cases which died in the first twenty-four hours, each of the remainder received an average of 18 bottles of saline. The giving of the saline and the provision of gastric suction was very difficult if pre-operative resuscitation of other battle casualties had to be done at the same time. It was essential to hold these cases at surgical level for 10 to 14 days after operation.

Chest cases, if they had to be transferred, could only be given a small amount of blood—1 to 2 pints—and this had to be given slowly at the rate of 1 pint an hour. Such a transfusion was only given for life-saving purposes. In all other cases it was found better to leave the patient alone and keep him warm, while if there was evidence of accumulation of blood in the chest, this fluid was removed. Great difficulties were encountered with chest wounds complicating wounds in other parts of the body. In many of these cases the blood loss had been so great as to make immediate transfusion imperative and such transfusion might always cause further bleeding from the damaged lung. In all chest cases plasma was avoided owing to the increased risk of haemorrhage from the lung.

Severe burns were common in the Desert, and in these cases large quantities of plasma were given in the initial stages, starting with 3 to 15 pints in the first 24 hours according to the extent of the burn. These cases showed the best results if they could be held at the unit when they were transfused. If this could not be done they benefited considerably by the use of travelling transfusions in the ambulance cars. The administration of plasma had to be continued until the loss of fluid from the burnt area ceased; usually this would be in 2 to 7 days according to the severity of the burn. After the first week blood transfusions were often required in severe burns owing to the secondary anaemia which followed the burn.

TRANSMISSION OF DISEASE BY TRANSFUSION

At the beginning of the campaign it had been considered that syphilis and malaria would present great difficulties, but actually no trouble was encountered with either. One case only of transmitted syphilis was recorded in a patient where freshly taken blood had been used. Kahn tests were done whenever possible, but probably these would not have detected a donor in the acute stage. Moreover, the arrangements for carrying out these tests broke down during the Alamein battle owing to the large number of bottles of blood required. Malaria was not a difficulty in the M.E. until the invasion of Italy and no cases of transmission of this disease by transfusion were reported. Instructions were issued, however, for testing the blood of potential donors whenever the disease appeared likely to become prevalent. All donors were asked whether they had had malaria and those who admitted having had the disease were not used.*

DUTIES OF TRANSFUSION PERSONNEL IN FORWARD AREAS

Close co-operation is necessary between the surgeon and the transfusion officer; although the latter has charge of the pre-operative ward, the former is responsible for the final treatment of the patient. In busy times the transfusion officer is almost invariably responsible for selection of cases for the surgeons and the examination of the cases by him will often give the first evidence of a missed abdominal wound or of a case of gas gangrene, the first indication of the latter condition often being the failure of a seemingly fit patient to respond to transfusion.

All cases which do not respond to transfusion should be seen as soon as possible by the surgeon as sometimes the only possible course is immediate operation without waiting for full resuscitation. Common causes of this failure to respond were over-morphinisation, when more and more morphia is absorbed as the circulation improves, fat embolism, which proved a relatively common condition and was not confined to wounds involving bones, intraperitoneal bleeding and, in cases seen late after wounding, a uraemic condition due to prolonged low blood-pressure resulting in renal damage. In the majority of cases seen within 24 hours of wounding the condition of 'shock' is due mainly to external bleeding, but other causes must be looked for, e.g. an abdominal wound, a retroperitoneal haematoma, or a small sucking wound of the chest which has escaped previous examinations.

Some technical points in connexion with forward transfusions are worthy of mention. Orderlies, including if possible one or two from the unit to which the F.T.U. is attached, should be trained in the assembly of apparatus and in keeping a transfusion running, and emphasis must be given to the necessity of avoiding touching the parts which come in contact with the transfusion fluid and with the patient's vein. The orderlies should also be trained in making accurate records of the amounts of fluid given, since this is most difficult in rush periods and requires a definite routine. The orderly should know how to keep the patient comfortable—e.g. the proper adjustment of the splint, keeping the patient warm, and giving him sweet hot tea.

---

* As to the risk of serum jaundice occurring after blood transfusion in Service patients *see* Civilian Health and Medical Services, Vol. I, pp. 86–88, in this series.

INDEX

Lightning Source UK Ltd.
Milton Keynes UK
UKOW06f1502081017

310624UK00002B/29/P